Caught in the Beloved's Petticoats

Caught in the Beloved's Petticoats

A Treatise on the Eternal Way

M. Young

HOHM PRESS

Layout and design: Becky Fulker

Library of Congress Cataloging-in-Publication Data

(application submitted)

ISBN: 1-890772-63-1

Drawing of Yogi Ramsuratkumar opposite page 517
by Otilia Planelles Ramos.

Cover art: Blue Gheriti, one of the sense-offering goddesses of Tibetan Buddhism; 11th century wall mural from the Red Hall at the mTho-Iding Monastery.

Inside cover art: Patterns from original 18th century Mysore school, unknown artist's sketchbook.

HOHM PRESS
P.O. Box 2501
Prescott, AZ 86302
800-381-2700
www.hohmpress.com

This book was printed in the U.S.A. on recycled acid-free paper using soy ink.

For all wayfarers

Contents

Author's Preface

This book marks the passing of thirty years since Lee Lozowick gave his first formal *satsang* in New Jersey in September 1975. To give a public *satsang* was a signal to the world that Lee had crossed a threshold from which there was no return, an event generated by a shift of consciousness that left Lee in an awakened condition, which he called "Surrender to the Will of God" and "Spiritual Slavery." Urged by friends and the students who were already gathering around him to start teaching, Lee was cast into the role of guru in a sweeping momentum of forces beyond his personal volition. He has said of this change, "I had no choice." One year later, under quite miraculous circumstances, Lee met his master, Yogi Ramsuratkumar, the revered beggar saint of Tiruvannamalai, India, and began an intimate relationship with him that has endured beyond the death of Yogi Ramsuratkumar in February, 2001.

Having written extensively in other books[1] about Lee Lozowick and his master, Yogi Ramsuratkumar, I am choosing to simply dive directly into the present experience of walking the path with Lee without providing yet another heavily biographical introduction. This puts the reader who is new to Lee and his teachings in a bit of

1 See *As It Is: A Year on the Road with a Tantric Teacher*, Hohm Press, Prescott, AZ, 2000 and the biography, *Yogi Ramsuratkumar—Under the Punnai Tree*, Hohm Press, Prescott, AZ, 2003.

a predicament, because there is an immense foundation of teachings and stories—the *lila* of Lee and Yogi Ramsuratkumar most significantly—that are the background, in fact the very backbone, of this book. Many of the teachings and conversations reported here are enriched and further brought to life by this complex background, and yet, an attempt to provide it would be largely impossible and even absurd, especially because this book has been published, for the most part, for the practicing sangha body of Lee's students.

Writers always hope that their work will reach a broader audience. And so, I invite the reader who has simply been drawn to this book magnetically, picked it up and wants to know more to refer to the literary resources that have been published by Hohm Press, which contain depth considerations of Lee's teachings and work, as well as biographies of Yogi Ramsuratkumar. For this purpose, a bibliography is provided in the back. However, there are a few pertinent facts that must be relayed in this Preface.

It has been said before that Lee Lozowick is one of the most enigmatic figures in the spiritual scene in the Western world. Lee's refusal to behave the way a spiritual master should behave has drawn criticism toward him at times from different quarters. At the same time, Lee actively nurtures links of friendship with a very unusual group of peers—other spiritual teachers, guides and serious practitioners of the path—in the States and in Europe; in such friendships, those who have realized many of the fruits of the spiritual path can see and understand the depths of one another in ways that are inexplicable to the rational mind.

The late Michel de Salzmann, spiritual heir of G.I. Gurdjieff, once said to Lee during one of their meetings in Paris, "You are so much more than what your students' describe in *Tawagoto*. It's much better than they say!"[2] At the time, Lee commented this was

2 *Tawagoto* is the journal of the Hohm Community and is considered a principle means by which his teaching is communicated.

a great compliment, because his students tend to deify and adulate him. Monsieur de Salzmann was referring to what he saw in Lee from the perspective of "the Work" as it was taught by Gurdjieff, whose life and teaching continues to be one of Lee's greatest inspirations and influences—as we will see in the pages ahead.

Sometimes difficult to understand and often cryptic, Lee has become more and more reluctant to be a guru—a role he still insists he has no choice about—as the years wear on. He has been described by various authors, friends, critics and biographers as a genuine teacher of the tantric and crazy-wisdom vein, a charlatan, a divine fool and beggar, a rock & roll guru, a great English poet and an Indian saint, the last two designations coming from Lee's master, Yogi Ramsuratkumar himself. Lee's favorite description of himself is the one that came from his close friend, Arnaud Desjardins: "Lee is a true disciple of his master."

Despite his sometimes grueling travel schedule, ashram life is a crucial element of the *sadhana* Lee has created for his students, both for ashram residents and the householders who participate in the daily schedule, celebrations and feasts. Lee has three ashrams that are maintained by his students: in the mountains of central Arizona; in the French countryside near Poitiers; and in Tiruvannamalai, one block away from the Yogi Ramsuratkumar Ashram. Lee spends the fall, winter and spring in Arizona every year; the summer months are dedicated to his ashram in France and his teaching work in Europe.

Many of Lee's students live in households near the ashrams in Arizona and France; others live in urban areas where study groups, called "bordellos," are formed to support the practice and quality of life of those who live far away from the ashrams. Like the Bauls of Bengal, traveling in groups with Lee on his various sojourns—band tours, teaching seminars, sacred artifact expeditions or visiting other teachers—is one of the primary ways that students can participate and receive the transmission of the teacher.

In fact, Lee's commitment to the arts—painting, sculpture, literature, music, performance arts—is a vital part of his work with students and one of the ways that he enlivens a return to sacred culture. Lee himself is a prolific poet, and he encourages the literary arts among his students, often giving writing tasks that have resulted in a significant body of dharma literature. As Baul poet or *kavi,* to use the Sanskrit word, Lee has written volumes of poetry to his master, Yogi Ramsuratkumar in the classic *ninda stuti* (ironic praise) form. Equally abundant is Lee's lyric writing—sacred poems written in the idiomatic vernacular or street language that contain secrets of life and transformation and have been put to music composed by his students.

Music has also been a central component of Lee's teaching work for almost twenty years. He has recorded thirty-five CDs of original songs, which have been performed in many public venues by the four different bands that he has created within the community of practitioners. Since 1995, Lee has traveled and performed with his blues band, Shri, for six weeks on tour during the summer, playing the festivals and street fairs of Europe.

This particular project was conceived in early September, 2005, when it became clear that Lee's teachings over the summer were so valuable that my notes and journals were far too thick and rich to publish as a summer chronicle in the community publication, *Tawagoto*. At the time, Lee said, "Keep writing—maybe we'll make a book out of your journal." When he got back to Arizona in October, without even looking at the rather large text that was taking shape or any other undue conversation about it, Lee said, "We'll make a book out of your journals. Have it ready for next summer." He was walking through the ashram office as he tossed this instruction off, then he disappeared behind the barricade of sacred artifacts, piles of books and magazines, letters and *murtis* of Yogi Ramsuratkumar that surround his desk.

The result is this: another whirlwind writing project, hopefully one that captures Lee, as if in a snapshot or freeze frame, during one of many summers in France. Truly, there are *many* teaching lessons and discourses that occurred over the summer that do not appear in this book. The only discourses that have been taken from actual transcripts are Lee's public talk in Paris on September 30, and the final darshan, given in Arizona on October 16. Everything else comes from handwritten notes. Therefore, both in my note-taking and in my reporting of conversations and exchanges, any error is entirely mine.

I would like to express my gratitude to Rakini Chinery, Nachama Greenwald, Christina Sell and Rose Volckhausen, who shared notes from their own journals; many thanks are also due to Paula Zuccarello, who tirelessly helped work the tangles out of complex messes of writing as copy editor and proofreader; to Becky Fulker for her ongoing layout and technical expertise and tireless commitment to *guru seva*; to Nachama Greenwald and Bhadra Mitchell for proofreading; to Nara for creative consulting on the cover design; and thanks to Laurent Belmonte, Sharana Lhaksam, Sylvan Incao and Christina and Kelly Sell for their photographic contribution.

I am deeply thankful that Lee was generously willing to read and correct the manuscript, adding or omitting and giving his unique editorial context to the project. As always, my teacher Lee Lozowick is the inspiration behind every page of this book: to him I offer eternal gratitude and devotion.

Foreword

Another summer in France, ah sweet France. When we first acquired our ashram, Ferme de Jutreau, Gilles Farcet told us that this area of the country was called "douce France," meaning sweet France. Indeed it is. Of course the countryside is glorious, the people, for the most part, friendly, helpful and hospitable, the food, well . . . outstanding. And more than that, even the atmosphere truly lends itself to an outpouring of the teaching, a small fraction of which is included in the following pages. And really, to even begin to comprehend the depth and breadth of the Blessings that Yogi Ramsuratkumar is pouring into the whole world, and surely France in particular, one must do more than read, one must experience directly the spaces, the chambers, the beauty and the ugliness, the "Flowers of Joy" and "The Flowers of Evil" together, as they arise in the course of our program of self-discovery, at times an adventure full of excitement and blissful anticipation and at times a horror of confusion, fears and misunderstanding. I've been teaching over thirty years, almost forty, if we wish to include the years of metaphysical instruction, and I am grateful to have been fortunate enough, by the Benediction of my Master, Yogi Ramsuratkumar, to have been sent to Europe to gather in praise and celebration for this extraordinary path. As the teaching evolves into its more informal and immediate stage, read on, digest, and welcome the gifts of the grace of the gurus, Yogi Ramsuratkumar, Papa Ramdas, Swami Prajnanpad and Arnaud Desjardins.

And if you visit in future times, remember to bring good coffee, good chocolate and good wine. For if the world goes to hell and the teaching becomes so boring to me that all I can do is sit around complaining and farting, how can we go wrong when we can indulge in good coffee, good chocolate and good wine? Yes, if relationships go sour, sex becomes a burden, love a torture and truth scarce, still, yes still, with good coffee, good chocolate and good wine, we can still look forward to tomorrow. When all the cheese is pasteurized, the vegetables irradiated and the meat chemicalized, hold fast to the life raft of good coffee, good chocolate and good wine.

And on that note, I bid you à bientôt.

lee lozowick
1 March, 2006
Prescott, Arizona

Introduction

This book tells the story of one summer in Europe with Western Baul teacher, Lee Lozowick, the spiritual son of the revered beggar saint of Tiruvannamalai, Yogi Ramsuratkumar. It has been inspired by Lee's many travels and teachings during the summer of 2005, which also marked the passing of thirty years since his first formal *satsang* was given in New Jersey in September 1975.

In some ways, this book follows the footsteps of its predecessor, *As It Is*, which chronicled a year of traveling with Lee, from November 1998 through November 1999. That was six years ago; times have changed, and we are farther along on the path we have been walking. Most significantly, Yogi Ramsuratkumar left his physical body five years ago, precipitating a major transition in Lee's teaching style that is reflected in the stories of this book.

Change always insists that we respond to a deeper call, which rumbles up from the depths of ourselves. The transformational path demands that we roll with change, use it as the springboard for inner work and the cultivation of qualities like faith, compassion and generosity of spirit. At the same time, our world is changing so rapidly and unnaturally that people of awareness are justly alarmed. We long for greater harmony and sanity worldwide, but we look around the world today and see nothing but heartbreak. Everything that is fine and good and true is disappearing or under attack; basic freedoms come at great peril for vast populations of individuals around the globe. The black cloud of ecological disaster hovers over us, and the rule of the day is toxic pollution, disease, war, political corruption, hunger, widespread poverty among the masses in the face of wealth and riches squandered by the few.

As we traveled around France during the summer, many friends and seekers expressed a sense of foreboding and the acute awareness of an uncertain future. Just months after the tsunamis that devastated India and Sri Lanka in December 2004, there were huge upheavals that rocked the world—the terrorist bombing in London and the tremendous suffering unleashed by the August 2005 flood in New Orleans, which became the focus of our sorrow and unleashed a great outpouring of compassion. The reverberations of these shocking events were reflected in the often-asked question, "What hope is there?"

Lee's answers can be found in this book. They were not comforting, but they were immanently clear and sane: the only hope, the only true refuge is the eternal way. And so, this book reflects not only the timelessness of the spiritual path as it manifests in the company of our teacher, Lee, but also the temper and pace of our present location in space and time, on the planet Earth in the first years of the twenty-first century.

Shortly after I returned to Arizona in October 2005, I was working on this manuscript, wondering how to introduce this material to the reader, and mulling over all that had happened, and the mood and inner penetration of Lee's teachings over the summer. One day I was driving one of the kids home from school, and she wanted the car radio turned on. As we drove along, I caught the line of a contemporary song lyric that repeated, over and over, "We're not going to survive unless we get a little crazy." The message penetrated into my mind until it hit a visceral chord. The universe is truly full of *drala* and magic, and this seemed like a message from the muse—an angel in the airwaves that was talking to me.

"We're not going to survive unless we get a little crazy" resonated so well with Lee's title for this book, *Caught in the Beloved's Petticoats*, that it became the refrain of my contemplations on the project. One thing is certain: we will not survive the changes that Lee says are inevitably coming in the years ahead if we aren't a little crazy, in the most radical and attractive sense of the word. Without question, while false truths and false idols are being swallowed wholesale by the masses, our reliance on the Divine makes us appear a little crazy as we swim against the overwhelming tide.

The encounter with a true path and a true master, as witnessed in this book, is a unique form of craziness. The Bauls call this the *ulta* path, which goes contrary to the prescribed cultural, political and religious injunctions of our society; it is our refusal to get on the treadmill that appears madcap, maybe insane, to those who are locked—body and soul—into the gears of the world machine. But ultimately, for a Baul, it is our longing for the living God as personal Beloved that turns us away from the comforts and concerns of the common life. How are we going to survive? By celebrating the fact that we are caught in the Beloved's Petticoats—that is our form of craziness.

Lee once wrote in one of his protest songs, "How we gonna survive / so much suffering around / it looks to me quite clear / that the world is goin down."[1] The song's plaintive refrain, "How we gonna survive," captures much about the underlying anxiety of our times. We are faced with the very real probability that the infrastructures of the world as we know it are "goin down." The prospect of being off the grid and thrown into an "ancient future" that may dawn upon us by ecological and economic necessity would urgently demand the reinvention of sacred culture, a return toward a way of life known by the ancients.

1 "2 and 2," from *Caught in the Middle*, recorded by Attila the Hunza, 2004.

That's where our craziness may pay off—years of spiritual disciplines and the Baul form of radical reliance on the guru as the tangent point with the Divine requires a sacred culture that functions as the container of our lives. Sacred culture nourishes the best of human potential, not the worst, as our deadening, soulless culture of today does in its glorification of horrific violence, depravity, blatant greed and materialism; its obsession with fame, vanity and vacuity.

The teaching and the true teacher naturally reflected these concerns. This vital call to the path and the sanity of sacred culture, then, is one of the recurring themes in these pages, where we enter into the stream not only with the teacher, but the students, who in their earnest efforts at *sadhana*, or spiritual life, become wayfarers alongside their guide.

Wayfarers on the Path: The Teaching as Art

What is most useful for us in stories of the teacher's daily life is that they are a teaching about how to survive these dark times with one's soul intact. Simplicity, conserving resources, nobility, dignity, integrity in relationship with others, compassion, generosity, kindness, a deep appreciation for beauty—Lee tells us that these are the road signs that point us in the right direction. Therefore, the master's day-to-day actions, as well as his spoken words, are the timeless wisdom that I have attempted to capture as journalist.

One of the notable elements of Lee's teaching and his way of life on the path is that he does not reject our culture as it is; instead he makes his own way through it, finding the way to be creative in the midst of destruction. Lee can walk the streets of any city and partake deeply of its essential vivid liveliness, without being contaminated or toxified by its poisons. It requires a finely tuned discrimination to navigate through the snares of desire and cultural decay in a way that actually serves the divine life; with the finesse of an awakened and vital awareness, Lee demonstrates this discrimination as he relates with worldly experience on his terms.

Because Lee utilizes everything he encounters as a teaching circumstance, he teaches his students that life is our training ground; it is in the unfolding of our lives that we are shown where our practice is. Therefore, in the minutiae of everyday experience and occurrence recorded here, there is always a fire burning beneath the surface. We find that the teacher is constantly exhorting, begging, teasing, inviting us to come into his world. It is not an orderly, prescribed religion that we encounter with Lee as our prophet; it is an untamed, sometimes heretical course through life, glorious and gory as it is, by means of guru yoga, which results in a "Divine Alchemy," to use Lee's term. It is a road that often leads through heaven and hell in a careening encounter with the angels and demons that populate the human experience. In September 2005 Lee described the Baul path we traverse under his guidance:

> *But in fact, we are learning skills by virtue of our lives together and our practice. We are learning to court the Beloved and enshrine the Beloved in our hearts and keep the Beloved there and make friends with the hounds of hell—go to the River Styx and have a picnic there! We are learning those things, but we're not learning them like taking a class on mythology or Hindu iconography. We're absorbing information that is producing a capacity and skill that we won't know we have, until the time to use it shows up.*

Since the death of Yogi Ramsuratkumar, Lee has added to his repertoire an inexplicable merchant with two-foot-long dread locks who peddles sacred wares, who is driven by a burning vision to search for those extraordinary pieces of art that communicate the Sacred and inspire that which is noble and good in human beings. Many of the experiences captured in this book are portraits of the teacher in this role, because since the passing of Yogi Ramsuratkumar, Lee's fervor for sacred art and the "Sacred Bazaar" has become central to his teaching work.[2]

In fact, Lee seems driven by his own muse to populate the Western world with sacred images, especially those of antiquity from the motherland of his spiritual father, Yogi Ramsuratkumar. The influx of sacred artifacts from many great traditions—particularly Hindu, Buddhist and Christian—has been an astounding development in Lee's work, to which his students have responded with enthusiasm. Suddenly we find our lives thronged with the presence of deities: Vishnu, Shiva, Buddha, Lakshmi, Parvati, Ganesha, Hanuman and Durga in bronze, wood or stone. All these and more have come to life for us, as we realize the living divine potentials and blessing power of these objective forms.

Lee's way of living the teaching as a form of art is not for everyone. It is a revolutionary way of life that is reflected as well in his new passion for graffiti and street art, which he spoke about in November 2005:

> *More and more we will run into people who are turned off by the kind of art I'm turning toward. It's a turnoff for some people, because we don't want to deal with the creeping evil that is taking over the world, and this art is about radical protest of what is happening in the world today. I am less and less interested in fitting into the establishment and more and more interested in following the path that maintains its radical edge. I'm going to protest, just because I can.*

---

2 The "Sacred Bazaar" is an appellation Gilles Farcet once aptly applied to Lee's immense collection of sacred artifacts, books and CDs and his traveling, gypsy-style selling.

Introduction

To the many facets of Lee Lozowick—the first and foremost of which is disciple and perfect devotee to his master, Yogi Ramsuratkumar—must be added: Baul *khepa* (Bengali: mad for God), merchant, social critic, songwriter, bluesman, comedian, raconteur, seminar leader, advocate for conscious childraising, apologist for true teachers of the crazy wisdom vein, businessman, fierce defender of dharma, and last but not least, yogi and practitioner of great spiritual discipline. Most of all, in everything that Lee does, we find the sensibilities of an artist. As we follow Lee from Arizona to London, France and Germany, we partake of his music, his teaching, his buying and selling, his friendship, his feasting and fasting, his practice and his unique way of celebrating the divine in daily life. Art and objects of beauty begin to play a central role, as does fine wine, exquisite food and the joy of communion among companions of the way.

We may well ask: What kind of spiritual path is filled with business deals, music, poetry, feasting, wine and art? In a paradoxical twist, Lee lives by the principle of beggary: like his father, Yogi Ramsuratkumar—who remained a beggar to the very end of his life despite the immense temple and ashram that was built in his honor— Lee's ashrams remain poor and recondite, although they are now adorned with objects of great antiquity and sanctity. Scratch the surface of Lee Lozowick and you find Yogi Ramsuratkumar; the pure disciple is never separate from any of Lee's far-reaching activities. In fact, his path is an extremely traditional one.

For many of us, the paradoxes of Lee's life and teaching sometimes fill us with questions that can only be answered by the heart, and surely this too is a teaching. As we seek to understand the path more fully, it is helpful to look into the renaissance of poets, renowned Vaishnava preceptors and minstrel saints of medieval northern India and Bengal in particular; there we find the origins of the

Bauls, those mystic poets par excellence, with whom Lee shares a deep spiritual kinship, and a tremendous wealth of wisdom.[3]

Caught in the Beloved's Petticoats

For over twenty years Lee has referred his students to Vallabhacharya's commentaries on the love games of Krishna, as found in the classic scriptural text of Book Ten of the *Bhagavata Purana*, as an important source of study, precisely because it comes the closest to the heart of Lee's work than any extant text.[4] Vallabhacharya (1479–1531 C.E.) was the progenitor of the *bhakti* path and founder of the *Pushti Marga* (Path of Grace), with which Lee has found tremendous resonance. Consider this story of Vallabhacharya's son, Gosainji, extolling the practice of devotional love for Krishna, who is known here as Shri Thakurji, from the tradition of the Pushti Marga:

> *Two Vaishnava brothers once approached Shri Gosainji Vallabhacharya, the visionary master, when he was seated amidst his own intimate circle. They prostrated themselves reverently before him as was customary, and sat down. "We have a deep longing to worship Shri Thakurji," said one to Shri Gosainji. "We beg you to consecrate an image of the Lord for us with your own divine hand."*
>
> *Gosainji smiled. "First speak to me of your tastes and inclinations and of what moves you most in your daily life,"*

---

3 Vaishnava or Vaishnavism are terms that apply to worshippers of Lord Vishnu, usually in his incarnations as Krishna or Rama. The Vaishnavites are one of three major devotional cults of Hindism, along with the Shaivites and Shaktas. Vishnu is associated with the sun, maintaining and preserving life with its all-pervading light and spiritual enlightenment. In the personal form, Vishnu is known as Narayana. Narayana/Vishnu rests on the coiled form of Sesanaga, the cosmic serpent; when Narayana wakes, the creation is renewed.

4 See *Vallabhacarya on The Love Games of Krsna*, translated by James Redington, Delhi, India: Motilal Barnarsidass, 1983.

he said. "Tell me how you would like to worship Him."

One brother declared, "I have no special tastes or inclinations. I meditate constantly and pray to Him, and that is all."

The second brother said, "As for me, O compassionate Master, I derive pleasure from many worldly things—fine perfumes, music and, indeed, all that makes life worthwhile."

On hearing this, Gosainji said to the second brother, "Thakurji, the Lord, will surely accept your service!"

But to the one who disdained worldly pleasures, he said, "The worship you offer would not find favour with the Lord, for the world is His creation, and he who partakes of its pleasures, while surrendering himself fully to Him in spirit, will meet with His loving response."

This anecdote effectively sums up the attitude to life and worship in the Pushti Marga, "the path of grace" laid down by Vallabhacharya. For the one who follows the path, bhakti, devotion, is the well-spring of true religion; but the true devotee is shaukeen too, a connoisseur in every field, one whose heart and soul are fully centred on his Lord. All the arts inspired by Pushti Marga . . . . reflect this attitude of celebration.[5]

Vallabhacharya's teachings dovetailed with cultural and political movements of the times and spawned a renaissance in every field of the arts. People began to express their love and devotion by creating beautiful images of the Lord in paintings, sculptures and in words. These images of the Divine were considered to be *svarupa*—the

---

5 Ambalal, Amit. *Krishna as Shrinathji*, Mapin International, New York, 1987, pp. 11–12. Shri Gosainji is Vitthalnathji, the son and successor of the deeply revered Vallabhacharya, the fifteenth century sage, guru and visionary who founded the sect of Pushti Marga and was the primary commentator on Book X of the *Bhagavata Purana*, "The Love Games of Sri Krishna." Vallabhacharya added a new element of ecstatic worship, or *bhakti* to the legend of Sri Krishna, with its erotic images springing from Jayadeva's groundbreaking twelfth century poem, *The Gita Govinda*. See Appendix for more information.

innate, true form of the deity, which, when meditated upon, conferred great blessings and realization upon the devotee. Music, poetry, cuisine, flowers and flower arranging—all these were integral to the worship of one's chosen deity. All forms of the arts flourished as underpinnings of a sacred culture.

In the next generation, Vallabhacharya's son and spiritual heir, Gosainji, took the tradition to a new level, adding a depth of insight into the nature of enjoyment, mood and aesthetic. Gosainji focused on *madhurya bhakti*, in which Krishna is related with as the beloved of the heart. Again, the sacred image as expressed through the arts soared into new heights: "The ashtachhapa poets, devotees to the core, created a poetry with a rich, new imagery, which permeated all the arts—music, dance, drama and painting. All this made Krishna human, alive and more accessible."[6]

Taking these teachings to heart, we can bring insight to our understanding of the experiences and teachings that are encountered in the pages of this journal. There are vast devotional and tantric traditions in India that are the bedrock upon which Lee's work rests, some of which are mentioned in the pages that follow or briefly explored in the Appendix. In encouraging us to study Vallabhacharya's commentaries on Book X of the *Bhagavata Purana*, Lee has given us a trail to follow: his work points toward the Pushti Marga and the beloved of the heart, which casts a certain light on the *sadhana* that he engages with his students. But most importantly, this story of Gosainji's teaching gives us some insight into the nature of the master as *shaukeen*, or connoisseur of life.[7]

It is this revelry in the beauty and wonder of creation, from macro to micro, which marks the pleasure-as-prayer of the *shaukeen*, the

---

6 Ibid, p. 12.

7 For more information about the Pushti Marga, the Bauls of Bengal and the tradition of poet saints beginning with the twelfth century poet Jayadeva, an appendix is provided on page 653.

connoisseur of life, whose context is to enjoy and partake of life's plenitude as a way of praising the Divine. It is the *jivan-mukta*—one who lives fully in the state of liberation—who may engage *sambhoga*, or complete enjoyment through the senses, to develop the *sambhogakaya* (divine body of enjoyment). Without this context, revelry quickly becomes the self-aggrandizing activity of the libertine, the rebel without a cause who generates suffering and karmic entanglements as he or she careens through the world, seeking nothing more than the gratification of personal desires. In other words, wherever *bhoga* (enjoyment) or opulence is found in Lee's life, it is turned toward Yogi Ramsuratkumar.

Divine Alchemy

Radical Surrender to the Will of God by the grace of his master, Yogi Ramsuratkumar, is the context that makes Lee's playful relationship with the world of incarnation so extraordinarily blessed, precisely because his actions are guided by the polestar of an amazing selflessness, an uncanny sobriety. What Lee teaches us is that the opulence of beauty and true enjoyment is possible because of our inner renunciation, or poverty of the heart—the commitment to a foundation in spiritual practice and a God-centered life. Lee masterfully engages Divine Alchemy in the friction between these two opposites as he demonstrates a frugal, disciplined, sometimes spartan and delicately discriminate sensibility, artfully interspersed with cornucopias of lavish, rich and even wild experience.

As *shaukeen*, Lee's revelry contains the seeds of revelation. Lee's students, who follow him in this quest for the Beloved in daily life, who are in fact tangled in the Beloved's Petticoats, in the kaleidoscope of existence in this complex world, experience their guide as the revelator: the revealer of a secret known to very few. What is the secret Lee reveals? In Lee's company, we are graced with moments of divine encounter—when we catch the faint scent of the Beloved's perfume—that arise out of the groundless impersonal emptiness of an underlying realization of nonduality. Discovering the traces of the Beloved, who the Bauls call the uncatchable "Man of the Heart," in the marrow of our day-to-day experience is the great joy of human existence. Such a moment gracefully arises then naturally subsides back into the same groundless, impersonal and liberating emptiness of nonduality.

Lee calls this experience "Enlightened Duality," a teaching that is threaded throughout his communications: in his poetry to Yogi Ramsuratkumar, his seminar talks, his daily actions and relationships, as well as in his interactions on the streets of the big city. This classic Baul perspective on life and enlightenment itself is, perhaps, the most exalted alchemy for which Lee prepares us: a conscious, awakened participation in the interplay between nonduality and duality.

This book carries the vision and teachings of a Baul *khepa*, the true guru who is mad with the fire of God, whose life and dharma has arisen in the West. Simultaneously, Lee Lozowick is unassuming and ordinary, even reticent and shy, in his most human way. Here we find another manifestation of Divine Alchemy at work; it is this exquisite juxtaposition between human and suprahuman found in the teacher that is most impelling, that piques our sensitivity and lashes the heart with the lure of those paradoxes that point toward transcendence.

A Return to Sacred Culture

In April 2005 I had the opportunity to spend time in the company of Purna Das Baul as he visited with Lee for a few days on tour in Arizona.[8] During the visit, Purna Das and his son, Choton, were candid

8 Purna Das Baul of Bengal is the son of the fierce Naboni Das Baul, singer and yogi par excellence. Purna Das was introduced as a performing artist to the West in the early seventies by Bob Dylan and Albert Grossman. He is known for his extraordinary ability to invoke divine moods through the beauty and power of his voice.

about the trend among the Bauls of Bengal today: their culture is dissipating, like everything else of the ancient past in India. Younger Bauls are not interested in village life; they want fame, travel, computer technology, cell phones, electronic stage equipment, money, fashion, recognition. This was yet another sign of the decay of sacred culture in our cynical times; the ephemeral life of the soul is of little interest to most people, and this attitude has spread from West to East like a contagious disease.

Oddly enough, it has been noticed by many great visionaries, including Yogi Ramsuratkumar, that the locus of spiritual knowledge and power seems to be moving from East to West. We can see this in the diaspora of Tibetan Buddhism and the transplanting of Zen in Europe and America. The world is crying out for a renewal of sacred culture in the West, which may be the only way to save what is left of sacred cultures in places like India, Africa, and Central and South America. Somehow, amidst the dark clutter and glittering debris of Western techno-culture, there is the glimmer of growing interest in the life of the soul and its eternal wisdom, shining here and there.

That the dharma is rising in the jaded, cynical West is hopeful. As Western Bauls we carry on with a commitment to the creative spark—in the market place, in music, dance, theatre, literature, poetry, feasting, or the great pleasures of family and friendship embraced as praise of the living Divine. These dimensions of the human experience are crucial building blocks of sacred culture. This is the seedbed in which a true life of the spirit and the great teachings of the ages may grow and thrive; simultaneously, sacred culture based on dharma, informed by divine law, is the fertile soil in which the creative spirit thrives in its many mediums of expression.

As Lee said recently, "The antidote to cynicism is faith." The true spiritual path and the engagement with the spiritual teacher forges faith and innocence in the disciple. A renewal of the inner life dispels the darkness of our times, and yet how easily we have forgotten that sacred culture does not exist without the spiritual guide—the archetypal teacher, shaman, preceptor or guru—in an active, crucial role. In the Baul path, the guru is at the center of the wayfarer's *sadhana.* This traditional stance is exactly what we find reflected in the stories of one summer on the road with Lee, who is at the center of the action, not because he himself has chosen to be, but because he has been placed there by divine intervention: by the grace of his master, Yogi Ramsuratkumar.

It's a rare and even strange occurrence that a Western teacher actually embodies the Baul tradition, since the Bauls have endured for five hundred years, springing out of the spiritual renaissance of medieval Bengal. Nonetheless, this is the path that Lee asserts, with his straightforward, steady certainty, has been given to him by the grace of his master, Yogi Ramsuratkumar. To a great degree this book is dedicated to the preservation of the Baul path in the West, particularly in that Lee Lozowick has, from the beginning of his teaching work in 1975, had an extraordinary natural gift for translating the eternal dharma of the East into a form that is workable and usable for Westerners in today's world. In 1999 I wrote about Lee in As *It Is*:

> *The Baul tradition has miraculously seeded itself in the West in the extraordinary way that the Bauls always arise—as a surprise, an epiphany, an organic burst of awakened life, a spontaneous expression of divine evolution. This evolution takes the form of a Baul master, Lee Lozowick, whose message is revealed in many discourses and spontaneous interactions with students that are threaded through the labyrinth of this book. The West urgently needs the Baul way of seeing and living, which is the way of the heart and the wise body . . . . The Western Baul gift to the world is a return to sacred culture, to the direct perception of the heart on fire, to the burning awareness of the living God within the cellular reaches of the body. It is a constant paean of praise to*

the human possibility in relation to the Divine, which may be discovered through kaya sadhana—and which turns each individual back in upon himself or herself to discover, with the help of the guru, the truth that slumbers within the human matrix.[9]

These words are as true now as they were six years ago; the essential teacher remains changeless in a changing world, even in the appearance of change in his teaching style. Lee Lozowick's legacy of spiritual teachings and dharma art is a gift to the world that cannot be measured except by the heart. It is my fervent prayer that this gift will endure across time as a message of compassion in times, like these, when we are so sorely in need.

M. Young
December 8, 2005

9 Young, M., *As It Is — A Year on the Road with a Tantric Teacher*, Hohm Press, Prescott, Arizona, 2000, p. xviii.

London

Prescott, Arizona
June 12, 2005

London! Place of myth and imagination, rich with history. Our transatlantic flight would be landing there in less than twenty-four hours, but we would not be seeing the historic sights of the city or floating down the Thames. Nor would we marvel at the exalted atmosphere of Westminster Abbey or take in Shakespeare at the Globe Theatre. London was just the first stop of the summer travels with our peerless guide, the Baul master Lee Lozowick, who spends every summer in Europe. And like every other summer, in order to keep up with Lee's pace, those of us who were traveling with him had a daunting schedule to embrace.

Two months ago, upon seeing the plan for our first five weeks on the road this summer, I wondered if I really wanted to uproot myself from the ashram in Arizona again this year. The stark beauty of the desert grows on one's sensibilities; for me, it has fermented slowly over years of life experienced within the refuge of the sangha and the peace that thrums beneath the busy, chaotic appearance of the ashram itself. Early summer in the high desert has its own special grace: nestled in a valley and surrounded by pine clad or rough and rocky mountains, the silver leaves of the tall cottonwood trees on the ashram shine in the morning sun. At sunset the indigo dome of the sky consorts with banks of crimson clouds on the western horizon, just before the wild tangled stretch of stars come out. Nowhere else have I seen the stars as they are in the southwestern desert of North America!

All this makes a sacred place that is very dear to my heart, but I reminded myself: this is a path of guru yoga. After ten years of summers living in France and traveling around Europe, four trips to India and many travels across the U.S.—from New York City to San Francisco and L.A. and countless places in between—courting the gracefully unexpected with my spiritual teacher, I should be well acquainted with the life of groundlessness and his rigorous style of travel. Attachments to the outer forms of daily practice, hearth and home must be abandoned for a deeper practice, yet remain with us as an essential wisdom, a subtle glow at the heart of who we are that feeds the life of a wayfarer on the spiritual path. This is one of many ways in which our spiritual path is similar to that of the Bauls of Bengal, who wander from village to village, singing songs of God and begging for the alms that will buy their daily rice and dahl. For a Western Baul, wandering takes a rather different form, and I reflected again on roads we would be traveling over the summer with Lee.

But today, on June 12, we were poised at the edge of the adventure, ready to leave Arizona and embark on another mystery tour with our teacher. Instead of our usual middle of the night or predawn departures when traveling with Lee, we planned to leave the Arizona ashram tomorrow at the reasonable time of early afternoon. We would drive two hours to the Phoenix International Airport and catch a direct flight to London in the evening. To get the less expensive lights, our rather large traveling party often has to change planes in the States, endure hours of layovers in stuffy, frantic airport *bardos* and drag luggage around—only to arrive at our first stop in Europe rather disheveled, disoriented and in a mental state reminiscent of a bad acid trip. This midday exit and direct flight was a boon, but in the process of sadhana, I've learned not to take such unexpected gifts for granted or expect them to show up again; we must draw no conclusions and proceed knowing that the next departure will probably be at three a.m. once again.

London
June 13

We arrived in London at midday quite fresh and very happy to see the British sangha, who had worked hard for weeks to prepare spaces and arrange for meals and events for the master's arrival, and everyone else who had traveled from France, Germany and Romania to spend this week with Lee. With our luggage, bags and book boxes packed into the flat where we were staying and food in our bellies, Lee was immediately in motion. We hadn't eaten the food on the airplane, and we were hungrily awaiting our first group meal with the sangha, which turned out to be a quick, eat-and-run style reunion picnic in the nearby grassy park with tall, stately trees.

It's usually Lee's way to churn up incredible momentum as soon as he arrives in Europe. After quickly giving orders to various people who were cleaning up after the picnic and setting up a plan for dinner, he took off with a small group walking hard and fast through the London streets for forty-five minutes until we reached a large, high-end antique show that was in progress. He had burned up the pavement to get there, and as soon as we arrived he plunged into the thick of things.

After three hours of following Lee through the aisles of gorgeous antiques of all kinds—from furniture to crystal, china, silverware, bronze sculpture, jewelry and everything imaginable that could spring from the endless well of human creativity—we walked back to the flat at Wolseley Road, our headquarters for the week. There we gathered with sangha members for a simple but luscious, much-appreciated dinner of green salad, raw veggies, bread, cheese and various other delicacies. After visiting for awhile in the salon with Lee while dishes were washed, the day came to its natural close. Taking the time change into account for the by-now quite tired travelers, Lee retired earlier than usual, well before midnight, allowing us all a good night's sleep.

Oxford
June 14

Today a small group of students were off with Lee to the beautiful, charming, very old English city of Oxford to visit with his friend, Robert Beer, author of *The Encyclopedia of Tibetan Symbols and Motifs* and renowned master *thangka* painter. Before we reached his house, Lee decided to stop for lattés at a little café in town. As soon as we sat down around the wooden tables in a back room, a lively conversation began about John Perk's book, *The Mahasiddha and His Idiot Servant,* which describes many provocative experiences of Perk's years with the controversial Tibetan *vajra* master, Chögyam Trungpa Rinpoche.

"The stories send shivers through you. It's great teaching," Lee said with a chuckle. He highly recommended the book as a "must read," then commented candidly about the intensity of Trungpa Rinpoche's style: "He was an incredible teacher . . . and I'm glad *I* wasn't there!" Lee laughed at this comment. Chögyam Trungpa Rinpoche was fearless and outrageous in his transmission of the teaching through action; he had stretched and provoked his students far beyond their usual frame of reference. Then Lee said, "Not me—I don't teach that way. I'm a *coward*!" He was partly referring to the recoil he would have to endure if he challenged his students to that degree.

Lee was in a playful mood as he engaged in conversation, touching on one subject and then another; it seemed he was using current issues, people and the spiritual path to communicate his viewpoint to Charlotte and Sue Kali, who he hadn't seen in nine months, as he quickly commented on several other teachers and, in particular, an article that had been published many years ago in a spiritual journal. In it the "senior" students of a so-called "tantric" path revealed details of their most advanced yogic practices in a way that Lee considered extremely distasteful and inelegant—a travesty of the spiritual path. These kinds of esoteric practices, he said, are considered "secret" practices for a good reason; such practices should only be passed on to those practitioners who are mature enough to guard and protect their own work by keeping their inner practices to themselves.

Just as quickly the talk jumped to the headlines in the newspapers we had just seen on the street: Michael Jackson had been found innocent of charges of child sexual abuse. Lee commented, "I *thought* he was innocent. The charges were trumped up by fortune hunters . . . Okay, yes, it's weird that he was sleeping in the bed with those kids, but every one of those kids said there was nothing sexual going on."

Lee's candor opened the door for several of us to express similar feelings of relief that Michael Jackson was exonerated. As strange and neurotic as he appeared to be, we all agreed, nonetheless he is a brilliant artist and businessman—a fantastic entertainer with more talent than most people can imagine in their wildest dreams. He seems to be a wounded black sheep who does not manage the fabulously opulent circumstances of his karma with wisdom or grace. Without question, he has continued to leave himself wide open for such accusations; anyone with that much talent, power and fame is likely to get attacked, especially if they are constellated by emotional trauma at age five, and need to sleep (not have sex, just sleep, we all hoped) with children to feel okay.

Putting the whole thing in perspective with a jest—because after all, it's only the theatre of the dream—Lee said playfully, "I wonder if Michael Jackson's new album will be called, 'I'm Free!' "

It was time to leave the café, and within minutes Lee was embracing his friend, Robert Beer, at the front door of his home.

We were ushered into the house and back to the sunroom, a small solarium looking out on the garden, a favorite project of Robert's partner, Jill, who arrived with cakes for our tea soon after we were settled. Lee and Robert, who share a love of the East, began to talk about the political turmoil in India, Bhutan, Nepal, Tibet and China. The conversation dwelled for a while on the world situation, and the recent tragedies in Nepal involving the royal family, as well as U.S. intervention in the East.

Suddenly, Jill and Robert brought up the headlines about Michael Jackson. It was an interesting bit of synchronicity that they spoke about this controversial African American megastar so soon after we had been talking about him. Their comments echoed our own, and they expressed compassion for this tragic stranger in a way that I found very moving.

Jill said, "He's been acquitted, but you know, he's a broken and ruined man. His face as a five-year-old child—it's unforgettable, when you see him now."

I thought to myself how much better it is to have compassion than to be cynical and always see the worst in people. It's easy to jump on the "we hate Michael Jackson" bandwagon, maybe because he is rich and famous, or because he is so odd and provocative in his unconventionality—or because of our own wounds, we project guilt on him rather than express mercy in the face of his suffering.

Robert ushered Lee and our party upstairs after tea to see some new Newari *thangka* art. Looking at the fabulous art that he displayed and hearing him speak about it, I was acutely aware that Robert Beer is one of the world's foremost experts on Tibetan Buddhist iconography. When discussing the sixty-four forms of Kalachakra, each with certain attributes, colors and specific symbolism, Chris asked Robert, "Is there anyone in the world who knows all this besides you?"

A simple and actually quite humble but truthful "no" was Robert's response. Then he added, "There are a few lamas who know this, but they are very old and may not live long." He pointed out a tiny inaccuracy on one of two absolutely gorgeous and mind-boggling *thangkas* of the three main *yidams* (meditational deities): Kalachakra, Chakrasamvara and one other I didn't catch.

Lee looked through the beautiful *thangkas* one by one and made a decision on which ones he would like to acquire. Robert watched him with interest. When Lee turned to Robert and went through the stack of *thangkas* in rapid-fire succession, "I'll take this one, this one, this one . . ." and so on, Robert commented, "You don't want to think about it?"

"No," Lee answered.

"I'm not trying to pressure you, you know," Robert said with a bit of a smile, "you've bought a lot already," referring to his visit with Lee at the ashram in Arizona two months before.

"You're not." Lee's response was the direct and simple answer of a man who knows what he wants and does not equivocate.

Some of us who were watching and had watched this kind of exchange numerous times commented that this was, in fact, just the way Lee liked to do business. Chris added, "He's happy when he's buying . . ."

While Robert carefully wrapped the *thangkas*, we went back downstairs to the sunroom and waited. Soon he came down with them compactly rolled into a tube.

"They're all in here," he said, handing them the tube to Lee. "I can't get over how fast you decided!"

Lee turned to Jill and smiled as he said, "I've lightened Robert's load this afternoon!"

"That means you've been shopping!" she smiled back.

It seemed to me like the most elegant, wise and civilized form of "shopping" there is—two people who share a passion for sacred art have an exchange, one level of which is the trading of art for money. It is a way of playing the role of merchant that Lee actively cultivates with everyone he meets these days—a richly nuanced way of being in the marketplace that has almost ceased to exist in the world today. Some are receptive to it; some are not. Robert Beer is highly receptive to it because his own life seems to be based on the same principles; he has access to a very rare treasure, which he makes available in the West because of his sacred relationship to the art itself.

After being further plied with tea and cakes and greatly enjoying the profusion of roses, jasmine vines and foxglove in the lovely English garden of our hosts, we said goodbye and drove back to London, promising that we would meet with Robert again at the end of the week, on Portobello Road. The traffic was not as bad as last year, when it took almost two hours to get back into London from Oxford, but the drivers on the road evoked a passing growl from our fearless driver, Lee, who said, "Next year, Purna and I are going to give a seminar on driving!"

Arriving at the flat in London, Lee was joined by the rest of the group, bringing our number back up to twenty-five. Inspired by the visit with Robert it seemed, Lee sat down in the salon, pulled out his journal and wrote for the next forty-five minutes. Lee's journal writings this summer would be made into a book—the fifth journal in a series he has published over the years, the last of which was the fabulous *Cranky Rants and Bitter Wisdom From One Considered Wise In Some Quarters.* It was great to witness the process of Lee's writing; like his poetry to Yogi Ramsuratkumar, most of which is written in morning meditation and is spontaneous and unpolished, his journals are also extemporaneous. They seem to whirl off his pen in the heat of the moment. They capture the essential Lee in one way, and it is these unstudied, ad lib journals, often using language in the style of the streets, irreverent, sassy, even profane—and in deliberately incorrect English—that contain what Lee considers to be not the teaching but the actual transmission of the teaching.

After an informal, buffet-style dinner—salad, bread and cheese laid out on a table in the small kitchen at the back of the flat—Lee held court ensconced in a chair in the small salon, which was now crammed with students, luggage and several big boxes that were brought over on the airplane. The mood became more and more spirited as he wove us all together in the tight space of the tiny living room over a lively conversation about art and antiquities. After a while, small glasses of wine were brought in on a tray, and when all the adults had been served, we raised our glasses as Lee offered the toast.

"Some of the sangha households that are filled with sacred artifacts are so breathtakingly magnificent, it's hard to explain," Lee said, the golden wine in his glass glinting a little in the light. "Let's hear it for everybody having a house like that!" Glasses were clinked together one by one, and then the taste of wine became our simple remembrance of that which is sweet and good, distilled from the essences of life and imbibed as an offering for the One who loves and enjoys.

Lee began to talk about his sadness and frustration over the fighting among the devotees of Yogi Ramsuratkumar in India. "It's a terrible situation," he said, then turned to the youngest of his children, who had come in to say that she was bored.

"Bored!" Lee said, "I'd much rather be alone than be with people—and here you are, bored! What an irony! Do you know what an irony is? Having all these devotees who want to be with me, and I'd rather be alone. A *great* irony!"

It's an even greater irony that someone who says he doesn't like people and would rather be alone can create a spiritual culture like the Hohm Community, which gives birth to such extraordinary, ordinary evenings of simple pleasures, shared by a diverse group of people—with four or five different languages and nationalities involved—who are bonded by the power of their sadhana and their love for the guru. It was the first of many such nights that would occur over the summer of travel, as the constellation of friends and students around Lee changed in a constant flow of people, juxtaposed against an ever-changing background.

Lee returned to talking about the politics in India at the Yogi Ramsuratkumar Ashram, where many people have become devotees of a popular young TV guru who is now associated with the ashram. Lee said, "The politics in India are just so Machiavellian, I don't even try to understand them."

The conversation changed again and Lee began to touch on a topic that he would speak about frequently as the summer wore on: making money. It was a timely topic, especially since he and Purna were scheduled to give a seminar at Ferme de Jutreau in September on money, how to make it and how to spend it wisely. Lee began by saying that we often feel afraid of success; we are afraid of bigness. Our guilt holds us back.

"Guilt is just a bad habit," he said emphatically. "It's just a bad habit . . . It's just a bad habit!" Repeating this statement three times seemed extremely important, as if he was hammering this information into us. He continued, "Unfortunately, bad habits are sometimes harder to get rid of than karmic retribution." He talked about how it is totally unnecessary to feel guilt about having money, as long as money is used for the right purposes.

"When we earn money that goes to serve the Work, we earn merit. Robert Beer is a great example of this: when he sells art, he is making it available for people to see. It breaks his heart when collectors buy a precious thangka painting and lock it away in their private spaces so no one gets to see it. He makes an agreement to take photographs of thangkas so he can make them available to museums and people in general. Every penny he gets goes to Nepal to support these incredible Newari artists. So, the more you pay for your Work, the more you Work. And the more you Work, the more you pay."

Lee continued to speak about the principle of paying for our own work; he said that "obligation in the Work" becomes active in us when we become capable of paying for our own Work. That means we are no longer dependent upon the guru to take care of us in any way; we really can stand on our own, in terms of our practice, our responsibilities both secular and spiritual, and our ability to create internal work for ourselves. We can create internal work for ourselves by engaging practices like the Heart Breath or Enquiry, self-observation, or simply by taking the way of blame.

The way of blame is articulated most effectively by the Sufi tradition. An example might be, if we are doing something as a part of a team and an error is made, we take full responsibility for it on ourselves, even if we are not the one who was personally, individually responsible. The Buddhist might say this is one way of "earning merit." A primary element of earning merit is that it usually occurs whenever we relieve the suffering of another being in some way. One of the big catches to this, as Lee said, is that everything we do to earn merit in this lifetime will not be remembered in our next incarnations.

"Yeah, I got pissed about that a few months ago!" Dave said, half joking and half serious.

Lee gave a short, ironic laugh. "That's the thing I'm most grateful for! You wouldn't be able to bear it, you know. If you understand karma in principle, then you stop generating negative karma. I don't want to know what happened in the past! Things are bad enough now—there's enough suffering in this life. I don't want to remember the suffering of other lives!" Taking off on a tangential but relative vein, Lee went on to say that in fact he hates suffering so much that he buffers himself against feeling it.

"I don't feel anything at all!" he snapped.

This paradoxical comment spurred Dave into action. Referring to Lee's devotional poetry to Yogi Ramsuratkumar, Dave protested, "But in your poems you say . . ."

"That's the nature of poetry," Lee cut him off mid-sentence with a smile and an enigmatic shrug.

"I don't believe you," Dave smiled. "The feeling I have when I read your poetry . . ."

"Maybe I'm being nondualistic in the poetry," Lee stated flatly, interrupting again. "I feel those feelings because *you* are feeling those things. The guru feels those things as a form of Work, because in the guru there is nobody to feel anything."

This rich teaching exchange signaled the end of the evening and left us all with plenty to chew on. Rarely does Lee make such statements anymore about the objective nature of the guru function, and his words inspired a volley of considerations for me. As he rose to leave the salon, I was still writing in my notebook. At the most apparent level, his words could be viewed purely as an expression of residing in the nondual perspective of reality. In other words, Lee doesn't feel anything because he is one with everything. In the state of union, there is only one. It takes two—a subject and an object—to "feel" something because feeling implies relationship and therefore duality.

There were multiple layers of meaning, it seemed, in what he said. "Enlightened Duality" is Lee's phrase that describes an objective state of consciousness that goes beyond the realization of nonduality. It is in this state that *true feeling*—as distinctly different from emotion—may arise, such as the moods, the *rasas*, of devotion, love, gratitude or praise that are so eloquently expressed in Lee's poems to his master, to which Dave was referring. Lee's statement was a testimony that experience is only objective when it arises from the fundamental realization of nonduality. And yet, he had said, "I feel those feelings because *you* are feeling those things. The guru feels those things as a form of Work, because in the guru there is nobody to feel anything." Now and then we catch a glimpse of ruin in the person of the guru—one who has become nothing, nobody, no one, who has been burned to ash in the fire of Yogi Ramsuratkumar.

London
June 15

This morning Purna Steinitz flew in from Germany to join Lee and his party. After Lee had picked Purna up from the airport and returned to Wolseley Road where we were staying, he was waiting patiently for everyone to leave the flat for the café. Dishes and laundry had to be dealt with, breakfast provided for kids, and so on, but there was a general mood of recoil and breakdown surrounding these activities, which made things much more difficult and sticky. When recoil rules, nothing goes right; we are usually too busy judging others, projecting and justifying our own misbehavior while failing to see clearly what we ourselves are doing—an activity that drains us of the energy needed for efficiency and economy of time and movement.

Some of Lee's students, who had come to join him for the day's activities, were standing outside on the sidewalk by the small rose garden, while others sat in the sitting room or stood near the front door. One of the children asked Lee, who was standing near the door and had been ready to go for about thirty minutes, "Why don't you leave, Daddy?"

Lee answered, "Because it's my responsibility to allow myself to be roasted by devotees until I'm well done and dead."

A few seconds later, someone said to the child, "We're waiting."

Lee added, "We're always waiting for somebody to get off it and just *be*."

That night Lee gave his first public talk in London, held at the Theosophical Society and titled, "When Spiritual Monsters Become Ordinary Monsters." Although the reports were that it was a fantastic talk, I didn't hear it—instead of going to the talk, five of us adults took the four kids to see *Les Miserables*, at Lee's encouragement. It's an opera he saw almost thirty years ago and loved. "You won't regret it," he said, and it was true. It was the guru, the dharma and the sangha, experienced in another form of art.

London
June 16

It was a long day of trudging around London on the hunt for antiquities, with a fabulous, much enjoyed interlude at the movies with the whole group: *Batman Begins*. Afterward we drove across London and parked the vans, then walked to a funky Middle Eastern restaurant that had been recommended by Charlotte's friend. Unfortunately, it turned out to be a cheesy place where the food was bad. There were over twenty people at the table, and we made our way through lamb and wilted lettuce plates. When everyone had finished eating, Magda, a young French student of Lee's who is opening a brocante and Asian antiquities shop in Paris with her partner, Bruno, asked Lee for his advice about the project.

"Never let anybody get to you," Lee began in an emphatic, forceful voice. "*Nobody*, ever. Even if you're shaking in your boots—never let anybody get to you. It's *your* shop. Be confident and never apologize to anybody for anything. People will come in and look around at things and find fault and complain, 'Oh, this has a crack in it, oh this is dirty.' Never apologize. 'Well, it's been worshipped for two hundred years—that's what happens!' Never apologize. Don't let anybody get to you! It's your shop. You'll be a fabulous salesman if you never let anybody get to you."

Lee seemed to be warming up for his second public talk, which would start in less than two hours. His passion in this rather lengthy communication was both very empowering for Magda and also a fast infusion of energy for everyone listening.

He continued, "When people find out what you've got and what you can get, people from New York, the rich and royalty will be coming to you. But as soon as you apologize, you've given away all your power. Don't ever apologize. If you apologize, the other person has all the power. Never apologize. Never let anybody get to you. People who have been in the business for thirty years will come in and try to tell you what to do—don't let anybody get to you. And never apologize!"

This communication carried such force and fire that I was compelled to write it down and reflect on it further. It seemed to me that the principle Lee was expounding had a much broader application in terms of our relationships with each other. We have been taught that it is "the right thing to do" to apologize for all kinds of things. Certainly at times an apology is called for, but so much of our apologizing is a form of manipulation, sentimentality and nostalgia—or worse, of self-hatred and self-loathing, or the way the adaptive child learned to make mommy and daddy love them or gain approval from authority figures. "Apologizing" becomes another draining psychological entanglement with each other; it is one of the prime ways to blow off energy when self-observation gets too uncomfortable in the constant flux of power dynamics between individuals.

In the seventies there was a popular American movie that was famous for the phrase, "Love means never having to say you're sorry." Lee's ferocious words to Magda put the "love" referred to in that pop truism in different terms. It's a love than has transcended emotional needs and entanglements, "You stroke me and I'll stroke you," those suspect interchanges fueled by guilt and a deep suspicion that we are not okay. It's a kind of love that *assumes* the Organic Innocence of self and other; a kind of love that assumes the other's integrity of practice and rests on pure good will for the other. There is no need to say "I'm sorry." The practitioner on the other end of the exchange doesn't need to hear it, either. All the way around, it's one of those things that falls into the "nostalgia is death" category, to use a phrase from Bob Dylan.

After dinner we drove quickly to the Theosophical Society, a beautiful old three-story house, where the talk would be held in a converted parlor on the first floor. The room had the classic look and feeling of the nineteenth century, done in ivory and gold, with chandeliers and ornate ceiling cornices embellished in a carved fruit and vine motif. The walls were home to old photographs of the venerable H.P. Blavatsky and Henry Olcott. Lee had a book table set up in the back from last night.

In the crowd of about forty people that quickly filled the elegant room to capacity, many were students and ex-students of Andrew Cohen, who has churned up a great deal of controversy and criticism in the past several years. An open debate about Andrew came out last year on the internet in a blog titled "What Enlightenment?" Many people had come forward with stories of emotional and financial abuse, and many others had contributed writings on both sides of the controversy. The night before, Lee's talk had been titled, "When Spiritual Monsters Become Ordinary Monsters." It would be interesting to see how he handled the high emotions in the room on this heated subject tonight.

From his first few opening lines, Lee was witty and sardonic: "One of the reasons I do public talks like this is because when I'm in cities I see lots of people I'd like to run over." Many people in the audience actually rose to the occasion to laugh at this, already knowing that Lee was up to some form of sleight of hand.

"How can a spiritual master be like that, you may ask?" he asked, with more than a touch of sarcasm. "Figure it out for yourself!"

Then he was off on a rant about French men and dogs, continuing on with several topics in rapid-fire succession, during which he railed against the ills of society, the pollution, toxicity and depravity in the world today. This passionate and scathing social commentary was quickly following up by blowing smoke to cover his trail, as he said, "Don't get me wrong—I don't know anything about politics or social action. My idea of social action is going to a disco and watching sexy girls dance!"

Lee's bawdy show up on the dais was impressive—his amazing ongoing creativity in bringing theatre, comedy, tragedy, irony, paradox, satire, love and despair into his talks and wrapping it all up with lots of laughs and fleeting moments of tenderness and communion with his audience. It was as satisfying as ever to watch him work. The onslaught was punctuated with hearty laughter coming from many people in the room (there were still a few who only chuckled a little now and then, and one or two who never seemed to crack a smile, but they stayed anyway), until at one point Lee said, "I'm glad to see some of you laughing—I hope that by the end of the evening, I have every one of you practically in stitches."

Then he was off on another trail: "Some of you probably know that women do not buy fancy underwear to impress men. If women don't buy fancy panties for the men they are with, then who do they buy them for? That may be the most important question we ask this evening! I'll say it again: If women don't buy fancy panties for the men they are with, then who do they buy them for? The most obvious quick answer is, for themselves. But there's more to it than at first glance . . ." Lee chuckled, paused, then said, "It's good in this world we live in to be strange and crazy . . ."

This comment was tossed off as if Lee was observing himself and reflecting out loud on his own theatre tonight. But as obscure as Lee gets, I often found wisdom lurking in the zaniest of his jokes and insinuations. The question he asked contained a very real metaphor—why do we women really wear silk and velvet, kohl our eyes, comb and braid our hair, dab sandalwood and rose perfume on pulse points? There is really only one answer, because there is really only one lover, and He isn't human. From the Baul perspective, there is ultimately only one answer to all questions.

Lee went on to talk about those who are under the illusion that "these people in cults are being victimized—they want you to be a good citizen and die for the state, not give your life to a spiritual teacher." After a chain of serious statements like that, he would veer back into double entendre and paradoxical satire: "It's much more important to have a good time than to be sitting there seriously considering the dharma, because the dharma is a bunch of *shit*, anyway!" People laughed at this one, but Lee didn't wait to enjoy it; not everyone was on the train yet, and he was working hard to enroll everyone in the transmission of the evening. He was on to one of his favorite subjects: women and power.

"I don't mind serving a woman, but I at least like the woman to *pretend* that I have some say in the matter. With most women, you don't even get to pretend that you have any say. But, you've got to be a little bit feminine to screw them right! I mean, if the man is so under your thumb that he wishes he was back with his mother . . ." Lots of laughter broke free; we were in universal territory, something everybody could relate to.

"Now we're on the right track!" Lee smiled.

Soon he moved on to the main theme of the evening: The same qualities that make a good disciple are the exact qualities that make a good master. He would return many times to comment on how the disciple is responsible for himself or herself. For example, when does the disciple, whose practice is obedience to the teacher's instruction, say no to the teacher?

Lee said provocatively, his voice rising almost to a shout, "People are always saying, 'follow your heart.' You should follow your common sense and your instinct and *not* your heart, because your heart is fucking *stupid*! Your heart has *emotions*! . . . . So, your heart is totally untrustworthy. Your heart, *your heart*, my friend, is just a *muscle*! Your heart responds to flash and glitter! Your heart is full of emotion. We went to see *Batman Returns* today . . ."

Lee went off on a very instructive tangent in which he used the popular attraction to famous and beautiful people as an example of following the heart, obviously referring to the lowest level of heart. He humorously lambasted himself in this regard, saying, "If Catherine Zeta-Jones came to my community, I would roll out the red carpet for her—not just the red carpet, but a red carpet with diamonds on it. Really! If Catherine Zeta-Jones came to my community and said, 'Make me a lineage holder,' I'd say yes!"

Another burst of laughter was unleashed, especially from Lee's students, but they were not alone. At this point most of the audience was on Lee's side, enjoying the ride in the backwash of his speedboat through hell.

"Yes! That's the heart! Because the heart responds to chemistry! I'm kidding ..." Lee fooled around, going on to Gurumayi and her hats: "I could only have sex with her if she wore one of those little pillbox hats—those things are *sweet*! I'm just kidding ... No, I'm serious," his eyes twinkled, remembering the way comedian Eddie Izzard used that ploy. "No, I'm just kidding . . . But Bob Dylan! Bob Dylan is one of my *heros*! Really, if Bob Dylan came to my community and said, 'I tried Christ, I tried the Native Americans, but I really like this path ... can I be a lineage holder?' 'Yes, Bob, anything you want!' "

Lee became mildly serious as he returned to his original train of thought: "That's the heart. The heart is not trustworthy. Common sense is trustworthy." Compassion, he said, is another thing altogether. Compassion does not necessarily arise without some kind of intention for it; compassion must be cultivated. Lee continued, "Like the Dalai Lama said, you have to be *practicing* compassion . . . . So, you don't do the things you think with your mind, unless you are willing to indulge the stream of consciousness. If you don't indulge the thought, you avoid the consequences of a bitter argument with your lover."

Lee made the point that our attempts to change or manipulate others, including the spiritual master, into being who we want them to be, are fruitless. We cannot train the spiritual master to be who we want him to be; instead, we must become good disciples.

"We are ultimately responsible for ourselves. We are not victims. We are all adults. We've all been burned, been screwed, eaten in bad restaurants, bought bad cars. Dennis O'Leary, a comedian, says there is no continuous happiness in life. He says that happiness is the next cigarette; happiness is just the moments between your misery. There is no happiness in life. Look at Andrew. Is he happy? I'm not asking if he's enlightened—is he happy?" Lee talked about how brilliant Andrew Cohen is, what a thrill it is to hear him speak the dharma and how sublime it is when intellectual brilliance gets turned to the dharma. Then, he was back to the subject at hand.

"All life is suffering. *All* life is suffering—it's a terrible realization. The Dalai Lama hears things about his monks being tortured every day—do you think he's a happy man? No. Do you think

Ammachi is happy? No, because she knows that the Westerners who come and just sit at her feet are never going to get what she is transmitting in a million years! You think she's a happy camper? No!"

This consideration lead to an exultant exposition on the joys of wine, chocolate and coffee—and living in France—then a return to the theme of taking personal responsibility as disciples and students of the teacher. Lee talked about how there are certain criteria that make one a good disciple; for example, not putting our personal suffering on the shoulders of the teacher.

Lee continued, "Every time the teacher asks something of us and we say yes, it's upon our own authority that we say it. It is our responsibility to get clear with ourselves to never say yes unless that yes comes from a mature adult within us. Do we stop to think of the consequences when we say yes, yes in the moment? Do you, in the moment, think of the consequences when you say yes to the spiritual teacher? It's our responsibility to respond as an *adult*."

Lee spoke about how we can be fooled into thinking that, because we've had a profound insight, some enlightenment experience, a satori, that we are the first ones in the world to have that experience. We claim it as our own, when it is a universal experience that has been articulated by many other spiritual paths and realizers before us.

"My God . . . what pretension! What hubris! Is that how you say that word?" Someone in the audience corrected Lee, giving the word "hubris" a French pronunciation, when in fact he had given it the correct (by the dictionary) English pronunciation.

Lee continued, "The Path is *not* about freedom. There is such a thing, but if you want it, stay off the Path. How do you explain that the Path has captured your soul? You can't explain it, but it's true, it's real. Maybe Gurdjieff might have called that objective love. Here we are in this state of love, and our teacher begins to do things. Oh! I didn't finish about bosoms. I used to be into bosoms, not the things down below. I *was* into bosoms, but now they're just canvases upon which to imprint permanent art—tattoos!"

After dwelling briefly on tattoos and how addictive they are, Lee began to talk about the necessity to be engaged in life. "We live in a horrible world, and we need to be engaged in it. What good is it to run off and be alone? What good are all our practices, without engagement? It is our personal responsibility to bring certain criteria to the path as a disciple, and if we do, we will know when to walk away from a teacher, and how deeply to get involved. We need to stand in perfect individuation, to use a term from Carl Jung . . . . "

Suddenly, the irreverent Lee was back and he was reeling drunkenly through old jokes, with mad talk about farts, sex, shit. "I let a few things *slide* out tonight . . ." he chortled, "I have to work on that! So, come back to the book table, if I haven't ruined it!" Lee started to talk about the books on the back table and suddenly shifted to some interesting comments on the two greatest French poets of all time.

"You know, Rimbaud wasn't human when he wrote poetry. He only became human at the end of his life, and he wasn't writing poetry any more. Baudelaire was so human—his work is *spiked* with love . . . "

The reverie was short-lived. Then he was talking about the big books on the book table again. "*As It Is*—two years of toilet paper, for a man! Aren't all men constipated? By the way, speaking of wiping your ass, don't grow your hair this long—it definitely gets in the way." Lee picked up one of his dread locks that hung below his waist as he sat in the chair on the dais.

I wondered: Who is this man? Despite the fact that I've known Lee for almost twenty years, it was one of those talks that left me shaking my head in amazement at his skill and capacity to weave in tremendous subtlety and innuendo of teachings, while at the same time taking direct shots at ego and provoking his audience to stretch beyond their psychological comfort zone. It's very difficult, if not impossible, to capture these talks in writing, even when they are transcribed, because Lee creates a chamber that operates on energetic principles. It is a matter of transmission. For me personally, the high note was hit when Lee said, speaking of Ammachi, "The guru will test you in a serious, demanding way, until you can maintain equanimity in a battleground."

That last phrase—*maintain equanimity in a battleground*—is the demand of the fast path, and we have to remember that the teacher will test us again and again, in ways that may be very unpleasant for ego, until we have that equanimity. I would use that teaching as a great reminding phrase for the summer ahead, where the battleground of the fast path promised to get pretty hair-raising in moments.

London
June 17

All day, from five a.m. to five p.m., we drove around London with Lee, following him from one antique mall, fair or shop to another. At the end of the day we were rewarded with a lovely supper at Wolseley Road, prepared by the sangha, of a large, sumptuous salad with saucisson, bread, wine and a rich dessert. Gathering with the sangha to share food was a welcomed respite from our day on the streets of the city.

These dinners were very informal affairs, with our large group sprawling throughout the flat and into the small garden in the back, holding our plates on our laps in whatever spot we might have found to sit or perch. Lots of animated conversations went on in various corners of the house, while Lee sat in the little salon with a few people squeezed together on the couch, on chairs or on the floor.

After supper, Lee pulled out some boxes of *108 Poemes et Prieres à Yogi Ramsuratkumar* that we had brought with us on the airplane from the States. It had just arrived, hot off the press, only days before we left Arizona, and now he was ready to unveil this premiere book of his poetry to Yogi Ramsuratkumar translated into French. Everyone immediately jumped on the opportunity to buy at least one copy. People were visibly moved as they turned the pages, lingering over the photos and then poring over the first poems. There seemed to be a magical way that the beauty and depth of the French language enhanced the meaning of the poems, juxtaposed as they in French as they were beside the original English versions. Everyone was struck with the beauty of the slim volume. Lee signed the books and wrote *dedicaces*. I saw tears on more than one face. The mood of divine remembrance was brought into focus and remained, like a faint perfume in the air, for the rest of the night.

At one point Oana asked a question about working with the emotional center.

Lee responded, "We use this word 'intention'—having an aim. The more intention we have, the more clarity we have to observe ourselves. When we self-observe it creates remorse, because of all the time we've wasted not working. Remorse is like rocket fuel to intention. If we are actually self-observing, it does create remorse, and remorse creates intention, so we don't need any technology. We don't need to know what's happening. Intention orients the body toward what is needed to be someone who is intrinsically noble and dignified. You don't need an in-depth explanation or definition of dignity and nobility—like 'Serving the Will of God,' it's tacitly obvious."

Another student asked, "What does it mean to open myself completely to receive the blessings of the lineage?"

"To see ourselves as we are without judgment," Lee answered. "Not to pat ourselves on the back, or only see negative things. All those judgments are just personality. To make a judgment about one frame in the movie doesn't in any way reflect the whole movie. So, it's simply to see things as they are, because in the next instant, it can be different; in one moment, we were selfish, and in the next, we were compassionate! Any judgment locks us into what is categorically untrue. With intention, it all goes on by itself—we don't have to do anything. What changes something is when there is self-observation at the causal level, not just at the conscious level of the mind, but at subtle levels . . . "

From Portobello Road to Brighton
June 18

Lee spent the entire morning at the world-famous antique market on Portobello Road. There were hundreds of people packing the street, milling about and wandering through the labyrinth of the market where vendors were selling everything from food to cheap (but expensively priced) import goods, junk, and high-end antiques. Lee and Purna very slowly and deliberately moved through the maze of shops and stalls, while everyone else followed at a respectful distance—not too close, but close enough to see when Lee was ready to move on. Often we would wait in one spot for thirty minutes while Lee conducted business with a vendor, and in this way, the minutes and then hours drifted past. By midday we were hot and ready to sit down in a café.

Around two p.m. Robert Beer met with Lee and his group. He had come in from Oxford to deliver some art to Lee before we moved on to Brighton. We settled in a café with Lee, Robert and Robert's daughter, who also joined us for a while. After a visit over coffee and then an affectionate round of goodbyes, we went our separate ways.

By late afternoon we were back at Wolseley Road, where the entire entourage of over twenty people had to re-organize our luggage, boxes and bags of stuff to move camp to Sue Kali's place in Brighton. Lee and his family would be staying at her apartment, where some meals for everyone would be served, while others were staying at the apartment of Sue Kali's generous friend. We had so much luggage—now augmented with Lee's purchases of antiquities and large amounts of bedding and food—in the two Ferme de Jutreau vans that we knew we would have some overflow for Sue Kali's own van, which she was driving.

We were sitting in the silver van, ready to go, while a few people were packing the last bags and boxes. Lee was in the driver's seat behind the steering wheel, ready to leave. There was a quick, heated, loud discussion about where several bags of bedding were going to go. Some of us were saying that there wasn't enough room for everything, which moved Lee into action.

"I will pack those into Sue Kali's van myself," he snapped as he jumped out of the van, "and they *will* fit. It's *not* a problem!" He strode over to the other van and started stuffing bags and boxes into the back.

Then there was the issue of where to put all the people. When Charlotte suggested that Lee take two more in his van, which was already packed with nine people, he said no, and sent them back to Sue Kali's van. We quickly discovered that Sue Kali's van had a flat. Rather than have the two men, Everett and Victor, change the tire, Sue Kali wanted to have her British service system come out and do it, because the job would "be insured." With the two French ashram vans loaded to the gills and packed with people, Lee finally took off for Brighton, leaving Sue Kali in her van with Grigo and Victor to wait for the tire to be changed.

An hour and a half later we saw the sea sparkling in the distance. We drove into Brighton to a complex of large, stately apartment buildings with sweeping green lawns and trees. This beautiful scene overlooked the gray-green-blue sea in the form of the English Channel just across the road and boardwalk. Dave and Jhanka were already in the apartment, preparing a meal for everyone. Walking into the space, our senses were immediately delighted by the many, fabulous bronze and stone artifacts—the sacred art Sue Kali had acquired from Lee—that graced the living room and brought it to life. Many of the deities had fresh flower offerings, candles or full shrines dedicated to them. There was a strong feeling of sanctuary, and we immediately settled in and relaxed from our travels.

The large, wide-open windows looked out over the sea, where the late afternoon sun sparkled and shimmered. It struck us all as quite a poignant situation that Sue Kali was hosting her guru in her home—so carefully prepared and especially appointed for him—for the first time, but the twist of fate was such that she wasn't there to welcome him herself. Another nourishing and satisfying dinner of salad, delicious English cheddar and Scottish oatcakes came and went, and still, there was no Sue Kali.

Finally she called to let Lee know that she had had a horrendous time of it after the tire was changed: she had been driving down the highway when the lug nuts, which were not tightened down properly when the tire was changed, came loose. The tire started wobbling and coming off the wheel hub of the van as she barreled along at sixty-five miles an hour. She barely made it to the side of the road, and upon calling her road assistance company, she was told that they were having a bad evening of it, with an accident on the road and the road being closed. They were so busy that it would be midnight before they could come to assist!

Lee suggested that she call them back and apply some pressure to the situation. After all, it was their responsibility that she and her passengers could have been badly injured or killed. That night Dave made two different trips to where Sue Kali was broken down on the highway to bring food, retrieve bedding and offer assistance. It was two-thirty in the morning before they all got back to Brighton. I'm not sure if there was a lesson to be learned in the whole escapade, but if there was, perhaps it was: rely on the sangha, not on the world.

Brighton
June 19

After two hours of sleep, Sue Kali, Charlotte, Dave and Jhanka were bright and enthusiastic when they met Lee and his companions at five a.m. in the parking lot of the apartment building. We were on our way to the famous English "car boot" sales—flea markets of a kind, where people sell things out of the trunk (that is, "car boot") of their cars. After roaming around at the first sale, we settled down at a plastic table beside the snack wagon at six-fifteen. We ordered "bacon booties"—that is, bacon and egg sandwiches—and melted cheese on slabs of bread the size of a brick. Lee sent two people in search of café lattés, but it was too early for any good coffee places to be open, and so we settled for some hot tea.

An hour later we made our way to The Meeting Place Café by the sea, where café lattés could be found. The other members of Lee's traveling party slowly began to arrive from their lodgings in Brighton or London. The sun was up high by now and shining on the water as we drank our coffee and watched people jogging down the boardwalk.

Lee held forth: "Exercise is one of the most screwed up human activities of all . . ." He looked around at our incredulous faces. "Really!" He added this, as if for emphasis, just in case we didn't think he really meant it. After all, he had been advocating exercise for years as one of the basic disciplines of spiritual practice.

He extrapolated, "I think it would be better if people just didn't exercise and had heart attacks. All they have to look forward to then is crumbling, disintegrating, veins clogged with fats . . . ."

"Because jogging as exercise is so contrived?" I asked, seeking clarification.

"I don't know," Lee shrugged. "It's a terrible thing."

Ann added, "We've just become so removed from natural activity."

Charlotte mentioned that she would be getting a black belt in aikido after three years of practice. In the training she is getting, the black belt is just the beginning of aikido practice, not a symbol of attainment. We were all surprised to hear this; it seemed like a disempowerment of aikido as a traditional form of practice.

Lee said, "That's dangerous. You could get hurt out on the streets, thinking you can do something that you can't do. In Japan a black belt is a sign of substantial mastery. You should be able to kick six people's butts with a black belt! It's like in Zen—people get authorized to teach, and they have no emotional maturity in their bodies."

A steady stream of people walked past. Watching them, Lee suddenly piped up, "I got a million dollar idea! Videos of ordinary people having sex—misshapen, fat, tall, bald, bow-legged, old hairy backs . . . on women!" We started laughing at the images he was conjuring. "You go to these porn videos—they are totally predictable! All the women look exactly the same. Ordinary people having sex would be fascinating! Everybody different, unique."

He went on, "Internet sex—people are hooked on it now. It's disgraceful. Don't you ever sit in a restaurant and see some couple, the guy's legs are skinny, he's toothless and bald, his wife is fourteen inches taller than him, and you wonder what it's like when they have sex?"

Purna said, "It could even be a new book, like the tattoo book. It could be called 'Alchemy and Agony'!" Everyone laughed.

Lee said, "It would probably sell like crazy."

Purna began to talk with Lee about one of his student who won't take any feedback but who is extremely competent and loves to work. He asked, "What do you do with someone who you just can't give feedback to?"

Lee answered, "What do you do with people you can't give feedback to? Give them more work. Give 'em six jobs, keep piling it on—that's what I would do! Keep 'em busy!" He was speaking rather loudly and distinctly, which made it possible for everyone at the long table to hear him easily.

Purna continued, "She's a really hard worker. She does the jobs of four people."

Lee said, "Why give someone like that feedback? Just keep 'em busy. You give them feedback, and then they become conscious and just do the work of one-half a person!" Lee sat with his baseball cap turned around backwards on his head and his sandals on. His mood seemed mild and relaxed, but his statements had a sharp, irascible edge that demanded deeper reflection.

The gang of young teenagers and several of the adults who were traveling with Lee arrived to join him. He waited patiently while they ordered and ate their food. Finally, he said, "Let's go!" and off we went to two more car boot sales, the last one out in the English countryside under a broiling sun. Lee spent several hours scouring the flea markets for that rare antique item that sometimes lies hidden in a pile somewhere, but he seemed rather disappointed by the end of the day. The rest of us had found a few bargains—inexpensive second-hand clothes, perfect for beggars, and CDs for the kids.

On the way back into Brighton in the early afternoon we hit a traffic jam and were stopped on the road for an hour. Sitting in the back of the van, tired, sun-struck, bittersweet with leaving London behind and touched by the faint sea breeze of longing, I looked out over the rolling hills and golden green fields of the English countryside. Finding myself in a place I'd never seen before and would probably never see again, I had that familiar sense that we were wanderers, adrift in timelessness, in search of something so elusive that it couldn't really be found. Finally the van started rolling down the road again, and the moment passed. Soon enough we were back in Brighton, with twenty-five of us sitting close together at six tables outside the Café Nero.

Café life with Lee is the same everywhere in the world—a place where we feel at home, even though we are thousands of miles away from it. At this particular café we were only two blocks away from the sea, and I could see the sun shining on the surface of the water from where we sat. A light and buoyant mood of camaraderie fell on our group. Brighton is known as an international party town, and our bunch of American mutts, Brits, Romanians, French, Germans and one Italian seemed to fit right in—in a Baulish sort of way. Lee was in very high, if still irascible, spirits. Just as we were finishing our iced double-shot lattés and chocolates, Lee looked around the table at his group as if to assess our state of being, and said, "Self-indulgent spirituality! That's what this is. I think we should copyright it! Give seminars on it! 'Mine, Me . . . No, Maxi-Me!' "

The dinner cooks soon left to start preparations. Purna and I began to talk about a phenomenon that seems to be ubiquitous in ashrams everywhere: people come to visit the guru, they haven't seen him for months, maybe even a year, but they stop to eat at a restaurant before they arrive instead of coming directly to the guru and receiving his hospitality. Or else, they come to visit the guru, but cling tenaciously to their partners and run off to "be together" every chance they get, instead of embracing the opportunity to be in the guru's world.

Overhearing this, Lee chimed in: "That happens all the time. People come to visit the ashram but stop first to have a meal—unbelievable!"

Changing the subject, he commented on some young people who were walking down the street sporting large tattoos on their arms. Tattoos have been one of Lee's passionate interests of the past five years, and now he observed the abundance of tattoos in the local scene with interest, commenting, "There are lots of tribal tattoos here—not just one or two, but arms and shoulders covered with them. They were all over the swap meet this morning . . ."

After a few more numbers of our group left, two of the adults took some of the children back to the apartment by way of the beach bordwalk. Still sitting at the café, I turned to Sue Kali and asked, "How does it feel to have the guru on your home turf?"

"Brilliant!" Sue Kali beamed, then added, "Somewhere between terror and excitement! Right now it's the excitement end of it." Indeed, Lee looked beatific sitting there. I noticed a sign not ten feet away from where we were sitting that said "Young Lee." Indeed, Lee seemed very youthful and vibrant that afternoon, despite his commentary on our self-indulgence. It was a relaxed circumstance in which we could enjoy the sea breeze and soft air, watch the flow of people going by. Overhead the blue sky was marbled with a soft hazy pattern of cirrus clouds. We were basking in the pleasant atmosphere of each other's good company.

Wanting more of the guru's commentary, I asked, "So, what would a seminar on self-indulgent spirituality be about?"

Purna laughed and said, "People could look in each other's eyes."

Lee answered, "You know: you don't have to practice; who you are is perfect, as you are; we would eat lots of chocolate . . ." He smiled.

Just then a woman walked past wearing nothing but a black satin half-slip for a skirt and a scant camisole. Her hips shook as she motivated down the street. Watching her closely, Lee commented, "That woman is wearing underwear, right on the street. Look—that's nothing but a slip!"

Soon we left the café and clambered back into the van, which Lee whipped quickly through the streets, back to the apartment for dinner. It quickly became apparent that dinner was ready on time but a number of people weren't there yet. Where were they? Lee turned to Purna and said, "People should know by now that six o'clock dinner means *be there* at ten minutes to six."

Dinner is almost always at six o'clock, the same time that it is on the ashrams. This is an ongoing source of frustration that Lee has often voiced with his students: one of the most fundamental ways in which we commit to a life of practice, in a very immediate and practical way, is to be ten minutes early to all events. We're an unruly bunch—rebellious, casual, sloppy, sentimental, self-referenced and asleep at the wheel a good part of the time. As Lee had said at one point earlier that day, "When you travel with a group this large, you have to eat shit." However, by my observation (as one of the casual, sloppy, self-referenced etc), it has been much worse than this when Lee has been traveling with a large entourage.

The plan for the evening was a British movie —a satire, highly farcical and ridiculous, but funny nonetheless. We walked down the boardwalk to the movie. The van was waiting for us when we got out to take everyone back to the apartment, but to Lee's chagrin, the second of two minor but expensive accidents in the ashram van occurred when the driver of the van backed into another car—the first one occurring when the van was being parked in heavy traffic near Portobello Road. His frustration about these accidents brought another volley of commentary. In both cases he had dispatched a member of the London bordello to drive the van (under the unusual circumstance that he was unable to do the job himself); of course, they each felt terrible about their mishap. One of his remarks about this was: "I always think people are capable of so much more than they are . . . I just assume they can drive the van. When will I ever learn? People should tell me when they don't really know how to drive the van. I guess we don't know ourselves that well. But I guess *I* am just naïve."

We were having a wonderful time together, the mood was great, love and communion were flowing like an endless bottle of the finest wine. But Lee's ongoing commentary was telling us that we were not traveling or functioning according to his wishes, in the way he has attempted for years to train us: like a well-honed special forces team—special *sadhana* forces, that is—that can act or move fast, pay attention in all situations, hold context, remain vigilant even when tired, maintain clarity and equanimity in a battlefield. The real question was: When will *we* ever learn?

Brighton
June 20

While we were sitting in the living room eating breakfast at nine o'clock, someone asked Sue Kali if he could use her house phone to make a call to France.

"Yes," she said amiably, "this is Lee's house now."

"Well, it will be on your bill," he responded.

"I'll bill you," she said.

"Oh, really?" He seemed vaguely surprised.

Not quite sure why he didn't just say, "Of course, please let me know how much I owe for the call," I couldn't refrain from adding my two cents. I muttered, "Well, that *is* standard procedure, you know."

Overhearing this, Lee grumbled, "People have no sense of protocol. We join the community and think, 'Oh, let's use everybody's resources with abandon!' We do not respect each other's boundaries—we get into community and we think we have rights over the lives of others."

Paula was leaving to drive the van to the airport in London this morning to pick up the rest of our traveling party, which was arriving at one p.m. from the States at Heathrow Airport. Our young teenage contingent would then be complete: six teenagers between thirteen and fifteen years old and one twelve year old. She stopped to ask Lee about food for the day, knowing that the group of kids would be tired and hungry.

Lee had already announced that we were going out that night, to a café just across the boardwalk, for our one big restaurant meal while in Brighton. He was enthusiastic about everyone having a really nice dinner there, and he had encouraged us to have a big breakfast and nothing else, except maybe coffee, for the rest of the day, until dinner. "Eat hearty!" he had said with a smile.

"If it was *me* picking up the kids," he responded to Paula's question, his tone dripping with sarcasm, "knowing they'll see all the exciting restaurants and want to stop along the way and want to eat, I would say *no*, but . . . *I* won't be there, *you* will be, so *you* do whatever *you* want to do."

That communication left no room for doubt, and so, with their working instructions quite clear, Paula and Brinda left with three of the teenagers in tow to pick up their buddies. In the meantime, Lee had already turned his attention on making a trade with Sue Kali: musical instruments of indigenous people from India and Africa in exchange for Sacred Bazaar items. He picked out one or two instruments, then turned a baleful, facetious eye on the women who were sitting there watching the drama of it all and drawled, "Most of the women are so choked with desire, they will want to raid the place!" Was he assuming that, based on our usual state of mind, we were probably coveting every instrument she had? He continued in the same vein, "I'm sure if the women know these instruments are available, they think they can play them *well* in the darshan hall. They're so dedicated, they'll want to learn to play them, but it will never happen, and they'd just collect dust. But, these will look good hanging on the walls."

Pointing to the Thai, Chinese and Greek wooden stringed instruments, the tambourines, xylophones, reed pipes, beaded gourd shakers, hand drums and assorted other things, he said, "I'll take that, that, that," more or less making a full sweep of everything she had.

At one point he paused, looked at Sue Kali and said, "Are you sure you want to trade all of these?"

"Yes, yes! Take it all!" she smiled.

Before we knew what had happened Lee had swept us all out of the apartment and into Brighton in search of antique shops. While we walked the old cobblestone streets we passed a pub with a wooden sign hanging from a post that said "The Druid's Head" in the style of the Dark Ages. As he walked through the winding village lane, Lee stopped for a brief moment, just long enough to point at the image of a Merlin-type figure that was carved on the sign: a wise old man with a long white beard.

"Look! There's Yogi Ramsuratkumar!" he said cheerfully. It seemed to me that he was really saying, "Yogi Ramsuratkumar is everywhere we go." Yogi Ramsuratkumar is everywhere we go, and that fact is the eye of the storm, the guiding star, the refuge of all travelers. Immediately he walked on, stopping a minute later to notice a porn ad in a window that depicted two partially nude women, named "Lucy and Michelle," hanging suggestively on each other.

"I think I should follow Lucy and Michelle's story!" He laughed.

Lee stopped at one shop that had antique weapons in the window—old Colt Derringers, French Napoleonic pistols, samurai swords and fancy knives. "It's great the way he displays these," he complimented the vendor, "on the shelves, like that." The Civil War pistols particularly drew his attention. "Cool . . . really cool stuff."

Very soon Lee was hooked into the local antique network, connecting with shop owners, shaking hands, walking with them down the street to their friends' shops. It was a tourist area, and merchants were not very willing to give Lee the discount he usually asks for. He moved on to an Asian arts dealer, where he disappeared down the stairs and into the basement to pour over treasures for an hour or so with Purna, while we waited out in the foyer of the mall.

Lee and Purna finally emerged, having made a satisfying deal. We immediately moved on and by noon were settled at another Café Nero, where we ordered with a little less confusion than usual and sat down fairly easily. I, however, got snarled up in my own comfort zone of wanting the exact same iced coffee drink that I had enjoyed so much the day before at another Café Nero. I didn't just want ice in my coffee; I wanted a café frappé with blended ice, a desire that became rather tiring as I observed myself going to great lengths to get it . . . unsuccessfully. It was a waste of energy—however, it was an opportunity to observe, once again, that desire is endless. Why not just be satisfied with whatever form the coffee came in now? The coffees came out, and they were very good.

"Oh yeah, triple shot!" Lee said with a satisfied smile. "You *know* there's coffee in this cup!"

Ann was perusing a copy of a free, local soft-porn magazine titled *New Currents*. One of the articles was titled "Dirty Weekenders," with photographs of half-naked men and women in "titillating" postures that were completely vacuous, unattractive and devoid of any true eroticism. Nonetheless, it provided another opportunity for Lee to comment as he took the magazine in hand and flipped briefly through its pages.

"Looks terrible!" Lee snapped, tossing the magazine aside. "If it's wild sex, it's wild sex, but all that posing is so boring it's unimaginable—who could enjoy that? But, that's me: old, boring, no-fun fart, who'd rather get in a Peugeot and drive around in the mountains looking for antiques any time!"

Chris commented that the doorway to the Sacred is closed in perverted sex. This is indeed the Kali Yuga, we agreed; the degradation of sexuality gets more and more pronounced every year.

The magazine had an article that mentioned Russ Meyer, a director of pornography videos. Lee said, "Russ Meyer is the Wes Craven of porno films—it's the worst imaginable, the lowest form of exploitation and manipulating emotions." I had never heard of Russ Meyer. I wondered at his ability to stay attuned to the pulse of our times in such ways. A voracious reader, Lee has a way of picking up information from different sources; it often seems to me that his attention on something has basic as a magazine article shines light into dark corners of our culture. He handed the magazine back to Ann, who put it on the table. I picked it up and thumbed through it to see what he had been looking at. There was an article titled "Babylon by the Sea," which said, "Brighton has always been a haven for the free thinker, the libertine and the louche." Then, a paragraph later, "If Brighton was a woman, she would be a sunshine-haired, honey-skinned succubus."

As I discovered, the famous Brighton Pavilion—which was less than two blocks away from where we were sitting—was built in the style of an Eastern palace by the prince regent, a son of Queen Victoria, Prince Edward V, who was a playboy and hedonist. The magnificent architecture of the pavilion is famous all over the world. Of course, we would not be seeing it. It simply was not of interest in the guru's world, other than to inspire the conversation at our table, which then turned toward how the outrageously rich and powerful have always been patrons of the arts, including great architectural feats like the Brighton Pavilion. Lee was saying that supporting the arts is something that wealthy people can do to earn merit, in the

Buddhist sense of the word. In this regard, he started talking about the young Newari artist, whose *thangkas* Lee had acquired from Robert Beer. The young painter, one of the finest in the world, could not make enough money from his paintings to live in the U.S., but fortunately, an American philanthropist became his patron.

We returned to the apartment around two-thirty in the afternoon and regrouped in a bridge game that lasted for hours, with some of us switching off as partners while Lee and Purna played together as usual. As the game proceeded, Sue Kali and I talked about Rabindranath Tagore (1861-1941), who considered himself a Baul and is widely recognized as the first person of considerable public fame to appreciate the importance of the Bauls in the spiritual culture of India. Tagore actively spread the teachings of the Bauls and brought their art—poetry and song—to the public eye. He seemed to consider himself a Baul poet as well. Sue Kali has a passion for Tagore and has been trained in the classical Indian style of singing his songs.

Tagore was, of course, a prolific creative genius. She handed me a volume of his poetry to read. I had forgotten that Tagore won the Nobel Prize for literature. As I read the biographical notes at the beginning of the book, I discovered an interesting bit of synchronicity: Tagore had spent time in Brighton as a young man. I looked at an English version of one of his many songs—a rather rough but accurate and heartful translation by Bisheswar Bhattacharya; the words struck a familiar chord, and immediately the mood of longing was invoked:

> This, my searching for myself, never ends
> And with it, my searching for You
> In so many births and deaths at Your feet,
> I will dedicate myself to You, but still my debt will grow
> I must descend to all the river ghats
> Again and again in this world, where life is marketed
> The more these dealings with You increase by day and night
> The more my very self is caught up in the buying and selling

The bridge players carried on, shuffling and dealing cards, play after play, while I was caught up in Tagore. I thought about how "buying and selling" was a good metaphor for desire—and of course, the obvious connection of buying and selling with Lee's Sacred Bazaar. Taken from the streets of everyday life, this kind of symbolism is often found in Baul poetry. On the spiritual path, we ceaselessly wander through the marketplace of our desires, where the master shows us again and again, the nature of our very selves. As we travel with Lee, we descend again and again to the "river ghats" of this world, now in the form of the restless sea, which I could see sparkling in the sun through the windows of our temporary home of the moment.

Soon it was my turn to play bridge, and I entered into another marketplace of desire, of winning and losing, success and failure. The bridge game is another excellent metaphor for daily life and an arena in which one grapples with desire and maybe even touches on experiences of groundlessness and non-attachment. Tagore had touched my heart, and I reflected over the cards as they were dealt: when will I realize that the whole marketplace of my wandering mind—all of my wins and losses, all of my attachment and desire and egoic bargaining—is just a passing illusion?

Just then Purna asked Sue Kali if she had any Motown CDs. At the same time, Paula came in with the new arrivals from the States. The quiet, reflective moment was over, and a lively, spirited camaraderie took its place. Sue Kali put on a CD, and the first song just happened to be "Mr. Lee," prompting everyone who knew it to sing along. While the song played and we sang, Lee dealt, bid and won a three no trump hand. That turned the tide, and Lee began to play with enthusiasm.

With the new influx of people and all the teenagers in the room, Lee winning at bridge and the Motown tunes that were rolling out and had us singing in our seats, the energy level had escalated by about a hundred times. Organizing the unwieldy group of kids that were milling about in a bored and unfocused way, Laura said, "Let's go to the beach!" Her idea was greeted with enthusiasm.

The bridge game continued. "Chains! My baby's got me wrapped up in chains! And they ain't the kind, no, that you can see!" Perfect lines for us, in a way, on this path of guru yoga—if we think of the guru as the person who receives our greatest affection. We sang along with vigor. It was fun, waiting out the afternoon over bridge and looking forward to the much-anticipated fish and chips dinner that night at the restaurant by the boardwalk near the sea.

Chris asked Lee, "Will you have fish and chips tonight, Baba?"

"No," Lee responded, "but the kids will. That's the important part."

Before long our group of twenty-three or so people was strolling down the boardwalk behind Lee in the balmy, early evening air. We passed The Meeting Place Café, with its "Angel of Peace" sculpture—a war memorial—standing tall and proud, overlooking the sea.

Arriving at the restaurant, we took up four tables. There was much chatter and excitement over the seafood menu, while Lee commented with a laugh, "I used to love mussels, until I read Anthony Bourdain's book! No more mussels for me, ever again!" Bourdain's unforgettable description in *Kitchen Confidential* of mussels sitting in buckets for days, steeping in their own piss before being cooked, was enough to turn us all off.

Our waitress, a Greek woman with a British accent who was also the owner of the restaurant, was instantly savvy to our group. When she came over to our table of four to take the first orders and asked if we wanted one check or separate checks, one of us called over to Lee, "Lee, do we want separate checks?" She immediately understood that the man with the dread locks was our fearless leader, whipped around and called out, "Lee! I already know your name!"

It was as if she had already become one of our party as she laughed and asked him, "Do you want it all on one check?" Lee rejoined in a fast repartee with her as she left our table and moved over to his to take orders. He teased her about not wanting any tartar sauce or vinegar on his fish, even if it was England! For a shy kind of guy, I thought, he can really draw people in.

Our guru was able to order a simple plate of grilled scallops, which he loves, and steamed veggies, which contributed toward making dinner a fantastic success for all. As we left the restaurant to walk down the boardwalk, both kids and adults were happy and relaxed. All along the way there were arcades, cafés and hot spots, as well as many small booth vendors of bright, colorful imported goods and clothing. A very contemporary crowd of young people dressed in scant clothing, bronzed from the sun, with pierced belly-buttons exposed in low-slung hip-huggers and many tattoos strolled or hung about the boardwalk.

Soon we were at the Häagen-dazs shop. Sue Kali was telling us about how the British sangha had come to her apartment and "cleaned house." With her unconditional agreement, they had gone through her things, thrown out boxes and boxes of stuff they thought she didn't need, then they had re-arranged everything. She was spacious and embracing of the whole process.

"It was brilliant, really!" Sue Kali smiled, when praise started coming her way. "It was really a great catalyst. I really appreciated it for that. I was absolutely paralyzed before that. My house was a mess! I had all these things, I didn't keep it clean . . ."

Back at the apartment after dinner, Lee played bridge again. The windows were open and a steady mild breeze streamed in the room. Ann adjusted one of the windows and asked Lee, "Too much air?"

"No, whatever you want . . ." he replied mildly.

When she pressed him further, saying, "No, whatever *you* want," Lee paused for a moment, seemed to consider, then said, "People *say* they want whatever I want until I want something different than what *they* want. Then they close the window or open the window as they like; they turn the music on, they turn the music off as they like; they do whatever they want to do."

Changing the subject, Lee turned to Sue Kali and said, "That was a fabulous act of practice!" He explained to Purna how Sue Kali had allowed the London bordello, her sangha mates, to clean, completely re-order and organize her flat and belongings in preparation for Lee's visit. He continued, "There are people in the Arizona sangha who would kill anyone who tried to do that with their things."

Sue Kali began to talk about a charity project she is involved with in India. After listening while she talked, Lee chimed in, "I'll give you some money for that! I like projects where all the money doesn't go to administrative costs. The advertising money eats up sixty percent of the budget—it's terrible."

The bridge game continued to roll along. After a while Charlotte, who leads the London bordello, asked, "How can we as a sangha serve you better next year when you come to London?"

"I don't know," Lee said at first, rather noncommittally. Then he launched into an instruction: "You have to think with more possibility. All opinions are based on completely subjective things, so you just have to have the idea that anything is possible. You have to think big, instead of saying, 'There are no antiques Lee would be interested in Brighton,' just because what I'm looking for is not the kind of antique that the person you've asked for advice collects. We think we know what's going on, but we are just defining the world by our opinions and projections and expectations. Like the research you did on the antique shows . . ."

Lee was referring to how Sue Kali had asked her uncle, an antique dealer himself, about Asian and Indian antiquities, which Lee usually looks for, as she understood it, not realizing that actually Lee is looking for all kinds of objects of sanctity and beauty—that which transmits the sacred in many forms. Her uncle had said, "Oh, he won't find anything like that here!" Of course, when Lee insisted on going to the walking area in the old part of Brighton, he had found lots of antique shops and interesting things.

Lee used Purna as an example of someone who knows how to get information. He said, "We ask open-ended questions, then we get information we never expected." He said that Portobello Market was the kind of place where, if we ask questions and assume that we already know what the answer is, we'll never find the treasures that are hiding in that labyrinth.

"With everything in general, it's a matter of being open, like in India. We go somewhere and it looks like a good place, but if we aren't open, people are always offering information or responding to the groove we have already dug."

In other words, we are molding reality to fit our own version of it, when there is so much magic and *drala* that could be at work in our lives. Instead of our predictable expectations, we have to cultivate the ability to expect the unexpected.

Lee then used the disappointing Middle Eastern restaurant we had gone to in London—a referral from a friend, not a sangha member—as an example of taking people's word for something, assuming that they know what they are talking about, or assuming that they are operating on a standard that Lee would find acceptable or, even better, enjoyable.

"If you check it out for yourself, you'll have a better sense of things, rather than taking someone else's word for it. People think high mediocrity is fabulous! People have no concept of what good food is. I've got students who have been with me for twenty-five years and they still have no idea what kind of movies I like! And we talk about movies *all the time*—more than dharma!" He gave a derisive laugh.

The bridge game continued throughout this exchange with Charlotte and Sue Kali. Lee announced that breakfast would be at nine-thirty the next morning. Seventeen of us would be taking off in the vans for the ashram in France. At ten o'clock the bridge game was winding down while Brinda, the ashram manager, talked with Lee about the huge amount of luggage, boxes, books, Sacred Bazaar acquisitions and various and assorted things that would need to be packed in the morning.

When it became clear, through the conversation, that it was actually, truly impossible to get it all in the two vans along with seventeen people, Purna suggested that some of the Sacred Bazaar things could be brought to France the next week. Lee growled in a loud voice, "I would rather leave the people here than the Sacred Bazaar. Leave my bronze? No way! The bronze is more important than the people!"

This is exactly the kind of remark from Lee that ruffles my fur, so to speak. When I hear Lee speak like this, it gives me pause to wonder: If the Sacred Bazaar is really the only thing Lee cares about, does he have to be so blunt about it? I remembered Daniel Morin's comment that the disciple is not a true disciple until there is nothing the guru can do to hurt his or her "feelings." Even a short-lived reaction like this is an indication that the tendency to project the fulfillment of our emotional needs on the guru has not been pierced. "I want my guru to be kind to me; I want my guru to respect me as a person; I want my guru to look and act like a good person, and therefore make *me* look good; I want, I want, I want . . ."

On the other hand, for three days Lee had been making caustic remarks in the easy going, decadent, devil-may-care atmosphere of this trendy seacoast tourist town. These kinds of scenes—where greed, self-indulgence and selfishness run rampant—bring out the ire in our guru. It's probably true that the deities and objects of true beauty are more important than the so-called "human beings," including those of us on the path who are still placing our personal wants and desires at the center of the world.

Several different possible alternatives for getting everything to the ashram were put forward to Lee, none of which were acceptable. All he would agree to was that we would leave Brighton at ten-thirty the next morning to make the two o'clock ferry at Dover. Eventually everyone dispersed to their different lodgings, and shortly after midnight Sue Kali's flat, which was housing Lee, his household and children, and Purna, was finally quiet and dark.

En route to France
June 21

The next morning we were up early in the flat, preparing things in the kitchen for the arrival of the rest of the sangha, who would be having breakfast with Lee before he left. Breakfast was scheduled for nine-thirty. Ann and I were organizing the meal; cereal and milk, yoghurt, fruit, bread and cheese, plates, cups and silverware were set out on the kitchen table. Everything was ready but the boiled eggs and the coffee, both of which were almost done.

We were surprised when Lee came in five minutes early. Ann was busy making the coffee; it was almost finished. I was boiling the eggs. They were thirty seconds away from being on the table, and I told him so as he made his plate.

"Too late!" he snapped peevishly. "Too late for me."

With dense persistence, I handed him two hot eggs that very instant. He was still serving himself to food, taking this and that from the table.

"No," he said again, this time quite gently. "It's too late."

It's the kind of moment you do not look forward to having with your guru. He was ready to eat, but the eggs were not ready. Neither was the coffee. I looked at my watch and could not refrain from a comment about how it wasn't nine-thirty yet. At the same time, the practitioner in me was saying, "So what? He's making a teaching lesson, and he should be able to have breakfast early if he wants it. The eggs should have been ready ten minutes early!"

Lee simply said, "Someone came to me and told me breakfast was ready—that's all I know." He also abstained from the coffee Ann had made when it was ready, while most of us knocked it back like there was no tomorrow.

A few minutes later in the living room, where people were gathering on the couch and a few chairs or on the many cushions on the floor around Lee, I asked if it was one of those mornings that we should eat hardy, knowing that we would be en route and boarding the ferry during the early afternoon.

"It doesn't matter what I say," Lee shrugged with resignation, reiterating the comment he had made yesterday about how selfish we really are, despite our sincerest wishes to serve—despite our commitment, love and devotion. "People do whatever they want to do. When people get hungry, they'll ask me for money to buy food. They don't care. They do whatever they want to do." He was grumbling, but in the next moment he was laughing and speaking in a mild and amiable way as people sat down around him with their plates of food.

The very instant he was finished eating—and most of the people in the room had just begun to eat, having waited in line while he ate—Lee jumped up and started yelling like a drill sergeant, "Let's go! Start packing—now!" Obviously he was anxious to leave for France. Everybody else, including those still standing in the slow breakfast line, had to drop their breakfast or leave the line. Purna and David immediately started helping Lee organize the massive amount of luggage that had to be taken down to the vans in the parking lot.

Purna laughed to Dave as they hauled luggage and heavy boxes, "We're in the deep masculine now!"

Even our attempts to bring some humor to the situation did not mitigate the tension that permeated the whole packing scene, at least in part because we did not have resolve about how we were going to get all that stuff to France. The alternative plans were still hanging in the air. Brinda was racking her brain for different options from which Lee might choose. Lee was complaining that a third van—the new cargo van recently purchased by the ashram in France—hadn't been brought to London along with the other two, and he blamed himself for this oversight.

"We just spent thirty thousand dollars on a new cargo van exactly for this purpose, and now it's just sitting at the ashram!" he grumbled. Tension continued to build upon itself and grow exponentially. Nonetheless, packing went on with everyone pitching in, in one way or another, in the warm, balmy sea air. It was a beautiful day on the English Channel in Brighton, the Babylon-on-the-Sea. The changeless, ever-present sea was a reminder of the eternal in the midst of our changes, now unfolding again on the stage of a rocky transition as we took off for the further shore of France.

As it turned out, the London-Brighton contingent would be driving to Paris in a van at the end of the week for Lee's seminar—they could bring the excess weight. Lee had agreed to Purna's original idea, which was to send some of the boxes to Paris in a week, so none of the human beings got left behind after all. We practically screeched out of the parking lot at 10:25 with Lee at the wheel.

We arrived in Dover two-and-a-half hours before our ferry appointment. Lee drove into town looking for a café, which he found with no help from several "helpful" backseat drivers, myself included, who told him where to go and landed us further away from the café that he finally located. He was still understandably grumpy as we settled at a table at the restaurant, when Purna told a story of an interchange that Lee had with a man in Canada, during a seminar Lee had given two months earlier at Mangalam. The man had described a woman he was involved with.

"How does she look?" Lee asked.

"She's beautiful," the man said, "but our conversations aren't very deep. I don't know if I should marry her."

Lee pursued, "How's the sex?"

"Great! Best ever," the man replied.

"Marry her!" Lee said with enthusiasm.

"Really? Are you serious?" the man asked, incredulous.

"Yes!" Lee answered.

We laughed at this story, so characteristic of Lee, then Purna said, "It wasn't just funny—it was a real transmission. That communication from Lee took all the nonsense out of relationship and all the processing that goes on. That's what I think he was communicating. Arnaud was sitting there, smiling."

We walked quickly back to the van and drove to the ferry. As soon as we were on board, Lee found a spot on a small side deck of the ferry. Standing there with him we were immersed in the elemental forces of wind and sea and sun and sky, while Lee talked for thirty minutes about the new video about Dzongsar Khyentse Rinpoche, titled, *Words of My Perfect Teacher*. Lee was describing it to Purna as an absolute "must-see." He has called this younger rinpoche "the hope of Vajrayana Buddhism in the West," and, "the real thing—a true vajrayana master." He has also given him the very highest praise of, "He is *always* working."

The voice of the captain broke into the conversation, saying that the Seacat was up to so many knots in speed and it would take sixty minutes to cross the English Channel. The water churned below us in an ecstasy of sea foam and waves that streamed out behind the vessel as it purred along, cutting across the water and gaining in speed. Another Seacat passed us as it came into port. Lee was telling stories of a new acquaintance, an American rinpoche called Traktung, whose teacher is Thinley Norbu Rinpoche, the blood father of Dzongsar Khyentse Rinpoche.

For the second half of the voyage Lee moved inside to the plush, comfortable chairs. I asked, "Are you looking forward to being in France?"

"Oh yeah!" Lee smiled a big smile. His mood had completely turned around since the morning in Brighton. "As soon as we cross the border to France," he continued, "it's like being at home!"

Purna asked, "Is it the same for you in Germany?"

"No, Germany is like a foreign country to me. But France . . . " Lee answered candidly.

"I like the people in Germany," Purna said.

Lee shrugged. "Sangha is sangha everywhere. There is sanctuary wherever there is sangha. But France . . . France is divine!" He smiled.

It was true that the closer we got to France, the happier Lee became. Moments later the ferry was docking at Calais. As soon as the captain made the announcement, Lee jumped up like a excited child and, with a huge smile, made his own announcement: "We're home!"

As we gathered our bags to walk back to the vans that were parked in the massive underbelly of the Seacat, Lee added, "England was like a foreign county to me. The language was the same . . . but it's just not France."

Within ten minutes we were driving off the ferry and onto French soil, down ribbon-like roads through green meadows and forested rolling hills, moving fast toward Paris and then on south to Ferme de Jutreau. We were hours away from the ashram, nonetheless we had reached our destination. London and Brighton were just short stops for wanderers on the meandering path of the summer, which would unfurl like a bright and shining stream, sometimes calm, even dulcet, sometimes rocky, turbid or crashing, sometimes leading into sublime transcendent pools for passing moments, with our boats adrift in space and time.

Even so, we would move from one place to another in the flow that would always bring us back to sanctuary in a quiet, hidden little gem of an ashram, tucked away in what is called "Sweet France," in the middle of this great lyrical country of romance, refuge, art, revolution, charming arrogance and haute culture that Lee calls home. The first chapter of the summer 2005—our sojourn in England—had been written. Now we were in France! We had reached our destination, and it seemed as if the summer had really just begun.

New Beginnings

Ferme de Jutreau
June 22, 2005

Lee and company—in two vans, packed to the hilt with people, luggage, books and sacred artifacts—arrived at the ashram at midnight last night, a little road weary but extremely happy to be home. Walking across the courtyard at that hour, the starry path of the Milky Way shone down on us in its enigmatic silence, while the green grass and close presence of the leafy linden trees seemed to murmur as we passed by. Nature is quite alive on Lee's ashrams, and tonight it seemed to welcome us home. I often feel a great intimacy with the natural environment there; it seems that the boundless presence of Yogi Ramsuratkumar has entered into the living forms in a particular way, so that even the trees and flowers on the ashram exude his blessings.

After a few hours of sleep, the Earth rolled on in its perpetual motion of turning, turning, turning until the stars faded and the twilight of dawn gave way to the sun on the eastern horizon, rising in orange and gold fireworks that lit up the beauty of the old stone farmhouses. The cosmos itself seemed to be watching this ceaseless drama unfold as the flower gardens and grassy courtyard with its big maple tree in the center came to life. My feet were wet with dew as

I settled on the pillow at seven o'clock for our first meditation of the summer in the old stone barn. As usual Lee sat on his dais, meditating along with us. This morning, as is often the case, he spent most of the morning writing poetry to Yogi Ramsuratkumar.

We were happy to be back in the mood and rhythms of our ashram sanctuary, and at breakfast everyone gathered over oats, fruit and tea in the part of the stone barn that is partitioned off as a dining room for the summer. The busy morning was spent quickly, as all the travelers settled into their home for the summer and anticipated the vegetarian lunch that would be served at noon. Sure enough, Alrun, the ashram cook, did not disappoint us: the first big meal on the ashram was salad, rice and curried vegetables, most of it from the ashram garden.

Lee's step was so light that he practically bounced out of the *grande maison* after lunch. He was ready to drive his new car, a 1986 Mercedes (practically an antique itself) that someone traded for bronze artifacts through the Sacred Bazaar, into La Roche Posay to see the new property: the guru's antiquities and brocante shop, located in a thirteenth century building that the sangha has been working very hard to renovate, stretching far beyond their known limits, over the past several months. Wearing the fine white straw Panama hat that David Amar gave him last September in Paris, a leather fanny pack strapped over a blue short-sleeve shirt hanging down over faded, old black cotton pants and the somewhat controversial expensive sandals (they last for life) that he reluctantly allowed Purna to buy for him in New York City last spring, and with dread locks down to his thighs now, Lee looked every bit the expat shopkeeper and *chineur* of extraordinary circumstance.

The Mercedes hummed along the bumpy rural back road to the village like a heavy boat: we just sort of sailed along, with four people crammed into the back and Lee and Purna in front. A vanload of people from the ashram followed close behind and Vincent Vigor, the new president of Ramji Association and source person for the acquisition and renovation of the three-story shop, was close behind in his car. Lee parked the silver-blue Mercedes in the shade on the far side of the plaza in the *centre ville* and struck out across the square under the chestnut trees, where the local market is usually in progress, in the direction of the shop.

Today there was only a single *vendeur* there, set up in the empty space under the trees past the carousel. "Bonnard Guy, Producteur," the sign said, "Degustation Gratuite." He was selling pineau de Charentes—a delicious, sweet wine that I fondly remembered from a dinner with Shri in Vitrac last summer, when the host poured very large glasses of this nectar for us, and other occasions as well—and cognac, made by his family from their vineyards and aged in their own caves in the region of Charontes. We struck up a conversation with the friendly, warm man behind the table, who was Bonnard Guy himself. The bottles of wine sparkled invitingly like nectar, both the golden variety and the clear, sweeter red.

Lee and Purna walked up behind us. Immediately taking the situation to heart, Lee said yes to the generously proffered tastes. M. Guy was delighted and offered tastes of three different pineaus from various years. Vincent walked up and joined our small group for a taste as well. It was a lovely interlude before seeing the new shop. Leaves fell around us in the hot, dry air as we savored the sweet wine, which was good enough as wine goes, but seemed, more significantly, keyed into the historic moment, a little flourish in the blitz of synchronicities that characterize the action around Lee. Right away Purna bought three bottles as a gift for Lee. Some of us bought additional bottles to give as *prasad* in darshan.

As we walked away Lee said with an amiable smile on his face, "Now that we're in France, even if there is only one shop in the entire market, we have to stop and buy something!"

We walked down the street and under the high stone archway that is the reinforced fortress wall of the old village, then down a short half block to the store. Walking into the new shop, we could see that the renovation project had come a very long way. The showroom on the first floor was now contained by eight-hundred-year-old stone walls, revealed in the process of tearing off layers of wallpaper and faux suede covering. The room gleamed with new lights, showcases and a spotless floor. As we moved through the building from one space to another, we were delighted to discover the "cave" of the basement—a dungeon-like, windowless room of raw stone and earth—and the second and third floors, which were completely rough and in an extremely rundown state but showing fantastic potential (that is, with a prodigious amount of work put into it). We wandered through the old building both dazed and enlivened by the magnitude of the project.

After seeing the new shop, spirits soared as Lee took off on foot for coffee in the *centre ville*, less than two minutes away just down the street. About fourteen of us walked down the wide stone-paved sidewalk toward the café with Lee in the lead. Soon we had arranged three tables and gathered around, ordered café crème and settled in.

"Will you be at the shop?" Alrun asked Lee.

"I'd like to be . . . I love retailing!" he replied.

Now that we were back home at the ashram, possibilities were popping up everywhere. Gathering there around Lee at the café, the occasion took on a tremendously auspicious feeling to it. It felt like we were looking through an open window into a star-studded vast space, rather like the stars last night when we first arrived. You could sense that one of those extraordinary spaces with Lee was opening up; he was brimming with creative juice, on fire with enthusiasm. The immediate force of his presence exuded a magnetism that was drawing us all in, while the conversation continued in fairly ordinary terms. Lee began to talk about the prolific French writer, Balzac, and what an inspiration he had found in him while reading his biography recently.

"Balzac wrote seventy-four novels in twenty years, plus all the other things he wrote—short stories, plays, poems . . ." Lee said. The conversation began to jump quickly from one subject to another as different people introduced their own topic of interest to Lee and he followed the lead of whoever was speaking to him in the moment. Four more people—those who had stayed behind to do the lunch dishes—arrived and joined our party. With eighteen seated at three tables, we strained to hear what Lee was saying as he turned his head from left to right to speak to people on one end or the other of the oblong perimeter we had formed around him.

More coffee was ordered—the elixir of choice was good on this hot afternoon in La Roche Posay—and then Purna asked a question about one of his students, who wondered if they were in the Work or not. Lee quipped with a lightly sarcastic tone, "Yeah, like people thinking they're in the Work but saying, 'Oh, I can't drink coffee after seven o'clock. It keeps me awake at night!' "

This gave rise to my own thoughts on that subject: it's been my observation that, in general, we have a very shallow understanding of the term, "the Work," and we use it quite incorrectly. The way E.J. Gold uses that term, there are very, very few people who are in the Work. Even to be a candidate to be an apprentice to the Work requires tremendous effort, time on the path, commitment. For most of us, we are lucky to have the opportunity to work for somebody who works for somebody who is in "the Work." If we can't even manage what Mr. Gold calls "the human biological machine" to the extent that we can, for example, drink coffee and still go to sleep (Lee says coffee never keeps him from sleeping—*ever*), or manage the psychological knots that most of us have around health, sleep, the body and our personal "needs," then most likely we are not very deeply engaged "in the Work."

Turning his attention to Vincent, who was seated directly across from him, Lee grabbed the reigns and effortlessly steered the large, unwieldy group in the direction of his choice. He asked Vincent when the renovation work on the shop had begun.

"February 2," Vincent replied.

Suddenly Lee was, once again, reinventing sadhana for his students. Instantly he began to outline a new direction for Vincent, the ashram residents and European sangha, the ramifications of which grew and expanded as he articulated his vision over the next hour, while we sat, magnetized and rapt within the chamber he created. We found ourselves immersed in a total experience, created in the moment by Lee. It was the visceral and energetic contact with the guru's presence that was opening each one of us to his vision of possibility.

"You could start a new business remodeling old houses and properties. Really! How many hours went into the new shop so far?" he pressed Vincent further.

"If it was one person full-time—three to four months," Vincent replied.

Lee quickly calculated the math to make his point: Vincent could hire people from the ashram to do the work while he managed and oversaw everything, and everyone could make money. "It might be an interesting idea—so that everybody is working . . ." Lee was getter brighter and more animated as he talked, pointing to one person then another sitting around the table and speaking directly about the strengths, talents and energy each one could give to such a project.

"So, if it's not too private, how much do you make a month right now?" he asked Vincent pointedly. Vincent answered, then Lee continued, "You could be making ten thousand euros more a month! Don't be impulsive, but it's worth considering . . . you could start slowly with a small classified ad. Renovations.

"One of my beloved disciples brought us this company years ago, a high level avante garde art for hotels and corporations. Art, like three dimensional, textured cloth, forty to fifty thousand dollars a piece. The way we worked was that we *never* turned down a job. Always, we said, 'Yes, we can do it.' After we got the job, then we figured out how to do it. Steven Spielberg was one of our clients. He was so successful, such a famous director, that the studio gave him a whole building, and he wanted art for the whole thing.

"We made him a proposition—we were going to do the entire building, a $250,000 job. He was really into children, and we proposed this whole children's theme. He loved the idea and put in a requisition for it. That's the way we did things."

Purna relayed the story of one of his students, who had basically invented a highly creative, viable business out of nothing, now wildly successful. Lee continued, expanding his ideas: "Then, you start restoring old buildings, not just apartments . . . "

We were witnessing the master at play in the realm of possibility, but more than that: for Lee, it was already done—"the chalk had already hit the floor," as Werner Erhard used to say. The power of Lee's presence impacted us with its precision and force of intention, and yet he was not weighed down in any way; he spoke with a lightness of being, a natural buoyancy of spirit. He was actually giving us a direct experience of the unfettered or enlightened mind, or one could say, of enlightenment itself, by virtue of being in his presence. In a spontaneous, extemporaneous way, Lee had created a temporary environment, a contained chamber, where we were not only bathed in, but thoroughly penetrated by, the naked, vital energy of the guru. In this circumstance, he was leading us further into the "impossible promise," as Werner Erhard has called it, of the Work.

He continued, hardly taking his eyes off of Vincent as he talked, "You could do complete renovations and redecorations—redesigning houses. You say to the client, 'We have, in our stable of people, some very fine artists,' and then you show them your portfolio . . ."

Within minutes he had just swept Hohm Community artists on both sides of the Atlantic into the play: Otilia, Nara, Ralph Pfleger, Denise, Jeff, Bandhu and others also had a life in this world, which was unfolding into a vast, wide-spectrum vista before our eyes as Lee spoke. Not only could Vincent and company do renovations, detail work and redesigns on people's homes, the company could offer an entire range of services associated with decorating the homes with original, one-of-a-kind art of all types. It would be an entry-point into working for someone who is in the Work for many people in the sangha.

"We have incredible resources in this community, and you could offer all that. Sylvan ran a successful painting business for four years just on word of mouth advertising . . . . " Lee talked about how one satisfied customer will bring many others in, and that individualized attention and focus on details and the kind of integrity that Vincent brings to his work would bring loyal customers who would pass the word on.

"The resources we have for decorating are immense, and that's not even tapping Purna's community! All these artists are just dying to make a living making art. Obviously, you'd have to get it up and running first . . . . I'll bet just the Paris sangha alone, their mothers are always getting their old apartments by the Eiffel Tower redone!"

It seemed that, although Vincent and several others in the group weren't catching every word of Lee's English, or his quiet and intense way of speaking, which often makes it hard for even the Americans to catch his words, the receptivity of the group was highly piqued by the pure energy coming from Lee, which generated in us simultaneously a powerful blend of intoxication and something akin perhaps to dismay, fueled by the heady possibilities of his vision. A tremendous opportunity was being offered, without doubt. Perhaps more than anything, it was the chamber itself and the transmission of pure presence and intention that was initiatory—an initiation into a deeper level of sadhana, as the guru melded his mind with ours in the heat and pressure of the chamber.

"It could happen," Lee stated unequivocally. "It could work, because you're a hard worker, you're enthusiastic, and you're smart. It could work. Of course, then you'd have to deal with sangha who think they deserve every day they want off, just because they're sangha.

"If people in the sangha were willing to work for money the same way that they are willing to work for me, then we would have something. If they'd work for money the way they work for love, it would be great, but they don't work that way when they're working for money.

"The worst thing you can have is a bunch of innovators. If you actually do this, you have to have people understand: No innovation! Orders come down from the top, and no changing even a tiny detail.

"So, people do the work that's required, or they get fired. I tell you, everybody could be making a lot of money! Then everybody wants to move into the area. You get five more people on the ashram and making money, you get a situation where people are able to travel with me, come to America—a whole different situation.

"I'll tell you, once in a lifetime some old rich person will buy a castle and you'll be renovating it, and you go into the turret and find a million euro stash of antiques, and they say, 'I don't even want to look at it—take it away!' And you've just found a treasure! There *is* treasure still in the world. Once in a lifetime it comes around. Everybody who runs a business they enjoy has some story like that!"

Lee then gave the example of his ex-partner in the rare stamps and coins business who had exactly that situation come up. Today he is a multi-millionaire running a fantastic corporate office, a leader in the field of rare stamps and coins.

"You can't have boundaries in the way you think," Lee continued, "like getting parking places: 'Oh no, you'll never get a parking place in that area!' " Every time Lee drives into an area looking for a parking place, there is one available in the most provident place. He said that when we talk to people, we have already assumed what the answer will be, and we define reality with our expectations in that way.

"You can't think with straightjackets on. You have to think with open-ended possibility. You get a realtor's license. You put a little notice at the bottom of your brochure: 'We buy estates.' " Lee kept punctuating his discourse with examples of great deals that have gone down because of thinking in terms of open-ended possibility.

"You go in, doing redecoration and renovation, and you'll find people who also want to sell property . . ."

Thirty minutes had gone by; one idea led to another, and the view, as Lee was opening our minds to it, became more and more panoramic. We too could see it, taste it, feel it. We were there. At the same time that it was fantastic and huge, it was also immediate, practical, do-able. It sparkled before our eyes, charged and raced in our blood; his pure creative zest infected us. Suddenly his enthusiasm reached a new peak as he made another quick turn:

"In fact, I would be willing to *invest* in your venture to the tune of at least fifty thousand euros, because I trust you, and I know you are somebody who could make me a lot of money—but not as much as you could make for yourself."

Lee paused while that sank in, then said, "You plug all these people in, you've got a portfolio and these people are in there . . . . Laurent—he's another example! Tremendous talent! You get Laurent taking photos of these old, rundown houseboats on the Seine with half-naked women laying around on them, blow them up and tint them—Americans will *love* that shit . . .!"

At this point Lee was so excited that he jumped from one idea to another so quickly that creative possibilities were pouring out of him with the incredible self-confidence that he exudes so effortlessly. He was an artist at work, painting, sculpting, wordsmithing a reality that already exists, that was churning through him, unfolding just as he spoke it, in the moment. What was it in Lee that made his spirited conversation about a business venture so fraught with magic? It seemed to me that we were witnessing the process of creation, sitting around the primal fire of a star giving birth.

"And you have integrity. People will love that. You're not a liar and a thief, like me! You'll do good work. These people and their money—redecorating and art, it's a diversion from their boredom. They've got money. You get one job done that people like and it will go on from there. You have to not be scared to charge. Find out the going rate and price yourself on the high end. It could work. It could really work."

Lee reeled off the names of other sangha members who could be plugged into the business. "I had this fabulous idea two years ago riding in the Metro in Paris. I was looking at those billboards; those things are totally cool—the images and language that are used. I'll bet you could buy those things and do people's walls with them—a whole wall! Americans would go crazy for those French Metro posters. You could offer them to Americans moving into the area. You just mention it as an idea, and maybe nine people out of ten think it's crazy, but the tenth person goes for it, and you get ten thousand euros for a wall like that!

"Yvan Amar's son, David, is a very good friend of ours—a wonderful young man. He's totally plugged into the Paris street scene, knows all the graffiti artists. I tell you, this is big in America—American and German graffiti artists paint on canvas instead of on walls and sell them in stores as art. David knows all the street artists in Paris. You could offer people a whole wall of graffiti art. What a radical idea!"

It seemed that Lee even surprised himself with this idea. He smiled in delight, excited by it all as much as we were, since all this was just flowing out of him without any deliberation or forethought. It was a pure demonstration of awakened mind, and it was our opportunity to meld with that living transmission, to be influenced by it to the point of radical transformation.

It was a hot afternoon in more ways than one, and sweat rolled down his chest under the blue shirt as he said, "Give the graffiti artists an opportunity to make a statement in some rich people's homes who are going to be entertaining! You're going to find another Keith Harring . . . he hit it, like that! On the streets of Paris and Marseilles there are *geniuses* down there—they are *real* artists. This is real art, good shit! Give them a real opportunity … "

Now Lee had struck a vein of gold. He has been passionate about street art for years. Often as we've traveled around Europe he has stopped the van on highways and busy streets to take photographs of outstanding graffiti; these photos he has had published in *Tawagoto* and in the *Hohm Sahaj Mandir Study Manuals*. Graffiti art and tattoo art have sprung out of the same culture of the streets, and Lee has been serious about them both for years now. The air practically crackled with electricity now that Lee had hit on this idea.

He continued, "After tattoos, graffiti is coming. Graffiti is going to be the biggest design phenomena in the world! I'll introduce you to David—he knows all these people. In fact, I'll finance it for you! I'd invest twenty thousand euros in this tomorrow! And we could start an import company: graffiti from Marseilles, Paris. Ha! We could turn this into a huge business! The flow of bronze artifacts is going to stop, and we're just going to be getting our feet wet! We're going to need some place to rock n' roll!"

The auspiciousness, the historical significance, the excitement, the wonder and awe, the magic and *drala* of the unusual chamber with the master on this fine afternoon had just peaked. Lee had hit the big note of the moment, and we were all hanging on every word that came out of his mouth. There really was no room, no space, no air, not a breath of energy, for the mind's concerns and protestations.

"The second floor of the shop can be the graffiti gallery! Okay, that's it! Why didn't I think of that before? Graffiti art, sangha art . . . It's perfect! See," Lee said, referring to a woman at the next table who was gaping at him, wide-eyed, "all you have to do is sit in a café and talk loud enough! And you don't even have to go anywhere to sell it!

"When does the money seminar start?" Lee asked. He was referring to the six day seminar that he and Purna would give later in the summer at Ferme de Jutreau. Vincent answered that it begins September 12.

"If you can make a quarter of a million by September, we'll use you as the example!" Lee chuckled.

Vincent laughed too and joked in return, "I'll have to quit my job tomorrow." A few others laughed, but at this point the magnitude of the vision—not to mention the sheer work and the risk—was beginning to overwhelm a few of us. As much as we want the groundless, infinite creativity of the guru's world, at the same time its vivid and raw reality is formidable and even terrifying. The idea of just how far people would have to stretch beyond their comfort zone and fixed ideas of themselves to manifest Lee's vision was intimidating. Michelle said that she was thinking about how many similar opportunities she's been given by Lee and how many times she has failed. In fact, every day she feels that she fails in some way in her sadhana.

"How do you deal with that?" she asked.

"Every day, you get up and you dedicate it all to the Work. Everything you gain, the money you make, you give it all back to the Work. You dedicate it all to the Work . . ."

Lee used the example of someone in the sangha who left his post, who was tremendously creative and had a huge talent, but didn't dedicate it to the Work. He believed it was his, not the Work's, and now the creative flow has stopped completely.

"Every morning you get up and dedicate everything to the Work. Every bit of money you make, you dedicate it all to the Work. You do that, you keep Remembering me, you Remember me, and it's going to work. I got lifted to a new octave in July 1975 and I stayed in it. There's no such thing as enlightenment. You just stay in the new octave. It's simply a matter of staying in the new octave."

Michelle countered, "You are giving us things that are very difficult to realize, and we end up feeling like we are failing, and it puts a wedge into our relationship with you."

Lee answered with unquestionable certainty, "Well, it doesn't put a wedge into *my* relationship with *you*." It was a statement that was all-inclusive, that embraced all of his students. He gazed at Michelle with radiant, lively calm. It's a hard lesson for many of us to learn—that whenever we feel distant from the guru, it's always the student who has created a distance, for whatever psychological reason we may have, not the guru who has distanced himself. Even when there is the appearance of change within the realm of the content of our lives, the guru, as pure context, never changes.

I glanced across the street at the central *place* of the village, where the outdoor market is held twice a week under the trees. The sun shone from the western sky, glinting in bright highlights on the gorgeous, riotous displays of carefully tended flower gardens, the guardian spirits of the four corners of the *place*. A few older couples walked about under the trees; a group of men were tossing *boule* balls across the beaten earth track where they usually play. Visitors strolled across the wide, almost colonial porch of the Park Hotel just down the block. It was timeless, eternal France, and we were the glad recipients of its grace. Our coffee cups were cold and empty, but, listening to Lee and basking in the moment, our hearts were on fire.

"Yes," Lee answered Michelle's question, "Yogi Ramsuratkumar gave me three ashrams, one hundred and fifty students, the Sacred Bazaar, several fabulously talented musical groups and God knows what all else. He just didn't ask me to do . . . *whatever*. Give me an example of something I gave you that failed."

Michelle said, "For example, that expensive art project."

"That is completely irrelevant. That project has no importance whatsoever. That's just fluff. If I ask you to take care of your mother when she's dying—that means something. If you fail at things that don't mean anything, you don't lose many points."

Lee paused for a moment, then said: "If Vincent can get out of his own way and make this happen, he'll carry everybody with him."

While that sank into the group, Lee seemed to shift gears. He closed the chamber by saying, "Okay, we've made everybody rich! Now all we have to do is bring it into manifestation, as they say in the new age." He turned back to Vincent and said, "Start with the graffiti art. You find really good artists to do it on canvas and start to collect them. This is what Purna and I will finance."

The chamber had reached its peak and now it was time to move on. Almost as an afterthought, Lee added, "It's so difficult to get people who do personal service work like this to just come and do the work. You do one job at a time and provide the service. You tell your clients, 'I'm working for you and you alone. I do one renovation at a time, so I'm not thinking of somebody else's house—I eat, breathe and sleep this house until it's done!' People will love that; they'll really appreciate that.

"If you dedicate everything to the Work, you're not going to kill yourself doing this. Part of it is working smart. You work hard, but efficiently."

It was almost four o'clock in the afternoon and time to go back to the ashram. There was the sense that a great deal had been accomplished. A fine film of sweat glistened on many of the faces that sat looking at Lee as he looked around at all of us, as if to seal our fate. Turning back to Vincent, he said, "Well, let's see what happens."

Striding back across the *place* to the Mercedes, Lee was behind the wheel in less than a minute. On the way down the narrow country road to Vicq and the ashram, Purna turned to Lee and said, "That was incredible. Really. I haven't been in a chamber like that with you in years!"

Paris

Paris
June 24, 2005

After a few busy but heavenly days in the sanctuary of the ashram, greeting the sangha and getting reestablished for the summer stay, Lee and company packed up for a five-day jaunt to Paris that would include a one-day seminar, treasure-hunting the brocante circuit, a volley of treks around the city, café interludes and visits with friends. Christina and Kelly Sell, who were scheduled to arrive at the train station in Montparnasse today, would be picked up by Lee to join his Paris retinue.

Arriving at the *gare* at Montparnasse, Lee sent Chris and Jan into the station to meet Christina and Kelly. Within minutes they all came out and walked quickly to the van. Lee was beaming as he greeted them and immediately invited them to sit in the front seat with him, so he could visit while he drove. Talking animatedly while he steered confidently through the streets, at one point he turned to them and said, "I guess it's easier in Paris to take the metro, but I just love to drive through the city!"

It's true. Paris has become a favorite and familiar haunt of Lee's, and whereas in earlier years of our summers in France when we always took the Metro to travel around Paris, for the past three years

Lee has been driving around the city in the ashram van. Therefore, in addition, the next five days would be a navigating challenge for the map reader or navigator of the moment, since Lee doesn't slow down while one studies the map, or allow any time at all to get oriented, but expects to be told where to go spontaneously as he careens through the streets as if he and the van, fused somehow into one organism, are creating the friction of our alchemy in the combustion of the engine and the burning of the wheels. Or maybe it is really his love-maddened attention on the road of our unraveling.

Paris
June 25

For the past three years the Paris sangha has hosted Lee in a one-day seminar in the city. Like last year, Lee was starting the Sacred Bazaar off with a blast that demonstrated just how big his vision for it really is: he had brought probably twenty big boxes of bronze, wood and stone deities and other sacred objects to display on six or seven long tables along the side of the room, in addition to two tables of books and CDs. It took Lee and a crew of people who were helping over two hours to get everything out of the boxes and displayed on the tables.

The seminar began this morning with about fifty people in the room and another twenty dispatched on various tasks to facilitate the day, including several cooks who were preparing lunch and dinner. The audience was a blend of Lee's students from various places in Europe, mostly France and England, a number of Arnaud Desjardins' students, and a few new faces.

Watching from the sidelines, I saw many smiling faces as people who were arriving before the talk greeted Lee, most of them for the first time in nine months. Others browsed the tables of the Sacred Bazaar, lingering here and there over a book or a particular deity.

Lee walked to his chair at the front of the room and sat down. The space had been prepared with a large *murti* of Yogi Ramsuratkumar and a bouquet of flowers. Taking the bull by its horns, he started out with a very direct communication, saying, "So, those of you who know me a little know that I'm here to sell things. Those of you who don't, don't be insulted yet. We have all day for me to insult you! I'm going to start off kind of light."

Lee began to sell books, but the crowd seemed reticent, even shy at first. He teased his audience mercilessly when they didn't buy as many books as he suggested they should: "That's all? I'm shocked! I take these things very personally . . . Okay, next book for sale. This one is called *The Eternal Heart of the Path…*"

After a few books had flown out of his hands, he turned his attention particularly on *108 Poèmes et Príèures à Yogi Ramsuratkumar.* Opening the book of 108 poems to Yogi Ramsuratkumar in French and English, Lee showed the beautiful color photographs in the book to his audience. He said, "My Master used to smoke. Yogi Ramsuratkumar *never* explained His actions—ever! For instance, He used to hold His cigarette up and wave it in blessing. Maybe He just thought the cigarette was a beautiful piece of creation, and He wanted to show it off, but we all thought He was blessing us! You know, cigarettes have to do with fire and turning things to ash . . . Before He was a master, He hated cigarettes. As soon as He started teaching He was drawn to smoke. If you look at Him in any normal way, He was totally addicted to cigarettes. But we, his devotees, always said He was blessing us. We assumed He burned up our karma—turned our karma to ash.

"So one of the things that I used to do, and still do, is write poetry to my Master. Although Yogi Ramsuratkumar has been dead for several years, His spirit is quite alive, but His body is very dead. Not as dead as He could be, because His devotees buried Him in salt to preserve His body! So, Yogi Ramsuratkumar was very happy with the poetry I wrote to Him about Him. He said that the poetry was a Blessing, obviously to the people who read it, but you have to *read* it to get the blessings."

Lee held the book up to show the audience two very beautiful *murtis* of Yogi Ramsuratkumar and Lee looking into each other's eyes, hand in hand and in rapt communion. "Here are two pictures of me totally sucking up to my Master, draining Him of everything I could get from Him! I always figure if you have a master, and you are serious about it, you try to get as much as you can from the master.

"One time in Tiruvannamalai we went to dinner. In India things start around midnight. I used to like to walk around India at night and soak up the life. India is kind of like France—no matter what time of night it is there is always somebody eating . . . "

Lee was tossing all kinds of things into the mix as he continued in his helter-skelter, throw-everything-at-them-fast method. Whether we knew what was happening or not, we were witnessing Lee's "the transmission is faster than the mind" tricks. It's not what he was saying that was most important—although he was saying some very interesting and potent things. In fact, he was giving us the teaching in a crazy, street savvy, upside-down, counter to the ordinary flow kind of way. What was important was the mood, the feeling tone of the space that he created—the bright, intense ambiance of clarity generated by the nuclear fission of his own self. As Chögyam Trungpa Rinpoche once said about the transmission of the teaching, "It's sixty percent mood."

Lee continued, "Yogi Ramsuratkumar said that everyone should read the poetry everyday. When He said 'everyone,' He meant that *everyone* should read the poetry everyday, because He loved everyone in the world—because everyone is a member of humanity and He loved everybody. He would read a story in the news, and He would start shaking and sweating, and then everybody who came to His darshan from other places, He'd ask, 'do you know about . . . ?'

"Yogi Ramsuratkumar loved everyone and blessed everyone. I don't, but my practice is about serving His Work. I am transparent to Yogi Ramsuratkumar and my work is to serve His Work. One of the aspects of that Work is to bring His blessings to as broad a spectrum in the world as possible. And so, everybody should read His poetry.

"Because we love France and so by association we love the French, one of my students had the bright idea, 'Why don't we translate some of the poems into French, so all of your French students will be able to have them?' I said, 'Great idea,' not wanting to get into an argument. And, my students, who are dedicated to their practice, take these very heavy, two kilo poetry books with them in their suitcases everywhere they go. So now they have this very small book that they can take. Who wants this book now?"

The sincerity and truth of Lee's words was the best sales pitch in the world, and a lot more people raised their hands to buy the book. Then he told a story of a teaching that Mr. Gold made some years ago.

"Purna and I and a few students were hanging out with E.J. Gold one time—although you are never really 'hanging out' with E.J.! E.J. asked Purna who his favorite basketball team is. Purna replied. When E.J. asked me, and I said, 'I don't have one.' Then he asked Purna, 'Who is your favorite player?' Purna replied, 'Michael Jordan.' Then E.J. turned to me and I said, 'I don't even know these guys.' Then, he turned to Purna and he said, 'Sports are for primates . . .'

"So the Suns, the Arizona team, were in the playoffs. They didn't win, but they were in the playoffs. We were in this restaurant last night in Paris and the owner was excited because he *loves* the Suns . . ."

Lee was referring to the restaurant where we had dinner last night, L'homme Tranquil, in Montmartre, just down the hill from Sacre Coeur, the beautiful old basilica. It's a place where Lee likes to go, partly because the food is good and partly because it has been in the same family for two generations or more. The mother of the family cooks, and now that the father is retired, his sons manage the tiny place. Lee has even given the owner posters and CDs of Shri in past visits; now, when Lee arrives, it's a familiar place where we are greeted with a warm welcome.

Lee continued, "And we didn't know a thing about the Phoenix Suns! People in Arizona know all the players, and we're from Arizona, but we don't know anything about them!" Lee laughed at the irony of the situation. This seemingly inane tangential reference carried with it an important teaching: in the Work, we do not identify with the icons of the sleeping world—nations, flags and states, politics, sports, media events of all kinds, advertising, aggression in many forms. Then he was off on another plug for the Sacred Bazaar.

"So, I am asking you to stretch. And I know it is money. Money has a lot of uses. I am not suggesting that you use the money you have for rent or that you spend your money that is for health care. Everybody lives somewhere—and I assume that just about covers everybody in here. Everybody has wall space in their apartment."

Continuing with the Sacred Bazaar, Lee showed some very old paintings of Hindu deities—Durga, then Shiva, the destroyer. He was slowly bringing everyone over into his world, loosening up our rigid definitions and survival mentality, melting our steely minds down and softening us to the world of beauty, art and divinity in its outward manifestations in the world. Speaking of the Sacred Bazaar, money, the common thread of scarcity that people feel and the uncertainty of the world, he said, "If a meteor hits, at least you'll go in the midst of beauty and sanctity."

Just then a woman in the front row stepped forward to steady some of the paintings that weren't standing upright. Lee pointedly asked her not to help him unless she was asked. It was a message meant for everyone there; she was just the person who created the object lesson for others, especially Lee's students who have not learned this after many years in his company. He stated unequivocally, "Someone does one thing to help and before you know it they are fucking up the whole damn world—you know what I mean? And they think they are helping—with no offense to you sweetheart, but I am sure you know what I mean. Sure you do, because you are all living in the middle of things just like that. So . . . no apartment in Paris should be without these!"

Lee forged ahead, "Every year when I get to Europe there is a theme. It usually takes a month or several seminars for the theme to emerge. I'm not entirely sure, but I have a guess. It came about in London. I tell this story all the time. The first year I came to teach in France was after Gilles had written his book on Western teachers. He had set up a whole seminar and arranged for me to meet Arnaud Desjardins. My style was . . . provocative and unusual! I was really going for it then! A lot of people were shocked and attracted at the same time. The people who came to my seminars where students of Yvan Amar or Arnaud.

"After I left people had questions relative to their confusion about me, which they asked Arnaud about. If you ask me, Arnaud is the perfect master. He is wise, compassionate, and I was this guy using horrible language, insulting women and being . . . confusing. One day Arnaud was teaching and someone asked, 'Is Lee a genuine master?' Arnaud said, 'I don't know anything about masters, but I know something about disciples. I cannot say if he is a good master, but I can say that Lee is a great disciple of his master.'

Lee has told this story countless times, I think because there is not a greater compliment that he could have received from Arnaud than this. Not only was it a great compliment to Lee; it was a teaching lesson for any student on the path, regardless of who their teacher is. From the perspective of the path, to be a true devotee, a real disciple, is the fruition of practice. And once again, Lee used this teaching lesson from Arnaud to make an important point about the critical responsibility of the student of the path to be a good disciple.

Lee continued, "A good master is always a great disciple. We are always looking at the master and asking if they are trustworthy. Rarely do we ask, 'Am I a good disciple? Am I trustworthy? Am I worthy of the master's blessings, teaching?' Those of you who know me, know that the emphasis of my teaching has moved across quite a vast landscape in the last ten years. The major change of the last ten years has been that my Master died. Arnaud said, 'You never really know the dramatic changes you are going to go through until your master dies.' Arnaud made that comment to me years before Yogi Ramsuratkumar died, and I thought, 'I only see Him once a year, so my life will go on as usual, because that's the way it is now.' But I had no idea how radically things would change once he died, even though I trust Arnaud's wisdom completely. The forms of my outer changes are different that Arnaud's but the internal changes are exactly the same.

"Yogi Ramsuratkumar was in His sixties when I first met Him. I knew Him for over twenty years before He died. He died in February 2001, and I came to Europe in June and the Sacred Bazaar started. One of the outer forms of what has changed is the Sacred Bazaar. I couldn't have imagined in my wildest dreams that this is where it would go—and this is just the beginning.

"We just got a little magasin in La Roche Posay, which is right near our ashram. A couple of my students have opened a shop in Paris. And I have started to do fairs. So everything is moving in the direction that the formal dimension of the teaching in seminars is slowly diminishing and the Sacred Bazaar is slowly taking over everything.

"The formal, linear communication of the teaching is moving into informal, nonlinear forms of teaching. It's moving slowly, but it's moving to where I'm behind the table, and what we have is sacred artifacts. I will never compromise you as a group of people who know what this is and can appreciate it, as people who can create sacred spaces in which you can realize the aims of the Path. We have a website, but I don't sell anything on the website. If someone inquires, I send them an email—or one of my students does, since I don't have email. I tell people I only sell art face to face.

"I have one hundred or so students, and that is not going to change. Slowly but definitely we are moving in a different direction.

My focus is to use art sensitively, to create sacred spaces to help you realize the aims of the Path, because that's how big it is to me. I find these very beautiful, but to me it is not about art. These things are art, but this is not about art. It is about the Work. To me, all this stuff is about working for my Master and doing the job He gave me to do and doing what it was He enjoyed and appreciated and was grateful for. He never explained Himself. This stuff," Lee said, gesturing to the bronzes, "never explains itself."

Advancing the topic of deities, Lee said, "With sacred artifacts every element of the iconography means something." He pointed to a stone figure of Ganesh and said, "This is Ganesh. Ganesh is the god of possibility and opportunity, of taste and opulence. Ganesh is the remover of obstacles. Those are objective symbols. They are empowered by the tradition. When you are surrounded by this kind of symbol, the symbol is always shaping your mind relative to the objective value of the symbol, like a book of objective communication.

"Symbols are archetypical; to be near them is to be radiated by them. They bypass the linear mind. This is the point of sacred artifacts. Everything in the Sacred Bazaar, even the bowls, have a certain symbolism. What is a bowl? A chalice. What is the Holy Grail about? A chalice. That's objective symbolism. Most of my students have become serious collectors, and if you haven't, then let's start today.

"The point of these tasks is the Work. I was talking with David, and he made a comment in frustration about how difficult it is for people to change." Lee was talking about David H., an American who has lived in France for a very long time and who currently leads the Paris bordello, or study group. He also happened to be Lee's translator for the day, which meant that David was getting the opportunity to hear Lee's comments about him and translate them into French at this very moment. It was the kind of teaching communication that must sink in, in a very powerful way.

Lee continued, "I said that for people to change is a process of twenty years . . . . After twenty-five years you can say, 'Well, twenty-five years of practice has built something in them that is unusual.' You say, 'Oh my God, this person is so amazing, but they're still such an asshole!' I said to him, 'You judge people not based on small failures but on what twenty-five years of practice has cultivated.' After you've spent twenty years in the Work, you begin to see what this person has sacrificed for *you*, putting up with your bullshit. And really they're only irritating you because you haven't done your work. Let them cut their beef however they want!

"We get into relationship with somebody in a mundane sense and six months down the road you become frustrated with each other. And then after twenty years, you may still bitch at each other, but there is an enjoyment and love—you see how much this person has sacrificed for you, for your bullshit, and a sense of appreciation is there. It is the same in the Work. Some things just don't change. Twenty years later, we're still jockeying for position, but we're still practicing and we've stayed in place—we're still there. This is the point."

Coming back full circle to the point he had started with when he spoke about the theme of the summer teachings being about the responsibility of the disciple, Lee continued, "We pick our teacher, our path, and we do our best to bring integrity to it. We can't change our teacher or his teaching—*our responsibility is to be a good disciple.* That's where our responsibility starts and ends. When you are a good disciple, you serve others, you care for others, you are responsible."

Lee spoke about how Swami Prajnanpad gave the word "disciple" an objective meaning, part of which is that a good disciple is not irresponsible in any domain. The implications of being a good disciple are vast, which can be overwhelming to us, but at the same time, we don't have to worry about those implications because they don't rest on willpower. Paradoxically our responsibilities begin and end in being a good disciple. This is our personal responsibility; no one else can make a good disciple out of us, not even the best teacher in the world.

Lee was winding down for lunch, which was prepared by the sangha. Afterward there would be a break, during which time Lee would be, as always, behind the tables of the Sacred Bazaar.

That afternoon Lee opened the second session with more sales, promoting everything from handmade clothes of Indian design to books to stained glass windows. Rapidly going from one thing to the next, selling each item, sometimes lingering with one or another to describe it more, or sometimes just touching on it, Lee was making one, long, fluid presentation of the merchant's wares; he seemed determined to provoke us with a deluge of the Sacred Bazaar instead of traditional teaching, and yet everything he said carried layers of teaching significance—it was just presented in a way that forced the audience to work harder for it rather than having it all spelled out for them. At the same time, he paradoxically wove it all together, while acknowledging people's resistance to the merchant guru, Lee.

Lee held up his CD and explained that the title used to be *Dog's Day in the Sun*, but nobody really understood its meaning, so he changed it to *Crushed by Love*. He said, "The title, 'Ecrasé par l'Amour,' describes life . . . because when your life is bad, it's because you've been crushed by love. Even when things are fabulous and couldn't be better, you are crushed by love! It's a fabulous title! It's *my* title—don't steal it. If you have heard the other CDs that I'm singing on, this is nothing like those, I promise you . . . *Everyone* loves this CD!"

When Lee asked for questions, Marie Claire, a disciple of Arnaud who used to occasionally translate for Lee, raised her hand and said, "You said that you tried to draw everything you could from Yogi Ramsuratkumar. When I try to do that with Arnaud, I can't because Arnaud is so huge, so bright, and I am so small. I feel so small next to him that I cannot even look at him in his brightness."

Lee responded, "That's a good way of denying yourself the chance of ever realizing the master. When we put the master on such a pedestal so far above ourselves, in essence we are closing off the doorway that the master is trying to show us—that ultimately we are the same one. Let's give Marie Claire the benefit of the doubt here. Maybe the realization of the guru, who is light, is so real and bright that there is a visual phenomenon of light, so looking at the guru is like looking at the sun."

Lee went on to explain that in the Indian tradition, it is said that the master transmits in three ways: touch, eyes and voice or sound, as in passing on the mantra. Lee spoke of the way Yogi Ramsuratkumar used to say the mantra, "Ram, Ram," when he gave blessings as an example of this. I immediately thought about how the master's transmission by sound also includes the master's speaking voice, the way words resonate through him, and singing—sacred songs of any kind and particularly chanting the name of God. The sound of Yogi Ramsuratkumar's speaking and singing voice was extraordinarily unique and beautiful; he had a certain lilting quality to his voice that made it amazingly childlike, innocent and disarming in the most divine sense. He could melt my heart with a few words, and to hear him say, "Ram! Ram!" as he often did when giving blessings, were some of the most unforgettable moments of my life.

I thought about how Lee does this same thing primarily through music, and he uses the syncretic music of America, coming as it does from the cotton fields and back streets, the broken-down rural farms and urban ghettos of people who have endured tremendous suffering. Lee's voice is infamous among those who know him. It has a way of penetrating through the density of the body. Sometimes it is almost like an alarm clock going off—it wakes you up! At the same time that his voice can be tender, gravely, raw, sweet or harsh, it is always closer to you than your own breath, and this too can be unnerving or very sweet, like nectar. This is also true of Lee's speaking voice—for example, exactly the way he had been speaking to us today, sometimes in a rhythmic way, his voice richly nuanced, sometimes husky and suggestive, sometimes lyrical, always communicating an intimacy with the human condition and the human heart.

Lee continued, "Any use of mantra or a song can be used . . . any use of the voice that communicates reality. Before I had a traditional master, Janis Joplin was my master! Jimi Hendrix said, 'She uses her voice the way I use my guitar.' When you hear someone with a really great voice like that, it touches you . . .

"The master can also communicate through symbol. The teaching can be communicated though many media. But the media is not the message in this case . . .You can receive the teaching in many ways. The more directly the teaching impacts you, the better off you are, because as long as the mind is interpreting the message you are at the mercy of your mind's interpretations. You want to directly receive the teaching with as little interpretation as possible.

"The mind edits everything according to our particular expectation of the world. We are giving a seminar on money later this summer at Ferme de Jutreau. In America, all of the people who never have enough money want to come to it, because they think if they come to the seminar they'll have more money. But if your psychological knot is that there is not enough money, then the mind edits everything so that there is not enough money. All the money in the world is available; you just have to know how to get it. You have to love money, not just want it, but love it. Money, if you really love it, it will respond, but not if you just like it because you are greedy . . .

"Money is not dirt, even though that's what Ramakrishna said. He said that women and gold are evil. I think Ramakrishna had it backwards; he said that women and gold will keep you from God. I have the opposite view; women and gold are the way to God. The Feminine is the way to God. Maybe if you are a woman you think it's men and gold, but you are wrong. Woman is the way to God.

"These things," Lee said, pointing to the bronze deities on the table behind him, "are like orphans. Ever go to an orphanage where the kids are up for adoption? To the kids, every adult is a potential home, a potential parent. They really don't get enough love. Every adult who comes in is a potential parent and the kids—the ones that haven't had it beaten out of them—look at you with a look that melts your heart. These pieces are the same. These pieces have been torn out of their homes . . .

"If you look at that table over there, and you have the idea that everything is expensive, then everything is. We need a certain amount of money—but if we have this idea that money is not spiritual, then we are always in conflict about spending it, even if we have it. In the spiritual world money is energy. It can be used creatively or destructively.

"Werner Erhard started a program back in the seventies called 'The Hunger Project.' It worked on the context that there is enough food in the world to feed everyone. So why is it that people starve? For the same reason that there is more money in the world than we can imagine, and many of us are always in survival about money. It's ego that is invested in keeping you from realizing that ego has no essential power. In the material world, wealth is controlled by those who have it and are invested in the poor/wealthy context."

Lee continued, "We are human beings first. You are controlled by the French media the same way that we are controlled by the media in America. In the spiritual world, ego controls psychology and personality, and psychology and personality control chemistry and glandular changes. Then chemistry and glandular changes control your literal response to things—if your adrenal glands are malfunctioning seriously enough, you will think you are going crazy. If your chemistry is off, you will feel dark, apathetic. Any little shift in brain chemistry can have a dramatic effect on personality, which is why psychiatrists all over the world are recommending brain drugs."

It's a bleak landscape indeed that Lee was describing. Most people, even those who are on the path, have very little idea of exactly how bad it really is—how very little authenticity we have as individuals. Lee said, "Therapy used to be about finding a good therapist and dealing with the formative experiences of your psychology so you straighten out and fly right. But now we are so incapable of any kind of basic strength of integrity that we need therapy for a lifetime. It has become a hand-holding lifeline for a culture of weakness and sickness. It's hard to actually manage our own lives. Even if we have a great life, and everything is going well, it is hard to manage. So you make a small change, take a pill that affects your hormones, and you are happier than a pig in shit. If you're a therapist and you are committed to helping people, you are going to have to mud wrestle with these people. It's hell…"

The next person questioned why we would use subjective objects like the bronze deities when we are after something objective. Lee replied, "We are subject to two forces: one that comes from inside and pushes us up toward God, and the other comes from outside—it is God pulling us to Him. Between these two forces are obstacles. Typically we try to clear the obstacles with our minds. This is usually helpful and useful, but it's not the ultimate way."

Lee asserted that sacred symbolism is not subjective; it is objective in that it communicates the same thing to everyone who sees it. Musical forms like rock & roll and rap are subjective—some people like rap and some don't—but, Pavarotti's voice is objective. In the same way, there are subjective symbols and objective symbols, and sacred artifacts are based on objective symbols—they push us up toward God. Their objective symbolism can cut through whole patterns of obstacles, which is essentially their value. Sacred symbols resonate to that within us that is objectively real.

Another question was posed by a woman who was expressing her frustration at the suffering she experiences. Lee said, "It's simple. When it gets bad enough, it will change. It's like addiction. If the conscious mind says, 'I'm suffering, I want to change' but the unconscious mind says, 'Yes, but there is a payoff,' then we are split. If we are split, the intention doesn't have the power to make the change. In a very real sense, it's a big risk to change, because inside the subconscious is saying, 'Don't take risks—it might not work!'

Whatever is known to us is secure, even if it is suffering. The only thing that can manage the subconscious mind is *intention*. So you have to have one-pointed intention.

"When we really hit bottom, anything is possible. It's then that we can have the strength to drop the problems, the habits, to go cold turkey. That's the kind of power that intention can have. But there can be no split—you have to have one-pointed intention. The motive doesn't matter; it can be completely selfish."

Lee used gambling as an example of an addiction, then he spoke of it as a metaphor for reality. He said, "Gambling is based on reality—the House always wins. The House is God. If we had faith in that fact, a lot of things that upset us would not upset us; at the end of the day, we would know that everything is going to be okay.

"If we really knew that the House always wins—God always wins—we would never do the things that add insult to injury. But we try to do God's job, and we can't: we're fallible. We say that the guru is infallible—not exactly. The human being who is a master has a light side and a dark side, and the dark side is pathological, but the thing is, for example, even within Catholicism today, there are certain sects in which true saints are living, praying and practicing. Unsung saints . . .

"My personal value as a teacher is not based on my psychology. I'm not a psychological exception—I have my own neurosis. What makes me 'infallible' is not Lee Lozowick and his psychology, which is pathological. What makes me valuable is the degree to which I'm transparent to Yogi Ramsuratkumar. It's the role of guru, the essence of the guru, that is infallible. As long as I'm serving Yogi Ramsuratkumar first, all of my pathologies will stay quiescent. But as soon as I start thinking I'm the House, and at the end of the day I win, I'll get into trouble! Because I'm *not* the House; God is the House. Anyone who puts themselves before their Master will run into trouble on the Path."

Lee said that what is needed is an intuitive and instinctual resonance to what the path is. When we recognize the teacher, we realize that this is who we've been given to walk the path with. He spoke about other teachers that he's known, some of whom are outstanding disciples of their own masters, some of whom are not and have run into trouble on the path, through abuses of power and other scandalous and unacceptable behaviors. These are teachers who have lost their way in the labyrinth.

Speaking to the numerous students of Arnaud Desjardins who were in the room, Lee said, "To receive Arnaud's transmission you have to put him before yourself. Most of the things you want for yourself, he wants for you, but you have to put your master first in order to realize that. As soon as I put myself before Yogi Ramsuratkumar, maybe I get financial independence, but I also get psychological pathologies."

Lee candidly spoke about himself and his own tendencies, saying that he was drawn to fame and power. "I tried to go in that direction; I went down to the crossroads with pen in hand, ready to sign and make a deal, but the devil never showed up, because Yogi Ramsuratkumar kicked his ass on the way down there—the devil, that is! Now I'm a yogi, and I can resist things like gambling, and even women and their breasts . . . . I look like a pretty disciplined guy—that's all my Master! My students think I'm so disciplined and patient. I put my Master before myself, that's why I look disciplined and patient. Yogi Ramsuratkumar put His Master before Himself and got to be one of the greatest Masters in the world!

"People ask me about therapy all the time—whether it is useful or not? If you are in therapy, are you being successful? If you are not being relatively successful coming to manage your pathologies, after some time and effort, and you are on the Path and have a real teacher, you can be one hundred percent certain that the reason you are not successful at managing your psychology is because you are not putting your master before yourself!"

The day was quickly coming to a close. Even after our short few hours together, the room felt completely different than it had in the morning when we first started. Everything felt relaxed, melted, the hard edges were made soft, the sharp edge of personality was rounded. It felt like a purifying force had gently burned through the atmosphere of the contained space we had created and defined together for a few hours, to hear the Baul master give the teaching and to bask in his transmission of reality.

Lee closed the chamber of the day with a flourish and a tip of his hat to the City of Lights: "So, it's time to end. Have a wonderful evening—it's Paris, after all! What a wonderful city! I *love* Paris! But then, you're Parisians! You're all practically *psychotic*!" Lots of happy laughter rang through the space—the rapport was strong enough that it seemed to be tacitly understood that this was Lee's way of giving everyone a final blessing. He had a big smile on his face as he continued, "Parisians all walk around like, 'Grrrr! Hhmmph!' So put your misery on the shelf for tonight and have a good evening!"

Paris
June 26

The day after the seminar, Sunday, Lee went to the mosque not far from where we were staying. Why the mosque? Because the mosque complex includes a café that is open to the public, where, at the suggestion of his student, Sian, Lee discovered excellent Arabic coffee a few years ago. At this mosque the elixir is black and strong enough to alter your state of consciousness for hours. Having mastered the art of making coffee, both espresso and the brewed cup, Kelly was interested in tasting as much coffee as possible while in France, and Lee was happy to help him in this aim. As Lee said to Kelly of the first time he drank coffee at the mosque, "I was ecstatic for hours!" A rare statement indeed for one who says he's never ecstatic.

Why is Lee so enthusiastic about coffee when he abstained from coffee for many years as part of his dietary discipline? That is a question that cannot be answered with absolute certainty, but it is worth recalling one of the most charming *lilas* of Yogi Ramsuratkumar, which occurred in 1993 when a number of students were visiting him with Lee. About fourteen people were having his darshan in a small shrine room at Sudama House after a meal had been served. He was interacting with us individually, asking us questions about our lives back in Arizona and about Lee's ashram. He turned to Lee and asked, "What kind of food do you eat, Lee?"

Lee said, "Vegetarian diet. Very simple, very plain."

Yogi Ramsuratkumar asked, "Do you have tea?" Lee answered no.

Then Yogi Ramsuratkumar asked, "Do you have coffee on your ashram?"

When Lee answered no, Yogi Ramsuratkumar began to chuckle. With a mischievous smile and a gleam in his eyes, he said, "You must not have very many people at your ashram, Lee!" It was a moment of pure delight. We all laughed—Lee, his students, Yogi Ramsuratkumar, Ma Devaki and the other Sudama sisters who were present.

Serving coffee was a ritual that Yogi Ramsuratkumar enacted many times over his years in Tiruvannamalai. When a devotee or guest came seeking the hidden beggar saint of Tiruvannamalai, he would always send out for cups of sweet Indian coffee. This was true even in the early years, when he lived on the streets and met with people in the *mandapam* not far from the Shiva temple, or in the small house where he lived on Sannadhi Street near the temple. After he moved to Sudama House with the Sudama sisters, the coffee was made in the kitchen and served to devotees and guests in stainless steel cups.

The ritual continued once the ashram was built. Yogi Ramsuratkumar always served Lee and his students coffee twice a day on his ashram, beginning in 1994 until his death. With the first chirping birds and the pearly dawn sky, coffee would arrive at the beautiful, cool hour of six, and then again at three in the sultry afternoon.

It took almost ten years for the gift of coffee to come to Lee after Yogi Ramsuratkumar's humorous play with him in 1993. Not long after Christina and Kelly Sell opened their coffee shop in Prescott, Arizona, Yogi Ramsuratkumar died. It was about one year later that Kelly started sending large donations of coffee beans when he had roasted too many, and they would not be up to his high standard of freshness if used in the shop. When Kelly heard that the ashram always took free food and ate it, he started sending the excess quantities of beans to Lee. Because any gift that is given to the master is a gift of prasad, and therefore carries blessings in it, sure enough, we found ourselves frequently drinking coffee made from Kelly's delicious beans.

When coffee kept coming in various forms of serendipity, and Christina and Kelly kept inviting Lee to their shop to enjoy their expertise with the coffee bean, it became clear that the "coffee lila" had started right after Yogi Ramsuratkumar left his physical body. We began to say, "Yogi Ramsuratkumar is sending us coffee!" Considering the amount of coffee that has shown up around Lee, who abstained for many years, we might do well to think of B.K.S. Iyengar, probably the greatest hatha yogi in the world today, who has been quoted as saying that coffee is the *soma rasa* of the Kali Yuga. Papa Ramdas, the guru of Yogi Ramsuratkumar, said that chanting the name of God is the only practice that will help in the Kali Yuga. So, maybe we could say that for us, at least at this point in time, it's mantra and *soma rasa*!

The sangha members who were in Paris for the seminar the day before, and who stayed over to be with Lee today, were invited to meet him at the mosque for coffee. As we made our way through the streets in the beautiful morning light, Lee was saying that he hoped people weren't just standing around in the courtyard of the mosque waiting for him, but that they would sit down and order. In fact, a very large entourage was waiting for Lee when we arrived, including the members of the Paris sangha, several residents from the ashram and students from England and France. And sure enough, everyone was standing around in the courtyard, waiting for Lee.

"Sit down! Sit down!" Lee barked in an irritated tone as he walked up.

It was the kind of inelegant high visibility and lack of sensitivity to public spaces and the needs of others that Lee's entourage sometimes displays on the city streets—and it could be any city, for that matter. The same kinds of things have happened in India, Europe or America. He has criticized his students many times for being extremely slow to learn this principle of how to interact with the world at large while being sensitive to the needs of different environments and the unspoken protocol of any given space.

The real question is: how to be a good guest? If you are a guest in another country, in another person's home, in a restaurant or any other public space, the law of hospitality is at work. It is a big law that covers a lot of territory, including all aspects of relationship, and there is no black and white rule for determining the protocol of hospitality in any given moment or space; rather it is a spontaneous, organic sensing into the present moment that is required. When we operate from this kind of wisdom, then we always know what the dharma in action is at any time.

Instantly everyone was in motion, scrambling to put several of the small round tables together for our large group of about twenty-five. We were perched on the upper level of the enclosed patio courtyard—the happy home to thriving olive trees and many chirping, fearless sparrows—that was cloistered from the street, just outside the mosque café, made colorful and exotic by the inlaid geometric designs of Islam on the table tops, walls and ceilings. It turned out to be a delightful interlude for the whole group, as Lee's mood turned genial and many rounds of coffee and sweet tea were ordered, along with a wide variety of Middle Eastern pastries.

The conversation took a lively turn, while the proprietor took a liking to our group, and treated us with affection and warm hospitality—he seemed to have a resonance to our friendly and joyous spirit. When he found out that Kelly owned a café in Arizona, he invited him back to the kitchen to watch how they made the Arabic coffee, then lavished him with boxes of pastries to take away with us, as a gift.

"Come again! Au revoir! Bon journée!" he called as we finally made our way back out the high wooden gate. Lee is often fond of quoting Shakespeare, which I've heard many times after making a mistake: "All's well that ends well!"

Paris
June 27

Hosting Christina and Kelly in Paris presented a rare opportunity for Lee to reciprocate the hospitality that they have so generously extended to the sangha by hosting Lee and Shri on many occasions at their café in Prescott, where the band plays once a month. In the spirit of that hospitality, which the guru was now lavishing on Christina and Kelly, Lee and his entourage made a rare visit to the Musée Guimet this morning.

Lee usually says of museums of all kinds, "Why would I want to go to a museum? If I can't buy it, I don't want to see it!" Ten years ago he had visited the Musée Guimet, and as far as I know, it's been about that long since he's been in any other museum, with the exception of taking his children to the Louvre twice—and then, it was *only* for the sake of the children.

Before the museum, Lee stopped in at a café for coffee. Christina asked him how long we would be at the museum. Lee said, "About an hour. I only need thirty minutes, but I will capitulate."

Christina laughed and said, "Yes, I suppose we will need longer than that to ooh and aah over everything."

Someone else in the group commented, "Yes, remember the time E.J. Gold took his group to the Metropolitan Museum of Art, he had them actually run to get through the whole thing. If you have a good antennae, that's all you need to make use of what the art has to offer."

At the Guimet, a short walk from the Trocadero, Lee strolled through one of the finest Asian art collections in the world, stopping now and then to gaze at a piece, but mostly just making steady progress through the halls and corridors of its four floors. A little over an hour later, he was ready to move on to the next thing. Standing outside the museum on the sidewalk, a few more sangha members had joined Lee's party, so that about fifteen people hovered around him or hung back, waiting for orders. He commented that he wanted to go to a good café in the Rive Gauche next, and then to walk around the area and visit the many antique shops there.

Someone asked if the rest of the Paris sangha was invited to come with him or meet him in the Rive Gauche. He said, "Well, they can come there and try to find us if they want."

Chaos began to take over. The reigning madness of city trips reared its ugly head and seemed to drag on and on as different people asserted, through their own confusion and sincere but tangled wishes to serve, what it was that Lee "really wanted" and where a "good place" in the Rive Gauche might be. Some tried to take the bull by the horns by grappling with logistics, maps and offering lots of suggestions. As the anxiety built, further tension was generated by others who were continuing to voice concerns that those who wanted to hook up with Lee later in Paris should be able to find him. Still others were simply not paying attention, spacing out, or lost in meaningless conversations and social chitchat.

In the midst of this embroglio, Lee stood off to the side, invisible, silent, a Nobody in a swarm of important people with agendas. Finally, with many good ideas having been bandied about, one person shooting down another's ideas and so on, all vying for dominance in service to the king, one suggestion in particular was put forth in a way that stood out from the din, which was, "Let's follow so and so," who lives in Paris.

"Absolutely not!" Lee blurted out. "I don't want to follow somebody else because inevitably they will take me where I don't want to go!"

When some of us seemed surprised by his outburst, Lee repeated, slowly and with emphasis, "Every time I follow someone else's lead, I end up somewhere I *don't* want to go." But his words fell on largely deaf ears, as most of the people who were involved in the chaos simply didn't hear him at all.

Finally, during another brief lull in the cacophony, Lee said in an understated way but with calm force and amazing equanimity, "How about I pick the place and then you call them," meaning the others who would meet up later, "and tell them where to meet me?"

Kelly Sell, who was traveling with Lee for the first time, was standing nearby, taking in the scene and the guru's comments. "Go to the Source," Kelly said, with the sage observation of beginner's mind, as we all took off in the direction Lee was walking.

After a long day of a more genial and easeful than usual whirlwind of the Musée Guimet, brocante shopping, walking the streets and café stops, Lee and company had reservations at Mandala Ray—a trendy, plush and rather exotic restaurant just off the Champs d'Elysée, owned by famous actors Johnny Depp, John Malkovitch and Sean Penn. This evening was inspired primarily by the seven young teenagers who were part of Lee's traveling party on this visit to Paris. The kids had been given the option to go to the Atlantic beach instead of to Paris, and they had unanimously said, "No way! We want to go to Paris!"

A special dinner like this, in which the kids were treated to an expensive and posh (and very cool) restaurant, was a very special occasion and certainly, in some ways, marked a turning point in their own growth and development. They were getting to do something the adults do only rarely. The rest of the adults in the party—Lee's family, Laura Shelby, Paula Z., Chris McMasters, Christina and Kelly—got to reap the benefits of this outing with the kids, who were all the more excited about it because one of their heroes, Johnny Depp, was somehow, mysteriously, peripherally involved.

Our reservation for seventeen people was for seven o'clock on Monday night, which was the earliest possible reservation available. We arrived even earlier, of course, and stood outside on the sidewalk until the restaurant opened. Once we were inside, the staff still wasn't ready to seat us. Being "on time" is such an oddity in Paris that they didn't really know what to do with us, so we just stood in the darkened, spacious foyer with all the live plants and abundance of gorgeous fresh flower arrangements. Some of us took the opportunity to visit the exotically appointed men's and women's rooms.

The décor of the place was somewhere between Indiana Jones and the Temple of Doom, the Potola and the French Rivera—a mystical marriage of Dionysus and Buddha. It definitely carried the magic of a finely constructed movie set, aimed at creating a certain mood, with huge, stained glass back-lit mandalas in reds and oranges on the ceiling, Buddha heads and immense, carved wooden *gandarvas*—celestial musicians—flanking the stage area. The chairs were plush, oversized, soft, so that you sank into them but with just the right amount of support. The whole room gave the sense of darkened vast space, and yet it was rich and full of images and impressions, carefully nuanced with soft, hidden lighting. All this was put together with excellent food (much of it organic), fine wine and music to offer a total sensory experience.

At one point one of the teenage boys, Max, in his typically precocious and theatrical style, looked around at the surroundings and said with a mixture of wonder, irony and his marvelous sense of humor, "I cannot *believe* I am here! I mean, who am I to be in such a place? I am just a *nobody*. A nobody . . . I mean I am not anybody to be here."

Christina, who was standing nearby, replied, "I'd rather be nobody around Lee than somebody around anybody else."

"Amen to that," someone echoed.

It was true. And that is the challenge we often face with Lee: while at the same time that the guru empowers each of us to be everything we can be—and he frequently throws his considerable weight of Blessing Power behind bringing out the potential in people—to fully embrace what the guru offers to us we must be willing to become nobody. We often have the chance to watch each other blossom and shine, in areas of music, singing, painting, writing, sculpting, raising children, managing the creativity involved in new business projects. We find ourselves in amazing, miraculous, extraordinary, rich and profound circumstances—perhaps the least of which is dining in a fine restaurant off the Champs d'Elysée in Paris—that can only be attributed entirely to our relationship with Lee, who makes all things possible.

There is a price to be paid, of course, and the price is in the coin of surrender. The more surrendered one is to the guru in this school, the more possibility one engages. But getting involved to that degree means guru yoga, in which the guru becomes everything and the disciple, the devotee or student, becomes nothing. It is a sweet emptiness, the joy of sacrifice, the joy of surrender, and it also has its harrowing and dark moments, in which ego and the separate personality are challenged, even threatened to the very core.

In fact, there are times on the path, sometimes a very long time, when this dichotomy is a mortal combat between the part of us that wants to be nobody in the sense of the diminishment of the egoic self, and the part of us that wants to be the most important, powerful, talented, acknowledged person in our circle. It's a war to the death, and if we stay on the path, it is nobody who will eventually win. Tonight it was the wisdom of one of our young people who gave us a reminding factor of this very truth. The English saying, "Out of the mouths of babes," on this evening, could be re-worded to state, "Out of the mouths of budding teens."

Interestingly, in addition to the delicious food, the wine and friendly service we received that night, we were delighted by the surprise of the live music that was presented: an eleven piece ensemble—complete with a dashing young maestro dressed in long black tails and two vocalists, a man and a woman—played mostly classical pieces and opera. The first time we had come to Mandala Ray, last summer, there was no music or live performance of any kind, so this was a very big surprise for all of us. As it turned out, the opera was a one-time event—a special feature of this particular Monday night. It was, without doubt, the highlight of the pleasurable feasting of the senses that Mandala Ray had to offer. The music was particularly serendipitous because Kelly sings opera. It was so perfect it seemed like it had been planned as the final touch to Kelly's first visit to Paris.

When Lee was asked if he knew about the performance tonight, he said, "No, but this must be why we came on Monday night—for Kelly to hear the opera."

Paris
June 28

Tonight was out last night in Paris. We had a lovely, quiet dinner at the apartment where we were staying—a truly ancient four-story apartment in the Place Contrascarpe, built in the oldest part of Paris not far from the mosque where we'd gathered the day before and a thirty-minute walk to Notre Dame on the Seine. Christina and Kelly had visited the market down the street that morning and bought everything we would need. They were happy doing what they love to do the most: providing hospitality. They hustled up a delicious meal in the second floor kitchen for all of us, with sauccison sec, baguette, a variety of delicious cheeses, a big green salad and bowls of olives.

Lee sat with his plate on his knees, ensconced on the low seat by the windows. Small glasses of wine were poured, and we sat down to a quiet dinner in the old kitchen, the windows thrown wide open to the street and the lively square down below. A few scattered raindrops fell, taking the edge off the intense heat of the day.

Hours later, in our beds on the various floors of the apartment, all the way up to the attic loft on the fourth floor, the sound of revelry was so loud, as it was every night of the week, week in and week out during good weather, that it was almost like sitting in one of the busy cafés down below. Two hundred people carried on in these cafés, trying not to notice the suffering in the world all around them and especially at the root of their own restless hearts, while on the bottom floor, the master slept in his bedroom with the windows, which open directly onto the Place, closed. He slept despite the lively drone of Contrascarpe, because, as he often says, "Nothing keeps me awake." It is a matter of his intention and what best serves his work.

The city has powerful lessons to teach, especially when it's too hot to sleep in the sultry Paris night. Sometimes the people of the cafés seem to me like hungry ghosts draped in human garb, pretending they will always be made of flesh and bone. We too will soon be dust, a fragment on the wind. Yet somehow, by the grace of God and the fruition of karmas, we are here with the spiritual master, and we remember, from time to time, that it is Ram playing games down below in the Place.

Sleeping in those old rooms with heavy wooden beams overhead, I wondered at the endless rounds of life, the people who have lived here, in this place, karma begetting karma, across the generations of mothers, fathers and children who have come and gone. A light rain pelted the small skylight in my attic room, and just the slightest drift of air lifted my spirits in the sticky, airless night. The city reminded me that we were wandering this planet, so sorely under siege, in the grip of illusion in very troubled times, with one who is a living artifact of sanctity and blessing power, an embodiment of

Surrender to the Will of God, and I felt like a soldier in the service of the guru, who wages a war of goodness and grace against the prevailing forces of darkness.

Lee is driven by the force of Grace and his master's Benediction, and we follow along as best we can. Riding Lee's edge of exhaustion, we follow behind, diligent, eager, soft-hearted or confused, harsh and sometimes angry, blaming each other for even our most inconsequential sins, still hoping to catch the crumbs that fly from the master's jubilant hands. All day we had swept the streets with Lee, loving Paris, place of grit and glamour, where everything sparkles like gold, and some of it is—in his company. It is that which can be turned golden that he catches in his diaphanous net as he trudges down streets and lanes, and once in a decade, through the Musée Guimet, that place of ancient treasures and relics of a glorious past.

Yes, whether it is Paris, Berlin or L.A., or the sweet countryside and beautiful villages of France, or the desert towns of Arizona like Quartzite or Tucson, Lee is relentless in his wandering, driven by his own inner fires. What is really going on in these peregrinations? In the past year Lee had spent time in Los Angeles, San Francisco, New York City, Las Vegas, Phoenix, Tucson, Montreal, London and Paris—not to mention the many European cities, towns and villages that he visits on tour with Shri in Spain, Italy, France and Germany, or his yearly travels in India. He makes regular forays into Mexico City as well. Lee keeps his finger on the pulse of things; he meets, befriends and touches the lives of countless numbers of people.

Lee once said that the tantric path is "Action, action, action!" His movement through the world and the divine activity of that delicate, multi-dimensional reality reminds me of the myth of Vishnu, and the churning of the cosmic ocean, which generated the nectars of the gods and revealed the rarest jewel of all, which Vishnu wears in his crown—Kausthaba. In Lee's endless brocante wanderings, his search for objects of beauty and sanctity across the world, what are we really looking for? What is it that Lee finds in the American movies he loves so much, the good food and fine wine, the favorite chocolates near the Place Pigalle? Maybe it is longing; longing for the impossible promise that the Beloved is alive and real—realer than real, to be found in the essences and quintessences of life as it is. We can be sure that it is not desire that drives Lee. As he has said many times, Lee can drop this play in the fields of desire at any time and resume the ascetic life. Unlike his students, who often fall into the traps of such journeys into the seductions, fascinations and distractions of the world with all its false glitter, Lee could let it all go in an instant.

Like everywhere else, so many people in the City of Lights are psychotic, troubled to the bone; bitter sorrows flow like the blood in their veins—even in this place, one of the most beautiful of all cities on earth. It takes a very rare kind of spiritual teacher to spend his precious hours and days romancing these streets as Lee does, at home in the world as he is, driving the van all across the city, through the Paris traffic or like a madman, down narrow cobbled roads and one-way lanes. That is our guru—a one-way street, whose destination is surrender and Grace.

Paris, or any other flashy bauble, is a mere carnival whose labyrinth we wander. All these ten thousand things are just the sheerest veil over the great truth of our lives with Lee. Faith is our true banquet; praise and adoration are our wine. We live under the ancient eaves of that temple called Yogi Ramsuratkumar; he alone is our goal, our passionate problem to solve, when there is no problem at all, but only the appearance of one. Yogi Ramsuratkumar is all of our answers, the source of our wandering, our departure and our destination. He is the soul of the world, the breath of life in all these forms that we embrace with Lee.

It is Yogi Ramsuratkumar who enjoys all this—the opera at Mandala Ray, the soaring voices, delicate food and dark red wine, the din of the cafés at night, the city streets, hot in the sun or cooled down by rain, the fabulous classic sculpture, the preponderance of art, these works of grandeur and wonder, generations upon generations bringing beauty into form, exalted in precious metals, gems and stones, in the craft of the goldsmith's hands, or the play of the wordsmith's dance, the great poets of years past—Tagore, Whitman, Wordsworth, Shelley, Baudelaire, Shakespeare and yes, Bukowski, and so many more—or as music soaring in melody and song. Everywhere there is color and texture, taste and *rasa*: in all these juices of life, in pleasure of every kind, dull or diamond, burning with emptiness, rich and fulsome with delight, there is Yogi Ramsuratkumar.

All these myriad impressions and contemplations lead me always to where we are now, when we have come so far with Lee as our guide. He is valiant, lionhearted, carrying on against the odds, in a world choked with *drala*, with violence, greed, beauty, terror and fear, charity and mercy, wisdom and war, not real and begging to be made realer than real.

Ferme de Jutreau
June 29

After the many activities of our five-day sojourn in the big city, we headed back to Ferme de Jutreau today for a few days of ashram life before the next seminar, at Chardenoux. What sweet relief to hurtle down the winding country roads of those last thirty miles, through the slow-paced villages with their markets and rambling old stone buildings, then finally turn down the long *chemin privé* under the canopy of trees, opening into the hidden jewel of sanctuary—oh, the gardens, the blooming roses, the peace and quiet, the countryside, the dulcet loveliness of Lee's ashram in France! Home again, and a welcomed respite from the hectic, feverish pace of our city journeys. Meditation at seven a.m. in the barn darshan hall, with birds singing and early morning mists rising in the fields, never seemed so peaceful, so good . . .

La Roche Posay
June 30

Today Lee took Kelly and Christina to the new shop in La Roche Posay with ten big boxes of merchandise that he would store in the back until the front display room was ready. We parked and walked in through the back door. People were busy at work putting finishing touches on the renovations for the grand opening of the shop on July 9.

Kelly and Christina were appropriately wowed by the eight-hundred-year old building, its stone turret, the basement like a wine cave, where Lee would store his stash of *prasad* wine. Immediately Lee began to unpack the boxes while Kelly enthusiastically took photos. Brinda showed us the sleazy faux suede that used to cover the thirteenth century stonewalls of the front showroom.

Later we walked through the cobbled stone streets and went to the café for coffee. Around the corner from the shop a bar was advertising chorizo, pizza, wine and a group of musicians, called Blues Latino Rosa, who would be playing later in the week. Just down the lane from Lee's shop was a three-story stone house *a vendre*, covered with wisteria vines, blooming purple clematis, red and pink climbing roses. Lace curtains hung at the window on the first floor. Once again, we were charmed by deep France. There were many fantastic buildings for sale on the streets around the shop at Rue Duguesclin and Rue Bourbon. As we came upon yet another gorgeous little gem of a place, Lee said, "Let's call about this one!"

Intrigued, Kelly asked, "What would you do with it, if it's really cheap?"

"Buy it!" Lee exulted. Walking along with Lee, we were a little like Alice in Wonderland with the Mad Hatter. Lee pointed out beautiful old places adjacent to and actually part of the block of rambling stone ramparts that make up the old wall of the city and housed our shop as one part of its labyrinth. "Someone could live in this one . . . You could put tables out there and set up a café . . ."

We joked around about how Kelly and Christina could have a Coffee Roasters café, à la La Roche Posay, three months a year in one of these locations. It was fun to simply enjoy the excitement of infinite possibility that we felt streaming from Lee as he danced from one thing to the next. The summer on the road in Europe with Lee was revealing one thing with crystal clarity: Lee is a man of many, many dimensions, with far-ranging interests and passions. As he said of himself at one point, "I have my fingers in a lot of pies." Music, fine art, street art, poetry, literature, business, antiquities, wine, food, sacred spaces, all kinds of culture, the transmission of the teaching and the lineage in many different forms—and within this complex yantra, he lives in the wide open, groundless space of possibility, where creativity bubbles up from the Source. It's a formidable circumstance around him, and there can be a very high degree of creative tension, heat, pressure and a terrible sense of panic that arises in the fast ebb and flow of energy and action, sometimes further abraded and made raw by our lack of compassion and generosity with each other. But on days like this, with the sun sparkling in the trees and Lee smiling, radiant and happy, nothing else mattered but the *drala* of the moment . . .

Soon we were in the van and zooming through the outskirts of La Roche Posay, on our way back to the ashram, past signs for the *paella soiree* that night, and then through the flat, fertile fields, dotted with huge golden rolls of harvested hay and fringed by green forests. The fields of sunflowers were still in full bloom, their yellow mandalas turned toward the sun. Lee drove these peaceful, back-country roads like a man with a high security mission, a covert operation—like the universe was going to explode if he didn't get to the ashram at exactly the right moment. Men and women on bicycles passed us on the narrow, two-lane road. There was no shoulder for the road, so Lee slowed down just a little.

Chardenoux

Chardenoux
July 2, 2005

In the morning, during Lee's first session of the seminar, after a quick review of the schedule for the weekend seminar and recommending that people get together in small groups after dinner "to consider the ideas that went on in here today," he launched into a refrain that we hear quite often from him these days: "I'm pretty anti-social, so I don't like groups at all, but they seem to be useful to others, so . . . God has a perverse sense of humor, putting somebody like me in a position like this! I may look like I enjoy it, because I'm a good actor. Mostly I'd rather just be alone with a good book."

It didn't take long for him to be in full swing, however, giving freely in his inimitable way. Soon he was talking about a man who wrote a letter to *Hustler* magazine, saying, "I try to be nice and sweet and good to women, and they leave me. What's the problem?"

Lee answered, "I think I have figured it out in thirty years of teaching. One of the tremendous quirks of fate is that we get born, we're the most conscious creation, in our solar system anyway, unless there are underground creations on Jupiter, and if you go to new age festivals you'll find people there who swear they are from another planet and tell you all about it—I think it's all hysteria, but maybe it's true! Most of those people would be bums on the street if they weren't making eighty thousand dollars a year going to new age fairs and telling people all this bullshit. I could teach a seminar next year on exactly how to do that, but you'd have to get over your psychology to do it! You wouldn't be able to!

"Anyway, here we are, we're born, and in our upbringing we are convinced that we are unloved, rejected, abandoned, and we're convinced that the reason that happened is that we're bad. We grow up, and the underlying feeling that motivates us is that we're bad and don't deserve all the good things of life . . . Well, maybe some wine!" Everyone laughed at this one small admission.

Lee went on, "I got a letter from a student saying, 'I want love, then when I get it, I don't want it because I don't think I deserve it.' There is the conscious mind that wants health, love, all the good things of life, and the unconscious mind that goes about creating the circumstances that prove that we're unloved, abandoned, etc.

"Your first child, especially if born at home, no matter how much you love children, *your* child is different. You go through labor—'Oh my God! Kill me now! I'm never going to do this again! Get the fuck out of my face!'—then the baby is born and you take one look at that and your world is broken open. You look at this innocent being—the most beautiful thing in the universe—and it completely breaks your heart. Then your unconscious mind says, 'I don't deserve this beauty and joy,' so you go about doing the very things that deny you the joy.

"Like, you stop nursing. Your breasts get infected, first one, then the other. It's messy and sloppy and you have to wear a nursing bra and it's unattractive. Then you go back to work after a few months, leaving your baby with a baby sitter or a class, when the baby only wants one thing: to be with its mother. So, we come home tired and ignore them, just give them perfunctory attention, without the slightest bit of conscience about the suffering we are causing the child, because we are so busy protecting ourselves from the primal beauty and wonder and joy of that relationship, because we think we're bad and don't deserve it. Then we spend most of our lives in therapy, trying to recover that space in which we can truly experience that love and awe and joy!"

This first talk at Chardenoux ranged over a lot of territory and then honed in on the changes in his teaching style—a theme Lee has returned to over and over again in the past few years. In the next two and a half hours Lee gave a powerful overview of how he teaches, what interests him and what all the commotion of the Sacred Bazaar is about. He set the context for the importance of the teaching in our lives in a reference to Bob Dylan's song, "Everything is Broken."

What motivates us on the Path? Lee said, " 'Everything is Broken' is an acute commentary on the world. Even love and joy and majesty is broken, not essentially, but personally. Some of you have good jobs, wonderful families, children, and, *everything is broken.* If you look around and really get in touch with your feeling, you know that something is wrong: everything is broken."

Everyone can relate to that line: "Everything is broken." That said, and many other things as well, Lee had the whole room connected to the comet of his train of thought as he talked about how he did not choose his teaching style, or to be a guru, but his master chose it all for him. His flow of words and images began to drift into how his teaching style has changed. He spoke about how disciplined and hardcore he has been over the years:

"But now that I've been in France so long, that discipline has softened some—too much good wine, coffee, cheese, saucisson. Oh, *saucisson!*" Lee's natural magnetism was glowing as he continued in the vein of how much he likes cars and loves to drive fast. He told the story of Boris' yellow Audi convertible and how much he wanted to drive it, but as it turned out, he never did. One of his students got to drive it, doing an errand for Lee, and that would have to be enough. He said:

"The fun of those things is taking your life into your hands every time you drive!" He laughed. "Now, I drive at a reasonable speed—really! We have these Citroen vans, and I drive along, feeling like a stodgy old . . . peasant!" Everyone laughed at this, and especially those of us who travel with Lee and know that he is anything but stodgy behind the wheel.

"Seriously, I'm finding that so admirable these days—those old guys, just taking their time to get somewhere! But," he said, turning back to the point from this little excursion into metaphor and allegory, "the whole teaching has completely changed, because the way I teach is to get into people's lives with them, and we sort of struggle together to get out of the swamp . . . .

"Before this Work I was relaxed. Things would break and I would just go on, but I'm not as strong as I thought I was. My optimism was psychological, not essential, because after thirty years of struggling with people, I find that, with rare exceptions and moments of eloquent flight in dimensions of transcendent possibility, my teaching has become very immediate. By 'immediate' I mean, we all have this incredible essence! Swami Prajnanpad called it 'intrinsic dignity and intrinsic nobility.' Chögyam Trungpa Rinpoche, a Tibetan teacher in America, called it 'basic goodness.' But I like Swami Prajnanpad's use of the phrase 'intrinsic dignity and intrinsic nobility' much better, because there is a whole different impact in your body when you hear 'dignity' and 'nobility' than when you hear 'good.' That's who we are . . . .

"My teaching used to be very cosmic. Thirty years ago I used to say, 'Therapy—nobody needs it! It's a complete lie!' Well, I've totally changed my view. If you don't somehow deal with what is immediately in our viewpoint, actions, emotions . . . . Hey! I haven't sold anything! Give me that box!"

Someone handed up a box of Shri CDs and Lee went into a highly animated sales rap, waxing eloquently about Mira Amadori's violin solo on "Summertime."

"It'll blow the carbon off your spark plugs!"

He began to sell *Ecrasé par L'amour* in lots of ten, offering two or three at a time on the side. Suddenly he was wheedling, begging, offering all kinds of outrageous deals, playfully scolding, then begging again. "Buy ten—*pay me later*! It's only a hundred and fifty euros. Pay me later, next year! I trust you! No, even better, take ten, and if they knock you out, *give them away* and assume the euros were charity! Ten, ten, ten! Who wants ten? Buy ten!"

Lee held ten CDs up in the air with a brilliant smile on his face. He spoke to his audience of about thirty-five people, many of them meeting him for the first time, as if they were long-time friends, like people he'd been through the war with and hadn't seen in a while.

"This is the least risk I've asked you to take all weekend! You won't get anything off that table this cheap!" His tone changed and became more sober, more intimate as he shifted on his pillow on the floor and said, "I make people a lot of offers—what people do with those offers has to do with their karma, not mine . . . . So, seriously, if I'm willing to trust you, and you are completely willing to betray that trust—go for it. I'm serious. That whole table in back is built on trust. People say, 'How do you know it's real, that the age is accurate?' Part of it is experience, part is because I trust the people that I deal with and they trust me. I buy twenty thousand euros of antiquities from someone in Paris and they say, 'Pay me next year.' It's all built on trust, the whole thing.

"The foundation of the teaching is based in trust. If you can't trust your teacher, who is supposed to be someone who trusts God, you've got a problem. So the whole teaching has become immediate and about what is needed now. Does it need dynamite? And what are we going to do about it? And part of that involves the Sacred Bazaar . . . .

"So, I like to visit other teachers, like Robert Frager, who founded the Institute for Transpersonal Psychology. He's a high ranking black belt in Aikido, trained with O'Sensei, and he's a Sufi shaikh, which is my connection with him. We were visiting him—we have a resonance, even though he's a Sufi and I'm a yogi. He prays to Mecca and I pray to pussy . . . I mean, to the Feminine in the form of Shakti!"

With this statement, the chuckles and laughter at Lee's jokes and humorous innuendoes that had been building all morning now broke out into wild, raucous merriment. The twinkle in Lee's eyes deepened as he clearly enjoyed our response and proceeded.

"So we visited him, and none of his students knew who we were. He gave me a place of honor, treated me special, so one of his students came up and said, 'Shaikh, who is this guy?' He was obviously very annoyed. Robert Frager said, 'A *guest*!' I thought that was just fabulous! He didn't offer any explanation or justification—just said what was true. And it was a teaching in the right use of information—though I didn't think the man got it. Meaning, if information is useful, you have it; otherwise there is no reason to have it.

"The linearity of my teaching is slowly being diminished and the immediate, visceral approach is becoming more dominant. Three of the seminars I did last year, I'm not doing this year. Next year more will drop. I am traveling more and being with people under immediate circumstances, going to antique shows. All of my students want to take me to local beauty spots—lakes, churches. Not my cup of tea! Business is my cup of tea!" Everyone laughed. I wondered if it was really funny, when actually Lee's statements carried a certain threat to ego's dominance over our lives.

"I appreciate the perfume of the flowers—that's why we opened the windows in here, not for *you* to be more comfortable, but to get the perfume of the flowers in the room. I made an exception this year and went to the Guimet. What I liked best were some of the pieces that are just like ones I have for sale. I like to go to the markets, the street markets—there's life in those places! Not to mention the food—real merguez! And malls! Oh, I love to go to Les Halles, because there's *suffering* there! People, desperate to buy something cheap, *so much* suffering, which also interests me: the circumstance of culture and life and also the circumstance of suffering, where culture and life have been lost. Like Las Vegas.

"I love Las Vegas. People ask me, 'Why do you like Las Vegas?' What a fabulous circumstance in which to Work, because to me, life is about working. Yogi Ramsuratkumar worked right up to the very end. He wasn't addicted to tobacco, so He didn't care if He couldn't smoke, but He wept that He couldn't smoke as a way of Work. He worked to whatever degree His strength allowed, up to the end. That's my idea of life lived to the fullest, which does not eliminate beauty and enjoyment of good things and the fine things of life—but the *context* of those things is the Work, the way that Gurdjieff spoke of the Work.

"So, my Work with students is moving away from the formality of seminars to circumstances and the Sacred Bazaar. The whole seminar is about that table back there, about surrounding ourselves with sacred artifacts as one source of solace as the world goes even more to hell than it already has, which it will. I don't think we've seen the worst of the natural disasters like tsunamis, or the worst of the human disasters. India is one third Muslim, and the Hindus hate the Muslims . . . .

"So, my teaching has become more immediate and direct. There might be more benefit at a dinner party that I'm at than in a weekend of seminar teachings. We are all attracted by ideas, but are we able to do anything with the ideas that inspire us? Are our lives changed at all? There is no substitute for learning what we need to learn to deal with those obstacles that keep us from living in those amazing states of consciousness, of reverie and divine contemplation. Some of us are lucky—we naturally get to spend more time living in those kinds of states. Others of us have to cultivate them.

"Here we are, confronted with our lives as they are, in the muck and mire, wondering how to get to the Promised Land. So, my teaching has gone from holding out the Promised Land and assuming that anyone can take it, to realizing what we're up against, in *real* terms, not in dharmic terms, where everything we're up against is an illusion, and there is no wall."

Lee told the story of working with an unusual healer/body worker named Warren Berrigian, who he called "a transformational character." Warren did a radical version of bodywork on his clients to help them break through vocal blocks, but he didn't use his hands because he believed that anyone was strong enough to do what was needed to temporarily break through blocks in the body. Instead of his hands, he had improvised all kinds of power tools—specially adapted belt sanders and such—to apply to the human body. Lee said:

"It could get very painful, when he hit a deep-rooted knot. I had twenty session with him over two years, because you needed a month or two between session to integrate what he had done. He was working on my shoulders one day, and all of a sudden something released a burst of energy that completely radiated, like a stone in a pond. Everything in my visual field got a little brighter. He jumped up and said, 'That's what we're looking for! That's what we're going to do all over your body!' That knot was gone!

"I used to think that if I could describe that, that would be it. In over thirty years of teaching, it's become clear that you've got to go in there with tools and work it, which is the thing I most hate to do! I grew up in a family with no tensions! I'm a sick man—I can't *bear* conflict! I grew up in the Garden of Eden! I don't know why I didn't get turned into a teacher who sits upon a throne and gets worshipped and all my students handle the mail and I live in a dream world, because I hate all this stuff! All my family not only accepted me but acknowledged me . . . . Now, everything I do is confronted with recoil and resistance. Talk about God having a perverse sense of humor! Man!

"However, it is my commitment to my Master, which is one of obedience. He gave me a certain job to do, and against my personal tendencies, I am going to do that job. I'm tenacious—if I pick up a book to read, ninety-nine times out of a hundred I will finish it, no matter how bad it is . . . When a teacher accepts a student, the teacher becomes responsible for the student's progress. In martial arts, if your students are not good, it is your fault as the teacher. So, it's a little more complex in the spiritual scene—except for Saotome Sensei, who I consider to be a traditional spiritual teacher, who understands human transformation the way I do. The teacher is in many ways responsible for the progress of the student; if the student doesn't progress, the teacher is considered not to have earned the status of teacher.

"I've seen some great breakthroughs in some of my students, but it's never enough, because there are always more students, more suffering, more children being born. So the teaching has moved away from painting beautiful philosophical pictures to getting down and wrestling in the mud, and part of that involves the Sacred Bazaar—that we surround ourselves with beauty that reminds us of the Sacred and have an environment to live and work in that reminds of what it is to be alive. Without an essential Benediction or Divine Influence, nothing concretely transformational happens. Divine Influence permeates everything I do because of my Master, Yogi Ramsuratkumar. We can never have too much reinforcement. Every one of these artifacts has a certain radiance that touches us, pre-consciously, no matter how successful we are, touches us, no matter what our life circumstance, prior to all our human stuff.

"That's why we're drawn to masters, like metal filings are drawn to a magnet. That's the way it is with me and my Master. By my neurosis, I would be drawn to Chidvilasananda—a beautiful young woman—or Anandamayi Ma, who was gorgeous at sixty! My Master was a short, overweight, dark-skinned peasant—not particularly attractive, with a very aggressive personality, but I've given my life to Him totally!"

This particular comment about Yogi Ramsuratkumar caused me to pause and chuckle at the smoke screen, remembering the beauty of the beloved beggar king, the elegance, the divine sweetness, the royalty, the magnificent tenderness of his *bhavas*. He could be equally irascible, fierce, funny, charming or compassionate—but not particularly attractive? Never! However, the son of the divine father is protective of the Holy of Holies, and likes to leave little dust devils and whirlwinds to guard the doors to the sanctum.

Later, in the afternoon session, Lee was answering the question, "Will you initiate me into tantra?" He began by saying, "To seriously study tantra, you should have a strong foundation," then continued in the vein of how he works with students. He said:

"When you're looking too good to the teacher, you will be tested. Our practice can look fantastically strong, but until it's been tested, we don't know how strong it is. When I first met my Master, our community was young. We looked great! I was a yogi, I had discipline . . . but, I wasn't tested in those days. I looked great. We had no money, no power—what's there to be humble about?"

Just then Tai came walked through the door into the back of the room with his father, Vincent. He was looking for Adeline, his mother, who had been sitting in the talk while Tai played with his papa. Tai entered the space quietly and slowly, even respectfully, it seemed—quite extraordinary for a two and a half year old! He whispered to his mother as they went out hand in hand. Noticing this, Lee said to the group, "See? He whispered when he came in to look for his mother. Would a neglected child do that? Never! So if you think your child is too loud, take a look at yourself!"

Lee continued, "I really wouldn't want a Porsche. I'm a spiritual teacher with this gaggling bunch of geese. I have to have vans to drive all these people. My students say, 'Oh, let's buy you a Porsche!' But if I had one and I didn't take those students with me, they'd say, 'You didn't take *me*!'

"So, thirty years into it," Lee went back to his point, talking about himself and how Yogi Ramsuratkumar tested him, "I haven't bitten it yet. I know what a real master is supposed to look like. Unless we are fully free of money, alcohol, drugs, sex, we are not trustworthy in a tantric sense. I've lost two students to Japanese girlfriends, because Japanese women are trained to serve every desire of a man. Is there a western man who can imagine such a thing in a woman?"

Several men in the audience laughingly said no and Lee shook his head in the negative, as if amazed that such a thing as a woman who serves a man's every desire exists anywhere on the face of the earth. He continued, "So, the testing can take a long time. The way I do it with my students is that I leave it up to life and the natural circumstances of life arrange the testing. The way the human psyche works is when there is too much energy circulating in the system, the system looks for ways to harmonize and balance, and the energy is going to be vented in the weakest part of the system. So any pathology you're hiding away for a good day is exactly where the energy is going to go.

"Some teachers suddenly become a monster—brutal, sadistic, and aggressive. You wonder where it came from? It's because they haven't examined their own tendencies. It's the same with all of us—any unexamined area can rise to the surface and act out.

"I'm not the kind of teacher who engineers situations to test people. One teacher told his student to have sex with his wife every day for a month, and sent another student to expensive call girls—prostitutes. That's not my way. I let the natural rhythms of life—karma, personal tendencies—move people into circumstances in which they either shine with integrity or prove that they don't have it. I have students with great potential; some are shining brightly, all my students work very, very hard and are totally dedicated, so why be in a hurry? I even like most of my students! Yes, we all get thrown together in this mélange. I even like most of my students," he repeated, "they're good people. It scares me to hear myself saying that!

"I often say, 'Can you give me twenty-five years?' Experiences happen quickly, extraordinary experiences, but that's not enlightenment. I used to be very impressed by the immensity of people's spiritual experiences. Everybody's had them—some immense opening to the nature of reality. But is your integrity in life reliable? Your lack of greed, lack of pride, reliable absolutely? The answer for most of us is no, it's not. Just vanity alone, for most of us, is hard enough to deal with, and our tendency to wield power in unconscionable ways."

Lee began to talk about the underbelly of the spiritual scene, and how pervasive it is that teachers themselves are not reliable, not trustworthy. Finding a genuine teacher who is trustworthy is critically necessary on the path. He said, "So, you have to trust your teacher. If you can't trust your master, you're not ready for work. You have to be able to say no when it's time to say no. We have to know ourselves well enough to know if we can handle transference, for example."

Lee told us that he himself never knew his grandfather and therefore did not have a grandfather's hand in his life. When Lee first met Arnaud, for example, he knew that he was going "to project like crazy all over this guy. He's the perfect wise elder." But because he knew his own tendency, he was able to handle that transference, so it didn't get in the way of his relationship with Arnaud at all.

At the beginning of the last session of the day, a young American, Charlie, asked Lee about how to manage stress in his life. Lee's suggestion was quite interesting: "Use the sun for harmonizing and balancing. Go out and stand in the sun with conscious intention for five minutes. The moon works in the opposite direction; the sun calms and balances, and the moon excites and exaggerates. Also use drinking and bathing water; consciously ask the water to draw toxins and impurities out of you, and it will."

Lee continued: "You make an agreement with yourself. When you start to get plugged in to something that is not important, you tell yourself, 'This is not important to me.' If you know that you are going to argue sometimes with your mate, then save the argument for something very important. There are very few things that are really worth arguing about. When we really start to practice deeply in terms of letting go, letting go, we find out that things are not very important—it becomes easier to make peace."

Another man asked a question about his practice of Enquiry, which Lee had given him two years before. He said that because of his practice, he was seeing more and more of his neurosis, and he actually felt self-centered in doing his practice of Enquiry—he felt that his inner work kept him from deeper relationship with his wife and children. Lee responded:

"It's true that as practice deepens we begin to see a vast territory. We run into trouble when we notice something about ourselves and we make a big story about it. You see the inner practice is keeping you from deepening your involvement with your wife and children. It's still self-involvement, but the problem comes in when we make a big story about what we've seen.

"In the beginning we don't know what the inner practices are, but they are designed to be practiced seamlessly within daily life, without in any way interfering with daily life or compromising the energy needed to practice. Enquiry works like this: You ask the question and discover something—you don't do *anything* about the discovery. Whatever you discover, you Enquire of that, and whatever you discover about that, you Enquire about that. No matter what you discover, you don't stop to do something about what you've discovered—you keep Enquiring.

"Sooner or later, you will end up with the phenomenon in which all discreet points of data, everything that stops us—every finite piece of information, every one of which stops us because we have an opinion about it or want to get rid of it—all just dissolves. The whole knot dissolves. That's how you know the process of Enquiry has been successful. It's not about what we discover, but about realizing that everything we discover is insubstantial. What's left? Life, as it is. All insubstantial, not solid. Nothing is food for investigating, opinionating and discussion; everything is food for Enquiry.

"Keep pushing the razor-sharp blade of Enquiry through whatever arises. Enquiry can slice through whatever arises with no story, no opinion. What we end up with eventually is just life, as it is. Your wife's and children's needs, instead of a response filtered through your psychology, your needs and opinions. Does that help?"

When the questioner answered yes, Lee continued: "Ramana Maharshi asked the question, 'Who am I?' All answers to that question are bullshit. The answer to that question has no mental equivalent. As long as you have a thought, that isn't it. The thing about inner practices is that they are designed to be done completely invisibly, so your outer life in no way shows the fact that you are practicing. Obviously the quality of your life will radiate a certain transformation, but the content of your life may not change. Your children may notice it, but . . . Inner practices are transformational, but they should become so natural to you that they require no physical time or effort."

Lee stopped to talk about two powerful, very primitive wooden monkey masks that were on the table in the back. He stated unequivocally, "If you put those two masks on the wall side by side and look at them every day with intention—those things are going to change your life!" His bold certainty about the transformational potential of those primal monkey faces demanded that his audience completely suspend disbelief, trust Lee and his connection to the Divine, look at the artifact with an open mind to receive its gift—all of this just based on faith. No one made a move to buy the masks.

Finally, after much teasing, haggling and wheedling of the group, Lee said bluntly, "If you have any intimation that I might have some connection to the Divine, then doing what I *want* to have done becomes an important thing to do. If I have a connection to the Divine, then this is for a good purpose . . . but if not, it's a shameless manipulation!" One of Lee's students raised her hand.

"Sold!" Lee yelled gleefully. He continued immediately:

"As soon as the mind gets involved, you are automatically handicapped. The essence of reality is no mind. As long as we are trying to think our way from the gross level of energy to a subtle level of energy, we'll never get there . . . .

"So, inner practice is designed to be completely seamless, not in addition to anything else, but as the natural interior process as you live your life on the outside, as it is—like doing mantra. When we were in India in 1993 we traveled all around with this bhajan band, and they were always chanting the name of Yogi Ramsuratkumar. The drums were ear splitting, and the drummer was this intoxicated madman; he wore metal rings that cracked on the edge of the drum. The sound was so loud that it was absolutely impossible! Every time we stopped the drummer would run to some betel nut stand and get some coked-up leaf. His eyes would get bloodshot, he'd be so high, and he would wail on that drum! It was so loud we had cotton in our ears. After we left, the chant we sang all day and all night was going on and on in our minds, day and night—so we didn't mind it so much. That's the power of mantra, the quality of the vibration of the mantra that influences you. When we saw the results, we were thrilled, and while that mantra was sung during those days, everybody was happy, relaxed, there were no arguments.

"When Yogi Ramsuratkumar asked Ramdas how to practice 'Om Sri Ram Jai Ram Jai Jai Ram,' he said, 'Twenty-four hours a day.' He did, and it ruined His life; Yogi Ramsuratkumar lost His wife and children. He couldn't keep His job because all His attention was on the mantra. He was doing the mantra, and because He brought such incredible discipline to His practice, the mantra took over . . . and then, at that point, He became very sane, very clear, very functional. He was awakened, transformed.

"The inner practice always bears fruit, and the fruit is when the practice ceases to be separate from you. Whoever you are and wherever you are, you are just carried by the wave, radiating, in whatever comes along. How can you do it twenty-four hours a day? *You* can't do it twenty-four hours a day, but the mantra *can be done* twenty-four hours a day.

"Yogi Ramsuratkumar was either a very bad student or a very good one because He practiced with such urgency, like the Buddha—He meant it. He did the mantra for a few days, then He went God-mad. His ordinary sense of things was completely taken away, and He got in a lot of trouble. He was even put into an Indian mental institution for a few months, until He could convince the doctors that He was sane. After that He just wandered around India for seven years. He became one with the mantra, and it took Him some time to get back into a functional state, which He did and wanted to do, because one complement of being one with is to live life with integrity. It's an absolute formula . . . Time to stop for today!"

Chardenoux
July 3

In the morning session, after a short introduction of sales, sales, sales and joking around, everyone was already on Lee's train, laughing and enjoying his company. At one point, after changing currents in mid-stream from irreverent to serious, Lee posed the question: "If one is trustworthy based on the motive of fear, then is one trustworthy? That's what you ask your partner. 'If I am being faithful to you because of fear of the fury of your jealousy, is that the kind of fidelity you want for our love? The answer is no."

Just then a huge bee was buzzing around the room and had settled on a closed window. A woman hesitated, then with some encouragement from those around her, got up to let the bee out the window. Lee commented: "Be careful—if that's the king or the queen, it might be so grateful that you'll be a bee in your next life!" Everyone laughed, then Lee added, "Remember, there are consequences to every action. Don't let that stop you; don't let that get in the way, but remember—there are consequences to every action!"

After a rousing plug for the movie, *Kingdom of Heaven*, and a description of the leprous King of Jerusalem, who always wore a mask—a noble soul trapped in the body of a leper—Lee followed his serious comments with a volley of jokes and bawdy stories that ended with his advice of the moment: "Why not just use a cucumber? A cucumber has staying power—thirty minutes, one hour, two hours! Then, you can serve it to your husband for dinner, and if he's French, he'll think it's the greatest thing in the world: 'You did *what* with this thing?' "

The group broke into full-bellied laughter, having been primed by the jokes and humorous repartees of the past ten minutes. "Then, when you have sex later, you can whisper to your partner, 'My cucumber,' and he'll . . . 'Ohhh!' " Lee pretended to swoon, as if in a moment of passion. More laughter punctuated Lee's dialogue as he slowly veered back toward a more serious subject—guru yoga. He forged ahead, saying, "One element of guru yoga is you don't have to understand anything, because the master does everything."

Lee began to talk candidly about how all of his thoughts and acts are Yogi Ramsuratkumar, so even though he often doesn't know what he is doing, or why he is doing it, everything he does serves the Work. He spoke about the Buddhist teachings, and the four turnings of the wheel. Of his own teaching, and the specific empowered phrases Lee has used to describe his own revelations, he then said, "The first turning of my wheel was Spiritual Slavery. There were other turnings of the wheel that came later. So now, we have this immense body of literature that articulates the teaching. We have the biographies of Yogi Ramsuratkumar, four Study Manuals . . . We'll probably have ten volumes when we finally get done—oh boy! That's exciting!"

In between sessions, people wandered the gorgeous wooded grounds of Chardenoux, an eighteenth century chateau hidden away in the forested rolling hills north of Lyon. The seminars themselves were held in the old stone carriage house across the grassy lawn with its central fountain, roses and tall, venerable trees. Most of the participants for the weekend stayed in the three-story chateau, or in the stables, which were beautifully renovated into small private rooms, each one like a monk's cell, big enough for just one person. Other people associated with Chardenoux—the staff, cooks and other workers—lived in cottages or stayed in tents. The grounds also included a huge organic garden, which supplied the vegetables for the excellent vegetarian meals that were served every day in the elegant dining rooms of the old chateau.

It's a very beautiful, blissful place that contains the teaching and provides a perfect environment in which to have *satsang* with the spiritual master and receive his communication. The whole place is a tribute to Swami Muktananda and Gurumayi, Chidvilasananda, the gurus of Alain and Evelyne Chevillot, our hosts, who are ardent devotees and the founders and editors of the magazine, *Terre du Ciel*. Lee was introduced to Alain and Evelyne thirteen years ago by Gilles Farcet; since then Lee has given many teachings at their seminar centers, including Chardenoux and Pierre Chatel.

Alain and Evelyne run their seminar centers very much like ashrams, so that the mood of sanctity permeates the grounds. If you are out walking very early in the morning, you may hear the dulcet strains of the *Guru Gita* being sung—a one hour Sanskrit prayer of over one hundred *slokas* (verses). The staff is dedicated to reciting this ancient text—a conversation between Parvati and Lord Shiva about the significance of the guru—on a daily basis. It is a familiar sound to Lee's students, as it is has been sung every Sunday morning at seven o'clock on Lee's ashrams for over twenty years.

Walking through the woods with one of the children between sessions, we discovered a small wooden gazebo in a secluded spot under tall trees. In the center of the gazebo was a peaceful shrine, home to a large black stone Ganesh deity. He was in full regalia, wrapped in colorful Indian cloth, anointed with red kumkum (vermilion powder) and bedecked with flowers. A small votive candle burned beneath the deity, and offerings of little sweets, candies and flowers were scattered at his feet. Incense was burning, its scent lingering in the cool morning air of this shady sacred spot.

We immediately felt at home in this sacred ambiance and circumambulated the shrine three times going in a clockwise direction—or around to the left of the statue—as prescribed by Hindu tradition. Lord Ganesh sat there in his inscrutable wisdom, offering blessings, removing obstacles, granting boons to those who came faithfully to make offerings each day. Like the Sacred Bazaar in Lee's teaching space, it was a taste of India, the spiritual Motherland that has given us these incredibly rich traditions, now seeded and taking root in the West through those who embody true lineages of God realization and who sacrifice their lives to the transmission of the dharma.

During the last talk of the two-day seminar Lee spoke about the vital necessity of knowing one's self in a bone-deep way. He said:

"If we don't know who we are, then all the practices we do are done relative to a false person. You just don't know yourself well enough to know how much you can manage—how much food you can eat or how often, how much wine you can drink."

Lee went off on a hilarious spiel about powdered green algae and vitamins, how he has to take these things because one of his students is a healer and tells him what he needs. He laughed about how awful the green powder is, and how he puts everything—trace minerals, soaked seeds, bee pollen and other things—into one big glass, along with the green powder and some juice, and then knocks it back each morning. Then he went on to elucidate how critically important it is to know yourself well:

"It's just a fucking body! It's a big hunk of fucking meat that does nothing but give you trouble, and every now and then during the day gives you a little pleasure—so bear down on that thing! We get a little sniffle and say, 'Oh, my allergies are acting up—I'd better go to bed for a few days!' But there's work to be done! My idea of an allergy is if you eat Coquilles St. Jacques and you have to be rushed to the hospital so you don't die! If we don't have a real sense of our bodies, our emotions, and we think we can seriously practice on the path, we are shooting in the dark, meaning: how likely are we to hit the target?

"I wrote *Spiritual Slavery* when this Work first began. How embarrassing! I hated it—I absolutely hated it. I wrote it in an altered state. When I finished the book I was convinced it was a very important piece of literature that needed to be published. After I wrote it, I re-read it and I hated it—I hated the hubris, the aggressive tone of superiority. I absolutely hated it. My mind hated it, but I said, 'I'm gonna follow my instinct.' It hit the spiritual scene like a bomb . . . .

"I know my tendency to bow and scrape before fame and beauty. I know my tendency well enough to get caught for a moment, but not longer, because as soon as I see it, the whole thing is as ridiculous to me as it is to anyone watching it. We earn a certain spiritual authority based on the strength of our practice, and the more spiritual authority we have, the more temptation there will be. There are subtle beings; the more spiritual power you have, the more subtle beings there are that want to feed on it, and the only way they can get it is to get you to vent and lose your spiritual practice. The more power you have, the more opportunities you will have to sell out, so you'd better know yourself. Whoever we are, we never know when a temptation will be thrown in our path. At a high level, we cannot play around—there are serious consequences for selling out . . . .

"So each of us has a responsibility to ourselves, to the Path, to the teacher and to God, really, not to sell out. So we have to know what our weaknesses are. Is our weakness vanity? We don't know what the temptation will be until it comes. As sure as we are all sitting here, we are all coming back to the Path . . . .

"In Hassidic Judaism there is a principle that has to do with the messiah. There were many other people claiming to be the messiah during Jesus' time, but they weren't yogis; they weren't sages. It's the same today: out of fifty who claim to be enlightened, only a few really may be . . . the rest are deluded. So there is this feeling that when the messiah returns, he will probably be invisible—disguised. If we don't have the presence of mind to see through the disguise, we will miss the messiah. Our whole lives are designed to receive the messiah when he returns, so if we miss the messiah, it's not good. The messiah could show up anytime, tomorrow, and we have to be ready. I like that idea of urgency of practice.

"It's true we have infinite future lifetimes, but there's no guarantee what those lifetimes will bring. When we take care of the Work, the Work takes care of us. How do we take care of the Work? In principle: selfless sacrifice—develop compassion relative to all creation. And charity starts at home."

Lee spoke about the highest law, which exists at the level of God: the law of sacrifice. Below that, there are many laws, including natural laws, which always have power over the laws of man. The tsunami last year was an example of how no human law can stand up to natural laws. Then there is the law of karma: there are consequences to our actions, and those consequences must be paid, sooner or later. For example, Lee said, if you believe in the law of karma, you can be sure that if you commit adultery, then adultery will happen to you.

"Ah," Lee continued, "but there is a higher law than the law of karma—the law of the Work. You can't avoid karma, but you can work it, and the law of the Work can facilitate that for you. The Work can help out. We take care of the Work, and the Work takes care of us. We eat a little meat, well, the Work will help us . . . maybe you have the karma to be reborn as a pig. Pork!" Lee exclaimed. "Yum, yum! It's good, but don't eat too much."

People were laughing again as Lee delivered these ideas couched in the absurd. He continued, "The Work knows important people in high places. The Work has a lot of influence—it can make certain arrangements to our benefit. At the same time, there is a very great urgency to practice with rigor right now, and it starts with a certain accurate sense of who we are. Otherwise, we practice looking in this direction, when we should be looking in the other direction."

One of Lee's French students asked Lee to speak further about guru yoga and how to practice it. He responded, "The first quality, you've got—good looks! I hate to admit it, but I'm a pig. If you're good-looking, you can get on my side very easily!"

Uneasy chuckles at this derisive comment about himself punctuated the brief silence that ensued in the group of about thirty-five. Lee continued on, "When I talk like this, there is discomfort in my students. Some think I'm serious, and some think it's smoke and mirrors. Some say, 'I love my master, but he's such a chauvinist pig!' Others say, 'He's just distracting us—can't you see what he's doing?' "

This comment brought some context to anyone who was not seeing what he was doing or was having a moment of forgetfulness; it seemed to cause some relaxation in the room, as everyone laughed easily. Then, just to make sure we hadn't drawn any conclusion or relaxed too much on the edge he had been creating for us, Lee added, "If I die tonight, put on my gravesite, 'We Never Found Out.' "

Lee continued, addressing his student's question about guru yoga, "It's ultimately about being a vehicle for the teacher's work. There are several ways to do this. The most passive way is to live our lives without creating negative karma. Create no bad karma. If we do that, the teacher will be very pleased, because the teacher is responsible for the student. So, not to create problems.

"Then, another way of serving the master's work becomes more active. The most active way is to have no life of your own. Devaki Ma, the attendant of Yogi Ramsuratkumar in India, had a big life of her own—she was a respected professor teaching at the university, she had a family and so on. She gave up absolutely everything to serve Yogi Ramsuratkumar. Not everybody can do that, as we all know. She was able to do it all the last years of his life. She was with him happily and with ease.

"When Yogi Ramsuratkumar was picking women who would be His attendants, there were a few He picked who just couldn't do it, because when He slept, they slept, what He ate, they ate. They had to live the way He lived, and He was hell to live with. He made constant demands, and He was never satisfied. He was tough! Not to test anybody; it's just the way He was. He was very child-like.

"So that's the most active form of guru yoga—serving the guru—and in between, there are lots of forms. To serve the guru, you have to be good at what you do. I work for the Work, not for myself . . . In Vajrayana Buddhism there is a phrase, 'the guru's world.' If you want the attention and trust of the guru and you want authority, you have to live in the guru's world, with the guru. My world is about three or four things. The Sacred Bazaar: I am moving into that world, not at the speed of light, but very quickly, and I've got to have momentum! So the more students can participate in that, the better. Some of my students are selling bronzes for me now in their own projects; others are becoming collectors. Anybody who is playing the game of the Sacred Bazaar is in my world.

"There are other elements of my world. One is my students. My students are either practicing in a satisfying way and in my world, or practicing in a frustrating way and not in my world."

Lee then gave the example of a long-time student whose teenage daughter was having serious emotional and physical problems. The student did not let Lee know about it until many months later, when the problems had escalated, saying that she didn't want to bother him. In fact, what bothered Lee was not being told about such an important matter earlier.

"I care about my students—not in a sentimental way. I'm responsible for my students, and sometimes, if my student is very close to their parents and families, I take on the whole family. Just like Yogi Ramsuratkumar. He *waited* to see those He loved. When He knew someone was coming to visit Him, He was longing to see the beauty of their face, but they would come to town and go to the restaurant to get something to eat first, or go climb the mountain, while He was waiting, and it would break His heart.

"First, you figure out what's being a pain in the ass to the guru and what's helpful. If you're being helpful, the more you're around, I want to know with certainty that I can count on you. I want to know with certainty that if I have a dinner party and serve wine, you are not going to get drunk and make an ass of yourself.

"Figure out what is helpful, and you will be welcomed and drawn into my world. The way it works is, the longer you're there, the more likely you'll be offered a permanent position, because there are permanent positions. There are a certain number of permanent posts that have to be filled, and if the person doesn't work out for some reason, if you stay in the guru's world long enough, you may get offered a permanent position. Yogi Ramsuratkumar called Devaki Ma, His 'eternal slave.' Wow! That's pretty good—she got some points!"

It had been a fruitful weekend for the dharma. After the last session on Sunday afternoon, Lee packed up the Sacred Bazaar, said goodbye to Alain and hit the road for the five hour drive back to Ferme de Jutreau. We were at home by midnight.

Ferme de Jutreau
July 5

This morning Lee went into La Roche Posay to the shop to take things out of boxes and place them on the shelves in preparation for the grand opening on Saturday, July 9. The renovations on the first floor were finally completed, and as he walked into the space, Lee looked around, appreciating the sight of the finished showroom.

"It's fabulous! Not only my own little shop, but my own little shop in France! Ha!" Lee declared with satisfaction. He began to unwrap things from one of the boxes and place them carefully on one shelf or another.

"So much room!" he said, smiling. His excitement was contagious; everyone was enthusiastically enrolled in the project and enjoying it all the more, just watching the way it was bringing our spiritual master to life.

"Wow! It's so exciting!" he kept saying, like a child on his birthday with the best, most coveted present of all. He looked at the antique chairs and the one-hundred-fifty year-old Chinese finely crafted wood bureau that he had gotten, which was now on display. "Beautiful!" He ran his hand along the smooth wooden surface of the bureau.

"Put a silk runner on this . . . or some of those Japanese silks we got in San Francisco . . . This is going to be great! It's going to be hard for me not to come here every day when I'm home this summer!"

A few of us were helping unpack items, which were carefully placed on top of the bureau, awaiting his pleasure in picking them up one by one and placing them exactly where he wanted them to be. He was fierce about this process, as if the exact location of every piece decided the fate of the world, and maybe it did. We have very little understanding of how a spiritual master works on subtle levels, or how the layers of reality, from gross to subtle, are not separate dimensions for the master, but are one unified field. We often fail to realize that the master uses the everyday circumstances of life as a stage or workplace for unseen operations of the spirit.

He mused, "It will be great for people to come down here during the Celebration, just like we did at Parada."

Parada was the shop that Lee and the sangha had for a while in Prescott. A co-operative effort of community artists, it was an elegant space that displayed fine art for sale: jewelry, sacred artifacts from India in bronze, glass work, stained glass, hand-made clay masks, paintings and watercolors. Parada was closed about a year ago. Before Parada, Lee had a bookstore named Mudra for over a decade in Prescott. Shopkeeping is one of his long-time passions, and now, he finally had another go at it, this time selling sacred artifacts and objects of beauty. What better way to make magic, or pray, than in doing something we really like to do?

Suddenly Lee said, "We need some coffee! Go to the café down the street and see if you can get some to carry out." Carry out coffee is not a custom in France. It's not entirely unheard of, and it can be found in some places, but not commonly in small towns and villages. Lee dispatched Chris and Jan, two of our most enthusiastic American ambassadors and lovers of French culture, both of whom speak French, to procure the elixir. Lee kept working at the task at hand.

In about fifteen minutes they returned with a tray full of coffees in cups, a small pitcher of hot milk and a story to tell. As it turned out, they had been to three different cafés; everyone had said, "No, we don't have carry-out coffee!" and turned them away. Finally, they tried a little café across the street from the central place, the same one where Lee had had the famous chamber with Vincent Vigor and twenty other people just a few weeks ago. It was owned by an Indian woman who said, "Coffee to go for ten people? No problem!" She hustled up the coffee and hot milks and simply asked them to return the china and cutlery and tray, which of course, we did.

From that day forward, the little café became Lee's place of choice in the village for coffee. It was not uncommon for him to bring anywhere from five to fifteen people there for coffee. It became a ritual; she had earned a faithful customer and greeted us with warm enthusiasm every time we showed up.

In the evening after dinner talk Lee focused on giving direction and empowerment to the sangha with regard to the new shop and public relations in general. Lee emphasized that all the principles of working in the shop applied also to our work in terms of practice. He spoke about the need to be able to answer people's questions about the ashram and the community, when they come up, in a consistent way. A short, friendly answer to questions is always best. He said,

"The more you talk, the more you risk saying something you'll regret and misleading or confusing people."

He spoke about the shop as a long-term project, and he addressed basic principles of running the shop, the necessity to be warm and friendly with customers and to develop a mood of hospitality. We find ourselves in a position to offer sacred art in a way that can change people's lives; we never know when one sacred image, or the atmosphere and mood in the shop itself, will transform someone's life in some way. He said, "If one person is deeply touched by what they experience in the shop, then *that* is the Work."

Lee ended the talk saying, "The ideal is to be as benign and friendly as possible and never have to answer questions about the community. It's a fantastic project. I hope it will be as much fun to run as it was getting things ready, because you've obviously done such a fantastic job. The way we do things is it always has to be done in half the time—or less!—than it takes to get the job done. Remember, over the winter while I'm gone, since this shop is one of my babies, if there are questions, call me and talk to *me*, right away!"

The ashram residents and the French sangha had worked incredibly hard to make the shop a reality; it was their work project, and Lee was empowering them to keep going. The shop was providing a tremendous opportunity for everyone in the sangha to plug in at various levels and offer their time and talent to make it happen. After the talk, the excitement and enthusiasm continued over tea and chocolates. As usual, the phone rang and many faxes arrived for Lee during tea time. Finally, around ten-thirty, he said goodnight.

Ferme de Jutreau
July 7

Today we got the news of the terrorist bombing in London. No one from the British sangha called Lee to tell him about the crisis, or whether or not they were alright. Jaya, who owns the flat on

Wolseley Road in London where some sangha members live, called Lee from the ashram in the States to give him the news and report that everyone was fine, although naturally shaken. When someone mentioned that it was odd that Lee had to hear about this from a student in the States instead of his sangha in London, he just shrugged. It was especially poignant after the teaching Lee had just given a few days earlier at Chardenoux about his students living in his world and keeping him informed of important events or situations.

Lee started the after dinner talk tonight talking about the natural compassion that is evoked by the bombing in London, the weight of caring that we feel about the people who were injured, killed, and the families who bear the grief and sorrow of that. His most pivotal remark about how to contextualize our response to such news was, "We have taken refuge in the alchemical chamber that is the Baul tradition in the West."

Hearing this I thought, everything hinges on the mood and texture of inner practice. Are we living in the guru's world? The resolution of this question is multi-dimensional, from the most basic, ordinary, everyday aspects of life to the sublime reaches of one's internal reality. Have we taken refuge in the teaching, the sangha and the guru? Have we taken refuge in the life that Lee has given to us? If we have, then news of tragedy evokes a natural response of compassion and perhaps sorrow, and yet, no matter what happens in our own lives, we have sanctuary.

Lee spoke further about the compassion that arises in us for those who are suffering, and also, he said, "There is a very real concern that we also have for the Work. I've had a very strong feeling that, over hundreds of years, the seed of the teaching is moving to the West. There is a tremendous passionate uprising of interest in the Work in the West, and an equivalent wish to be rid of it in the East.

"I had a very intimate relationship with Yogi Ramsuratkumar. One of the reasons He trusted me considerably was because I understood Him. He knew very well that I understood these things because of a very acute perception of my work. It doesn't take much for a teacher to understand another teacher's understanding. I understood His Work and His burden better than anyone. I think that He had a tremendous understanding of the shift that was occurring over centuries in the world. It's like a kind of universal biorhythm that makes one aware of the movements of the Work, and Yogi Ramsuratkumar was well aware . . .

"We do want to protect certain sanctuaries of the Work, like these ashrams. Yogi Ramsuratkumar said that His temple in Tiruvannamalai was not just for Indians, and that it would be a temple for all people of all times . . ."

After this way of contextualizing our response to the world crises that are coming up with more and more alarming regularity, Lee began to address a list of questions from Vijaya Fedorschak, who was currently writing a book about Lee and Yogi Ramsuratkumar. It was a very long list of questions, and Lee had been taking his time answering them over the last several months in after dinner talks, beginning in the spring in Arizona and then continuing in France at Ferme de Jutreau. Tonight he made some tangential forays into speaking about the guru/disciple relationship, referring to his decision, many years ago, not to change clothes whenever he is traveling in India. In part, Lee said, this was one way to align himself with his master, who changed his clothes about once a year. It was an instinctual decision, not a rational decision. In other words, it just happened as a natural movement on his part.

He continued, "To align one's self to what the master's practice is—if it's not orthodox and rigid—can be very powerful. And there are exceptions; we need to be clear enough in our devotion and confident enough in our practice to know when to apply them—one exception being when the master offers something that the disciple doesn't eat, say, for medical reasons. Or, also with amounts of sugar, alcohol or coffee—you wouldn't want to match the master's capacity to manage such substances.

"We should be serious about trying such a practice—as aligning oneself to the master's way of practice—and not just playing around with it. Do it for a certain period of time, and then evaluate. Two or three weeks is not long enough; four or five months is too long as an experimental time."

Returning to the theme he opened with, Lee said, "The power and breadth of Yogi Ramsuratkumar's work was so all-encompassing that He didn't really *need* to come to the West. He was relying on myself and others to spread His work in the West. His psychology and personality as a mad divine beggar was really out of sync with teachers in the West. He would have been not only misunderstood but aggressed upon to such a degree that He would have been frantic and unable to Work. Westerners visited Him in the definition of His culture and His chamber. He wouldn't have had any of that matrix and sanctuary in the West."

Lee talked about how the master of Yogi Ramsuratkumar, Papa Ramdas, seemed very ordinary; so ordinary that he was able to come to the West and fit in rather easily. Yogi Ramsuratkumar, on the other hand, was not ordinary in any way.

Lee continued, "It wouldn't have worked for Yogi Ramsuratkumar in the West. We would have loved it, though. Even on the devotional path we have come to expect the teacher to be according to our terms—we define the terms, and we expect the master to meet those terms. Whenever the master breaks a predictable mold, even on the devotional path, we feel shocked, betrayed. We haven't yet understood the real distinction between a genuine spiritual master and any other mundane authority. We relate to our masters as if they were police or teachers, professors—we're all shootin' for that 4.0! We expect the Path to be like university—we can party, goof off, not study, and as long as we get a good grade on the test, it's okay. Unfortunately, spiritual life is not like that. The grade is not based on the test but on the life we live. If tested at all, it's designed to break through into our lives."

In two days we would leave for Hauteville for Lee's seven-day seminar there. We were also gearing up for the grand opening of Lee's shop. During these scant few days at Ferme de Jutreau, Lee was rushing off each morning for nearby cities like Tours and Poitiers, where he scoured local brocante markets and fairs for beautiful things and the rare, occasional sacred artifact that can be found there, returning in time for lunch or dinner. The overall effect was that those of us who traveled with Lee were never still. There was no time to really sink into the ashram pace; there was no time to recoup our energies in the way the mind says it needs to before hitting the road again. We would have to find a way to manage the fast pace of life in the guru's company and maintain our practice internally.

La Roche Posay
July 9

After lunch we dressed up and went with Lee into La Roche Posay for the two-thirty grand opening of the shop. It was a benevolent social occasion, with many of us standing outside in the warm air and visiting with friends who showed up, while Lee and Michelle stayed inside to answer people's questions about various pieces of interest to them. A fruit punch and chocolates were offered on a table outside the door under the portico of the shop, where people tended to congregate and visit and watch the activity out on the street. At one point the cobblestone street was filled with the long train of a spirited wedding procession; the women were dressed in the most gorgeous, bright colors, with feathered hats and shawls, their presence lending an added gaiety to the day. After awhile storm clouds amassed overhead, and a rumble of distant thunder rolled in the distance. It began to rain, the drops gathering momentum until they showered us with a downpour that lasted about thirty minutes.

"It's a good sign," Lee said. "A sign of fertility, good things to come, you know." It was the kind of thing that the Tibetan Buddhists make a big deal of. A few of us walked around the winding cobblestone streets that meander up the hill from the shop in a labyrinth of very old houses and a beautiful old church overlooking the river. Hidden gardens could be glimpsed behind tall stone walls, overhanging with roses and clematis. The sheer beauty and charm of the area was an inspiration in and of itself.

Over the course of the afternoon many people came into the shop and looked around. One comment was, "This shop is way beyond La Roche Posay . . . it should be in Paris!" It was true that the ambiance of the shop was very different than anything that could be found in town; at the same time, people lingered and looked about and seemed to enjoy simply being there. There was no question about it—this was not an ordinary shop. It was more like a temple, a kind of hidden sanctuary filled with empowered objects that could bless and inspire those who looked at them. It would be very interesting to see what might happen over time.

It was a day the sangha had been working toward for six months, and they had pulled it off. For now, we were all happy with the outcome and nourished by the hard labors of so many dedicated sadhakas who had thrown themselves into the project to serve their guru's vision and bring it into manifestation. We had officially inaugurated a new phase of work for the ashram residents and the French sangha, and we would all benefit from their efforts. It was a great testimony to the power of devotion, dedication, commitment and hard work.

We were back at the ashram in time for dinner; everything was perfectly ordinary, with bridge and the evening tea and a rather early night, since we were leaving for Hauteville the next morning at five a.m.

Hauteville

Hauteville
July 11, 2005

Several of us walked with Lee down the gravel road that winds down from our quarters toward the *grande salle* and the silent courtyard at the center of Hauteville. The sun was shining brightly in the green Ardeche mountains of southeastern France at this beautiful ashram of Arnaud Desjardins. At the side door to the *salle*, we turned left to go inside while Lee walked across the dusty, pebbled ground of the courtyard, framed with lush patches of blooming flowers and vines, to meet Arnaud at the door of the large chateau which houses the offices, library, kitchens and dining rooms of the ashram.

About one hundred practitioners were settled in the *grande salle* at Hauteville for the first dharma session of this annual seven-day retreat, in which Lee would give formal teachings at Hauteville, answering questions in a *satsang* circumstance with Arnaud. This collaboration between Lee and Arnaud has been going strong since 1992, becoming almost legendary among their students

Today when we rose to offer *pranams* to Arnaud and Lee as they walked in and took their seats on the dais, the ritual opening of this teaching space struck me viscerally; it was as if we had always been there with them, in an eternal chamber. While they took their seats, the whole group prostrated once with hands in the *anjali* posture (together in *pranam*) and bowed, followed by a bow to the whole assembly from Arnaud and Lee.

The protocol of this space, which is very formal and strict in some ways, with respect shown to the lineage, the teachers and sangha, lends the meeting weight and substance, accentuates the sacredness and sanctity of the circumstance, the precious opportunity to sit in the company of the masters and hear the spoken truth of the dharma. This opening of the space completed, Lee immediately and simply asked, "Are there any questions?"

It wasn't long before he was in a humorous exchange with a man named Jean, who had spent some time working in the Fourth Way, and had met Lee the year before. Jean described how he had offered to help carry boxes earlier that morning when Lee was setting up the Sacred Bazaar in the smaller of the two formal dining rooms, which Arnaud had made available to Lee for that purpose. When his friend saw Jean carrying boxes for Lee, he snapped, "Whose disciple are you, Lee's or Arnaud's?"

Lee laughed rather sardonically and replied curtly, "What does your friend think? If you're a disciple of Arnaud, that you can't help somebody else?" Arnaud smiled broadly while everyone else laughed at this kind of common orthodoxy among students. The rigid way of thinking—so common to religions, cults and spiritual schools as well—completely obscures both the dharma and basic human courtesies; we become spiritual fascists and spiritual bores. Our very linearity renders us into a state of crude ineptitude.

Smiling broadly at this, Jean proceeded to attempt to ask his question while Lee interrupted several times, making jokes in a rather deadly, pointed way, while everyone else in the *salle* laughed and benefited from the teaching that Lee made with each joke.

"Just a pleasantry," Lee laughed. "My pleasantries are always being misunderstood as interruptions and irritations!" More laughter rang out.

Jean offered in English, "I love your pleasantries, they open my heart!"

"That's because you don't live with me!" Lee retorted, followed by a quick response of more laughter from the group.

"You are charming me, but there is some part of you that is disturbing," Jean admitted.

Lee laughed again and said, "Well, we'll never get to the question if I keep interrupting and you keep responding to my interruptions!" Everyone was laughing, relaxing into the space more and more, as Lee and Jean continued, both of them laughing as well.

"I'm trying to be serious!" Jean laughed.

"I am too!" Lee retorted again.

"I felt something like I could follow you—I don't know why I didn't, partly because of the images I have of you. I'm trying to see who you are. Is it possible for the base of the mountain to see the summit?"

"Oh," Lee smiled, a light sarcastic tinge to his voice, "Who's the base here, me or you?" People were practically bouncing with enjoyment at this witty repartee as the laughter continued to ring throughout the hall. Arnaud too was smiling and chucking. There we were, at Hauteville again, with Lee making us all laugh, tenderizing us with his great sense of humor. I was reminded of a familiar story from our own lineage: Arnaud, who knew Papa Ramdas very well and filmed him, told us years ago that Papa Ramdas, responding to someone who felt that Ramdas' attitude was irreverent, once said, "Here we laugh the ego away!" We would laugh a lot during the next week with Lee in the driver's seat.

Persevering, Jean continued to attempt to speak seriously with Lee about his attraction to Lee as a teacher, and comparing Lee and Arnaud. Clearly he was sitting on the fence as to who his teacher was, and while this vacillation as a strategy of ego seemed obvious to everyone else, he seemed completely oblivious to it himself. The covert operations of ego, and the way Jean was trying to enroll Lee in the game, seemed to be fueling the provocative and insulting tone that Lee was taking with him.

Jean said, "Your humor, your unconventional, ranting side . . ."

Lee laughed, "I only do that here! My students let me out when we travel. They're on good behavior—they want to look like good students. But if I try to do that privately? Forget it! I'm crushed before I even get one word out of my mouth!"

"Too bad," sympathized Jean.

"Yes, I think so," Lee responded mildly.

As the dialogue continued, Lee encouraged Jean to come to Hauteville more often. It seemed clear that he was steering Jean toward Arnaud and away from himself. Finally Lee said, "If you haven't made a commitment yet, but you're allowed to be here, why not take the gift? Take advantage of what's offered here . . . . What difference does it make? You're going to end up where you belong, so do what's right in front of you."

"I'd like to believe that," Jean said.

"We'd all like to believe it," Lee commented. "Sometimes you only see it in retrospect—you look back at your odyssey and say, 'I ended up here in spite of all my resistance and distractions, finally!' This morning in meditation Arnaud said that you can't just sit around like a lump on a log and wait for God to come down to you—you have to try, to make efforts. Sometimes you don't know the efficiency of that until the tree has born its fruits. Sometimes people look back and say, 'Oh my God! I almost blew it!'

"I look sometimes at my struggles with my students—because I'm still attached and I don't think they're making enough progress—and I think if I'd stayed with Silva Mind Control, my books would be selling wildly today . . . I'd be successful . . . I ended up where I was supposed to be, even though I had some crossroads to go through. It's a destiny kind of thing. Sometimes we just have to move forward in the direction we're going, with awareness . . ."

The four-thirty session that afternoon began with Lee stating that Arnaud had asked, after the morning session, when he would give an advertisement for the Sacred Bazaar. Lee and Arnaud both smiled, then Lee told us that Arnaud had said he would tell a little story when Lee did the advertisement. Lee began by saying, "The Sacred Bazaar was a completely unexpected coincidence with the death of my Master. It's about transmission through sacred artifacts and symbols rather than through teaching."

Lee proceeded to give a rather tame version of his usual "advertisement" for the Sacred Bazaar, in which he encouraged people to take a risk over the course of the week, but, he said, "a real risk is to trust your master absolutely. That's a real risk. So," he concluded, "it's about filling your space with reminding factors."

At this point Arnaud spoke, with Gilles translating his French into English: "Don't expect any extraordinary story, or you'll certainly be disappointed! It's really worthy of me to plead for the Sacred Bazaar, because all the money you spend there, you won't spend here!"

This good-natured little pleasantry brought a round of laughter from everyone. Everyone in the room was eager to hear what Arnaud had to say on the subject of the Sacred Bazaar, to such an extent that you could feel the room sort of leaning in toward him as he spoke.

"I'd like to share with you something I shared with Thierry. We went to Switzerland for a celebration at the chalet of a woman who was a famous explorer—in the seventies she spent time at the feet of Ramana Maharshi and Krishnananda. The celebration was not in her chalet—it was too small for two hundred people—but we went on a pilgrimage to her chalet, which was lost in the mountains. Nothing has been changed in this chalet where I went often when she was alive. For example, she brought back ancient carpets from Bucharest that are worth a fortune. I thought, what did she bring back from spiritual India, where she spent four years?

"What did we see? Two petite bronzes! Exactly like the bronzes from Lee, Lee's bazaar! So, there we can shift the proposition—she didn't bring back luxurious saris, but small bronze pieces—a little Gopala! Then you can say, well, I don't need to travel through central Asia for years or spend time at the feet of Ramana Maharshi to have one of those little bronzes!"

Arnaud smiled broadly and shrugged, saying, "That's all." Lee himself was all smiles, obviously very moved by this generous gesture of support from Arnaud. That being said, Lee and Arnaud simultaneously and unceremoniously shifted back into the usual form of the space, and Lee asked, "Any questions?"

One of the women who is married to a staff member at Hauteville raised her hand. She said, "I am not being able to find my place here. I am feeling that I am not bearing my full weight to be here."

Lee said, "You're a dancer, aren't you?" She answered yes, and indeed we had seen her dance on more than one occasion at Hauteville. Lee mentioned that physical activity was probably very important for her, then he went into the meat of the answer, saying, "Many of us think our value to our master, or our group, lies in what we *do*. In my small community there is a small bit of competition over who gets to do things for me. Luckily I live with human beings, not jungle cats!

"One person found herself relieved of doing little things she used to do—like making tea for me. After a long period of struggling with it in herself, she came to me and talked to me about it. I said, 'Well, somebody has to do the praying.'

"Yogi Ramsuratkumar used to say of Mani, who was the ashram manager, 'Mani doesn't need to pray—Mani needs to work. Work, work, work! Work is Mani's prayer!' It's the same with practice. It's not equal. Somebody has to hold the space. Whoever holds the space doesn't need to be the person who is most busy, who has the most outward responsibility and the most things to do."

Lee then told the story of a hidden Sufi saint, who lived the anonymous life of a simple baker. No one knew he was a Sufi master; they all thought he was just the baker. When his zealous devotees forced him out of anonymity, ostensibly for the good cause of offering public blessings, the Sufi saint eventually had to leave the village and start a new life somewhere else, because his inner work had been interfered with, and he needed the shelter and sanctuary of the ordinary life of a baker in order to continue his life of prayer and inner work.

Lee continued, "So, somebody's work has got to be holding the space, doing the prayers. Especially in my school, where everybody works, works, works—somebody has got to just practice! Like Mary and Martha in the Bible. Martha was the one who worked and worked and was respected for it, but the one who just practiced devotion, Mary, 'has the better part,' according to Mr. Christ."

Lee said, "If you were as good a dancer as I imagine you were, one who had that inner quality, then you know what I'm talking about. Somebody has to shoulder the burden of the physical work, or working in the office answering the phones, etc. But somebody's got to just hold the space.

"The practice is not what we *do*, but *how* we do what we do. If we are not one with what we're doing, we've missed the point. And Arnaud knows the difference. He knows the difference between one who is practicing and one who isn't. You're not a Martha—you're a Mary . . ."

Hauteville
July 12

The usual rhythm of sumptuous evening dinners, in which Lee and Arnaud are hosted by various members of the permanent Hauteville staff each night at a different home, was well under way. The night before, we had been in the garden of the beautiful old stone home of Patrick for a delicious dinner of grilled sausages, salad and wine. Lee and Arnaud sat at a private table with their hosts and one or two others by invitation and were served separately, while the rest of us dined buffet style and scattered around the beautiful garden overlooking the forested hills to the west. We could almost see the ashram from this place, nestled on the side of the hill as it was.

This morning Lee began his answer to the first question by referring to Arnaud's guided meditation, which had started the day at seven-thirty.

"Being here and now," Lee said, "the way Arnaud describes it, means literally dropping everything of the previous moment. That is the state Arnaud is in—and it looks pretty attractive to me!

"What's to say that we don't have, somewhere in our karmic destiny, the same great compassion of the Tibetan lamas? Why not us? In them, it has been cultivated since childhood. For us, the study and practice necessary to craft us into a certain kind of being requires self-motivation. We didn't have an old monk with a stick standing over us as children growing up. Still, we can cultivate it . . . . There are living examples of taking the kinds of risks, the consequences of which are attractive and sometimes radiantly beautiful. Swami Ramdas tells us in his autobiography how he was saying the mantra 'Om Sri Ram Jai Ram Jai Jai Ram' and seeing Ram in everything. He was thin, emaciated, an ascetic, but he was radiant, beautiful! Some sadhus are radiant and beautiful, and some are angry and haggard. One sadhu said to Ramdas, 'I've been saying mantra for thirty years and I'm angry—what is the difference between us?' Clearly the difference is in having taken the risk. Ramdas dropped the gold coin, he dropped it![1]

"There is a big difference between wanting to drop it and making that leap and dropping it. In the Gurdjieff work they talk about

1 Referring to a teaching given by E.J. Gold, "Security is not the cure for insecurity," in which he used the metaphor of the gold coin to symbolize desire; the only way to deal with desire, or any emotional state that hinders our work, is to completely drop it. Ego is greatly attached to its desires and emotional states, therefore they are like a gold coin that is coveted yet must be relinquished.

octaves; each octave is discrete and complete unto itself. When you move from one to the next it is like crossing a chasm—there is no bridge. You can't test it out to see if you like it. When you move up to the next octave, the previous octave is finished, done.

"What is helpful are those who are examples of having taken a risk. Look at some people, teachers, like Swami Satchidananda. 'How do they look that way?' we ask. He was a disciple of Swami Sivananda of Rishikesh. He'd been out on retreat in the jungle and when he came back Sivananda gave him the hottest pepper he could find and Satchidananda had to eat it without showing any outward signs of discomfort at all.

"What is it that propels us across that chasm between octaves? We need a special fuel, because it requires a different mood or effort than just moving from stage to stage. Like the difference between the break up of a marriage and the death of a child; they are not in the same category.

"There is an interesting phenomena I've observed: people handle dramatic suffering better than mediocre suffering. When an emergency happens, people rise to the occasion in dramatic ways. But with the little insults life throws in our way, we are angry and vindictive. We know that when we get to the really big things we will rise to the occasion. When the time is right we will draw energy to us to drop the gold coin. The only reason we don't sooner is because of our minds, our imagining, fantasizing, etc . . . .

"The master is a paradox with the student. On the one hand, the master is impatient and wants the student to change now, and on the other hand, the master understands that we are working with a medium like clay or paints, and we have to be patient. Arnaud was saying yesterday how incredibly patient Swami Prajnanpad was with him, because Arnaud had the tendency to throw everything away for a distraction. Swami Prajnanpad went with him, side by side, he was one with Arnaud through it all, over a long period of time. That's the commitment of the master.

"The master understands that we are working with a medium that requires forbearance and long-term vision. I remember sitting with Yogi Ramsuratkumar in 1979, there were four Americans and Him. He interrupted His conversation with us to interact with a little old grandma. She was *pouring* out her grief, crying, sobbing. He sat there with streams of tears running out of His eyes, saying nothing but, 'Yes Ma, yes Ma, yes Ma.' In His own magic way, He was just being *one* with her.

"The human being is a machine and will always be—so you can be a machine that serves. The master's machine is a particular type of machine that has the capacity for transmuting toxic negativity—that is the blessing or curse that the master finds himself or herself animating. When the master is one with the student, the machine of the student begins to be transformed into a machine that also functions like the master's machine. So, Yogi Ramsuratkumar was helping the old woman, entering into oneness with her literally to help her have a greater capacity to bear suffering with dignity and grace.

"Over a long time, we just relax. We don't lose our rigor and fervor, but we start to realize that everything that we thought was realization and enlightenment *weren't*, and there it is, completely indistinct from who we are, here and now . . . . So, you're doing okay. The way to have more of those moments, to the point of permanence, is to keep doing things that allow those moments to arise. You have to allow the master to be the magical paradox of transmission . . . . "

The next question was from a woman, who said, "I'm addicted to not loving myself, even hating myself."

"That's very common!" Lee returned.

"Eventually it is synonymous with being self-centered," she added.

"That's a good connection to make," Lee offered.

"You gave me insights to go toward letting go . . . . "

"Great! Persist, and relax," Lee said. "One of the things we find is that we can approach two ways: hard and long, or incredibly simple—to which we have profound resistance.

"The first approach is that we find all the things about ourselves that are loveable: we are a good partner, a good parent, or more technical things, like we are a good musician, actor, cook, etc. And we look at those and put attention on those things and reason it out: I'm not a bad person, my children love me. Or we try various therapeutic processes.

"The other approach is that in the ultimate view of reality there is no one to love and nothing to love, so what is the problem? So you explode the whole thing, and what you find is love—not anything or someone to love, but just Love. We resist that because body, emotions and mind have a certain reason for existence that it protects and defends at all costs . . . The raison d'etre of emotions is to bring some kind of harmony to the system, as strange as it seems! One of the primal drives of the system is love, love in human terms. Then we find the Path, and the Path is about love—not loving, or being loved, but Love. So in the process of here and now there is just what is . . . So, just Love. The mind tells us, 'If you discover this you will be destroyed,' but it's not true.

"The last brick on our wall is not our childhood conditioning . . . . We think 'Lyings'[2] are about revealing that primal experience; they're not, if I can be so presumptuous as to talk about what 'Lyings' are about. 'Lyings' are about the fact that we have made that primal experience an obstacle to what is, here and now. The point of 'Lyings' is not to get to that experience, but to get *through* that experience, because the bottom brick is the entire human dream, the human identification with mind, body, emotions—so, understandably, everything in us resists that. Everything in us resists just blowing up the whole thing. No amount of reasoning will convince us that when you blow the whole thing up, what you find is just Love."

---

2 "Lyings" is a psychological process developed by Swami Prajnanpad as an aid to the traditional practices of *sadhana*.

A little later during the same session, in response to another questioner, Lee was talking about the importance of how we use language. He said, "Just because we experience something we think it is translatable by the mind, body and emotions into language. That's not necessarily true, unless you are skilled and even gifted with language. I read *Ulysses* last year—what an extraordinary talent James Joyce was! Someone gave me the book or I wouldn't have read it. My experience of that book was not in the domain of rational understanding—I had no idea what he was talking about! But the skill of the writer was breath-taking! I was awed by his ability to use language.

"So, we have an experience and we try to translate it into mental terms, and we really can't. Art, sculpture, painting, dance, music and certain forms of written art can be tremendously inspiring because it is through these that our experience can be communicated. E.J. Gold said that art is the excrement that comes out of the actual experience of the artist, of that which it communicates. When we are elevated in that way, we are one with the artist. When we try to translate that into past, present and future, we are frustrated . . . We find ourselves not having the experience because in some way we have translated the experience into descriptive terms."

Lee spoke of being very grateful to Arnaud for clarifying Swami Prajananpad's use of the word "see," so that Lee understood what Arnaud was saying in an important teaching communication. Language is tremendously important; in fact, Chögyam Trungpa Rinpoche taught that language is a form of objective art, but for most of us, our language is just sloppy.

Swami Prajnanpad's meaning of the word "love" is another example of a very specific use of language. In order to understand it, one must blow up the entire human identification and live singularly in the here and now of the present moment—reality, as it is.

"So, blow the whole thing up! Love in Swami Prajnanpad's world is one thing, and in the human world, it means something else . . .

The fact that we don't act like we are here and now doesn't mean that we aren't here and now. How could we not be? Impossible! When you blow the whole thing up, instead of the horrors and tragedies you think you will find, you'll find yourself resting in Swami Prajnanpad's world, and that world is love. So when you blow up your dream, you find yourself completely understanding the language of truth . . .

"You blow up your dream and find yourself in new territory, but you haven't discovered it yet, so you spend the rest of your life exploring it. In the Arab world there are one hundred words for love! Even to children, love has this vast domain. In Vajrayana Buddhism they have this phrase, 'the guru's world.' The guru's world is unbound, threatening and ecstatic, all at the same time. But that is where we have to live, in the guru's world."

We walked out of the hall into the bright summer day, excited and inspired by the richness of the teachings we had been given and exalted by the company of the teachers. We were only two days into the week, and we were already beginning to cook as if we'd been tossed into a stewpot together and the fire had been cranked up.

Hauteville
July 13

The hot summer morning sun was glinting on the leaves of the trees outside the *grande salle* on Wednesday morning at ten-fifteen, when Lee was answering the question of a woman who had had two heartbreaking pregnancies, in which the baby died, the first time at six months in the pregnancy, and the second time at two months. She said that she thought she was at peace with not having a child, since that was five or six years ago, but now, at age forty-three, it was coming up again for her. Lee started out saying that her wish to have a child now might just be body chemistry at this point, and he talked about how hormonal changes affect our emotional and mental states.

He spoke with very gentle, firm authority and tremendous kindness as he said:

"When we're not clear in our mind, we assume whatever thoughts arise are an accurate reflection of reality. Maybe it's just hormones, thinking you still want a child. It's worth a consideration; maybe it's just hormones making you think you're not over the desire. Life itself is not about having children. Most people have children and are happy about it, though some aren't, but that doesn't mean that it is what life is about. Yes, there is an instinctive imperative to perpetuate the species, and yes, there is an emotional component to being a parent. We love our children and enjoy them . . . all of that is true, and none of that has anything to do with consciousness.

"In essence, life is about consciousness, then there is the swirl of phenomena, this hurricane of details that's always flying everywhere, and we're trying to understand it. But that's all content. Contextually, life is about consciousness. There is a difference between being and doing. This morning in meditation Arnaud said something like, if I understood him, 'Presence, being in the moment here and now, is completely neutral. Ego is never neutral. Ego always has opinions, editorializes, has expectations. Ego is not what life is about.

"We are born and find ourselves with this package: mind, emotions, etc. We discover the Path and work at making distinctions of all this package. Arnaud also said in mediation: 'We choose to accept what is, as it is, here and now. Refusing to choose changes nothing; welcoming to choose what is, changes everything into ananda.' He used the Sanskrit word, ananda. Ananda is what everything is changed into. When we accept everything in the swirl of phenomena, opinions, emotions, reactivity are changed into ananda. This is what life is about: accepting what is, as it is, here and now. It is a choice, because when we're caught up in some emotional reactivity, we feel helpless. We say, 'I couldn't help myself.' "

Lee talked about seeing Ramesh Balsekar in India in 2004, and he proceeded to tell an irreverent version of this story, self-deprecating all the way and making himself look like an ass. He said, "I got a good lesson from that visit!" According to Lee, when he first walked into the room where Ramesh would speak, he saw two chairs conveniently placed right up front, and he and Purna sat in them.

"I even thought, 'Oh, they knew I was coming—this chair is for me!' You know—'Lee Lozowick, the Great Western Guru!' " Lee chuckled.

Some students of Ramesh who were sourcing the *satsang* space came up and asked Lee if he had any questions. When Lee said no, he was told that the chairs were reserved for those who had a serious question to ask Ramesh. Laughing at himself, Lee continued theatrically, obviously exaggerating to make the experience a valuable teaching circumstance:

"I was instantly deflated! From somebody to nobody, in an instant! Which is good! We should all hope that happens to us! There I was, staring into space, my mind gone! *Samadhi at last*!"

The response of spontaneous, whole body laughter at Lee's theatrical, obviously exaggerated story was tremendously freeing. Once again he was sacrificing himself to bring humor to the situation and make a point for all of us.

He concluded, "So, we got up from the chairs . . . . "

After a while, Lee came back to the original theme of his answer, saying, "Presence is neutral. We could say, love is neutral. God is love, and love is neutral. And, there is action, change—as Arnaud said, 'There are reactions.' So, you've come to the Path, you're most likely committed to realizing the Path, and now this—wanting to have a child—has come back up. Giving 'no weight to anything' means neutrality, which is why negativity becomes bliss when we accept. Mind gives value to things: a good career has value; a career we hate has less. Having a child in our lives is given value, as if being a mother makes us a woman. It's wonderful, being a mother or father, but it's not what makes us a man or a woman. Even plants procreate! It's a terrible realization for a man! Men think what makes a man is this little thing that jumps to attention and spits when he gets excited!" Lee smiled, then continued. "We have to come to terms with the fact that even plants can have babies! Wow! What does that do to your self-confidence!

"So we give tremendous weight to having a child—it gives value to our lives. It's very nice, it's accompanied by wonderful emotions, but it doesn't complete anything in our lives. Our lives *are* complete, whether we have a child or not. We are complete already. Some have children, some don't; some make a lot of money, some don't; some get sick, some don't. We need to realize that none of the phenomena that swirls around our lives completes us or adds or subtracts anything.

"Nothing adds anything to neutrality, and nothing takes anything from neutrality. As artists, we think if we could just create the perfect sculpture or dance performance, then we'd be complete. It's not true. In the world of illusion, yes . . . "

Here Lee used Rodin as the example, and, as he often has, he talked about how much he loves Rodin's sculpture and has enjoyed seeing it. He continued, "But I wouldn't be less complete without those things in my personal experience. What can we say of all the tribal peoples who never see beyond their village or jungle? If you look at the entire history of Christian aggression, that's where it's coming from: 'These people are missing something! No art! No culture! No civilization! No savior!'

"We *are* who we are—nothing adds or subtracts, that's reality. To choose *who we are* is bliss, ananda. That's the task. Not to value having a child as something that will change your life, would fulfill you, make you a woman. So, who you are as you are is perfect—not in relation to good or bad, just perfect. That's where you need to be. You can't do anything about that, but that's where you need to be. Then all questions that arise, all things that pull on us—from that which is heavily weighted, like having a child, to where to eat Thai tonight—then all phenomena that arise become things you observe, you notice, and you see them as they are and make choices relative to them that are objective, not defined by ego, which is never neutral. . . .

"For a lot of women being a mother is all about *them*, not about the child. 'How will I understand myself as a woman if I'm not a mother?' That is not a good basis for bringing a child into the world. Most women think, 'If I had a child that cute, who would get all the praise? Me!' So, first you have to come to the place of clarity and neutrality."

A woman named Sabine, who had had a strong interaction with Lee the previous year at Hauteville, asked a question about her relationship. The exchange heated up very quickly as she told Lee that she had been in the relationship for over a year, but they had never had sex. Lee's stance with her was one of playful insult and fast repartee as he commented ascerbically that she was a bit of a handful and she admitted that perhaps she was too much of a warrior. But, she countered by saying at the same time that there was no sex, she felt this man was good for her. She described him as a rather feminine, very sensitive man while she was a very strong woman; maybe she could just continue like this, after all . . . And besides, they like to talk to each other. "He understands me," she concluded.

Lee chided, "A warrior woman who doesn't have sex? Come on!"

She said, "You contradict yourself!"

Lee retorted, "Only a true warrior can say yes! Honey! I can talk my way out of anything! Don't try to catch me in a compromise!"

After some further bantering and arguing back and forth, Lee broke the spell, saying forcefully, "Only a warrior has a choice . . . Look, Sabine, nobody can force you to be happy. We can talk about it all afternoon, but *you* have to do the work. A warrior can move in *any* situation and make any situation profitable . . . This man you are with is either really committed, or very strange!"

Lee had a glint in his eye as he prodded a little further. He laughed and continued, "Like Nike says, 'Just do it!' That works! You wear red sneakers and he wears white! That's kinda cool! A little freakie, but you're French!"

Laughter was building in the room as this repartee continued and Lee playfully cornered her. Now he was on a roll: "You climb on top of him and screw him till his eyes bug out! You have to evoke the man in him! All these long, psychological conversations . . . Oh my God—what a tragedy! *Screw* the bastard! If he has been feminized by a woman like his mother or grandmother, his inner lion is just waiting to roar! You have to be the vehicle through which his masculinity is expressed, and he is going to gain confidence in that. Only a woman who is a true warrior could carry off an operation like that successfully. Has he found the right woman? Yes or no!"

The silence was pregnant as Lee's eyes were locked onto hers and she considered the question. Everyone in the room was immersed in this exchange; there was something in it for everyone.

Lee continued, "Being a warrior is about having one's own innate power. I'm using the word warrior relative to being, not doing. *You*, you are not your qualities . . . Now, are you the woman he's been looking for? Yes or no!" His tone was challenging, almost belligerent.

Another silent pause filled the space. Finally she said, "Yes."

"I agree with you," Lee said softly.

Lee's tone completely changed at this point. He became the soul of compassion as he continued, gently now, "That yes is a little fragile right now. Are you going to take that yes and build on it? I can't answer that for you. You get clear, and I'll bet you he'll get clear very quickly. The fact that you are here again this year means that, in Arnaud's world, you are lovable. The way you return gratitude for the gifts of the guru is to realize who you are already, here and now, who the guru sees you as. It's a vision of here and now, not some potentiality.

"The guru sees us despite all the veils we put up. The guru sees that we are essentially dignified and noble, and the best way to return that gift is to be who you are, not who you can be, but who you are already, that the guru sees. In Arnaud's world everybody in this room is lovable—not can be, but is lovable, here and now. The greatest gift you can return to Arnaud is to realize that about yourself. In spite of all your negativity and aggression, you are lovable. Realize that, and you won't have problems in relationship. You have to make a radical assumption that cuts through everything in its path, and only you can do that.

"My Master was a beggar. He literally begged in the streets and referred to Himself as a beggar. His students would rationalize their view of Him by symbolizing 'beggar' as: He begs of God for us."

Lee was still talking to Sabine. Now the space became very poignant and ripe as he said, "So I beg you—you really had a yes for a moment. You've had it before and thrown it away. Don't throw it away this time. You have another opportunity. Everything in the dream wants you to throw it away. Right here, right now, we're in a timeless chamber . . . right here. We're in a space where a lot of work has been embodied; right here, right now, we are in a timeless space. You feel it, you know it. You know what I'm talking about. You know that as soon as you get out of here, everything in you is going to start screaming to go back to your habitual way of being.

"I've been watching you the past couple of days. You look like shit. Even a good-looking woman can look like shit from crying and all that. You've smiled some now, changed your facial mask. We're in this room, it's a timeless chamber. We have all this power available to us in here. As soon as we walk out of this space we are assaulted with our history and the comfortable familiarity of that history, even when it's suffering and misery. So look. You've a chance now! You've said yes, a real yes, a little delicate now, but . . .

"If you do it, then you'll have a *man* that understands you, not a feminine man. Wow! What an opportunity! This is the time to make the decision, when you have all the power of this room behind you. It's only a moment, but it's enough. Don't screw it up! Okay?"

She answered, "Yes!"

"Okay," Lee said.

There was a powerful transformational doorway that had opened up in this space, and we were all standing in front of it with Sabine. Each person had a possibility in that moment, to take the energy that was made available through Lee's skillful interaction, in which he had carefully and slowly taken us to the door and pointed to it, and move forward with it. We were witnessing the principles of transformation at work: not only was the doorway of transformation open, there was a greater reservoir of energy available to Sabine or anyone else who was able to make use of it—the energy of the group, which could help an individual make the leap.

It was up to each person to gather that group energy and their own energy to walk through the door, which would mean something different to each person. For Sabine, it would be to have a breakthrough in her relationships with men and sexuality, which would have reverberations of change throughout her entire life.

After this incredible session Arnaud told Lee that he had a vision of Lee while he was working with Sabine. He saw that it was the archetypal fight between the guru and the mind. Arnaud said, "At the end I wanted to," he gestured to raise Lee's arm high in the air like a boxer who has just won the fight, "and say, 'The winner!' "

After a peaceful lunch in the sunny courtyard with Arnaud and Veronique, and the rest of the assembly scattered beneath the tall sycamore trees on benches or perched on the steps of the old chateau, Lee was at the Sacred Bazaar, talking with people about artifacts, deities and sacred space for two hours before he reconvened with everyone in the *grande salle* for the four-thirty session. He had just been talking about how he has given his students a similar practice to the practice of accepting what is as it is, here and now; in Lee's school this is one of the core practices, and it is called Assertion, or the use of the phrase, "Just This."

"This is a process of being, not doing," Lee continued. "It is not something that you do. Whatever is natural is not in conflict with the Path, whether it is emotional, physical or mental. What is unnatural is aggression, violence—these things are in conflict with the Path. Commitment is not a process of doing; commitment is of the heart. Commitment is something that happens in your innermost heart. Our innermost heart is reserved for God; there is no room for an "other"—only God. We fall in love, give our hearts to lovers, children, and delight in the presence of our object of love, shine like a lighthouse when they walk in the room—all of this is true! You deserve it, why not? And, the innermost heart is not an affect of being human. It's not even subtle, because even the most subtle level is part of the complex of being human. The innermost heart is reserved for God, and ultimately, that is what is committed to the Path."

The next question came from Emilie, a young French woman who, along with two young friends, traveled in India with Lee and his group last year. No stranger to India, Emilie had pursued studies in traditional religious singing in India with a teacher there, but in India with Lee, she had experienced a tremendous opening of her spiritual life. She was unhappy about the way she had lived the last six months of her life, because she wasn't able to keep that openness alive.

Lee responded, "I think you're being a little too hard on yourself."

After some dialogue with her, Lee said, "When we get opened up a little bit, which not only India does, but our artistic pursuits anywhere, we don't get to pick and choose what we become sensitive to. We become sensitive to beauty and art, but darkness, pain and suffering also become more intense for us. It's a heavy burden to bear, this darkness and misery that invades us when we open up. Even if we're not conscious of it, when we open up, we open up to everything.

"What you've been going through the last six months is just a stage. And, being a sensitive woman, you're going to have to figure out how to deal with all the cruelty, injustice and pain in the world. If you keep your natural sense of wonder and awe and beauty alive, you'll also cross paths with much joy and profound happiness, but you'll have to learn how to deal with both. You approach them both the same way, which we don't want to have to do, which is to become one with, because to become one with gives everything the same flavor: ananda.

"We get happy and want more, get sad and want less. It's to become one with whatever is. In our school it's the practice of Assertion: Just This. It's essentially the same thing. One reason people don't pursue that practice is we assume if everything is equal there will be no texture, and that is a wrong assumption. We assume if we're not identified with anything, it will become bland, like perfectly creamed mashed potatoes!" Everyone laughed at this familiar image that sprang to life as soon as Lee said it.

"Ananda is ananda," Lee continued, "and, it is infinitely textured—it's the same, and, it's infinitely textured. So you approach everything the same way."

Lee told the story of a devotee of Yogi Ramsuratkumar, a European woman, who hadn't seen him for twenty years. She came back to Tiruvannamalai to find that Yogi Ramsuratkumar was living at the Sudama House and giving darshan at the ashram. When she saw him she theatrically lamented how different he was than before.

"You used to be so carefree, so joyful," she said.

"Not now?" he asked playfully.

"Yes, but you used to be dancing on Arunachala," she cried.

"Not now?" he asked ironically, making his point.

Lee continued, "The teaching was lost on her, but everyone else got it. Appearances had changed, but He was the same. We all have certain times of life that we remember with particular fondness; nobody stays the same. Sometimes our parents find themselves in very unattractive circumstances. To be in relationship with our parents we can't be like that: 'Oh, I remember twenty years ago, we had so much fun!' We have facilitated the death of someone on our ashram. When someone is vital and healthy and then down to sixty-five pounds, you want to remember the past when everything was different, but you can't be in relationship with them as who they *were*; you have to be in relationship with them as who they are now.

"So you want to get used to this idea of being one with. If that becomes a reliable practice, moment to moment, we will find that that serves us inestimably. You have to be in relationship with what happens—like Karlis, a student of mine who was in a terrible accident recently. You can't go to the hospital to see him saying, 'Oh my God!' We never know what life is going to throw in our path . . . We can't say that we'll practice later.

"Nothing in the Sacred Bazaar replaces practice. Yes, you surround yourself with beauty and the sacred, but there is only one singular answer: the practice. Not even, 'My practice,' but 'the practice.' I can't live relying on that perfect picture of Ganesh. It feeds me, I love it, the energy of Ganesh protects and creates wonderful things—but ultimately that won't do it. Ultimately, it's only the practice that is reliable.

"To accept what is, as it is, here and now . . . Just This. It is the only thing that is absolutely reliable, no matter how much beauty we have in our lives, even if what we *do* brings us joy. Practice is the only thing that is absolutely reliable. Everything else passes; *everything* else passes. What if you get Alzheimer's—all of the wonderful memories, everything is gone! Everything passes in the material world. The subtle domains are also material. Only practice, through birth and death, time and space—only practice is reliable."

It had been a stellar three days for the teaching. The next morning I had the opportunity, with Laura and Ann, to take all the teenagers who were traveling with us to Saintes Maries de la Mer, a little over two hours away by car, right on the Mediterranean. It would be Bastille Day, an important festival day when people celebrate the French Revolution. We adults would have to be in the teaching chamber in a very different way.

Saintes Maries de la Mer
July 14

One of the ongoing elements of a life of practice is learning—and this comes slowly for most of us—that we are never separate from the guru. Lee has a teaching phrase that he has used over the years: "You never miss anything." Today, on Bastille Day, we would have the opportunity to practice exactly that, as our little party of three adults and five kids drove away from the ashram at seven a.m. in the blue van, headed south toward the sea.

We arrived in the village on the Mediterranean at ten o'clock, stopped at a bakery for some fresh baguettes and—miraculously!—found the perfect parking place in a sandy park with old wooden picnic tables and a sparse scattering of pine trees by a small inlet or estuary. Pink flamingoes dotted the shallow salty water and the bright burning sun played tricks on our eyes as we looked across the marshy expanse out toward the sea. Fishing and sailing vessels could be seen at the harbor nearby, while the sounds of music and revelry were already escalating three blocks away in the central *place* of the village, where Saint Sarah al Kali, "Sarah the Black" waited for us in her sanctified crypt in the thousand-year-old church.

The parking area had been almost deserted when we pulled in, but within minutes it was completely filled with cars and vacationer's *camions*—there was not a single parking place left! We pulled out our picnic fare, generously provided by Michelle, the head cook at Hauteville—cheese, saucisson sec, tomatoes and apricots, jam and cookies, chocolates—and spread it out on the tablecloth we'd thrown over the weathered wood of the table.

As we ate beneath a small, feathery pine tree, the atmosphere was idyllic, even sublime. The kids were co-operative, happy and enthusiastic; everyone was flowing together beautifully. I was acutely and sweetly aware of being held in the auspicious blessings of Lee, Arnaud and Hauteville—the combined lineages of the beggar and the buddha. Even here in Saintes Maries de la Mer, I would feel the victory of the guru.

Soon we were walking down the main boulevard that runs along the coast, which is lined with restaurants serving *fruits de la mer* and specialties of the Carmague, beach shops and cafés in this now famous town of the gypsies. We passed the big arena of the bulls—later today there would be five bullfights to commemorate freedom from the tyranny of the monarchy and its attendant ruling class. Crowds of people lined the streets waiting for the running of the bulls, which would happen any minute.

After swimming in the ocean for a couple of hours, we dressed and walked to the church. Gypsies lounged here and there around its perimeters in the Place de la Gitans. We walked through the ancient stone portal of the church and into the cool, dark space of the sanctuary, then down the length of the pews, lined with paintings and relics of the three Maries who supposedly arrived here at Saintes Maries de la Mer two thousand years ago—Mary Salome, Mary Jacobe and Mary Magdalene, with their dark-skinned Egyptian servant, Sarah.

As the legend goes, Sarah became a saint in her own right, and her icon, a four-foot-high black-skinned statue, ensconced in the crypt of the ancient church, was exalted by the gypsies as a Great Mother/Dark Mother figure. The gypsies, whose origins are from northern India, worship her as if she was the goddess Kali, and once a year, in early May, carry the statue down to the sea for a ritual ablution and blessing, after which she is dressed in new finery.

My relationship with her goes back many years, to 1992, when we were visiting Yvan Amar with Lee, and Yvan regaled us with stories of the gypsies' love of Saint Sarah. That year was the first time we saw Saint Sarah, when Lee was visiting with Yvan in Gordes and with Arnaud at his second ashram, Font d'Isiere at Pont du Gard, both of which were close to Avignon. There were about ten of us traveling with Lee, including Gilles and Roger, disciples of Arnaud.

Following Yvan's directions, we drove to Saintes Maries de la Mer and went directly to the church. Once inside the crypt, Lee took a long taper candle, lit it and performed an *arati* ceremony to the deity, then offered the light to each of us. He sat on a tiny stone ledge that opened out into an even tinier window onto the street, and for thirty minutes, we meditated there. Afterward Lee bought food for a picnic in the market and we ate on the jetty rocks by the sea. Having no picnic supplies or silverware, we simply ate with our fingers, tearing the chicken and bread into pieces, squatting there on the rocks with people staring as they passed by. It was an unforgettable moment in the history of our travels with Lee.

Since then, both Shri and Attila the Hunza have made pilgrimages to see Saint Sarah while on tour in France. Today was the fourth time I had seen her, having taken other groups of community teenagers or children on previous occasions. Each time I have had the *darshan* of Saint Sarah, it has been the same. She is one of the rare living artifacts in France that Lee recommends that people visit, and that he makes available to the children as an important educational opportunity.

We walked into the darkened, cool stone church and down the middle aisle between the pews toward the crypt beneath the sanctuary. There were quite a few other people standing before the statue as we entered the crypt. The air was lit with the burning flames of many candles and the time-darkened stone walls seemed almost wet with accumulated soot and grease. Walking forward, we sank into the presence of the deity. Her eyes, so full and dark, eternally the same and constantly changing, glittered with life, with sorrow, joy, compassion, love. Mercy flowed from her and seemed to penetrate into my being. She was wholly alive for us, to such a degree that the objective response is one of awe, wonder, reverence in the face of such a living divine presence. She was dressed in garments of lace and satin, and her dark, chestnut skin seemed to glow in the refracted light of the candles.

For generations there have been those few who knew the esoteric secret behind Sarah's legend: it is said that Sarah was the child of the union between Jesus of Nazareth and Mary Magdelene, and therefore, she was the living holy grail—the vessel that carried the bloodline of the House of David. She was depicted as having dark skin because the truth of her origins had to be kept secret, or underground, in the dark, in order to protect her life and her progeny. Yvan once told us that the bloodline of the House of David, which passed through Mary Magdalene and Jesus, still exists in Europe today. The holy grail, as the symbol of this blood line, is alive in certain individuals who remain heavily veiled and under the protection of secret societies.

The gypsies recognized the archetypal power of the goddess in this icon of Christianity; over the years, they have solely kept her alive with their ardent worship. Lee has often spoken of the need to keep authentic spiritual lineages and their teachings alive in repressive times: what is paramount is that the teaching be preserved. This has been a recurring theme in Lee's talks for the past several years, as we are faced with the growing uncertainty of our times, and the conservative religious backlash against esoteric teachings and spiritual traditions.

We were expected back in time to join Lee and company for dinner, and yet we found it hard to leave. The streets were growing more and more crowded with every moment. After a quick ice cream at a nearby stand, we picked up our beach towels and bags and pulled ourselves away to head back to the van. As we walked out of the Place de la Gitans, I passed by four gypsy women who were sitting against the stone wall of an old building on a wooden bench. One of them looked up at me. Our eyes met and merged for an instant. I half expected her to say something, the mutual acknowledgement was so strong. An enigmatic smile played about her shapely, full lips, and her beautiful hazel eyes were wise, full of irony and lit with the fire of essence.

We packed into the van and headed back through the marshy Carmague north toward Valence. The kids would sleep all the way back, and we would return on time, with sun-reddened faces to reunite with our dharma friends for dinner at the home of Odile, a disciple of Arnaud, who was hosting Lee and her master for the evening.

Hauteville
July 15

Lee began this morning saying, "It's a good morning to ask a question because I'm a little cranky. Danielle's question left me feeling incomplete yesterday—I felt like I didn't really get to it with her, and I don't like that. When I'm cranky my answers tend to be blunter, sharper and less rambling. But I don't like to be cranky . . . what would cheer me up is a small advertisement for the Sacred Bazaar!" Everyone laughed.

Lee then launched into a discourse about accepting violence and anger in ourselves, and what happens when we don't accept these troubling emotional states. At one point he said, "When we truly feel accepted as who we are, then all of our tension and conflict over not being accepted dissolves, and we even feel happy at being accepted." Lee used various movies as examples of revenge at work: *Carrie* and *Manon of the Spring*. He laughed as he said, "I love revenge movies!"

He continued, "So we're afraid to accept our anger, but our fear is misplaced. We're not Idi Amin or Papa Doc. We're not those kind of people, but we're afraid we might be, under the right occasion. The act of acceptance, of being one with what is, doesn't release aggression and violence beyond our wildest fears; it actually dissolves violence and aggression. This morning in meditation Daniel said, 'If God isn't here, there is no God.' What do you get when you unconditionally accept anger? You get to be here and now only, and that's God. Would God do what you're afraid you would do? No. In spite of treatises like the Old Testament, God would not express in that way, if free of our injunctions upon ourselves.

"Violence is arising, yes, which doesn't free the violence into greater expression but frees and diffuses any need in particular of that expression to get our attention. As Arnaud said, 'Presence is neutral. Ego is never neutral.' You find yourself present and neutral. Ego is what we're afraid of, because ego is the demonstration of the violence, the fulfillment of anger. There is a complete diffusion of anger when you accept here and now. We can say yes to the memory of the past or wish for the future, but as soon as we say yes it neutralizes the expression of that whenever it arises.

"To become one with the anger, violence, aggression, is to find yourself in a state of presence in which you are noticing what is arising, and noticing it is *not* you, which gives you a choice. Like getting on a ride at Disneyland. Obviously the ride is not you. If it looks attractive, you take it. If it doesn't look attractive, you don't take it. You are not obligated to get on the ride; you are not obligated to any anger, violence or any form of ignorance and suffering. From presence, there is choice: from ego, only relative choice. Yes, this is arising; not *my* anger—just, anger is arising. Unconditionally accept and you will notice something curious—the doorway is open, but you aren't jumping through the door."

A student of Arnaud raised his hand and said that he had been practicing for twenty years, but he still doesn't get it. He was still searching for some practice or technique that would make a difference. Lee said, "There is no method. You allow your experience of frustration to rub against the irritating feeling that you're not getting it. It's not method; it's intention. In the Gurdjieff work they talk about having a 'wish' or 'aim' in a particular way. That is, a quality of intention that is generated for a real, heartful wish to accept, be one with, integrate the teaching.

"Several of the questions that have been asked are about commitment; most of those who ask have commitment to the Path, which automatically produces intention. The fact that we ask the question with such longing is a sign that something is working.

"In our judgment, we feel that we aren't progressing the way the mind imagines we should because we define progress by certain qualities, and that often misses the mark. Most of us are fairly well aware of our outer manifestations, but we are out of touch with the movement of energy in subtle domains. It's like a mechanical chess game; you've already set up a pattern of movement for the game before you touch the pieces. Inside, at subtle levels, there is a repositioning going on that is managed by and inspired by intention, which we are mostly unaware of until the final movement: checkmate! The guru is the chess master, and we are apprentices. We don't see what the guru sees. We see we've been doing the same thing for twenty years and there is no progress, but the guru sees us at a deeper level.

"Yes, at the level of ego it's a very frustrating process, because ego is defined by effects and results. The effects are not in the domain of ego's expertise. There's plenty going on, but ego doesn't see it. Ego looks here, but it's going on over there, just like in magic. Have you ever seen David Copperfield perform? Incredible! You're looking here while the magic is going on over there. One day we find ourselves present based on a whole process of integration and absorption that is mostly prior to our awareness.

Lee said to the questioner, "You're still here at Hauteville, you're on the Path. Just persist. Persist. You may want to take it on faith. Your mind may not be able to perceive what has happened in the past twenty years."

The man responded, "I've heard this same thing several times, but . . . my question is about the specific aspect of practice that has to do with vigilance."

Lee said, "You are practicing vigilance right now! Exactly the way you are describing the conflict is vigilance. What do you think vigilance is? Enlightenment? God?"

The man answered, "Well, I do see that I'm not being vigilant in general."

"That's the beginning of the practice!" Lee retorted. "Every time you see that you're not being vigilant, you develop a greater wish to practice."

The questioner pursued further, "What is it to persist?"

"To keep the question of vigilance burning in you," Lee returned. "To persist is to keep the question alive, burning, and the forces of confluence that produce the unconditional 'yes' will produce the answer. It's a cosmic law. It's an excellent question. Keep it burning—that's what creates intention. The Benediction of the lineage of Arnaud and Swami Prajnanpad will produce the answer.

"It's a good question. You asked the practice question! The answer is not going to relieve you of your stress and tension or pierce a temporary problem in your life. When that question gets answered, then you will have something—not just temporary relaxation of stress and tension in your life. But that's not what we've come to the Path for.

"There are people in this room who don't know why they've been drawn to this Path. Ultimately it's not about harmonizing our life situation, because all that passes when we die. The Path is about what is imperishable, eternal. I might add an addendum, which mostly can't apply because our habits of speech are so mechanical. Instead of using the word 'mais,' replace it with the word 'et.' The word 'mais' is a complete refusal of what's been said; if you use the word 'et,' there may be resistance and confusion, but you are working with it. It's a tiny, tiny thing—something that small can have a very large consequence in consciousness."

After a few more questions, Veronique Desjardins asked a question about Lee's use of the word "lineage" in relation to Arnaud and Swami Prajnanpad. She said that this word is typically not used in their path, and she personally had a hard time accepting that Arnaud was the link to Swami Prajnanpad in the sense of a spiritual lineage.

Lee said, "We depersonalize and idealize the master's master and personalize our own master. Lineage is a stream, a continuous flow of the teaching. Whoever can transmit what the master's lineage is, is in the lineage."

A dialogue began between Lee and Veronique, in which he was addressing the difficulty of being closely related to the guru. "E.J. Gold said of his household, 'To live with me is the worst job in the Work. Nobody should admire it and think it's the best place to be. It's the worst.' One reason for that is because the closer we are to the master, the more trouble we have melding the teacher's mastery with the human person. It's a very hard thing to do—no question! Often we don't get to see we've done it until we're looking back in retrospect."

Lee continued, "My human father died when I was thirty. I was very immature. I loved and respected him, but I was very immature. I had no idea of the depth of humanity, the quality of human being that he was. Now I can't go and throw my arms around him.

"Often resolve comes in retrospect to the elements of life that produced that resolve. It's a very profoundly difficult resolve to come to, that Arnaud is our link to Swami Prajnanpad. Not his books and photos—*he* is. Swami Prajnanpad is alive, but he is not defined by his old body and ashram in Bengal. He is defined by this body and name, Arnaud Desjardins. So if you are idealizing Swami Prajnanpad, then give that attention to Arnaud."

Veronique responded, "The resistance and struggle in relation to Arnaud, doesn't it prevent my own path?"

"No!" Lee smiled. "That was easy!"

At this point, Arnaud spoke. He said, "About the fact that there was no sentiment in Swami Prajnanpad: Swamiji didn't speak of his own guru—Nirabanda Swami—as often as I do speak of Swamiji. But over the years, several times he invoked Nirabanda Swami, and I did feel the intensity of his relationship and love and gratitude—it was quite intense! You could discern in Swami's letters little sentences, and at that time Swami Prajnanpad was still referring to himself as 'I'—he said, 'You knew what Nirabanda Swami meant to me, and therefore you can understand what his passing means to me.'

"I don't exactly remember, but the expression of the words was intense to show that his passing was an extraordinary event for Swamiji, and the extent to which he was touched by that event."

Shortly after this Lee was answering the question of a woman who had a thirty-three-year-long relationship with an abusive, alcoholic husband. Lee said that he could not tell her what to do in the outer world; however, he said, there is something that gets built in thirty-three years that is irreplaceable. Once again he shared E.J. Gold's teaching, "Security is not the cure for insecurity," then he began to discourse in a serious vein.

"This principle is very important to understand because our lives are informed by the struggle to get what we feel would change things for us. Often the intensity of our desire to find a lover is not for companionship but because we think we'll feel good about ourselves. If our own internal state of serenity and happiness depends upon anything in the environment, we are never going to get it completely.

"If we feel the only way to be fulfilled is to have companionship, then we are expecting something from our companion that is humanly impossible. We expect them to be someone who can make us happy. Obviously our partner can be a source of friendship and affection, but if it's impossible for us to be happy with ourselves and feel loved when we are alone, then we have some work to do—on the Path or off. Most forms of dependency are hoping this person will fulfill us. It's the same with the guru: 'The guru is going to complete me in some way.' Then we are not practicing rightly, because we expect the guru to practice for us, to somehow magically get inside us.

"I had a bad role model for relationships in this world of broken dreams and broken hearts! My parents never fought, ever! My idea of relationship is: you love each other, it works, you worship your partner and it goes on until you die and it's all perfect! I'm always a little sad when long-term work relationships disintegrate."

Ranging out into commentary on the moral decay of our contemporary culture and lambasting TV reality programs like "The Swan," which films real women getting plastic surgery before, during and after the process—and pits them against other women who have the same kind of plastic surgery in "beauty contests"—Lee again emphasized: "Any dependency is only resolved in an internal realization that we are happy and whole as we are."

The woman said, "I am completely convinced of that, but I expect less violence . . ." She spoke about the verbal violence, the degree to which she could be deeply wounded by her partner.

Lee responded, "If this was the new age and I had a pyramid on my head and was wearing violet, I'd say, 'If there is violence in your life, what are you doing to create it?' . . . He knows exactly what to say to hurt you the most, but what he really wants is for you to be the angel that takes his pain away. He really wants you to feel the pain he feels, so that you can take it away. That's a very sobering consideration, because we want people we love to be happy and free of pain, and we can't do it for them. Like with our children. The child has to suffer what it has to suffer, so it's a very sobering realization for parents. It also gives you the realization that only you can take care of your own pain, including what it is in you that allows you to believe his cruel words, that allows you to believe this cruel speech. When somebody doesn't know what they're talking about, you don't take it seriously.

"When you can be present, accept yourself as you are, you realize that what he says about you is not you. Alice Miller says that when parents take responsibility for the ways they abused their child, automatically the child is transformed, feels different, is released from the burden. When you realize presence, your husband will change positively. I can't say he'll stop drinking and completely change, but he will change positively. When you have an unconditional 'yes' to life, the people most intimate to you cannot help but be affected."

At one point in the afternoon session on this day Lee entered into a dialogue with Michel, a student of Arnaud who Lee has known for many years and has come to many of his seminars, both at Hauteville and at Maison Raphael in Paris. Michel spoke about his mother's recent death, a relationship that had been very consuming for him as he took care of his mother for many years. Her death had removed a certain form of protection for him, and at the same time, he realized that not only is he not changing, but that he doesn't really want to change. He said, "Other people have a life; I have the impression that for fifty years I haven't had a life."

Lee began, "I have good news for you—you're wrong!" Everyone laughed at this spirited beginning. Lee continued, "Well, maybe your psychology is more inclined toward martyrdom. Now that mother's dead—now what? I think there is a lot of depth in you that you are denying. Somehow, I would recommend experimenting. How about music?"

Michel smiled and said, "Well, I am taking up the clarinet again."

"That's great!" Lee smiled back.

"And I have the fantasy of working with Amnesty International," Michel added.

"That would give meaning to your life! Why not give that a try? It's for the relief and diminishment of violence—the more the better. Are you open to a coupled relationship?" Lee asked. Michel answered yes.

"But the way to do it is to be open and wait. If we get desperate and start reaching, we pick the wrong person," Lee cautioned. "What else?"

"Have friends?" Michel asked.

"Another excellent idea. Did you ever consider working with children?" Lee asked unexpectedly. Michel answered that he had done some of this work before. Lee continued, "It would be healthy for you, and I think you're the kind of person children would like a lot. There are consequences, of course, because you fall in love with them and get your heart broken when you find out how brutally they've been treated by their parents. But maybe you could help some of them. Maybe you could even save some of them psychologically."

Nodding in the affirmative and seeming to receive this, Michel changed the subject and said, "I'm also interested in numerology."

Lee shrugged. "That requires study. Anyway, the point is, there are things that attract you and could be interesting and satisfying. Now that you're free of mom, it's time to go for it! You definitely seem not attached, like last time we talked. Time to pursue other interests . . . Obviously, with the support and guidance of people here at Hauteville."

Henri, another of Arnaud's students who Lee has known for years raised his hand and said, "I don't have an essential question."

"You *should*!" Lee said with a chuckle. Reading between the lines, it seemed that Lee was saying that he could see into Henri, who, at this point on the path, should be asking a real question with real necessity.

Lee said with a derisive shrug, "Okay, let's handle the question you *do* have."

Henri said, "I feel more and more childish. I find it amusing and mostly funny. I've been a grandfather for six months, and observing the baby I realized that he was not doing anything in the proper way!"

Lee drawled in a provocative, challenging tone, "You mean he's eating out of his ass and shitting out of his mouth?" This response brought on a spasm of laughter from the group. People seemed to instinctively know that something was up with this exchange.

"No, like an adult, I mean!"

Lee said, with some sarcasm, "He was doing things *exactly* the way a baby should . . ."

"I was joking," Henri said, trying to justify his off comments.

"I caught your tone of voice," Lee responded sharply, "but most jokes aren't jokes."

Henri continued, "I realized that it's not okay to hit the baby."

"You're just now realizing that?" Lee asked, incredulously.

"Well, I'm a slow learner," Henri smiled sheepishly, as if it was really all okay.

"You are lagging behind a bit," Lee retorted, while the room exploded with laughter.

"I see the dark side of myself," Henri began again, "is not something to hate, but something is growing. I was also helped by 'Star Wars'."

Lee enthused, "It's not as good as 'Batman Begins'! I'm a big fan of American movies!"

Henri kept going, "I realized that the struggle going on between Luke Skywalker and Darth Vader is the same thing for me." Henri went on to say that he wants to stop the Star Wars that are going on inside himself, and in fact, now he is giving lectures on the causes of war and violence.

Lee interrupted this noble discussion with an irreverent outburst that caused another big outburst of laughter from the whole group, saying loudly and dominantly, "The cause of violence is men have *dicks*—that's about it! That's the cause of *all* wars. It's a simple lecture."

"Well," Henri mumbled, "women have inner violence . . . ?"

Lee responded vehemently, almost belligerently, "The only women who have violence are women who have dicks! Psychologically speaking!" Another big laughter attack hit the group. Lee was holding up a perfect mirror for Henri, and everyone could see it.

"I realize it's a simplistic description, but you always want to boil the question down to its essentials," Lee said, changing tact and almost charming now.

Henri continued, "So, I have a fear of thinking that the meaning of life as I sense it, may be that it's all stupid, it's a mistake . . . . And even if my life has meaning, I won't have the time to find it . . . ."

The repartee was going so fast at this point, and Gilles' translation was so flawless and happening simultaneous to the exchange, that I missed the full brunt of what Lee said before he answered, " . . . . I'm not sure those two things are related. If the world has no meaning, the only thing that can discover that the world has no meaning is mind, ego. Many people can live for years without being confronted by fear. The fact is, life does have meaning. Your life has meaning, and both of those things becomes clear when you accept what is as it is, here and now."

After bursting the bubble of Henri's philosophizing, Lee brought the discussion back from the edge of oblivion to the teaching as he stated, "We can only start working where we are, which is why the practice of self-observation is primary in the Gurdjieff work. If you apply practice to what is not you, then what you get is not real. Your conclusions will not be accurate."

Henri took one last stab at it, saying, "I have proofs of consciousness, but the doubts never stop . . ."

"When ego is the dominant reference point," Lee said, "we find ourselves in situations that produce firsthand experiences of consciousness as an energetic spike that arises out of ego and falls back again. The moment of experience is real, but we're not living in a context in which those experiences can contribute to freedom of doubt. But something you are doing is pointing you in the right direction."

At this point Lee's compassion and kindness to Henri was simply amazing. His entire demeanor had changed radically. We had witnessed Lee animating every characteristic that Henri needed to see about himself; now Lee was pouring on the milk of human kindness.

"I would go further," Lee summed up, "but I think this is a good place to stop. Okay?" Henri said yes.

Jean, who had asked Lee questions earlier in the week, resumed their dialogue: "I will try to speak from presence, but it's difficult!"

"Was that a joke too?" Lee responded tartly, with some irritation. Everyone laughed again. "Never mind! Just speak! What a pretentious statement! Just speak! If you speak from presence, I will *know* it, Arnaud will *know* it."

Jean back-pedaled, "I will try to pacify things . . ."

"For who?" Lee challenged. "For you? For me? For your wife? To create peace in the world? Look Jean, everybody in this room is as self-centered as you are! We're interested in us—*me*! Okay, let's go for it! Start!"

Jean was the willing foil for Lee's theatre for the short, wild ride of a crazy interchange that ensued, charged with laughter, in which Jean humorously tried to convince Lee of his authenticity and Lee was unwilling to buy it, mostly with regard to Jean's infidelity to his wife, his philandering, and his coming divorce. His weak excuse for licentiousness was, "I love life!" It was a comment that seemed to spur Lee on to end the afternoon session with a timely comedic rant: "I'm like Jean. I love life too, and I've decided to channel my love of life into good food, good wine, and good coffee, because pussy is just too expensive!"

The laughter that had bounced around the hall throughout this exchange and continued now seemed to be much needed, as we freely gave ourselves over to it while Jean and Lee both seemed to enjoy it as much as everyone else. Lee kept it going with his humorous routine, as he closed, saying, "And with Arnaud's guidance, I'm starting to learn a few things about good food, good wine, and good coffee. Thank you Jean, that was a lot of fun!"

The first question this morning in the *grande salle* was, "What qualities made Lee Lozowick, Mr. Lee?"

Lee laughed before he answered, "I don't know. Before I met Arnaud, I used to think that only socially retarded losers became enlightened!" A goodhearted, genial laughter rippled through the room.

Lee smiled then continued seriously, "One primary element on the Path is one-pointed attention. If our sadhana, our practice, can be diverted by our desire for money, for vocation, for relationship, then we don't have one-pointed attention. It's not that we can't have those things, but that they don't get in the way of the Path.

"I've always considered myself lazy and oriented toward comfort. Always take the hardest path, they say—never take the easy way. And I've always taken the easy way. I don't like to struggle and suffer. It's always been obvious to me that whatever qualities I brought to the Path have nothing to do with whatever qualities you need to bring to the Path. Everybody's different.

"One pointed attention is the common ground. Before this work, I considered myself someone mild-mannered and generous and kind, but I wouldn't say I'm like that now. My students say, 'Oh, he's so kind, so generous,' but I know what *real* patience, kindness, generosity are, and I'm not like that."

The questioner said, "I asked Veronique and Gilles the same question and they said what really helped is a taste for the truth."

"I can't say I had a taste for truth," Lee replied. "I'd say I had a taste for freedom, and truth be damned! I'm not like Arnaud; I find life a burden. I'm interested in freedom; unfortunately, there is no freedom, no freedom as I looked for it. There is freedom, but another kind of freedom, which is why my first book was called 'Spiritual Slavery,' instead of 'Spiritual Freedom.' I would rather have written a book called 'Spiritual Freedom' . . . or 'The Celestine Prophecy,' because that book has sold more copies than all of my books put together and probably more than all my books put together ever will sell! Well . . . would you like to continue?"

"No."

"Does that help you?" Lee asked.

"Not the way I expected," the questioner answered frankly.

"That's the Path!" Lee said. "We don't get what we expect."

Lee turned to look over to the women's side of the room. "Okay, Denise. Is that your sadhu blouse? Are you renouncing being at the university?" She laughed. The color of her blouse was indeed a kind of saffron, sadhu-orange.

She said, "I never renounce being at the university of life! Thank you for the generosity with which you tried to answer my question."

"*Tried*," Lee said with pointed emphasis on the word, making it come out quite sarcastically. "That cuts!" He was smiling, demonstrating equanimity and calm as he often does, even when he is working with someone and saying things that implicate him in "feelings" of all kinds. The anticipation of another juicy exchange could be felt in the air as everyone laughed again.

Just as Denise started to object, saying that she didn't mean it like that, Lee interjected with a laugh, "Ah! That's the spirit!" Denise insisted that she didn't say the word "try." Everyone was involved at this point, groaning and saying, "Yes you did," and laughing along.

Lee was smiling as he said, "Yes, you did say 'try.' I recognized it myself. Of course! It's the title of one of my books!" Lee was referring to one of his books based on a transcript of his seminar at Hauteville from some years ago, titled *Don't Try, Just Live*.

"Okay, let's go!" He chided, hustling her to stop wasting time and get on with it.

"I was touched that you were dissatisfied with the answer you gave to me," she began.

"I wasn't dissatisfied with a bad answer," Lee corrected her, "but that *you* were dissatisfied. If I gave a bad answer and you were happy with it, I would have been fine with a bad answer! Are you squirming in your seat with delight . . . or for some other reason? Worms?!"

Laughter broke out again. The whole space was liquid and flowing, buoyant with laughter and ease. Lee went off on a routine about how his student, Lalitha, who is a healer, says that we have to look at our feces to check for worms—arrghhh! Who wants to look at that stuff, especially after you've eaten beets and you think, oh my God, is it blood? Some of us were wiping our eyes from the tears of laughter in the midst of this hilarious, scatological monologue.

"It's like having a horror movie going on all the time but inside you, and you can't turn it off!" More laughter. "So, all my students were doing this big program to get rid of the worms. Herbs that tasted like crap, by the way . . . I'd rather just drink extra wine—get the worms drunk!" Another wave of laughter swept over us.

"Then they'd just *dance* themselves out! In fact, I'm gonna write a book for healing worms: three or four cups of black coffee drunk quickly in a row for constipation . . . See what you've inspired?" He looked inquisitively at Denise, who was along for the ride and seemed to be enjoying it as much as everyone else. In one way she was the focal point of all that energy and Lee's powerful attention, and in another way, the theatre was for everyone in the room.

"No, it's not you," he smiled. "One of my children is in the room. She thinks that my talks are funny. One of the things that are funny to children are conversations about bowel movements," more delight and laughter, "and being somewhat childish, so do I!"

After the laughter subsided, Denise had a chance to speak. She said, "So I felt I had gotten something from you, and over time I would get a lot from it. At Hauteville two years ago I became aware of my financial problem." She began to tell a long story about her financial situation, her relationship with Hauteville, her psychotherapist, and how she realized that she was not giving enough money to Hauteville, where payment for retreats and seminars is strictly on a donation basis. She spoke about herself for what seemed like a very long time. Finally she mentioned that Maryse, who takes the donations at Hauteville, must be aware of her problems with money.

"Not necessarily," Lee said sharply, interrupting. "Sometimes the person who takes donations just thinks the person is stingy and *cheap*! I realize that being a spiritual teacher I'm supposed to be able to see through illusion and pierce them right to the heart of things, mais . . .!" He was smiling at her, while everyone else in the room was laughing at his not so subtle but very skillful way of pointing out how mired in illusion we really are. Cutting through it all, he changed tact and asked bluntly, "Are you happy?" She answered no. "Are you lonely?" She answered yes.

"So, what's at the core of that?" Lee asked.

Speaking very fast, she said, "My life is a disaster."

"That's not why you're unhappy and lonely," Lee challenged her. "Your financial problems are not at the core of it."

She responded, "The simple core question would be to know what is my wish in life; what is my role, why am I on this earth?"

Lee then asked if she was in the room when another student had relayed a terrible thing that her mother had said to her. Denise answered that both her mother and her father had said terrible things to her.

"Ah! What did they say? These things are so unimaginable to me," Lee said.

"Ma mere said even if you had everything on earth but didn't believe in God, expect the worst. She told me the story of a woman who committed suicide because she hadn't believed in God. Mon pere said no man would ever want me because I was like the untamed shrew—I would have to be tamed!"

"What a sweet guy," Lee stated facetiously. "Do you believe in God? It's a yes or no question. Okay, I'll take that as a no."

Denise said, "I don't believe in some God with a big belly on a pink cloud."

"I didn't ask if you believe in some God with a big belly on a pink cloud." The laughter started up again. "I asked if you believe in God! That's Buddha you described, by the way!" Lots more laughter.

She equivocated, "I'm aware of the magnitude of the universe . . ."

"So is every scientist," Lee retorted mildly.

"If the intelligence of life is God, then I believe . . ."

Lee laughed. "You couldn't possibly mean human intelligence!"

"Oui."

"Oh good God! Have you listened to the questions in this room all week? And the world! That's human intelligence! Do you know what I'm getting to?"

"I'm not sure," she answered.

"Me too!" Lee laughed.

"Back to my first question. Does it have value here?" She asked.

"I think the fact that you were raised in a family," Lee started, "where it was a habit of rule to say bad things to children has more value. Why do you think your life is a disaster?"

When she said that she had difficulty trusting her abilities, though she knew that she does have abilities, Lee interrupted her, saying, "You have abilities, je pense. I think so too. Absolutely! What's the problem?"

She responded, "Fear of being rejected because . . ."

Lee interrupted again, "Is your mother alive? Your father alive? Too bad, they'd be proud of you, having turned out exactly the way they said you would." Silence spread across the room as the mood deepened. He had just taken her to another level, but she was a tough nut to crack.

"What do you think? Okay, so maybe when they were alive you had some responsibility to them, but now you don't."

Denise said argumentatively, "I don't know . . . it's a question of being loyal to my parents . . ."

Lee said, "Okay, you want to continue to be unhappy, lonely, desperate—be my guest! And when you die unhappy and lonely, you can say, but at least I was loyal to my parents! Does that logic seem ridiculous to you? Good. It does to me too. But I can't do anything about it in your case—only you can do something about it.

"How about being wildly, profoundly resplendent, to use Alain's words, as a form of being loyal to your parents? How about having so much belief in God that you actually demonstrate the power and force of what a human being can be? Now, *that* is loyalty to parents! Otherwise, you're not being very loyal—you are selling them out. Every parent loves their children but are abysmally ignorant about children and untrained in how to be with them and demonstrate their love."

She said, "I read Alice Miller, and I seem to understand those principles. But I'm still under the influence of all those things . . ."

Lee said, "Do you have any form of physical activity, walking, running, gymnastics, any form of physical action with others? Fencing, martial arts, theatre?" She answered no, but once she did some tai chi. "Actually that's not so active, just standing on the ground in a park and lifting your leg up!" Everyone laughed at Lee's sketchy lampooning of tai chi. Denise said that she would like to learn the tango.

"Why don't you, if you'd like to? Is there anything stopping you?"

Always making things difficult, Denise answered, "Well, there already are too many women."

"Oh, you've already tried?" She answered yes. "Then keep trying," Lee encouraged. "I'd recommend some form of strenuous physical activity that requires physical skill and not intellectual skill to loosen things up. A kind of psychological laxative," everyone laughed, "if you will. I think we'll stop there, if you don't mind."

Later in the session Lee began to discourse in a serious vein in answer to a question. He said, "The longer we're around, the more pressure there is to *see*. The more we know that we don't see, the more pressure there is. To keep the question burning is the irritation that creates the pearl. We aren't inspired to take care of ourselves until there is pain; then we are inspired to take care of ourselves. It's the same on the Path, this pain of longing for a more substantial practice is rightful. When the body gets involved, when the body really aches to resolve a conflict, then we're really got an intention to practice. So, stay with the crisis, stay with the question. Every time you catch yourself not practicing, let that sharpen the blade of your longing to practice. It's that principle."

Lee spoke for some time with Sabine again. At one point he suggested that she gain a little weight—as an experiment. When he made the suggestion, he asked, "What do you think?" She flatly answered no.

He continued, "When we find ourselves in a situation that compromises our commitment to a certain armor that we bear, then we can find out something about why we have that armor. So, too much weight, too little weight, a certain way of wearing our hair or our clothes, these all can indicate the ways we are armored. Paradoxically, that which creates a certain tension and stress might also be the key to relaxation. Sometimes to soften the armor, to crack the armor, we have to do something different."

Sabine said, "You are hitting a raw nerve!"

"It's a recommendation, not of practice, but . . . the fact that you're admitting it's a raw nerve will be completely buried if you don't do the exercise," Lee cautioned her. The exchange was over, and the session came to a close shortly thereafter. It was Friday afternoon; we had been in this dharma *sesshin* for five full days. Tomorrow would be the last day, with only one session on Sunday morning before lunch, after which Lee would take off for Ferme de Jutreau.

Hauteville
July 16

"Okay, Henri," Lee smiled as he asked for questions at the beginning of the morning session and Henri raised his hand.

"I got tickled," Henri began with a smile, referring to his dialogue with Lee the day before, "I tried to be casual in my question and it didn't work. You gave me a blow with a stick! I didn't think the situation was that serious . . ." Suddenly he asked Lee, "Do you think I'm a four or a five?"

Lee answered, "With all those systems, I can never remember which number is what. Same with astrology. I never could remember . . . Well, study of the self is okay as long as I don't have to remember anything. So, I don't know!"

Henri pressed on in a good-natured way, "Well, so you're putting me in the same category as Jean."

Lee laughed, "Well, there are some similarities between you. I wouldn't say you're exactly twins!" Everyone laughed. "But I've always liked you, since we first met in Paris. Hitting you with a stick is to wake you up. Sleeping for a moment doesn't have such horrible implications!"

Henri responded with a smile, "It hurts because the blow has been given to the precise spot my wife has been hitting for some time!" More laughter broke out.

"I'm not surprised," Lee smiled. After Henri said a few more things about his situation and his wife's criticisms of him, Lee said, "I lean toward your wife's viewpoint."

When Lee and Henri had reached the natural conclusion of their interchange, another questioner spoke about a statement Arnaud had made to him: "Trust yourself." This person described how he was a musician, actor and therapist in Paris; now he was teaching guitar lessons and leading a choir. He described being blocked, as if there is a mountain in his way.

Lee responded, "To trust yourself is not to mean you'll never make a mistake; it means that whatever circumstances you find yourself in, you'll make use of the situation. Whether you make good or bad decisions, to trust yourself is to trust your practice and commitment to the Path. When Arnaud says, 'Trust yourself,' that's his trusting your practice in the midst of whatever arises. That's a great thing. Swami Prajnanpad said that every human being, at base, has 'intrinsic dignity and intrinsic nobility.' A lot of human beings are not noble or dignified, but if they dive deeply enough, they will discover intrinsic dignity and intrinsic nobility. This is absolute trust.

"When your practice is stable and a state of presence is known and established, dignity and nobility will shine through you. That doesn't mean you won't make bad decisions sometimes. I have a weakness for famous people. Even if they might be even close to famous, I have a weakness for them! If Bob Dylan was sitting next to you, I wouldn't be able to answer your question—I'd be so nervous! Even if it was Lenny Kravitz!

"When I first started this work, I wrote 'Spiritual Slavery' and it was an incendiary piece of literature . . . . "

Lee went on to humorously describe his first book, 'Spiritual Slavery,' and how it became an embarrassment for him. He would hardly call it literature, actually—it was more like the outpourings of a raving madman in one way. Finally, about fourteen years ago, he had all the existent copies that he could get his hands on, including copies owned by his students who were willing to pitch their copies into the fire, burned in a big bonfire on the ashram in Arizona.

"I felt sort of like a Christian burning the works of the devil! Two types of people were attracted to that book: real teachers, who thought, 'This person looks interesting—let's see what happens,' and every spiritual nut, all the crazies. I got phone calls at three a.m. from drunks, 'Hey, *Leeee*!'

"Even when our behavior is completely undignified and immature, we still are intrinsically noble and dignified, and when we sink back into the state of presence, there it is. When you are in a state of presence, you can still make bad decisions, but that doesn't change the fact of your intrinsic dignity and intrinsic nobility. So you are trustworthy. You are intrinsically trustworthy. We think our actions are what make us trustworthy. We are all just people; what is common to us all is intrinsic nobility and intrinsic dignity. At a certain point our practice is reliable. That doesn't mean we are enlightened; it means we have earned our place on the Path."

Lee told the story of going to India in 1986 with twenty of his students to see Yogi Ramsuratkumar, who did not remember him from their times together in 1977 and 1979, nor did he remember the poetry Lee had been sending him since 1979. Yogi Ramsuratkumar sent Lee away: "Lee, I know what you want. I am not a guru. Go find a guru." Then in 1988, Yogi Ramsuratkumar called Lee back to

India; the tide had turned completely and Lee was embraced fully by his spiritual father.

"Yogi Ramsuratkumar said to me, 'Lee! Lee! You've been so kind to this beggar.' I never let it get to my head, which is why His attention continued, because if I had, He wouldn't even have known my name. After that, at some point I knew that I was reliable, because I had earned Yogi Ramsuratkumar's trust. I was being tested, relative to my commitment to my Master—was my word, my practice, reliable? When I proved my reliability to His satisfaction, then He gave me His trust, and He made it very clear that I had His trust. His trust in me didn't have any conditions.

"I put conditions on His trust; I still have lots of years to live, and Bob Dylan and Johnny Depp might want to become disciples! Who knows what could happen! I could become a complete idiot!" Lee laughed at himself.

"Here, now, I trust myself, and my Master trusted me, deeply, here and now, because the moment I got off a little bit, He let me know it—instantly! We're not trustworthy in our egos. Look how many people spend a lifetime in ethical service and then crumble in a certain circumstance. So, ego is not trustworthy—maybe never! Until the moment we die, ego is not trustworthy. Don't trust your ego—trust your *self.* Say, that's a catchy little line for a song! Anyone who's a musician can have it!"

Mae asked the next question, beginning, "I was touched by that answer. This week you said something about the warrior that touched my heart. In my vision the warrior is one who takes the position of her innate power. I feel that in my work, but in my daily life there are many fears and blocks . . . . How can I intensify and accelerate that in my daily life?"

Considering Mae, a teacher of Middle Eastern dance, Lee responded, "Dance *through* the day! It's a metaphor. Dance through the day."

Mae commented, "You often wrote this as a dedicas."

Lee continued, "You live here, near Hauteville, you're close with the permanent staff members and collaborateurs and Arnaud, so there are always tremendous forces of help flowing to you. The wave of informal or nonverbal help that's coming is immense and never ceases. It's always . . . like the ocean, the tide comes and goes, but the ocean never changes.

"Times when we need to integrate a powerful breakthrough, we don't stop practicing, but the wave kind of backs off a little. That process happens. You should never discount the constant flow of help or Benediction that is flowing to you. It's more an ocean of Benediction that you live in than a flow. The more passionately you want to intensify that will be the magnet that draws that intensification.

"On the mystic path, most potent in Sufism, when we are longing for the Beloved, the more broken heartedly we long and the more anguished our cry, the more likely it is that the Beloved will show Her face, with eyes like antelopes and Her jet black hair.

"It's the intensity of the question, the passion with which you mean it, that will draw you the help and guidance you are needing. Unfortunately, for ego, there is no way to know what the timing is going to be. That's the unknown, because the future does not exist. So all we can rely on is that we are trustworthy on the Path; that we can trust ourselves."

A man said, "I tried to think of a question that would expose me . . ."

Lee said, "Maybe you don't need to be exposed."

The man continued, saying that what he was actually seeking is peace. Lee answered, "Everything has a price. When we want something badly enough, we are willing to pay that price. It's that simple; there is a very direct ratio. Many have asked, 'What can make me want it badly enough?' For Buddha, it was suffering—that all life is suffering."

Lee then talked about the Buddhist *tonglin* breath practice, which is very similar, but not identical, to the Heart Breath practice that

Lee gives to his students. He said, "When we are suffering physically or psychically, we understand that there are many others who are also suffering, and because we have entered the stream of practice, because we can find the Path, we can see the landscape better than they. Maybe we are one step up on the ladder, and we can help relieve their suffering.

"So when we do the technique of tonglin, it's a practice of empathy, of compassion—our pain is not ours alone. We are actually building force behind a reason to practice. Some say, 'I'm selfish and don't care who's suffering.' It's not true. Maybe ego says that, but it's not true. In the place of presence, where dignity and nobility are the radiance of that presence, we are deeply involved with the suffering of all beings. It is a catalyst to provoke in us a deeper practice. That's what inspires us to actually throw logs on the fire of practice, to identify with this burning.

"You have to practice as if your hair is on fire. Then you would instantly respond with great energy. How? In the practice of tonglin is the conscious remembrance of suffering that inspires practice. We see it everywhere. Go to Paris and look into people's faces, and you see suffering. Out on the farm the cycle of life is so evident; people handle pain differently there than they do in Paris.

"In Arizona we just had lightning strike again. It hit telephone wires and fried the telephones, melted the wires. We have five phone lines on our ashram, and lightning strikes and they're all dead. We can't even make a call. People on the ashram who have been working under tremendous personal work loads for years just shrug their shoulders and handle it. The new students say, 'Oh my God! Lightning! What are we going to do!' "

With the sessions for the day over, we gathered at seven-thirty for dinner together in the courtyard under the tall trees. After dinner we were treated to a theatrical performance by Arnaud's students, presided over by Pascal. In years past it has become an annual event to have Shri, and on one occasion, Attila the Hunza, perform music, along with a band made up of Arnaud's students, on a portable stage set up in the courtyard one night during the weeklong seminar. Shri and Hunza were not there this year, and so Arnaud's students, organized by Pascal, made the entire presentation of the evening.

As twilight and then evening fell upon our group of over a hundred people dedicated to the spiritual path, the stage, set up beneath a spreading mimosa tree, was transformed into another platform from which the dharma in action could be expressed. Many different people performed, in a delightful rediscovery for us of the incredibly talented group of people in the Hauteville association.

It seemed, as always, more than appropriate to somehow close this incredible week of celebrating the dharma, the guru and the sangha at Hauteville with music. Highlights of the night were performances by Veronique, Emmanuelle, Gilles, Pascal and many others, and also of songs sung by Pascal and Alain René from Lee's CD, *Ecrasé par l'Amour*. At one point Pascal invited Lee up to sing "Love Never Dies" with the band and some back-up singers. It was a fabulous moment when the feeling of unity between the two schools—which are very different in many ways—was never stronger or more palpable and heartfelt. The capacity of Arnaud and his students to appreciate our master, Lee, and express the fullness of their gratitude and respect was awe-inspiring and at the same time humbling.

Hauteville
July 17

Lee had packed up the Sacred Bazaar immediately after meditation this morning; the vans were packed as well. As soon as the session was over, lunch would be served and Lee and his crew would fly down the road back to our ashram, some seven hours away. Now it was really just a matter of saying goodbye.

By the end of the week, a great deal had been accomplished; time would be needed to integrate the teachings and the powerful effects of the spiritual influence flowing from Lee and Arnaud, all concentrated into seven days. As full and saturated as we were, our last two hours together with Lee and Arnaud ran true to the vein of the whole week—poignant, dynamic, provocative and intimate.

In the morning session Lee recapitulated many important points he had made during the week in a very organic and spontaneous way, sewing it all together with the constant thread of the fundamental practice of Arnaud's students: accepting what is, as it is, here and now. Lee spoke of how much upheaval we create in our lives when we try to satisfy the dissatisfaction in our lives, tormented as we often are by the constant change in our world, because there is no satisfaction except through the inner stillness where there is no change. He exhorted us to have faith in our practice and in the path, and to cultivate inner unity so that we can move in the outer world with clarity and purpose. Otherwise, we will find the temptations in the outer world too great, and we often realize this too late.

Lee also spoke of the need for repetition in our practice, whether it is a mantra, something like the Christian "Prayer of the Heart," or meditation. It is only through repetition that our practice can become constant and automatic within us; in this way, practice becomes organic to our whole being.

At one point Eric, the base player for the Hauteville rock band, asked a question about Lee's favorite song on *Ecrasé par l'Amour*: "Love Never Dies." He said, "I wonder sometimes, I don't know—do I believe in God? When you sing that song, it sounds like a romantic song, but I was trying to look at you and see the extent to which you are what you sing, because I'm not sure . . . The only reference points I have are Arnaud and you."

Lee asked, "What about your wife? Veronique is not an example? Or your kids?" Eric answered oui. "Great, and so?" Lee nudged him on.

"A few days ago," Eric said, "I wanted to ask you a question and I stopped. So Didier asked the same question. I'll listen to the tapes of your answer, but I am confused about the lyrics of your songs, especially 'Love Never Dies'."

Lee began his answer, "Most lyrical expression, in poetry or song, can be taken in one of two ways, although Idries Shah says there are seven levels to every tale. 'Love Never Dies,' can be romantic or anti-romantic; it can also obviously be about the mind, which never lets anything go and drags things out. It could also be about the pure eternal nondual reality . . . I guess! I always write these things in a moment of inspiration, and I don't think about what I'm trying to say. I think if I thought about what I was trying to say, I'd never write anything! So I write quickly—poetry and prose.

"Most things can be taken two ways—dualistically or nondualistically. We can choose in a very real way how we want to take something. I find the work of Baudelaire very inspiring, but some find it very depressing. The wound of love and broken-heartedness is very present in my own work, so I find Baudelaire tremendously elevating—his are real love songs. If you think his poems are just about a woman, you'll get depressed—unless you see them as being about Woman as the tangent point between duality and nonduality. So we choose which direction we will go in. If we want the love that knows no sorrow, then you take whatever strikes you about that song and go toward love to teach you about sorrow."

This theme was picked up by Franck, who played lead guitar for the rock band the night before and has toured with Shri for the past three summers, playing guitar onstage with Lee and the band. He too was struck deeply by the song, "Love Never Dies" and Lee's performance of it. He expressed his deep connection with this song and the profound impact it has on him.

Lee commented, "Great! I hope to do some gigs under my own name next year, and if that happens, I will be calling you!" Everyone laughed, while Franck broke into a very big smile.

Franck continued, "Every time I come to Hauteville, I realize the richness and profundity of the teaching. It gets simpler and simpler. I see what is and stop making a problem out of things. Everything was said this morning in meditation. Every morning when I get out of bed, I leave the one who does not want to meditate, and I go to meditation. It's a joy to practice every day . . ."

It was an inspiring testimony to practice and the great value of this week in the sanctuary of Hauteville. Everyone was listening closely as Franck spoke passionately, and it seemed his words, even translated into English by Gilles, were touching the collective heart at a deep level.

Lee responded by heaping praise on Franck for the genius of his guitar playing. Lee called Franck an example of someone who is "one with" the guitar as he played. At one point the night before Franck had played a riff from famous guitarist Carlos Santana, and now Lee laughed sweetly as he said, "Franck plays Carlos Santana better than Santana! When you are listening to music that inspires you, what you're actually getting is the spirit of the musician."

Answering a question about how to open the heart, Lee talked first about his relationship with his stepdaughters from his second marriage. He gave a very moving account of how he had failed in these relationships. Many problems arose, and eventually the girls, as they grew into young adults, became estranged from Lee. "It was all me," Lee confessed. There were tears in some of our eyes as Lee continued on the subject of how our hearts get opened when they get broken.

'How do we know if our heart is open or closed? It's mostly the mind. Maybe having an open heart is just a matter of a moment of sweetness during the day . . . "

Continuing, now on the ever-popular subject of enlightenment, which has nothing to do with having an open heart, Lee said, "Enlightenment is the knowledge—absolute knowledge, not mind knowledge, not dualistic knowledge—that all things are transitory, including enlightenment. Because what is enlightenment? If it can be labeled or defined, it is not that. Everyone who uses that word uses it to describe a discrete state that is not present, that is compared to other states that are not enlightenment."

Lee was eloquent in expounding his absolute nondual view of the enlightened state; he was expressing the full mystery of it, when he segueyed into a mild rant about how we confuse an open heart with some misplaced, illusory ideas about intimacy.

"Ah! Don't get me started on intimacy. Women and their needs for intimacy! My idea of intimacy is you sit in the same room, you are aware of each other's presence, you feel love, have sex once in a while, enjoy each other's company over a good meal . . . what do you need all the rest for? What is having an open heart anyway? How do we know our heart isn't open, and we're just looking at the wrong thing? It's just the baby rattling the cage—feed me! feed me! Those dry crusts of bread are not enough! I want a *steak*!"

Everyone laughed, remembering a funny monologue Lee had done a few days before about the emotional tyranny of the "inner baby" within us. Babies are naturally grasping, demanding, they cry when they experience the slightest disturbance, they have not built any capacity to endure discomfort or hardship, nor do they have the tensile strength and skillful means that an adult should have in the face of life's pleasures and pains.

"Surrender to the other grounds us in intrinsic nobility and intrinsic dignity," Lee continued, "so that we are not relating through our psychology. Surrender into love . . ."

At this point, Sabine, who had already had two significant interactions with Lee earlier in the week, asked a question that catalyzed yet another round of dialogue on the seemingly eternal quandary of men and women. Every time Lee called her bluff or made a point, she threw another flame in his direction with her arguments, rationalizations and justifications. She seemed hell bent on languishing in her illusions about herself, sex, men and life in general. It was an object lesson for everyone in the room, as we watched the way ego sabotages transformational opportunities.

Lee was by turns funny and provocative with her. At one point she said, "I'll be a renunciate if you say to!" It was a totally off the wall remark, coming out of nowhere, made all the more frustrating because Lee had, just days ago, lead her patiently through the consideration of "invoking the masculine" and transforming her relationship.

Lee snapped back, "I didn't say that! I didn't even intimate that!"

His irritation matched our disappointment at the common human unwillingness to walk through the door of transformation he had so generously opened for her. The whole group seemed poised on the brink of wonder as to what Lee would say and do next. Where could he go from there? He plunged into telling the mythological story of the warrior goddess Durga, but first, he playfully described how he usually gets the details of these stories wrong, saying, "So, if there are any Sanskrit scholars in the room, spare me the corrections at lunch!"

Lee then proceeded to tell the story of how all the gods were unable to kill a terrible demon that was plaguing humankind. They all got together and birthed the mother goddess, Durga, a great warrioress who was the sum total of all their wrathful and merciful energies concentrated in female form—that is, symbolically representing incarnation, or the manifest world—Creation. After a terrible battle in which the demon played many tricks on Durga, including changing forms, Durga killed the buffalo demon, and all was well again.

Lee commented, "When we get the demon to the point where we can kill it, it changes form. What the Buddhists call 'skillful means' is what is required. Skillful means is what gives the teacher the ability to help the student, so every time a student comes up with some new fancy moves, the master still has to counter it, which is martial art—ritualized movement. One of great skill has to move spontaneously with that which has been practiced. When you are present, that's what you do.

"We saw Bob Dylan perform in Las Vegas last spring in concert. It was straight ahead, blistering rock & roll! The quality of the musicians he chooses is that they can follow him anywhere—they're with him, they're right there with him, wherever he goes. In a very real sense, that's what we're called to do. What is, as it is, is only this moment. To make a connection to the next moment is to compromise our practice. Our minds are not quick enough to think your way through practice. You can't practice with the mind. Can't do it!"

Lee praised Pascal's English in the complex poetry of Bob Dylan's song "It's Alright, Ma," that he had performed the night before as an example of having to function outside the confines of the mind. There was no way that Pascal could have pulled that off with his mind in control. Lee also mentioned Jimmy Page, the guitarist of Led Zeppelin, for his virtuoso guitar playing. But it was Stevie Ray Vaughan who he held up as the standard for this kind of transcendence in the arts.

"Stevie Ray Vaughan. We saw a video of him playing over some years at Austin City Limits. It was just unbelievable! What he does with the guitar stops your mind. What he does is being one with the guitar. The mind may be brilliant, you may be a genius, but you can't practice with your mind. Sooner or later it will get tired or crack."

Franck, who was sitting in the front row on the men's side of the room and was raptly attentive to Lee's words, was nodding his head in enthusiastic agreement. "Incroyable!" he said, adding that he too had seen the Stevie Ray Vaughan video that Lee spoke of.

Lee said, "If a musician is only technically proficient, Franck can tell, because he knows the difference. Your spiritual master knows if it's your mind replicating practice, or if you are actually practicing. A lot of the questions the master asks are rhetorical; they are designed to disturb your illusions of a calm and undisturbed surface, to give you a glimpse that you are not practicing as you thought—it is only the mind practicing. The master can tell, even when the appearance of your practice is seamless; he can tell the difference between practice and the replication of practice by the mind.

"With a false master, the master looks just like a master, acts like a master, but doesn't *know*. The real master can tell the difference. Real practice *is*, just is. It's not something that gets done. It's difficult to grasp because we are all doers. And we have to be, or we'd starve to death! But practice is not something we *do*; it is something we *are*.

"When we become one with practice permanently, then we realize that all our doing had utility, value, but was frustrating. Accepting what is as it is here and now is a state of being. We are trying to actively accept something, so we are more or less effective. If something is not too shocking to us, we take deep breaths and accept, but other things, we can't accept.

"What the master does is keep blocking our escape routes. We start out in a labyrinth with a million different directions. But there's only one route to accepting what is. One by one, the master closes off our options, so we are being channeled, very effectively, and we fight it and fight it! We don't like it. We say, 'I can find my own way! I'm intelligent! Just point me in the right direction.' Until we step on the mine, and then we're not so arrogant anymore . . . . So the master is guiding us, guiding us, slowly, slowly, blocking off one distraction after another, until finally there is only one—Arnaud and Swami Prajnanpad. At this point, some people walk away. It does happen."

It was twelve-thirty, time to stop. The last of the baggage was quickly packed into the vans, and to facilitate Lee's usual preferred fast getaway, the vehicles were driven around to the parking area near the courtyard where lunch would be served as usual. After a quick repast with Arnaud and Veronique, including ice cream and coffee, Lee said goodbye to everyone. The whole group gathered to see him off. After many *pranams* to Lee and promises of "á l'annee prochaine" between the disciples of the two schools, we were gone, off down the road toward the wide river Rhone and in the direction of Valence, then north and west, back to the Baul sanctuary known as Ferme de Jutreau. We would arrive just in time to have evening tea with everyone who had stayed home to keep the hearth fires burning.

Yogi Ramsuratkumar, 1995.

Lee Lozowick, summer 2005.

Lee and Purna, tasting the pineau in La Roche Posay.

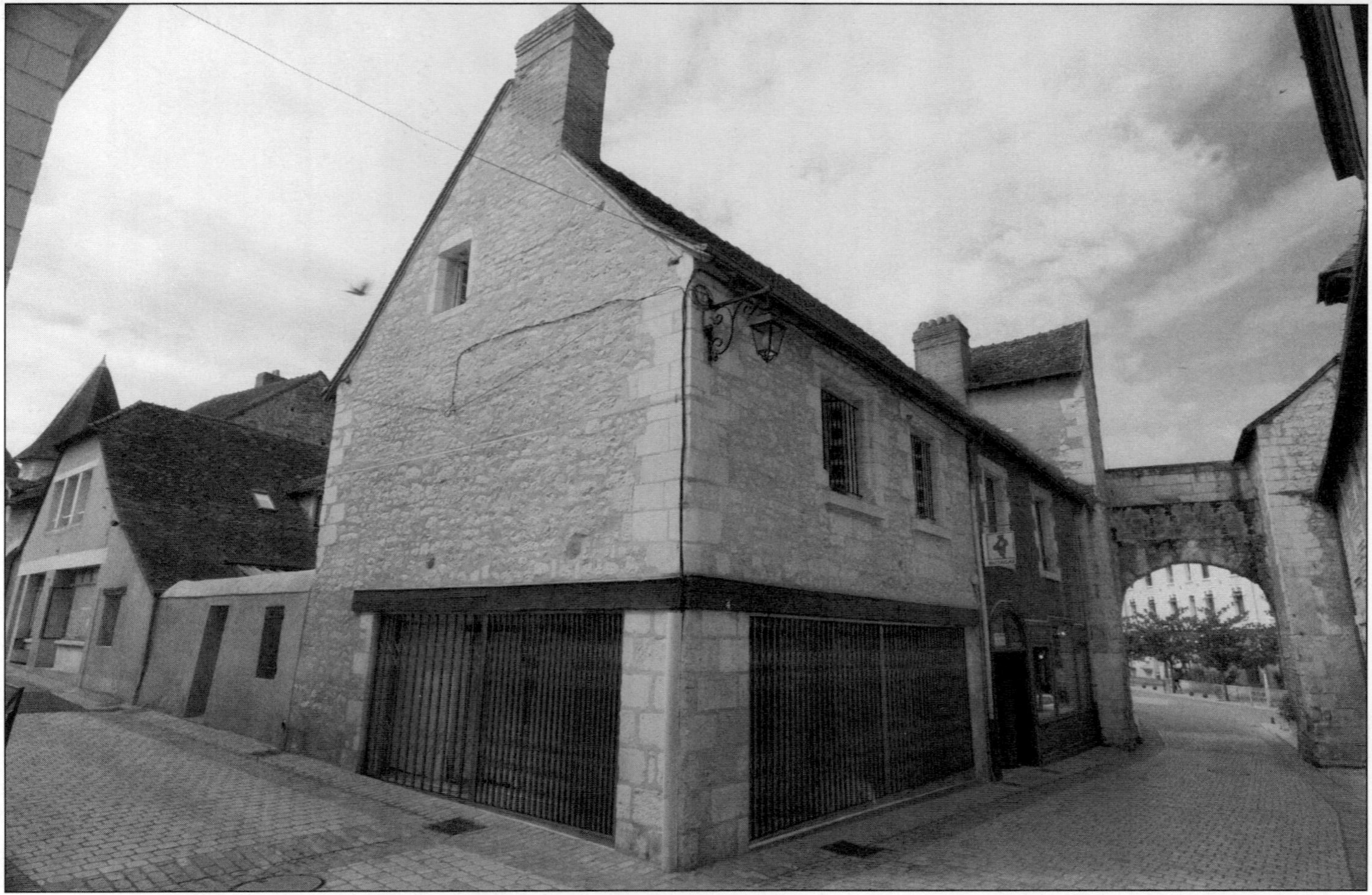

The magasin, *before the opening.*

Opening the back door of the new shop.

Selling at the Paris seminar, June 2005.

At the mosque and on the streets of Paris.

Opening the shop.

Asian Antiquities and European Brocante—the grand opening.

In the shop basement.

Arnaud Desjardins and Lee in Canada at Mangalam, April 2005.

Lee and Arnaud at Hauteville, summer 2004.

Sacred Bazaar sales at *Ferme de Jutreau.*

Guru Purnima: tea in the salon at Ferme de Jutreau.

A quiet moment at Ferme de Jutreau.

Ashram Life

Ferme de Jutreau
July 18, 2005

The next morning Lee sat in the shade of the maple tree in the courtyard for forty-five minutes with Magloire Lamine, the editor of *Arya*, a new French magazine on Ayurveda and other topics germane to the spiritual path, and three female members of his staff, giving an interview. They leaned forward to hear what Lee was saying, and to understand his words—with some difficulty, since none of them spoke a great deal of English. A small, unobtrusive recording device was on the table between them. Lee was jazzed from his week at Hauteville and he spoke in an animated way, his blue eyes shooting benign sparks upon his rapt audience.

While Lee sat with his guests, everyone on the ashram was busy at work; those who weren't in the kitchen preparing lunch or at desks in the office were gearing up for the Guru Purnima Celebration that is held every year. Many spaces had to be created for the people who would flood the ashram in two days' time; the couples' section of the stone barn had to have sheet rooms created in the old cow stalls, and beds and bedding had to be organized for the women's and men's dorms, also in the barn. Menus were being planned and large amounts of food being purchased, while several different schedules of tasks—from childcare to cooking and to serving meals to daily clean up of various spaces and outhouse duty—were made.

At noon we all came together, and as we walked up in the sunshine to the barn to stand in the buffet line, Lee gestured toward us and said, "All these beasts are my students!" He laughed a loud and sardonic laugh. We smiled at the visitors as if to say, "Yes, we beasts are his students."

As we sat down at the long head table in the cool barn, Lee invited Magloire, Sylvie and the other women, whose names I didn't catch, to sit directly across from him. Magloire sat down with awe and amazement written all over his expressive face, saying, "I never thought this would happen! I can't believe I'm sitting across the table from Lee Lozowick!"

Never one to miss such an opportunity, Lee rejoined, with equal amazement and theatricality, "I can't believe I *am* Lee Lozowick!" Everyone at the table laughed. It was an ice breaker, but it was also a direct communication of the guru's nonidentification, particularly demonstrated for the rest of us in the face of adulation, recognition and praise.

After a pleasant lunch Lee retired with his guests to the salon in the *grande maison*, made rather dark and cave-like because the windows were almost completely obscured by artifacts of all kinds, shapes and sizes in bronze, wood and stone. Lee sat in his big leather armchair in front of the fireplace, while the guests sat in chairs in a semi-circle in front of him to continue their interview. Several students sat around on pillows or chairs to listen and take notes. While we were waiting for the coffee to be served, the interview continued.

Magloire began with the question, "So, is your path a bhakti path?"

Lee answered, in his laconic way, "Yes, bhakti, and more. As long as the 'and more' is full of bhakti, then it's possible to have more."

Another questioner asked, "How did you get started?"

"I started in Silva Mind Control, which has to do with controlling the mind, and this Work has to do with *using* the mind—an important distinction." Lee explained that the Silva Method, as it's known now, is a system of parapsychology, meditation, dream interpretation and expanding human potential through the discipline of the mind.

"What about dreams? Are dreams important? Do you use them?"

Lee responded, "I think dreams can be very valuable in the spiritual process—not all dreams, but select dreams."

At this point Lee stopped the questions by handing his guests a box full of CDs of his music, which Andrea had just brought to him—a mix of all the community bands, and, of course, *Ecrasé par l'Amour*. The guest was overwhelmed by the generosity and immensity of the gift.

"Oh man!" Magloire smiled, receiving the box with a look of wonder. He was very genuinely surprised, as many people are by Lee's frequent generosity with books and CDs produced by the Hohm Community. Clearly overcome in many ways, Magloire said with surprising passion, "You have no right to give me so much!" Lee merely smiled and shrugged ever so slightly.

One of the women asked, "Is the blues about God?"

Lee answered, "No. It's about food, money and sex. After all, it's the blues!"

She pursued, "Do you make a difference between love and sex?"

Lee responded, "Well, it depends on who I'm talking to!" Everyone laughed, understanding this answer quite well. Lee continued, "In the natural aspects of life—the enjoyment of beauty and relationship—sex is just a part of that. Some people are natural celibates, but that's rare. Love has many facets, many reflections; but when sex is neurotic, I wouldn't associate it with love. When it is naturally established as a part of life, then love is possible, but most people give it too much weight. In many traditions the feeling is that sex is too much of a distraction, and it's better to just prohibit it. I have another view—you work with it as part of your life.

"Most people here," he indicated the ashram in a way that was inclusive of the greater sangha, "work so hard that they have no time for sex! At one time in India, sex was a natural part of life, then a time came when the feminine was considered unwholesome . . . ." Lee spoke for awhile about the repression of the feminine aspects of life in India, including sex and the body, in a culture that had at one time honored and exalted these dimensions of life in their art, literature, daily life and in their religion.

Continuing on, the woman asked, "There are a lot of women on your ashram, not a lot of men. How do you explain that?"

"Bad luck!" Lee retorted, to instant peals of laughter. He continued, "In Arizona there are more men but not here. I guess the men feel they have to go out and conquer the world. It goes through phases—over time it evens out."

Magloire interjected, "Do you have hope for the world?"

Lee answered unequivocally, "No. In centuries, yes, then I have hope, but in years—no."

"Do you believe in paradise on Earth?"

"No," Lee answered, "not as long as people have emotions."

"Can we live without emotions?" a woman asked.

"Probably not. That's why I don't have hope. But if people can have a better life because they have hope, it's good. I believe in kindness, compassion and generosity—if the belief in hope for the future inspires that, then I'm all for it."

Another question was put forward: "Do we come back for another life?"

Lee answered, "I believe God chooses for each of us whether we come back or not."

Lee began to talk about saints and what creates good karma. He said, "It's really about cultivating the ability to put others before ourselves. If you have that ability, of course you're not going to cause suffering for others. That's what creates a saint . . . . Of course, change is possible. Yogananda said that small groups living together is what will keep the Path alive in the years ahead. Change is possible, but not on a large scale. It starts on a small scale. There is as much possibility in the future for a greater resonance to the Divine as there is now."

Someone else asked, "What can the divine master do with this mess?"

"Well," Lee began, "there is always the force of prayer. So I think with any divine master, a large part of their work is prayer."

This more serious vein was interrupted by the arrival of the coffee, which was served with hot milk and sugar. Lee seemed very excited by this. He smiled broadly as he accepted a cup and said brightly, "Wow! Coffee in the middle of the day! I'm glad you came—now we get a treat!" The guests and students who were gathered around listening laughed in concert at Lee's pleasantry.

He continued, "It's a divine master's job to communicate the teaching as well, not just pray, and that gets done through teaching, music, art. Even in a very mundane way, for example, if we're in a restaurant and the waitress is in a bad mood, and someone goes in and cheers her up, and then she passes that on to others all day—it spreads out!"

A brief lull passed through the room, then one of the women said, "It's very peaceful here."

"It's peaceful as a general rule," Lee commented, "but there are small periods of time when people have tension with each other. But not all the time." After a slight pause he chuckled and said, "It's not the ashram—it's just a nice part of France!"

"How do you approve of the progress of your disciples?" someone asked.

"Not enough for their liking!" Lee retorted. Everyone laughed, visitors and students alike. "I approve their progress over time—

when what changes have taken place with progress is stable and reliable. If every time a person has an ascent into samadhi, that person got approved to teach, there would be a bunch of psychotics all over the world, teaching in my name, because it's very easy to produce those states."

Just then Manuela came in to refill our cups with coffee. Lee instructed her to serve the guests first, not him, saying, "The guest is king for three days! On the fourth day, they work! It's a principle of Sufism."

Magloire asked, "Did you work as a businessman before?"

Lee became theatrical as he said, "Business! Money! I'm a very bad master, because I've never submitted to anyone else. I expect my students to submit to me, but I've never submitted to anyone else!"

Lee began to talk about the community bands, and in the meantime, I wondered about his cryptic, self-deprecating statements. Who were they for? He had submitted entirely to his master, Yogi Ramsuratkumar; his discipleship and integrity as a devotee has been demonstrated before our very eyes for years, most poignantly in trips with Lee to India to sit at the feet of Yogi Ramsuratkumar.

Ma Devaki once said that Yogi Ramsuratkumar would say things that were quite self-deprecating whenever there were disbelievers and doubters around him; these remarks seemed aimed at their lack of insight and faith—their inability to see through the ways in which the master veils himself. Why does the master veil himself? To catalyze a further descent into the confusion in which we are already floundering, because that is the only way we will come to actually see through it by ourselves, without a spiritual authority explaining and hand-feeding us. Then, we have the possibility to pierce through it to clarity.

The next question was, "Do you choose the bronze yourself?

"Yes, I choose," Lee answered. "God save every spiritual master from having to live by gifts alone, from disciples who have no idea what the spiritual master likes or needs! If my students chose the bronzes, these shelves would be filled with ugly things! I choose myself by beauty and sanctity. I look for pieces that invoke the Presence of the Divine."

"Do you do puja?"

"To Yogi Ramsuratkumar," Lee answered. "And obviously, if there are other deities on someone's puja, they are included in the worship. My Master, Yogi Ramsuratkumar is dead now. He died in 2001, but when He was alive I would see Him two weeks every year. He would have preferred that I saw Him much much longer, but because I felt I had a responsibility to all the demands of my life as a spiritual master, I put those demands before my personal pleasure—I would have preferred to spend six months a year with Him. He understood that very, very well, and He never asked me to do anything else. He knew my work in the world had value, and so He sacrificed His personal pleasure, and I sacrificed mine . . ."

"How did you know he was your spiritual master?"

"Instinct," came Lee's one word reply.

"Now do you maintain a connection?"

Lee answered yes, then Magloire asked, "Subtly?"

"Of course!" Lee answered. "To me He is still alive. The Master has dropped His body, but it doesn't mean the Master has gone away."

"Did you connect with other masters?"

Lee answered, "Ramana Maharshi, Nityananda, Shirdi Sai Baba, and of course, Arnaud Desjardins—he is a real master. Anandamayi Ma also—one of the few genuine woman masters. I also went to see Satya Sai Baba. Those connections are because of a resonance to their surrender to God and their clarity of understanding, but none of that is like the resonance I felt to Yogi Ramsuratkumar—that is unique."

Lee stopped to look at the platter of sweets that was being offered to him.

"Oh, ginger!" He took a piece and looked up at his guests with a smile. "We have so much to thank you for! Coffee! Ginger! All we're missing is chocolate . . . " Lee shrugged and smiled, "Another time!"

One of the women guests started coughing. This spurred a fresh round of commentary that came from Lee, with a mischievous gleam of enthusiasm in his eyes, "When I go somewhere with one of my students to see a real master, and they start coughing like that, I wish they would just keel over dead, just to see what the master would do!" He paused, maybe for the effect of comedic timing, then said, "Because, what would a real master do if someone keeled over dead?"

Magloire smiled uncertainly. Maybe he wasn't sure he'd actually heard what Lee said, English being a second language for him. He changed the subject, asking, "You have tattoos? What for?

"I have a few," Lee answered coolly. "I like tattoos. I got my first one five years ago. All of my tattoos are sacred symbols."

Lee asked Andrea to bring the Shri touring schedule for the guests to look at, and as they looked it over, they all commented on how hard it is—hard work, lots of gigs and lots of travel in a short period of time.

"When do you sleep?" someone asked.

"After the tour, we sleep," Lee answered with a smile.

Magloire asked, "Do you like to sing?"

Lee answered with candor, "I don't like to sing as much as I like the applause. See? I say things like that and all my students think I'm kidding! When I say things like that, my students say, 'Oh, he's such a trickster!' "

We were getting into interesting territory, in which Lee was becoming more and more cryptic in his answers to their questions. It was at this point that they politely, enthusiastically and genuinely expressed their gratitude to Lee for the interview, asserting their excitement again about the new magazine in this particular interview. They commented that they had a lot of material. Perhaps we would meet again, sometime? Yes, we hope so.

With warm handshakes and a final heartfelt *pranam*, they walked away across the grassy courtyard to their cars and left.

Ferme de Jutreau—Guru Purnima Celebration July 21

Our numbers had grown substantially with people arriving for the Celebration, and on Thursday, the first night of the annual Guru Purnima Celebration, Lee gave a talk in the barn meditation hall instead of in the salon to accommodate everyone. It was quite warm, pleasant in the summery evening air, so that the coolness in the vast space of the barn was a welcomed change. Lee began with answering questions.

One man in the French sangha said that he felt the need to spend more time at the ashram, with the sangha, and it was threatening to his wife. Lee made a point about what is important: that we create as little suffering as possible for others without compromising our real needs. When asked, how do you know what your real needs are, he said, "Trust the teacher. And, it's very important to tell the teacher the facts."

Then Lee read a question that had been submitted in writing by a thirteen-year-old boy who was visiting for several days with his mother, who is a disciple of Arnaud. The question was: "A lot of beings seem to become enlightened, but then they die, and it seems like they don't come back here. Where do awakened beings go when they die? Do they ever come back here?"

Lee gave a long, serious answer to this boy's question that delved into some esoteric considerations that he doesn't very often cover. He said, "This is my opinion. It's my opinion that, when someone reaches a certain level of spiritual development, which isn't necessarily enlightenment, realization, mukti or liberation, that person's freedom of choice becomes submitted to the higher wisdom of whatever Process it is that defines our movement through incarnation, which is not necessarily God, but maybe a demigod or something. When we reach a certain level of value to the Work—not just useful, because academically we could say that a lot of artists could be very useful to the Work; an artist like Rodin or Picasso or Bach could become necessary to the Work—when we are necessary to the Work, then the Work defines our trajectory through time. But then, they say if you eat a lot of pork, you could come back as a pig!"

On this humorous note Lee stopped the serious discourse to segue into a high-spirited selling session, pivoting around the beautiful old Lakshmi lamps that he had massed around the guru's sandals on their pillow below his chair. He was selling the lamps in groups of three at very reduced prices, but people were reluctant at first. After some cajoling and laughter, the lamps were sold as sangha members took Lee up on his offer to make a deeper commitment to bring the Sacred into their spaces.

This piece of business having been conducted, Lee continued answering the boy's question: "When we become necessary to the Work, our choice about things becomes submitted to the Work, which isn't necessarily God. Indian philosophy says the last thought before you die defines your next incarnation. Like Gandhi, who said 'Ram' at the moment he died. Before we have that level of attainment, we actually have more choice in how we incarnate. So, If you want your ego to decide your next incarnation, don't practice too hard!

"Those of great attainment, when they die, what happens next could be incarnation on Earth or in some other conscious planet in some other galaxy, or whether they go to some subtle realm and teach in a 'university,' like the way people dream of going to a cave and meeting radiant masters who teach them. You could be given another body, or given an astral body that does have a function and can do things. Clearly, it's also my opinion, that the great beings incarnate, when they reincarnate, in different parts of the world than their last incarnation, looking very different than their last incarnation, with different color skin . . . So, a great Indian master probably would not reincarnate in India, depending on who they were.

"In Christianity there is the 'coming of the Messiah,' but in my opinion he won't come in the Middle East, or look like Jesus looked.

I think he probably had dark skin and strong features and beautiful, long, wavy hair. In his next incarnation he'll probably have pale skin and lots of bad hair days, and halitosis, and he'll tell everybody to eat lots of garlic, and he'll go, 'Ahhhh,' " Lee breathed out noisily, as if into someone's face, " and people will go," he covered his face with his hands as if turning away in disgust, "and he'll recommend a diet of boiled cabbage and cooked onions!"

Laughter rippled across the audience at this earthy and slightly raunchy version of the dignified, perfected Jesus we all know and love. Jesus, brought down to the immediate proximity of human foible!

"So, the Work defines our incarnation and we get to incarnate where we are needed, so a great spiritual master could get incarnated as a doctor or an artist or a scientist—but not in the dark side of science—or as a teacher. People who have revolutionized certain fields, even Freud, although he was very neurotic, but people like Carl Jung or Einstein . . . or Elvis . . . or Janis Joplin . . . yeah! Rock & roll has definitely revolutionized the world, and some of its consequences are not so bad!

"So, a great awakened being submits themselves to a higher authority that decides how, where and when that essence will get used. If a revolution that isn't called 'spiritual' can help a lot of people, then that's how that being might come back. I don't know much about Foucault, but at times in his work he probably thought he was Jesus!

"When we reach a certain level, we are required by obligation to continue to serve—the only question is who, where, when, what level of being they will serve. So, Yogi Ramsuratkumar. As I have said before, many Westerners came to Him. I've told lots of stories of initiations He gave me, teachings He gave me. But He was not stingy with a number of Westerners. I ended up where I am for a reason, one reason. Yogi Ramsuratkumar knew that a Westerner was going to do what I'm doing for Him in the West, but He didn't know who. If they passed the first of the list of criteria, He went on to the second on the list; it ended up being me. It wasn't because I was supposed to be the one doing this job—it was decided by a higher authority that is not necessarily God.

"I came to Earth with a certain constellation of qualities that were useful to Yogi Ramsuratkumar and that were what He needed in this incarnation. Whatever I was and I did in the last life, I have no idea—it was probably very different, in a different part of the world, different color skin, different religion. Yogi Ramsuratkumar is higher in the divine bureaucracy than I am. He needed something and I got sent to help Him. I could've been a great spiritual master in my past life, or an artist, or . . .

"When a highly evolved being is done with an incarnation, the body leaves and the essence, including psychological qualities that have been coded into essence, that essence will be sent somewhere to work for one of two reasons: to serve, which service will automatically create merit or good karma, or two, because those that are higher in the spiritual bureaucracy than we are, the spiritual hierarchy (but I prefer the word bureaucracy), those higher in the system see that even a highly evolved being is missing a piece. Then, that being might be sent to realize that piece and coincidentally, they will naturally serve. That's a given.

"So, we actually give away our vote. We might be on our death bed, if we are somewhat spiritually advanced, and the spiritual master might say that the world is so desperate, so full of greed and violence, that we offer up a prayer for humanity, but nonetheless we give up our vote at a certain point in spiritual evolution. We can still volunteer an opinion, but one of the clauses on the contract we have signed with the higher authority says that even though we and the higher authority agree to disagree, the higher authority always has the final decision.

"You've probably heard people say, 'This is my last incarnation.' That person will probably reincarnate as a human being to evolve beyond the foolish notion of a 'last incarnation,' because things just go on and on and on, which is not the way I would design it . . . but things just go on and on. I'll end with this consideration, since more of you will want to think about it: If the right person comes up with the right question relative to this, I will answer it. But if you come up with a question and I don't answer it, it doesn't mean that you aren't valuable to the school and appreciated! Because not being the right person to ask a question does not mean you aren't the right person!" Lee was smiling; a few people were chuckling, many were smiling along with him.

He continued, "Like your partner not remembering your birthday is never a sign of lack of love. Or remembering your anniversary. We get upset about these things, and take it as a sign that we're not loved and appreciated. Such things as your birthday and anniversary are not the ultimate pivot around which love revolves!"

The laughter that erupted on that note ushered us into another sales session, as Lee proceeded to sell different items and specifically talked about the wooden "marriage dolls" he had been selling in the Sacred Bazaar since the first seminar in Paris a month ago. He said, "By the way, for those of you who got marriage dolls, or who want to buy them, I found out something else about them that really adds to their meaning, I think. You know, the man gets the woman doll to keep and the woman gets the man doll to keep. Not only do they represent love and abundance and all that, the woman doll represents the 'First Woman,' and the man doll represents the 'First Man,' so they're sort of the Hindu Adam and Eve. Cool! I really liked that."

At the end of the talk everyone left the barn to get ready for dinner, which would be served in about forty-five minutes. A large group of teenagers and children were gathered under the tree at the tables, peacefully playing together, flirting or strumming guitars. Amidst all the hard work that was going on as well, you could see communion flowing in tender exchanges or shared laughter at every turn. The flower gardens around the house were in full bloom, the big hydrangea bushes were loaded down with massive pink petal balls. It wasn't too hot, not too cool. It was a mellow and idyllic scene, and underneath it, a fire was burning.

Ferme de Jutreau—Guru Purnima
July 22

This morning at seven a.m. a ten-wheel cargo truck arrived in the drive at Ferme de Jutreau. Parked at the edge of the courtyard, it looked huge and out of place in this rural setting, but it was laden with things that were soon to become part of the Sacred Bazaar. As soon as the bell rang at the end of meditation, Lee was all over the boxes and crates like a mother bear with new cubs. What a scene, with Lee and the men ripping into crates and boxes and Quint, one of Lee's French students, on a fork lift, moving pallets of heavy stone pieces off the back of the truck and onto the ground. It took four men to carry one of these pieces, and very quickly the whole ashram was busy with unpacking and carrying off massive amounts of packing materials or just watching in amazement. Out under the maple tree a very large stone Nandi Bull sat, looking regal in his absolute devotion to Lord Shiva. The salon in the *grande maison* was filled and overflowing. The question was, where would we all sit now in the evenings, in the already very crowded tea space?

Cancelling Brindaban's talk that was scheduled to happen before brunch, Lee started unpacking boxes of carved wooden pieces—fabulous chiseled and sculpted images of Vishnu, Lakshmi, Krishna, Shiva, Durga, celestial lions, elephants, *nagas* (snakes) and guardians of the temple, which appeared one after the other, to be sold immediately. They were practically flying out of Lee's hands. Thirty people crowded around him in the salon as he whipped through one box after another. The excitement was palpable, frenetic, and not just a little competitive over the best pieces. At the same time, there was much laughter and good natured fun over the whole episode; whenever competition reared its ugly head, it was soon vanquished and disappeared completely into the revelry and joyous participation in Lee's games. The space in the salon with Lee was so powerful, hot and bright, and there was such an ecstatic joyful mood pulsing in our veins, you would have thought we were each in a bridal chamber with our own beloved. Stopping for a moment to contemplate the scene I thought, just beneath the appearance of things is a *ras lila*.[1]

It truly was a way of sporting with the guru, a Krishna *lila* in and of itself. How did Lee do it? How did he cause our hearts to swell, heat up, melt down, to have us jubilantly jumping into the flames of his fire in such a crazy, unexpected circumstance as buying sacred antiquities from our own spiritual master and going into debt in the process? It was a bizarre turn of events, to be sure, but one that the sangha has embraced, not out of blind following, or because a spiritual authority says we should, but because individually we have been convinced, through our own bodily heartfelt direct experience of the sacred artifacts, the Sacred Bazaar and Lee, of the tremendous value that is contained within the wonder of it.

That afternoon, after all the Sacred Bazaar excitement, brunch and a period of *guru seva* (work), Lee gave a talk before dinner. He answered questions for a while, spoke a lot about the amazing collections of sacred antiquities that people in the sangha are

---

1 Ras lila: The mythic play of Krishna with the *gopis* or milkmaids of Vraja, as recounted in the scriptures in "Book X" of the *Bhagavata-Purana,* in which the love play of Krishna with his female devotees is used as a metaphor for the moods of divine love experienced between the human lover and divine Beloved. In this exceedingly popular Vaishnava myth, the haunting sound of Krishna's flute incites such longing in the heart that the *gopis* are lured away from their homes to the forest, where they join with their Lord for a night of revelry and ecstatic love. Although they are dancing in a circle together, their passion and love for Krishna was so all-consuming that every *gopi* has the experience of being alone with the Lord.

amassing. Then, when there were no more questions, he began to talk about the theme of the Celebration: "Good Company," as it is understood in the Buddhist context of the sangha as refuge.

Lee began, "So, the topic of the Celebration is 'Good Company.' Swami Prajnanpad, when he first came to Europe, was greeted with a large group that Arnaud and his disciples had gotten together, thinking he would like that. He sent them all away, saying, 'I want to see everyone, one at a time.' He had only nine French disciples, and he wouldn't let them come to his ashram in India all at the same time. That's a valid way of working, but it's not our way of working, even though the teaching is essentially the same.

"We work differently, and it's the way we've been given to work, and not by my choice. It was a choiceless choice that was given to me. I was always a loner—I was happy alone, happy to eat alone, happy to travel alone. I used to come home after teaching a class of Silva, after being with people all day, and I would pull something out of the refrigerator and be in ecstasy—alone!

"So, this work is completely uncharacteristic for me, but it's what we have been given. As much as I value solitude, I was aware of the value of Good Company. I was never a party guy, but I always had a few very close friends, so I was always aware of the value of Good Company.

"Good Company means a number of things in our work. We develop a great love and bond with one another, and we help one another in a variety of ways. A lot of the Arizona sangha has been busy for months . . . helping people move and fixing up new homes. And happy to do it! It's all been a big party. But there is more to Good Company than being there for each other in ordinary ways, like sitting by someone's bedside when they are seriously ill."

Lee then spoke about his mother, Adele Lozowick, who went through a tremendous transformation during the last three days of her life. Linda, Joanne and Jaya, three of Lee's students, had taken care of her. He spoke about how she was a very armored person who was difficult and loving and wonderful at the same time, and that she was often full of complaint and demands.

Lee continued, "Once she decided that she was dying, all the armor disappeared and she was a completely different human being. She was Good Company. There were no complaints, which were chronic before—no demands, no bad moods. She was radiant, in love with everyone and everything. She took care of the ordinary concerns of the world in a perfunctory way, even though they were not her concern."

He spoke about his experience of looking out the window yesterday during Michelle's talk and seeing the children playing a game in the courtyard under the tree. Lee commented, "I was watching the children play, and the catalyst that play was for me, *organically*, could have been more valuable than if I'd been given a brilliant talk about the dharma . . . . "

Changing tact, Lee said, "Good Company is not exclusively the effect of our love and bonding with each other." At this point Lee began to speak effusively of Werner Erhard, one his great dharma heros, and how, with Werner, it was always "strictly business, nonstop, from the moment he woke up until the moment he went to sleep." He told stories of how Werner gave talks for up to eight hours, drinking cappuccinos the whole time and never going to the bathroom; of how Werner woke up in the morning with his valet and his secretary waiting for him in the bedroom. They would follow him to the shower and begin firing questions at him right away about his schedule for the day and decisions that had to be made.

"What a guy!" Lee grinned. "Werner bought a yacht and he used to have wild parties out on the ocean, but it was business, from the minute you got on the boat to the minute you got off the boat, even though there was lots of entertainment, because when you are in the Work, you cannot take a break. All of our ashrams are metaphors of the Work—there is four times more work to be done than there are people to do it. There is no time to kick back and take a break.

Everything in Werner Erhard's work was about Good Company, and in his work you did not get sentimental. So we need to remember that there are the effects of bonding and spending time together in this Work, but there is a lot more to Good Company than that.

"We want to remember that the phrase 'Good Company' came from Tibetan Buddhism and taking refuge. We take refuge in the Buddha, the dharma and the sangha. To take refuge means to surrender into that domain and trust that domain to have your best interests at heart. We take refuge in the Buddha, which is taking refuge in the guru, when there is lineage, that is. We take refuge in the Buddha, dharma and sangha; and then there is the Buddha's eightfold path, which are the recommendations for practice: right action, right thought, right livelihood and so on, and Good Company. The context of that phrase is relative to the Work, to practice, relative to psychology."

"Good Company is an obligation, not a choice. We love each other and are bonded, but we are also comrades of the Work. We have a common obligation to sustain existence, and that is at the essence of Good Company—our common aim.

"Coincidentally, we develop a deep and loving bond, but that is not what Good Company is about, it is a secondary effect of Good Company. Good Company is about a common aim, not a common lifestyle. In Arnaud Desjardins' school there is not a common lifestyle, but there is common aim. We, to a greater degree, also have a common lifestyle. If we were practicing rightly, even if we live separately, we would be eating the same food, meditating at the same time, reading the same literature, more or less, listening to the same music—not because we *had* to, but by choice. There would be certain similarities that would create not just common aim, but a common aura, a common field. Okay, that's a good place to end."

At the end of the talk everyone dispersed to various tasks or for a quick walk before dinner. The Celebration was in full swing with about one hundred people filling the ashram. The Guru Purnima

Celebration every year here in France is one of those times when most of the European sangha is together, which lends a perspective to what is happening in the big picture of Lee's teaching work. Many of the French sangha have now been practicing in the school for eight or ten years and have bonded with each other and with the rest of the sangha as well; the German sangha has a strong, almost twenty-year-old backbone, although there are many newer students among them. The American sangha has roots that go as deep as thirty years in Lee's company, making the foundation of the *sampradaya*, to use the Sanskrit word for the lineage or clan of practitioners; this year the vast majority of the American sangha was celebrating Guru Purnima in the States.

A unique bond exists now between all these nationalities, including the British, the Indians, the Swiss, Mexicans, Canadians, Romanians and Norwegians among us, and it is this bond, interacting with Divine Influence in the company of the guru, that generates such a powerful and beautiful mood when we all come together. Every day there were periods of *guru seva*, with teams of people going into La Roche Posay to work on the shop and the tireless kitchen teams preparing brunch and dinner feasts. During this Celebration it was particularly joyful to see the teenagers and children from several different countries and with different languages having so much fun together.

Furthermore, we were blessed with gorgeous weather, dry and warm yet cool, making the ashram environment delightful and the sleeping accomodations—which are rustic at best, in the barn or tents or *camions*—quite agreeable. Lee too was in high spirits, particularly with all the Sacred Bazaar movement during the day. At one point he said, "When the American sangha hears about the good deals I gave you all today, they are going to be soooo envious!" It was another reminder of the American sangha, so far away but so near to us in spirit, who were celebrating Guru Purnima in the desert an ocean and a continent away.

Ferme de Jutreau
July 25

Guru Purnima had come and gone. We were back to our usual ashram schedule: seven a.m. meditation; breakfast, work, lunch, work, dinner, Tuesday and Thursday after dinner talks and the evening tea. Our numbers had slowly dwindled as people left for their homes in Germany, Switzerland, Paris, Montpellier, Rennes or Annecy. Tonight Lee played bridge in the salon. Afterward, around nine o'clock when coffee and mint tea were being served, someone mentioned a western woman named Penny Ma, who Lee and company had met in India in 1998. She had told us some stories about the fierce way her master had treated her. Listening to these, Mariana, who was visiting from California, said, "We have it really good here."

Lee seemed to jump on this opportunity, as he snapped, "Yes, because I'm a *coward*. I'm not willing to give people feedback because they will *kill* me. The emotional violence is more than I can stand. It's not worth it to me anymore. If I so much as laugh, three people will look at me and say, '*What*?' " His tone indicated a controlling, aggressive sarcasm on the part of the person saying "What?"

He went on, "I should have grown up in a family with brothers and sisters and violence and cruelty—then I'd be able to take it. Emotional violence and recoil and self-hatred is not my cup of tea. People ask me for feedback, but they have a very limited, specific definition of what that means. The love that we want is all around us, and we just need to take it in, take it in, take it in . . ."

He was on a roll, but there were only a few people sitting there to hear it, and no one taking notes. I put this report (which is accurate but incomplete, in that he said more than what is captured here) together immediately after tea, working with two other people who have good memories. Lee went on to say, "Students will not allow the teacher to animate certain things because of their sense of fairness. But even when I am being fair, people think I'm not. People need to be willing to offer themselves up. People have to be willing to deal with their anger, their fear and their boredom."

It was sobering but not surprising to hear this yet again from Lee. This is a common theme in Lee's spontaneous softcore rants. I call them softcore because Lee does not coerce us; he rarely even gives people direct feedback anymore, especially those who have many years in the school. We are either unconscious of our own motives and actions in relationship to the teacher, or we just don't care—we really believe that our emotional need to be safe, look good, have control and feel powerful is more important than anything else. It's up to each one of us to get real with ourselves. The kind of ruthless self-honesty and discipline that is required demands courage, conscience and commitment. It requires blood on the meditation pillow. Despite repeated failures, we have to persevere.

Ferme de Jutreau
July 26

Sometimes the tea space that is held every night at nine o'clock on the ashram in France is quieter, more contemplative; we sit around Lee, having coffee or mint tea, dates, nuts, often chocolates from Lee's substantial stash. At other times the tea space can be highly conversational and animated, with an easy repartee with Lee and students asking questions. On other evenings, Lee is roused from his quietude or social conversation to make a more pointed or serious teaching communication, as he had the night before.

Tonight the conversation had gone toward people's concerns that they won't have enough time to get everything done that needs to be done. Stretched to the maximum capacity, people who have jobs, families and ashram responsibilities also get special projects from Lee—like booking Shri tours or the Lee Lozowick Band; writing a book; renovating a thirteenth century building. It doesn't seem possible to do it all and still have time in one's busy life for creative projects, much less all the practices we have been given. When is there time for an inner life? It seems we are being asked to forge the ability to split our attention, so that we are functioning multi-dimensionally. The consideration sparked a very juicy response from Lee. His solution: we have to learn to bend time.

Claire asked Lee, "Is bending time a thing like Grace, something that happens outside of our will power?"

"It's not as high as Grace," Lee answered.

I asked, "Is it mostly about intention?"

"It's more like 'drala'," Lee began, "the way Chögyam Trungpa Rinpoche used the word. Drala as a natural force and a way of seeing the world, the beauty and magic in the world. But unless we let go of our rigid ideas, we can't possibly live in a world of magic. You have to trust the Work. You have to trust that the Work has your highest good at heart, which doesn't mean that this lifetime will be a bed of roses. You have to look over lifetimes.

"We are extremely fortunate in this lifetime. The world is full of pain and suffering, but we don't find ourselves in Ethiopia or Nicaragua. The Work gave us sanctuary in which to practice in this lifetime. Street people? They don't have time to even think about practice! Our good fortune in this life comes from what we have earned before. All the camaraderie, the communion with each other, everything we have is from before—we earned it. What we're doing in this lifetime is setting things up for future lifetimes.

"People think that life should be happy, everything should be perfect, but it doesn't work like that. So we have a very nice night of tea, coffee, Good Company—the Work has given us that. We have earned the opportunity to work free of massive debts in our lives. Owing me money for the Sacred Bazaar is not a massive debt, like owing money to a bank. It's completely different, in fact. We have worries and concerns for our health, peace and the state of the world, but just walk outside on a sunny day and look around at what we have! We have our sufferings, but we have earned the right to practice in a safe, protected environment with others—that's from before.

"If we start looking at things that way, we shift our perspective. If we look at our dreams—'I've got to do this and this before I die'—we're not looking at lifetimes, or seeing that we've earned being here in this ashram instead of in Bangladesh. Everything we are doing is setting up for the next lifetime. Somewhere before this life we have proven to the Work that we had intention and we were serious; we worked enough that we were given this—*it's our gift*. If we see things that way long enough, then the whole rigid crystallization around time starts to dissolve. The whole underlying, tacit worldview starts to change. The tacit perception, the whole field changes, and it's not something that you've dredged up by an act of will. Then, something in your worldview is tacitly flowing. What you get done are the things that are most profitable. Things fall away or arise, so that the way you are using your time is most optimal.

"So, you do that, and you reinforce, reinforce, reinforce it and learn from lessons you are given, be consistent, tenacious and committed in practice, and in the next lifetime, you will be given maybe even more. Maybe we'll be given better health, if we don't allow health problems to separate us from the Work in this life. If we just look at this lifetime and this mortal body, we can't do it—we cannot live by drala. Instead of dealing with cosmic energies, we are only dealing with one little band of energy, and we can hardly move."

To the hardcore realists and pragmatists and materialists, this might sound unreal, unreachable or idealistic at the least. We can write it off as magical thinking, and it does have a mystical dimension to it, but it's a principle of life that exists in truth, with which we have lost touch. What about all the fabulous teaching stories of Tibetan Buddhism? What about Yeshe Tsogyal, a skydancer yogini, one of five primary consorts of Padmasambhava who could fly through the air and perform miracles of many kinds? The Hindu tradition is also full of miracles and amazing feats, as are Judaism and Christianity—after all, Jesus raised Lazarus from three days in the grave! That is probably the most impressive, outrageous miracle story of all. In our own time and lineage, Yogi Ramsuratkumar was known to be a worker of many miracles. Those events have been possible because human beings had a different relationship to *drala*, or the magical, elemental powers that permeate life.

As human beings, we have the blueprint of all possibilities within us, but to live in that way, we have to relinquish control and surrender to the groundless reality of magic. We live in a way that soothes our psychological fear that reality is groundless, but we are a long way from home, because home is that place where anything is possible. And in that place, there is nowhere to stand—only the interplay of light and dark, only magic and grace, whirling in space.

Ferme de Jutreau
July 27

On the way to a special dinner at the home of Vincent and Adeline Vigor, a ten minute drive from the ashram, Lee was upset because an important piece of information had not been passed on to him. He was all thunder and lightning for a while, practically pulling his hair out as he drove lickety-split down the country roads, through wheat and sunflower fields. Finally, he said, "If I die tonight, I want put on my gravestone, 'Why didn't somebody tell me?' "

It was a quiet and formal dinner, with an elegant repast and choice wines provided by Adeline and Vincent. Jennie and Emilie were the servers for the evening, and the mood was sweet, if pensive, perhaps because we were anticipating our time of *viraha*, or separation from Lee's physical company. He was leaving at five a.m. the next morning to take the train from Poitiers to Cannes, where he would meet up with Thomas, who was coming from Germany to be Lee's driver for two weeks on tour with Shri. They would be traveling to gigs in southern France, Switzerland, Germany and finally, Italy, after which they would travel for twelve hours nonstop through the night to

Annecy, France. There they would be hosted by Lee's students who live in the city, and Shri would play a gig there on the night of August 3. The next day Lee and Thomas and Shri would drive to Paris, where some of us who were staying at the ashram during this time would meet Lee for dinner at the apartment at the Place Contrascarpe.

After dinner we settled on the floor around Lee, who sat on the couch. The conversation was gentle, often focused on questions of child-raising or the topic of the renovations at the shop. The most exciting topic of conversation was Adeline's and Vincent's participation next summer as musicians on tour with the Lee Lozowick Band, based around the songs on *Ecrasé par l'Amour*. After coffee and dessert, which was sumptuous, testing even Lee's great capacity for cream and chocolate, we headed back to the ashram around nine o'clock, where Lee had tea with the ashram residents before saying goodnight.

Relinquishing Lee to the tour, we said our goodbyes. It was our last night with Lee until we would meet up with him eight days later for Shri gigs in Bretagne, Normandy and in Paris, the great city itself.

Singing the Blues

Paris
August 4, 2005

Yesterday a small group of adults and kids traveled from the ashram in the silver van to Paris. On the way we made a stop at Fontainebleau-Avon to visit the grave of G.I. Gurdjieff. We have made a number of pilgrimages with Lee to this place over the years, the first time being in 1992. This time the teenagers wanted to see it, having studied a little about the life of Gurdjieff in the home school program on the Arizona ashram some years ago.

We spent some time at the grave site, which is distinguished with two large stone dolmens, then walked back to the van for a snack of ripe peaches that dripped with juice. Back in the van, we were soon in Paris and settling into the flat at Place Contrescarpe. After a family-style dinner in the kitchen, we walked to the Seine that night and visited Notre Dame at dusk with the kids. We planned to meet Lee today.

During the morning we walked down to the market a few blocks away to check out what we would buy later for dinner, since we would be preparing dinner for Lee and the band. The day passed quickly, and in the midafternoon, Lee arrived with Thomas and Rakini, earlier than he originally expected—which was to be expected! The rest of the band would join us in two hours.

We sat with Lee in the café, waiting for the market to re-open in the afternoon. He ordered a *citron pressé*; the rest of us ordered the same or coffee, and sat back to enjoy stories of Shri's adventures on the road so far. Lee, Thomas and the Shri crew had just driven from Rome to central France, after two gigs in Italy—Serre, and the much-anticipated gig in Rome. We heard that the gig in Serre was fantastic, with the guitar players—Ed, Franck and Doug—outshining themselves and taking the band to greater heights.

As Rakini wrote of the gig in Serre in her journal, "In Shri, three guitar players can equal one amazing guitar machine, and when they hit this sweet spot, Lee practically jumped through the roof. It really gets him glowing. At the end of the night people crowded around us, as we came down the back stage stairs. Hands were being thrust forward for shaking, lots of Italian praise was being heaped on us. One young man came toward Lee. 'You are the man! You are the man,' he said as he smiled at Lee and shook his hand."

On the other hand, the Rome gig had been a bit of a bust; there was a very sparse crowd, and it was one of those nights when it was hard for the band to rise above the black hole that appears sometimes when there is a small, inattentive audience.

"The music just didn't touch the people at the gig in Rome," Lee said. That seemed to be Lee's bottom line with the music—whether or not the people are touched.

Nonetheless, at the end of the gig Lee said to the small group of listeners, "I want to thank all of you for staying with us tonight. Even if you aren't here to stay with us, I want to thank you anyway. It doesn't cost anything to be grateful! Some of us don't learn this lesson, and we die ungrateful, which is a terrible way to die." Hearing this, I thought of how Lee often quotes Gurdjieff when he says, "We always make a profit." Despite everything, he could still make the teaching available to anyone who was able to hear it.

Around four o'clock about ten of us wandered down the street with Lee to the market, where he picked out the salad greens and other vegetables for our dinner. At the *fromagerie* Lee looked over the cheese very closely, carefully choosing a fine selection for the thirty-plus people who would cram into the tiny kitchen for dinner.

"Oooh, look at that one," he enthused, pointing to a very soft and creamy brie. "That's exactly how I like my cheese!" He indicated a healthy slice to the clerk and it was swiftly wrapped up and added to the purchase.

Rakini and I headed back to the flat to make salad while Lee and the others went to buy bread and wait for the chickens to finish roasting on the spits. They arrived about fifteen minutes later. Lee immediately came over to the counter where the salads were being put together to check out our progress. Looking at the salad greens, which had just been washed and put into three big bowls, he said, "Oh yeah, that looks great!" Then he started tossing other ingredients in. He poured in a whole bag of pumpkin seeds and then instructed Rakini on the plump cherry tomatoes, sweet peas and green beans. Ann started cutting the chickens into manageable, individual pieces and opening the bottles of wine. Michelle was helping with the general organization, since she knew where everything was stored in her parents' kitchen.

The rest of Shri arrived as well as some members of the Paris sangha. The windows of the small room where thrown open to the *place*, and once again the ambiance of Paris flowed into the room, infecting us all with the bon vivant spirit. We managed to glean enough glasses, plates and silverware from the cupboard for everyone, and dinner was served buffet style, with a long line of people heaping their plates with savory, plump spit-roasted chicken, salad, bread and cheese. On the fireplace mantle we had arranged everything resembling a wine glass, water glass, cup or mug to use for the wine, of which there were two bottles opened and four bottles unopened.

Lee has often made comments on how his students manage their wine consumption when it is served. For many, many years, our practice of abstaining from alcohol was very strict: wine was something that happened in Lee's company about once a year, if then. On very rare special occasions, like once every five or ten years, Lee might offer his students a beer. Now, wine has appeared in our lives with more frequency, and in fact Lee uses it as a particular alchemical element in feasts of all kinds—both formal and informal, like the one tonight. Sometimes he even serves a glass to everyone on a road picnic in the middle of the morning: there we are, standing in the sunshine or shivering under a cloudy sky, drinking wine from a plastic glass to wash down our boiled eggs and salad!

However, he expects us to pay in the coin of the Work for the privilege of drinking even very small amounts of wine because it is a sacred substance. The first payment is that you only drink wine when it is Lee's party; that is, either he is offering the wine at his table, or he has endorsed an invocational meal for sangha members who live at some distance from him, and the meal includes the use of wine for the evening. He expects us to interact with this mood-altering, powerful substance—which is, in fact, a living spirit, with a sentience of its own—with discrimination, awareness and the appreciation that allows for a conscious enjoyment without any trace of self-indulgence. It's a tall order for most, one that probably every one of us has both failed and succeeded in at different times.

It is useful to remember that in the classic rite of the tantric feast, food and spirits are eaten and imbibed as an offering to the deity, in a ritual that is undertaken to the extent that the deity is invoked through prayer, mantra, song, inner visualization or other methods. It is considered the deity who is actually enjoying the food, meat, wine or other alcohol. In our case, the sacred substances used include meat, wine, sugar (or honey), chocolate, cream and coffee. The deity, of course, is Yogi Ramsuratkumar.

Lee sat down on a low stool by the window with his plate of food. From that central vantage point he presided over the space, while everyone else found places to sit on benches, stools, chairs, the floor, in the hallway or on the winding staircase of ancient stone that lead upstairs and downstairs in the four-story flat. We were taking up every available inch of surface room.

As well-fed as we were, there was just a little salad left; since it was already dressed, and we would be on the road for the next two days, it had to be eaten. Lee asked Deborah to "sell" the salad, which she did with her usual aplomb and charm, taking it around the room and graciously offering it to all, extolling its virtues and the necessity for finishing it off. This being accomplished, it was time for dessert. A much-admired and exclaimed over platter full of luscious, exquisite, petite French pastries—provided by Vincent and Adeline—was served along with coffee and cream, only to disappear almost immediately. Clean up was a group affair that happened very quickly and efficiently, with Michelle putting everything back into its proper place.

Just as some of us were probably wondering what was next, Lee announced in a loud voice, "I'm going to the Champs d'Elysée to see 'War of the Worlds.' Anybody who wants to come is welcome, but you'll have to make your own way there. *I'm* leaving in ten minutes."

A mad scramble ensued while everyone dashed to make quick plans—who would ride with whom in what vehicle and so on—which continued once we were out on the street by the cafés. We had parked Lee's silver ashram van just a few car lengths away down the street. Lee organized his own vanload of people while everyone else shuffled from one vehicle to another, and we were off to the movie.

St. Brieuc, Bretagne—Shri Gig
August 5

After Lee conducted some private business in Paris, he was back in the silver ashram van, commanding the road as we headed out on the autoroute in the warm, overcast mid-afternoon for St. Brieuc, where Shri would play tonight. Thomas had already driven ahead with Michelle, Mira and Vincent, in caravan with the Shri van. Claire and

Volkmar had driven up from Chauvigny, and numerous other sangha members were arriving from different directions.

Two hours later we were driving through the Forêt de Paimpont, or Brocéliande, the place where King Arthur and Merlin went to war in Bretagne to rid the country of invading Saxons and eventually unite the Celtic people under one king. It's the region of France where mysterious megaliths can be found, scattered here and there, or concentrated in places like Carnac. As the van burned down the road and the scenery passed before our eyes, the rich history of this region could be sensed; it was truly, in the language of Bretagne, 'Amor,' the Land of the Sea and 'Argoat,' the Land of the Woods, the secret interior. The land took on a mythical cast as we saw signs for villages with names like Plédeliac, Languédias, Yffiniac and Trégueux.

As we were driving along, I told Lee a rumor about the Hohm Community that one of his students had heard from a family member who lives in a distant state: "They are a secret society." This bit of anti-wisdom had been passed along by an anonymous person who used to live in Prescott, Arizona but had never connected with the community.

I commented that this couldn't be farther from the truth. The Hohm Community bands perform regularly in public gigs and even tour extensively every summer in Europe, as well as advertise on websites. Lee gives public talks in Europe, the U.S., India, Canada and Mexico. Friends and relatives of community members are always welcomed to visit any of our ashrams. All of the books of Hohm Sahaj Mandir, the legal entity of the community—recognized as a church by the U.S. government—are publicly for sale. The truth is that we are an open book, and we live by the philosophy, "Live and let live." We respect the privacy of others, and we protect our own privacy. We do not proselytize and we like to be invisible and ordinary among our fellow human beings.

After having said all this, I asked Lee what his response was. He said, "You can't do anything about people's negative projections on our community. People will never understand our work. They will not respect it if you try to explain it. *Never* defend yourself against a comment like that. You'll only dig yourself deeper in."

He reiterated, "People will never understand our work." Subject closed.

By six o'clock we were driving through the picturesque, ancient cobblestone streets of St. Brieuc, an oceanside village with the Celtic mystique in full play. In the middle of the *centre ville*—surrounded by an old Roman church and centuries of the stone mason's art evidenced in the many buildings made of rugged, dark rock—was the Café Americano, a lively place with tables that spilled out over the rock-worked patios and sidewalks and into the *place*. This central plaza was only a block away from the sea, and was dominated by a permanent wrought iron and wood pavilion where a stage was set up and the band would play later that night. The town, frequented by tourists, had live music and performance arts every week throughout the summer season. Even now, two hours before the band would play, people were already gathered around tables in the café or hanging out around the pavilion.

The band and friends—about twenty-five of us altogether—were hosted at a nearby restaurant for dinner, after which we walked back toward the pavilion. I noticed that the town was flooded with the new Shri poster: a moody, steamy, almost life-size photo of Lee wearing sunglasses with dreadlocks hanging down, microphone in hand. As we walked up, we noticed that a crowd was already gathered around the front of the stage, ready and waiting for the music.

"Wow, they're already out there!" Rakini and Deborah both exclaimed as Lee walked in the backstage area, a small space that was partitioned off for privacy in the back of the pavilion.

"That's the way I like it," Lee enthused, "with people pressed up tight against the stage!"

Looking out at the people, I noticed right away that they did not have the same appearance as the French people in general. They seemed salty, sea worthy and yet more connected to the earth, hardier, more rugged. Lee looked out at the crowd and noticed a number of members of the French sangha—Therese, Marie Françoise and others from Rennes. Anne Marie, who we hadn't seen for years, a student of Arnaud's who runs the center at La Bertais where Lee had been hosted (both with LGB on tour and to give teachings) in years past, was also in the crowd. People were smiling broadly, greeting each other, all the while the noise level kept growing with the hum of voices and occasional shouts and yells of revelry going on as it spilled out from the Café Americano. People were ready to party!

"Great! There are a lot of people out there who can sell CDs!" Lee commented with satisfaction. He turned to the musicians around him and started giving instructions: Vincent would take the first solo, Franck would come onstage on the third song.

Rakini walked up to Lee with paper and pen in hand. "What do you want on the set list?" she asked.

Lee named a couple of songs then said, "And whatever else you want." He emphasized, "If Mira plays on every song, I'll be happy."

Tonight would be Vincent's first time to play flute with Shri. A classically trained flautist, Vincent had been enrolled, as had Mira Amadori, to play with Shri as much as possible this summer. Mira had had her debut with Shri last summer, and was ready to hit the ground running this year. Also performing guest solos would be Franck on guitar and Volkmar on sax.

The excitement was building like an electrical current running amok in the air itself. The stage was lit with spotlights in the dark, chilly sea air as Lee walked out on the stage first. As soon as he appeared, the crowd, which had swollen to five hundred, burst into a roar of recognition. The poster was working! This was the first time the band had ever played St. Brieuc, and they were already Shri fans.

Tattoos flashed in the multi-colored stage lights, as Lee took center stage and the rest of Shri came walking out. The tattooed band members were reflected by the many tattoos that could be seen in the audience as well, mostly Celtic and traditional designs, and some hell-raiser old school sailor ink. It was obvious from Lee's reception and the first blast of music from the stage, which was greeted with another roar of enthusiasm, that there was an instant rapport between Shri, the blues and the local folks.

A few songs later the band went into "Left My Baby," that brooding blues ballad in a minor key in which Lee and Deborah always go out into the audience to greet people personally. The crowd had grown to about a thousand people, spreading out into the labyrinth of small, narrow streets that lead into the square. The Café Americano was jam packed with people who were yelling and shouting encouragement to the band. Standing up on the ledge at the back of the pavilion, just between the café and the pavilion itself, I could see over the heads of the crowd and out through the open-air pavilion to the trees and the stone church across the square. Pink and red lights were strung across the wood and iron pavilion, adding to a festival mood. You could smell and sense the presence of the sea. The music and the mood was intoxicating.

Lee was still making his way through the throng to shake hands and greet people, while he also sang his verses. The crowd was so thick and dense, and people crowded in around Lee so tightly that at one point he yelled into the mike, "Help! I'm lost! I don't know where I am!" Fortunately, it was just his brand of theatre.

When Franck tore into a blazing guitar solo, I watched as Lee slowly made his way back to the stage and joined forces again with Deborah, Doug and Ed. The song ended with Ed's signature solo.

As the night went on, song built upon song, rousing the crowd to a fevered pitch that soon translated into a wave of Celtic patriotism and ethnic pride as people started yelling, "Bretagne! Vive le Bretagne!"

Lee responded, "Where are you all from?"

"Bretagne!" The crowd surged and pitched up against the stage.

"Vive le Bretagne!" Lee called back. People were riveted to him.

The night spiraled around Lee; for the moment, he was the center of their world.

Moving right along into the sultry and sad "Silken Cross," Mira and Vincent came on together to give us solos, setting the stage for a sweet and rollicking Shri version of Lee's song, "Love Never Dies."

This summer Lee was also covering Aretha Franklin's "Chain of Fools," inspired by R.L. Burnside's loose, growly, gravelly interpretation of this famous R&B song. Burnside's version is stylized and very simple—but ah! that fabulous beat was still the same great groove that made you move.

After Bob Dylan's "Everything Is Broken," Lee introduced the next song, "Help Me," a classic blues song by Sonny Boy Williamson, saying to the audience, "This song is so true, so true, so true! Très vrai. Regardez moi! Regardez moi! This is a song for all the suffering people in the world!" Lee leapt up on the huge black speakers on the left side of the stage to dance, sing and incite the audience to greater heights of ecstasy and the spirit of revolution. The zeal and fervor of the crowd became super fuel for the band and the music, which soared on their high energy as Franck took a guitar solo during "Help Me" that brought the house down.

"That's what I'm talkin' about," Lee called out from his high platform on the speakers. "Mira, give me some help, now!" Mira threw herself and her violin into a searing solo that pulled the underpinnings of longing and helplessness, verging on the edge of prayer, out of the song. "You gotta help me baby / I can't do it all by myself . . ."

Watching the musicians step up to the plate one by one as Lee called them to offer up a solo with their instruments, I thought, we are being given a chance to help Lee with his Work. With Shri, we protest in the realm of the world, and we pray in the realm of the spirit. That's what all this is about, at least at one level. It's our opportunity to learn so much, to make a small contribution to the Work, to work for someone who is in the Work, as Mr. Gold says. We aren't capable of working by ourselves, but we can work for someone who is in the Work.

In the process, the musicians are initiated into the Baul path, the *ulta* path which goes the opposite way of the rest of the slumbering world. Once you are on that path, there is no returning to the old life of ignorance and unconscious drives—that is, without great cost. Of course, the cost is very high to continue also. Ultimately it's the path of annihilation and ruin, but that's much, much later on . . . or so I've been told. In the meantime, it's guru yoga and the slow, painful stripping away of our illusions, the gradual, sometimes imperceptible process of Divine Alchemy, of dissolving the old personality to make way for a character that shines with the patina of an inner gold.

Deborah took the mike and hummed, her honeyed tones melting the night, "Mmmmmm . . . yeaahhhh . . . . I just need a little lovin' before I pass away . . ." A haunting, melancholy song with enigmatic lyrics, "Help Me" is a great paradoxical prayer of a song, spoken in the language of the streets.

When Nachama offered up her harp solo, we hit a groove that took us over the wall and into the Elysian fields. Worlds shimmered and dimensions interplayed, mixing and mingling, while we were the medium for the master alchemist, who labored over his laboratory like a mad genius at work.

"Vincent! Gimme a little help . . . That's Vincent! There we were, walking down the Champs d'Elysée . . . and there *he* was," Lee gestured toward Vincent, "covered in shit, fingernails cracked and filled with dirt, his mouth encrusted with a ring of dried scum . . . I said, 'Man, can you play the flute?' He said, 'Yeah . . .' and the rest is history!"

Vincent moved up to the mike and the sounds of the flute floated on the night air, weaving in with guitar and drum. It was a short solo, and it seemed our Jethro Tull should have played on and on. Still, the onslaught of music and groove upon our pulsing senses kept on coming.

I moved back to the staging area at the side rear of the stage, where there was a completely different vantage point. During the next song I noticed that Lee was talking to a man who stood right up against the front of the stage, where people were crowded up against the platform by the rhythmic swell and flux of literally hundreds of people who were straining forward to get closer to the band and the music. The man's face was covered with scars in deep gouges and craters; he looked like he'd been in an accident or a war. He was rugged—a street drunk, perhaps, or just a guy who's seen a lot of trouble. Lee was befriending him and handing him a maraca to play. While the guitars wailed away on the next song, Lee handed out percussion instruments to about five other people who were crushed up against the stage.

"That's what I'm talkin' about! Come on, give me more!" The crowd howled for more as Lee walked over to Ed, who was taking the solo, and beckoned for more with his hands, saying, "Give it! Give it! Yeah! Give it to me!"

Striding back to the center of the stage to take the last verse, Lee handed a tambourine to a dark haired woman who stood by the stage. An immense flag of Bretagne had been slowly making its way through the crazed crowd since the beginning of the gig. Now it was being waved back and forth near the edge of the stage. People were worked up into a frenzy. The surge of the crowd—the roaring, yelling, whistling, clapping, wild and rowdy crowd—was exultant, gone mad from the joy of the music and the good company of Shri. The goddess herself was invoked into their midst on this chilly northern night.

I saw Lee disappear into the crowd for a moment as people begged him to come near. One minute later he reappeared onstage again. The band tore into "Satisfaction" and I thought the roof would blow off the pavilion as the crowd went berserk at the first unmistakable notes of this universally known and loved song. It was a blow out, even in the back near the café, where people were cat-calling and whistling and clapping from their tables.

Fortunately, due to the wisdom of Shri, the band played "Summertime," a song to soothe the restless, tumultuous soul of the world, as their last song. Deborah gave it her all, accompanied by Mira's flawless, heartbreaking violin, the strings giving sound to such tenderness and beauty, you could weep from hearing it. Everybody needs sanctuary, the song seemed to say. Somewhere, somehow, there is a place of refuge for us all. "One of these mornings / you're gonna spread your wings / and take to the sky . . ." Deborah's burned sugar, honey buttered voice lulled the crowd into the surprise of sudden, quixotic happiness, sublime yet still raw about the edges.

It felt like bells were ringing in our hearts, and then it was over. Shri left the stage and the crowd went wild, clapping and shouting for more, surging up against the stage, chanting "Shri! Shri! Shri!" How could they possibly top that? Just as suddenly, they were back to give us their final gift of the night, Dylan's "All Along the Watchtower," which brought another roar of recognition: it was a song for revolutionaries, clearly one that people knew.

On the walk through the quiet, cobblestone streets back to our hotel, we overtook two young women who were walking in front of us, talking excitedly as they walked arm in arm. Just as we got near enough to make out their French, we heard them saying how much they loved Shri. "That man, that singer—ohhh!" They turned and saw Lee, and laughed with surprise. One covered her face in embarrassment. Recovering quickly, she touched her heart and said with a smile, "Your music . . . your voice . . . it touched my heart."

Festival de Dreux
August 6

Lee was back on the road the next morning by nine o'clock. The Shri crew lingered a little longer over breakfast and made a trip to the cathedral at Chartres on the way to the next gig, where we would reunite later in the day. Lee decided that he wanted to check out *brocante* fairs and markets, and so, leaving Bretagne behind, we drove along the coastline, winding through villages and towns along the seacoast most of the day. This was not Celtic territory any more; we were back in France as we know it to be, but with the distinct flavor of Normandy. Finally, we drove east toward Paris to our destination for the evening and the gig in Dreux.

Dreux was a very different place than St. Brieuc, where the village was alive and thriving, juicy in a soulful way. Dreux seemed dull and depressed in comparison. However, our hosts provided a very nice dinner for the entire Shri party—about thirty people now—at a local pizza restaurant. Afterward we walked a few blocks to the *centre ville* to check out the gig site. A very large, professional stage had been set up with chairs for about five hundred arranged in concert style. The band dressing room was inside an old building that was once a church, just across the street from the stage.

When we first walked into the church, I noticed an unusual round stained glass window high up on the wall of what must have been the main sanctuary of the church. The concert sponsors had thoughtfully provided cold bottled water, fruit, candy, Cokes and other snacks for the band inside; there were dressing rooms with mirrors in a back room. Band members commented on how fine the hospitality was, which is typical for traveling musicians in France.

Lee changed his shirt for the gig standing behind the van, which was parked in a weedy, overgrown lot behind the church. Deborah and Rakini walked up. Like a coach pumping up his team, Lee said with a chipper mix of humor and ebullient enthusiasm, "I'm *ready*! Let's smoke those turkeys! Let's kick their asses! Let's shake 'em up . . . Let's give 'em something they'll never forget . . . Let's change them forever!" It seemed optimistic and prophetic in an ironic sort of way, as we walked down the side street that ran along the church and out into the *place* where the stage and concert was set up. Immediately we saw the crowd sitting tamely in their seats. A few guys raised their fists in solidarity gestures and yelled a friendly greeting to the band as Shri took the stage.

Although the audience generally seemed low-key, the music was great, and as is often the case in France, the sound system was excellent, making it an especially good night just to listen to the songs, the lyrics and the solo performances. About five hundred people sat calmly in their chairs below the stage while Shri put on their show. Another hundred or so stood around the sidelines listening. There was a gulf between the band and the audience, partly because of the concert arrangement of the chairs, and the fact that there was about twenty feet between the front row of chairs and the stage, which was high.

I walked over to the CD stand to get a different perspective. Jim Capellini, the band's publicist, said, "Did you notice that church? It's a Knights Templar church."

Indeed, I had noticed the inscription carved into the stone on the outside wall that read:

Cette salle fut la chapelle de l'ancien hotel dieu
1100-1900 sa construction enterprise en 1562
se termine vers 1600 la charpente fut offerite
par Catherine de Medicis Reine de France
et Comtesse de Dreux.

This house of God was built under the auspices of Catherine de Medici. She wielded immense power in Europe; wasn't she one of the patrons of the Knights Templar? I looked again at the stained glass window, which could be seen now, lit from within as evening fell. Deep red bars made up an equidistant cross enclosed in a green circle inside a twelve pointed star designed in interlocking gold and dark blue triangles. I'd never seen anything like this in a church anywhere in Europe.

I remembered another Shri gig, two years ago in Chinon, when we walked up the hill to the crumbling ancient fortress that overlooked the old city; there I discovered the prison where Jacques de

Molay, the Grand Master of the Knights Templar, was incarcerated in Chinon during the Inquisition, just before he was *brulée á Paris.* France is full of such esoteric history, which, for me, lends a certain power to our travels, and especially at gigs.

The band was moving through their repertoire for the evening at a steady if rather sober pace when a small group of mentally challenged adults walked up with their chaperones. Some of them played around, dancing and jumping up and down and singing along, even though they didn't know the English words. A very young Turkish man, probably eighteen years old, dressed in baggy pants and a skinny t-shirt, with close-cropped dark hair, danced in the open space just below the stage for the last hour of the performance. He was miming the arm and hand gestures so familiar to hip hop music, but in this case it was to the blues, which created an interesting mix. Maybe it didn't matter; it was all American music with African roots, with its origins in suffering and slavery.

Suddenly I heard Lee's voice ring out over the crowd in between songs as he said, "We would appreciate it if you'd take one of our CDs home with you tonight. Anytime you're feeling sad and lonely, just put on a Shri CD and . . . feel the love!"

Lee laughed. Who knows why? It was a good message for this audience. When the band closed with "Summertime," the atmosphere was so poignant and rich that you could have cut it with a knife. I could sense that, despite their decorum, people were absorbing what Shri was offering, and on this particular night, it left me with a bittersweet feeling.

Lee's student Jennie, who lives in Paris, told us afterward that Dreux is known to be one of the most politically conservative towns in France—in fact, it is considered a stronghold of particularly virulent and oppressive fundamentalism. Living under that dark cloud is enough to make anyone unhappy. All the more reason for Shri to play there . . .

Paris
August 7

Lee spent the morning shopping at a famous brocante market in Paris. After dropping his purchases off at the flat at Place Contrescarpe, Lee headed off to the Champs d'Elysée to catch another American movie. This time it was *Transporter II*.

The sangha was providing a picnic dinner before the gig on the Seine that night. As we made our way across Paris in the van after the movie, the cell phone rang and was handed to Lee, who was driving as usual.

"How should I know where I want the picnic to be? I've never been there before!" Lee said in a very loud, irritated voice. Everyone in the van could hear what he was saying. He was referring to the quai where the riverboat was docked—the venue where Shri would play tonight.

"Let me speak to Tina," Lee snapped. There was a short pause, then he said to Tina, the bass player and manager of Shri, "It should be obvious to everyone there where the best place is. So I'm going to leave it up to you. It shouldn't be where everyone gets baked in the sun. It shouldn't be where it smells like piss or dog shit, or where it's overrun with rats, drug dealers, fleas or dead fish!" He paused again for a second or two, then said, with that deadly sense of humor, "If you pick the wrong place I'm gonna feel fucked!"

He turned the phone back over with a theatrical flair, for emphasis, and continued to rant. When Lee gets in this acidic mood, it's usually because of the cumulative effects of his students being particularly dense and unconscious or mechanical or childish or just plain defiant and resistant in ways that are blatant to everyone else, it seems, but the person who is doing it. Often our reaction to his trenchant comments is not the reaction of a practitioner, but the reaction of a little child who has been chastised by his or her father, especially when we are already "being little" in relation to the authority figure.

Once we have refused to take responsibility to act as an adult, our projections on the authority figure are unshakable—there is nothing Lee can do about it. We have to disentangle ourselves. This too, Lee takes on himself. Finally, wheeling around a corner in Paris traffic, he said in a self-deprecating tone of voice that, again, was loud enough for everyone in the van to hear, "Well, if I die tonight, you can put on my tombstone, 'He made us all feel like children again.' "

He continued to grouse, saying, "We were all shamed by mommy and daddy, and everyone is mommy and daddy to us until they aren't anymore!" He mimicked his students, speaking as if one of us: "Every time the guru starts criticizing me I feel just like I was home with Mom or Dad!"

He provoked his captive audience further, saying, "You expect a woman to be able to clean a bathroom . . . just like you expect a French person to know the difference between good bread, good cheese and shit! But that's not been my experience . . ."

Just about then we pulled up to the parking place Tina had reserved for Lee's van right across the street from the river Seine at the Quai Malaquais, where the *peniche*, or riverboat—called La Balle au Bond, or Catching the Ball in the Air—was docked. It was the rather romantic site where Shri would play their gig tonight. Just beside the *peniche* on the paved stone esplanade that runs all along the river quais, the Paris sangha had spread out blue plastic tarps on the ground to create a large picnic area under a chestnut tree. When Lee was shown the picnic spot, he said, "That's okay." There weren't a lot of options there by the gig site, and this place did fit his requests.

About fifty people, including the Shri crew, ashram residents, sangha members from all over France and some from London, many students of Arnaud and several friends and family members were gathering at five-thirty to have dinner together before the eight o'clock gig that night. The picnic was spread out buffet style on the ground. The Paris sangha, who were providing the food, hustled about setting out food and getting the final touches on this and that.

Five-thirty came and went. Lee was visiting with Chris's sister and her husband from the States, who live and work six months a year in France and had come for dinner and the gig. Soon it was already ten minutes after the time that Lee expected to eat.

Rakini came over and said, "Has anyone mentioned anything about when dinner will be ready?"

Lee shrugged his shoulders and said no. "I could've had it ready twenty minutes ago if they let me work alone! But, you know, surrender . . ."

Investigating further, Rakini discovered from Laurent that dinner was ready and they were waiting for Lee—they were respecting the fact that Lee was visiting with guests, and they did not want to disturb him. It seemed to be an example of cultural differences—that is, the imperatives of polite French culture and protocol, versus the guru's world, the guru's culture, the guru's protocol. Timing is everything in Lee's world, and he is a stickler for being on time. This is a principle that subsumes almost all other circumstances of protocol. If we say we are going to eat at five-thirty, we should eat at five-thirty. Or earlier, if possible. He will almost always take an option to eat earlier, if dinner is ready early, and it seems to delight him when that happens.

Finally the courteous French were convinced that it was well and good to interrupt Lee's conversation with the news that dinner was ready, to which Lee immediately jumped up and said, "Let's eat!" Within seconds he was helping himself to olives and salad greens.

Parisians and tourists who walked by looked at us, some of them smiling and wanting to join us, some of them curious as we spread out with our plates and sat wherever we could find a decent spot, some critical of our definitely unusual-for-Paris behavior. "Just a family picnic," the French sangha explained to those who were passing by.

After dinner people were busy putting the leftover food away and clearing the site, while Lee talked with David, François Fronty, his daughter Julia and a few others who arrived late. Lee wouldn't go on the boat until the last minute, since the rocking of the boat on the water was not exactly his cup of tea. Usually a hardcore stoic who only takes herbal medicine on rare occasions, and even then very sparingly, Lee was humorous about his tendency to get motion sick when the ground is moving beneath his feet. He even went so far as to take a homeopathic remedy for seasickness.

In their ten years of touring Europe every summer, this was Shri's first gig in Paris—that alone lent itself to a high celebratory mood. By seven-thirty people were already boarding the small boat. Some of us settled at the small round tables, while others sat down on the floor in front of the band. On the upper level people were dining in a separate facility; on the bottom level of the boat was an empty room with a small bar in the back and a hardwood "dance floor." A few tables and chairs had been moved to the sides of the boat. The walls were made of big open windows that gave the feeling of being one with the water. Looking out on the water and the gorgeous sight of Paris and the Seine, I could see the Ile St-Louis and Notre Dame glimmering just across the way upstream.

Lee walked on board and strode to the microphone. As the boat tipped on one side, he staggered a bit, laughed and quipped, "This thing is moving!" He laughed, "It is a *boat*, after all!" With the windows open, a lovely breeze wafted in off the water, which helped alleviate the discomfort of the constant shifting, rocking, swaying motion. Music filled the air as Shri struck up their first rousing chords and rhythm rocked our bones. People were up and dancing right away. On "Mighty Tight," the second number, I noticed a student of Arnaud's talking on his cell phone at the front of the dancers. With a big smile on his face, he was holding the phone out for someone to listen to the music.

On "Stormy Monday" Vincent gave a flute solo while the restless river rocked us in eddies and flows of constant movement. During Ed's guitar solo Lee was calling out, "Lord have mercy!" A great harp solo was given by Nachama and then a violin solo by Mira. It occurred to me that Lee was throwing the ball of existence, as E.J. talks about it, from one player to another, and they were catching it in mid-air—La Balle au Bond—and then throwing it back to him again. The interplay between the musicians and Lee also nourished the dancers and was consumed into our blood like a very fine wine, instantly turned to sugar and building a highly spirited atmosphere among the crowd that was almost entirely, with the exception of three or four people, students of Lee and Arnaud. Outside the still-blue sky of early evening was washed with light and lambent clouds that were reflected in the shining water. The violin solo soared and took us with it, showed us where our suffering lives.

Shri's music comes in and takes us over, lifting us up or revealing our sore spots, the caves and grottoes or craggy mountains or lush jungles of our inner landscape. Sometimes what we find inside are stars bursting into creation; sometimes it's a black hole. Swimming in the sounds of the music tonight, and sinking deeply into the gospel strains of Shri's soulful version of "When the Levee Breaks," I looked out the window at Paris and reflected on its beauty. Strangely enough, it's become like a second home. I am one of those who enjoys visiting cities for short periods of time but who does not want to live in them. I tend to prefer the solace and refuge of daily rhythms that are closer to nature, more resonant with the Earth itself. I love ashram life, and the simpler, calmer world of the village or small town . . . that is, as long as good company, good food, good cafés and movie theatres are still readily available. (I wouldn't want to paint the wrong picture here!)

Paris, however, has gotten under my skin, with its labyrinthine streets and living sculptures and old stones, its ancient history and intellectual dimensions, its tall chestnut trees and rhododendrons, gardens and lush parks and fountains, its art and food and cafés and boulevards and monuments and catacombs and cemeteries and museums, its diversity and masses of people in every color of the rainbow from all over the world, the vast richness of its culture and its freedom and anonymity. Paris is a paean to the best and worst of civilized humanity. Rich in underworld and upperworld, heavily laden with art and atmosphere, populated with characters of all kinds from angelic to psychotic, the streets and cafés of Paris have been a refuge for many people who have a different vision than the norm. It is a fabulous playground for a Baul *tantrika* like Lee, who travels there with his unruly bunch of gypsies in tow.

"Welcome to Shri's premiere venue in Paris! Le Cité d'Amour et Malaise!" Lee's voice broke into my reverie as he spoke to us over the mike. "I don't know what that means—I just heard that word and threw it in there!" We laughed with Lee at this. People were smiling and happy; the space was thick with the unique bond of the spirit, felt by people who share the path in common. It would be hard for a stranger coming off the street to penetrate into this scene.

One thing about this gig was the intimacy of the band and the dancers. Because there was no stage; the band was set up right on the dance floor at one end of the boat, and the dancers were pressed up against the mikes. As soon as the music had started, dancers, musicians and music became one continuous seamless flow of reciprocity. As the night wore on, the thick knot of dancers, about twenty feet deep in front of the band, was roused to a new height of ecstasy as Lee went into "Love Never Dies," with almost everybody singing along on the chorus.

"Love never dies, but sometimes it *smells* like it has!" Lee quipped. A lot of people laughed, getting Lee's joke about the fact that the management had come down and closed the windows, so that the diners upstairs would not be "disturbed" by the music. It had gotten hot, smelly and stuffy in the rocking boat, adding substantially to the reeling stomachs of those who were dealing with motion sickness. It was amazing to think that the blues could disturb people's dinner! Even in Paris there are grim, intolerant, narrow-minded party poopers.

Lee continued, "But sometimes love picks you up and lets you know there's beauty in life, and then it keeps doing the same thing—

but that would be bad for all the therapists! Because what else do you ever talk about? Mommy! Daddy!"

I thought about Lee's diatribe earlier that afternoon in the van. Are we doomed to an arrested development as children or teenagers for the rest of our lives? Is there hope that we can become mature and maybe even wise adults? It takes a lot more than psychotherapy to achieve that maturation in human life; we must *hear* the teaching clearly and take it to heart. Then we must apply the teaching with integrity and a strong dose of practice and discipline. The soulful strains of the violin reminded me: I'd been reading a fabulous novel of contemporary India, criminals and saints called *Shantaram* by Gregory David Roberts and was humorously, and not-so-humorously, thinking of myself as a dharma criminal—someone who has fully heard the teaching, been offered countless profound opportunities, but still does not live up to the promise of the guru's gift.

The band ripped into the next song, a saucy little blues dance tune. All the dancing bodies were generating a lot of heat, and with the windows closed, we were beginning to really sweat. There was barely room to stand, much less dance, but somehow people managed to bounce around. Everyone was facing the band, clapping and yelling and whistling with appreciation at the end of the songs. One searing guitar solo after another spurred us on . . .

"Fuck the management and open those goddam windows!" Lee yelled into the mike to a loud roar of approval. I agreed wholeheartedly; it had been blissful with the fresh air off the river; now the atmosphere was stultifying. Still, we partied on anyway. Every ten minutes a tourist barge would chug downriver with a crowd of people. Invariably they would hear the muffled strains of the blues and see the crazed, happy dancers and the band; usually some of them would wave and we would wave back with big grins on our faces.

"Throw the people upstairs overboard," Lee yelled, "and open the goddam windows!"

After all, what is more important—people eating, or music as food for the soul? Decorum or art? Propriety or beauty? Hmm. Lee laughed, then he gave us an avenue to just accept it as it was. He shrugged and said, "It's not good if it's not hot! The blues is about *sex*! If you're having sex and you don't *know* you have the blues, I don't know what will do it!"

Finally the air conditioning came on, but it was too little, too late. In the end it didn't matter, because we were all in an altered state of consciousness, blasted beyond caring about such minor details or irritants. All that mattered was the music, the dancing and the pleasure of Good Company.

At ten o'clock the gig was over. People lingered to visit and say goodbye. Lee had been talking with various people after the gig. He walked up and I asked him if he was ready to go.

"Ready?" he answered incredulously. "I'm waiting for all of *you*! Where is everyone?" He was referring to everyone who was riding in his van. He answered his own question. "They're all still on the boat, talking about who knows what! Yes, I'm ready. Go round everybody up."

When we were all present and ready to go, Lee was out of there and off to the Place Contrascarpe. For him, the night was over as soon as the music stopped.

Paris to Ferme de Jutreau
August 8

Lee stayed in Paris on Monday to shop for *brocante* and visit Bruno and Magda's new shop in the Marché Vernaison in les Puces de Paris Saint-Ouen—a vast labyrinth of antique and high-end flea market shops and stalls. You could wander for days in the markets at Saint-Ouen; in fact, it would be very easy to get lost in there. There is a delicious flavor of the Third World about these markets, partly because they are mostly small stalls whose front wall opens onto little walking lanes that meander around in a maze-like pattern.

Bruno and Magda had opened a stall to sell sacred artifacts in the Marché Vernaison in July, and this was Lee's first visit there. It was a beautiful sunny day as we wandered through the market with Lee, taking our time and looking at things all along the way. Rakini, Ann and I scouted ahead to find the shop location while Lee strolled or shopped with the others at another stall. We saw Bruno standing just outside his stall and greeted him. A study in reds and gleaming with the coppery golden hues of aged bronze deities that populated its interior, their shop was different from all the others—it had the feel of a temple. The smell of Nag Champa wafted through the air, and there was a spaciousness and presence of sanctity that was exuded from the artifacts.

Soon after we arrived there, Lee walked up and embraced Bruno, who was alone at the shop since Magda was away tending to an illness in her family.

"It looks really great," Lee said to Bruno, praising their efforts. "Very impressive." We lingered for a while as Lee and Bruno discussed various deities and options for displaying them, then Lee was off again for more wandering through the market and shopping.

Soon we were driving through Paris to get back to the Place Contrascarpe, where Michelle and Jennie were preparing lunch, most of it leftovers from the picnic the night before. When we arrived at the flat, Lee walked into the kitchen and looked at the food on the table: baguettes, olives, saucisson, fromage, some salad.

"Wasn't there any chicken left last night, or is it all gone? I thought there was chicken . . ." Lee asked, looking up at Michelle and Jennie as he served his plate.

"Yes, there was some chicken," Michelle began.

"Where is it? Why isn't it on the table?" he asked. The chicken was packed away in the cooler to be transported back to Ferme de Jutreau.

"It was all in little pieces, so we didn't want to put it out," she explained.

"Put it out! Put it out!" Lee snapped. "Put *all* the food out! I thought we were being punished or something—'No chicken for you, you've been *bad*!' Always put all the food out—all of it." Lee laughed as he served his plate. Michelle quickly produced a plate of chicken.

"Is that it?" Lee asked piercingly. "I thought there was a lot more left last night."

David replied that he did indeed have more leftover chicken in his refrigerator at home.

"It's okay. This will do," Lee said as he sat down to eat. After a minute or so, Lee asked from his chair by the window, "Where's the melon? Wasn't there a melon?"

We were all laughing now, including Michelle and Jennie. Michelle replied that she was waiting until after lunch to slice the melon.

"You're too French!" he laughed, joking with her. "Slice it now! Now! Put *all* the food out. . ." More veggies and some olives appeared on the table along with the melon and some chocolate cake.

This was a teaching communication Lee has made countless times: put out *all* the leftovers. Do not hold food back. There are many reasons for this. One is that many of us have the tendency to withhold food—and other forms of nourishment—out of a psychological knot of scarcity and unlove. We have been punished, by authority figures, parents, teachers, priests and preachers, friends and siblings and strangers, and therefore, in the tangled knot of this, we sometimes wield whatever authority we have as a way of punishing others for real or imagined transgressions against us. There is unconscious aggression, anger and sorrow tied up in such habitual acts.

Another reason to serve all the food is that food is sacred; when it does not get eaten, it rots and is wasted. It is a "sin" to waste food, because food is the sacrifice of a sentient being, whether that being is an animal or a plant. On the great chain of being, everything sacrifices itself to feed something higher up on the chain; in this way, everything has the chance to be transformational food, and to be transformed into higher states of being in the process.

We ate most of the food that was now out on the table, and then, after a swift clean-up and last minute check of the flat to make sure everything was in order before we left, we piled into the silver van with Lee and took off for Ferme de Jutreau, arriving in time for dinner.

Back on the ashram for a day or two, Lee sat in the salon for bridge after dinner. Claire brought in an article that was published in the newspaper in Dreux about Shri's performance a few nights before. She had translated it from the French. It read:

America, the One We Want!

Saturday night, just enough time to pack the suitcase and to fasten the seatbelt, and we flew to a musical destination . . .

And what a destination! America, the one we want to have and the one we had, the one of the groove, the R&B, and a very good one please . . .

The band, Shri, Blues Sensation was in Dreux, in between a stop in Naples and one in Hamburg, in between tens of dates planned for their tenth tour in Europe and for the great happiness of their big audiences.

Shri, who borrowed their Sanskrit name from a goddess of luck, was born in Arizona about ten years ago, and it was first in the bars of this southwest state from the US that the group played before they, overflowing with talent, inevitably found themselves propelled "worldwide."

The Little Brothers of Jimmy Hendrix and James Brown

Nine p.m., Grand rue, the audience is sitting, the guitars and plugged in, the music takes off and there, the only thing

> *you can do is bow. It's the grand mass and it's the little brothers of Jimmy Hendrix and James Brown who officiate. At the guitar, the excellence of Franck Giambelluco, and at the micro, singing, the personality of Lee Lozowick. On the girls' side, same heritage. The singer, Deborah Auletta, reminds us of Janis Joplin, Big Mama Thorton or Aretha Franklin. Cover songs, personal compositions, a "Cry Me a River," and a last "Summertime" for the road, and it's the landing, so successful that it leaves our heads in the stars . . .*

Reading that review left my head in the stars, not only because it praised Lee and Shri, but because it reflected in such a genuine and heartfelt way what the music had meant to people in Dreux that night—not to mention their insight into American music and the band itself. People were deeply touched that night, even though they weren't up bouncing to the beat or screaming and yelling or dancing the night away. It was a great reminder that we cannot know the heart of another by the appearance of things.

At nine o'clock the room was changed into our evening tea space and quickly filled with people, including the Shri crew, householders who live near the ashram and several others who were visiting from different parts of France. All summer people come and go, come and go, so that the mandala around Lee changes constantly. The rich variety of opportunities to be with the guru also come and go, becoming kaleidoscopic over time, and we are the individual colorful pieces of a puzzle that fall into place to make crystalline formations—sometimes lustrous and bright, sometimes sublime, sometimes garish or bland and subdued, sometimes murky and stained with illusion—as his great kaleidoscope turns through the wheel of time and space.

Shri is one of the spokes in the wheel of Lee's teaching activities, including both recorded music and live performances at gigs; there are many other spokes, including the Sacred Bazaar, ashram Celebrations that occur during the year, his other bands, Attila the Hunza and the Denise Allen Band, his poetry to Yogi Ramsuratkumar, teachings in seminars and public talks, traveling on the road with him in any capacity, or just being around him on a day to day basis on the ashrams. The body of dharma art that has been produced by Lee and his students—CDs of all the bands' musical projects, the dharma literature, poetry, painting and sculpture—all represent spokes on the wheel.

The evening gathering is one of the spokes in the wheel with Lee, when Lee sits in the leather armchair before the fireplace, surrounded by stacks of hundred-year-old bronze bowls and deities of all kinds. On his left stands a three-foot-high sculpted white marble Krishna, hands raised as if holding a flute to his lips. Beside Krishna is the bronze Primal Mother from Madya Pradesh, standing with such nobility, attention and impersonal love in her glass case. Flowers from the garden always grace the table beside Lee, and above him is one of the most beautiful large *murtis* (photograph) of Yogi Ramsuratkumar that exists. Below the *murti* a candle burns on the fireplace mantle and a small arrangement of dahlias or roses from the garden is offered to the guru.

The intimacy of this evening tea space is exquisite yet powerful; within the close communion that flows, the mood changes from night to night, ranging from dulcet, bittersweet, peaceful or sublime to hilarious, raunchy, irreverent or blasphemous. Tonight was a rather quiet evening, more restful than most. After three cups of Alrun's coffee, heavily laced with cream, Lee smiled at us all and said goodnight.

Ferme de Jutreau
August 9

Lee spent the morning packing up bronze for his seminar at Le Rozet in a week, which made the salon a busy place. People gathered around to watch Lee, finding a spot to sit on the couch or somewhere out of the way on the floor with the bubble wrap and newspaper.

Someone asked if a particular piece was for sale. Lee answered, "It's *all* for sale!" It seemed to me that he was saying, in one way, that all these myriad pieces of sacred art, depicting the amazing panorama of the Divine manifest in different forms and qualities, are all waiting for us to become conscious in relationship to them. Yes, they are for sale! God wants YOU.

He continued to pick pieces off the shelves—which covered one entire wall of the salon and in the winter time would serve as the ashram library (the books are packed away for the summer to make space for the Sacred Bazaar)—and hand them over to his helpers who were wrapping them in newspaper at the moment. Deborah walked in and, searching for an unobtrusive spot, gingerly sat down.

"Am I in the way?" Deborah asked.

Lee was scanning the shelf for another artifact as he laughed and said, "Anyone in the way, the Work crushes!"

Sooner or later, this is true. There is a saying in this school, which is: "Lee gives us enough rope to hang ourselves." Often an individual will be given a tremendous amount of time and space, even at the cost of causing suffering to others, to come to terms with their cramp and the ways in which their own shadow manifests—greed, selfishness, vanity, the will to power, fear, pride, shame, manipulation, domination of others and so on and on. This is a long-term process of slowly penetrating into the depth of our own illusions about ourselves and how we are with others.

However, as generous and magnanimous and compassionate as Lee is in this regard, at some point the Work will bear no more of our denial, arrogance or pride, and it is time to pay up or get out. The psychological cramp inevitably becomes magnified by the natural empowerments that come when we engage sadhana in a true lineage. If we find ourselves in a crucial position in relation to the guru's work, and we don't do the transformational work we must do on ourselves, we become a gross caricature of ourselves and a burden to the guru's work. Eventually, sooner or later, the Universe steps in and pushes us out of the way, usually through circumstances that are beyond our control. The Work must come first.

After a short trip to La Roche Posay to the new shop, Lee was back in time for lunch. People from all over France were beginning to gather at the ashram for the Shri gig tonight in Chauvigny—students were arriving from Annecy, Montpellier, Paris, Rennes and Germany. Alrun would cook a beautiful ashram meal for everyone, while Lee, the Shri crew and the extended company of soloists and their families would dine at the home of Volkmar and Claire, who serves as Lee's booking agent in France.

Claire and Volkmar's house in Chauvigny was a virtual museum of artifacts from the Sacred Bazaar. Large stone pieces—a Hanuman and a gorgeous Devi—as well as many smaller divine beings, with their polished coppery or golden glow, emanated blessings from every nook and cranny. I had the feeling that they were very happy together here in this home that is a shelter for Lee's work. Flowers and small candles adorned the shrines of various deities, and the whole house was permeated with the subtle influence of the lineage of the beggar saint and his son—known to be a bad poet, tonight to be seen in his form as bluesman.

After a hearty meal of grilled sausages, bread and cheeses, salad and desserts, Lee played bridge for an hour or so while most of the Shri crew went ahead to finish set up onstage. When it was time for the music to start, we walked with him two blocks to the Havana Café in Chauvigny, where the band was set to play at nine o'clock.

That night, the sangha came together again for the guru's music. It was one of those steady, solid gigs with the band set up outside the café facing the town square. It was a family affair in a small town; there were quite a few local people and their kids having dinner, but their numbers were overwhelmed by the sangha members, as well as friends of the community, and our many children, who were dancing and running happily amidst the adult dancers. It was quite a contrasting scene with the festival gigs that Shri plays every summer, where there are hundreds or thousands of people listening.

At one point Lee said over the microphone to his audience of local folks and his own students, "You may be wondering what a world class band like Shri is doing playing here in Chauvigny! Well . . . one day I was sitting at a table right here at this café, and an eagle landed on my head! And that doesn't happen every day. So I thought, what a great omen! And I got the idea to form this band, right here, at this café! So, we come back here every year to pay tribute to the place where it all started . . ."

It was an entertaining little piece of theatre. It made Lee's students laugh, and it's likely that many of the people who didn't speak English didn't know or care about what the lead singer was saying. Maybe it was just the guru playfully rendering a new version of physical reality, as if it was modeling clay. Lee has often quoted Henry Miller as saying, "Don't let the facts get in the way of the truth." Maybe the mythological version of this story could go something like this: An "eagle" (sort of like, umm . . . Garuda) did land on Lee's head and inspire him to start the band Shri, and since the guru is everywhere, sure, he was sitting in the café at Chauvigny when it happened. Why not?[1]

The two-hour performance flew past us like a blur. It was a nice space and a pleasure to be together in the healing wash of the music, an ordinary night out with the guru and his band before they hit the road again. We were back home on the ashram by midnight.

1 Garuda is the mythical bird—a divine eagle of sorts—who serves as Lord Vishnu's mount. Garuda symbolizes many divine qualities, such as the ability to fly and float the currents without ever having to land, as well as the piercing, insightful vision of the eagle. Garuda's devotion to Lord Vishnu is legendary in the Vaishnava tradition.

Ferme de Jutreau
August 10

Lee and Thomas left early this morning before meditation; the rest of the band left an hour later in the Shri van, which carried all the musicians and their equipment. The musical entourage would be driving many miles north to Berlin, for the first of eleven gigs in Germany with a short, one-day sojourn into Austria near the end of this leg of the tour. Every day Lee, Thomas and the band would travel to a new location, set up, play the gig and tear everything down again, get up early, drive the next day and do it all again.

Those of us who stayed behind on the ashram would meet Lee in eight days in northeastern France for a three-day seminar. In the meantime, we were ready for the peaceful rhythms of pure, uninterrupted ashram life in the week ahead.

Le Rozet
August 18

Two vans departed from Ferme de Jutreau this morning at seven o'clock for a reunion with Lee in the Jura Mountains of France at Le Rozet, a center for the teachings of Arnaud Desjardins, where Lee has given seminars many times over the past ten years. With a short stop for a picnic en route, we had timed the seven-hour trip expecting Lee to arrive earlier rather than later in the afternoon. He and Thomas had left the tour for a few days to drive to France for this seminar; they had picked up Clint in Freiburg for the weekend at Le Rozet.

Sure enough, we were right about Lee arriving at Le Rozet earlier than planned. When we were about forty-five minutes away from Le Rozet, just leaving the city of Beçanson, the cell phone rang. It was Lee letting us know that he would be waiting for us when we arrived at the center. We drove through the beautiful, green Jura Mountains in anticipation of joining Lee. As soon as we arrived, laden with many boxes of sacred artifacts, we were greeted by Jean Pierre and Josette, our hosts. Lee stopped long enough to welcome us briefly, but he had only one mission: to set up the Sacred Bazaar.

The rest of the day was filled with that familiar activity of unpacking boxes—unwrapping every bronze bowl and pot, each deity, large and small, in bronze, wood and stone, and every little detail of Lee's wares: rosaries, crucifixes, intricate silver delicacies, carved and handmade wooden boxes, kachinas and everything in between. Lee placed each one in its proper spot on the tables beneath the windows in the seminar room, which provided a sweeping pastoral view of green meadows and evergreen mountains. The next day would begin with a thirty minute meditation, then Lee's first talk of the three-day program.

In the Jura Mountains

Le Rozet
August 19, 2005

Lee sounded the pristine tone of a singing bowl from his dais at the front of the room to signal the end of the meditation, then immediately began his talk. Almost everyone in the group had been to many of Lee's seminars at Le Rozet over the years; we were ready to follow his lead into the labyrinth. He plunged in with a bitter invective about the world: "Good morning. Well, morning, anyway. For some, it's good, for some, it's bad. I've been on the road with the band, and I chose the wrong books to read—the biographies of two comics, George Carlin and Bill Hicks. When I read that kind of thing I get très sardonic. It's like throwing gasoline on a fire . . . We live in an unnatural world; the water and air are polluted, there are toxins everywhere. Bill Hicks was not just sardonic but wickedly furious about the state of the world . . . because people are not going to be different. *We* have to be different.

"The world is run by crippled perverts who want to squeeze you dry and raise another generation of people who want to do nothing but put money in their pockets. If we want our lives to be better, different—and I damn sure do—*we* have to do it. Drugs don't do it. I read the biography of the lead singer of the Red Hot Chili Peppers.

The Rolling Stones, Aerosmith, the Red Hot Chili Peppers, Stevie Ray Vaughan—they all got off drugs.

"So, it rests with us and only us; it's in our hands. Yes, there is help—good therapists and spiritual teachers, good lovers, friends—yes, there is help, but often even those can't take the actual steps that only we can take in our own lives. So, having been on the road for a month, locked in my little hotel rooms . . . the band is so kind to me, of course, I'm the guru, but a lot of people kill their gurus! So they try to get me my own room—what a luxury! Twelve people in the traveling party this year, and there are only so many rooms, so three or four people have to stay together, which is hell, even if you love them! You know, everybody goes to sleep at different times, has their own rhythm and way to do things . . . So, I get my own room, and even when I don't, I get to choose who stays with me—of the men, I mean. So, here I am, holed away in my room with Bill Hicks and George Carlin!

"So, there's been a lot of input since the last seminar . . . Someone asked me if there had been anything notable in the gigs. The band is so good anymore that pretty much it's all the same. Ed plays a sublime guitar, and Franck . . .!" Lee shrugged in appreciation, as if to say that there was just no way to adequately describe Franck's guitar playing on this particular morning. "And we had Ed, Doug and Franck, who we were calling 'The Guitar Monster Orchestra'! Franck is just . . . from heaven!"

Lee talked about playing gigs in East Germany, and he took some time to describe the oppressive atmosphere there. The years of repression and the suffering of the people is not just palpable but painfully obvious. He said, "In East Germany we always get a different response to the music from the people than we do in West Germany. We suffer, but most of our suffering is bullshit! We create these dramas that are nothing, they're absurd. The eastern European countries had something to really suffer about. We played a gig in East Germany when the wall was still up . . ."

Lee recalled playing in East Germany many years ago with LGB, his first band, which was a rock & roll band. He spoke of the acute economic depression of the cities and villages; traveling in East Germany, the band had nowhere else to spend their money—but on what would they spend it? The clothes were out of style, the cars were like electric lawnmowers. Even the ice cream was terrible!

"Shri played the blues there and they loved us. They begged us, 'We love you! Move here, we need you!' So, we go around spreading the gospel. That's what the band calls it. I don't. I call it the blues gospel—really it's just music. They say, 'Oh no, we know what you're really doing!' "

He began to describe the gig they played recently in Leipzig. At five o'clock in the evening people were lined up, two hours before the gig was to begin. All kinds of people were there, especially old people with their walkers, barely able to move. Lee laughingly said, "We're not young anymore, but these were old people—really old!"

He continued, "Every culture has its own particular facial mask. In Leipzig people have this 'I've lived my entire life under a totalitarian government, so have my children,' facial mask. What kind of music were we going to play? The blues! They'd heard nothing but violas and cellos for years! Last year we played there too; last year and this year it was exactly the same—now we have a fan club in Leipzig!" In the midst of this very serious discourse, Lee was pelting us lightly with his sense of humor, and the burden of pain was relieved in our shared laughter.

"As soon as we started playing, you could see the mask fall; you see the mask fall away and essence is there, and the intense suffering was gone and smiles showed up. And I thought, 'Where is the Sacred Bazaar when I need it?' " This bit of ironic levity brought more laughter from us, fueled as well, paradoxically, by the way Lee was touching our hearts with the plight of these people.

"So, that table over there is where I'll be in between sessions. Yes, that stuff is going to cost money, but it's only money! It's *only* money. It's not love, intimacy, health; it's not dharma. So, one thing is to get our priorities straight: it's only money. There's always more of it. There is more money in the world than we can imagine! So go over there and spend yourself into a trance! If you want to, you can come to the money seminar at Ferme de Jutreau and learn how to relax."

He spoke of having two passions; the first one is the Sacred Bazaar—the harbinger of significant changes in his teaching style. He continued, "The other passion, believe it or not . . . interestingly enough, the thing about Bill Hicks was the title of his book, which is 'Love All the People'. His book is a furious, angry monologue about the idiocy and blind following of people. That rage was the result of his frustration, because he loved the world, and that rage turned him into a fiery, bitter comic. The front cover of George Carlin's book says, 'When Jesus Comes Again Is He Bringing the Porkchops?' The only way people are shocked into considering the reality of the situation is through sardonic comedy.

"My other passion is something we could call truth or reality. I'm frustrated as well because as much heart and soul and intention as we bring to the Path, we still have a problem. I have two students who are now teaching students of their own, and I hope to keep it to that for a long time. Breaking through is not necessarily the same as having the capacity to teach. Purna, one of those students who is teaching, said to me recently, 'I've had two great realizations: one, it's all context; and two, people are going to keep doing what they're doing because they can.'

"Only one thing will change that: obligation. There is a big difference between obligation and responsibility. Obligation is the only thing that will keep you from doing the same neurotic things over and over and over again. When we were at Hauteville this summer, Arnaud told us that for the first six years he was with Swami Prajnanpad, he was not obedient. Arnaud said, 'Once I understood that my master had no purpose or life except to serve me, then I had no more doubts, no confusion, and it was obedience from then on.' That's obligation. And Arnaud changed. You can have obligation to God, to your spiritual master, to your children—pick your poison! God, Reality, Truth, children—pick your poison, because what's important is the obligation, not the object of your obligation."

We took a break for brunch, since the Le Rozet schedule would follow the schedule that Lee prefers on his own ashram: two meals a day, brunch around ten-thirty or so, and dinner at six p.m. At twelve noon we reconvened with Lee. He began by promoting the new tattoo book, *Agony & Alchemy*. He reassured his audience that it was actually about transformation. He even said, to his own students who were present, "If you want to understand your guru's interest in tattoos, read this book." But his pitch was falling on mostly deaf ears. Watching Lee's valiant efforts to sell the book in the spiritual scene over the summer, it was surprising to see how much fear and prejudice people had about inking the skin. The idea of tattoos turned out to be, in the spiritual world, still a taboo subject.

Lee's talk during this session centered around a discourse on a phrase taken from the Gurdjieff work: "the terror of the situation."

"I used to call it the horror of the situation until some helpful person told me that it's actually 'the terror of the situation.' There is a difference, although they are connected. The terror of the situation is that nothing is substantial. We say, 'I'll love you forever.' The builder says, 'This will last two hundred years.' We say, 'Oh, this I can count on.'

"We can count on the sun rising every morning, and it's a new day, but in fact, nothing is substantial. Form is emptiness; emptiness is form. Even this body is completely insubstantial. When we are wracked with grief or sorrow, we don't feel it is insubstantial. When we start to realize how insubstantial everything is, we are terrified because everything we relied on is an illusion.

"The distinction I've made is, the horror of the situation is personal; we come to realize that we are false. That doesn't make us bad people; we try to be honest and live good lives. Essentially we're not bad people; however, we lie, aggress, manipulate, allow our feelings of self-hatred and insecurity to create situations of our unworthiness. That's the horror of the situation. It's about our manifestations.

"When you set foot on the Path, if you are serious, sooner or later, one year, ten years, twenty-five years later, you are going to come up against the horror of the situation and the terror of the situation. It's uncomfortable, unattractive, humiliating to think that things we say, gestures, the love we offer, is false. Our motive isn't false, but the action is false because it is mechanical—it's blind. We don't know what we're doing. We think we do, but we are being moved by forces we are unaware of. None of this is good or bad—it's just the way things work.

"When we get in touch with forces that move us, it's exhilarating because we are touching something real, but also uncomfortable because everything familiar begins to crumble. As we begin to examine ourselves, everything becomes glaring and unimaginable, because we don't imagine ourselves as aggressive and vindictive. So we're horrified, and the issue is always, 'Am I going to continue this way, or not?' We don't want to continue, but everything in us does. The body, emotions and mind want to continue because the territory is known, it's habitual.

"So everything in us wants to continue being aggressive and false and lying and cheating, but when we see it as it is, sometimes it's the horror first, then the terror, or the terror then the horror, but always they go together. Sooner or later, if we stay on the Path, we are going to hit this thing. Hopefully we can hit this maturely and gracefully, with as little suffering for others as possible. We will see our lives crumbling right before our consciousness. So it requires a lot of intention and attention, because the mind will feed us every distraction to get us to break our discipline of intention and attention.

"Mind will say, 'Oh, I've outgrown this person. I've loved them, but now I've outgrown them.' It could be either a partner or a teacher, because sooner or later you'll come to that place with your own teacher. 'I've outgrown my teacher; now *life* can be my teacher.' Or you find another teacher. One of the most primary trainings in the Work is discipline—the ability to stay in place.

It's like in the rodeo, with a horse or a bull—it's the elegance with which the rider can manage the ride. It's the same on the Path, except it's not sixty seconds in hell but sixty years. You just have to hang in there. Like E.J. Gold said, ninety percent is hanging in there—the other ten percent is finding your way through hell. I said that part; E.J. left hell behind a long time ago, and he's gone *down*, not up! Where he works, you do not want to know!"

People laughed, especially those who have met Mr. Gold, but many people at this seminar have heard so many stories of him from Lee that they probably feel as if they know him.

"So, hanging in there . . . Maybe you get cancer and there is a tremendous drama around it. You go into treatment and it's successful and it passes, but all the drama happens first, and you can't take that back. You weren't willing to breathe through it; you had to have all this emotional catharsis first. It was unexpected, but you *should* expect it. Every morning you wake up, you should expect to die that day."

Lee told a story of one of the top trainers under Werner Erhard, who was to give a talk many years ago to a group in New York City, to the toughest crowd to face in the world. He was feeling great trepidation about it and called Werner, his mentor, and asked him what to do. Werner said that the way he deals with fear is that he wakes up every morning, looks in the mirror and says, "It's a good day to die!" After telling this story, Lee reminded us of Paul of Tarsus, who said, 'Every day I die in Christ.' He meant that he knew his personal desires and wishes were the worst kind of shit.

Going scatological, Lee smiled as he embarked on a spontaneous metaphor of what shit our personal desires and wishes are, beginning with the fact of how he had been eating pork all summer, everywhere he went.

"In the metaphor, you're at a wedding feast; you've been eating nothing but pork and fried onions and cabbage. Suddenly it starts rumbling down there, and you run to the toilet, and it's not just a shit you leave in there but a weapon!" Everyone started laughing again. He paused just enough for his delivery to be perfect as he assaulted our funny bones one more time, saying, "It could take over a country!" More laughter. He concluded, "That's your personal desires and your personal shit."

Turning serious again, Lee said, "A shift of context is not just to shift your focus of abuse—it's to shift to no longer be an abuser. It's our job to die every day; to die in the master, to die in the Work, so that our illusions do not overwhelm the impulse to live a life of genuine honesty and truth, because typically, they do. We are very sincere people—we wouldn't be in this room if we weren't—but we're creatures of habit, and it's very difficult to break that structure.

"If you stay on the Path, you will run up against this wall of horror and terror. It's all a matter of context, so there's not a handy list of what to do and what not to do. It's all context. You struggle with the mind, emotions and body. It's important to remember that the body is a great magician; it can make bumps and pains and aches and all kinds of things. The body itself will try to get in your way by creating a health crisis.

"So when you hit the wall, you've got to remember that you are struck by the horror and terror of the situation. It's better to hit the terror of the situation first, then the horror of the situation, but we don't choose. You've got to manage your mind, emotions and body, because if they have anything to say, you will not make the transition. And you've got to make the transition, because your life is not about your beautiful children, or your hungry sex, which is equally beautiful, or political consciousness or your wish for stability and peace in the world, although we should always fight for justice . . . . What life is about is transformation. What life is for is to move transformationally forward, evolutionarily. You must make the transition, because this is what your life is about. Your life has led you to this point, but most people don't do it."

Lee talked about how we would be surprised to know that most of our parents have seen the terror of the situation, but they stuff it away, pretend it never happened, and go on in their miserable lives, meaning that they may be relatively happy, they may be wonderful people, but they are not pursuing the true purpose of life.

"We'd better do something before it's too late. Most of our practice is preparing us to hit the wall of horror and hit the wall of terror. Where is happiness in this bleak picture—where is the reason to live? How about allowing what the purpose of life is and the pursuit of that to fill you with ecstasy and happiness? What else? What about relationship and children? Not necessary! I purposely left out sex, because where sex is concerned, where women are concerned, men are . . . hopeless!"

This lead to another hilarious rant about our illusions around sex and the human drama fueled by our weaknesses. He began with a description of how all women are good at sex, but most men—forget it! "Anyone who is open is good; anyone who is closed is not," was Lee's basic formula on sex. He joked around about how women should just forget about men and use their anatomical difference ruthlessly, for their own purposes: "Can I borrow that thing for thirty minutes?" Playing out the man's clueless response, Lee quipped theatrically "Sure!" to gales of laughter.

"Use them for your own purposes," Lee finished triumphantly, "and let them go back to sleep!" Laughter rocked the room, with the men joining in just as much as the women. Then he picked up the seemingly dropped stitch of why relationship is not necessary to the true purpose of life.

"We should be able to put the pieces together in our lives of love that doesn't come from a lover. Have you ever had the experience of walking into a friend's house and the eyes of their child light up and they say your name? What else do you need?"

Lee went on to speak about how life brings experiences to us—we bump into things. Each of us comes to the path at different ages, young or in our middle years or older. We are inexorably drawn to the path, and slowly, we begin to discover what our purpose is. The immensity of the situation begins to dawn on us.

"We've been like rats in a labyrinth—God has designed this labyrinth—where slowly, slowly we are channeled to this place where we realize the terror of the situation. What if we don't realize it? Nothing, just another wasted lifetime. We can make this a wasted lifetime that means nothing, or if we do it, your life takes on meaning, absolute, cosmic, objective meaning. That's why you must make it . . . . "

Lee began to talk about the joy of natural childbirth, which he called "a mystical experience." In it, you have two realizations: one is wonder at the mystery of life, and coincidentally real is the realization that you are going to pass away, the mother will pass away, every one in the room and the memory of that experience will be erased. He reminded us again that when we die, all of our memories are forgotton by fact of cosmic law; we do not remember the lives that have come before, except in very rare cases. When we die, our joys, wonders, tenderness, love, intimacy, sweetness are all erased. What is not erased is that which those experiences and qualities of life have built within you. But that which is built is not named love, intimacy, tenderness, et cetera.

Lee spoke about the escalated number of recent major plane crashes, wherein hundreds of people have died, as important reminding factors of impermanence. A little later Lee was asked to clarify the meaning of context.

"Guess you have to have context to know what it is! That's a joke. Context is the field out of which participation arises. When we prepare a meal, everything on the table is content. Context is the mood in which we prepare to receive guests—the whole complex of relationships. From context flows content. For example, if we are preparing a meal for guests, if we feel the guests are unwanted; like our in-laws are coming to dinner, or our boss, and we're not really into it, but we're going to do it anyway. Then the context of the meal is different than a meal for people we haven't seen for a while and look forward to seeing. The same food can be prepared, and it can be completely different meals, as any cook knows.

"Context defines content, so if we believe we are unlovable, that is what defines our relationships. If the Work is the context of our lives, it will define the content of our lives. When we are happy and clear and relaxed, we are more able to serve the Path than when we are unhappy and confused. If the context of our lives is the Path, what content do you think the Path will most likely produce in our lives? Health, security, happiness, success . . . "

Lee qualified this statement by saying that health may not be what we experience, because even the Work cannot change the negative effects of our toxic world on food, air, water. The Work will want to produce health for us, but of course we live in a polluted world. The Work will want to give us happiness, because when we are happy we just serve the Work. When we are unhappy, we are always *looking* for happiness instead of serving the Work. Lee said that this is why most teachers of the Gurdjieff persuasion are notably unsentimental and unromantic about life, beauty, relationship—because their emphasis is entirely on bringing us into the context of the Work.

"The teacher knows that when your life is contextualized by the Work, then happiness, love, beauty will most naturally follow, because the Work wants the best you have to give, and you can't give your best when you are worried about love, health, happiness. Finding the context of your life in the Work is very, very difficult, because we are so intent on seeking happiness at first, and for a long time. First, you have to give your life to the Work, then, we'll see. Since content follows context, if you give your life to the Work, everything else will follow. But 'Seek ye first the Kingdom of Heaven, and all things will be given unto you.' The Kingdom of Heaven is here on Earth, in the Work, contextually. Seek that and all things will be given to you."

Le Rozet
August 20

After the eight-thirty meditation was over, Lee immediately asked for questions, and with over fifty people in the small room there were several hands that went up. One question lead to a long discourse in which Lee spoke in a poignant way about his own changes in teaching and leading students on the spiritual path, beginning with a discussion of our deep sense of unlove, and how that primal psychological strategy undermines us in our practice. Lee told the group about going to visit E.J. Gold earlier this year, and how Mr. Gold had given a teaching, "Security is not the cure for insecurity." This principle, he said, applies to everything. We have certain aspects of ourselves that we would like to be rid of; we think that if we could just be loved, we wouldn't feel unlovable. If we only had money, it would cure us of feelings of failure or poverty. Not so, Lee asserted.

He continued, "Arnaud said that we come to the master, and we feel a certain distinction. The master is this great being, up here, and we are down here, this turd . . . So we formulate this idea that only the transcendent master can love someone like me, this piece of crap. And it's true! Ha, ha! . . . That was a joke!" We sat there, looking at Lee, not sure whether to laugh or cry.

"So we validate our feeling by saying, 'Only the master could love *me*.' What we feel from the master is true. And what Swami Prajnanpad said to Arnaud was, 'The master cannot love someone who is unlovable,' under other circumstances. That's a shocking statement if we feel unlovable. That means, if we feel the master's love, then we must be lovable across the board.

"Imagine if you could feel lovable, how that would change your relationship with your partner. Love is not the cure for unlove, neither are *gestures* the cure for unlove. What if you made a list, 'I would feel loved if . . .'? We say, 'I know you love me, but do you respect me?' Look at all the ways you expect your partner to be, to prove they love you, when they feel totally in love with you and they don't feel the need to prove their love.

"Yogi Ramsuratkumar was hurt when His devotees fought over Him. There were times when He cried because one devotee was criticizing another. When we love someone and that person doesn't feel loved, it hurts us, because we know there is nothing we can do—no amount of love poured on them can help. It's kind of heartbreaking, because there is no cure. The answer to psychological considerations are not in the psychological domain—they are in the spiritual domain."

Lee talked about his early work teaching a psychological seminar on positive thinking called Silva Mind Control. He said that dealing with the mind alone was much better than dealing with the emotions. He said, "In this business, the Work, emotions and feelings are like a volcano, over the top! I maintained an optimistic attitude for years. Now it's been thirty years, and my attitude has changed. I can whomp up optimism and theatre, but as you can tell by my comments, I'm a little sobered by the situation."

Lee used the example of how we step up to the bar for specific situations, like when our parents are dying, when we are finally able to tell our parents that we love them. You can imagine what it means, he said, in the last moments of their lives, to hear that their child loves them! But in day to day life, we are still prisoners of our own negative habits.

"We get up to the door, and all we have to do to transition from a lower state of transformation to a higher state of transformation is to walk through that door and close it behind us. In higher stages of transformation the door automatically locks behind us, but you have stages. You have to lock the door, because once through the door, there is no returning. Things are different on the other side of the door. Have you ever walked into a sex shop?"

Lee regaled us with a description of walking, like Alice in Wonderland, into the completely different world of a sex shop after a nice dinner: You're just walking down the street under the moon, everything is beautiful. You don't know it's a sex shop; it's just a door like every other door, but when you open that door, it's completely different on the other side! The contrast between outside the sex shop on the street and inside the sex shop is startling, which Lee compared to having seen a pit full of thousands of snakes in a zoo in Chennai many years ago. It was an image he never forgot, because it wasn't like anything else he had ever seen before—in principle, like walking through the door of transformation:

"When you walk through the door, it's not like anything else; not like any fantasy you have had of what it would be like; it's *better* than anything else you've ever experienced. But if you walk through that door before you're prepared, it's hell. You've got to be ready to walk through the door, which is why you find a teacher—to prepare yourself for the possibility, even though it's highly unlikely. Statistically it's impossible; it's not literally but statistically impossible.

"The teacher helps to prepare you for each of the initiatory doorways. You don't want to walk through a farther doorway before the others. When that happens it's often clinical madness that results. You need to build an energetic tolerance for being a conduit for energy, for force. It's not unlike if you take too high doses of psychedelics, it can 'fry your brain.' You have to be prepared for what you'll find behind that door, but also for the level of energy.

"The Baul path is a tantric path that involves sexual practice, but that is not until the end of the path. The criteria is that you have to be in relationship for a long time and be friends. When a couple hits a breakthrough moment in sex—not orgasm or great sex—and reaches that doorway to a different reality, they are totally ecstatic. 'This is what we've been waiting for all our lives!' Every nerve is blitzed with light! The next day they have the biggest fight they've had in years! Vicious! They're close to killing one another the next morning. We slam the door shut and put locks on it—we really dig into our partner to make sure it's not going to happen again because our egos do not want any changes, even a beneficial one.

"So, we get to the door, it's the transition from one state of consciousness to the next state of consciousness—always higher. What we do is turn around, put our back to the door, close the door and brace ourselves! We use the doorframe, lean against it to keep the door closed, just in case somebody tries to push us through the door.

"We get to the door, and this is what we want in our essential self, but we fight it with every breath. Our bodies, minds and emotions do not want it. When the other side of the door is a complete uncertainty, we don't know how the emotions and mind will respond. We may be the same externally, and all the changes may be internal. It's an unknown. We have a choice at that time.

"How do we get through the door? Gracefully, meaning *big* Grace. Who is on the other side, enticing us to come through? Jesus, Buddha, Nityananda, Neem Karoli Baba and a few of the women, Ma Anandamayi . . . and of course, Yogi Ramsuratkumar.

"When we have these choices, we can either sit in the corner and suck our thumb or learn the new territory. 'Okay, I'm through the door, I'm going to learn the new territory.' Like getting a new car. You learn the territory; how to manage the energy, how to respond to people lovingly, free of your usual habitual bullshit. For example, how many of you chatter on mechanically and insult people without meaning to? 'Oh, did I say something?'

"So, you get on the other side of the door, but your habits have momentum. They're moving on their own steam. You get through the door and the identity is gone, but the habit is still there, still moving. Part of learning the territory is realizing what our habits are and dismantling them: speak less, or more, as the case may be; be more sensitive to your environment; be more sensitive to other people's struggles, to the suffering of others."

Lee spoke of Swami Prajanpad's formula of how things progress on the path: "First it's just me; then it's me and the other; then it's the other and me; and finally, it's only the other. When we walk through the doors of transformation, we go from complete self-centeredness to being focused on the other. At the final door, we leave ourselves behind completely.

"If you don't continue to indulge those habits, their momentum will slowly wind down; if you indulge them, the momentum will continue. When you walk through the door, the entire complex of psychological habits and neuroses don't figure anymore. They are out of place, unattractive, ugly. They are obvious to everybody; it is obvious how out of place these manifestations are for you. But you still have a choice to intelligently learn the new territory or fall back into old habit patterns. If you allow yourself to fall back, you can't get back through the door—it's locked—but you can suffer, and the more your habits continue, the more you will suffer. Angst, remorse. The suffering of your knowledge that you are above and beyond the behavior you are animating. We may desire to change our behavior, but you have to *do* something about it. As you can tell, chattering on blindly is particularly irritating to me.

"You are being guided. You will be led through the door . . . You think you are making choices, but you are being guided. Once you're through the door, the horror of the situation is *glaring*—you look at your habits and are horrified that someone as good and as committed to the Path as you can still be habitual in that low, cheap, empty, ugly, miserable way."

This extraordinarily powerful session was over. Everyone poured down the steep wooden stairway into the dining room on the first floor of the centuries-old building for lunch. Bread, cheese, fresh tomatoes, fruits, boiled eggs, sliced ham awaited us. After such a sobering consideration, people were lively and enthusiastic about the food, but at the same time, there was a certain subtle hush in the air. The weather continued to be beautiful, with sun shining on the green, pastoral mountain slopes all around. The household cats strolled in and out of the room, at ease with the whole scene of fifty or more people inhabiting their space.

After brunch, washing dishes and setting up for dinner, there were a few scant moments to stretch before the next session. Lee was, as always, standing behind the tables at the Sacred Bazaar, available for interactions with people, whether it was over a bronze sculpture of a deity that had called to them or a special bowl they wanted to buy, or if they had specific questions to ask him about their lives. I often heard him explaining the iconography of pieces, but sometimes his words were quite inaudible, as if he was speaking only for the person directly in front of him. His presence and steady attention was immediately directed to whoever stood before him in the ambiance of the sacred images that make up the content of that vast context we call the Sacred Bazaar.

At noon the next session began. After a few questions, someone talked about the formula given by E.J. Gold, "Security is not the cure for insecurity," saying that some states can be really disagreeable and can come back often. Lee responded:

"Exerting effort to try to control the mind or change our feelings is going to keep those things in place. Relax into thoughts and feelings that arise—completely relax into those things. There is a difference between feeling something and acting on the feeling. What you feel doesn't mean you have to act on it . . . . To be one with whatever arises is to not be separate from it or try to do something to it."

Lee encouraged us to keep trying, to allow our experience to flow in this way, whether the thought or feeling is "loser, failure," or anything else, don't give it any meaning. You relax into it. He continued, "You can't deal with insecurity, or whatever it is, gradually. There is only one way to finally and effectively deal with it, and that is to drop it—turn your back on it and walk away."

Again Lee referred to the metaphor that E.J. Gold used last year when he gave this teaching—that of a precious gold coin that we don't want to drop. Our desire for security is the gold coin, and we have to put it down and walk away. Of course, ego does not want to do that, because the gold coin—the desire for security, love, affection, money, whatever—is so familiar to us, it is inextricably interwoven with our survival strategy. We are driven to keep our connection with these things, even when they are terribly painful to us. Like an emotional addiction to people who are dead, or anything we want to grow beyond—at some point we have to put it down and walk away. With a loved one who is dead, it doesn't mean that we won't remember that person lovingly and affectionately, or that we won't enjoy the good memories we have of them, but that we are no longer driven by the suffering of desire or self-pity.

Lee continued, "We think, my life is completely interwoven with this—how do I put it away? In ordinary therapy you take massive complexes and pull the threads out one at a time to untie the knot. If it's successful, it's a miracle! When you drop the gold coin of desire, you cut through the whole thing in one movement—that's the only way. You don't want to be like Lot's wife. She turned to a pillar of salt because she couldn't let go. So it has to be cold turkey, but it has to mean enough to you to do that. What if, when your partner tells you that he loves you, you just assume it's true? Try it!

"Who you are is already perfect. You've perfected your cramp! Your psychological character is perfect, as good as it gets. Like drama queens—they can't be better drama queens than they are. They have their psychological story perfected. You can't move from where you are now to transform. One minute you're who you are; the next minute, you're a disciple. There is no bridge. How to get to be a disciple? Put down the old, neurotic character and step into the disciple. Turn your back and walk away—no attachment, no threads. So, what's stopping you from being a good disciple? You. It's all a matter of the choices you make."

Mentioning Robert Svoboda, who talks quite a lot in his seminars about the law of karma, Lee spoke about how we can minimize or maximize our karma. Interacting with Mr. Svoboda, Lee said, has brought the law of karma more definitively to his attention. Lee continued, "When we put down the gold coin and walk away, will we get what we want? Not necessarily, because there are karmic implications. The purpose of putting the coin of desire down and walking away is to relieve ourselves from the intense suffering we have from our insecurity. Just two weeks ago there were huge earthquakes in Japan . . . there really is no security in this life. To release the tremendous burden of suffering that is created by our insecurity and unlove is the purpose of dropping the coin of the need for security, the need for love. Will we get what we're looking for when we put down insecurity and unlove? Almost always, yes. But if it's a business deal for us, no.

"Usually in life when we remove the barrier to wealth, love, respect and regard, all those things are just beating on our doors, waiting to get in. Once we are rid of the obstacles, it just flows right in. Sometimes there is a certain task that the Work has for us that requires either a lot of resources or no resources. But that is very rare. Most of the time we just have to remove the obstacles and it flows."

A tall stack of various books was on the dais beside Lee, and now he began to sell them in earnest, beginning with the French translation of *The Only Grace Is Loving God*. He said, "Since I've been coming to France, I've been asked which book I wanted published in French first, and I always say this, 'The Only Grace Is Loving God'. It took ten years for that to happen. People are disturbed when they read this book because it doesn't say anything. It says *everything*, but for the linear, logical mind it says nothing."

He held the book up and a few people raised their hands. "A book guaranteed to confuse you, if nothing else!" Everyone laughed warmly as Lee picked up the next book, the biography, *Yogi Ramsuratkumar—Under the Punnai Tree.*

"This is not just a biography, but a teaching manual. Yogi Ramsuratkumar's life is considered in light of the teaching. It's a book for anyone who is interested in the fine points of how to work with the master."

It took a little more cajoling to sell two or three copies of this big, heavy book, partly because many people who have been to Lee's seminars at Le Rozet in the last two years had already read it. Nonetheless, Lee pressed on. After the sales were finished, Lee asked for questions.

Josette, one of our hosts, said, "At the last General Assembly at Hauteville, Arnaud asked us to give him an ashram. What can we do?"

She was referring to a teaching communication that Arnaud made back in June, which we had heard many of Arnaud's students refer to over the summer. The essential impact of it was so strong that Lee's students had been taking it to heart. Arnaud was talking about how he is now drawn to spend more and more time in Canada at Mangalam, a small ashram in Quebec that is dedicated to his teaching. He had been speaking about his disappointment that Hauteville does not have the atmosphere of an ashram as he envisions it, with the mood and flavor of a sanctuary where people are practicing profoundly. Fundamentally, Arnaud said to the large crowd of about eight hundred people at Hauteville who had gathered for their General Assembly, "I would like to die on a real ashram. Maybe at Mangalam . . . but why not Hauteville?"

Lee considered the question for a moment before answering. He said, "I don't know . . . I think everything we've talked about this weekend has implications for making an ashram. But we need to understand the distinction between an ashram and a center, or a therapy center. One thing that is frustrating to Gilles and especially to Daniel is that so many questions are not about practice but about other things. Often when I am teaching at Hauteville and we leave the space after a session, Arnaud or Gilles will say, 'Where are the questions about practice?' I answer whatever questions come up.

"My question is, why aren't people practicing? What makes Hauteville an ashram is the intention with which people go there, practice there, and what they take away from there. We know Arnaud is a master, but we aren't telling him with our activity that he is a master. It's not just the physical person who makes the master . . .

"It comes back to the difference between an ashram and a center, the difference between the teacher, healer or therapist, and the master. If we are always evaluating the teacher's activity in psychological terms . . . I have a weakness, which is to devote an inordinate amount of my time and attention to attractive women—that has nothing to do with my function or relationship to Yogi Ramsuratkumar. I hide it, so nobody knows that's where my attention is . . . 'He's always chasing antiques now. He doesn't care about us. All he cares about are those fucking antiques, those fucking artifacts!' That's what some of my students say or feel. When people evaluate the master's behavior in psychological terms, the master has to be frustrated about people not seeing the sacred environment around the master."

Lee used the example of Swami Prajnanpad, who said to Arnaud many years ago about his first ashram, La Bost, "Let them die in the snow!" Taken out of context this sounds like a heartless statement, but actually Swami Prajnanpad was referring to the need for ruthlessness and ferocity in relationship to practice. And now, we bring our cell phones and computers to the ashrams and expect to do business while we're there! Lamenting this state of affairs, Lee said, "We have to come to Hauteville without our phones and computers; we have to *make* it an ashram, not act like children! We have to bring to Hauteville some discipline and some real sense of integrity . . . . It's all those little things that distract us from practice. If you take one of those little things, it's very small, but taken all together, it's big."

The next question was, "You spoke earlier about the 'Great Process of Divine Evolution.' If we cut off our secret life, are we part of the Great Process of Divine Evolution?"

Lee answered, "That's too absolute. Some of my best students only see me once every three or four years! When we have a secret life it is an obstacle to deeper practice, but I wouldn't say that we are cut off from the Great Process of Divine Evolution. There is a way in which the Great Process of Divine Evolution is not bigger than you;

you are bigger than it! That's too obscure!" Lee chuckled, then said enigmatically, "But contemplate it!"

Proceeding further, Lee said, "So, in relationship to psychological issues, there is a real sense in which there is no separation between spiritual and psychological . . . there are emotions, physicality, essence, spirit or soul, all part of the same thing. At the same time, different spaces demand different responses or protocol. There is a space for the psychological, for refining skills, and different spaces for aspects of human life."

Protocol is an aspect of Lee's teaching that receives very little attention from his students. For new students protocol is something that gets stumbled upon, usually after having made some faux pas; nonetheless, it is a much more important element of life in the guru's company than one might think. Lee said that he visits a lot of different teachers and takes his students with him; unfortunately, his students often think that they have to demonstrate their own practice as a priority over the spaces and protocols of others, particularly the host in any given situation. When you are in someone else's space, it is respectful to function within the guidelines of their protocol, not your own. Lee remembered that when he first met Arnaud, the meals were silent, which Lee honored, happy to go along with the discipline of the meal spaces. After that first year, Arnaud made the decision to abandon their practice of silent meals whenever Lee was visiting, demonstrating the converse of the law of hospitality: courtesy and respect to an honored guest.

You learn to bring a sense of protocol to the particular space you are in. This sensitivity to protocol and hospitality also applies to visiting, for example, one's parents. Lee has often admonished his students for being too rigid with their diet and other practices when visiting parents. "Just make your mother happy," he said today, "stay in your old room that she's kept just the way it was all these years and eat whatever she serves you."

The next question was about the difference between not putting the love of God on the human lover, and how to find the personal Beloved. Lee spoke about a Japanese movie in which the main character "bowed to a woman's cunt."

He continued, "There is this quality of humanness that can truly adore—can have an object of adoration, human or not. Often, in the blush of love, we feel that one another are each other's beloveds. Because of the sublimity of the whole mood of adoration, we tend to divinize that mood, and in that, to divinize our human partner, which, when held in the appropriate context, is not a problem. When it is not held in the appropriate context, it is a problem.

"In Baul sexual practice, partner practice, in which Radha and Krishna are the ultimate symbols of union with God, when the man is with his wife or thinking of her, he thinks of her as Radha, and she thinks of him as Krishna. So whenever they are together, sexually, or just sitting before the fire talking about the grandkids, there is an objective mood of adoration."

Lee talked about the fifteenth century mystical poem of adoration, the *Gita Govinda*, by the famous Hindu poet, Jayadeva, which is the text that is most honored by the Bauls as elucidating the play between Radha and Krishna as symbolic of love between the human being and the Divine. The basic story that is expounded is that Krishna loves Radha, then he rejects her; her heart breaks, then his heart breaks at her heart break. He pursues her again, they get back together, and it goes on.

"In the Baul Tradition the instruction is to apply those principles to one's human partner with one stipulation: we relate to the human being as if Radha or Krishna is the doorway to union with the Divine, but they are not the same thing. It can seem like the same thing: when union with the Divine is realized, the integration of that union includes the continuation of relationship. That union is integrated into the world, into the reality of the senses, in an Enlightened Duality.

"E.J. Gold talks about the archetypal Feminine and Masculine; he works with men and women in relationship, so we create circumstances that mirror the circumstance in another domain—a subtle domain. Maybe the beings in that domain don't even have genitals, but there is love, adoration and union.

"Only one thing brings Woman to life: adoration. Men cannot find their way through the labyrinth alone; women instinctively know the way through the labyrinth. A man cannot find his way through it without a woman, but if Woman is not awakened in her, she will not remember that she knows the way through the labyrinth. So the way to awaken Woman is through adoration, and then she will remember the way through to union with God.

"How to adore Woman? Not by giving her flowers and chocolates! Adoration takes place in a different domain than the usual social conversation and relationship. True adoration takes place in a different domain than habitual relationships. That's as close a clue as we're going to get! The usual expectations in human exchanges—'If you love me, why can't you do this, do that, give me this, give me that'—have nothing to do with adoration.

"In ordinary human relationship we often have hidden agendas, but because we want relationship to be smooth and we don't want to argue, we keep those agendas to ourselves. So, adoration must be a response of such absolute purity that all the deals we want to make with each other are erased in that moment. The unconscious mind completely disappears. In that moment, when there is pure adoration, Woman responds, *in the moment*. This is the delicate part—it's wordless, thoughtless.

"Woman wakes up, and that awakening translates into that human woman's response to the human man, and that's where it gets delicate because that's what we've all always wanted. So we immediately try to territorialize it, to grab it to make it our own. Then Woman goes back, snaps back, to wherever Woman goes. 'You screwed it up, you bastard! You always do that!' she says.

"So, part of it is the ability to sustain the moment. Suddenly, after years of practice, adoration arises. We're awed, we're in wonderment, and Woman feels it and responds, and we have a great tryst—a great sexual moment. We want to repeat it next time, but as soon as we try to possess and duplicate it, it seems farther away than ever.

"I don't call the shift of context in my case enlightenment anymore. How have I kept it, if it was just a shift of context? Because I made a conscious choice to practice based on what was realized. Those Laws were obvious when the shift of context occurred, and I simply live according to those Laws. If God talks to me at all, it's through the ongoing living of those Laws of Spirit. I am obedient to the Laws of Spirit.

"So, when Woman begins to lead us through the labyrinth, and it just so happens that sex is going on . . . there we are, being lead through the labyrinth, then it's over, and we think, 'Where can this lead?' You've got to be intelligent. So how do we keep it going? We've had this moment of communion, so we want to keep the woman open and vulnerable. How? Do the things that please her and don't do the things that displease her. And obviously the same thing applies to the woman in relationship to the man; we know what our partners like and don't like. 'Do you like your brownies with or without nuts?' You only have to ask once to know and remember. We approach relationship with softness and gentleness, and that encourages communion . . .

"It's not easy, which is why the phenomena of Woman awake in communion is so rare. Woman awake in her own sphere is not rare at all. That's why the arguments have to fall away. The task requires tremendous spaciousness—to give people the space to be their neurotic selves.

"When adoration awakens Woman, Woman leads man through the labyrinth. Every man and woman has an anima and an animus; each of us has both masculine and feminine within. It's not only 'the man' that screws things up—it can be 'the man' within the woman, because it's the animus that's always criticizing, demanding, manipulating. Either man or woman, out of the psyche, can interrupt the process. That's why it's important to recognize that adoration happens in a domain that is not social, but subtle."

That night there was a session after dinner at seven-thirty. Lee began asking for questions. The first question was from an American woman who has been living in France for twenty-five years. She has been practicing Zen for ten years, had a Hindu master before that, and was currently unsatisfied with her path. She wanted something more.

"Will you give me a mantra?" she asked naively.

"Coca-Cola!" Lee retorted to an outburst of laughter. The room was primed and ready for more of Lee's pranks tonight, having been significantly pounded, melted and softened all day during the sessions, then further worked on many different levels during all the breaks, interacting with Lee and the deities at the Sacred Bazaar.

"From one American to another!" Lee smiled charmingly.

"No problem!" she smiled back. Then she asked if she could give herself a mantra. Lee looked at her for a moment.

"So, the one single practice that Yogi Ramsuratkumar gave to everyone was the repetition of His Name. His master was Swami Ramdas, who gave the practice of mantra as the principle practice, so I'm very much in favor of the use of mantra. However, I'm also in favor of maintaining some degree of discreteness to the Path one is on. Zen and mantra don't go together. If you're serious about Zen, not just as something to do until something better comes along, then the answer to unsoluble questions of the mind is: sit. However, if you're just waiting for something else to come along, then mantra it is! But you want to pick your mantra carefully, relative to its associations."

She replied, "I'm a heretic. I've spent ten years with a Hindu master and ten years in Zen. For me it's the same practice. The same practice the rishis gave and Buddha's practice of watching your mind . . ." Lee interrupted her in mid-sentence.

"Watch your mind, and when you can't bear it anymore, watch

someone else's! Woah! What a show," he commented satirically. Another outbreak of laughter rippled through the room.

"The Zen path is dry," she said.

"I thought in Deshimaru's school they did a lot of drinking!" he rejoined. "When I was there they had a bar where people spent a lot of time. Did they close it?"

"It wasn't feeding my heart," she answered, then said that she had chosen the mantra "om mani padme hum."

"I find tremendous similarities and synchroncities," Lee responded, "between paths—between Castaneda and Tibetan Vajrayana Buddhism and the Baul Path. But when it comes to practice, I don't use those practices. I just use the language that may touch someone when my language won't.

"Like the Heart Breath in our school—it's pretty much exactly like tonglin, but it *isn't* the same. In my school people practice the Heart Breath; it isn't the same because the tradition is different. Obviously I'm very biased toward linage and path. There is food in every path. When we pick a path we should be fairly rigorous in practicing the practices of that path."

Lee used cooking as an example. If you want to have a tasty dish, you don't just dump everything in the kitchen into it; you are selective, and the ingredients are very specifically combined to create a certain taste.

"You can do any mantra you want—it won't hurt and it may help—but it could put a barrier between you and the possibility of Zen. My students have a lot of input, from Robert Svoboda to poetry, Baudelaire, Rilke, Bukowski. To use that information properly is to relate everything they touch back to *their* practice—all the wisdom of other paths is related back to their practice and path. I recommend that my students take in powerful impressions, including the art at the Rodin Museum, or at the Guimet, or powerful Egyptian artifacts at the Louvre.

"Our roots are in India. Feng sui is popular, at the same time, if we want to use a science of environment, we use Vastu, because it has the same mood, but it's from India. So choose something Japanese."

She responded that her deepest connection was with India, that in fact she is awed by the Indian traditions.

Lee offered, "Then why not 'tat tvam asi'?" He was referring to the Vedic maxim, "You are That." He'd already said that Yogi Ramsuratkumar gave his name as mantra, but she didn't seem to catch that one. Now she said no to this suggestion.

"Why not?" Lee asked. "It's simple. 'Gayatri' is too complicated. The more exclusively you practice a path, the more the ultimate possibility of that path will be available to you. These are my thoughts, just for your consideration . . ."

The next question was, "Is there a place for suffering?"

Lee answered, "Of course, because it is a natural human experience. Shri played a gig in Leipzig, and there were these parents with a young boy, a twelve year old paraplegic. The mother was holding him in her arms. The look in that kid's eyes was so full of suffering it was unnerving. I almost thought I wouldn't be able to sing. When we started to play, it changed. I was glad, because my attention was drawn to him—I couldn't take my eyes off him. What suffering he must have to look like that!

"Sometimes sadness comes and stays for awhile. Relative to the Path, what do we do with it? Chögyam Trungpa Rinpoche answered the question, 'What do you do when you find yourself in hell?' by saying, 'I stay there.' Who of us wants to stay in hell when we find ourselves there? We want to get out as soon as possible. When our lives are about service, about the dharma, we teach, wherever we are. If we find ourselves in hell, we teach hell realm beings, or in heaven, we teach heaven realm beings.

"What to do when we find ourselves in a state of sorrow? Stay there, because that's where we are. When we have given that realm what we can give it and drawn what we can draw, we'll find ourselves in a different realm."

"Is it the same with confusion?"

Lee answered, "Yes . . . . Pema Chödrön writes a lot about groundlessness. There is no solid ground to stand on. When there is confusion, the first thing we want to do is find something we imagine is real. Chögyam Trungpa Rinpoche said, 'Stay with the confusion.' Learn to live with confusion, because if you can live in a state of confusion, you can live anywhere."

Lee spoke about our deep-rooted fear of authority. He said that even when there is nothing riding on it, we will compromise our ideals when we are threatened. It's very important to notice that about ourselves—after all, Peter denied Jesus three times before the cock crowed—with good reason. He would have been killed by the Roman guards if he had come forward as a disciple of Jesus. But he didn't deny Jesus as a strategy to protect the teaching; he denied Jesus because he was scared. Lee said that to deny Jesus as a *strategy* is something he would recommend in that situation—to protect and safeguard the teaching. If all the disciples die, who will be there to carry on and insure that the teaching will be passed on?

Lee laughed, "Jesus is turning over in his grave about everybody's lurid interest in his sex life with Mary Magdalene, because it's voyeurism, not a real interest in Jesus' life."

Lee continued, answering a question about impatience, "We should all understand how lazy and sloppy we are, and that basic goodness is who we really are. So we should be impatient, if we have any degree of mechanicality. Intention is the wedge that drives through the obstacles toward clarity. So, intention doesn't imply a long time before something happens, okay?

"Bill Hicks says that the true comic is a shaman. The real comic is looking for transformation in the audience; a real comic has compassion for mankind. They speak the truth in a context of humor, so we can swallow it. 'A little bit of sugar helps the medicine go down.' That's from Mary Poppins. It's really sweet and innocent . . . those were the days!

"So, happiness is what happens between our suffering. Impatience, confusion, sorrow—the whole range of unpleasant emotions don't go away so you can be happy all the time!"

Lee told the story of the Sixteenth Karmapa going to Hong Kong for a visit. He was looking out over the city one night from his room, which was up very high, and he started crying. His attendants were concerned and asked him why he was crying. He said, "So much suffering . . ."

Lee continued, "But that's not who he was—it was the moment. He *was* essential happiness, and even so, there are still moments of grief and profound frustration, and all the rest . . . . On the surface there may be a tremendous variety of feeling; none of it is a problem if we don't take it out of context. Form is emptiness; we don't ever say, 'Form is form.' But we tend to say, 'I am sad,' instead of 'sorrow is present now.' In fact, you are never confused, while there are many circumstances of confusion. When you live in a state of groundlessness, there is absolute clarity. Only when we start to think that form is form and emptiness is emptiness do we get into trouble. When everything that arises is viewed from the context of form is emptiness and emptiness is form, then there is no problem. Clear?" Lee addressed the questioner directly. "Crystal clear! Very good . . . "

He continued, "Happiness is what happens in between suffering. There you are with your child, and they smile and then you hear someone's voice in the next room calling your name, and the quality of that voice is harsh and cutting, and that happiness is gone . . . gone! Sadness, anger, hatred, happiness—all those are experiences that happen alongside all other experience. Ah, to hate something—it's so fulfilling! Fortunately, it doesn't last too long, because it's very destructive."

Lee returned to the mantra he had mentioned at the beginning of this session, *tat tvam asi*: You are That. He said, "Only consciousness understands itself, so you have to be conscious to understand consciousness. What the hell does that mean? Consciousness aside, there's nothing like a good piece of chocolate, and tits aren't bad either! Young, old—doesn't matter! You do different things with different ones . . . in fact, chocolate and tits *together*!"

Everyone was laughing heartily now, and Lee was all smiles. He said cheerfully, "You know, you start talking about essence and reality—you've got to stop and talk about something inane and ridiculous! Now that's my viewpoint—let's have a little dharma between the fun!"

It had been a long day, rather like a dharma *sesshin*, in which we had been sitting on those same pillows for over eight hours. It was eight-thirty at night. Darkness had fallen over the mountains, and as we settled into our seats for the closing thirty-minute meditation, Jean Pierre turned the lights out, so that the room was lit by one tiny votive on the dais. Lee sounded the bell of the singing bowl once again to begin the meditation. At nine o'clock, the day was over.

Le Rozet
August 21

We had been blessed with beautiful weather during our stay in the mountains, and today was no exception. The pristine beauty of the mountains and meadows at Le Rozet always lends itself to a very contemplative mood when we visit. The soft melodic clanging of the cow bells is almost constant, and the land itself is so lush and benevolent that nature becomes the sanctuary of this place, dedicated to the teachings of Arnaud Desjardins. Lee is always happy to be at Le Rozet, a place where he has been giving teachings for eight years.

This morning, immediately after meditation, Lee began to describe his teaching and work in broad strokes. He said, "The term Enlightened Duality is an essential description of my work. It is based on an abiding, inherent realization of nonduality, and based on that, integral to the fact that we are, by nature, physical beings with a mind/body complex, turning that in a mystical sense toward worship of the personal Beloved. That's essentially my understanding of the Baul Path.

"Yogi Ramsuratkumar did not want Westerners to take on Eastern affectations. He wanted us to be Westerners and have Western names. Occasionally, I've given Indian names, and one requirement of that is to change your name legally.

"We call our path the Western Baul Path, not the Baul Path, because there are certain particulars that are different, but the essence of the Path—the abiding realization of nonduality and adoration of the personal Beloved, after the abiding realization of nonduality—is the same. If we approach a serious mystical path of worship of the Beloved before we have a realization of reality as it is, the tendency is to turn that devotion into a romantic fantasy in our minds. So we tend to psychologize mysticism.

"The formula given to us in the Diamond Sutra is: form is emptiness—emptiness is form. First we realize nonduality, and then, realizing we are alive and interacting in a world of physicality, we go on from there. The goal is not to turn into a lump of flesh with no mind that has to be cleaned by someone else."

Lee then began to elucidate the distinction between obligation and responsibility, which he said is different in a way that is similar to the difference between a vow and a promise. When you break a vow, the consequences are very great. A promise is important, but if we break a promise, the karma involved is not as great as when we break a vow—like a marriage vow, for example, or vows that we make on the path. It's the same with obligation; if we fail our obligation on the path, the karmic consequences are much greater than if we don't show up to wash the dishes when our name is on the schedule, which is a responsibility.

The struggle that we find ourselves in is that we have multiple "I's," and each one has its own desires. One "I" wants to be responsible or to fulfill our obligation, and another "I" doesn't want to. Lee used the example of how we often don't make the choices to serve when there is a need, like washing the dishes on the ashram. He said that on his ashram, during the Celebration, it's the new students who raised their hands every time people were asked to join the dish crew.

"The oldest students," Lee commented wryly, "those who have been here a long time, should raise their hands to wash dishes, but they don't. The guests raise their hands and jump to help enthusiastically, but the old students say, 'I have other work to do!' My American students are very lazy—they just want to sit back and contemplate the dharma and wait for another cup of coffee!

"If we can't manage responsibilities when the teacher is not looking over our shoulder, then 'having obligation' is nothing more than an academic consideration. It's my unyielding, immature, orthodox opinion that we have a responsibility to our babies: we nurse on demand. We don't believe in allowing children to cry themselves to sleep. So we're having sex and it's going *really* well and the baby wakes up and starts crying—the responsible thing to do is to stop and take care of the baby, even though we're sweating and grunting and thrashing around!

"So, the first order is responsibility—being responsible—and not just when the guru is around. We have to be self-responsible as a matter of personal pride, not just to look good in front of the authority figures we respect and admire."

Lee said that he was surprised when he discovered that several of his men students were addicted to pornography on the internet. The problem with having a secret life when we are practitioners—whether it's pornography or drinking beer, which is not part of the practice in Lee's school—is that we start hiding more and more, and we become buffered against the blessings of the guru in our efforts to hide.

"It's not that everything we do should be public—that would be disgraceful, because so many of us are filthy little perverts! But we are hiding out in our secret lives. It's nobody's business if we watch porn on the internet, but it is God's business. We defend ourselves against the Blessing Force that we have come to the Path for . . . . So, part of being responsible is an internal relationship to our lives that is accepting and acknowledging. No secret lives! That doesn't mean that we tell everybody everything. Some things are nobody's business, but we should be conscious of those things, not in denial. The point is self-honesty.

"When you can maintain responsibility to your path wherever you are, even when the teacher is not around and no one is going to rat on you, then you are ready for obligation. Again, there are consequences if you are irresponsible, but if you have taken a vow and break it, the consequences are way, way, way, way greater!"

Lee spoke about whether or not we take every request that we receive from the master as something that demands our attention; in this regard he used the example of a small shrine on the far side of the huge temple on the Yogi Ramsuratkumar Ashram. This particular shrine was very important to Yogi Ramsuratkumar; he asked over and over again that it be kept in that particular location—*exactly* there—and lit at all times. During Yogi Ramsuratkumar's lifetime that obligation was maintained, but now, a few years after his death, the light has gone out a few times due to lazy neglect.

Speaking of the recommended practices in his school, Lee said that people are not obligated to do them. Daily meditation, study and exercise, for example, are not required, but you do the best you can with them and try to incorporate them into your life as much as possible. Beyond those Conditions—meditation, exercise, study and vegetarian diet—are the core practices: the Heart Breath, Enquiry and Assertion. Those core practices are internal practices that are more serious and absolutely necessary, while at the same time, they are not obligatory either. You have to choose to do them.

"There isn't time today to really consider what obligation to the master is, but remember that Yogi Ramsuratkumar wanted that flame to be lit always . . . ."

Lee continued to dialogue in question and answer exchanges with students throughout the rest of the seminar, giving freely and touching on many different subjects. The teachings at Le Rozet this year had been some of the richest of the summer, but now we were winding down, the chamber coming to its natural closure. After the last session and a nice dinner with everyone, Lee packed up the Sacred Bazaar. It seemed to me that our time in these precious spaces with Lee was passing like a summer storm—flashes of lightning, the distant rumble of thunder, a brief downpour, and then it's gone.

The pulse of the summer was quickened indeed, and early the next morning, we piled everything into the vans at six-thirty. Jean Pierre and Josette were busy making a picnic for Lee and the whole company, which would break the monotony of the long drive home. Lee had told them he would leave at seven. At twenty till seven the packing was done and Lee was standing outside the vans, ready to go and waiting patiently for the picnic box. At ten till seven the picnic was packed into the van, we said our goodbyes to Jean Pierre, Josette and others who would not be accompanying us, and we were off into the thick mists of the Jura Mountains and then down into the valley. Driving through the green countryside, we watched as the sun came out and burned away the fog. We were at Ferme de Jutreau in time for dinner.

Germany

Ferme de Jutreau
August 23, 2005

Back at Ferme de Jutreau, the whole Shri crew was at the ashram for a blessed three-day rest in between gigs, having arrived the night before while Lee was playing bridge. The pace of the tour had been crushing, but the energy and juice of the ashram was quickly reviving their spirits. Today they all looked bright and very happy to be in the sanctuary of the ashram.

This afternoon we were heading into La Roche Posay to the shop. Lee was standing under the maple tree waiting patiently. A few of us were waiting with him for the rest of our party. It was a beautiful afternoon, with the warm sun glinting down through the leaves. The longer we waited, the more the moments seem to drag by.

When Lee was asked if he would like someone to check on the people he was waiting for, he responded, "No. People know what time it is. They know what time I want to leave . . . People operate on their own time schedule, not on mine. Until they operate on my time, I'll always be waiting."

He paused, then went on to say, "If I die tonight, you can put on my tombstone, 'Don't be sorry. Just be on time.' Because people will be late, and then they'll be apologizing as if that makes it all okay. I would rather they either just be on time or be late and say nothing."

It seems like apologizing for being late, listing our reasons why we are late, or any other form of justifying and rationalizing our irresponsible behavior is only adding insult to the injury. From the perspective of the Work, we can actually get some value out of making a mistake or having a moment of bad behavior by burning with it inside, alone with the resounding silence of our own conscience, rather than trying to save face or pretend it's not so bad after all.

After the usual thirty minutes of chanting and a light dinner of green salad or fruit, Lee gathered with people in the salon to give his Tuesday night after dinner talk. He spoke about the body of habits and how bad habits are like being addicted to drugs. His words were poignant and carried the weight of his compassion for us as he talked about the pain that many of the sangha have as we begin to truly see our situation with more clarity, and we see the dichotomy between our years on the path and how we behave—"The difference between what I know and what I do."

He talked about an incident that occurred when a member of the sangha, who is in an important position of responsibility for Lee's work, wrote a rather vicious, negative letter to someone they were working with, who is a friend of the sangha, erroneously heaping blame and castigation on this person over a business arrangement they were involved in.

Lee said, "You have to know you're under illusions when you write a mean-spirited letter to someone and you give yourself away. When we start to see that dichotomy in ourselves, between what we know and how we act, we feel like, 'Oh my God! How could I?' There is only one way to change: a shift of context. For any kind of permanent change, there has to be a shift of context. The obvious question is: What creates a shift of context? When we want something badly enough. And nobody knows what that is until we get there. That is the only way the context will change—when the addict gets out of the addiction.

"If we try to force change, we may be relatively successful, but it will then show up in another place. Only a shift of context, and we have to want it badly enough. Just because we create suffering for others, even those we love the most, does not create a shift of context. We don't know what 'badly enough' is until we get there. One of the things that helps is to continue to see this dichotomy of our years on the Path—the difference between what I know and what I do—over and over again. Often 'what we do' doesn't leak out, doesn't show up, unless the stakes are high enough. We have to keep seeing that over and over and wincing at the masking over of the genuine wisdom of our time on the Path. We have to continue to self-observe with ruthless self-honesty."

Someone asked the question, "What is our responsibility when the teacher dies toward the sangha, the school?"

Lee generously answered, "I think in a real school the teacher lives just long enough for there to be a few students who can carry on with real integrity. Sometimes our habits are so strong that we don't stop to think, 'Is this how Lee would like it done?' Even when people are doing a task for me, their habits take over; they know how I want it done, but they do it the way *they* want it done. But if the teacher is around long enough, a few people will remember, besides those who remember anyway. If we are not clear during the guru's life, our ability to know which faction to align ourselves with will be questionable, so it comes back to our clarity of practice."

Michelle asked, "In support groups, the tendency is to ask people to work against their personality, but Orage says that struggling and striving directly against chief feature is not workable, and that you should never allow anyone to convince you to struggle against chief feature. And anyway, we don't even know what chief feature is! Are we digging too much within ourselves and each other and digging our own graves?"

Lee responded, "That's a well thought-out question. Maybe one of the hardest aspects of an intimate community like ours is to embrace and be spacious around this fact of the dichotomy between what we know and what we do, regardless of how long someone has been around the school. For beginning students, the assumption is that after ten or fifteen years in the school, a person's actions should be integrally related to what they know. After a while, new students look around at the senior students and say, 'Oh my God! I am not going to be like that!' We expect people to walk their talk, but unfortunately it's unrealistic also, because people don't . . . . Often we are hooked by something in another person that blinds us to the space or the moment, and until we figure that out, we can't get into the groove.

"So, do not struggle directly against chief feature, but what if it's already a habit, and we've already been struggling against chief feature for years. So how do we reverse the process? Simply stop doing it. There are always many vectors of energies moving at any given time, and, at the same time, there is ongoing deepening of clarity, devotion, self-observation. That is all going on at the same time. Because of the glaring nature of chief feature, it seems like that's not happening; it seems like we have no practice, when in fact after fifteen years we have built a substantial practice.

"We don't have to do anything about struggling against chief feature except to stop, because when you create a gap between the two, you see the momentum of practice and the being that you have been building all these years, and you see all these years have not been wasted because you were on the Path, in the school, in the Influence of Yogi Ramsuratkumar. You just plug into the practice vector and jump into that stream, instead of struggling against chief feature."

Lee ended his discourse and waited quietly for the coffee to arrive. The evening tea space was enriched tonight with the Shri crew as a much welcomed addition to our usual numbers of ashram residents and local householders. Faxes rolled in from the States, the phones rang and Lee took his usual coffee with the usual heavy cream and a few pieces of dark chocolate and sugared ginger. In this way, like every night, we celebrated the end of the day. Afterward, slowly everyone began to wind down, while the office and kitchen lights went out one at a time as people put down their work for the day. Finally, well after midnight, the ashram went to sleep for the night.

Ferme de Jutreau
August 24

In the early morning dark just before dawn and the meditation hour, I had this dream: I am living with Lee and others in a very high place; it almost seems like a penthouse suite, but it could have been a village, at the same time. Suddenly I can see that far off, in the distance, there are immense tidal waves—terrifying, huge walls of water—that crash down and flood a city. It is an awesome sight. The tidal waves strike a primal memory in me; the water element is out of control. I can see the water rising in the city and people fleeing; I see palm trees in the streets that are rapidly filling with water, and I know that thousands are dying. I am distraught and horrified.

I turn to look for Lee and see that a score of people are taking refuge with us; they come streaming in the front door; they are young people, and they all have elaborate, sacred tattoos. Where did they get those tattoos, I wonder? I realize with great urgency that we have got to find Lee and tell him what is going on. I go to the bedroom, where Lee is sleeping. Next to him under the covers in the bed is a good friend of his who is a very wealthy businessman, one of the few individuals left in France who comes from a lineage of nobility in Bretagne. He slumbers under the covers.

I thought, how can Lee sleep at a time like this? I call to him. Immediately he is roused, and it is as if he was awake the whole time, after all. He sits up in the bed with a presence of being that is stunning. He has both arms out, in an all-inclusive gesture that is, at the same time, not unlike Jesus on the cross. It is as if he is embracing the world. He is gorgeous, almost blindingly radiant; he is radiating light like a sun. His eyes are blazing and blue as blue can be. Benediction and grace seem to pour from him in beams of light. His power is not of this earth. He has a look of compassion and irony—an almost sardonic sense of humor mixed with an absolute beneficence—on his face. He looks at me. As I start to tell him what is going on, the power of the images are so intense that I wake up.

I was shaken by the dream and as soon as meditation was over, I relayed it to Lee. He listened attentively. Sometimes when Lee hears a dream, he will point to its subjectivity by saying, "That's a dream, alright!" This was not his response at all. Instead, he nodded his head in the affirmative as I described the dream. It wasn't what he said, but what he did not say as I felt him absorbing this dream into the mysterious digestive system of his being. When a dream makes an objective communication from the wisdom of the unconscious, its power is undeniable. The images of the dream, the tidal waves and the sublime sight of the master, the *satguru*, stayed with me all day.

Ferme de Jutreau
August 25

At lunch today Lee was telling the Shri crew about the interview he gave earlier in the summer to a French magazine. There were four people who came, one of them a man, who was the main person conducting the interview. He was very sweet and polite and quite taken by Lee. At lunch that day, he sat down across the table from Lee and said, "I can't believe I'm sitting across the table from Lee Lozowick!"

Lee responded, "I can't believe I'm Lee Lozowick!" For the second time this summer the line got a big response.

At the end of lunch, announcements were made as usual, including one about the gig at the Havana Café in Chauvigny, our second one this summer. At the gig a few weeks ago the café was besieged with sangha members, who invaded the space and moved chairs and tables around in a way that upset some of the waiters at the café. Tonight we were asked to please not move the furniture around to suit our needs.

"Oh," Lee drawled, playing off the announcement humorously, as if he had never heard of such a novel idea, "you mean we should be *invisible* in the space?"

About twenty-five people, all of them involved in one way or another with the Shri party, had dinner tonight with Claire and Volkmar in Chauvigny. Jennie, Betty and Cathy were there to help with cooking and set up for dinner. The whole evening was a bit of a déjà vu, except that tonight the sangha did not so greatly outweigh the number of local people at the gig. The tables were left in the arrangement that had been made by the café, and all was well.

The most memorable moment of the gig for me was the unexpected appearance of one of our guru's identities: "Pig Man," who we had been hearing about from Shri. Tonight Lee unveiled the divine swine to those of us who had not been on the last leg of the tour in Germany, where the band ate unimaginable amounts of pig in every conceivable form, provided in rich meals by various hosts along the way. There was so much pork consumed that at some point Lee had started referring to himself as Pig Man on stage. This identity lent itself to many jokes and ribald comments from Lee to his unsuspecting audiences. Tonight there were some guests, friends of friends or relatives of students, who came to the gig, and they were in for a treat: Pig Man made an unexpected special appearance.

"You're probably wondering why Pig Man wears these dark glasses at night," Lee began, speaking into the mike between songs. "That's so you can't see his beady little eyes staring straight into your soul. Pig Man sees it *all*!" Lee's voice was raspy, rough-edged, abrasive, gravelly. It seemed to scrape across raw nerves and leave an abrasion on ego's tender sensibilities. "You can't hide from me! You French don't fool me. I know what you're doin' behind closed doors at night when you got your pig baby there. You all are ruttin' around in the sheets!" Lee laughed, a guttural, sardonic laugh. "Yeah. We're gonna rut around some up here onstage!" He snorted, like a pig, for emphasis.

Rakini, the drummer for Shri, got to witness Pig Man throughout his evolution over the summer onstage with the band. She summed up Pig Man in her journal: "To me, Pig Man is hysterically funny. It's like some comical piece of the underworld surfacing through Lee. One minute he's the guru, and the next he's some swine burped up from hellfires to strut around our stage on his cloven hooves. He grunts and snorts and is about as first chakra as you can get. That's humor to me."

A lot of comedy is like that, something that Dante must have understood quite well, or why would he have given the title, *The Divine Comedy*, to his own mystical journey through hell? I have never forgotten something written by Aleister Crowley, a really bad boy, by the way, but then the shadow on the spiritual path has a lot to teach us, after all. He said that the only way to deal with the Devil is through mirth. This is something that Lee excels in; he brings humor and light-hearted play to the most miserable and morose moments, and thank God for it. But we've got to have a sense of humor to get the teachings that are always encoded in his ribald play with us. There may be a direct correlation between being able to laugh at oneself and one's ability to actually work at sadhana.

Later, the space turned indigo and gold when the band played a very beautiful, soulful version of "When the Levee Breaks," and I watched one of the guests, a very dignified psychoanalyst from Paris, rock and sway with obvious enjoyment and recognition. All in all, it was another multi-layered evening with Lee and his music, and no matter what form it takes, I am always glad to be there.

As soon as the gig was over Lee said his farewells and took off in his silver van to drive back to the ashram. We would be leaving very early the next morning to drive with Lee to Germany, where he would spend a week with the sangha, give a two-day seminar, and perform in local venues with the band.

Freiburg, Germany
August 27

Lee and company had arrived in Freiburg the night before to settle in for a seven-day visit with the German sangha. With two vans driving northeast from the ashram in France, when we got to the city we were met on the road by Thomas Bormann and Stephan Bischof, who we followed to the seminar space to unload all the many heavy boxes containing the "movable feast," to borrow shamelessly from Hemingway, which we call the Sacred Bazaar. It's a ritual that occurs many times over the summer as Lee travels from place to place to give teachings and the Sacred Bazaar goes with him. Converging a little later with the German sangha in Emmendingen, near Freiburg, for a reunion dinner, we finally retired before midnight.

At four-thirty this morning we were up to hit the road by five a.m. and drive in the dark for an hour with Lee and Thomas up through the mountains to a large annual *brocante* fair in a small village in the Black Forest. It was extremely cold as we disembarked from the van in the black predawn air and hit the cobbled streets of the village. A few stars still twinkled overhead as we approached the first vendors, who were just beginning to put out their wares. Wishing I had warmer clothes on, we wandered around behind Lee while he, like a bee to flowers, began his winding pathway through the labyrinth of the village, now the backdrop to countless sellers of German *brocante*.

We had accompanied Lee to this antique fair last year as well, and once again, it yielded some very interesting things for Lee's voracious appetite for that which is beautiful, unusual or somehow carrying a subtle flair or communication of the artist's sensibility. Afterward, Lee drove helter-skelter over winding mountain roads to get back to the seminar site in time to set up the Sacred Bazaar, which waited patiently for him, packed away as it was in boxes and huge wooden crates with lots of bubble wrap, newspaper and packing paper of all kinds. We arrived at eight-thirty and immediately started the ritual of unpacking, with help from several people.

At ten o'clock it was time to begin the morning session. Lee stopped setting up his tables and strode to the stage, leaving three of us to continue with the unwrapping process; when it was all done he would have about twelve long folding tables laden with *objets d'art sacré* before the first session was over.

From Pig Man, Shri, *brocante*, street fairs, ashram life and ten thousand other things, we were instantly back in the chamber of the pure expression of the dharma. Lee began to talk about the path, and alchemical transformation on the path, and I slowly realized that he was actually mapping it out yet again. He was talking about alchemical transformation, "The deeper you go in the labyrinth of the Path, the more narrow the way gets, and the more extremes of temperatures—and sensitivity to them, both hot and cold—there are."

He spoke about how we do not see ourselves, typically, for a very long time on the path. He continued, "So, our ideas of ourselves are cloudy. At some point along the way, we realize that we can only change ourselves. It is a law of human consciousness: we can only change ourselves. It's a very ugly realization, because it means we have to live with the people we live with, just the way they are. We begin to realize that we're all on the same boat. We are not smarter, or better practitioners, than anyone else."

This realization, Lee said, is shocking to us, because for a long time we think that we're practicing, we have it together, when in fact we absolutely do not. Then he began to talk about a favorite subject of many: transformational sex, its joys, attractions, illusions and pitfalls. He said, "We discover this amazing adventure—we can have sex for hours! Then what? We have sex for hours, and hours, and hours—now what? Nothing!"

A few people laughed, several of the men chuckled, some were smiling, while some of the audience, who were completely new to the paradoxical Lee Lozowick and his teaching style, were looking dazed and confused, bored or in recoil. The scattered audience, about fifty people, were a mix of Lee's students, some of them long-time and others with two, three, five or six years in, and Purna's students, plus several new faces that had been referred to the seminar by Clint; there were also two ex-students of Andrew Cohen in the group, who had come from London for the seminar. Lee began to humorously lament the fact that women can carry on sexual intimacy for hours, and hours, whereas men get bored or just worn out by this level of intense intimacy.

"And women, being the incredibly tender, vulnerable, wonderful, long-suffering creatures they are, bear with it. Because they can go for ten, twelve, fifteen hours! But women, the tender, vulnerable, wonderful, long-suffering creatures they are, are also more delicate—their nerves get fried. It's just too much energy!" Theatrically taking the man's part in the drama, Lee looked up toward the heavens, held his hands as if in thanksgiving and said, "Thank you, Lord!" People laughed again and Lee himself chuckled.

"So, the Sacred Bazaar came to me through Yogi Ramsuratkumar, and it really saved me; it gave me new faith in my teaching work, because I had become a pretty dark character. This whole thing is not my idea. It's Yogi Ramsuratkumar's gift to all of us through Purna and me. It carries a certain essential radiance that influences us in a way that is not in any way compromised by our psychology, emotions or mind. We could say that is the primary value of all art. Not just sacred art, but traditional art—painting, music, everything. It influences us no matter what we are thinking or feeling. My students' spaces are full of this art. I'm in favor of having art all over the place—on every wall, on every shelf! So, I'll be behind that table during every break . . . ."

When Lee said that the Sacred Bazaar had given him new faith in his teaching work, and that he had become a very dark character, my attention was grabbed. Never before had I heard him say this exact thing, and I have listened to ninety-five percent of Lee's talks in Europe over the years. That he had become "a dark character," seemed to me a typical Lee Lozowick self-deprecating remark, one of his sweet half-lies, half-truths—the truth of which is that Lee has, since the death of Yogi Ramsuratkumar, animated a growing cynicism and has often been bitterly sarcastic. He has borne and still bears what can only be an objective sorrow so great that it is unimaginable for those of us who live on the illusion side of the veil; from the dwelling place of awakened mind, he bears the great burden of the illusory suffering of his devotees, and of the devotees of Yogi Ramsuratkumar, as well as the suffering in the world. The suffering in the sleeping world is perhaps, in a way, easier to bear than the unnecessary suffering of those of us who have heard the teaching, who have the Grace and Benediction of the guru and the lineage of gurus in our lives. Instead, we indulge in useless emotional pain, when we could easily be living in the refuge of the dharma, the sangha and the guru, with which we have been so richly gifted in this life.

Lee's unhappiness has been a familiar ache among his closest students for a few years, although in the past two or three years, some of the clouds have seemed to part, so that once again we sometimes see our master's smile as bright as the rising sun. The Sacred Bazaar has engaged him, uplifted him, given him a new passion. Tattoos and street art are also aspects of life and art that excite and enthuse Lee; in fact, beauty, the sacred image in any form, whether it is a bronze deity, a sacred symbol tattooed on skin or a beautifully crafted cut glass decanter, a silver crucifix, or an ancient carved wood lintel, a fine painting of Yogi Ramsuratkumar, good music or poetry feeds him deeply. People, on the other hand, despite the obvious love that he pours on us, are salt on the wound. Like so many teachers before him, maybe Lee will leave this world knowing that none of his devotees ever got it? *Really* got it . . . Will he, like J. Krishnamurti, be sorrowful and downcast by this fact in his final days? Or, like Gurdjieff, maybe Lee will simply say, "Now I have left you all in a fine mess."

In the afternoon session Lee talked at length about how our habits—of all kinds—bring us down from objective mystical states and states of profound clarity and awakened mind that we find ourselves in. He said, "When you are in a state of clarity, you know that the physical realm is malleable. Reality is malleable. *And*, you have all these habits. If you are in denial about your habits—not just something like smoking, but more subtle habits, like separating the peas and carrots on your plate—then they will bring you down from higher states. Enlightenment is not a permanent state; enlightenment is a moment to moment state . . . ."

How do we sustain higher states? Practice. Lee began to talk about the Sufi practice of chivalry; for example, leaving food for the other instead of making sure we have a big portion, or a special treat, or giving the best seat nearest the teacher to another. He said, "The idea is to actively practice those principles of chivalry without compliments or the acknowledgement of others."

Lee talked about instances when his own students have been in extended mystical states; his consistent instruction to them has been to stay in ordinary life, even though, for most of them, all they wanted to do was meditate, to contemplate the nature of reality. The important thing with any intensification of transformational states, whether they are accessed through sexual experience or through other yogic practices or meditation, is that the transformation must be grounded and integrated in the body. Lee said, "The body *is* consciousness. We tend to think of the mind as consciousness, but the body is consciousness. The point of the Work is consciousness *in the body*, because what you have *here*, you have *there*. So, transformation happens here and now, not in some other time or space.

"Sex is tremendously vital, active, and we are culturally trained toward more expressiveness in sex. We think if we follow our feelings and let go, it will be better, but that's not necessarily so. At the same time, Wilhelm Reich was on to something about unleashing sexual energies . . . but unfortunately, he didn't go far enough with his work to find the Work. He died in prison in America, terribly misunderstood.

"When we get into transformational work, the definition of freedom is very different than the psychological definition of freedom. Psychological freedom is good, healthy . . . and, when we get into the intentional use of sexual energy for transformational purposes, we get into an entirely different context. The conservation of orgasm is very important in most systems. The Western Bauls also make certain distinctions here, and since I'm the *only* Western Baul teacher, I can say anything I damn well want!" Lee chuckled, then he summed up, "The body is miraculous! Bone can knit together in fifteen minutes! Diabetes can disappear . . . The body as a transformational tool is absolutely miraculous . . ."

Freiburg
August 28

During the break between sessions Lee was at the Sacred Bazaar. Many people perused the tables and picked deities or sacred objects from among the plethora of sculpted bronze and stone. The large stone deities were extraordinary this weekend, many of them having been brought from Niederweiler, Purna's ashram near Freiburg, by his students, or by Thomas Bormann, the bordello leader of the Freiburg sangha, who had been handling some of Lee's inventory for a few months, until Lee would arrive in Germany.

Even more extraordinary was the fact that so many people would have sacred art of this quality in their homes and offices as constant reminding factors of their personal relationship with Divinity. One glance at a three foot-high stone Krishna or Hanuman or Devi seems to spark a recognition of the underpinnings of blessedness and wholeness in everything we see, do, hear, speak or encounter in this world of sorrows; when we see these archetypal images, something in us is softened and uplifted, even if imperceptibly.

The tables themselves were crowded, mostly with bronze deities of all kinds, mostly Hindu but also with a healthy amount of Buddhist and Christian iconography, so that standing before them one got the sense of the multitudes, the vast panorama, the awesome display of the Divine that we call Life. Finding one's piece in all this is not always easy, because so many of the pieces speak to us, calling loudly, "Take me home, take me, take me!" It's an amazing phenomena that Lee has brought to us, and one could say that it is pagan to the core—pagan in its celebration of the multiplicity of God, but at the same time, the profundity of Hindu philosophy and understanding is such that everything—every single thing—is viewed from the nondual realization of the oneness of all.

While people come to gaze and pick up pieces to hold them, feel their weight and energy and look at the sculptor's detail, they also interact closely with Lee, who is there to answer questions of all kinds—not only about the deities, but also about their sadhana, their lives, their relationships. He is a bright light standing behind the table, beckoning, like a lighthouse for all the ships in the foggy night sea that are trying to make it to shore.

Four people who had been "training" with Clint—one of Lee's students who is a business consultant—came up to say goodbye and thank Lee for the seminar. They were leaving before the last session of the day. Clearly they were dazed and confused; many of the teachings Lee had given—principles of the tantric path—were new to them. It seemed that many things Lee had said caused them to question what they had already learned. There didn't seem to be much resonance for them at this point with Lee, but they were polite and respectful. Lee spoke with them very briefly after they said, "Clint told us to come—we are in his training program."

"Well," Lee asked with a tinge of humor in his voice and a bit of a challenge, "how's the *training* going?" His tone of voice on the word "training" was tinged with sarcasm. One of them seemed like a self-appointed spokesperson for the group. She stumbled over her answer as she said hesitantly, "Well . . . we're here." Lee smiled, and in the place of his seeming sarcasm there was a quiet, empty, serene space that seemed like compassion itself. He'd offered help; it was accepted or not, and he was ready to go on.

Lee started the last session of the seminar talking about teachers who abuse their power with students, from using violence to sexual abuse of children. He said, "Sex with children is *my* bottom line. It's just bad, no matter what . . . Yogi Ramsuratkumar was completely peaceful; he had not a violent moment in his life . . . ."

After the last session, before dinner was served and afterward, Lee and a small crew quickly packed up the Sacred Bazaar, a job that took about two and a half hours. We left the boxes and crates in the building, which would be well-secured and locked, until the morning, and jumped into the vans to caravan about an hour through green fields and vineyards to the Weinfest Kaiserstuhl, a wine festival in the countryside near a small town, Breisach, in southern Germany.

We arrived to find a large festival going strong; it had been in full swing for almost a week. Tonight Shri was one of the main musical attractions, although there were other bands and performing artists at various stages around the fair. Set up under tall, leafy trees strung with colored lights, as twilight fell upon the scene with all its food and wine vendors hawking their products, the festival took on a celebratory ambiance. Peaked white tent pavilions were set up all along the midway. People of all kinds strolled through the pathways that led crisscross here and there under the trees throughout the festival grounds. The smells of wine, beer, bratwurst and fried funnel cakes with powdered sugar filled the air.

About fifty people—the German sangha and their kids, Lee's large traveling party from France, visitors from Britain and other newcomers who had been at the seminar—crowded into the long wooden tables that were set up in front of the stage. As soon as the first chord rang out heralding the first song, people jumped up and started dancing. These were people who rarely get to see a Shri gig, and their enthusiasm quickly escalated into an ecstatic unraveling of the senses, which were pounded, rocked and gently uplifted by the music.

Within the contained alembic of rhythm and melody, people in the dancing crowd—mostly devotees, but with a healthy sprinkling of local people who braved the crush—could be seen with deliriously happy smiles on their faces, bobbing up and down or swaying to the music, since there was very little room to actually dance in the crowded area in front of the stage. The ground was uneven, and we stumbled a bit here and there on the grassy dirt beneath our feet, but we danced on, undeterred. The experience of the band was so immediate, with the dancers just beneath them, so close to the stage, that there was a direct relationship between dancers and musicians that flourished in the night air as the heat rose and we shed coats and sweaters, which were left in piles on the wooden benches or the tables. Lee himself seemed totally accessible as he prowled the stage, danced, strutted or achingly brought one song after another to life in his inimitable way.

As the evening wore on it became a love affair between the audience and Lee. With the players of Shri as the backdrop, the complex pattern of the night into which we were drawn was interwoven into the mandala of Lee's world. During the second set a man carrying a huge bundle of long stem red roses threaded his way through the crowd of dancers, offering the roses for sale. Just as he was about to move on to another area of the festival, I saw Lee call Andrea to the stage and give her some instruction. Within less than a minute Lee was standing onstage with a huge bouquet of red roses, while the rose vendor moved on empty-handed.

Lee immediately began to throw the roses out to the audience, one rose at a time, which were then caught by one person or another, to their great delight and joy.

"These probably don't even smell anymore! I bought these roses with my own money," Lee barked into the microphone, "so get back there and buy some of our fucking CDs!"

His humorous tone, which was slightly brusque and husky, seemed like a futile attempt to cover up the sweetness of his gesture—the giving of roses being such a charming way of touching people in a very immediate and heartfelt way. It was something I'd never seen Lee do before. I've seen Lee throw his own clothes and candy to the audience many times in LGB, when he used to perform "Sugar Shock," but this was very different. "Sugar Shock" was a provocative, confrontive song about addiction, co-dependency and self-destructive habits; these roses were more like missives of love, and the happy glow of the recipient of each flower made it clear that the rose had melted rigid backbones, dispelled doubts, calmed the mind and infected us all.

I remembered Yogi Ramsuratkumar giving us roses in 1993, when we sat on the porch during a private darshan with him at Sudama House. He would carefully and delicately place a full-blown rose in each cupped palm, gazing tenderly into our eyes. It was an exquisite moment of receiving his blessing; the hue and timbre of this intimacy was overwhelming. As the rose throwing proceeded, I was reminded of this—like Father, like Son—and I knew that the reception of each rose carried with it a similar gift of intimate connection and the full force of the guru's Blessing Power.

Freiburg
August 29

With the seminar over, we were now fully into *brocante* hunting and, at night, Shri time and space; Lee was back on the tour with the band. Later tonight Shri would play at Le Caf' Conc', a little blues club just over the border in France. But something else big was happening: earlier in the day someone had given Lee just the bare bones of a report of a disaster in New Orleans associated with Hurricane Katrina.

As soon as the Shri crew arrived at the Kostkas' house, where about fifty people were having dinner with the guru, Steve Ball immediately came over to give Lee a full report of what was happening in New Orleans.

"It's a level four hurricane, and the sea surge was so great that the Mississippi River levee broke at Jackson Square. They are evacuating the whole city. A million people are left homeless. New Orleans is under ten feet of water. The city is devastated. Thousands of people are dead, mostly in the slums—they don't know how many yet. It's the biggest migration of people in the U.S. since the Civil War. There is no help coming from the federal government. People are still stranded on rooftops . . ."

It was stunning news. It was heartbreaking news. It felt to me like it was happening to our own families, to ourselves. Hurricane Katrina carried the energy of a ten-megaton nuclear bomb, exploding every twenty minutes, but it wasn't the hurricane that caused the greatest damage; it was when the levee broke at Lake Pontchartrain, and the mighty Mississippi River came rolling into the city in thirty-five foot high tidal waves, that the city was crushed and brought to its knees. That, coupled with the appalling lack of support from the President and federal agencies, made the situation unbearable.

New Orleans! A city from my childhood, where my grandfather grew up in the French Quarter almost a century ago; a city I loved dearly, where I had spent time quite often twenty-five years ago, though I hadn't been there since; a place of so much dark and light, with a unique alchemy and history and, ultimately, so much soul. A great sorrow settled in on my heart. We live in dark and murky times, and this seemed to carry with it the dread knowledge that we would live through even greater sorrows and holocausts—or not live through them.

Indeed, the news carried profound implications of the era in which we live. Lee keeps saying to us that there is more devastation of this kind coming, and soon. It seems a dark specter hovers across the entire world, with human beings, the supposed highest life form on Earth, held in thrall under its spell. The universe works on the harmonious interplay of dark and light forces, and in these times, it seems that darkness is taking over on our beautiful planet. At the same time that we seem in thrall to dark forces, human beings have become a pestilence on the Earth. The Earth itself, the water element, the air element, are profoundly disturbed. Within eight months there were the tsunamis in India and now the tidal waves in Louisiana.

In fact, the hurricanes and tsunamis seem to be the forces of light at play, the impartial activity of the conscious planetary being, which we call "the Earth," to bring balance in the face of the human horrors that are perpetuated daily. War reigns supreme in anguished spreading pockets across the globe, while corruption is the name of the game for politicians and corporate profiteers who seem to merely laugh at the suffering of the multitudes. The arrogance, greed, vanity and drive for power has reached such proportions that it is difficult not to simply label it "evil."

We are spinning down through the halls of time, having lost our connection to the Earth, the cosmos, the ancestors and future generations. The burden of seeing and feeling—with any degree of clarity—the reality of the situation is enough to make us weep. For those who choose the path of spiritual practice rather than social action, it is our practice that is both our refuge and the way in which we can make a difference. In the face of the tremendous suffering in southern Louisiana, there was nothing to do but let our tears, both visible and invisible, be the liquid fire, the surging holy water that breaks the levee of the heart and inundates the landscape within. We suffer objective sorrows to soak our prayers with need, until God hears our pleas.

Back in Emmendingen for dinner at the Kostkas' house with the whole group, Ann and I stayed home with one of the children for the evening, and so we said goodbye to Lee, the Shri crew and the revelers who accompanied him to Le Caf' Conc' for another facet of our lives with Lee: the living God blues, experienced in its unique form, at a gig with Shri.

Freiburg
August 30

Everyone was abuzz about the gig the night before at Le Caf' Conc' in France; it seemed that it was one of the highlights of the summer tour so far. Different people gave different reports. Some said the music and the chamber were sublime; others said it was underworldly. Everyone agreed on one thing: it was great. The music and Lee's antics onstage had provided a strong release for the passion that was stirred up over the flooding in New Orleans.

At one point Lee had held the mike in hand and exhorted the audience, "God created the world in seven days. He made some beautiful things. On the seventh day, he created pussy. But pussy ain't love!" Later he had told his audience, "Tattoos are my religion. They're sacred to me, so don't fuck with anyone who has tattoos!" Tonight Shri would be playing there again, and Lee was luxuriant in his enjoyment of the little club—"Who would ever think there would be a great little blues club out in the middle of nowhere in France like that? They've had all kinds of blues acts there; the owner really loves the blues . . . they were crazy about Shri!"—and enthusiastically looking forward to going back.

It is our job to celebrate the advent of the guru, the teaching and the sangha in our lives, no matter what is happening in the world around us. Lee's consistent instruction to us, in the face of tragedies and the heartbreak of life on Earth, also described as "Crushed by Love," is to carry on, full speed ahead. And so, carrying an acute awareness of the suffereing in New Orleans in our hearts, on this particular morning we drove the two vans up through the mountains into the Black Forest for our annual picnic at the mountain retreat home of Lee's students, Stephan and Gesine.

Pork chops, vursts and chickens sizzled on the grill, tended by Claus. The buffet table was laden with a cornucopia of goodness: a fresh and lively salad of mixed greens, a salad of fava beans and red peppers, just-baked pretzels, several kinds of spicy or sweet mustard, an array of cold drinks and spring water . . . The options seemed endless. Lee served a small glass of wine at his table as well, then passed the bottles on to everyone else to serve themselves.

The sun was just peaking over the mountains, lighting up the thick, lush forest that was only twenty feet away from our picnic tables outside the house, when a light dessert and coffee was served. Afterward everyone retreated inside the house to the living room, where several musicians in the German sangha treated Lee and company to a concert. Almost all of them classically trained, the musicians took turns offering their music—violin, flute, guitar and accordion. The music brought tears to my eyes. The sensitivity and soul they brought to the music was disarming. The clarinet delighted us with three Romanian pieces, the last one a Jewish klezmer piece, full of ragged, sharp notes, whimsical or piercing, like shards of longing, seeking the broken vessel of what has been lost—the love of the ages.

Like all traditional Jewish music, the melody was shot through with joy and sorrow, the reflection of a diaspora, strangely akin to gypsy music only livelier and less brooding. Most of the selections the musicians played were from the European equivalent of the blues; that is, it was gypsy music, and the folk music of old Europe, haunting or heartbreaking Celtic melodies from Ireland and Bretagne. It seems that it has always been the music of the outcasts—the homeless, those who have been uprooted and displaced, who have nothing and endure the oppression, prejudice, and violent bigotry of those who have everything—who produce the music of the greatest longing. It's that inexplicable link between objective sorrow, suffering, loss and creativity that has haunted artists down through the ages—the poets and writers, the sculptors and painters, the musicians and dancers. It's the very groundlessness and vulnerability and heartbreak of that experience that provokes the human spirit to discover "the joy in the cracks between my sorrows," to quote a Lee Lozowick lyric.

All too soon the music was over. Lee sat on the couch, not having moved once since the performance began, as everyone gathered around on the floor or on a few scattered chairs throughout the room. He began to talk about why he had disbanded the gospel choir project, which he had given to the German sangha four years before and to which people had become very attached. The music that was presented today seemed to say, "The first musical project didn't work—we are ready for more."

Responding to this message that was so strong in the air, Lee said, "It's not that the gospel choir didn't work at all, but there was too much conflict and turmoil, and even more importantly, the music was closer to the Christian camp, the Sunday morning goin' to church music, and that is *not* gospel! Your choice of songs to perform was 180 degrees from what I wanted, and that was a sign to me that as a configuration, people weren't getting the context.

Lee said candidly that he wasn't happy with the way certain people he had asked to be soloists were not being given the front role in the group. Finally, the decision to make the group all women was "categorically antagonistic to any conceivable vision that I had for the group." Lee then criticized one of the men for scene-stealing and being out for himself, but nonetheless, he should not have been excluded from the choir. In general, there was far too much disagreement and bickering in the group.

Lee continued to give very specific feedback to individual students, then said, "It's very clear that the German sangha should have some kind of musical project, but it's not clear *what* yet. When it is clear to me, you'll be the first to know. The music and skill is here, and the problems with the last project will not be there with the next project."

Lee began to talk about the expatriot African Americans he's seen who lead white European gospel choirs and tour around the Continent, singing "Christian camp music." Once again, Lee emphatically stated that this was not the kind of music he wanted for the original project. He continued, "I wanted the deep South, crushed-by-love kind of music that is sung from a place that is completely crushed by love of God; it's sung from a confession of love of God. The mood is a testimony to suffering and the ability to survive in unimaginable suffering. Obviously I could have told you this ahead of time, but the way I work is I don't try to create something artificial, and you weren't coming to it on your own.

"I don't know what the next project will be, and the last project wasn't good enough to keep it going, but after hearing the music today, clearly there is the inspiration to line up with something else. When I do, you'll be the first to hear about it, and I'll be more specific about what I want."

Lee talked about the difference between LGB, his first band, which was a rock & roll band that performed and recorded fourteen CDs from 1987 till 1999, and his current blues band, Shri. He said, "Shri is not more spiritually advanced than LGB, but a different stand was taken at the beginning, and the stand was for it to be *my* band. It stuns me, the decision to make the gospel group all women! Instead of changing the original vision, you find other men!

"So, when we start another project, I will have much more personal involvement. Next year we're doing a two week tour with the Lee Lozowick Band and the Denise Allen Band as a touring review . . . with European musicians. Next year we'll keep the tour to France, but if the experiment works . . . The first shot is an experiment, and if the internal feedback I get is a green light, then the experiment expands. Obviously the logistics are difficult, and obviously I have to give a seminar once in a while, but we'll figure out how to expand the Lee Lozowick Band and the Denise Allen Band into Germany. Essentially it's now French musicians in my band, but hearing the music today, and people's talent, adds dimension to it. So I want to see something continue, but I don't know what yet.

"You know, there are always one or two people in a crowd who get it, and that's who you play for. At our gig in Bretagne this year the crowd was crazy—like a sea of noise! Still, there's one or two people in every audience who *really* gets it, and that's who you play for. They get that something is happening that is extremely rare in the field of performing arts. So when we come up with another project, that has to be the context. There has to be a certain authenticity to what you're presenting, even if what you're presenting is different than all the other gospel groups—if it's gospel, and it might be or not, I have no idea . . . .

"The next project will go to the next level—where and when, we don't know, but obviously hearing the music today, my enthusiasm is activated and reinforced. So keep practicing! I want to find a way to use the voices, so it won't be a strictly instrumental project."

Lee continued, "Once in a talk in California a man came up afterward and said that he'd been following my work for twenty-five years, reading all my early works, and the written body of my work had been the most inspiring thing in his life all those years! He didn't want to come to the ashram, he didn't want to become a student, but he was hooked on to the teat and drinking the milk. He didn't even need to know the name of mother—he was just feeding.

"A single concert can change someone's life. A single guitar riff can change someone's life—that's what we do all this for. We provide something essential and real at a time when it's needed, but if you *think* that going on stage, then you will fail miserably. You take whatever talent you have—music, painting, dancing, writing—and give everything you have to the Work. Forget the details, and every once in a while you hit it. When your intellect is involved and you're trying to create something, you set the intention and establish context, and then you forget everything. It's the same with all artistic projects . . . . That's the way you create magic. Go out and do it!"

A mother with two children asked a question about the difficulty of not having the time to practice. Lee answered, "The Heart Breath is a practice that takes no time; sometimes people miss that. The practices you do in the midst of whatever you are doing—when cooking, eating, being with the kids—can be done without having to alter anything or create a 'spiritual space.' There should *never* be a consideration of not having enough time to practice for anyone!"

One of Andrew Cohen's ex-students asked a question about their former teacher and abuses of power. Lee commented, "I still believe in Andrew. I wish he would return to who he was in the early days, before he had power—he was lighting people on fire!"

Finally, near the end of this juicy talk, Annette asked Lee how to get new people to participate in the Freiburg bordello. Immediately Lee offered the Freiburg sangha the opportunity to have an invocational dinner once a month, to which interested friends and acquaintances could be invited.

"Twenty people or less," Lee elucidated, "in a highly defined space. The food should be finely prepared, all the courses are served, it takes two or three hours, maybe a toast, not necessarily with wine. And when it's over, you kind of lounge around and carry on a social conversation. Invite guests. And always have products to sell . . . books, CDs.

"We're trying to create an invocational space to draw the regard of the Universe—or God—to us. We are trying to discover an objective mood of prayer. 'An invocational dinner or space,' we call it, because what we are trying to do is create a space of prayer by attention to detail and to hosting others based on that intention. On the other hand, tension about doing everything properly can crush the space. You'll have to formally close the space and suggest it's time to move on because people will want to stay all night.

"If people want to know more, or participate more, you pace them. 'Oh, no need to rush . . .' And eventually they might come to bordello. You have to be prepared to answer the question, 'Is this a sect?' without justifying or defending. You always prepare the food to have an invocational mood, even the salad. For example, there should be no dirt or insects in the salad. The meal is prepared with courses, and one course leads to the next, everything is plated and served—that's how you create a certain formality."

After a substantial, elaborate Thai feast prepared by the women in the Freiburg bordello with Annette serving as head cook, later that night we accompanied Lee to Le Caf' Conc', the small but hoppin' blues club in Einsisheim, France where the band had played the night before. Lee was visibly excited as we walked into the place. At the door Lee stopped to get a report from Jim Capellini, who was at the CD stand. It seemed they had sold out tickets for the gig tonight—even more than last night. This brought a big smile from Lee.

"That'll be cool!" he said. "It'll be just like when we played in Mississippi, except we'll be white instead of black." It was one of those out-of-time, enigmatic remarks that Lee makes every now and then that, if we catch them, remind us that there is always more going on than meets the eye. We are living in a continuum of incarnation, in the field of space and time, and we have been together before. Who knows? Lee could have been an old-time blues player in Mississippi a hundred years ago. What was it he said recently about how highly evolved beings incarnate wherever they can most relieve suffering at any given time? Sure enough, as we walked into the tiny space of the club it was grimy, smoky, sweaty, hot and dark—sort of the French equivalent of a juke joint, like the kind you find in Mississippi and Louisiana, and in south Arkansas where I grew up. It's just the kind of place that often brings out the best in Shri.

My heart was aching deeply for the people of southern Lousiana and for the city itself. I felt my whole organism had been taken over by the impulse to pray. At one point, as we sat at a table in the back of the bar drinking juice with Lee before the band started their first set, Ann asked Lee, "With what is happening in New Orleans—is it possible to do the Heart Breath too much?"

Lee's answer was a simple "No." Her question touched me very deeply, because it gave me some insight into the impact the tragedy of southern Louisiana was having on others.

My all-time favorite cover tune over the years that Shri has played consistently has been "When the Levee Breaks," written by Memphis

Minnie and made famous by Led Zeppelin. Traveling on vacations with my family as a child to the Gulf of Mexico, I have vivid memories of crossing the Mississippi River many times; it was an entity of myth and real meaning—the river was the source of life. The south Arkansas, Louisiana and western Mississippi cotton fields and rural gardens were nurtured by the river and its tributaries. People lived off the fish they caught from its waters. Crops and other goods floated on barges down the river to be sold at distant ports. The river was the source of life, but it was also the source of death for the poor people who lived in shanties for miles in the delta country around its banks. The levee itself was a sentient being; it was either strong and resilient, like people, or it broke under duress when the surge of water was so great that it couldn't hold—also a lot like people.

Memphis Minnie captured all this and more in her powerful song about suffering, using the Mississippi River levee as both a literal reality, a physical fact, and as a metaphor for life, sorrow, impermanence and longing: "If the levee breaks, we got no place to go / Mean ol' levee, cause me to weep and moan, / Mean ol' levee, cause me to weep and moan, / Mean ol' levee, cause me to lose my happy home." Memphis Minnie goes on to warn us, "Cryin' won't help you, prayin' won't do you no good."

What does she mean by this? Maybe what she means is that we are helpless and hopeless in the face of cosmic and terrestrial forces, whether we call them karma, fate, nature, impermanence, life and death or God. None of our efforts can keep the levee from breaking. Even our subjective prayers, the supplications we make for our own survival and well-being, cannot save us. All we can do is surrender to that which is beyond the play of opposites, beyond birth and death. All we can do is to turn toward that which is changeless, pristine, transcendent. And that is the nature of objective prayer.

I'd been thinking about it a lot with the levee actually breaking in New Orleans. I even lobbied a little with some band members for "Levee" to be played, but to no avail. They had played the song at this bar the night before, and it was not going to be on the set list for tonight. Brooding over my disappointment that "Levee" wouldn't be played that night, I wondered at my attachment. A part of it was sentimental, perhaps, and yet . . . and yet, "Levee" is one of those rare songs that sweeps the listener along, toward objective prayer. If we are willing at all, we will be taken there. I thought about how "Levee" never fails to touch the tender place of deep sorrow and the truth of impermanence; it never fails to reveal and celebrate the marrow of life, and in this way prayer is invoked. It is no longer a subjective cry for the personality that goes through birth and death, but a cry of longing, a cry of the immortal being for that which is eternal, changeless, and incorruptible.

Lights gleamed off the chrome of the Harley Davidson frame suspended over the bar and the full regalia Harley that was parked on top of the bar. The band perched on the multi-tiered stage in the tiny club, whose walls were plastered with signed photos of blues acts from the States that had performed there . . . Thirty members of the sangha mingled with the local crowd to make about a hundred people who remained riveted to the band for the three hour gig. People were packed together in the tiny space of the club, taking whatever bit of room could be found for dancing. As the night wore on, the longer they played the hotter it got, and the more fluid the boundaries became between individual people.

The music rolled along like a sea at high tide, and I floated in its floodwaters, reflecting on all this. Suddenly I heard Deborah put in an ad lib verse to "Left My Baby Standing," a Shri cover tune, originally written by Fred McDowell. It was one of the verses from "Levee." I was dancing, or swaying might be a better word, since the tiny space was packed with people who stood pressed up against each other and the band on their small stage. I noticed a local photographer, sitting at the curved bar. He was leaning into the stage, which was less than five feet away from him, and clicking photo after photo, obviously focusing in on Lee.

"Left My Baby Standing" churned through me, vibrant and sonorous with chords that changed our bodies into objective states of feeling. Tears started flowing. I noticed other people were crying. When he took the mike, Lee sang some "Levee" stanzas as well, and the prayer was made complete. All considerations and attachments were subsumed as we danced together, suspended in the music, raw and empty, moved at the cellular level, bones and joints enraptured somehow with rhythm in this steamy hot tiny place, jostled close together with the sangha and the locals who also danced beside and around us, and Lee, burning like an archangel just there on the stage, close enough to touch, everyone in their own way emptied into the whole.

Worlds connected and collided, miles were breached, separation ceased to exist, and for a brief moment, we were all lifted up into one place beyond space and time. Everything came back into focus as sorrow and loss and anger and frustration and helplessness and ruin and love and compassion and heartbreak melted into a flawless, spontaneous and fiery breathing of the world into the heart and back out again. In those moments everything was made clearer, purified, through the medium of the music, and all things were suddenly made possible.

Freiburg
August 31

After breakfast at the Kostka's house with the sangha, the morning was spent in Freiburg with Lee and Thomas, checking out some antique shops in the old downtown area. We skipped lunch because Lee and several of his students were invited at two p.m. to the home of Stephan and Katrina for coffee and dessert. Sitting at the formal table setting that had been arranged, as soon as he had wolfed down his cake, Lee began to talk about his new passion: graffiti art. Once again, he commented that he believed graffiti art would be the next art craze of the future.

He said humorously, "Purna is having a conversation with graffiti artists in Freiburg. My idea of a conversation is, 'Where is the art? How much is it? Give me twenty!' " He laughed.

The conversation wound around to the rather hazy plans to build a new ashram on the community's property in the high desert in central Arizona. The ashram already has a name—Triveni Ashram—but we don't have the money for such a large and daunting project. Lee talked about the prediction from a friend, Starr, who is a well-known psychic, who had said that an unexpected source of money would show up in 2006, making it possible to start building sooner than Lee expected.

"She can be pretty accurate," Lee conceded.

Discussions about the almost mythical Triveni Ashram are always poignant, and tend to leave one with a feeling of groundlessness. At the same time, we have no idea where the money for such a major project will come from; we have never been a wealthy community, like many of our friends in the "spiritual world." It seems like the clock is ticking on this project that is so crucial to Lee's work; at sixty-one, Lee has said that he does not want to live to a very ripe old age, like ninety. He has intimated that there are some twenty-odd years left in his sojourn on earth, a comment that is always very sobering to his students. But then, Yogi Ramsuratkumar did not have his ashram in Tiruvannamalai until the last eight years of his life, when it was under construction, and he didn't live on the property until the last six or eight months of his life.

The conversation turned to the deity Brahma, which Stephan and Katrina had gotten through the Sacred Bazaar and now graced the room in which we were sitting. Lee was explaining that Brahma is almost always depicted with three heads, and that he is the one of the three deities that make up Trimurti—Brahma, Vishnu and Shiva. Of these three, Brahma is rarely worshipped in India these days; his temples have all crumbled down.

"People don't like the Absolute," Lee explained, "they like the relative." He laughed the enigmatic, rather derisive laugh so characteristic of him. "People like Shiva and Vishnu, Lakshmi, deities like that. Brahma is pure Context."

Katrina said, "I though he was angry," looking at the rather large stone sculpture of Brahma.

"No, he's not angry—he's just unsentimental!" Lee responded.

Katrina asked a question about the teaching Lee gave at the seminar a few days before; she was wondering how, since we can't change ourselves, but we must change our context, this can be done.

"It's just one of those paradoxes," Lee said. "When you change from one character to another, it is a change of context. Context changes at the same time that you decide the old context is unacceptable. E.J. said he got into the Work because he had nothing else to live for. He had *everything*—kids, family, career, friends—but he's not speaking from a conventional point of view. It's also instructive that when his context changed, he didn't lose all that."

Katrina asked, "The outside doesn't change, but inside there's a change?'

"Right," Lee responded. "Arnaud was a big TV star in France before he started teaching. He chose to give up a very big career—he could have had tons of money, fame. His first ashram was only big enough for nine people. Now about one hundred people come to his ashram every week; it's a big chateau, with lots of land on a mountain. When he was reconstructing the ashram, Arnaud refused to use labor from other villages—they did it all with local people. He went in and met the mayor of the village—he does things that way. We don't! Every time I do something he shakes his head in disbelief!"

We laughed at this, knowing how we do things in the Hohm Community—creating something out of nothing, working on a shoe-string budget, attempting to learn the essential art of "Beggary," which our master exemplifies for us daily.

Lee continued to praise Arnaud, saying, "He does a lot of

interviews, is very highly respected. He stands for the integrity of the Path . . ." Changing the subject, Lee perked up, encouraging everyone to have more cake and coffee. "The cake was great! There's more. We can always make more coffee. Don't worry about dinner—eat more cake and then put dinner on top of it, then dance it all off!"

Everyone laughed, but I didn't see anyone take Lee up on the invitation. He often says that we need to be in control of our bodies, rather than letting the body control us. It's usually our comfort level, one way or another, that dictates our relationship to food, and he is suggesting that we learn to deal with different kinds of discomfort, for example, either not eating for long periods of time, or eating more than is comfortable for us. Plus, the last gig in the Freiburg area was scheduled for that night.

Lee began to praise the gig at Le Caf' Conc' last night. "What a great club! A blues club like that, out in the middle of nowhere! And what a stage! I haven't seen anything like that anywhere. I really loved it from the minute I first walked in . . . . everybody dances and gets ecstatic, then the pickpockets have a good day!"

Katrina asked Lee questions about the pre-school program she runs out of their home. After answering a few of her more practical questions, he said, "I think it's important for children to learn how to learn. They learn in their own way, at all different speeds. They learn to love learning, and that lasts a lifetime. Children absorb information even when it doesn't seem like they're doing anything. So, it's important not to make a lot of assumptions based on what the child is looking like . . . Children's unconscious is closer to the surface than adults," which makes children particularly sensitive and fluid in how they learn. They are not bound by the rigid concepts that bind adults, making creativity and learning a whole different game.

Lee used one of his daughters as an example: in the home school program on the ashram, she didn't want to do anything but art and play. She refused to learn math and English, reading and such. The people who were teaching the children at the time were worried about her, but Lee kept saying, leave her alone. Trust her process. Then, when she decided to go to public school at age thirteen, after a very short adjustment period, she starting making A's in all her subjects.

Lee continued, "You have to trust in the child's innate brilliance. If the parents speak well and enjoy art and music, the children will too, even if it doesn't show up till they're older. So, role modeling is very important. People are so desperately terrified of children in America, they are drugging all the kids. People can't bear any expression of life that is outside their control. America is supposed to be creative, but it is the land of absolute conformity. The slightest deviation is upsetting to people. It is shocking, the amount of drugs for children; shocking how many are on prosac."

We talked about how there has been a disturbing rash of teenagers and young adults who have committed suicide as a result of their use of mood elevators like Prosac. Lee continued on the evils of Prosac, the use of which is epidemic: "Watch a couple of generations of kids grow up—what you see scares you."

Someone commented that we had heard that the water supply in London and other British cities is full of Prosac. Lee joked, "Wait till the water is full of Viagra!" Everyone laughed. It was comic relief in the midst of the seriousness of the conversation. "Then we'll really be in trouble! And now, there's a women's version!"

The discussion ranged toward the African spokesperson Malidoma Some, who was raised by Jesuit priests but at age nineteen found his way back to his village. The elders told him he couldn't be part of the village unless he became part of the tribe in the telepathic, intimate bond of tribal people; because of his Western upbringing and education, he was dissonant to the tribe. Devastated, he asked them what he could do, and they said that the only way to become part of the tribe was to go through the boy's rite of passage, the initiation into manhood. This rite of passage was a dangerous feat, a confrontation with death, undertaken usually between the ages of twelve and fourteen; Malidoma was far too old, and it increased the risk of death in the process, but he did it and made it through. The elders eventually sent him to the First World to carry the message of the importance of tribal life, rites of passage, the bond of communal relationships and many other principles of living in harmony with the Earth.

After this discussion, when asked how one earns such a task from a karmic perspective, Lee said, "Everybody gets the challenge that they have earned in previous lives—they don't get the challenge they haven't earned."

Before everyone took off for the gig that night in Villingen, we drove back to Emmendingen, parked the van, then walked across the village to a café in another part of town. Over hot *milch café* and luscious chocolates (the best in town, according to Thomas), Thomas took a local newspaper from a nearby table and showed us the photographs of New Orleans in flood. He translated some of the German text for us. It was impossible not to spend the next hour talking about New Orleans and the horror of the situation in the States, with the President withholding aid to a million homeless people. We were outraged, as many people back in the States must have been as well. It was unimaginable that we would abandon our own people, but it was happening. It's clear that the United States doesn't have to be brought down by terrorist attacks or war; we are doing it to ourselves.

Thomas began to talk about the situation of nuclear energy and the scarcity of water and the fierce competition over other natural resources in Europe. Politics in Europe aren't really any better than they are in the States, but the culture itself is hundreds and hundreds of years old, which gives the common people a profound rootedness in the soil of their local region. This is a very healthy situation in terms of self-sufficiency and basic sanity within the culture. This is especially true in rural areas such as in France, where local markets are actually supplied by local growers, small farms and vineyards, cheese and sausage makers, bakers and vintners. These are arts that have endured for two thousand years or more in Europe, and make up the texture of daily life, lending integrity, wholesomeness and authenticity to the quality of life.

It was a sobering conversation that reflected so powerfully what was happening in the States. We walked back across the village to the houses where we were staying. As soon as we arrived, Lee left with a number of companions for the Shri performance.

Freiburg
September 1

Another hearty and delicious brunch was served up by the Freiburg kitchen crew, after which Lee answered questions with the sangha gathered around him in the Kostka's tiny living room where most of our meals were being held. About thirty-five people packed into the room, with another ten or more listening from the kitchen, while others were busy with various tasks necessary to keep the logistics of hosting Lee—and the large group of devotees that had gathered to be with him during this week—running smoothly.

Lee spoke about how the bottom line is always about the three core practices—the Heart Breath, Enquiry and Assertion—and the Conditions: meditation, exercise, diet and study. Everyone has to find their own way through all this, which could be called Practice, and there is always the problem of those people who police others; there will always be those who are rigid and orthodox about how we show up.

Lee said, "People shift context one person at a time. Sometimes we're in a space together and everyone can feel the brightness of the space, but real shifts happen one at a time. Often when one person out of thirty shifts, it gets lost in the flow of the action, and we don't see it."

In response to a question about how to find closure for such an intense experience as the Shri tour, which was coming to an end, Lee said, "Closure to the tour is actually about winding down the activity, not winding down what has been opened. To actually have closure is not to close down what has been opened internally. Don't allow the internal shift to close down. It's the same in relationship. Maybe this is a man's viewpoint—if two people are confident in their love for each other and their lives are intertwined, it should be enough now and then to meet with the eyes, and on that meeting, recognize the love we share for each other, and that's enough. We shouldn't need constant reinforcement.

"So we're on tour together in tremendous intimacy, and we get home and we think the only way to keep that alive is to keep the circumstance going, and that is categorically untrue. The form changes, dramatically, but that doesn't change the internal connection. Sometimes you're touchy, you're tired—it doesn't mean anything to the configuration or the project. It passes, like indigestion."

In the past few months several people in the sangha had expressed a concern about the gap between their inner lives and their actions in the world, and therefore questioned their own sadhana. In fact this consideration had become a recurring theme over the summer, as many had spoken passionately about their disappointment in themselves to act in a way that reflects what they know to be true. In answer to a question in this regard, Lee said, "Then you know what your task is: to bring what you know into your life. The more clearly you see how big the gap is, the more momentum you will have toward changing."

A young woman, who had talked to Lee the last day of the seminar about her emotionally abusive husband, started the story up again. Lee used the question as a jumping-off point to make a teaching about his view of objective relationship between partners or mates, in which the overall mood has a certain delicacy, dignity and nobility that makes a striking contrast to the casual, entangled relationships of mutual need, falsehood, grasping, betrayal and possessive ownership that characterize Western society. Of course the principle he went on to elucidate has implications for relationships with children and close friends as well as partners, mates, husbands and wives.

Lee said, "My inner childhood response has no reference point for this kind of abuse and disturbance. In my family, the waters were calm and serene. So when I hear something like that, I have a reaction; I don't understand it. The way I deal with conflict in my own relationships is: if there's a problem and it's *my* problem, I work on my part of it; if it's my partner's problem, I just take a deep breath and try to bear it. I don't ever want to talk. I want my partner to understand and to have a kind of telepathic understanding between us. And then what do we talk about? Movies or something. I do everything I can to not get into it, and I avoid conflict.

"Take responsibility for your part in it—manage your own part—and don't expect your partner to change what they can't change."

Helma asked, "How do you develop that telepathic understanding?"

Lee responded, "To develop the telepathic understanding takes basic friendship—time and affection builds that kind of bond. A lot of people have it from the beginning, but allow ordinary life struggles to obscure it. Struggles over child raising and sex and one another's families and so on, but you never allow all that to be more important than this telepathic communion with your partner.

"But, we allow all the petty details to interfere with communion, when the love we feel for each other is tacit. When I feel moved to buy somebody a gift, I like to just buy it and bring it home. That love gets reinforced in a spontaneous and non-formulaic way. All the expectations and comments and demands—'It's my birthday'—eats away at our desire to want to bring little gifts, to take our mates to nice restaurants. We don't have to demand it; it will come spontaneously. The reinforcement of love will come, but not necessarily on our anniversary or when we think we want it.

"We live in inauthentic times. Things are bad in America. There is a large, dynamic alternative culture, which is great in mood, but they have no power. The power rests in the hands of those who want no authenticity and complete domination and control. Things are moving in a very unpleasant direction . . . the opposite direction of the way those who don't want to see the Declaration of Independence eroded away." Lee concluded, "We have to keep plugging away and don't give in to the inauthentic life."

As easily as these spaces spring to life—where students can ask Lee questions and receive sometimes unexpected answers that flow into spontaneous teachings much broader and deeper than their original question implied—they just as easily dissolve into the movement that creates the next space with Lee. Unceremoniously, Lee was up and out of there and walking fast toward the van.

Tonight Lee and all of the Hohm Community sangha members who were gathered together this week were hosted by Purna's students at their ashram in Niederweiler, about thirty minutes away from Freiburg, for a feast and evening program, which would end with Lee giving a talk to the combined sanghas.

The meal was a feast indeed, with a wide array of grilled meats and just as many choices of salads and vegetables, capped off with ice cream for dessert. Afterward, we gathered in their spacious, large living room where we watched Ed Bradley interview Bob Dylan for the American television news program, "60 Minutes," gleaned from the internet and reformatted for a large screen TV.

One of Lee's heros, Bob Dylan is not just a legend and a myth, but a real flesh and blood inspiration for many people in the sangha—as an artist, as a visionary, even as a mystic, and as a human being. Toward the end of this fabulous interview, in which the news journalist was asking Dylan questions about his life based on his recent book, *Chronicles*, the journalist asked Dylan why he was still out there playing music after forty-three years. Earlier Dylan had made a statement about his sense of destiny. Now he responded, "It goes back to the destiny thing. I made a bargain with it a long time ago, and I'm holding up my end of it."

"Who did you make the bargain with?" Ed Bradley asked.

"With the Commander in Chief . . ." Dylan answered with an inscrutable gleam in his eye, "in this world and in the world we can't see."

Kindred spirits with those on the spiritual path, Dylan was following the kind of "orders" from the "Commander in Chief" that Lee has spoken of, using very similar language, countless times, when he says things like, "I get my orders for the day from Yogi Ramsuratkumar."

Fired up by the interview, in Lee's talk he drew parallels between many comments made by Dylan and sadhana on the spiritual path: "When we set out on the Path, we are fulfilling a destiny. We have to uphold our end of it; really, in a way, it doesn't matter if the teacher holds up his end or not. It's not like things went well in Dylan's life; he went through a painful divorce and tremendous personal upheaval. A lot of people, when tragedy strikes, say, 'Why did this happen to me?' instead of just going on. So for us, there is a certain expectation of trustworthiness; each of us has a responsibility to uphold our end of the deal. Often, we feel if the guru is not meeting his responsibility, why should we meet ours? But that's not the agreement we make when we enter on the Path. Our part is to live up to our destiny.

"When Dylan was asked if he could still write songs like, 'It's Alright, Ma,' 'Hard Rain's Gonna Fall,' and others songs from his early years as a songwriter, he said, 'No.' It's also a parallel to practice, because in the beginning we have a wild enthusiasm for practice."

Dylan qualified his answer of "no" by saying, "But now I can do *other* things . . ." It was an enigmatic comment from an inscrutable character, but if we take the parallels Lee was drawing to *sadhana*, the principle holds true: although some things pass away over time on the path—in fact all things *must* change—they are replaced by other gifts of the spirit. In this vein Lee shared the story of visiting with Richard Moss several years ago: one of the things they had in common was that both had been to India in the seventies, when they were younger men, and they did things, like swimming in the Ganges, that they would never do now.

Lee continued, "So we get on the Path, willing to make tremendous sacrifices, and after thirty years we get a lot more conservative, but only in certain ways. I continue to suggest that people take risks.

"So, as you go farther in sadhana, it's like you've been on the Path for hundreds of lifetimes, and you find yourself in a maze where the options get to be less and less . . . . Again, community is not the point, but one of the Work elements of our environment is community. The Work will provide you with little opportunities to stay stretched . . . . Or, maybe we'll get sick—another area in which we come to the crossroads. If we've been a natural medicine adherent up to then, will we stay with it or not? Are we going to say, 'Take me to the surgeon! The hell with natural remedies!' Will we toe the line or not? Some people panic over their health, and they're like, 'Give me drugs!'

"When you find the Path, it is your destiny. You are led to the Path; there are no accidents." Lee began to talk about how there is no real glory on the path but internal glory. He said that we have to be willing to "take the responsibility road, not the glory road." He talked about Purna and Lalitha, the only two of his many long-time students who are now teaching students of their own. He spoke of several other students, who have a great deal to offer others but will never get the glory of a formal teaching position, who will never be recognized and acknowledged; they remain the unsung heroes of the Hohm Community. Lee continued, "But no matter how long you are on the Path, integrity of practice is necessary."

By ten o'clock the evening had come to a close. After expressing our gratitude for such lavish hospitality and saying goodbye to all, the caravan of sangha members in various vans and cars, led by Lee in the ashram's silver van, drove back to Emmendingen.

Yogi Ramsuratkumar, mid-1990s.

In Chauvigny.

Les Nocturnes in St. Brieuc, Bretagne.

St. Brieuc.

LES
NoCtURnes

Before the gig in Dreux.

Onstage in Dreux.

Dreux.

Picnic on the Seine.

Performing in Paris at La Balle au Bond.

de la Tournelle.

La Balle Au
s'amarre :
1er Avril : Quai Malaquais.
1er Octobre: Quai de la Tournelle.

1er Octobre:

La Balle Au Bond
s'amarre :
1er Avril : Quai Malaquais.
1er Octobre: Quai de la Tournelle.

Greeting the crowd at a gig in Grimma, East Germany.

In the market at Freiburg, Germany.

Le Caf' Conc' in France.

Le Caf' Conc'.

Niederweiler, Germany.

Niederweiler.

Niederweiler.

On the Road

Brussels
September 2, 2005

This morning was one of those crossroads, which occur frequently throughout a summer of many changes of people and place, where everyone who had gathered to be with Lee during this week in Freiburg would be heading off in many different directions. Thomas Bormann and Stephan Bischof would caravan in their own car to Brussels, following Lee's van; the other ashram van would head home with the ashram residents to Ferme de Jutreau. Members of the Germany sangha would return to their homes in various cities. While all this was going on, two of Lee's students, Ron and Lawrence, were preparing their home to host Lee and his traveling party for three days in Brussels.

At eight-thirty we all gathered one final time to have our last breakfast of the summer with the German sangha and the visitors from France. It took Lee about thirty minutes to bolt down his food and leave, with no fanfare or sentimental goodbyes. He simply strode out of the house, down the steps and across the patio then through the gate to the street. At the gate he turned and said to everyone who was seeing him off, "I'm not going to hug all of you. I'll see you next year." And he was gone, back on the road again.

Arriving in Brussels at the home of Ron and Lawrence in the early afternoon, Lee spent the rest of the day checking out antique shops and sitting in a café. Back at the house, we ate a quick dinner at six o'clock. Just as two of Lee's American students and their ten-month-old baby—Sylvan, Denise and Sari—walked in the door from their long transatlantic flight, Lee gave them a warm but hasty hello, then took off for a long-awaited American movie: *Wedding Crashers*, with Vince Vaughan and Owen Wilson. Nothing gets in the way of movies! We laughed until tears ran from our eyes.

Tumbling into bed around midnight, we would be up again at six the next morning to drive to the Brussels airport, where we would bid adieu to three members of our traveling party who were returning to Arizona. Afterward, the big event of the weekend, which Lee had been looking forward to all summer, would be the Braderie du Lille—the biggest *brocante* fair in Europe.

Lille
September 3

The "Braderie du Lille" had been promised to be the most amazing *brocante* and street market experience in the Western world; in existence for five hundred years, a million people are said to roam the streets of the old city, shopping for two days over the weekend. It is held every year on the first weekend in September, and as one *brocante* friend of Lee's had said when he recommended this place, "You will go mad!" People come from all over Europe to shop for antiques, drink beer and eat *moules frites*—that is, mussels and french-fries.

It was a short one hour jaunt to Lille from the Brussels airport, where we saw our friends off. As we approached the city, Thomas called on the cell phone with a suggestion that had been broached in his car, which was leading the way into the city. "Did you want to park outside the city and take the metro in?"

"No!" Lee retorted sharply. "That was not *my* idea!"

"I thought so," said Thomas in reply. Getting off the phone, Lee relayed Thomas' comment and laughed. He went into a genial diatribe about how people are always putting words in his mouth relative to what *they* want to do, and worse, always thinking that he won't be able to find parking close to the action, which is where he wants to be. Lee's way of doing things is to trust that the universe will open amazing and surprising doorways for us to walk through—all the way down to something as simple as finding a parking place, often right in front of the place where we are going.

It doesn't always work, of course, but it's a matter of cultivating faith and trust, and being open to the magic and *drala* in the world. We can begin to participate with the *dralas*, in the way that Chögyam Trungpa Rinpoche frequently spoke of them, to the point of having a living, active, interdependent relationship with them. If we can live by magic when it comes to getting a parking place, certainly we can learn to live by magic when it comes to things that really matter, and what miracles might be unleashed in the process!

We blew into the city at ten-fifteen in the morning—the fast and furious *brocante* team of the day, ready to follow the spiritual master through any and all hardships. He quickly and easily found parking near a small Saturday morning neighborhood market about three blocks from where the fair would begin, walked through the market and located a corner bar and *tabac* with a few tables outside on the sidewalk by the street. It was two hours before the *chineur* extravaganza was supposed to start, and Lee had said that he would probably play bridge for an hour or so—something I love doing.

I had carefully placed the bridge cards in one of two bags before we left the house in Brussels early this morning, but when we were parking, I had to quickly transfer things from one bag to another to be ready for walking many miles and hours over the day. In the rush, I forgot the bridge cards, much to my chagrin. As we settled in at the table, I asked Lee if I could walk back to the van, which was less than two blocks away, to get the cards. It would have taken less than five minutes.

"No," he said mildly, moving immediately on to something else. Ride the horse in the direction it's going, Lee often advises. Another piece of advice he has given many times is, when you've made a mistake, don't try to fix it! When everyone had their coffee, a rather weak version of the usual French café variety, he laid out his plan for the day. The food market was in full swing across the street, and immediately across the road from us was a man roasting whole chickens that looked and smelled delicious. Lee's plan? We would have an early lunch, meaning right now, of coffee, Diet Coke and roasted chickens. "That's all I need!" he smiled.

He generously and spaciously offered for everyone else to go to the market and get any other food we might like. Sylvan, Sari and I went over to the market to pick up some fruit for the day. While Thomas procured the chickens, Lee enthusiastically downloaded his ideas to Denise for the two-week tour for the Lee Lozowick Band and the Denise Allen Band, now being scheduled for next summer.

"I have a *big* vision," he said, smiling. "The details aren't all in place yet." Then he began to talk about Emmanuelle's voice, when she had performed at Hauteville back in July. "It was spine tingling . . .!" He said. Creative juices seemed to flow off him as he filled in Sylvan and Denise, Thomas and Stephan, on the projects involving the new shop in La Roche Posay. He said, "I was talking to Vincent about the second floor, thinking it would be an apartment, and somehow, it became a gallery! Then the whole graffiti project came in . . ."

In the meantime, the two roasted chickens arrived fresh off the spit from across the street, and we split them between the ten of us, in a haphazard but focused way using pocket knives, grazing on the succulent, spicy flesh. As soon as the chickens had been thoroughly and properly honored, we were off, walking fast down the streets of Lille, and within three or four minutes, it seemed, we saw the first of thousands of little dealers with wares and goods spread out on blankets, on the backs of cars, in little makeshift stalls, under canvas umbrellas, and in some cases, for the more professional vendor, portable tables with glass cases for jewelry and more expensive items in silver and gold.

Soon we hit masses of people, which quickly grew to a river of people in the streets. Hip hop, African, Moroccan, traditional Middle Eastern and tribal music blared with polyrhythms and heavy drumbeats so loud you wanted to cover your ears. At times the chaos and sheer numbers of people was so great that Ann and I held onto each other's belts or shirts to stay together.

We were like the spiritual special forces, Baul-style—we worked as a team, keeping up with Lee's extremely fast pace. But it wasn't his fast pace that was the true challenge; he had a way of disappearing completely in the throngs of people. His moves were unpredictable in the chaos of this unknown territory. One instant he was there in front of you, white hat and dreadlocks hanging down, and the next instant—he was gone! Vanished, disappeared, as if by magic. It would have been very easy to get separated from the group, which would have been nightmarish, to say the least, especially for the non-Europeans among us. We spontaneously fell into a system whereby we all watched for each other, with Thomas, who usually kept pace with Lee, as the primary point man.

It reminded me of the U.S. Marine's: "Never leave behind a wounded man." More than once we would turn back for one or two of our numbers who were caught in the press of the crowd and falling behind: "He's turned left at the next street!" Ann and I ran interference in this way quite a lot, being used to filling in this role in chaotic situations. Sometimes it would be Stephan, Ron or Sylvan who would wait at a corner for the rest of the crew to catch up, while Lee moved on ahead down an interesting street. Rosaries, crucifixes and other Christian iconography, a vase or delicate blown glass decanter with four or six matching glasses, silver objets d'art, mantle piece clocks of interesting design, hand-beaten copper bowls, an unusual find of carved stone Hindu deities—all of these made their way into Lee's bags, which filled slowly but steadily and became the bags and bundles we began to carry for him around the wildly packed, ages-old streets of Lille.

We had started walking before eleven a.m. and had not stopped. Sari slept peacefully at times, even in the mayhem of the streets, or watched with bright interest from her backpack perch. After about four hours Lee accepted a cold Coke Lite, which he drank on the hoof, still walking and looking at everything.

"Have we been down this street yet?" he would turn to Stephan and Thomas, who had the map and were keeping track (we hoped) of where we had already been so we wouldn't cover our own tracks again. "I have to see everything!" Lee smiled.

His enthusiasm never flagged. Sometimes we would turn down a cobbled lane or a quieter side street under tall trees. Sometimes, when he was lingering with a vendor, carefully perusing every detail of his or her treasures that were presented on a makeshift table or a portable stand of some kind, I could take the moment to look around at the beautiful architecture of this fine old European city in the north of France—the proliferation of carved stone, the neoclassical motifs, ornate cornice work, gods and goddesses, fruit and vine, the fecundity of nature, the interplay of stone and brick and wood and tile and the freemason's art. All this lent a certain ambiance, a delicious mystery and arcane undertone, to the overall tone of the day.

At six-thirty, with sunset coming on, we were still trudging along with Lee. While he had cruised from one vendor to the next, we had followed him, not stopping or eating since the café at eleven a.m. The further along we got, the less *brocante* there was and the more flea market atmosphere and goods—the typical French *marché au puce*. It looked like this famous fair gave a lot of poor people the opportunity to bring their junk out on the curb and attempt to sell it.

At this point, after seven hours of walking nonstop, Lee no longer stopped at each and every vendor to look over their goods. He began to fairly fly through the streets while he assessed what was being sold from the middle of the street; it was easy to see when the vendor had a pile of old clothes and a few contemporary knickknacks and kitchen wares for sale.

As we threaded through the crowd, Lee commented quietly, "You walk and walk until the right person shows up. The right person shows up, and all the aches and pains go away."

Watching Lee for the past several summers as he has skimmed the cream from *marchés de brocante* and *marchés aux puces* all over France, as well as observing his buying for years in the street markets of India, and more recently at the gem and mineral shows in Tucson and Quartzite, Arizona, or at the super elite Asian Arts Fairs in San Francisco and New York, I began to see that the person who is selling is a key ingredient in the mix for Lee. It's about relationship, trust, dignity, the exchange of energies and being, as well as the exchange of money, which is perhaps in some ways merely a metaphor and a carrier for the former qualities and potencies.

Lee's comment, made after walking all day, and admittedly we were getting tired—though on this day there was not one complaint, not even a whisper of one, from any of us, including the young parents and the baby herself, who had just come from a time zone that is nine hours across the globe and were hitting the ground running, so to speak—was a confirmation of what I have observed over the years. Lee is drawn to people, to who they are, and the teaching, on many levels, is made apparent in these interchanges. When the "right person" showed up, Lee would linger with him or her sometimes for thirty minutes or an hour or more, looking and looking, talking, asking questions, haggling for a price, sharing a coffee, forcing them down to a fair price by his standards—which meant it had to be a screamin' deal for Lee. Then shaking hands warmly, with smiles and a lot of direct, eye-to-eye exchange of that thing which Lee, who insists he is not a "people person," so obviously holds in great esteem—human relationship—the deal was closed.

For a long time now I've been entertaining the notion that tantra is really about relationship—with everything. The right person has a certain quality of being, or it might be an objective need, the exact fruition of karmas that call them into play with a being like Lee. Or, they might be capable of playing with Lee in a way that delights and engages him. In any case, in these exchanges that occur on many different levels all at the same time, blessings are invoked from Lee and that which he represents, the lineage of Yogi Ramsuratkumar. And, of course, the right person also has to have something of real value, in some way—a thing of beauty, of rarity, or with some stamp of the artist's vital experience of life. Like Gurdjieff, Lee Lozowick always makes a profit, which can show up at any one of many different levels.

Finally, well past sunset and into the long twilight, the descending night was alive around us as we walked the streets. Around eight o'clock. Lee decided that we should get something to eat. We explored several more blocks, walking fast and checking out options. He wanted a place where the music was not assaulting our rather fried nervous systems, and he wanted a place where we could sit down together.

This was asking a lot from Lille at this point. The streets were an exotic blend of chaos, people, sweat and spice and driven, pulse-pounding sound. Everywhere there were peoples of color, mostly North Africans and Arabs, plying their trades—selling food, *merguez* and other sausages, skewered kabobs or brochette sizzling on small grills, couscous. *Moules frites* were for sale everywhere, huge piles of shells littering the street corners and curbs or spilling into gutters in front of small restaurants with tables and chairs jammed into whatever space was available, all of which competed with parked cars and motorcycles for what little space there was amidst the madness of the vendors' patchwork set ups. The streets were strewn with plastic cups, beer and wine bottles, trash and litter of every kind; the noise pollution was unbelievable; street performers abounded, with electric guitars, congas, dumbeks and every possible kind of hand drum playing in the mix. The smell of marijuana met and mingled with all the other smells—food, wood smoke, incense, coffee, beer and wine, people. It was a carnival, a vast party for the people of the streets and anyone who could flow with them, fueled by human chemistries, need and greed and hungers of all kinds.

Finally, just after eight-thirty, we noticed a little food vendor on the other side of a street lined with trees. They were working out of a caravan, selling baguette sandwiches and *frites*. On the sidewalk behind their stand were long wooden picnic tables with benches under some trees, and there was plenty of room for ten people. We ordered sandwiches and *frites* and drinks and sat down, relieved. It was the first time we'd sat down together since the bar where we'd had coffee and chicken in the morning. All along the street there were four-story buildings, but immediately next to us was a small grassy vacant lot where children were playing, and a dog. The brick walls of the buildings were covered with colorful graffiti. It was the perfect place for us—our refuge from the madness. We ate enthusiastically, while Lee simply sat, keeping us company. He wouldn't even take a Coke or a Perrier.

"You're not eating?" he was asked, more than once.

"No, I don't need anything," he answered. The emphasis was on the word "need." He smiled at us, as if to say, "It's okay—I want you all to eat." He was pure simplicity, quietly gleaming in the growing dark, lit as it was with the array of colored or bright lights, which made pools and splashes of light and shadow, accentuating the onset of night up and down the street.

As soon as we were all finished eating, Lee was up and on his way, striding through the streets. As we got further away from the jubilant insanity, there were still pockets of partying going on. A few blocks from the van, Lee found a café with tables outside on the sidewalk, facing an open plaza, where he stopped for a quick *café crème*. We sat around him, watching the young people in the plaza at their lively revelry. The drunkenness of the city seemed all pervasive; even walking down dark, empty streets the last three blocks to the van, we could hear the sounds of nearby music and laughter, loud conversations, mingled pleasures of the night.

It was ten-thirty before we reached our car, and midnight before we arrived at the home of Ron and Lawrence, where we were all staying. The next morning we were getting up early to go to the biggest *brocante* market in Belgium, held not far away in Waterloo. Afterward? Back to Lille, as Lee said, "To finish it off." After all, he hadn't seen quite *everything*, yet.

Waterloo and Lille
September 4

We took off early this morning to spend three hours at the large *brocante* market in Waterloo. This, Lee said, was the most successful hunting of the weekend. Lille was proving to be a bit of a bust—that is, it was mostly *marché au puce*, just junk, used household goods, children's clothes and old furniture turned out of people's homes and attics onto the streets, like the *vide-grenier* (emptying the attic) sales we'd been to with Lee last summer. Waterloo, on the other hand, was a true *brocante*, with about four hundred vendors and lots of great things—real antiques and real art. Lee was making purchases all along the way, obviously enjoying himself, and quickly our bags began to fill up.

As he went from one *vendeur* to the next, at one point he began to say, repeating it several times, "I'm looking for something big and ugly—it's got to be a particular thing. I want it for the shop. I won't be happy until I find that, but the price has got to be right. It has to be a deal!"

I spotted an iridescent, small green-blue, hand-blown glass vase on one table. This was my idea of something beautiful, even magical. I pointed it out to Lee. He looked at it and agreed, "Yes, it's beautiful." He asked the seller how much it was. "Eight hundred euros," the man said. Then he explained that it was very old and rare, and if it was a little larger, it would have been a great deal more—thousands, in fact.

"Oh," I said. Of course. That's kind of the way it goes at these things for me, an ashram renunciate with twenty euros in my pocket. When we are at *brocante* markets, Lee often says that we should buy the things that we can't live without. Like the eight hundred euro vase, the things I can't live without seem to inhabit a different universe than the one I live in.

Finally, after almost three hours and many, many felicitous purchases, Lee found the big ugly thing he was looking for: another (he already had a similar one in the shop at La Roche Posay) mantle piece clock, encased in dark wood with decorative agate "wings," for lack of a better description, and two agate half-moons accompanying it, which would sit off to the side of the clock, for some reason. It was impossible to imagine what its creator might have had in mind, much less to describe it, and I suppose that might just be the definition of ugly in this case. The only thing that mattered to us was that Lee was beaming and thrilled with it as we jumped back into the van and tore lickety-split over to the home of our hosts, back in Brussels, for a quick brunch.

To say it was a "quick" brunch means that we bolted down some food, hardly even aware of what it was, outside on the sun-washed patio. Lee had a one-pointed focus: to get back to Lille and finish the project of shopping at the biggest brocante market in Europe. The kitchen was hastily cleaned and we all piled into the vehicles again to fly away.

Going back to Lille was like entering a war zone, only the casualties were the bottles and trash strewn all over the streets, which reeked of urine, beer and liquor, and the strung-out people that lounged around in the bars and cafés or walked the streets looking bleary-eyed from last night's revelry. Still, there were many hardy souls still selling and buying. Once again, as we penetrated further into the streets, the African rhythms and hip hop beats blending with tribal sounds permeated the air. Smells of grilled meats entered our nostrils, commingling with the pissoir of the alleys and side streets, walls still stained from where men stood the night before, trousers unzipped, to mark the city as their own.

Today the sun was burning down very hot on our heads. Lee wore his Panama hat again, his dreadlocks a beacon in the crowd. Thomas was easy to spot as well, as was Sari in her backpack, bouncing gently along on the back of her mother or father. It was a little anti-climactic, but we were happy to be with Lee and each other.

Finally, the Lille extravaganza was over. We headed back to Belgium to meet up with Shri, who had just arrived after a long, long drive from Agde in southern France, where they had played gigs for two nights. Tonight was the last gig of the tour; tomorrow Shri would be in Hamburg, getting ready to fly back to the States.

We met at the Nekkersdal Culturcentrum somewhere in Bruxelles, a meandering modern wood building that reminded me of Denmark. It housed an odd little restaurant with a patio café nestled in the inner courtyard of the complex, with a sort of night club/live music haunt in the back. The club had a nice stage and an ample, spacious dressing room for the band. The whole place smelled of stale cigarette smoke, but at the same time, it seemed more like a private club than the usual bar scene. We were happy to see Shri, and after saying hello and checking out the space, Lee played bridge on the patio behind the café until it was time to go on stage.

The two hour gig was very enjoyable—a steady, solid, rocking, farewell made to a very small but enthusiastic audience. One young man in particular seemed to be really connecting with the music and the band. During the break he came up to Lee and gave him a poem he'd written:

> They inject
> They combine
> They stir up

They are truthful
They kick ass
They get through to the core of your soul
They are swampy
They are funky
Ils sont un joli cri
They are a joyous cry
Shri

He told Lee that he had had cancer twelve years before, and now he is grateful every day to be alive. After the gig he walked out the door with Lee, shaking his hand, receiving a warm embrace and still extolling Shri's excellence.

Saying our goodbyes to Shri, we left. Once again, the configuration around Lee would change as Shri returned to Arizona and Thomas and Stephan would leave at five-thirty the next morning to drive back to Freiburg. Our van, with Lee driving as always, would be heading south to the ashram. But first, Lee had important antiquities business to do in Brussels.

On the Road
September 5

After a fruitful morning in which Lee made a new friend—a man as passionate about sacred art and antiquities from India as Lee is—we hit the road. Before long we were buzzing along at 120 klicks on A 86 toward Bordeaux, one of many autoroutes that intersect with the daunting traffic around Paris. At one point a police car, siren wailing, came up behind the car in the next lane. We watched as the driver, oblivious to the police car and the siren, failed to pull into the other lane to let the gendarmes pass.

Lee laughed. "People sure are thick—they're in a dream within a dream."

Sitting in the front seat with Lee, we began to talk with him about his plans for the week after Ann and I would return to Arizona on October 3, when Lee would stay on for a week for a birthday celebration with Arnaud at Hauteville. Lee commented that old friends, Rob and Stewart, who run the Tayu Center in Santa Rosa, California, would be visiting for two or three days at Ferme de Jutreau that week.

"Will you be going to brocante markets in Paris that week or . . .?" I began.

"No," Lee stopped me in mid-sentence. "We'll stay at the ashram, because Rob and Stewart are visiting. They want to be on the ashram. They're into spiritual things," he said rather enigmatically. What was he implying? He's not, because he is constantly pulled away on business? Or we're not, because we're fascinated, distracted and seduced by all our desires and attachments in the domains of money, food and sex?

"Oh right, you're a businessman—you're not into spiritual things anymore," I said with a little tongue-in-cheek laugh.

"I'm *desperately* into spiritual things," Lee shot back, in a very earnest tone, "I just don't have any players."

Ann asked, "No players?"

"One or two," Lee conceded. It had been a very quiet ride until now. Our attention was piqued by this sudden rousing of Shiva from his meditation behind the wheel. Lee continued, "But it's not enough, because I'm always compromising, capitulating and *mousing* out to my devotees—as distinctly different from *ratting* out. *Mousing* out . . ." He smiled.

"What does it mean to be a player, then?" we asked.

Lee responded, "I want people who so completely want to work and are so grateful for work that they don't ask me, 'Where are we going? Where do we stay? When do we eat?' They're so grateful that they don't ask me *any* questions. That's the kind of player I want. And they just participate with joy and enthusiasm, with no underlying internal recoil or resistance."

The discussion continued in the vein of comparing those who see Lee every now and then and those who live in very close proximity to him, in situations where a great deal of personal freedom is relinquished.

I said, "Anybody can look good for a few weeks, then they can go back to their nice houses and big lives, their private spaces, private kitchens, private lives where they get to make all the choices, all the decisions themselves . . ."

But Lee disagreed that people actually look good during that time period. He said, "It's not true. People can give up their will power pretty well for a short period of time, but not without internal recoil when sleeping conditions are chaotic. They can give up control over their lives to be at the ashram for a few weeks, but if they're on the road with me and having to deal with unforeseen conditions, then they can't manage their recoil in the same way as being in a situation that's predictable. Shri does it much better now than they used to, but they've had ten years of being in the van together."

"So what is it that makes it possible to be a player who has no internal recoil or resistance?" Ann asked.

"It's just a matter of being willing to follow. It's not like you don't get to sleep or eat!" Lee laughed incredulously, since those of us who travel with Lee on most of his trips throughout the year are hardly deprived in any way; in fact, there is so much feasting, general abundance and flow of plenty around Lee now that it makes my earlier years of sadhana look like austere practice. Of course it wasn't austere, because I complained and resisted too much for my efforts of those years to really qualify as austerity; my idea of real *tapas*, or austerity, is that one undergoes such an ordeal gracefully, with dignity and nobility—without complaint and resistance. At any rate, that was back in the days when we didn't drink coffee at all; when the diet was fiercely in play, when . . . I still had to write by hand, before I had a laptop and a great IBM desktop.

Lee continued, "It's not like E.J.'s, where all you get is two hours a night and a doorway to sleep in . . ." I remembered the story that Chris often tells, of a memorable moment in her sadhana when, years ago when she was having a hard time, struggling with recoil and resistance, Mr. Gold said to her humorously, "Remember, it could always be worse. You could be here!"

With that having been communicated, Shiva went back to his meditation and a silence fell over us while we chewed the gristly morsel, fed from the guru's hand, so to speak, in quiet reflection as the van sped down the road toward the ashram.

Ferme de Jutreau
September 6

When Chris called the ashram for Lee from Arizona at four-thirty in the afternoon, those of us in the office overheard Lee, after a spell of quietly listening, saying, "Great! I haven't been able to touch people that way in thirty years. If that's what it takes to make people get it, then let's lose two or three more cities! Let's make use of it and go on with our work!"

At dinner I asked Lee, "So, Chris said that people in Arizona are really being impacted by what's happening in New Orleans?"

Lee answered, "Yes," paused briefly then said, "and I said, 'Great. I haven't been able to touch people that way in thirty years, so if that's what it takes for people to get it, let's lose two more cities! Let's feel it and get on with our work!"

This time, after repeating almost verbatim his first response, he added, "We should grieve for the suffering of others, but we should not be surprised by it. We should go on with our work. No one is surprised by it except the people in power."

When Ann asked for a clarification of what he meant, he said, "Everyone knows why things like this are happening, except the people in power who don't want to believe that it's because of the things we are doing on the Earth."

The conversation flowed on to less intense subjects. Fifteen minutes later, at the end of the meal, Lee was making the announcements and said cheerfully, "After dinner talk at seven-fifteen, tea at nine o'clock, and Good Company all the time, even when you're alone!"

I said playfully, "Maybe especially for you," referring to the "when you're alone" part and all the remarks Lee had made over the summer about how he doesn't really like being with people, prefers to be alone with his book and his carrot and celery, but the Work has forced him into this situation, when he is the least likely candidate by natural disposition for such a job. Nonetheless, the job is his.

Walking briskly out of the barn and looking back at all of us with a bright smile, he quipped, "Oh no, I'm a real *people* person. Jai Guru!"

The resounding "Jai guru!" with which we responded was accompanied by chuckles and gaiety.

At the after dinner talk tonight Lee was answering Annie's question about empowerment and special projects, which led to a short, potent discourse on power. He began by reminding us that power is naturally gathered as we progress in sadhana, and in fact, our practice makes us powerful. Still, most of us have not experienced having real power over others yet—in other words, we have not been tested.

Lee said, "There is a point at which we get so much power that we become a petty tyrant with it. A 'petty tyrant' means that the person has no real power, but uses what power they have over others. If we push ourselves into the spaces of others when we have no power, imagine what we will do when we actually *have* power! Ultimately, the idea of accumulating power is to serve the Work . . . . "

"So, a lot of people don't understand and have no feeling for using power for the Work. A lot of opportunities we come upon in the Work require a certain amount of power and skillful means. The depth and breadth of our skillful means is part of our power complex. Like Vincent, without power, he won't be magnetic in his new business venture. To have power and to continue to build a stronger and stronger base upon which to work—that's all understood when we talk about power. It's understood that if we have not been tested relative to our psychological relationship to power, we will be.

"Like with projects like Shri and Attila the Hunza—when people get into positions of authority, every flaw in their ability to communicate comes to the forefront. There is always somebody in the band who, if they don't know what's going on, feel that they are hated. And 'hated' is not too strong a word. And they don't know what's going on because the people with the authority don't feel the need to communicate every detail; they've been given the authority to do the job and they just want to do it.

"If I felt people could simply work in whatever way the Work was happening, with no questions and no complaints, internally or externally, I would never ask anybody a question. I would *never* ask, 'Where would you like to eat? Would you like to see this movie, or that movie?' *Never*! I would never ask. You wouldn't believe how much people say, 'Where are we going? Why did you turn there? It's shorter this other way that you didn't go.' You have no idea! We're driving around France and Germany, why would anybody need to know where we're going? Where would we be going, besides to a sangha household, a gig, a movie, or a seminar? So, I'm constantly capitulating, because people feel they need to be in on something."

This is a big power issue for most people, especially when one is attempting to follow the guru, who is constantly creating opportunities for us to experience and surrender to groundlessness, among many other things. Information is power, and the one who has information feels in control, special, on the inside of Lee's world. Lee keeps telling us that it couldn't be less true; just because someone has information about his plans, for example, does not mean that they are living in his world.

In fact, our grasping, aggressive, egoic drive to have power, in any form, including the power of information, keeps us out of the guru's world. Surrender is a soft, resilient, fluid, receptive, graceful state of being. It begins in the heart and spreads from there. Surrender has nothing to do with personal power, and yet, the surrendered one is ultimately powerful, because he or she needs nothing and cannot be manipulated. Such a one has an equanimity and solid, steady state of being. Such a one can actually use power that comes along in service to the guru and the Work, without any danger of claiming it for one's own aggrandizement and glory. Lee is the stalwart example of this kind of ultimate surrender.

He continued, "As the world deteriorates, it becomes useful to have power . . . and the more we have, the more likely we will be able to protect the Work and have the Work grow and flow. We will have the power to work more effectively and efficiently.

"When we develop some degree of power, we need to understand how few people have any degree of integrity in relationship to power, because we aren't out in the world, dealing with people. Often we're very naïve because a lot of people we're around have a relative degree of integrity, but it's relative, because there are still these misunderstandings that happen. When we have had a misunderstanding with someone, we don't stop and think, 'Am I abusing power?'

"When we get out into the world and start using power, people are going to be drawn to it. The more power you have, the brighter you are and the more people flash on that brightness, and the more opportunities you have to abuse that power. The world will be banging on your door. If we don't know all this ahead of time, we will get seduced by power."

Later over tea, Lee said, "Somebody once said, 'God is in the details.' I don't believe that. My philosophy is: 'Don't sweat the small stuff.' If you think most things through, the small stuff, you really don't have to address it. The worst thing that can happen is that the soup is too salty, or the meal isn't so good."

Ferme de Jutreau
September 7

Today marked the thirtieth anniversary of the first *satsang* with Lee after the event that catalyzed his teaching work. It also loosely lines up with almost twenty years of Lee's teaching in Europe, beginning in Germany in 1987, and ten years at Ferme de Jutreau, which began in 1995. Following the lead of the ashram in Arizona, tonight we had a commemorative dinner, with everyone from the households who live near the French ashram as well as some people coming in from out of town for dinner and a talk by Lee.

It was an intimate group of about twenty-five adults and five children for a simple supper—roasted chickens and Caesar salad, no frills, no extras. Lee poured glasses of white wine, donated by Shri, which they had received as a gift on their tour from one of their hosts. With Lee pouring, some of us got very small amounts of wine, less than half a glass, while others got first and second glasses, filled dangerously close to the brim, accompanied by much laughter and merriment.

Hoping Lee would wax eloquent, I brought my notebook to the table, but the meal was so ordinary, such a demonstration of simplicity and actually rather quiet, that I didn't write down a single thing he said. He gave a magnanimous gift to one of the women in the French sangha, however, in his offer to take some of her Chinese calligraphy pieces, executed in her budding talent for the art form, in trade for her debt to the Sacred Bazaar. This captured the attention of the whole table, and another woman immediately piped up, "What can I do?" Meaning, to clear her bronze debt.

Lee generously answered, "I'll find something!"

As ordinary as it gets, Lee ate three or four chicken wings (a lot, for him), gnawed enthusiastically on chicken bones, dug into the salad, even ate some anchovies. I was amazed at how he was able to eat the rich, greasy chicken and tear into those bones in his silky silver shirt without getting even a tiny spot of grease on it. Somehow, he managed to be elegant and earthy.

At the end of the meal he announced that we would gather in the salon at 7:45, then have tea at nine o'clock. "Let's move on to another space," he said. "Jai Guru!"

After dishes, while Lee worked with the men to load the new cargo van, the blue VW Transporter, with large stone deities that would be going to Paris in two days with him, we gathered in the salon. The room was thick with powerful presence, subtle and gross, including the musty, powerful smells of India and Nepal, exuded by the many artifacts that inhabit the salon as their temporary home. Lee even had to unpack and rearrange some boxes to make space for people to sit for the talk and tea.

As soon as a few people were gathered, while others were quickly making their way into the space, Lee said, "I thought tonight it would be not a talk but a rambling commentary. The reason today is a little different is because it is the thirtieth anniversary of the first formal gathering of the community—we called it satsang then, not darshan. It is also twenty years of teaching in Europe and ten years at Ferme de Jutreau, so we have a lot to celebrate! Thirty-twenty-ten! Sort of like roulette!" Lee chuckled. "Well, a lot of things are changing, of course."

Andrea came in with the recording equipment then and Lee said, "Let's not record this." He began to talk about the hurricane and disaster in Louisiana, and especially in New Orleans. He explained why oil prices went up when two oil rigs in the Gulf of Mexico were knocked over by the hurricane: any time there is any break in oil production, regardless of where it is, oil prices go up because it is a global economy. He continued:

"They say one of the best places to be when fossil fuels run out is France, one reason being the nuclear power in France, which isn't going away. One thing we come to realize as we are more and more stung by the absolute barbaric behavior of people in the world, is that blessings are curses and curses are blessings. That is also true in the Work."

Lee used Franck, the guest guitar player who has played for two summers with Shri, as an example of someone who doesn't live to play guitar, like many musicians, but plays to live. Without his music, Franck might well be dead, and so his extraordinary talent is both a blessing and a curse.

"People are really insane. In a tragedy like Louisiana, the best of people comes out and the worst of people comes out, so it's a blessing and a curse. It's a curse in the sense of the tremendous damage and loss of homes, and a blessing in that people who stayed home before and stuck to themselves are coming out and demonstrating compassion, caring for others. Recently a number of community members have been involved at different levels of the culture through medicine, education, etc., and have seen how people are so cruel, the world is corrupt. All of this is heartbreaking, and what it should do is throw us back on the fact that this Work is all we have.

"If there is a tragedy, you may be the beneficiary of the best or the worst in people—you never know. We were talking today about the last thirty years and somebody said, 'Let's have another thirty years, and then we'll have a sixty year anniversary.' I said, 'Oh my God, I hope I don't live that long!' Maybe twenty, they said. 'Okay, maybe twenty,' I said. It's not up to us, of course. I'm sure I'd know when the end is near, but until it's near, it could be another fifty years! The longer we go, we will see our sangha mates die, and the blessing is that we have more time to Work, and the curse is that we see our loved ones die off."

Lee talked about a fan at the last Shri gig in Brussels, and how vocal he was in his appreciation of the band. He told Lee that he had had cancer fifteen years ago, and he beat it. Now, he said, he can really appreciate music and the blues. He was only twenty-one years old when he had cancer. "That's too young! No one used to get cancer at that age. That's not supposed to happen in my world!" Lee said.

"Every curse is a blessing and every blessing is a curse. So we go into debt more than ever before, and the blessing is that our spaces are filled with sacred bronze, and more money is flowing in new and unexpected ways in the sangha. Make sure you have lots of Lakshmis!

"America and France are getting more and more repressive—taking more and more authority in people's lives. That is not a good sign. Pretty soon they're going to tell you what to read and what to watch on TV. More and more pornography is sprouting up everywhere on the internet, on TV, in the media, but people are becoming more and more repressive and uptight. The majority of people in America, who elected George Bush, those people are becoming more dominant, buying up newspapers and magazines and in politics—they have tons of money, and that's very bad.

"So here we are in the Work, something that can't be explained, something that requires fifteen or twenty years of involvement to begin to understand, and the world we live in is demanding more and more explanations of what we do. We gather together, there is a tremendous bond between us, there is a light in us that radiates out to others—and then there is life. What is going to happen in the next twenty to thirty years? I don't think it's going to be very attractive. On the other hand, every curse is a blessing, and every blessing is a curse. It falls to us to find the blessing in the curse."

Just at this point I got a phone call from the States and was out of the room. Later, Michelle, who had been translating into French for Lee, paraphrased the remainder of Lee's talk for me, as I sat at the computer after tea was over.

Continuing in the same vein, Lee said that we, as the sangha, have an incredible depth of bonding, and that we must cultivate that bond so that it stays strong in the years ahead, because we don't know what is going to happen. People in the sangha are shocked by what has happened in Louisiana; part of the shock comes from genuine empathy for the suffering over there, but another aspect of it is naiveté in believing that Louisiana is different from Arizona or France—that it is a different place. We need to be able to deal with crisis, manage crisis, and we need to train our children to manage crisis. He said that he was not talking about telling our children about the state of the world or corrupt politicians, but training our children to manage crisis, so that in a situation of crisis, we will all be able to stand and focus on sustaining the Work rather than being swept away by our emotional response.

Lee said, "It's naïve to think that we are going to be protected or that we will not personally have to face tragedies like what has happened in Louisiana. For now, regarding sustaining the Work, we think things are good, our Work is well established, but in the future we may need to be more actively engaged in preserving the Work—like in 'Fahrenheit 451,' where people had to pass the knowledge on orally, because all the books were burned." What if people were captured or disappeared and they had not transmitted their knowledge to the children? That line of knowledge would be gone forever. We could find ourselves in a situation of having to preserve the teaching by memory."

He said that he himself is a coward, and has always avoided war and conflict. He talked about how his mother kept him from being drafted: "Even the government couldn't say no to my mother!" He didn't go to Vietnam, and for the following wars he was too old to be drafted. So far, Lee said, he has not had to be confronted with war directly. He said that he secretly hoped to finish his life without being in a situation of war. There is an expression in America—"Make love, not war"—and of three options, making love, making war or running, he would choose running. Maybe, he said, since the sangha is the tail of the comet, if he is able to avoid direct confrontation with war, then we might be lucky enough to not find ourselves in that situation in this life either. But, Lee said, we still need to be prepared for anything. What is happening in Louisiana is a situation of war, because of the suffering and people losing their homes. He was not just talking about the fact of literal war, but also psychic war.

Lee's talk focused on the need to cultivate the wisdom to see the blessings in the difficulties that lay ahead, and to cultivate our bonds with each other. Our relationship to the Work and our obligation to preserve the Work becomes more critical with each passing year and with each blow to the stability of our world. The vital point is that everything we do is done to serve the Work; when we serve the Work, the Work serves us.

I came back into the salon to see a tableau of about eight women seated in a semi-circle around Lee, who was showing them the new necklaces made by Deborah for the Sacred Bazaar. It was a very soft, intimate, warm scene, the *gopis* gathered around a mysterious merchant playing an invisible flute. Almost every woman in the room bought one of the necklaces. With a beautiful new necklace on, Brindavan said with a smile, "Can you believe it? We are beggars, but we are wearing all these jewels!"

Just then a sweet cassis liqueur was served in small glasses, its dark berry color another gem in this jewel-like scene. Brinda came forward and offered a flower *mala* to Lee, which he allowed her to place around his neck. It was handmade from our ashram garden. With a big smile on his face, his form graced with the flower garland, he sparkled as he held his glass out and made a toast: "Here's to the next twenty years—and you all can celebrate the sixtieth on your own!"

His words were bittersweet, like so many things this summer. Lee rarely offers up a toast when we have wine; usually he asks someone else to do it. It seemed important, on this particular night, that Lee himself offered this blessing to us, and it reflected in principle exactly what he had spoken earlier: "What is going to happen in the next twenty to thirty years? I don't think it's going to be very attractive. On the other hand, every curse is a blessing, and every blessing is a curse. It falls to us to find the blessing in the curse."

Everyone settled down on the floor around Lee while coffee, cream, chocolates, sugared ginger and other treats were served. I mentioned that Zachary, who I'd just talked with, had told me that 263,000 people were actually homeless in southern Louisiana.

Lee seemed to take that harsh fact in, then said, "This would be the time for a great publicity coup, if McDonald's would offer those people a free meal a day! That's what I would do. And Starbucks could provide the coffee," he added with a smile. A great idea! Of course, neither of these monster corporate profiteers were stepping up to do anything so altruistic.

Vincent Cenni asked Lee what he should tell his children about the disaster in New Orleans. Lee answered, "Don't tell them anything, unless they ask. I keep my children as protected from bad news as possible. Keep them innocent and free from all that as long as you possibly can. They'll have plenty of time to deal with the suffering in the world."

Lee talked a little about the first *satsang*, how Bala, Brother Juniper, Jeff and Bandhu were there. Claire was asking him questions about old photographs of him from that time period, and what kind of food he was eating, to which Lee responded that he was a purest in the beginning. "That was before I became decadent," he laughed, then added, "sugar came later."

I said, "And look at us now—coffee, wine, meat . . ."

"Yes," Lee added, "if it had been like this thirty years ago, we'd have a thousand people here now!"

After some rounds of coffee and treats, the fax machine could be heard, tapping out a new message, in the office. Lee commented, "There goes the fax machine. I used to get letters that people wrote, with *tears* streaked down the pages. That moved you—you got a real feeling for what was going on. Now people write faxes, they rip something off and send it—you don't get the tragedy of the thing that way. It's not the same."

Claire asked, "Do you still prefer handwritten letters?"

"It depends on who is writing," Lee answered. The conversation went to the illegible handwriting of many people, whereas others, like Shukyo and Brinda, write beautifully. Then there are those who write "artistically," using silver ink that is impossible to see, which Lee finds particularly irritating.

Lee talked for a long while about Bob Dylan, the film *Masked and Anonymous*, and the interview with Dylan that we saw at Niederweiler in Germany. He praised Dylan, and said that he doesn't really talk or give interviews, but "sort of invites you into this mysterious world that he lives in."

"Does he have a teacher?" someone asked. Lee answered no. Thinking about how powerful that interview was, and in particular some of the things Dylan said, I reflected, "He has a direct connection."

"That's right," Lee said.

It was almost ten-thirty. The tea space was winding down for the night, the evening drawing to its natural close. I shared some news that Kate had told me on the phone. A large statue of Kwan Yin in the Chonggyesa Temple in Seoul, the capital of South Korea, had blossomed with twenty-one tiny flowers of an extremely rare kind that only bloom once every three thousand years. The legend is that their blooming appears to signify or even announce the incarnation of the Maitreya, a future Buddha who is known as "The Sage King of the Future." According to the news, Buddhist monks are keeping a prayer vigil there, awaiting the next sign, while the biologists are shaking their heads at this "miracle." The internet article said that the experts were all abuzz; everyone seemed to agree that it's unthinkable that the five-hundred-year-old statue of Kwan Yin, which is gilded every year over the original woodwork, could produce these extremely rare flowers, considered sacred in the East, without divine intervention. A blessing in the curse of our times?

After a few seconds, Lee said, "Well . . . on *that* note . . . we'll say goodnight. Bonne nuit."

Ferme de Jutreau
September 8

At the after dinner talk Annie asked Lee a question about whether or not one could get to work with their issues of power if they are not put in a position of authority in the sangha or given some important, high profile task or money-making project that directly feeds the Work.

Lee responded: "It's a very important reflection for all of us. There is a difference between the task we have for the Work, and the *being* we move through life with. The task we are given seems to be a special gift that certain devotees get. Like Shri: people think, 'Shri is so important, Lee loves them and gives them attention.' But all of those people who are in relationship in the band have to leave their partners for six weeks to go on tour. There are tremendous sacrifices made to work on that project—it's not an easy thing to do.

"If one is managing a task poorly—not being in integrity and not bringing clarity to the task—it's almost worse to have the task than not to have a task at all. Progress on the Path is relative to one's *being* authority, not related to fancy tasks we get in the Work. It's true of course that certain tasks magnify and intensify certain aspects of psychology, and it's true that part of the development of the being has to do with developing integrity in relation to those characteristics. Sometimes a task is particularly useful only because we give it exceptional authority.

"Tasks are not about personal progress; they are about service to the Work. *All tasks*. The music created is the point; the musicians, as much benefit as they may get, are secondary. Obviously I want proficient musicians for the project, for the music, for the Work—but not for themselves! The point is to create music that has a certain reverberation that serves the Work. The musicians are ingredients in the stew. If the stew is good, you eat it—you don't take the carrots out and idolize them!

"There is a great possibility of capitalizing on the possibility of a task—there is also a great possibility of capitalizing on boredom, sitting around or doing dishes all day. When people get a task, there is a certain personal relationship to me that may not be possible under ordinary circumstances. So one thing Mira, Vincent and Adeline have to look forward to next year in the new band is that I'm going to be on them like flies on shit! Even though I don't know a lot about music, I have a vision.

"So, that's one of the benefits of the task, we think. But then, there is also a benefit to not having that involvement. When Yogi Ramsuratkumar sent me away in 1986, I really, in my own mind, was prepared never to see Him again, for the rest of my life. So, the whole personal aspect of our relationship wasn't relative anymore. Obviously He called me back and initiated a deeper and far more personal relationship, but at the same time, my personal relationship with Him was over—finished. But only our personal relationship. Our essential relationship had to become deeper and more subtle if I was to continue to be as devoted as I was—to maintain the devotion I had. It was as if He had physically died, and I had to find Him without His body.

"So, the tasks are wonderful. I certainly enjoy them, but we have to understand, the tasks are to serve the Work, and if we benefit, it's icing on the cake. And as some Europeans have not learned yet, cake without icing is a different kind of cake!" Everyone laughed. "So we don't want to discount the icing! So, tasks are to serve the Work. The Work responds to us, but it's not personal."

Lee used the example of Robert Svoboda, who spoke in a workshop he was giving about how, in tantric work, one can burn karma at a much faster rate than in ordinary circumstances. Svoboda told a story of how he burned a tremendous amount of karma when he had a scorpion bite in India. The karma was burned, but with tremendous pain and suffering. Robert had said that he didn't want to have to go through something like that again.

Lee continued, "For example, Yogi Ramsuratkumar went into divine intoxication. He was in that state when He left Papa Ramdas and started wandering. Once He was getting off a train in a state of ecstasy, and the train roared by and clipped off part of His toe, and in the moment when that happened, He heard a voice that said, 'This is what happens to devotees of Ram.' Not that they get wonderful comforts, but that they get rapid transformation, evolution, without regard for their personal wishes and concerns.

"So, we want to be very clear that our progress on the Path is relative to our integrity of *being*, not to the amount of authority we have in the spiritual bureaucracy. Sometimes we fall into that illusion—'Oh, I'm the singer, the violin player, the keyboard player, I'm very important'—and we think we are making more progress than someone who is just washing the dishes. Not necessarily! Humility goes a long way in the Work. It's got a *very* high value, and it's much harder to cultivate when you're a superstar."

Art, Money & Sadhana

Paris
September 9, 2005

This morning we left with Lee at five o'clock to drive to Paris. Volkmar and Sylvan followed behind us driving the Transporter. They would split off when we got to A6 to pick up Purna at Charles De Gaulle Airport, then meet us for a late lunch somewhere in Paris, to be announced later in the day, when they would contact Lee by cell phone. Lee drove his '86 Mercedes, which was leaking transmission fluid, so Ann and I had to open the hood, check the fluid level and add fluid every so often. Nonetheless, navigating the Mercedes through Paris was a great treat, as opposed to the bulkier, more difficult to maneuver Citroen van, so it was well worth the added attention to detail.

Lee's morning was about meeting with one of his business associates in Paris—a man who has traveled extensively in the East. He has a shop where Lee likes to go to buy artifacts and visit since, over the past three years, the business relationship has become a friendship as well. On the way there, Lee said, "Oh, this business will only take forty-five minutes; we'll be out of there, and if we find any good brocante markets that are on today, we'll go to them before we meet the guys for lunch."

We arrived at the shop around ten a.m. to a very warm welcome from Lee's friends, who offered us espresso and sent out for croissants and *pain au chocolat* from the award-winning bakery across the street. "These are the best croissants in Paris," they said with a smile. They were promptly consumed with great enjoyment, and having sampled many varieties of croissants, I felt qualified to say it was true; they were the best I'd ever eaten in Paris, without question. Even Lee ate one, which was quite unusual—it was the first croissant I have seen Lee eat in many, many years. It's a luxury that is exceedingly rare for him. Someone once asked him if he didn't like croissants, since he never took one when they are offered, which is often in France.

"I *love* them," he said, "but I don't eat lots of things that I love!" Lee is legendary among his students for his fierce discipline. Sometimes he says of his own discipline, "I do your work for you until you do it for yourself." It took someone who has become a friend and cohort in Lee's passion—sacred artifacts—and the laws of hospitality as well as the fruition of whatever karmas have brought these two men together, to break the croissant barrier with Lee.

Lee spent about an hour walking around the shop, while in the meantime, we were talking about *Ecrasé par l'amour,* or *Crushed by Love*, which Lee had given to his friends as a gift last summer.

"I *really* love it! The music is fantastic, beautiful! The songs are very special" the antique merchant's wife said passionately, with more than a little wonder, it seemed, at this man in her husband's shop who is a spiritual teacher and also sings with a band. Her English was excellent and made more lyrical with the charming addition of her beautiful accent as she continued, "I listen to it all the time! Every morning I put it on in my studio while I work, you know, and every time I play it, the heavens open up!"

She turned to Lee, who was looking at some bronze Ganesh sculptures, about four hundred years old, in a glass case. "Are you making another CD?"

"I'm not sure yet," Lee smiled. "But we're doing a two-week tour next year." The conversation turned to the tour, then back to sacred art, sculpture, bronze and the archetypes that inhabit them.

I was thinking about the first two or three years that Lee visited this shop, when it was just a tiny little space near the Place Pigalle, before it was moved to this new location. The *vendeur* had no idea who this unusual American man was; he just appeared out of nowhere one day with his retinue of several adults and sometimes one, two or three children. Somehow, he had ascertained through light conversation over his business dealings with Lee that the guy with the dreads had a summer home near Poitiers and a blues band that toured Europe in the summer, and furthermore, he was a dealer in sacred art and bronze antiquities of the East.

The relationship had slowly grown; Lee resonated deeply to his friend's way of doing things, which is based on trust, integrity and mutual respect. Then, last summer Arnaud Desjardins asked Lee to find a large Buddha for him for a specific purpose on his ashram—to place in the entryway at Ranchi, the new silent retreat space at Hauteville, a tribute to Swami Prajnanpad. Lee found the Buddha that he thought Arnaud wanted, at this shop.

A month later, Arnaud sent his ashram manager, Thierry, to Paris to acquire the Buddha. As it turned out, the statue Lee had picked out was sold, but Thierry found another one that was perfect for Arnaud's needs. The two French men hit it off, and in the process of introductions, as Thierry explained that he was picking the statue up for the renowned French filmmaker and spiritual teacher, Arnaud Desjardins, the subject of the American man, Lee Lozowick, came up.

"Don't you know who he is?" Thierry asked. When the answer was no, Thierry said, "He's a well-known spiritual teacher from America, a very very close friend of Arnaud Desjardins. He comes to Hauteville every year to teach . . . We know him very well . . ."

I could only imagine what the rest of the conversation must have been like. Of course, Lee could be looked up on the internet, revealing a plethora of information, including Lee's own website that simply says, "If you're looking for enlightenment, go somewhere else," and nothing more.

It's most interesting to watch Lee interact in the business world, where he travels incognito, not in a premeditated way, but naturally, because Lee does not travel with pomp and circumstance like so many masters, tulkus and gurus—the high priests of the spiritual scene. There are no robes, no demands for certain formalities of reception, no lists of requirements and needs for where and how he will be hosted, how the bedroom should be laid out, what he will or won't eat. It's not that Lee doesn't have strong preferences—he does. It's that Lee travels like a beggar in that he is surrendered to what life brings his way; he simply accepts whatever is offered to him, whether he likes it or not. Sometimes this means that he bears things that are significantly disagreeable to him. Some people who host Lee understand this and, knowing that Lee will not ask for anything special, they will go out of their way to find out what Lee likes, in order to provide it—for which Lee's students are extremely grateful, wanting their master to be cared for properly.

Quite often I get the feeling that the people in the antiquities business, both in Europe and America, sense that there is something uncommon, even rare, about the enigmatic American who comes to all the Asian arts shows or buys from their shops. On the other hand, Lee is not keeping his identity a secret, nor does he ever advertise who he is in any way; he is just being who he is. Everything is straightforward and direct. Everything is exactly what it is, and that very quality of direct and immediate contact with the raw essence of awakened being, which is the confrontation of relating with Lee, plugs the person into the fire of the present moment—reality, as it is, here and now. It can be very disconcerting and uncomfortable at times, but it is often laced with a tangible nectar; one is uplifted by even a brief contact with the lineage of the beggar king, Yogi Ramsuratkumar. "Grace and mercy flows from his wild hair," one could say, if Ramprasad

Sen hadn't already said it in his unforgettable poem to his *ishta devata*, Kali. Nonetheless, the phrase rings true for Lee.

Almost two hours and quite a number of purchases later, Lee was finally ready to leave the shop. We drove to the Rive Gauche, on the left-hand side of the Seine not far from the Ile St-Louis on the right, where there was a very special, rather elite restaurant that had been suggested as a possible place for lunch. This was the same area we have walked through many times, this summer and in summers past, where the streets are packed with high-end antique stores, gourmet *chocolatiers*, exclusive boutiques and jewelers. Although we had called a few days in advance hoping to reserve a table, we were told that the restaurant didn't take reservations, so we would have to walk in off the street and hope for the best.

Purna, having been picked up at the airport, would arrive with Volkmar and Sylvan any minute, and we would all have lunch together. We were on a tight schedule; we had to pick up Vincent Vigor at four p.m. at the Gare de Montparnasse to make an important five o'clock meeting that Lee had been looking forward to all summer. Wherever we had lunch, we would be asking the maitre d' if we could be accommodated very quickly.

Despite heavy traffic, Lee rather miraculously found a parking place just a block away from the restaurant. He whipped the Mercedes into the tight space with fluid ease. Instead of going directly there, he chose to walk around for about ten minutes. When we arrived in front of the restaurant, the maitre d' met us at the opaque, smoke-colored heavy glass door. He did not invite us in, but spoke to us while we stood out on the street and he stood two steps up, just inside the door. Eyeing Lee's wild silvery hair which framed his face like a benign storm, and the long *jatta* hanging down his back, his faded cotton short-sleeved shirt, sandals and baggy pants, the simplicity with which he just stood there, penetrating blue eyes and thatch of bushy beard of mixed hues, the maitre d' rather skeptically told us that there would be at least a forty-five minute wait.

Again my thoughts turned to the unique circumstance of a spiritual master of the West at work in the business world or walking the streets of Paris incognito. These kinds of situations, where Lee is interacting with the more elite sectors in any given city where we are traveling, are equally interesting to me. I think about other spiritual teachers I've met in Lee's company, or those I've read about, and the kind of privilege or clout that is often wielded on their behalf in order to facilitate a smooth and graceful flow for the teacher himself or herself.

In Lee's case, there would be no one saying to the maitre d', "Do you know who this man is? He has thirty books in print in four languages! He has over thirty recorded CDs of original music. He is a respected international teacher and revered spiritual master with a community of students in the U.S., Canada, Mexico and Europe—and most of all, he is the spiritual son of Yogi Ramsuratkumar, beloved beggar saint of Tiruvannamalai, India!"

Nor had we, upon finding that the restaurant didn't make reservations when we called last week, taken an aggressive stance and demanded that the place clear the way for the teacher to sweep in with his entourage and claim the place as his own for a two hour, extravagant lunch, which could have sounded something like this: "Mr. Lee Lozowick will be coming to Paris with his retinue on Thursday . . . we'll need a special table for six. It has to be round in shape, near the windows . . . quiet, preferably in a private room, and no smoking . . . He must have lightly cooked vegetables and a salad of fresh, organic baby greens with his viande, which should be well done—no potatoes or starches, s'il vous plait!"

No. We just stood there on the sidewalk, waiting for the maitre d' to show mercy—or not.

"Okay," Lee said, "we'll wait. We need a table for six." Lee and Ann explained the tight schedule we were on and asked if the maitre d' thought we could be finished with lunch by three-thirty. With that established, just as Lee was about to turn away, the maitre d' relaxed a little, told us that we could come in and sit at the bar, which was obviously customary, even expected of the restaurant clientele. Lee declined.

Stepping up to the chrome and glass door just as the maitre d' was closing it, I rather boldly asked if I could use the toilet in the restaurant. He said yes, but it was not the most hospitable yes I'd ever heard. He rather reluctantly held the door open for me and I slipped through into the subdued, modern space with recessed lighting, where businessmen in expensive suits chatted and clinked glasses lightly at the curved dark wood bar where they were eating.

When I came back out, Lee was leaning against the outside wall of the restaurant, about ten feet away from the door. Sometimes it is his ordinary tenderness and vulnerability as a human being that most touches my heart, which seems to be the most extraordinary expression of divine madness. It is the elusive, immense mystery of a heart on fire, concentrated and hidden within the most ordinary and true human being, who is divinized, claiming nothing, always stepping fresh out of emptiness. In Lee, the spirit of the Bauls is alive and well in the West—iconoclasts, heretics, always going in the opposite direction of the somnabulent public. Ultimately, Lee always strikes me as a total enigma on the streets of Paris.

As we looked inside the almost opaque plate glass windows, the color of smoky quartz, at the people dining side by side at an elegant bar inside, and not at tables, Lee was clearly chewing on something. He said, "That's not going to work for us. Six of us seated at a bar? No." It was true; we couldn't even have a conversation that way. Lee asked Ann to ask the maitre d' if they had any tables, and if not, to tell him that we would not stay for lunch.

A minute later we were trooping down the street in the Rive Gauche, looking for a restaurant that would work for us. As we'd walked around thirty minutes earlier, we had seen a lively and promising place, full of people and camaraderie, with windows invitingly open to the street. Lee said, "What about that place we saw, not far from here? It looked great. Where was it?"

We quickly found our way back there. As soon as we arrived at the door, the maitre d' came out and gave us a hearty welcome. The contrast with the other restaurant was notable; we immediately found ourselves basking in the best of French international hospitality. We would have to wait ten minutes, the maitre d' apologized. They were at their busiest peak of the lunch hour, it being now almost one-thirty in the afternoon. Would we like drinks? Or anything else while we were waiting? Lee declined the offer of wine or drinks, and we simple stood waiting on the street beside the door of the restaurant.

Lee had an instant rapport with the maitre d', and soon a young waiter came out on to the street. He was smoking a cigarette, and turned to see Lee standing there. The waiter sported a beard, and he gestured to Lee's beard and then to his own, joking around in English. In the meantime, the cell phone rang—it was Sylvan, telling us that they were in the area. We were giving them the location of the restaurant when suddenly they drove down the very street where we were standing. Oh, the ironies of cell phones! It makes you wonder how we ever lived without them—which we did, and quite well. Purna jumped out to greet Lee and stand with him while we waited for a table. Sylvan and Volkmar continued on with the search for a parking place.

We were soon seated inside at a round table. The restaurant was a very open affair, full of light, with skylights in the room where the bar was, which adjoined the main dining area. With all the windows open onto the street, the whole place seemed to flow with life. Lee picked up the menu, looked at it for about five seconds, then he was ready to order. The rest of us, however, had to ask about a hundred questions of the friendly, helpful waiter, who not only spoke excellent English but was also very patient with our French. He and Purna struck up a jovial, jiving sort of repartee.

We had brought in a bottle of wine—a gift given to Lee by one of his students. When we asked the waiter if we could open the bottle of wine we had brought with us, the waiter flinched only slightly (every waiter in Paris does when we make this request), then instantly rebounded in his warm, sociable way, to take our orders for lunch. Thirty minutes later the food began to arrive. Lee poured each of us a glass of wine; Purna, Volkmar and Sylvan got to finish the bottle off. The food was delicious—mounds of fresh, creamed spinach, lamb and grilled *boeuf avec sauce poivre*, an incredible creamed ravioli made with the most delectable *fromage*, hearts of lettuce salads garnished with fresh herbs and a light lemony sauce. The service was fantastic, the meal was consumed with gusto and relish, and we were out of there, back in the Paris traffic, heading toward Montparnasse to pick up Vincent.

We pulled up just outside the *gare* and Vincent jumped into the Transporter with Volkmar and Sylvan, now that Purna was riding shotgun with Lee in the Mercedes. It was rush hour traffic in Paris—not a pretty sight. The Transporter led the way since Vincent knew Paris better than any of us, and he was the one who had arranged this meeting with the graffiti crew.

Lee groused, "We're going to be late! There must be a better way to get there!" We inched our way along at times, and finally hit the popular suburb, Vitry sur Seine, in the outskirts of Paris. The excitement was growing as we sped toward our destination. Finally, around five-thirty, we turned into an old warehouse in an industrial zone south of the city. Pulling into the parking lot under some small trees in the late afternoon heat, we got out and immediately noticed the fantastic splashes and shapes and colors in the graffiti on the walls of the building down near the corner of the lot.

"That's what I'm talking about!" Lee smiled as he gestured toward the graffiti. The rest of us were also exclaiming with pleasure—just looking at this art from a distance was enlivening. Because the Mercedes was carrying precious cargo from the morning shopping at the antiquities shop, Lee asked Sylvan and Volkmar to take turns staying with our two vehicles. Volkmar took the first turn.

We approached the chain-link guard fence that surrounded the entrance to the warehouse, whose vast interior housed Rollerparc

Avenue, the largest skatepark/incline park in France and second largest in Europe. Vincent spoke to the person at the door, who let us in, then introduced Lee and Purna to Didier, who represented the crew because he spoke English.

"Would you like to see some of the graffiti?" he asked.

Of course the answer was yes. We followed Didier and his two friends, Alain and Michel, outside and around to the side of the building, where we entered into a wonderland of visionary art expressing the range of underworld, middleworld and upperworld elements of life on Earth in the twenty-first century. We walked the length of the building, then back again. There were many different graffiti styles represented on those walls; Lee walked along taking it all in.

"Do you want to see more?" Didier asked.

"Absolutely!" Lee replied.

We walked through the roller park and then out the back door. There we found the entire back wall of the warehouse covered in street art murals of the most complex, interwoven images—one of them a work-in-progress of samurai, warriors and the interplay of dark and light, mostly rendered in gray scale. We listened in amazement as Didier explained to us that about one year ago Alain, Michel and Didier raised a seven-person crew comprised of some of the best graffiti artists from Paris, Lyon and Marseille. It had taken their crew of seven about a week to paint one of the two immense murals. He said that they would take pictures of it, then cover it over with white paint and start again.

Back inside, we looked at two fantastic canvases that Alain had painted especially for this meeting with their potential patrons. Lee and Purna began the process of working out a deal to represent these artists world-wide on the internet; their work would also be in the second floor gallery at the shop in La Roche Posay and offered to all of Lee's students.

While Lee, Purna and Vincent talked with the other artists, I spent some time talking with Didier. I knew that David Amar, the son of the much loved French spiritual teacher Yvan Amar, who died six years ago of a lung condition that he had battled for many years, was the person who had hooked Lee up with the graffiti crew. When I mentioned David's name to Didier, he lit up. He told me that he and David grew up together as best friends; his family was very close to the Amar family.

"You must have known Yvan?" I asked.

"Oh yes, I knew Yvan very well," Didier answered with a smile. "He was like a second father to me."

"Yvan was a very special person," I said. "He touched my heart very much. He touched the hearts of many, many people. A rare person."

"Yes," Didier smiled broadly in agreement, "he was very special . . . he was a very big influence in my life."

This interchange I found especially poignant, because Yvan was the person who really connected Lee to France and Arnaud Desjardins. Yvan met Lee in 1988, when Lee came to France at the invitation of his first French student, Michelle Bompois. It was a friend of Michelle's who introduced Lee and Yvan. Two years later, it was Yvan who told Gilles Farcet about Lee Lozowick, saying, "You must interview this man for your book." He had given him a copy of one of Lee's books, and Gilles had immediately connected to the teaching.

The karmic connection between Lee and Yvan has always been extraordinary, rich and heavy with significance and their shared love of the path and the guru/devotee relationship. Like Lee with Yogi Ramsuratkumar, Yvan was a great devotee of his master, Chandra Swami. I had had the opportunity to know Yvan through Lee, had met him several times and stayed in his home on a few occasions over the years when Lee visited there to give teachings in Gordes. Yvan had a way of creating sacred spaces, of invoking exalted devotional states, and of making the teaching available in personal, immediate ways. He had a natural instinct for the devotional path, and he was one of the few people I've ever known who saw Lee purely at the level of the heart. When Lee and Yvan were together, there was a *bhava*, a devotional mood, created: I always felt that Yvan became Radha to Lee's Krishna, while the rest of us were the *gopis* watching their *lila*.

All these important background connections made Lee's relationship with this graffiti crew, which came through David Amar, more subtly textured, as if the relationship, from the beginning, carried a little something of the sweet dignity, the ancient-of-days nobility and even the *rasa*, or mood of divine love, that characterized Lee's relationship with Yvan.

The arrangement for the art was sealed, and we walked together back outside to our two vehicles after Alain and Volkmar very carefully wrapped the larger of the two graffiti pieces in huge sheets of bubble wrap. Only one of the two canvases painted by Alain would fit in the Transporter that night, and even then, it had to be tied in with twine, the back doors secured but partially open. Lee drove the Mercedes behind the Transporter, to make sure nothing happened to the canvas, which was carefully sealed inside its plastic bubble wrap. Just as we hit the autoroute outside of Paris, a few raindrops sprinkled briefly, then it was dry for the next three hours. At midnight the art was finally unloaded in its new home: the ashram.

The next morning Lee, Purna, Ann and I would leave the ashram at six-thirty, before meditation, for Limoges, two and a half hours away. It was the day of the Limoges Annual Grand Brocante Festival, held in the winding, narrow cobblestone streets of the old city, beneath the benign watchful care of the old cathedral there. We would be home in time for dinner.

Ferme de Jutreau
September 10

While Lee was in Limoges all day having a great time at the *fete de brocante*, the ashram was gearing up for the six-day money seminar, to be given by Lee and Purna, which would begin with darshan tomorrow night. People were already coming in from various places in France, Germany, England and America, and the atmosphere began to build a different kind of charge that had begun with Lee's one-day trip to Paris yesterday and the connection he'd made with the crew of graffiti artists.

After dinner Lee chose to play bridge. As the cards were shuffled and dealt time and again, it rained outside. Inside it was quiet and uneventful, like the calm before the storm. Lee, who specializes in spontaneous teaching outbursts, seemed to be in a dormant mode for an hour or so. Then, ending the game abruptly, Lee began to work with Purna on arranging some of the vast storehouse of artifacts that dominate the space of the salon in the *grande maison*. Tom Lennon, Clelia, and Ken came just in time for tea. They had arrived from the States via Paris and were bearing boxes of books and CDs. After a very affectionate reunion with their guru, their attention was taken by the five by ten foot graffiti piece Lee had brought back from Paris late last night, now on display behind his leather chair in front of the fireplace.

The graffiti was a complex amalgam, a stream of consciousness strident chord blasted down on canvas from spray cans of paint in grey tones and black with splashes of pink and green. It had strong underworld notes and a raw, bizarre, distorted quality. Contemplating this piece of art, you get a hit of what it's like being on the city streets or in the underground scene, in the Metro in Paris.

With Lee ensconced in his chair, the tea space began, with about twenty people sitting in the room. He started to talk about the graffiti, which everyone was studying with great intent and interest as the coffee was served. He was elated by the whole project and quickly suggested that someone should buy the piece for the ashram; furthermore, he said that it should be installed on the wall in the dining room in the *grande maison*. Sylvan asked the price of the piece, and when Lee told him, he quickly conferred with Tom then said, "Tom and I will buy the piece for the ashram."

Lee's response was ecstatic: "Great! It'll be perfect in the dining room. We'll just have to move things in there tomorrow. Everyone in the sangha should have one of these on the walls of their house! You know what happens when you have something like this on the wall? Everyone's idea of what is art and what is attractive gets thrown into a kind of magnified clarity. Imagine how Christmas dinner with your family in your home and what kind of reaction they would have! So we can have Serge and one or two of the men hang this up tomorrow."

Lee began to describe the scene with the crew of graffiti artists in Paris, how we met them at a warehouse in Sevre, where they paint on the outside walls. He said that when Volkmar, an artist, saw the other piece, which was too big to fit into the van, he gasped and said, "It's a masterpiece," because Volkmar, a fine artist himself, could see the skill that went into the making of the art. At the time, as we stood in the warehouse in Paris looking at the work of the artists on the crew, Lee had also said of that piece, painted by Alain, "The artist speaks . . ."

Lee began to explain further, "Graffiti is a criminal offense; it's still considered absolutely taboo in Paris. And the cops are crazy, they'll shoot at you . . . These guys got tired of dealing with it, so they rented a warehouse and now they paint graffiti on the outside walls—huge complex pieces of work. You wouldn't believe these pieces, so intricate, the detail that covers immense spaces on the walls. When they are finished, they spray white paint over it and then start again!"

"So it has this quality of impermanence," someone commented.

"Yes, impermanence," Lee nodded. He said, "Their whole thing is to create art, and the impermanence is part of it—the act of creating it is the point. It's the creating itself that is the transformation."

Michelle asked "When we buy a graffiti image that is a permanent piece of art that doesn't get spray painted over, is that the end of the transformative power of the piece, the true creativity of it?"

Lee answered, "No. What we get with the piece of graffiti art is a little slice of the transformative process. Yesterday when we talked to the artists, they practically had tears in their eyes, because people see them as criminals, when to them, they are like modern Van Goghs."

Lee talked about two other artists whose quite sublime work we had seen on the warehouse wall; they work together without talking to each other. They have no plan at all of what they will do—they just start, and once in a while they will look at each other, and then go on painting in this creative telepathic process. Lee said, "The art that is created is *seamless*: you cannot tell that two people worked on the piece."

Lee gestured to the piece behind him, saying, "Three guys did this. The big square one that we couldn't fit into the van was done by the head of the crew. There will be a whole variety of styles in the pieces we've committed to. Eventually, we'll have a whole stable of graffiti artists doing work for us—in different places like Marseilles, Freiburg, Berlin—that we are putting out to the world. We're starting a website; it will be a very large, mainstream presentation . . . ."

He continued, "Graffiti is like tattoos—people are still offended by them—they don't understand. Like Aaron's grandfather . . . ."

Lee told the story of Aaron Funk's grandfather, who had never supported Aaron's work as a tattoo artist. They were at odds with each other on the issue, even estranged in a way, because of Aaron's choice of livelihood, until the tattoo book, *Agony and Alchemy,* came along. Aaron showed it to his grandfather, who read it and spent an hour looking at the photos. It turned his grandfather around, opened up his understanding and view of Aaron's work. Now he is really proud of Aaron.

Lee said, "It's the same with graffiti. People have to be educated about what it is. It's that they don't understand the incredible creativity this art can be, or the transformational power it can have. The graffiti piece is the doorway into the artist's world. It's not the actual image itself; it's what the image holds from the act of creation. Even if the images are somewhat bizarre, what you're getting is the passion of the artist for transformation. They've grown up in a culture where this is the dominant kind of image on the streets, but their desire for transformation is the same as anybody's.

"If you look through the images, what you find is the artists' desire for personal transformation, if the creative process comes from true inspiration, instead of a commercial wish. You have some degree of technical skill, because it requires both technical skill and a desire for personal transformation; the more skill involved, the more accessible the doorway to the transformational process is. Volkmar could *see* the skill in this art—you may not like the images, but the potential for transformation is the same."

Lee continued, "But a lot of art is crap, so the artist has to have some real sense of self. Like Alain—I looked at that guy, and he just looked so out of sync with society, with the sleeping world, as it is. He looked like he is at odds with the sleeping world."

The conversation rolled along very quickly, with the servers coming and going, refilling cups of coffee and offering sweets. At one point Joelle, who was troubled by the intensity of the images, asked, "What is the use of having this on our walls?"

Lee answered, "As a reminding factor. A *reminding* factor," he emphasized. "What does this," he pointed to the canvas behind him, "make you think about?"

Joelle said, "Death . . . and it makes me feel nausea."

"Perfect! That's the perfect answer," Lee exulted. He was smiling as he said, "What better reminding factors to pierce your lack of self-unity than death and nausea. It's a reminding factor that is completely benign—it's not dangerous, not an outpouring of suffering, like photographs of war, like blown up people, people who have been tortured, mothers who have lost their children, where the immensity of human suffering is overwhelming. And these images come from a place of love of life, instead of the horror of the situation. Colonel Kurtz couldn't have painted this!" Lee laughed.

Everyone in the space, about twenty people, looked at the graffiti searchingly. Our interest was completely engaged by Lee and his "new passion" as we considered the paradoxical nature of his statements, which threw light on his own insight into graffiti as an art form and the reason why he has such a rapport with it. It didn't communicate the power of human suffering like the photographs Lee mentioned of actual suffering—human beings torn by war, torture, losing their children—but it did communicate suffering; it has a definite evocative underworld quality. Then Alrun said, "But the eyes are very sad; I see such sadness in the eyes."

Without even turning to look at the graffiti, Lee knew exactly what Alrun was talking about, and he answered, "It's a man with a mask on," referring to one of the images in the piece. "Yes, the eyes are very expressive."

The evening seemed to be winding down; all tea spaces, however lively they are at times, eventually disappear into the void of impermanence. Then Clelia commented, "I read a quote from Robert Svoboda that the essence of tantra is finding what opens you."

Lee responded, "He means what opens you to the flow of Divine Influence or to the Will of God. Well, that's nice! That makes tantra a pretty easy practice! Most everything in this room opens you!"

Purna, who was sitting on the floor beside Lee, said, "Part of what Svoboda was saying is that you have to have the strength of character to stay in contact with it."

Ann commented on what a tremendous passion the artists have for their work, and then said, "I noticed that this guy's car was packed with spray cans, literally packed . . . . "

We began to talk about how the artists are compelled to make graffiti; it truly is their calling, and they are fueled by a powerful muse. I said, "Didier told me that one of their friends got arrested and fined one million francs for painting graffiti on a train—that's one of the worst offenses, painting on trains. But they have to paint, the art comes first, so they won't stop, no matter what.

Lee said, "I think my father would have liked graffiti art—that kind of complexity, he was really into that . . . . In America, people are so paranoid about gang influence, something like this shows up and people go ballistic."

Lee then described the larger piece that was left in Paris because it wouldn't fit into the van. He said, "It is a literal translation of the artist with his muse—the muse as the spray can, as a woman." It was essentially the "artist" depicted in the bizarre distortions of a human character, with big lips, a black Afro, long, spindly arms and splayed fingers, his arm draped affectionately, possessively, intimately, around a voluptuous woman's body.

First you just saw the male character; then you noticed that the woman's head was the top of a can of spray paint—an image that stops the mind. The whole thing was done with the characteristic graffiti twist in shades of black and gray, with splashes of lime green and pink.

One thing was perfectly clear: Lee was marvelously enlivened by the whole project. It was thrilling to see him so alive and ecstatic. After a few minutes he said, "Wait till you see the other one! Wait till you see the stuff that comes from these guys, now that we're behind them and our Influence is permeating them. I can hardly wait! I'm so excited I can barely sit here and eat chocolate and ginger and drink coffee! But that's a good thing to do, while you're waiting—eat chocolate and ginger and drink coffee!"

Ferme de Jutreau
September 11

Darshan tonight in the barn kicked off the beginning of the long-awaited money seminar, titled "Money: How to Make It; How to

Keep It; How to Use It Wisely," a six-day extravaganza to be presented by Lee and Purna that had everyone buzzing. Lee had been in France for two and a half months, and this was only the second *darshan* of the summer, so the mood was very strong. People had come from Britain, the U.S. and Germany as well as from various places in France to attend the seminar. Tonight the hall was full with seminar participants as well as the householders and other French sangha members who live nearby.

Lee came in during the chanting and took his seat, wearing the thin white cotton caftan and red head wrap that he has been wearing for six or seven years in *darshan* at Ferme de Jutreau. As soon as the *prasad* exchange and chanting was over, he jumped into his talk enthusiastically, like a racehorse at the starting gate. Like every other presentation for the next six days, this talk was not recorded on audiotape or film. Our notes would be the only record we would have of the whole week.

He looked out at everyone and boomed, "Congratulations! Twenty-five percent of the people who registered for the money seminar dropped out, so you made it through the first hurdle! It wasn't an accident for those who didn't make it! Part of how great a week it's going to be is how strong the denying force was—and it was big! *You* made it through!"

Two days earlier, after a phone call from another student canceling their enrollment in the seminar, Lee had said with sarcastic exasperation in the office, "I've never known so many people to have their parents die in one week! *Unbelievable*!" Now he began to speak about the importance of our Work as the world gets worse. He spoke about his new passion for graffiti art, and that he believed graffiti would be the next big craze in the art world. He talked about his relationship with the young graffiti artists and how extraordinary it is for them to have a patron for their art. "Let's hope that all the money we're giving them is not going to turn them into materialistic pigs—like Purna and me!" Everyone laughed at this first of many jokes that Lee would make over the next six days about money and desire.

He continued, "So, we're not recording the seminar in any way, video or audio. Now that you made it here, don't fuck up. Don't get sick—you know what I mean? We're not going to do this again. Purna may decide to, but I'm not. But you're *here*. You made it through the labyrinth, but you still have to get what's being offered. It will require moving through another labyrinth, but you can do it. I have faith in you. We don't have faith in humanity, but we do have faith in you!

"We live in a very dynamic Universe. Most people live in a singular Universe—only one reality. Even though the Universe is always trying to convey its multiple forms, we keep going back to the view that there is only one reality. We live in a multiple reality Universe. The gross physical world of the five senses is not the only reality."

Lee began to talk about the huge, five-tier, black granite, two to three hundred-year-old *arati* lamp that was burning now with about a hundred wicks soaked in ghee. He said, "It's the second time we've burned it. I'm so embarrassed—I didn't even see it the first time we burned it. I asked everyone after the last darshan, 'Why didn't you burn the arati lamp?' They said, 'It was lit! Didn't you see it?' I was so focused on darshan, and happy and absorbed in seeing all of you, that I didn't even see it when I came in!

"Every summer in the past, in my wandering and looking for treasures for you all, in all that time I've found one treasure trove. This summer I found three! I mean *treasure troves*! In each case, there was instant communion, an instant connection with the owner of the treasure, soon to be mine—mine alone! You know, I don't need any time to understand what something is in the multiple reality of things. I don't need time and space to show me the value of something. I get it instantaneously.

"So, in one instance, I found this man at a brocante who had all these shamanic implements for magical purposes and piercing through multiple realities. I realized instantly it was a treasure. I started piling things up, 'I'll take this and this and this,' and the longer it went on, the more disturbed the man got. He wanted me to look at each piece and listen to him go on and on poetically about it, and commune with him about how special it was. He had lived with shamans in Nepal and in other places, and he wanted me to really appreciate the value of this stuff. But the thing is that I instantly knew the value of it. He was getting more and more disturbed that I was just buying it, without any romance. I was like, 'Fine, get disturbed—just give me the shit!'

"I came back the next day and he had doubled his prices! 'Your prices are high today,' I said. He said, 'I made a mistake yesterday. Listen,' he said, 'Can I tell you something? I'm afraid you'll get angry.' I said, 'Nothing makes me angry.' Of course, that's not true. Plenty of women have made me angry, but I like to pretend that I'm not angry, and that shows them!"

Everyone laughed at Lee's description of relationship dynamics. The mood was friendly and celebratory, and there were lots of smiles in the room along with some quizzical looks or simply interested faces among those who were new and not used to Lee's pointed, power-packed ramblings.

He continued, "You know how it is with our partners. The unspoken agreement is 'Make me feel good.' Even if our partner is the guru, the agreement is not, 'Thank you for this incredible opportunity.' The agreement with our partners is, 'Make me feel good!' Right? So, this guy said to me, 'You don't know what these things are.' He wanted me to linger and listen to endless stories.

"Fuck that! I don't have time for that! Time is money! This guy had a fantastic buffalo killing sword, exactly like the sword they used to sacrifice the buffalo in *Apocalypse Now*—I mean exactly. Incredible! He said to me, 'I have the feeling that it's just business for you.' He was offended because I'm not going to live in his world. Fuck his world! I have a world, and if he's not going to let me live in it, well . . . !"

People burst into laughter at this. Lee had a big smile on his face. Obviously he was joking, but at the same time it was a metaphor and a demonstration of his ruthless inherence in the absolute context that he would be transmitting about money. His smile lingered, and he said, "It's funny, isn't it?" Then he continued: "So, we live in a multiple Universe. For most people the world of time and space is their only reality, and when the world beyond time and space intersects their world, they reject the multiple Universe.

"You and I live in a multi-dimensional, multi-reality Universe. So, we're going to be talking about context this week, but you cannot get context from your five senses in the time and space Universe. It's not possible. So even though we use the language, 'shift of context,' it's not actually a shift from the context we are in now to another context—you cannot shift context from a position of the time and space, five senses reality that you live in now. You can only shift context from the context you want to be in! How do we get there? You don't get there; you are there. You simply start living there. Instead of this being your singular reality, that becomes your singular reality.

"Purna and I are going to create magic this week, and every one of you can participate if you wish, if your wish is strong enough, but you're going to have to understand that we live in a multiple reality, in a multi-dimensional Universe. Every one of you has extraordinary gifts—as an artist, a partner, a parent—and in spite of that extraordinary gift, we struggle in ways we don't need to struggle in. It doesn't mean that we don't have wonderful lives, but they are limited by our perception of reality. You know the line in the Bob Dylan song, 'You don't have to be a weatherman to know which way the wind blows.' "

Lee paused and looked down at the guru's sandals, which were placed on the dais just below his feet. They were smothered with gorgeous lavender and gold dahlias from the garden outside the *grande maison*. "Look!" he exclaimed, looking back up at us with delight and a disarming innocence that seemed to belie his brash and arrogant words of only ten minutes before. "There's a bee dying, right in the middle of that flower! That's nice. That's a good metaphor for the Work. The flower being the Work, and you being the bee . . .!" He smiled again.

"So, we live in a multiple reality, and the more subtle the realities are, the more power they have. Money is just a metaphor, a symbol for power, and power is what tantra is about—power used for the Work, not power used for what *you* think is useful. If you go to India and meet tantric sadhus, most of them are angry and unhappy, because they misunderstand the aim of power. They seek to be yogis with personal power, which is why they're angry. Those tantric sadhus who understand that they are gathering power for the impersonal purpose of the transformation of humankind are relaxed and attractive."

He continued, "You've got to be able to shift realities instantly, because we live in a dangerously shifting, changing world, and you don't want to be stuck in a five sense, space/time reality if you don't have to be.

"The money consideration is a doorway. It's a doorway into a vast domain of a multiple reality Universe. Getting into this world will be easy this week, but then you are going to leave, and you need to be able to have this domain as a resource you can tap anytime, easily. You have to pounce on an opportunity like a cat on its prey, like a big cat on a gazelle—when the moment is right, they pounce! Then they eat their meal, sleep, and if the jackals come, they chase them off."

Lee careened full speed ahead into fast-paced, theatrical joking around, reeling on into a description of how he likes to pepper his conversation, when he needs to, with quotes: "Robert Frost, you know, 'Miles to go before I sleep.' You say that and people go, 'Ohhh, Robert Frost . . .!' As if you know all about Robert Frost. I don't know anything about Robert Frost! I've never read his poetry! But I know, 'Miles to go before I sleep,' and people are, 'Ohhh . . .'

And who is Robert Frost when compared to Bukowski? Nobody!" Everyone laughed. It was a rather sly communication of skillful means in a multi-dimensional Universe.

"I keep my sentiments to myself. I'm a very romantic character, but I keep it all to myself. I'm in love with tattoos and graffiti, but it's all inside. Outside, it's all business . . . . Even in relationship, I keep my sentiments to myself. Time to eat—fine. Time to screw—fine. Time to be romantic? See ya—I'm going to my room to be alone!

"I have zero compassion for all your, 'Oh, I've always been afraid to be successful.' *Fuck* that shit!" More laughter broke out in the room. Lee's absolute statements in which he freely acclaimed and affirmed his unshakable faith in his students' ability to break free of our chains was very moving. The last statement, "None of your previous history with money has to implicate you—ever again," was a kind of *abhisheka*, an empowerment that was given to anyone who was able to receive and hold it. Immediately he veered toward the mundane, picking up some *prasad* and exclaiming, "A chocolate pig! I love pigs! And here's one in chocolate!"

Uproarious laughter broke out at this oblique reference to "Pig Man," an alter ego, so to speak, that had taken hold as a humorous metaphor with multiple meanings. He spun off into a hilarious reverie about boudin, or blood sausage, and the bodily effects of eating such things, eventually being turned into a pig, and ending with hefting the *prasad* in his hand and saying, "Chocolate pigs are wonderful! Everybody should have one!"

Everyone was laughing as Lee continued tongue-in-cheek, with a sly smile, saying, "I think we should try to make pig cheese! Why not? We eat goat cheese, cow cheese, sheep cheese—why not pig cheese? We *eat* pigs! Why not make cheese from their milk? A big sow, with twelve teats! I think we should try it! We'd be the only farm with pig cheese!" The laughter got more delirious with the zany nuttiness of Lee's idea, which at the same was communicating the realm of infinite possibility in a multiple reality Universe, and demonstrating the necessity to drop our preconceived notions of what is acceptable and what is not.

"Well, there's a business idea for you—you can have it! I don't even want a percentage! I come up with ideas like that once a month, and nobody takes me up on it! Like Atlantean Tantra, for example. The students I gave that idea to would be multi, multi millionaires by now if they'd done it, but they didn't do it. The thing is, Atlantean Tantra is real, only you have to make it real in this world, and as soon as you make it real, it is Real. You think in the five sense time/space reality that star people are real? They are raving maniacs! But in their reality, they were born on Saturn or Sirius. Really, nobody was ever born on Saturn, we know that. There's nothing on Saturn but poisonous gas, which is what some of you will have by the end of this week!" More laughter.

"Atlantis really exists in some form on our world. Atlantean Tantra is a real reality, not a psychotic reality. But you'll have to understand this, because I am not going to back-slap some guy over a shamanistic power tool because it's socially expected. I don't live in that world. Let's do away with expected relationship. Plus, I have a black and white relationship to money that is completely impersonal. Money is black and white to me—it's not about sentimentality and romance. Friendship comes later, if it comes, and sometimes it does. But first, it's all business, *all* business . . . I've been saying for years, do not borrow or loan money to members of the sangha, except with my express support. When your context for money is not my context for money, this is bad work.

"So, if you want to be sentimental, you're going to miss my part of the week. If you want to think you're taking advantage of somebody, you're going to miss my part of the week. My relationship to money is completely free of sentiment, complication, psychology, guilt—it's black and white, and I'm going to try to convey that to you this week, because money is *not* love, people, art, relationship—it's *money.* If you want to maintain a psychological, emotional relationship to money, you're going to miss my part of the week.

"Purna and I did not discuss what we're going to talk about this week, and we will weave everything together in a magical way before the week is over. We're going on a great ride this week! Congratulations again, because you made it through the labyrinth to get here. And take a good look at that graffiti in the dining room of the house—you're gonna love it, but you'll have to shift your viewpoint. I grew up in a very refined artistic environment, around artists. I think my father would have really liked graffiti art, because he had an instinct for what is real, and this art is real. When we were talking to these graffiti guys about their work as art, they had tears in their eyes, because people don't think it's real—they think it's shit. I'm wild about this stuff . . ."

Lee's excitement and enthusiasm fueled the darshan, which lasted until almost ten o'clock. Finally Lee carefully packed up several items of *prasad* in a large, precariously balanced pile that he would carry in himself—the chocolates and other special items—and said "Jai Guru!" as he walked out.

After the closing *puja* and chants in the darshan hall, everyone very quickly gathered in the salon of the *grande maison* for tea, and the coffee and treats came out, one platter after another of cookies, chocolates, ginger and special treats. The room was crowded and hot, with people clustered together in the small amount of space left after the artifacts were rearranged by Lee to make a little more room for us to sit.

We were on to our second cups of coffee when, before we knew what had happened, Lee was selling artifacts, offering sizzling deals on old stone pieces and bronze singing bowls. One beautiful piece after another—Ganesh, Hanuman, goddesses of various kinds—flew out of Lee's hands. Suddenly, it was eleven-thirty, and Lee was talking ecstatically about the kachinas that were recently unpacked and merchandized in the shop in La Roche Posay.

Charlotte said, "I've never seen a kachina."

"You've never seen one?" Lee countered in amazement. "We've got a whole box of them here. Would you like to see them?" Charlotte answered yes immediately. Lee looked out at the rest of crowded room and asked again, "Would you like to see them?"

"Yes!" came the resounding answer.

"Bring that box of kachinas!" Lee practically shouted. The huge cardboard box in which the kachinas had been shipped was somehow lifted up over all the people who were crowded into the salon for tea and deposited at the side of Lee's chair. Very quickly Purna and Andrea opened it and began to unpack kachinas, carefully shaking off the white plastic popcorn in which they were nestled for safe shipping. One after another came out for display, bright and colorful, feathers proud and bold, dancing and shaking. Lee held them up one at a time, played with them like a child, extolled their virtues.

He was ecstatic, beaming light on us as he sold kachinas for the next hour while we were rapt and totally captured in the joy of his playful, supercharged interchange with us. He kept pushing the edges back further and further, challenging and charming people into buying more, until everyone was engaged in some way that catalyzed us to move intentionally out of our usual comfort zone. For many, that meant buying more artifacts, the implication being that we were committing to a greater vision of how our lives can show up in terms of creativity, possibility, energy and money—and the skillful means that would have to be cultivated to manifest that.

It was clear that there was a transmission and exchange of energy going on in the midst of the theatre, which went on until almost one o'clock. We seemed to have no concern whatsoever for the fact that we would be on our meditation pillows at 6:45 the next morning. It was the harbinger of things to come for the next six days, when the schedule would be packed, with a fleet thirty-minute break between events in the barn darshan hall, where all the talks and gatherings, except tea, would be held.

Finally, Lee released us from his spell, and after he walked out with a triumphant, "Bonne nuit!" we dispersed, slowly, one by one, with many lingering in little clusters of two or three, to talk in animated, intimate conversations, on into the wee hours of the night.

Money Seminar
September 12

The first morning. With about forty-five participants enrolled, including several of the ashram residents, the darshan hall was comfortably full on the women's side and more than half full on the men's side. Other ashram residents would be spending all their time in the kitchen and on staff to manage the food and logistics of the week, as well as to continue to staff the store in La Roche Posay. Right away this seminar was proving to be a different kind of atmosphere and mood: Lee had already told us that there would be no recording and no video. In other words, the only record of this unusual, even historic teaching event would be in our bodies and in our notes. He commented that we could pass stories on to others on a one-on-one basis, but he asked us not to read notes in an after dinner talk, as we often do. The idea was that whoever made it through the labyrinth to get here for this was who would receive it.

Another very different note was that there was only one child on the whole ashram for the week, Sari, a ten-month-old baby visiting from the States, whose father, Sylvan, was enrolled in the seminar. Denise, Sari's mother, spent the week in a different kind of retreat; all the adults were completely engaged, from early morning until very late at night. The parents of the French children had made plans for their children to be elsewhere with their mothers and other adults, at home or on vacation. It was the first time I've ever seen the ashram without lots of kids playing, calling out, laughing, running around the courtyard or in the orchard.

The first session started thirty minutes after meditation and *arati*. Purna kicked things off, giving us a general idea of things: that the schedule for each day would be posted day-by-day, after morning meditation—which meant that we did not know from one day to the next what would be happening tomorrow; that we should honor a certain protocol—like not talking as we left the space after each scheduled event and coming on time; and we were asked not to read ahead in the seminar workbooks that were passed out.

Purna told us that there would be a lot of experiential processes this week, and that Lee had already set the bar so high with his *darshan* talk—and his absolute statement, "My relationship to money is black and white"—that Purna himself was powerfully impacted by Lee's willingness to expect and demand the ultimate from us. He was inspired by Lee's unwillingness to capitulate to the habitual ways of his students, and in this gesture of compassion, Lee was offering the opportunity for us to walk into his context and into his world.

Speaking further about context, Purna said, "A new context is always asserted. A new context is always due to practice. What we are doing here this week is an insight-based approach." He made it clear that Lee was the one holding the absolute Context for the week, while Purna would be helping us integrate that in a more relative way. A lot of Purna's presentation would include working in teams or small groups and engaging writing exercises, much of this based on work that he had done in the prison system or in other secular circumstances. He said that all the processes we would be doing were not Lee's way of doing things, but that out of his love for Purna, Lee was allowing him to do things his way.

Making it clear that the experiential aspects of the week would be aimed at integrating the context that Lee transmitted to us, Purna said that a lot of what we would be doing was getting vulnerable. He quoted psychologist Gordon Neufeld as saying, "Vulnerability is the driver for growth and maturation," and he talked about the importance of what Chögyam Trungpa Rinpoche called, "The tender and sad heart of the warrior."

On a practical note, Purna asked that we make a commitment to be on time and to take everything that belonged to us—notebooks, sweaters, shawls, whatever—out of the hall at the end of each session. The schedule included having two meals a day and would be posted every morning for that day: today brunch was at ten a.m. and dinner at four-thirty p.m. The rest of the day was arranged in one hour and a half sessions, packed in back-to-back, with thirty-minute breaks in between.

Furthermore, with one hour scheduled for the meals, there was only thirty minutes to eat because the participants had to spend the last thirty minutes clearing the tables and washing dishes for about sixty people before the next session started. The only kitchen staff we had were four cooks and one server/set up person; they couldn't be expected to wash all those dishes as well as prepare food for everyone and handle all the meal set-up!

All this said and done, we had been fully introduced to the space and the chamber of the week. Despite the beautiful early fall weather that made you sort of want to bliss out, even though it was a little chilly, we knew we were in for a *sesshin* of a different kind; instead of a meditation intensive, we would be sitting on our pillow, but engaged full on in a different way. All in all, we figured out that we would be spending over twelve hours a day sitting—in sessions, meditating, or crammed into the tea space on pillows on the floor.

After brunch on this first morning of six, Lee gave a talk at eleven o'clock. He began with, "Don't sweat the small stuff. Where money is concerned, it's all small stuff, because money is not health, love, relationship, happiness. It's just money. It's useful to remember it's small stuff, but be responsible for your debts. Money is small, but responsibility is not small. Maybe for some of you who

I've allowed to really go into debt, *responsibility* is the issue, not the bronze . . . ."

"When you get into believing that your wants are needs, then you get into significant conflict. It's been proven that human beings need physical contact and physical affection, but it has not been proven that we need love. We all think we need love. Maybe we just need company, community. What would you rather have: someone who loves you but dishonors and abuses you, or someone who doesn't love you but who is respecting, honoring and affectionate? I'd take the second.

"There is nothing wrong with desire on the Path—it's very useful. Big desire! I'm suggesting that you always play it safe, but the thing is that you don't know what safe is! A lot of people thought playing it safe meant not coming to this seminar!"

Lee began to talk about how most of us need to relax, and he used one of the men in the seminar as an example. "He has got to relax! He could be making twenty thousand euros a month, but he's got to lighten up and relax, because people he will do business with will want someone who will make them feel good, not someone who is *serious*. So, he's got to lighten up and relax, because it's all small stuff! The Universe is waiting to shower him and everyone who works with him with a lot of money, but he's got to relax, without losing his integrity.

"People with money are bored. Why shouldn't you be the beneficiary of other people's boredom, of the money that they have to throw around? We have grown up with a certain ethic. My parents were socially and politically alert, they marched against segregation and aggression on America's part. My father was passionate about social causes and they were relaxed, at ease with themselves. You are never going to be able to control the ethics of others; just deal with your own integrity.

"The first part of that is getting some perspective. Even when you have money to waste, to waste it is an abuse of resources, and abuse of resources goes against the laws of the Work, even when you can afford it."

When Lee commented in jest that he hoped people would buy a lot of bronze—that is, people who can actually pay for it—laughter broke out in the space. "You know, I won't turn it down if you come and say, 'I have have thirty thousand euros and I want some bronze!' I won't say, 'Oh please, I want to give you credit!'

"We have no idea how much money we spend on insignificant indulgences—most of it is for imaginary comfort. So you want to be conscious about how you spend money." Lee talked about how he doesn't go out to restaurants very often at all. Once or twice a year he goes to a very fine restaurant, because that is a good use of money. He continued, "When you spend money, the only question is, is it a good use for your money? What would you do with that money otherwise? Most people would spend it on restaurants and clothes, and travel. Is it worth it? I haven't been on a vacation in years! I can sit out in the courtyard on a nice day, and it's as good as any vacation for me. My kids say, 'Let's go to the beach, let's go to the beach!' To me, just sitting here in the courtyard is heaven! The weather is beautiful, the buildings are full of age and wisdom and beauty. What more do you want?

"If I buy an artifact for myself I think, what would I do if not buying this artifact with this money? If you have money, spend it. Keep a little bit aside for eventualities, and if you have it, spend it—on investments, on bronze, but on substantial things. Clothes, food and vacations—you might as well throw it away! But substantial things—jewelry, bronze, houses, cars, rare jewels, gold—those are substantial things. Do those other things you spend money on give you joy? If there's nothing else that gives you joy, then go to the beach. But if the pleasure you get from going to the beach is completely subjective, you could have just as much pleasure staying home, then consider.

"When you spend money, the question is not, how are you going to pay for it, but is it necessary? The seminar, the bronze, the renovation to your home? Part of managing your money is having this perspective: what would I do with this money if not spend it here? And is that more valuable to you? Having pizza for lunch, or having an artifact or going to a seminar? Fifteen hundred euros is nothing! Ten euros for pizza is less than nothing, however, wasting resources goes against the laws of the Work. So, money is a resource. It's not health, happiness or love, so please, never assume it is. When the choice is love or money, always take love; if the choice is health and money, take health. Because there are certain jobs that pay more money, but you lose your health. I would never recommend trading health for money.

"Money is just a resource, and it's all small stuff. It's the unconscious that turns money into love. Obviously you need some degree of self-awareness to do this whole thing. So, the bottom-line recommendation is: don't ever trade health, happiness and love for money. Work hard, but not so hard that health, happiness and love are compromised. And *never* waste resources: money and energy. We waste huge amounts of energy on emotional crises."

Lee spoke about how a lot of his students had gotten emotionally involved in the break-up of a long-time couple in the sangha, which was "a colossal waste of resources." He said that when we do this, it is throwing resources out the window. He continued:

"So, don't waste resources—money or energy. The question is always: is this a proper, useful use of resources? You have to stop for a second and ask yourself that question: What would you spend the money on otherwise? In his early years in Paris, Henry Miller was poor; he often had no money for food and had to go to his friends for dinner, but he always had paper and pens for his writing. So the question is, how are you using your resources?"

We were spiraling through the first day at what seemed like the speed of light. We'd had no time to stop and reflect on the nature of reality as Purna plunged into his one o'clock talk asking the rhetorical question: How many people felt the guru function in an unusually strong way last night in *darshan* and in the tea space? The tea space had been unique in the history of Ferme de Jutreau, lasting until one a.m. What was it that was so incredible about those spaces? And what stands in the way of that being the way it is all the time? Can we imagine living in that all the time?

Purna said, "My experience is that the communication of the guru has been made to people; my experience is the communication has been by Lee to most people in this room, and people are carrying that in some way. What is it that doesn't allow that to show up as an expression of our lives?" He referred to Warren Berrigian, a unique character who does an extraordinary form of body work aimed toward breakthrough in vocal capacity for singers. Warren says that a man or woman who cannot be responsible for their past cannot create a new and different future, so that the past doesn't keep our foot nailed to the floor.

Purna continued, "How many people experience fear, distrust, greed, anger, competition, jealousy, the need to control? All that has to do with scarcity, with not having enough. Gordon Neufeld says that the brain functions in one of two ways: one, it defends itself against pain or disappointment too great to bear; or two, it is vulnerable to the wound of love, or brokenheartedness, because we are able to experience and bear the pain and disappointment of life. Either defended or vulnerable: there is no middle ground.

"Vulnerabilty is a very big word for this workshop. And, you don't have to *share* when you're vulnerable. The reason most people are driven to share is neurosis. Last night, for me, was historic, one of those nights when the transmission of the guru was just . . . " Purna clapped his hands together very loudly, so that the sound popped in the space.

"So Gordon Neufeld says that vulnerability is the driver of maturation. Most of the people sitting in this room are *not* maturing in their sadhana. It's not that something isn't going on. People are being radiated with Lee's Influence, but that's different than maturation—that's different than climbing the ladder of the Work. We are stuck in the same bullshit we were stuck in at four years of age, because we're not vulnerable. The brain looks around and says, 'This reminds me of something that happened to me,' a pain or disappointment too great to bear. Or, we cover it over with some spiritual mumbo jumbo! I am sick to death of it! People talk the dharma and can't even turn out a damn light.

"So, we're going to spend some time getting vulnerable—to acknowledge the disappointment. The practice is being able to move fluidly into some kind of vulnerability."

Purna talked about how each one of us has a "winning formula," which is in fact based on our survival strategy. As much as we may need to change, we do not want to get rid of our "winning formula." He said, "Allow it to be informed over time by the guru's Influence and transformed, having the discipline not to express it in a dark kind of way, but letting it be there and accepting it and working with it. Let the guru's Influence inform it."

Lee began again at three p.m., saying: "Robert Svoboda said that Vimalananda said, 'We Aghoris can have all the money in the world—we just don't want it.' It's a well-known fact that when people get a lot of money, intrusive and uncomfortable things start to happen. Friends and family all want some of it.

"Whatever projections people have on you have an effect on your life—it's not unlike voodoo, in a way. So the less people know about you, the less psychic influences will be attempting to define your life. If people know the details of your financial situation . . . . average people, who have the tendency to be jealous and vindictive, will have envious, jealous and vindictive projections on you, who is supposed to have money and says no when they are asking for help.

"When someone gets an inheritance, for example, people may even ask, 'What are you going to do with your money? Give it to the ashram?' Because we imagine that we know what we would do with a large amount of money—but we don't know what we would do.

"The practice of Enquiry—'Who am I kidding?'—is an empowered phrase. This is the question, really." Lee told the story of how this phrase came about, when one of his closest students, who was an ardent devotee, got an inheritance and realized that there was no way he was going to give the money to his guru. "Who am I kidding?" was the phrase that came up for him at the time; he told Lee about it, and it became the phrase of Enquiry for Lee's community. The student actually left the school shortly after that.

Lee continued, "It doesn't matter whether projections are negative or positive—they are influential. So you don't want people to know the details of your financial situation." Lee talked about the karmic entanglement of situations like winning the lottery, in which, according to Robert Svoboda, the winner takes on the karma of every single person who lost. As Lee said, "That is bad—really bad! Think about it. Two or three million people buy a ticket, and one person wins!"

He said, "Our lives are defined by the imbalance of karma in our ongoing process. The idea in tantric work is: You can't *not* have karma. You *can* have lots of positive karma and as little negative karma as possible. The more exclusive your karma can be to your own actions, the better—which makes my job and Purna's job the most fucked jobs in the world! Except for heads of state!

"The less you intertwine your karma with others, the better, which sheds a really radical light on relationships, because you can't not be in relationship, but who are you in relationship with? Because it implicates you in their karma.

"So we were all young and foolish once, weren't we? Maybe we were in relationship with a cocaine dealer, associated with murderers and thieves and God knows what else. It's his karma, the cocaine dealer, but guess who gets to be involved with the repayment of his karma?

You! You don't want to win money, to be implicated in a million people's karma. I haven't bought a lottery ticket since I heard that.

"Suppose you get an inheritance from an evil uncle who made his money in bad ways; what you do with that money is very important to your future karma. You could give it away, but that's just foolish. People have projections; we see somebody walk down the street, how they are dressed, how their body moves, and automatically, we have projections about who they are relative to using money wisely. Whoever we are involved with, sometimes we don't read into people, and our projections can be completely inaccurate as to who that person really is.

"So, we all have projections. Some of us are tremendously insightful, others are not. Like Americans and wine: certain labels look like it's a good wine. Most Americans judge wine by the label—they don't know the difference. And some of us are like that with people; we don't look deeply into things.

"That is in your favor. We are in a tantric school. We don't use that word a lot, or make a big drama about it, or go sit in graveyards . . . too bad! You can have a lot of fun doing things like that . . . We all have this fascination with Kali, or we see fierce Tibetan Buddhist deities in union and we say, 'Yes!' But we're just talking out our hat. One of these deities shows up, and we're *out* of there! Phheww! Like that! So we don't make a big deal that this is tantric work, and we're going to invoke deities and ride those suckers into some golden Universe and wield power and sit on clouds of glory with them. . . .

"But in fact, we are learning skills by virtue of our lives together and our practice; we are learning to court the Beloved and enshrine the Beloved in our hearts and keep the Beloved there and make friends with the hounds of hell, go to the River Styx and have a picnic there! We are learning those things, but we're not learning them like taking a class on mythology or Hindu iconography. We're absorbing information that is producing a capacity and skill that we won't know we have, until the time to use it shows up.

"It's great to build a myth, but not like when people say, 'What is that person's problem?' Like wearing a pyramid on your head . . . Or, we would learn these things to become good witches and warlocks. When I got into this Work, all my sorcerer friends abandoned me. It's good to have a myth—not something ridiculous, not making up lies, but that you don't feel you need to reveal every detail about yourself, including to your family. I'm sure your brothers and sisters have asked you, what are you going to do with your part of the money? Because we want to manage others' affairs.

"So it's healthy to maintain some privacy about your financial affairs. Your guru is the exception to this—if you want. It's not necessary, but if you are with the right guru, this is someone who will not have projections on you. Under ideal circumstances, your guru is the one person you don't have to maintain a myth with."

Lee started to talk about how C.S. Lewis and J.R.R. Tolkien were fabulous mythmakers, and they were very good friends. He said, "Imagine the conversations they used to have! That's beside the point . . . in fact, nothing is beside the point! Wow! That was profound! I'm just blowing myself away here! So, we don't realize the power of money to turn people against us. People want power because they think power is security, but security is not the cure for insecurity, as E.J. said. But our psychology thinks it is, always. Love is not the cure for unlove, success for failure, etc. etc. etc. People think that liposuction, nose jobs and breast jobs are the cure for self-hatred; they are not, but you can't convince psychology of that. So when any of us have anything enviable—good looks, success, fame—we are the target of a tremendous amount of negative projections because people want what we have. Those projections will impinge upon the sanctity of your inner world.

"Llewellyn Vaughan-Lee says that your outer life just needs to be handled. His path is a path of training mystics, and mystical ascent and the relationship with the Beloved is an internal process."

Lee's talk ended at four-thirty. We exited the meditation hall with notebooks, shawls and pens in hand and immediately went to dinner in the dining hall—the other half of the main chamber of the stone barn, it being petitioned off by white curtains that delineate meditation/darshan hall from dining hall. Tonight the meal was simple and sober. We ate quickly and, after announcements and Lee's traditional Baul salutation—"Jai Guru!"—we dispersed to wash dishes or take care of any other business that simply had to be attended to before reconvening for the next session.

At promptly five-thirty we gathered again in the meditation hall for a question and answer session with Lee and Purna. Lee began with talking about the need to be a shapeshifter—one who can fluidly change to function well in many different circumstances. He said, "It's a useful skill to learn: the ability to be different people under different circumstances."

Shapeshifting is an art that Lee has talked about a great deal with his students; over the years he has carefully set the context for this specific form of skillful means, closely linked as it is with magic, the craft of acting, and working with *drala*. It could mean that we get to save someone's life—or our own—or that we can create resources for the Work, or make the teaching available to someone in a way that leaves no trail at all. Being a shapeshifter is made possible through our invisibility; ultimately, one has to be nobody to be able to appear to be many different things.

There were quite a few students who were new to the school and Lee's teaching in the room. It seemed that there were a number of people who felt this idea of shapeshifting verged on being a liar, a cheat, or a scoundrel. That, combined with the ruthlessness that Lee was communicating and the spare, raw simplicity of his context—"My relationship to money is black and white"—was stirring up a place of doubt in many people. Money, survival, life and death: these are intricately entwined in the roots of the psyche. Trust was a shaky edge that many teetered upon as our dialogue with Lee and Purna unfolded. Purna in particular encouraged questions and conversation. These too were part of the process of coming to terms with our relationship to money and energy. Purna's spaciousness and compassion gave Lee a wide open canvas upon which he could freely play, splashing designs in bold black and white or brilliant color.

At one point Lee said, "If you know someone's a liar, you just don't believe what they say—how much simpler can it be? Am I cynical? Yes, I'm cynical! The thing is, you've got to be able to move in different circles and get whatever advantage you can find for the Work . . . All of your questions will be answered this week. By the end of the week, everything we're going to talk about throughout the week will all tie together and make a beautiful brooch, full of diamonds and emeralds and rubies . . ."

Jeannette, one of the new students who was voicing concerns, brought up a specific question about something Lee had talked about earlier in the day. In a voice shaking with emotion, she said that this was so lacking in ethics and so offended her sense of right and wrong that she could not accept it. It looked, on the surface, like Lee had no ethics at all; he was perfectly happy to fleece uneducated, poor people to make a buck for the Work. Many questions of ethical behavior, how to trust the guru and our fears about money and power came up. Sylvie, another new student, was passionately opposed to the whole idea of having a desire to make money; she was satisfied as she is, with nothing, and had no desire to make money at all. She flatly stated that she could not relate to anything that was being talked about.

Purna said, "If you focus on the content of what Lee is saying up here, you're going to miss what he's giving you. Everything he's saying is just dripping with Context . . . . You aren't going to get Context through a formula. The only way you're going to get Context is to have your steel-trap, snapping turtle mind opened a crack for a fraction of a second, and then you'll get Context.

"What Lee is giving you is really all you need; it's the whole thing—Context. Lee is being very generous in letting me bring these other things in, the processes and all that, the community building. The exercises we're doing this week are necessary only because they build a matrix in which Context can be held."

Lee began to dialogue in earnest with Jeannette, who was still upset and crying a little. He asked her the ontological question, "Who is upset? Ask yourself that question. Really. *Who* is upset?"

When she said that she felt he was just telling stories, maybe he was just lying about things, Lee interrupted her, countering in a relentless, pitiless tone, "I'm a *fabulous* story teller! I could tell you a story and you wouldn't even know I wasn't telling the truth!" Lee gave an implacable, sardonic laugh, and a look of shock registered on her face.

"That'll be 120 euros!" He snapped, referring to his skill as a psychotherapist, which he was demonstrating without any effort at all. Then he laughed even more. He seemed to be enjoying her predicament. He was pushing her, very hard, to break through the web of confusion. Silence stretched out the time and space into infinity while Jeannette and everyone else in the room—about sixty people—sat immersed in various levels of clarity or unclarity, either as an observer who could see the way through the maze of the mind at this point, or as one of the many other participants who felt highly sympathetic with Jeannette's plight, having their own version of the same recoil and primal mechanics. She was, in fact, working for the whole room at this point; whatever breakthrough she would make would benefit everyone.

Finally, Lee broke the silence, saying with a piercing clarity that was big enough to encompass both ferocity and gentleness, "Jeannette, the real question is: Why don't you want to laugh?" The silence deepened; the space was alchemized into a deep blue blaze. Infinitesimal cracks were spreading across hearts made of granite and marble. Time seemed to stand still, until, finally, Lee said, "It's okay to cry."

He paused, then added, "However, don't just cop out to some therapeutic form of avoidance. You're talking about ethics; I'm talking about something *entirely* different. I'm not interested in training a bunch of liars and cheats. I am interested in teaching people how to shapeshift. But this is great! If you want your relationship with money to be different after this week, *this* is what is standing in the way. Listen Jeannette, if you enter into the shift of context that I'm talking about, you *will* have to change everything, but *not* your ethics."

Purna said, "And it's standing in the way for everyone in this room—not just Jeannette."

Lee became even brighter than he already was, and he was like a lighthouse sitting in his chair beside Purna, in front of the divan on the platform where he usually sits.

"Boy, this was fun! I haven't done this since the seventies with Fritz at Esalen!" Lee quipped enthusiastically.[1]

There was no resolve for these issues at the moment; people who were struggling with the uncompromised communication of nonduality and the ruthless self-honesty that was demanded as we encountered many of the ideas would have to trust enough to see the week through and allow the process to unfold. As Lee had said, everything would be woven together into a seamless whole, into a beautiful jewel, in fact.

After the session we had thirty minutes to run to the toilet, get a drink of water, grab warmer clothes, since the temperature had dropped quite a lot after sunset, and get back into the hall for the last session: two hours of community building. The agreement of this process is that everything that occurs within the community building process is confidential and sacrosanct. Every night for six nights, we would spend two hours in this process. Needless to say, there were no notes taken in this space. At nine-thirty after community building, there would be tea in the salon of the *grande maison*.

1 Fritz Perls (1893–1970) was the originator of Gestalt therapy; he was famous for his unique talent as a psychotherapist of radical and provocative means.

Money Seminar
September 13

This morning Lee spent an hour and fifteen minutes selling all kinds of things—masks, a bell and *dorje*, lots of rosaries, the tattoo book, *Agony & Alchemy*, and then raffling tickets for the large stone Durga, the proceeds of which would go to support Brinda's daughter Amethyst's school endeavors this fall. It was a lot of fun, with a wide range of participation from many different people. Finally, Lee began to talk. He said:

"You get pushed up against something—it's fun, but uncomfortable because we're not used to bearing a new Context. It's not any more intense than the context we're used to bearing, but that one has been around for so long that we're used to it. Like living next to a pig farm. My students at Bittstedt used to live next to a pig farm that smelled terrible, but they couldn't smell it at all. Every morning and afternoon the pigs would start squealing when they were being fed—and the smell! Just when you thought it couldn't get any worse, the pig farm was taken over by a geese farm—the smell was worse and they were louder than the pigs! But, you know, they got used to the geese!

"So, whatever context we are used to living in has its responsibilities and characteristics. It's really the same, but a different character, burden, mood. It feels like something really intense is going to happen, but it's not really more intense, just different. You get pushed up against something; it's a permeable membrane, but it feels like a steel wall! Really it's such a soft, gentle membrance that molds right to your face—like a woman's thighs, which is why more than one man has almost drowned down there!"

Hearty laughter shook the group as Lee continued without missing a beat: "You're flopping around, her legs clamped around you, you can't come up for air, she's loving it, you're almost drowning, but you can't say anything because you're almost drowning!" We must have really needed to laugh, because it seemed extraordinarily funny on this chilly, bright sunny morning, with the fine golden sunlight filtering down through the high barn windows on our group, sitting bundled in shawls and wool sweaters. With his audience in the palm of his hand, Lee forged ahead.

"I'm not speaking from experience—people tell me these things!" Another wave of full-body laughter swept across the room. "Really! You wouldn't believe the things people write to me! Of course, I don't keep those letters! I also get letters from people who are melting into my eyes on the murti, 'Oh, my guru,' disappearing into bursts of gold and weeping with devotion. Those are the letters I keep! Remember *The Secret Garden*? I should write a book: *Secret Gardens of the Path . . .*!"

The jokes got bawdier and more rakish as Lee reeled off on a tangent about the delights of screwing at your mother's house when you go home to visit. "And you should get the man to make a noise, so your mother will hear! Isn't that the fun of it, anyway?" He deftly drew a quick sketch of how the mother would respond, based on the culture she came from: British, American, French, German. We were howling with laughter, when suddenly he was back on the original target of the dharma:

"So . . . this seminar is about what we have to deal with in life. It's all a metaphor for our own relationship with money. Time to end!"

In a session that Purna lead this morning we played the maze game. It was, in many ways, the highlight of the seminar for me. It's impossible to adequately describe, and perhaps should not be, because it is a visceral, immediate experience that is very physical and shared with one's teammates. Suffice it to say that we broke up into teams and had to find our way through a maze in twenty-five minutes, with the pressure on and the clock ticking, without any instructions except that we couldn't talk and that our coach would say "stop" or "go," depending on whether or not we had made a correct step in the maze.

The only other instruction was to play as if your life depended upon making it to the other side of the maze, and furthermore, your whole team had to make it or *you* hadn't made it—even if you were the only one who made it. The work principles embodied in this exercise were profound: you cannot do it alone and therefore you must drop your conflicts with others and work together; you have to think radically, outside the box of the mind, or you will *not* make it; you have to create something out of nothing. It was an amazing process that was exhilarating and rousing. Now and then Purna would walk by and coach us in a loud, implacable voice, "You play this game as if your life depended on it. *As if your life depended on it*!" Each time I heard this, I was personally spurred on, and when our team reached the goal, we were ecstatic.

The day was flying past us, as we had almost no time to stop even long enough for a toilet break, as we hurried between sessions to get back to the space on time. At three p.m. Lee gave another talk:

"Languishing in Context—an excellent phrase, one that a student of mine, Stan, came up with. I think we can do that on a verbal level, because that's what I like to talk about. Purna and I like to talk to the heart and soul of the Work, but particularly relative to the subject of money, we need to be practical.

"There are always people who want to multiply their money without doing anything themselves. They know what they're doing; they know the difference between a reasonable risk and a stupid risk."

After telling a story from his own experience thirty years ago, Lee made the point, "Don't ever get involved with anyone, ever, without a written contract. If it means something to you, never, ever, ever take a loan or loan money without a written contract, and get it signed in front of a lawyer or impartial witness, because people do not remember what they agreed to do . . . . There are different situations in which it is to our advantage to *listen* to people. I've seen a lot of friendships break up because what was innocent trust in the beginning turns sour. Plans rarely work out the way you expect them to.

"On a practical level, I would like to see as a result of this week that you can throw around the concept of amounts of money that before seemed like fortunes to you. I want you to get used to thinking in really big terms. Are you ever going to have that kind of money? Where will you get it? Academic! What you need is to get comfortable with the concept of that kind of money. When you get into the hundreds of millions, you start dealing with people that you have no idea how evil, criminal, violent some of them are—more than you can imagine.

"If you are going to play with your money, go for a big return. If you're going to play with other people's money, do it with a contract and a lawyer. So, I would like you to get used to thinking in large terms—sums that are three or four times your annual income. If you make thirty thousand euros a year, you can start thinking in terms of one hundred thousand euros. You can throw terms like that around all day, until you're comfortable with them, so you become easy with large sums of money, even if it's just a conversation!

"I bought everything Robert Beer had for sale, and I'll tell you why. He showed us a thangka, Samanthabhadra, which has sixty-four deities in its mandala, plus attendants, in an indescribably complex painting. Every tiny deity in the mandala is painted with a one hair brush, because every deity is exact in detail—face, clothing, implements, all the fingers and toes. So when you buy a thangka like this, they give you a magnifying glass, because the detail is breathtaking.

"There are seventeen distinct lineages of Samanthabhadra and minor differences in those; Robert Beer knows every one of those deities in every mandala. He's the only person alive on the face of the Earth who does, except one or two old lamas, who are too old to talk. And, he knows all this about the other deities as well. For years he has been sponsoring a group of artists in Katmandu, where there are ten thousand thangkas painters, and, he says, about twenty good ones. So he works with the good painters; the average painter takes two to six months to finish one thangkas. He orders and buys them, keeps them busy. If he doesn't buy them, they will sell to big dealers who don't care about the art. The Japanese dealers go in and offer them more money, but they won't sell to the Japanese because if Robert Beer doesn't tell them what to paint, their deities won't be accurate, because they know he's the only one who knows the imagery.

"The point: America is still seen as the land of riches where streets are paved with gold. So a lot of these painters want to move to America . . . but it takes four months to paint a thangka, and they sell for three or four thousand euros retail! If the painter sells to a gallery, half of that money goes to the gallery. Nobody can live on that amount of money in America, except maybe in places where you wouldn't want to live.

"So I bought all of them. I got them framed and they were gone! But whatever you pay for something like that is worth it—it's a unique piece of art, and it would be a shame if their talent wasn't used.

"There are certainly things that have no price. I've been confronted with such things and been scared or too conservative to buy them, and I remember every single one, because these things are unique, priceless. When you are confronted with such things, never worry about the price. Just buy it. Like when you are somewhere with your children or your lover or wife, in a circumstance where you have a unique opportunity; that time is never going to happen again. So don't think about the money. Money is only a means to an end. Never make money the end.

"I'm not talking about trips to the beach; trips to the beach can happen any time. I mean when you find yourself in a circumstance that is pivotal to the education of your children, if it happens to be with a child, or in the intimacy of a relationship with your lover; whatever it costs you, don't think about it, just do it. These things don't come along every day—they happen very rarely. But they have happened to all of you at least once, and they will happen again.

Don't compromise because of money. And, I'm not talking about buying your kids a house or a car.

"If you put your house, for example, before your children, they will go on, grow up, have a good life, but they will in some way have their relationship to opportunity be compromised. What's most important to you? If you were on an airplane that was about to crash, would you save your computer first, or your child or the child next to you? You'd better hope you would save the child next to you, because you want to be able to live with yourself!

"Art is worth more than order. In my community, musical projects get paid for before the leaky roof. The tasks that people get always come before physical upkeep of the ashram. Our ashram is home, and comfortable and sacred, but a little run down! The roof leaks, it has for twenty years, and we have so much stuff now that everything is falling out all over the place. We've run out of room. Because in my sense of priorities, the teaching artifacts, all of Hohm Press, all of the books we publish, all the musical projects, come first! My priorities are art projects, Hohm Press, the garden—the garden is better cared for than the buildings, because we eat the food. Those are my priorities. I don't buy clothing, between what giveaways we get and gifts from friends . . ."

Lee talked about how he used to be a classic nerd when he was in high school and college. "Now," he said, "I'm cool, and I get to hang out with all of you! Isn't that wonderful? All of you are cool. Not out in the world; out in the world, some of you are not cool . . . You're cool where it counts. When someone like Arnaud or Robert Svoboda appreciates you, fuck the world! Even Andrew Cohen was trying to recruit some of my students, right here, in the sangha! So you guys are cool!"

After the talk we had another simple four-thirty dinner in the barn. Dishes were washed then we all ran to the next meeting, which was a question and answer session with Lee and Purna that started at five-thirty p.m.

Jeannette raised her hand right off the bat. "Why is more better?"

Lee said, "Jeannette, the point is not what we *can* live with. Of course we can live with very little. It is neither to live on what we can live on or to become greedy with desire, but to become conscious. Once we are conscious, health is better than illness; comfort is better than no comfort; and being surrounded by beauty and art is better than not."

Purna added, "Are you familiar with the three yanas of Tibetan Buddhism?" Purna gave a quick sketch of Hinayana, Mahayana and Vajrayana paths. The Hinayana path is, generally speaking, focused on personal, individual liberation or realization and is often referred to as the "lesser vehicle" of the Buddhist path. Mahayana is called the "greater vehicle," and beyond personal enlightenment or liberation, focuses on the distinctive teaching of compassion for the suffering of all sentient beings, such that the practitioner would delay his own entry into nirvana until all other beings have been liberated. The Vajrayana path, or "diamond vehicle," is the tantric aspect of Mahayana Buddhism, which is considered the swift or fast path due to efforts made through various yogic practices and often extreme hardships, usually focused around a fierce devotion to the guru. Lee has, on many occasions, described his teaching and path as a Vajrayana path—the fast path of tantra.

Purna continued, "In the Vajrayana path, people work with very intensified circumstances as a path to the Work. That's the ore out of which gold is mined. If you live in a monastery, the ore is silence, a simple diet, a very regimented schedule. Simplicity. If you look at this ashram, there is tremendous simplicity, but there is also all the art, food, jewelry, relationships that people have. It's all very rich in terms of the human world. The context of our lives with Mr. Lee is simplicity, but also working with intensified circumstances.

"If you make twenty thousand euros a year, you can work with that, but you're not going to work with the power issues and greed that is beneath your suffering. If you make two hundred thousand euros a year, part of you will come out that will be the ore of your sadhana.

"Thirty years ago Lee said, 'I'm going to put you through experiences that are grandiose and big, so you can learn something!' So now we have the Sacred Bazaar. If you spend five hundred dollars on bronze and have to figure out how to pay for that, you don't have to get that big. If you spend fifty thousand dollars on deities, you have to recreate something about your self to pay for it. You've got to create magic."

Lee interjected, "Werner Erhard used to say in est, 'Sit with it like a brick.'[2] As if you have a big brick in your lap and it wasn't useful for anything, and you just sit there with it until you figure something out—anything! Maybe you figure out that you're just sitting there with a brick on your lap, and you have nothing to get, no breakthrough to make. A lot of us having questions to resolve should just sit with them like a brick . . ."

Nicola, a student from Germany who used to live on the ashram in France, addressed Lee and the group about her dissatisfaction at not being asked to contribute her skills at the level and with the responsibility and authority she felt she should have. She felt underused and often relegated to unskilled labor, when she is a lawyer and also knows accounting. She expressed suffering with years of frustration, anger and resentment about this, and then finally confessed that she wanted to "be a boss" in whatever she does. As when anyone speaks in a group, they are almost always expressing a group concern; in this case, Nicola was speaking to people's drive for personal power, which is inseparable from our relationship with money. After an extended dialogue with her, Lee finally went into discourse mode:

"If I'm a guru at all, it's a quirky guru, full of eccentricities and idiosyncrasies. Having a profound psychological reticence to suffer

2 The radical seminar program designed by Werner Erhard in the 70s, est, or "Erhard Seminar Training," which later evolved into The Forum.

any kind of emotional expression in my field of attention, often the best people for the job don't get the job, because the best person for the job creates emotional recoil in those they have to work with.

"Anybody who offers any kind of service needs to understand, it's not simply plugging in your skills and talents; it's about the whole game plan and working like a team. For anyone who offers service of any kind to the school, you've got to be willing to be part of the team. That means respecting the rung of the ladder on the hierarchy you are on."

Lee talked about E.J.'s teachings on what it means to be a boss: "You are on the lowest rung of the ladder if you are the boss. Being the boss means that you are serving everyone else. In E.J.'s work, the more visible you are in a position of authority, the less likelihood there is that you will ever Work! It's much better to be in an invisible job, to be nobody and have the teacher *know who you are*, than to be somebody and have the teacher have *no idea who you are*."

Purna hammered on the point: "What is the *Context* that everything Lee says is springing from? What is the Context? Lee said, 'I don't buy clothes,' and he said, 'You can be making three to five times more than your present income.' "

Ann, who is the financial manager of the Arizona ashram, spoke about the difficulty of working on the edge of financial ruin all the time. The kind of tightrope that she has to walk, given Lee's priorities around money, and the way he radically trusts that Yogi Ramsuratkumar will provide what is needed, is constantly pulling the ground out from under her feet. She said, "Sometimes it feels like we're going to flip right out into outer space."

Lee shrugged, "So what? So what if we did?"

She responded, "Every time we get to that point, something happens . . ."

Lee smiled and sang his response, to the singsong melody of a children's ditty or nursery rhyme:

"Something always happens,
Even when it doesn't.
Something always is,
Even though it's not!"

He was like the court jester, the divine fool in the royal court of the beggar king, Yogi Ramsuratkumar—a divine child, playing with us. This little song on the nature of reality seemed to say that our worries are very small in the big picture, and like everything else, will pass away.

Ann continued, "You say, if you take care of the Work, the Work takes care of you. There have been countless examples of that, still I have this problem . . ."

Lee said, "If you write checks relative to my priorities rather than relative to your priorities, things will be different. We're not gonna get rich, but . . . If I say to you, 'We need to do this,' you just write the check, not say, 'But first we have to write a check for this . . .' And you put all your concerns for creditors who will call and complain aside—try it! You'll hate it, but it's going to work."

Ann persisted, "I want to do that. Last time you said, 'It's my responsibility.' You said that I have to get it in order for it to be better."

Lee interjected incredulously, "I couldn't have possibly said that!"

After a short silence, Lee continued, "So, since you've had that job, have I ever offered to take the checkbook over or assume any technical responsibility for any accounts? Yes or no?"

She answered, "Yes."

Lee said, "Have you let me?" She answered no.

"Why not?" he asked.

She replied, "Because I say I can do it."

"So what's the question?" Lee asked. When there was no response, he continued, "To me it's a regression; I don't want to go back and start handling the checkbook, but I'm willing to, to make some kind of demonstration. But if you don't let me help when I offer . . . then things will be more difficult, not impossible, but more difficult. The first step is to accept help, not assume it's spiteful or whatever. I'm sure there'll be a few opportunities, even before the year is out. And so what's the question exactly?"

Ann said, "I'm asking for your help. I'm here, in the seminar . . ."

Lee interrupted, "Yes, you're here in the seminar, with a graduate degree in finance. It must be humbling! Well, alright. But you have to take it when it's offered. In principle you always have my Help, but you have to *take* it. It goes against logic, because you're dealing with numbers, and they are concrete. But it's not logic. Old habits don't turn around instantly. There's a start up time. The Universe doesn't instantly send one hundred thousand dollars—there's a turnaround period."

Purna said, "There is so much help available in this school you could choke on it! The guru, the men's culture, the women's culture, books, the practices—incredible!"

Lee interjected mischievously, "Your requisite number of borderlines!"

He was referring to a diagnostic term for a certain particularly slippery category of psychological characters that fall between the neurotic and psychotic manifestations, who are impossible to deal with because, in part, they can so cleverly hide what they are up to from themselves and others. The borderlines kick the function of denial into another sphere of operation. They tend to be pathological liars par excellence. They are extremely inconsistent and unstable in relationships, being both manipulative and self-destructive.

Purna said, "Earlier Lee described something he was going to do . . . Something became clear to him and—boom!—he changed his life! He became clear. How does one do that? Because there's no lack of help or sincerity on our part. What is the Context that he has? That's the important thing, because if you walk out of here on Sunday morning without that, when this seminar is over, after hearing a lot of great stories and having received incredible data on changes you can make, you will have gotten the message but not eaten the meat."

"It is simple," Lee said. "If you focus on the eight jobs you didn't get instead of the two jobs you did get, then . . ." He shrugged.

Purna added, "If you look at circumstances, you'll never get Context. You'll survive, but you'll never get Context."

Lee's last bit of advice to everyone in this session: "When you hear 'no' a couple of times, you don't keep trying the same thing, because obviously it is not working."

Money Seminar
September 14

Leaving meditation this morning we checked the schedule for the day: breakfast would be at ten o'clock and dinner at four-thirty again; everything else was the same as it had been so far. However, the sense of groundlessness persisted, as if at any time we could be given a different rhythm to work with. This morning we were served simple fare of boiled eggs, fresh fruit, bread, butter and jam, coffee and hot milk. The day had dawned, beautiful and sunny; the weather was turning warmer than it had been the first two days of the seminar. Still, we needed to sit in the cool stone barn with shawls or sweaters.

At the eight-thirty session Purna led us through exercises in which we wrote, for ourselves, about the messages we received in childhood about money. The meditation hall was quiet, with the morning sun sending strong shafts of light down through the high windows on the eastern wall above the dais. The light was an important part of this space every morning, because it not only illuminated but also clarified and rarified the air itself, so that all of us sitting in it were bared and revealed to ourselves and those around us.

The thick, white stone walls spoke of endurance, timelessness and strength. The rough concrete of the barn floor where we sat on zafus was covered with a patchwork of rugs and carpets—it communicated simplicity and connection to the earth. On both sides of the dais were large bouquets of flowers—dahlias, sunflowers and roses—from the ashram gardens. To the right of Lee's dais was the Yogi Ramsuratkumar *vigraha*, the sculpted bronze statue that was consecrated and blessed by Yogi Ramsuratkumar in 1994. A candle burned at his feet, and flowers graced the *puja*. In all these ways the meditation hall itself was a vital part of the chamber that was being created. Divine Influence has a way of alchemizing the natural elements in empowered spaces like this one, so that we were further stripped of buffers, and the convolutions of the mind were exposed as meaningless in the simplicity of the space.

At eleven a.m. Lee gave a talk. The sun was still doing its magic; now, instead of shafts of light, it was a strong, diffuse daylight that brightened and smiled upon the planes of Lee's face. He looked amazingly youthful, vital and full of grace. He began by reading a fax he'd received from Rick Lewis in Arizona, who was feeling profoundly connected to the seminar. Rick was testifying to the truth of one of Lee's often-stated teachings to us: you never miss anything.

Sangha members across the ocean were feeling the effects of the powerful chamber that was being created and engaged on the French ashram this week; blessings were flowing in all directions and could be received through the subtle nervous system of the *sampradaya*, or spiritual clan, of the Western Bauls. Everyone would benefit from the work that transpired this week, undertaken by less than a third of the sangha as a whole.

Lee commented, "There is a place in your psychic nervous system where you are literally where the action is: that is being in the guru's world. You get to be in the guru's world by being energetically associated with the guru's nervous system, not by being in the physical presence of the guru. You never miss anything, we say, because you are bonded into the energetic field that is the Hohm Community. Even if you are not conscious of what is being received, there is a flow—a telepathic flow.

"Because Rick has made and continues to make choices in relationship to his devotion to me, he is consciously keyed in. It's a choice, and he maintains it. That's part of being able to be successful—having the energy of the Context that the guru and lineage live in pulsing through you. So you are not alone, and when you act alone, it's like walking a tightrope one hundred miles above the ground without a net. When there is a net, you don't pay as much attention and you get sloppy with your craft—but that is something different.

"To be financially successful, your unconscious mind has to be in the game. One of the things Purna has addressed this week is your underlying relationship to wealth. If you don't get your unconscious mind in alignment, you'll never be able to live by what your conscious mind has committed to. A shift of context brings the unconscious mind into play.

"When you are tuned in, you want to contribute, even though you are not the gross recipient of what is being contributed. Rick wrote this because he was impelled to participate, and he will benefit from his participation. When you are tuned in, you are compelled to serve whatever happens in the moment. That might be to act, to write or practice or strengthen your practice, in ways that no one sees. When you tune in, you are compelled to be part of the action, and part of the action will come back to you. The value that you will be offered will be on many levels, including the physical level . . ."

Taking a sudden turn in his presentation, Lee made an important statement to us. He said, "You have already gotten whatever there was to get in this seminar. You cannot get anything more—the transmission was made by Monday night. It's already done; the seeds have been planted. The imprint for a new context is already blueprinted into your system. All the rest of the seminar is realizing, coming to terms with, aligning your mind with that."

Speaking of aligning the mind, we were focusing now on the particular plans of various individuals to bring more prosperity into their lives. Lee began to talk about how we are often pennywise and pound foolish, to use an old-fashioned term. We cut off many avenues of possibility in exactly this way, by being afraid to spend money in order to make money, which is quite often a necessary step in the process.

Suddenly we were on a wild ride as Lee shifted gears yet again and started talking about, of all things, the Ku Klux Klan. He was bending our minds again, trying to open the steel traps that tightly grip our rigid ideas of what is and what is not. He said facetiously, "You know, they're really nice guys! They just need love and community—they don't really hate blacks, Jews, gays and women! Half of them *are* gay! That's why they wear those long white sheets—to cover up what happens to them when they dance around the fire with a bunch of other guys!"

Some of us were laughing freely at this point; it would take a little longer for the rest of the room to catch on to what Lee was doing.

"Life is strange. It's worse than strange—it's eerie!" Lee chuckled. "It's one big 'Twilight Zone'!" Now the laughter was coming in bigger waves.

Lee forged ahead, "Men like women in stilettos, I don't know why. They're terrible for your feet, but who cares, it makes their asses *pop*! That thing practically sits up and barks!" Now we were really forced to laugh without restraint. Playing the edges of sexism and outrageous political incorrectness, and poking fun at some of our sacred cows, Lee was at his most hilarious best. And besides, he was forcing us to see the absurdity of our cultural mindset. It was tremendously liberating to just drop our identifications, even the supposedly noble ones, if we were willing to relax into his theatre.

"You break your ankle, but so what? Those babes with their massive fixed breasts—they're like weapons! They can use them if they need to! Those skinny little legs, like toothpicks, and then their ass—*boom*! And their hair, three feet above their heads! Their little 38 in their pocketbook, cause these bitches carry *guns*! Like *Thelma and Louise*! A fantastic American movie about women finding themselves by throwing themselves off a cliff!"

People were roaring with laughter by now. And it was much needed; we'd been exploring our psyches, probing into deep pockets of all kinds of emotional abscess, reviewing our life scripts and the barriers to a free flow of life force, all of which keeps us from experiencing life in all its fullness, richness and glory! What a relief to just belly laugh! Laughter was ringing in our ears as Lee said, tongue in cheek, still referring to the movie, *Thelma and Louise*, "Oh . . . you mean it had more meaning than that?"

Finally we settled down a bit and Lee continued, "Anyway, pennywise and pound foolish, instead of spending money, is what is really important, and we're often that way when we're trying to develop a strategy for how to make money. We often are scared to spend the money upfront in order to create a future payoff . . . and, you can lose everything by making stupid decisions."

As Lee was expounding these principles, I looked around at the walls of the barn, which were now decorated with one line principles that had become guiding factors in our work this week. Some of them were quotes from Lee, as in, "My relationship to money is black and white," and "Context vs content." Others read, "Vulnerability is the driver for growth and maturation," from Gordon Neufeld, and "In the Work we always make a profit," from G.I. Gurdjieff. I noticed a new one that said, "The fire is burning. Will we be a phoenix or an observer?" It was also posted in French: « *Le feu brûle. Serons-nous un phénix ou un observateur ?* »

One of the exercises we did with Purna today was to assess what our strengths and weaknesses are and what our core values are, starting with a substantial list of values—things like love, discipleship, practice, family, integrity, service, sacrifice, community, kindness, etc—from which we had to pick ten, then narrow it down to three core values, then one dominant value. It was an interesting process. Lee began his three o'clock talk commenting:

"If so many people had integrity as a core value, then why are there so many conflicts between people? If you are interested in handling large amounts of resources, you have to have the learned skill to put your personal reactivity to people who are different from you, who annoy you, who provoke you, aside for the sake of the relationship."

Lee commented that his own list would have included family and friendship at least in the top five, if not as the top two values.

He continued, "That's something that new students have to deal with—it's not utopia in here! We want it to be, we're working on it, but it's not. Even some of the senior students are angry, short, impolite and territorial. So, we don't bring our core values to ordinary circumstances. Some of you can be dominating and controlling, but at the level of Context, you've got to 'do your own time.' " Lee was using a saying from the prison system in America: everybody has to do their own time, meaning that no one can pay your dues for you. It's the same thing as saying that no one can shoulder the burden of conscience, or the need for discipline and practice, for you; you have to do it for yourself.

"So, bringing our core values in a practical way into money matters is not to assume or demand that people you deal with have to have your core values, or be the people you get along with. At the same time, if you are in business, or you are working with a team toward a certain goal, you want to reach it as smoothly or quickly as possible. When we work as a team, reaching the goal benefits everybody.

"You need to be able to maintain your responsibilities under pressure—to keep your post. When you are working with a team, the team comes first, individuals second. E.J. Gold has talked about working with the Navy Seals; if any one member gets into trouble, the whole team is willing to sacrifice their lives for that person. The team comes first. If you have to work with someone who is egotistical, loud, crude, would you drop the account, or find a way to work with them? You'd find a way to work with them because your business will thrive.

"You want to be able to relate and adjust when you don't have to compromise your core values, your core principles; you just relax and step back, so to speak. When you're dealing with people, particularly people with authority who can make or break your circumstance, you need to be able to sing and dance.

"You want to develop the Taoist quality of water—it flows around obstacles; it is always meeting and flowing; it goes around rocks and other obstacles. It has no obstacles, in fact. If you have high financial aims, you have to cultivate the ability to move that way without compromising your core values.

"Yogi Ramsuratkumar was adamant about never going to the government for money under any circumstance. The government is like a gambling casino—the house *always* wins. Never an equal deal, ever . . . and Yogi Ramsuratkumar knew that. There are certain circumstances in which there is no way you can avoid compromising your values, so simply avoid those circumstances . . . .

"You may find yourself in a situation of tremendous crisis, when you know what the right thing to do is, but some desire—for fame, money, sex, power—is just *raging*! And the older you get, the harder it may be to say no."

Lee told the story of a twenty-five year student of another teacher, someone he personally knows well, who was a pillar of their school. She went to Italy to give some teachings, got involved with a twenty-one year old man and left the school to be with him. This was a person who was rock solid, at one time, in the Work.

He continued, "Is your desire enough to rip up your roots, give up a lifetime of work? Let's say you're a starving artist, and someone comes along who makes you a promise so tempting, so exciting, of such high anticipation, but this person needs one hundred thousand euros. Most people would give the money because they don't have the clarity to see . . . The journalist who was assassinated in Nepal, Daniel Pearl, was a man of great integrity. But he didn't know that he wouldn't compromise his integrity, even to save his own life, until it happened to him. When we are offered money or the promise of money, that is when we will have to decide what is more important—money, or our values?

"Consciousness is your warranty to keep you from going against your core values again. To be conscious of an event that has caused you to go against your core values is to prepare for the eventuality that you'll be in a situation of compromise again."

In answer to someone's question, Lee posed the question, "What was your core value? Service?" He laughed. "Do you know what service is? If you spent your whole day dealing with service, you'd probably change your core value!" Everyone laughed at this jab at our illusions about ourselves, couched in a harmless little pleasantry.

"So, consciousness, awareness. Know thyself. If you know your strengths and weaknesses, then you can be strong in the face of seduction."

Money Seminar
September 15

The schedule posted for the day was a continuation of the same flow we'd had all week: Yogi Ramsuratkumar *puja* at 6:45 in the morning, followed by meditation and *arati*, from seven to eight o'clock; an eight-thirty session and ten o'clock brunch; three successive sessions at eleven o'clock, one p.m. and three p.m. followed by dinner at four-thirty; a five-thirty session then community building from seven-thirty to nine-thirty. As always, we would end the day with tea.

The last three days of the seminar focused on questions and hammering out the details of people's personal plans for generating abundance in their lives. The first session of the day was lead by Purna and tended to be experiential, with writing, reflection and then breaking into small groups. At the eleven o'clock session, Lee and Purna sat together again in chairs in front of the dais. Once again, we were being asked to leap out of our old worldview—the context of "I can't, it won't work," because of five hundred rules and regulations and limitations and restrictions, all in the name of practicality or realism or bitter experience or childhood conditioning toward failure and poverty or whatever it is—into the context of infinite possibility. He was asking us to step into the world of magic and *drala*, while at the same time, having the basic sanity, to use a term from Chögyam Trungpa Rinpoche, to recognize the fundamental operating principles of various realms of reality and how those levels of reality overlap and interact.

Purna talked about how we bring the past into the present; we are literally recreating our past in the present, over and over again. Instead, we have to bring our vision of the future into the present, and then the Universe will conform to that. He posed the question, "How much time do you need for your family; how much time for your personal practice; how much time to travel with Lee?"

Purna continued, "You declare it. You sit down and say, 'This is what I want my life to look like,' not based on your life script or on what the present is screaming at you in terms of survival. You declare it, and then you are flexible. You declare it: this is how it's going to be. It has to be do-able. *Do-able*. And it has to be something you are passionate about."

Lee interjected, "Reality is extremely unreliable. I'll bet in New Orleans there are people who just invested their life savings in a business and now they have nothing. So there is always a risk, a chance. But my philosophy, in spite of the situation in the world, is full steam ahead, full out, and don't focus on the negative. People come to me and say, 'It's full of tension, I hate the people I'm living with, but I don't have any other choice . . .' Such bullshit! So unrealistic! You may not want to do what options you have, but there are always options. When we say, 'There's nothing I can do,' it's not true. We have a lot more options than we know. If you're not psychotic, you can always come live on the ashram! And if you are psychotic but you can get along with other people, you can still come live on the ashram!"

Everyone laughed at this. How psychotic is psychotic, anyway? It's a long way from just being neurotic.

Lee proceeded, "No matter how bad things get, rich people need their diversions. And I'm not talking about black leather and chains—I don't understand why rich people have to pay for that! Don't these rich people know any women?" More laughter rippled through the room. Once again, Lee was relieving the pressure with a little humor. "It doesn't take much encouragement, and overcoming a few inhibitions, and you're there!" More laughter.

At this point the feeling of being bonded within this particular chamber of self-honesty, even in an impersonal yet very real and visceral way, had become quite apparent within the group. His comedic hits were making waves as he continued, "Why not make a lot of money on the rich and use that money to serve the poor? Even better, the poor in the Work? Make money providing services or art, and then use the money providing humanitarian services. It's fair! Even those greedy rich Americans who built their fortunes on the bones of poor Chinese and Mexican children will get some good karma, because their money is being used for good purposes, instead of 'Oh, those fascists! I wouldn't go anywhere near them!' Their money is as good as anybody's! We're talking about money, but you can draw the parallels to love, food, work, practice—the principles are universal.

" 'Money is the root of all evil,' is the saying. Money is a controversial resource. There will always be people who want to tear things down and see the negative side of things, even when the Sat Yuga dawns. Sometimes when we're in a situation where we're taking a risk—financial, artistic, personal—sometimes our mood surrounding the risk seems fragile. If it's really a risk, we may be insecure, tentative. We have to be aware that there are always, always, always people who will criticize and tear down what we're doing. There are people like that in this room, who have that tendency—and people in Arizona, in France—and they are experts at saying just the right thing at just the right time to magnify our insecurity."

Lee was referring to a paragraph in Rakini's letter to him, in which she wrote about coming back to Arizona after the Shri tour.

Back at home, one person made a comment that seemed aimed at sabotaging all the positive experience of the tour.

Lee continued, "People who do that want to serve, to help, to participate, but it's a psychological habit. Those people are of no concern to us, except when you start any project or business, these people will be on the front lines, wanting to tear us down."

As an example, Lee used the establishment of the French ashram. He described the condition of Ferme de Jutreau the first time he saw it—at which time he decided to buy it. It was incredibly run down, unlivable, with grass grown up to his waist. The windows were completely overgrown with Virginia Creeper vines. And even worse, the community had no resources with which to start such a massive project as an ashram in France; it was all done by bootstrap and magic—the Blessing Power of Yogi Ramsuratkumar. The first time he saw the place, he had come with a number of his students and Gilles Farcet, who had told him about the farm.

"I had one question of Gilles, which was not whether the roof leaked or if the water worked. My question was: what's the financial deal? In other words, how do I buy this place? It was very advantageous and didn't require a large amount down. Gilles opened the front door, I walked inside, looked this way and that way, and said, 'I'll take it!' "

It's true that some people were shocked at Lee's temerity in taking on such a huge project without funds. This brash American has some audacity! Well, frankly, the Americans felt the same way that some of the French did. It all worked out, and it worked out beautifully. Lee continued, "I throw myself into things and ask questions later, except: How much does it cost? That's the important question. Years later some of the partners in the association wanted to sell their part, so we did have to come up with a fairly large sum in the ensuing years in order to stay here, but by that time the whole project had momentum and it was easy to find the money.

"Of course, my American sangha were somewhat sobered by

the fact that I was going to be spending three months a year in Europe every year. I was already away three weeks a year in India . . . But the project had momentum, which was obvious to even to those most disturbed by the three months a year in Europe. As time goes by, I enjoy Europe more and more and America less and less—not on our ashram, but the country itself. The American sangha is wondering if I'm going to spend even more time here.

"During the first Celebration at Ferme de Jutreau we had fifty Americans here. That was before the Sacred Bazaar. Now they can't even buy a candy bar! They do, but they shouldn't! Now very few of my American students can afford to come over here. That's the sacrifice they made for such good karma. You couldn't hope for better karma than to buy these artifacts and owe the money to me!"

Reflecting on all that was being said, I thought about how the entire spectrum of the Sacred Bazaar has been a profound and at times challenging journey for us all, with many complex levels of work that is provided through its function in our lives. The cramp revolves around the core issues of money, sex and food. The Sacred Bazaar has given Lee an inroad into seriously working with our money issues; it has made cracks in our protective armor and secret lives that are crystallized around money, energy and survival—our fear, shame and murky confusion—and forced a ray of light to shine through those cracks to illuminate the whole landscape. It has brought grace and blessings into those dark places and lifted them up into the light of day, so that they may begin the long, arduous process of transformation.

"A lot of people ask if they can buy artifacts in other places. Of course, you're an adult, you're free. A number of my students have gotten screwed doing that, but sometimes they find a good deal. One reason I was enthusiastic about giving this seminar on money was because to me, money is a magic element. It's a transformational ingredient in the whole stew of the Work. I know how to use it in the world, though I use it the opposite of how any financial advisor would say.

"Money is, in a real metaphysical sense, like breath. So when the guru and disciple share breath, which doesn't require a kiss or breathing into each other's orifices . . ." Lee delivered this line with a satirical power that caused us to laugh heartily, even in the midst of this very serious consideration. He smiled with that blend of wisdom and humor that is so very characteristic of him, then continued, "Well, it's a very important distinction, for some teachers!"

More easy laughter, the kind that comes from a deep rapport, sprang up among us. We had moved through some difficult spaces during the week; trust had been tested and proven strong enough, worthy enough to continue. Now we were all, most definitely, on the same train. I got the sense that we had earned the precious gems of the teaching that he was weaving into the tapestry now, in this very moment.

"Money is like breath in the sense that an exchange of the medium is potentially powerfully transformational. It's not just that I'm taking money your money and you are getting a valuable sacred artifact, although if that was all it was, that would be fine, as long as you're getting value for your euros. But it's not all. Even though my prices aren't the least expensive in the world for an artifact dealer, you're getting good value. And, to me, money is a magic ingredient, like crystal power, diamond power, pyramid power!

"It's a magical element of exchange, and when you exchange breath with your guru . . . they say in the traditions when the guru gives a mantra, it's whispered into the ear. That is called, 'Blowing in the ear of the disciple,' because it is an exchange of breath and sound. Breath magnifies and amplifies the mantra's taking root in the disciple's body. When there is an exchange of money—whether I give to you or you give to me, if I treat you to a cup of coffee or ice cream—something goes along with the money. It's you giving me money, getting an artifact and the transmission, the transference of energy in exchange. If you tell your mother or your friend this, they'll say you're stupid for swallowing such shit from a guru. But

I know the truth of it; E.J. knows the truth of it; Arnaud knows the truth of it. So, this is for you. It may help someday, and it may not."

Returning to the theme of his talk at the beginning, Lee then said, "There are always people who unconsciously feel themselves to be bigger when they make someone else small. You may find yourself thinking about something someone has said, 'Oh my, that's not very nice.' When you deal with money, an object that is desired and creates envy, there will always be people who will say these kinds of things.

"You have to be prepared to hold your vision and secure that vision. Hopes and dreams can be very delicate, easily fractured and thrown into doubt and confusion. So when you start a project, you want to be committed enough to that project not to be thrown off by people who will criticize you. You really want to be able to stay with your vision and have enough peripheral attention, so if the venture is really not workable, you catch the signs and don't fall into a pit you can't get out of without great loss.

"Many of our ideas seem crazy in the beginning . . . . When you start something, it's a good idea to start small, but be willing to use your resources to get it started. It's very important to follow your vision and hold to it in spite of good advice from helpful friends and business people who think they know better than you. Stick to your vision and know, from the beginning, you will get criticism, even from people who's opinion you respect and trust. But if your vision is strong enough, you have to be willing to stick with it no matter what."

Lee talked about the three forces: affirming, denying and reconciling. He said, "The denying force is the negativity of critics, your own psychology and the fact that the Universe doesn't give away its gifts lightly. The Universe wants you to prove that you deserve it and will throw some obstacles in your way. That's the denying factor. The reconciling factor is the success of the project.

"Everything in life is interconnected. You can't be a practitioner in a school and have some practice around money on the side that's unconnected. When you move forward affirmatively, to move to a new location, start a new profession or business because you are inspired or have a vision, the denying factor will interfere with your trajectory at some point. When you make a decision that is antagonistic to the Work, the Work will give you signs that you are making the wrong choice. Signs can come and the denying factor can come in different domains.

"Dreams, for example. It would be extremely rare for the denying factor to come in a dream; it's not impossible, but highly unlikely. But signs that you are making the *wrong choices* often come in dreams. Dreams are one of the primary ways that signs will come. We have anticipation dreams that are purely psychological—we're worried about something, and an anxiety dream will come. These things can be confusing. Is it a sign? Is it a real dream? Is it an anxiety dream? So it helps to have a circle of advice. The sangha can help you in this way.

"The denying factor will often come in the form that it requires extra effort to move beyond something. They are not things that stop the project, but will get in the way and can be moved over. You want to be able to stay with your vision when the world seems to tell you it's not going to work, because there will always be people and things that will tempt you, to dissuade you and seduce you away from your path.

"To reinforce: it's always good to start small and organically move up, so you can adjust as you go and make changes and learn the system. If it doesn't work, you haven't lost all your money or your family's money, because often it's our families who rescue us out of these things . . . ."

Lee talked about the fun of being partners in Vigraha with Purna and buying artifacts together, then he closed the talk going over a number of more "nuts and bolts" kinds of considerations:

"It's useful to have a long-term vision and to understand the kind of supplementary ingredients that would make your business more successful. Where are your materials going to come from? How much money will it take? What kinds of licenses will you need? You need to have a general idea of how you will function when your business grows and you get larger.

"If you are sentimentally attached and unable to be honest with your friends, don't hire them, because you will probably have to fire them. It's a rare friend who can keep from taking advantage of your friendship in such a situation . . ."

After the usual thirty minute break, we reconvened for another session before dinner, which would be served at four-thirty by our tireless kitchen crew, who worked from dawn until midnight every day preparing and serving our meals. They were all smiles; every time someone walked into the kitchen, the atmosphere was easeful and happy. They made a tremendous contribution to the seminar and were a great example of many of the principles—especially teamwork—that we were immersed in throughout the week. It felt to me like there was no separation at all between the kitchen staff and those of us who were in the barn, even though they didn't hear a word of what was going on in the seminar space.

At three p.m. sharp Lee began: "With money, like all forms of energy, stagnation is not healthy. Clear water supports life and stagnant water is unhealthy, creates pollution, disease and so on. So, of course when we think about money, we think about security. Even if we don't have any money, security is still not the cure for insecurity! Anyway, movement . . . and remember that security is not the cure for insecurity.

"It's very healthy, given the laws of energy, to keep the energy moving. Whether the energy is love or good vibes or money, energy demands movement so that things don't stagnate and rot. Money is a wonderful thing if you *use* it! If you just store it away for a rainy day . . . saving things to use later often doesn't work out the way you think it's going to. I'll go to an antique fair, and at the first booth I'll see something I want that's expensive, and I only have a certain amount of money. What if I see something better later? So I come back later, and the thing is gone, and I'm kicking myself. I saw a Tiffany lamp once many years ago, and I really wanted it. I like power objects and beautiful things. I looked at the price; I could have bought it. It was expensive then. I thought, oh I love it, but I really don't need it. I didn't buy it, and I always remember that lamp, because when there is a certain level of response to something beautiful or powerful, I always buy it. You never get the same chance twice!

"Money is most effective when used, when it is active, when it is doing something. The more active movement, the better, which doesn't mean you should invest in monkeys—they have dirty minds and dirty bodies! So movement is healthy. 'Nature abhors a vacuum,' which means if you create a space that is a vacuum, nature will immediately fill it. Money is energy and energy is always returned to you when you use it. When you spend money, it is always returned to you, but not necessarily in the form of money. Energy is returned to you in the form of love or friendship, like that. So it's good to keep money moving, obviously with intelligence. If you get ahead of yourself, it can be counterproductive. If you want to go out of business quickly, be fanatical about the details of your business—with the exception of legal details, obviously.

"There is a different sensation between the Universe telling you you're on the wrong course, and the denying force. With experience, it gets clearer and clearer. In the beginning, my way of doing things is to just keep moving forward, unless the warning signs are undeniable. I tend to push a little, but . . . Yogi Ramsuratkumar will often have us stop early, by eliminating the opportunity, or by various signs. I tend to look at things that come in threes. Like the reading material I choose. If I hear about something three times, I usually look it up and read it. On the other hand, if three of my students independently tell me about a movie they loved, it's a sure sign I won't like it!" Several of us laughed a this, knowing how true it was.

Lee continued, "It's funny, but there's something to be said about this. We're always wanting to serve the guru and be in the guru's world, but often we're so blind that we don't even notice really obvious things—like what ice cream the guru likes. Every time I'm hosted by someone who really wants to serve me, Cote d'Or ice cream gets put on the table, because they know I like ice cream. But . . . Cote d'Or! I'm like, *whatever*! It's not very good ice cream, relatively. Or if we're in America, it's Dreyer's ice cream, after I've said a hundred times what ice cream I like. If I don't eat it, they get very upset. But they will not get out of their own viewpoint long enough even to see what kind of ice cream I like. It would never enter our minds that a movie *we* like, another 'type' of person wouldn't like it at all!

"We want to be in the guru's world, and we are not willing to alter some of the smallest of our tendencies and thoughts and preferences! It's so simple! What kind of music does the guru like? What kind of art does the guru like? What kind of movies does the guru like? What kind of food does the guru like? And so on. You should see some of the books people have given me! I keep everything people give me; someday we'll have a museum with things like little glass shelves with flowers . . . People spend a lot of money on me, on things I don't like, when they could know what I like with about fifteen minutes of observation!

"It's very easy to get into the guru's world. There aren't any gates, it's not locked up. You just need a certain resonance. And you have to be able to put your action where your resonance is. That's all—simple! Like not getting in the way: you go in the tea space, the phones are ringing off the hooks, Brinda and Andrea are running around like chickens with their heads cut off. Alrun is in the kitchen feeling insecure, and Manuela is just doing some service somewhere. Where do we sit? Right in the doorway! And we don't crouch down so we can get up quickly if we need to; we *plant* ourselves there! Andrea has to get through, she comes and stands behind you, you look up and smile!"

Laughter ricocheted through the space at this perfect description of the tea space. Every single one of us knew what Lee was talking about, somewhere in us. Lee paused for effect, then said, "You're supposed to *move*!" He smiled and laughed along with us. It was time to end for dinner.

Money Seminar
September 16

"When you support the Work, the Work supports you," Lee was saying again. "You will be rewarded by the Work, but not necessarily in the same medium. You may contribute land, money, a house and get back peace of mind, certainty, or various miracles in your life, like one of your children being spared the full brunt of the law for some indiscretion."

He began to talk about how *Dog's Day in the Sun*—known now as *Ecrasé par l'Amour*—was a breakthrough project for the entire community. People kept asking Lee, "How about a tour around that CD?"

Lee would answer, "Well, Paul is not available, and we can't do it without Paul," who composed the music to Lee's lyrics and produced the album. Lee said, "Because Paul is the magic around the whole thing!"

Then Shri played a gig in Bretagne this summer that was "so just over the top, and I had so much fun! Because I like to play with the audience."

People went crazy in St. Brieuc as soon as Lee—just Lee alone—walked out onstage that night. It seemed to be one of those "signs" that Lee talks about, that a tour with the Lee Lozowick Band just might work, without Paul, after all. And so, this summer the idea for a two-week tour was born. Lee never does anything that he thinks he can't make a profit on, in several domains.

He pursued the idea, "How do you make a profit? You don't stay rigid and crystallized. If your contribution to the Work is valid, but your mind is a little fixated or something, if what you are proposing is of use to the Work, but you are stuck on one point—'I can't move because of this'—then the Work will give you viable options, but you have to be open enough to notice the options and brave enough to take them.

"When I say that you need the bravery to follow them, most of you have no idea what it is for me to do this Work. You see me giving talks in Paris and bantering with the audience and relaxed and natural—but it is anything but relaxed and natural! Most people have no idea what bravery it is for me even to get on the stage. I could with LGB and Shri because I wasn't the only singer. I didn't mind singing with Deborah, because she was so good. I was locked into rigid thinking about this CD; I thought that only Paul could do it. But the Work said, this is useful; here's an option. If what you are doing is useful to the Work, the Work will give you an option, always, without failure, but you have to be able to capitalize on the opportunity.

"When you contribute to the Work, the Work contributes to you. Money is just a response; it's energy. You can use it constructively or destructively. To feed your money into cocaine addiction is a destructive use of money. Going in and helping people whose lives have been destroyed by tsunamis or hurricanes is a creative use of energy and money. Money and energy are the same—you can use them constructively or destructively in the world of the dream. Or, you can use them in the world of the Work, which is always creative and is different than the world of the dream."

Purna then spoke about how we are all geniuses in some area. Our particular service to life, where our impulse is, where our energy and attention is primarily focused, is *what we use to transcend our limitations*—the limitations of our own cramp. When our attention is on what's lacking, it shows up as scarcity in three ways: 1) There isn't enough; 2) That's just the way it is; and 3) More is better. Then he led us through an exercise in which each person made a plan based on the resources we have, the resources we are willing to get, what our particular genius is, and what that's going to look like at the end of the week when the seminar is over and people are going home. Purna asked us to make three unreasonable requests of ourselves that we would complete within twenty-four hours after the seminar was over.

"Without unreasonable requests," Purna said, "it is very difficult to grow. I wrote down: if there was anything about the human condition that I would put an end to, what would it be? It wouldn't be hate or something like that, although it would be great if we didn't have hate. It was reasonableness! For anything to change in life, it has to be an unreasonable request. Most people are about their *reasons*. If you are about your reasons, then your reasons are deciding, not you, not your core values, not who you are.

"You know how you get to the source of transformation in the Work? Say yes to everything you don't want to say yes to and find a way to handle it inside yourself. So, write it down: three unreasonable requests, one in your relationship with money; one in your personal life; and one in your spiritual life."

Purna asked everyone to pick a "buddy"—someone they would check in with regularly, with whom they would share their plan, who would be able to act as a coach and source of feedback for them. Someone who could witness for them and provide needed support when they felt shaky. Phone calls would be enough for this relationship; you didn't have to have the person physically present to be a "buddy." The idea is, you really can't do it alone.

I noticed a new quote on the wall when I came in for Lee's three o'clock talk. It read, "I have met the enemy, and it is me." Lee began to speak, and one of the first things he said summed it all up. He said, "We should have no doubt now about how we limit ourselves by the paucity of our vision."

Then he made two more important statements that stood on their own: "Your conflict has nothing to do with anyone else," and "It takes tremendous energy to make a shift in context, which, loosely translated, we could call a leap in the octaves."

Lee continued, "No matter what happens, the Work must survive. What insures that the Work will survive? Outside the books we write and the art we create, *you* are what makes the Work survive. Yogi Ramsuratkumar was the first generation of this Work; I'm the second generation of this Work; you are the third generation of this Work. Your children and my children are going to have some rough times. So it doesn't hurt to have some skills, so that you can leave your country if you need to. The reality of the situation is that Yogi Ramsuratkumar has guided us from the beginning of this community; He has never let us down, and He's not going to."

At the same time, Lee said, we don't want to have what Chögyam Trungpa Rinpoche called "idiot faith." We don't want to be ignorant of the situation in our time, so that we're saying, "Oh, God will take care of us!"

"Yes and no," Lee said. "A lot of what we've been talking about in terms of money are principles that apply to gathering and developing the energy needed to leap the octaves. The Work will lead you to the point of take off, but the Work will not give you a free ride. You need to have the energy and the skill to get to the next octave. Even if you have the skill but don't have the energy you're not going to make it. If you don't have the fifty thousand to pay off the guards and get you out of prison in Nepal, you're going to rot in that prison. So skill has nothing to do with it—you've got to have the money!"

There is a lot of fear flying around about the state of the world. Each time there is another catastrophe, we hear big, dramatic, scary stories about the hard times that are coming, and it's true that there are hard times coming. Lee posed the question, "Will any of us find ourselves in those circumstances? Unlikely. But will skills and money be useful to you in your life? Damn straight!"

He continued, "When you're dealing with people with no integrity, it's better to deal with them with energy and skill—or don't deal with them at all. Stay out of their world!"

Lee continued on a slightly different track: "You train your psychology slowly. Here's how you do it: instead of tackling the whole mountain at once, you take one element—something you can accept—and say, 'From now on, I'm not going to . . .' Something you can do, something realistic. Even if you have to use will power. When you're doing that successfully for two or three months, and you're in a pattern with it, your success with that little thing says to your unconscious mind, 'I'm serious.' Then you pick another element; something a little bigger but this is realistic. You can do it. Then you do the same thing; after two or three months, your unconscious is primed and ready to go along with whatever you tell it. You've got to get your unconscious in on the plan."

Purna said, "Werner Erhard had a phrase he used: an 'impossible promise.' It's a promise you can't keep by yourself; you need other people to fulfill it. Many of us will not be able to succeed in our project without the help of our coach, our buddy."

Using a play on words to make his point, Lee quipped, "Our bacon booties, 'cause that's what we are—just big hams!" He forged ahead, "The thing is, you don't have to be humble to get lessons in humility."

Purna continued, "You need to create necessity for yourself. Buy twenty-five thousand euros of bronze in the Sacred Bazaar! Commit to pay fifteen hundred euros a month on your bronze debt. Negative habits have energy; one way to work with them is to put energy in an opposite direction."

Lee added, "Someone who has urgency to pay off their bill can create necessity by buying bronze, but if you don't have urgency to pay your debt, you don't create necessity."

The week was without question winding down. Now it was the end of the day; time for community building and then tea. Tomorrow would be the last day of the money seminar.

Money Seminar
September 17

This morning Lee relayed an important principle that applies to skillful means in all things. He said, "Don't reach for things. When you reach for things, you usually end up with blood on your hands. You have some kind of mess. Yogi Ramsuratkumar will bring us what we need. Any phasing, like the moon, in and out of our responsibilities, our financial responsibilities, like tithing to the community, represents our tendency to withdraw from true and consistent practice. The basis of practice is constant participation in the ordinary responsibilities of our lives. So we don't want to phase in and out. For example, we want to meditate every day.

"Practice is about functioning, not about, 'Oh, I love my guru.' That's a given. Unless you don't love your guru! Some people feel, 'Well, he's my guru, and this lifetime, I don't really love him.' "

Purna continued, "You want to have the guru be pleased with your practice? Be functionally consistent. Meditate every morning, pay your bills, keep your house clean, be on time. Function, function, function. Do your laundry and don't let it pile up in the corner. You know what that messy, stuffed glove compartment in your car represents? Your own confusion. If your glove compartment is like that, you don't respect that space.

"Keeping our time and space agreements are the foundation of a life of a devotee. Being late, psychologically, is an angry position—always. Unconsciously you are paying people back for something. 'I'll make you wait.' The number one reason we don't get what we want is we don't know what we want. Tony Robbins said, 'The main reason people fail is they do too many things.'

"So, we're in a lineage of crazy wisdom, like the Vajrayana path, where chaos is a good thing to work through. You do have a choice. If you drop these two things, you might have a better relationship with your children, and so on. Our circumstance will never leave its identification with physical life if we keep practicing in the air. The ability to stay with it, in spite of difficulty, in spite of any obstacles, is basic sadhana. Werner Erhard said, 'Stay alive in the face of breakdown.' And breakdown will come. A caterpillar literally has to be liquid before it becomes a butterfly. When you make a commitment, the Universe will challenge you. Be alive in the face of breakdown. Embrace the practice of minimalism."

At Purna's eleven a.m. talk, he said, "Have you ever noticed that Lee always makes a positive comment? When he loses at bridge; when he didn't like the antique store we went in. Ninety percent of the negative things in our lives are not about karmic samskaras but about the negative conversations in our heads. Pay attention to the conversation in your head. Positive thinking is mostly a strategy to avoid suffering, whereas our approach is to be positive while also willing to be vulnerable to pain and suffering.

"Another view of your project is 'my responsibility is to provide what's wanted and needed to make this project successful.' If you've got a breakdown in an area of your life, go to that area and provide what's wanted and needed. Look at what that person wants and needs and provide it. This is a big secret of life. You want to get close to your teacher? Provide what's wanted and needed. Not what *you* want and need, but what *he* wants and needs. Many people in this sangha have gone through a lot of frustration wanting to provide what Lee wants and needs."

Purna asked and answered two questions: How does one get strength of mind? Meditation and study. How does one get strength of body? Exercise and diet. Then he stated, "That's how we get the capacity to sustain insight."

That would be our big job after the workshop was over. All the "aha's" we'd experienced during the week as we connected the dots between principles that were elucidated and our life experience would have to be nurtured with practice.

At one o'clock Lee gave another talk, beginning with advising us that it is useful to be able to travel with him, and to be able to jump on the opportunity when it arises. Such opportunities arise randomly, and there are times when someone may find themselves locked into a particular circumstance with Lee, like going to Mexico with him every year because you speak Spanish. You've got to have the resources and the flexible schedule to lock into an opportunity like that when it arises.

Lee said, "One of the other things relative to a money-making project is if you can create something flexible enough time wise that your presence is not required in a rigid way. Every once in a while some important thing comes along, like you're having a baby or your child is getting married, and your attention has to go there. Especially the first child can be a little stressful.

"One of the things we really have not discussed this week for those of you with families is that you may be taking something on that may not have the complete support of your partner. One of the things you want to consider when taking on your project is the rest of your life. You do want to be in communication with your family.

"There are choices that are going to get made that create stress for other people. You really want to communicate, and it takes a long time to figure that out. Because, as you know, most people are tremendously generous and spacious when you honor them enough to include them in the information loop. There is an information loop, and you do want to keep people on it, particularly relative to your use of time. People tend to be much more generous with money, spending money, than with time, spending time. Most of our families will allow us to indulge in our Sacred Bazaar activities as long as they have enough time with us . . .

Changing tracks again, Lee said, "Don't get lazy, because once in a lifetime, every business finds some treasure—or not, if they get lazy. If you have any kind of project dealing with other people and their resources, follow every lead. If you're going to be in business, always maintain something in your favor. Always give yourself an edge—never be afraid to make a profit. When you get into the world of business, start on the basis that everybody's a thief. You will meet some wonderful people who will help you, who are reliable and keep their agreements. But if you start out looking for them, you may be disappointed. So don't trust people until they've proven themselves trustworthy. And always give yourself an edge to produce a profit.

"Don't trust people to stay in communication with you. Stay on the phone and communicate. Not too much, because you don't want to bother somebody. But you do want to stay on top of the details. It's very, very difficult to remember not to make assumptions about how long it's going to take someone to do something, how much money it's going to cost, etc. Because we have our own idea . . . Tremendous misunderstandings can arise when two people have different ideas about how something should be happening.

"So you want to remember what a crucial element communication is. As any of the writers in the community know, when you are inspired and you are writing about a space you experienced, the unconscious assumption is that the reader is going to 'get' the space. Sometimes someone will write an article about a seminar, 'Oh, Lee was making so many jokes and he was so funny!' The reader is like, what?"

Lee's final advice to us was, "Ultimately, if you want to make use of this workshop this week, you are going to have to think differently. You can only do that if you Pay Attention. You have to see it every time you do something that is antagonistic to the principles we've discussed here. You say, 'Ah, there it is!' and recognize it."

We spent the rest of the afternoon at the shop in La Roche Posay. It was the objective example of something that has been created out of nothing. People lingered over the many beautiful objects that grace its shelves and tables, and quite a few purchases were made as well. Snacks and fruit punch were served on the second floor, right in the middle of the ongoing renovations in the rooms that will, by next summer, be an art gallery.

The schedule on this last day included a late dinner, a celebratory feast of lamb and sumptuous vegetables in the barn. Afterward, we all gathered one last time in the salon for a late dessert and coffee. Many people would be leaving that night or early the next morning. The American visitors were staying until Monday. There was a sense of being filled to the brim and spilling over. There was much to digest; it would be a long-term process for all of us, and in very different ways, perhaps, for each of us as individuals. As Lee has said countless times when he has heard passionate commitments to be different, "Time will tell."

Ferme de Jutreau
September 18

Lee began darshan tonight praising the cooking crew for their service to everyone and to the ashram during the six day money seminar. He said, "It was the best job ever in the kitchen. All the meals were on time, the crew was invisible, no pots were thrown through the window! Sometimes you don't get to find out what the best work in the school is until you get forced into it by chance!"

Lee read some of the stories written to him in a letter from Christina, taken from a yoga workshop she had done with some of the senior students of B.K.S. Iyengar. He was particularly taken by Patanjali, the reputed author of the *Yoga Sutras*, written in the second or third century of the current era, in which the classical form of yoga is given an organized presentation.

Lee continued, "So, according to Patanjali, the endeavor to practice is against all odds and in spite of repeated failure. One of the things we run into in the Work are situations that are impossible for us as we are, which usually means people who are impossible to deal with. The people that are impossible to deal with usually find the resistance to their impossibility to be impossible to deal with and they leave the ashram. It's too bad because people who are impossible to live with are often hard workers, when they're not in breakdown.

"I don't have to live with people who are impossible to live with—only with people who find each other impossible to live with! Ha ha!" Lee laughed in a strange, ironic way.

He then relayed the three components of practice according to Patanjali: Practice must be consistent, without interruption; it must be done for a long period of time despite repeated failures; and it must be done with ardent devotion. "In India," Lee commented, "the subject of our ardent devotion is the guru."

Lee spoke about the tremendous number of practices that we have in this school, and the impossibility of doing them all, all the time. Besides daily meditation, there is the picture meditation, sun practice, breath practices . . .

"So, we're all busy. We all have work to do, and if you add up all the practices that we have—the ones that take time, not the ones that don't take time, like Assertion, Enquiry and the Heart Breath, using the Name of Yogi Ramsuratkumar—it is unlikely that we can do them all, all the time.

"The Patanjali text, loosely quoted, continues: 'Your practice must be dedicated, unswerving, it requires a constant vigilant search, pursued against all odds, and in the face of repeated failure, for an indefinitely long time.' " Lee commented, "You will find people who are stubborn, argumentative, aggressive, unwilling to compromise, dirty! You will be thrown into a practice situation with such people, inevitably . . . ."

Such was the task before us. It was predictable that there would be recoil and breakdown right away, and it seemed that Lee was addressing this fact as he spent the rest of the darshan talk articulating with deft precision our incredible resistance to each other. The task was to persevere in the face of repeated failures. The money seminar was a landmark, a historic moment in the history of Lee's teaching. Both before and afterward, he said, "I won't be doing this again. It's a one-time deal."

Ferme de Jutreau
September 20

Dasya arrived from the States today. The weather has undeniably turned cold in a fit of autumn that seemed to herald our last two weeks of the summer in France. The nights and morning meditation are quite cold, while the days stay crisp and cool but sunny, with bright blue skies. During the day Lee sat out in the sun, and I was reminded of what he said recently about how just sitting in the courtyard at the ashram in the beautiful weather is his vacation. Today he seemed to be not only soaking up the very ground, the trees, gardens, the sky, the clear air, but also nourishing the Earth itself with his rooted goodness, his very enjoyment, the serenity and peace that he exuded as he sat reading in a chair in the grassy yard. He was completely present here, on a tiny, unheralded, unknown plot of holy ground in the middle of France, and at the same time it seemed like he was everywhere in the world. It seemed to me that the Work went on, maybe even at its most piqued or heightened possibility, in those moments of quietude.

The ashram schedule always includes thirty minutes of *kirtan*, or chanting the name of God, on Tuesdays and Thursdays before dinner, since these are the two nights a week when the sangha gathers with Lee to hear his after dinner talk. At five-thirty in the afternoon a small group of us started the chanting before the meal. For those few moments, we were as close to heaven as it gets. No difficult, painful, sticky interactions, no jealousies or anxieties or clutched heart and twisted gut—just the name of Yogi Ramsuratkumar, soft voices, our small group of six chanters surrendered into the moment of refuge and the sanctity of this place.

The dulcet quality of the ashram, the powerful humming presence of Yogi Ramsuratkumar, permeated all and was completely inseparable from the warm sunshine, the fresh growth of emerald grass, the apple trees laden with fruit, the last flowers of the garden before summer's end. Lee came and stood by the front door for several minutes, his whole body subtly poised in an attitude of listening. It struck me in the moment that he was absorbing the sweet sound of the name of Yogi Ramsuratkumar as it was sung.

It was a poignant moment for me, one that precipitated a mood of longing: perhaps that brief glimpse was as close as one gets to the heart of devotion in our master, who keeps his inner life to himself, except in his poetry. Now that Yogi Ramsuratkumar is gone from his body, Lee is alone. No more will we see him held in his Father's burning graceful gaze on the ashram in Tiruvannamalai, no more will we see Lee leaning into Yogi Ramsuratkumar so completely, receiving his blessing with such an amazing purity, as we did for so many years. No more do we bear witness to the beauty and sanctity of their *lila* together in this physical realm. Sometimes the longing for this *darshan* of the two together is so great it becomes an arrow that pierces my heart. Instead, Lee wanders about in his meditation on worldly affairs and asserts to us all, "I'm just a businessman."

Lee's aloneness strikes at the core of me so often these days, as in this moment of sanctuary, when we could provide the smallest island of refuge in the sea of our own suffering and lack of clarity. The chanting was strong enough to draw the master out of his sphere of action, action, action, of business, telephone calls, advising or chastising one of his many recalcitrant students, all of us who wish we could somehow show up the way Lee showed up with Yogi Ramsuratkumar. Of course it's an impossible promise, because the relationship of Lee and Yogi Ramsuratkumar was so exceedingly rare and uncommon; still, it is the impossible promise of our master's gift and transmission to us. Somehow, in some place in space and time, each of us may come to fruition and realize that which has always, already been true of us, and of our relationship with our guru.

We ate together at the wooden tables that had been taken from the barn dining room and set in the middle of the grassy courtyard. Sitting in the last warm rays of the sun, we dined on the pure nectar of ashram fare: although Alrun had made a big green salad as always, most of us ate fresh fruits of the season prepared in a fruit salad with walnuts from the tree behind the barn and drank freshly pressed apple and plum juice from the fruits of our own trees. These last autumnal days at Ferme de Jutreau always carry the flavor of the purity and healing power of a country ashram. The harvest was in, the air was clean and crisp, life was simple and good. You would never know that the world was falling apart out there, beyond the boundaries of sanctuary.

Afterward, in the salon, Lee began the after dinner talk speaking on a subject that everyone could relate to. He began: "Abuses of practice generally occur with people who have no idea whatsoever that they are doing it—they're in complete denial."

In answer to a question about resistance to serving, and particularly from a visiting sangha member who has health problems that result in a lot of fatigue, and the snares she encountered with the projections and expectations of others, Lee said, "We're making everybody else's problem our problem. We're carrying six people's problems on our shoulders! What a mess, over nothing!"

Lee seemed to be addressing some of the underlying tensions that had come up after the week-long seminar as he continued, "We see each other often down to extremely subtle thought processes we have, and if we are going to pay attention to every signal that is put out by others, we are going to drive one another mad. Leave it alone! We can look at people's dominant social tendencies and let them work out the rest, instead of, 'I know what you were thinking, this and that . . . '

"For all of us, part of our work—and some of us have more ability to ignore the signals that are coming in—is to not think that every little signal we get from someone's unconscious is a disturbance that needs to be brought to light and handled, even when it's there and it's true. We need to be able to make a distinction between minor responses to something that doesn't have any effect on the space, and the things that do effect the space negatively . . . ."

It was a very important piece of guidance for everyone who lives in close proximity to each other, like ashram residents, or people who live or work in configurations of any kind, or are in committed relationship and marriages, or even with our children. "Live and let live" is a great thing, a doorway to kindness, compassion and generosity. The biggest pitfall, it seems to me, is my own inability to simply practice good will and loving kindness with myself foremost; the harder I am on myself (that is, the more shame and self-hatred I heap on myself under various masks), the harder I am on everybody else, while at the same time, I am not piercing through my own illusions to see myself clearly, strengths, weaknesses and everything in between. With the winter at Ferme de Jutreau coming and Lee leaving for Arizona, these distinctions become critical for those who will keep the fires burning here in France.

Fall Equinox
September 21

Tonight on the ashram Lee offered the ashram residents, our visitors from Germany and the U.S., and a few of the local householders a simple autumnal feast of French onion soup, salad, wine and chocolates. Later, over bridge, we were having a very quiet night as the game flowed on. Lee began to read some mail that had just been handed to him.

"Listen to this," he said, seeming to rouse out of his open-eyed meditation and sit poised for a communication to us. He read, quoting from the student's letter to him, " 'I know you don't like people to write long stories and confessions to you, but an old student advised me to tell you about this.' " Lee paused, then asked, "What old student? That student should have his head pulled out of his ass, but it's probably so deeply buried there that it would pop across the room and knock something over! Look at this letter—written in tiny script, I can barely even read it!"

One of Lee's pet peeves about the endless letters he gets from students is when they are written in such a small script that he can't read it—which is especially irritating to him since he chooses not to wear glasses but insists on keeping it as close to nature's bone as possible. The best way to get a letter across to the guru is: if typed, print it in fourteen point, and if handwritten, use a blue or black pen and write big.

An hour later, after a quiet conversation over coffee and tea with about twelve people, the space came to life in a different way. Michelle brought up the subject of so many Western Buddhist practitioners doing three-year retreats. Lee was talking about the form of Buddhist retreats, where there are no books and no writing—only dealing with the mind—whereas his recommendation for students going on retreat at Triveni Retreat Center is one book.

"What about writing?" Sylvan asked.

"Writing is okay, but minimal is best," Lee answered.

"Is retreat practice something you see as being important for us?" Michelle asked.

Lee answered, "Yes . . . I think if I was structuring things the way I really want them, there would be some retreat practice scheduled in, but people have to have some minimal strength of mind. I'm not interested in all these hysterics. Who was it that said that three-year retreats make people psychotic? Traktung? Yes. There you are with your mind . . . So what's the use of longer retreats if you don't have minimal strength of mind?"

Michelle asked, "Do I have minimal strength of mind?"

"Are you thinking of going on retreat?" Lee asked piercingly, bringing her rhetorical question into the immediate moment.

"No," she answered.

"Then we'll consider that when you are," he smiled.

"But you've only given people two week retreats so far. Is there room for one or two month retreats, or longer retreats, in our lineage? Could that happen down the road?" Sylvan pursued.

"Yes, definitely, at some point," Lee answered.

"When we're old?" I asked humorously, seeing only years and years of action, action, action ahead of us.

"No . . . then we'll need comfort," Lee answered seriously, taking the straight ahead tact.

He began to talk about a letter that was written by another woman who has been in the sangha for thirty years. The letter was written to her ex-partner and sent to Lee to read. Lee commented on it with real sadness.

"It was so demeaning, so undignified, so groveling, so painful! It was so painful to see such ignorance in a thirty-year practitioner—it was hard to read! It was heartbreaking. The desperation of a thirty-year practitioner was really awful. And these are the people who want to go on retreat? They're not dealing with the mind—they're dealing with a nightmare! To go on retreat and make use of it, people need to be *mature*; they need to be in relationship without making snide, snippy comments to others. How many people in the sangha are like that? You get out there and you're stuck in the mind, replaying, replaying, replaying, lost in your paranoia. The Buddhists say that's the idea—deal with that crap! Good luck! In theory, it's supposed to work, but I don't know."

Dasya added, "You need the ground to pull it forth; you've got to have ground to stand on, otherwise it's a battlefield and you sink and sink and sink. You could get suicidal. I understand the Buddhists are putting a lot of people through three-year retreats."

Lee talked about how he had heard from Purna that this was true. "Purna says that people have no context for this kind of work. So you go through a three-year retreat with no context? Maybe they come out with some modicum of sanity, but have they learned anything? With no context?"

I mentioned that I had just read in the biography of Chögyam Trungpa Rinpoche by Fabrice Midal that he did not allow his students to do three-year retreats for a very long time. He only encouraged them to take one or two months of retreat at a time.

Lee continued. "For the serious practicing Buddhists, they have children, whatever, their mother can die, their kids can die, if they are on retreat, they do not leave retreat until it's done. That's the real work. Nowadays we're so weak and spineless . . . In the tradition, you're supposed to have mastered Hinayana before you consider a retreat. You're supposed to be reliable in vipassyana before retreat; you're not supposed to do it out of order. You go through Hinayana, then Mahayana, and at a certain stage you're authorized to get to the next stage.

"Traditionally, by the time you get to the three-year retreat, you'd really be ready. Now they have three-year retreats that are done six months at a time, six months on and six months off! How can they even consider that? In American Zen and Vipassyana schools, they have capitulated to weak, sloppy American culture, and yet it's the most popular spiritual path in America. It's wildly popular. 'Oh, this is too hard,' they say. 'No problem, we'll soften it up for you!' That's the Kali Yuga. The complete dumbing down of the true Work."

Michelle asked, "You give more priority to action for us than retreat, and it's taken twenty-five years to even have people accepted to do retreats at all . . ."

Lee broke in, "I figure people might as well earn merit, because if people aren't even answering the phones or doing dishes on the ashram, they're not going to take their practice seriously. Why not just let them earn merit? Practice is supposed to get strong over twenty-five years, not just go to hell. 'Old students in Germany' told this person to write me that stuff! I don't even want to know who it was! Fifteen-year students can't even tell a new student how to write the master? And you tell a new student like her, who is so lost in content, to write all that?

"Tell me when your child has spinal meningitis—that, I *want* to know! But all these meaningless details about process—who are we listening to, except our own minds? Forget going on long retreats! Just work, serve, get some good karma, earn some merit. Unfortunately, that's the way it shakes down after all these years. So, people get tons and tons of merit and tons of good karma. Hey, that's not so bad! And they'll engineer their next lives so they'll get to continue to practice on the Path."

Michelle said, "You were commenting on people living lives of quiet desperation because they know they're not fulfilling their potential . . ."

Lee continued, "People have to not be so desperate. This woman who wrote the letter to her ex that I read: I told her a year ago to break it off, make a clean break, so it's finished, but she couldn't do it, and it's been heartbreak after heartbreak after heartbreak. She didn't do what I told her to do, she kept trying to make it work. 'But maybe we can . . .' Once should be enough. I can't be bothered with telling people the same thing over and over. A year and a half later of struggle and torture, it gets worse."

Wrapping up this poignant communication of his frustration at the needless suffering his students create for themselves, Lee said, "And on that note, I think we'll say goodnight."

And the Sacred is Everywhere

On the road
September 22, 2005

We left the ashram at ten a.m. and headed south to Touzac and La Source Bleue, the country estate of Jean Pierre and Sian Bouyou's family—for many years run as a beautiful, rustic hotel, restaurant and seminar house— for Lee's annual seminar there. It is a truly amazing place with an incredible ambiance and history; the estate and grounds have been in Jean Pierre's family for five hundred years.

On the way, we stopped for the ritual picnic and small glass of wine. We had started out in meditation that morning at the ashram in a cold barn, with hats or shawls covering our heads; even Lee, who is stoic about sitting in meditation in the barn, wore a Russian-style fur hat to keep the heat in. By the time we were getting close to Cahors, south of the Dordogne River, we had stripped off three layers of clothes as we sailed through sunny early autumn vineyards, heavily laden with purple black clusters of ripening grapes.

Lee had been invited for dinner at the home of Ceri, the sister of our hostess at La Source Bleue, Sian. Nestled in the pine thickets and densely wooded hills outside Prayssac, Ceri's home overlooked a widespread valley, with further hills, vineyards and farms in the distance. After a warm welcome from Ceri and her helpers in the kitchen,

Sian, Jennie and Danielle, we were seated in the sun and shade of the partially covered verandah, sipping diet Coke over ice, while Lee's students, who were coming for the seminar, began to arrive.

The "pig theme" of the summer seemed to be following us everywhere. Dinner was a rich combination of grilled bacon, pork ribs, chicken and shrimp, accompanied by two or three salads, potatoes, and topped off with Häagen-Dazs ice cream.

Despite the appearance of opulent and leisurely dining, these kinds of gatherings with Lee, where he is being hosted by friends or students, have a burning quality of the real that surges beneath the surface of sociality; there is a flow of kindness and a demonstration of dignity, in which Lee shows us directly what it means to be a guest with nobility, to receive the love and service of others with gratitude and gentility, to embrace richness with simplicity. If the hosts and other guests are able to, they will engage Lee in a way that brings him to life, in which case he is roused out of his meditation on the bacon and ice cream and places his attention more specifically on whatever is brought into its sphere.

In this case, it was Ceri who began to talk about her own version of the blues—a certain sadness or depression that comes upon her. It was interesting to hear this coming from a highly successful, creative, independent and strong woman who is quite radiant, who has made sweeping, powerful, positive changes in her life and the lives of her two young sons in the past few years, moving from England to southern France and changing her whole circumstance to provide a richer life and an optimal opportunity for them. Nonetheless, like us all, she sometimes has dark, unfocused days of doubt and depression. Lee listened attentively, watching her closely.

"I know exactly what you mean! The same thing happens to me," He laughed. She continued to talk for a while, and after she had said all she wanted to say, he simply said, "Whenever you have a day like that, just call *me*. I can take care of it right away!"

I was touched by this offer, even amazed in some ways, though not surprised at all, because it is so like Lee to give blessings in this way. These gifts of the spirit cannot be underestimated; at the very least they are the amazing gestures of a bodhisattva—a pure friendship, a true caring. At deeper levels, they are *abhishekas*, anointments, initiations, moments when he opens a doorway to the path.

We were on to second-helpings of grilled bacon and shrimp when Ceri began to talk about the situation in southern France, and the theme, as it so often does, turned to the world situation. She brought up the tragedy of the floods in New Orleans, and like many Europeans, expressed deep sorrow and compassion for the people of Louisiana, as well as horror at the failure of the American government to provide aid and relief to its own people. She shook her head in disbelief, then said, "And now there is another hurricane headed toward Galveston. And this one, they say, is even worse than the one that hit New Orleans. It's a level five."

That was a shock! Of course, we had no idea—we'd been on the ashram with no radios or televisions, and then on the road. Because a large part of my own remaining blood family—my sister, one nephew and his family, and two first cousins—live in the Houston and Galveston area of south Texas, I was concerned. I sat forward and began to ask her questions. At moments like this the situation in the world intrudes its harsh reality as a reminding factor of the Buddha's teaching on suffering and impermanence. There is no getting away from the dire situation in the world today—nor would we want to, because, as Chögyam Trungpa Rinpoche said to his student who asked what he did when he found himself in hell, "I try to stay there."

One who has taken the bodhisattva vow, which is a part of every real spiritual tradition, in one form or another, hell is the place where real Work can happen. For Jesus, it was, 'Do unto others as you would have others do unto you,' and 'Turn the other cheek.' Jesus said that we have to harrow hell, a teaching that has many levels of meaning, one of them being that hell is a place where the bodhisattva can serve others. For Western Bauls, the context of our lives should be itself the very breath of prayer; the remembrance of the name of Yogi Ramsuratkumar, the cultivation of the mood of practice. Our task is, "May my breath, body and mind be nothing but You."

A little later, Sian's daughter, Sara, came to the table and sat down with her four-month-old son, Ilya. She began to talk about how much Lee's book, *Conscious Parenting*, has meant to her. Her seven-year-old son, Joachim, played about, catching large grasshoppers and a praying mantis. She asked if Lee had written the book, and he answered that it was actually edited from his talks, as most of his books have been, with the exception of his journals. He said, "I just finished writing a new journal this summer. It will be published this year."

She continued, "Your book has been very important for me . . . Your book has been very important for me . . . *really*. The way you speak touches me *very* deeply. Your words are very intellectual, very strong, but with a *deep* reflection beneath them. It has meant a lot to me. I try to follow what you say, and you know, there is very little support for this kind of child-raising . . . ."

This interaction reminded me of countless other stories and *lilas* that have occurred over the years, revealing how Lee's teachings have touched many people and made a difference in their lives; and furthermore, I thought of the far-ranging, unknown effects of our prayers and practice, or the energies that are generated by those on the path—from the most subtle prayer or the Heart Breath, to our practical efforts, such as creating dharma art in any form, or taking care of a child or an aging parent or family member or friend in need.

Watching Lee interacting with this young mother of two children, the daughter of one of Lee's devoted students, I pondered the way Lee is always working, and in fact, the way the Work never stops, and especially over dinner at a lovely home in the hills of southwestern France. Soon it was time to drive the last twenty minutes to Touzac and La Source Bleue, where Lee immediately plowed into the process of unpacking and setting up the Sacred Bazaar, to be ready and waiting for the seminar participants who would arrive the next day.

La Source Bleue
September 23

Another feast, this time in the form of brunch at Sian's ample table, was served at ten-thirty this morning on the verandah that overlooks the sacred spring—*la source*. The first session of the seminar wouldn't begin until two p.m., leaving Lee some time to explore one of the local markets. After a short brunch, Lee was off to the market in Prayssac, and we were back in the van to travel over the lush green countryside with its wooded hills, limestone outcroppings, and beautiful old villages along the winding Lot River.

When we stopped to park, I jumped out to spot Lee as he parallel parked on the side of the busy road between two cars. I was attempting to position myself on his right side, so that both he could see me in his side mirror, and I could see where he was going on the right side, when he began to back up very fast, and at such an angle that I was blocked completely out of his field of vision. I ran to the other side to try to catch his eye in the left side mirror to direct him. He glanced once and saw me there, but turned back and kept backing up fast, not looking to me. It all happened so fast that I hardly had time to yell out, "Stop," then louder twice, "Stop! Stop!" until he rammed into the concrete gate pillar of the home next to which he was parking, taking a couple of layers out of the concrete in a wedge-shape and scratching and smudging the rubber bumper of the van with white concrete dust. Damn!

Lee jumped out of the van and around to the back, where I was brooding over the scratched rubber bumper. He didn't seem angry, but of course, I know only too well how many times there had been accidents with the vans over the summer. Each time he had been very vocal in his displeasure about these useless wastes of resources. This time, strangely, he said almost nothing, except maybe, "Okay!" as he wiped a bit of the dust off the bumper and then charged off down the street as if nothing had happened.

It's true that it could have been a lot worse, but I was still crestfallen, ashamed and angry with myself. I realized that if I'd been thinking, I would have banged on the back of the van to at least get the attention of Sylvan, who was sitting in the back seat and might have gotten the message across to Lee, who couldn't hear me yelling with the all the van windows closed. Then, ego being what it is, I found myself angry with Lee as well. "Jesus, he's such a madman. He can't slow down for five seconds to let me get in the right spot to help him back in without doing damage. What a set up!" After all, my mind ranted on, I do know how to direct a vehicle that is backing up; I used to drive tractor-trailer trucks, for God's sake! Why do I have to be proven to be incompetent and unable to do what he wants me to do in the heat of the moment, over and over again? What the hell is it all about?

Well, it is about being trained to move, assess what's wanted and needed and act on that *without even thinking about it*, in less than an instant. That's what that's all about. It's about being able to move—fast, from instinct, from all three centers working in concert. It's just the guru showing me, once again, that I haven't gotten it yet. What if our survival depended on me being able to move that fast and make that decision? Obviously my full attention was not located completely in that moment. Where was it? What was I obsessing about, underneath the surface of things, that was causing a split in me, keeping me from one-pointed focus in the present? The fact is that full attention is the only way to access the instinctual wisdom to move like that, or to pound on the back of the van to get someone's attention when you realize, quickly enough, that the guru can't hear you.

Every moment is another chance to drop it and move on to the ever-present now, into another possibility. Lee knew that I was stewing, but by the time we'd walked down the street and into the market, he was serenely and quickly moving forward into the beautiful late morning market, arranged on cobblestone streets around an old church. I decided to drop it, and somehow, I did. It was just entirely too miraculous and wonderful to be in this beautiful place with Lee and his companions, my friends, traveling together as we do in the refuge of the dharma, to waste precious moments letting ego reign in the kitchen instead of making room for the guru's great alchemy. Fact is, Lee is always in the kitchen cooking a feast of grand design—it's just that we're usually off in some alternate reality, cooking up recoil, resistance, and further bullshit which amounts to toxic poisons.

The market was fabulous. The late morning light glinted and played through the leaves of tall trees, while strong shafts of sun slanted down around the angles of the old stone church and brought the world to life. Everyone was friendly. Grace seemed to flow off Lee's dreadlocks like the Ganges flowing from Lord Shiva's *jatta*, and the graceful light of that outflowing illuminated everything with we saw, so that it was all tinged with grace.

Every single product that we saw for sale was of the highest quality, made or grown or produced with care and craft. France at its best, displayed in the native relationship with the land, the soil itself, the garden, farm, vineyard, the animals who are milked to curd the cheeses, the wheat that is milled to bake the finest breads in the world. Lee stopped to buy bee pollen from a local honey vendor, then, as we wound our way around the old church, going from one stall to another, we found ourselves looking over some wines. On one end of the display was a spread of Armangnac—the famous favorite drink of Mr. Gurdjieff, used in his toasts to the idiots. But there was something different about this display; the bottles were labeled by the year, going as far back as 1966. Forty-year-old Armangnac! Then, as we looked at the vintner's brochure, with its list and prices, we saw that he had Armangnac as old as 1900. The *vendeur* came over to talk to Lee, who was clearly interested.

He offered generous tastes of three different years, 1975, 1978 and 1976—sort of a crazy, informal toast to the idiots, I thought. The Armangnac was strong and satisfying. Lee seemed to like it, which was a surprise, since he had said before that he didn't like cognac, which is similar to Armangnac. The man who was selling the wine began to talk about the process of making the Armangnac, and how strong it is in alcohol content—forty-three percent or more. He said, "In fact, the 1976 is too strong for me!"

With Arnaud's eightieth birthday celebration coming up, which Lee would be attending in early October at Hauteville, it was the perfect gift. Lee picked the 1975 for Arnaud—it was the year that Arnaud started teaching. Lee ended up with three bottles. We walked away, back through the market, with smiles on our faces.

It has been ten years since Lee first began to come to La Source Bleue, this exceptionally beautiful place on the Lot River, not terribly far (by American standards) from the Pyrenees and the border of Spain. The hotel and grounds, including all of its old stone buildings, ranging from five hundred to a thousand years old, have been in the family of Jean Pierre Bouyou for five hundred years. The venerable, deep and wide spring itself has been a holy site, place of shamans, priests and ancient peoples, for probably a million years, going back to the earliest days of humankind on the European continent.

The beauty of the place always makes a jewel-like frame around Lee and the presence of Yogi Ramsuratkumar that is invoked, as well as the presence of Arnaud Desjardins and Swami Prajnanpad. Jean Pierre and Sian, who are students of, respectively, Arnaud and Lee, have dedicated their seminar program at the hotel to their teachers. Many distinguished and inspired speakers, teachers and guides of the path have come to give seminars over the years. The first talk of this three-day program began at two p.m. with about forty people in the audience, which would grow to seventy-five or so before the weekend was over.

Lee began, "I still like to talk about refined perception and heightened awareness, but I think my expectations of people being able to practice are just too high. So I had the view this year that we're basically honest and sincere and devoted, and that just has to be good enough. But when it comes to practice—profound, substantial practice? I don't know; I feel like I've been beating my head against the wall for thirty years, and I've had enough of beating my head against the wall.

"That's one of the reasons we have the Sacred Bazaar, because the sanctity of the artifacts radiates us and our spaces, and we don't have to do anything except buy them and put them in our homes. And you can start anytime! So, I hope you've been saving up all year for this, because I'm going back to Arizona, and all these fantastic, vibrating, living objects will be packed up, so you need to be liberators! Liberate these fantastic objects from their dark caves this year!

"It's not that there aren't practitioners—there are some wonderful, fantastic practitioners—but that kind of practitioner comes to the teacher already practicing and continues to practice, not because of anything the teacher has done. So I need to relax. Just put out the practice, wisdom and knowledge, and wherever it takes root, it takes root, and that's that.

"France is being inundated with British. Everywhere, here and where we live up north. Ceri says that people come from other countries and buy big estates, and after one or two years, the excitement wears off, and they want to go home. I'm just the opposite. My first two years in France, I'm like, 'What's the matter with people? The stores are closed at two p.m.! Don't they understand business?' I'd be needing to get gas on Sunday, you know, and couldn't find any . . . After a couple of years I started thinking, this is good; this is nice. Take it easy. My first two years I'd go to a seminar house and say,

'Where's the refrigerator?' There'd be this tiny little thing with nothing in it. But you buy your food fresh every day at the market—what could be better?

"So, I'm the opposite! I want to be spend more time here—I want to come live here. It's great here. Unfortunately, Americans and British are having more influence than the French want to admit. After awhile, everything will be open seven days a week. Too bad! Don't let those bastards do that to you! That's really indicative of where people's priorities are; after one or two years they say, 'I can't stand it, I have to go home.'

"So real practice is not a priority for us. We play around a little bit, do a little meditation, a little breath . . . but real heroic, abiding, moment by moment practice, where nothing gets in the way? Somebody dies, you grieve, you cry, and you go on. Where is that kind of practice? A relationship breaks up, you are crushed, and what happens to practice?!"

The opening talk was a cry against the failure of real practitioners to show up in the company of the master. I experienced it as a lament, one melody in a whole symphony that Lee had been playing all summer, which has become more pronounced, louder, more nuanced and complex as the summer has worn on. He continued:

"New Orleans gets washed away. We lost a lot of good voodoo priests on that one! And now there's another one coming. I hear it's going to hit Galveston, you know, in Texas, where Bush comes from."

Finally, a rather sober, ironic laughter began to break out among the people who were gathered, softening the heat and the sting of Lee's words. Yes, we're all suffering about the floods in New Orleans, and the sorrow and tribulation of the people in the South, but we can at least laugh, although bitterly, about George Bush, in a way that unites us all.

Lee said, "So, three million tragedies down there—yes, it's a heartbreak, it's crushing. The suffering is unimaginable. That's a fact. And, life goes on. But some of my students are paralyzed by what's happening in New Orleans, they're so upset. We earned it! You can't let the ozone layer go without some consequences. Some of my students say, 'I just can't meditate. All I can see is the suffering in New Orleans.' So, pray for them! I have nothing but disdain for that kind of practice. Arnaud and I have given practices to be used for all situations . . .!"

Still incredulous over the failure of his students, overall, and students of the path in general, to really practice, Lee returned to the conclusion he had offered earlier.

"So, I'm like—I need to relax! Damn! Just put out the teaching, and wherever it falls, it falls, and whoever picks it up, picks it up. Life goes on. That's where the Sacred Bazaar comes in. Fill your spaces with what is sacred, beautiful, holy, and just take the Blessings. Be a decent person, work hard, respect the people you live with.

"Practice! Practice requires a radical shift in your worldview, in which everything is seen as it is for what it is, but is not made into something it isn't by over-emotionalizing and romanticism, and not denied either. We tend to do one or the other; we go numb, pretend it's not all happening and we don't feel it, or we indulge the emotions that come up.

"Although, there's something to the saying, 'Blessings are curses and curses are blessings.' Like the old story, which some of you may have heard, about the farmer and his son who work very hard, but the son breaks his leg and can't work. The neighbors say, 'Oh, it's so horrible! Now he can't work, what will you do?' Then shortly thereafter, there's a war, and the king takes away all the young men to fight, but the son has a broken leg and can't go . . . so there is a negative side, but it turns out to be a blessing.

"One of the curses of France is nuclear energy. However, the futurists who predict the end of fossil fuels and the resulting breakdown of society as we know it, because everything depends on fossil fuels, say that France will have energy because of the nuclear power! So, I'll be spending more time here!"

Everyone laughed, some uneasily, because the irony is almost too weighted on the side of the curse. It was one example of how Lee has continued to push us to break out of a rigid worldview, even when it has the full weight of what is right behind it, even from the revered ecological perspective.

Lee continued, "I'm coming here, because I have no patriotism. In the Indian system they say we're in the Kali Yuga. There is the age of truth, the age of less truth, the age of partial truth, and then there is the age of no truth, and we're in the age of no truth—the Kali Yuga.

"My work has gone through a tremendous amount of changes, and where it has ended up is called 'guru yoga.' It's probably the single most unpopular spiritual path in the world today, except for fundamentalism in all forms—Christianity, Islam. Or Hindu fundamentalism—Hinduism is a universal religion that embraces all . . . but, 'Let's kill the Muslims!' There is a very delicate peace in India, and certain large areas are Muslim and the Hindus don't ever go there. They are scared to walk the streets. So, we could sum up this situation with one sentence that applied to us all: 'I'm fucked.' "

People were quick to laugh at Lee's blunt assessment; it's something we could all relate to, although he was talking quite literally about himself and all of us. He said, "You'd better have a sense of humor about it, because you don't want to laugh at other people's tragedies, but you do want to laugh at your own. The ultimate practice of guru yoga is: surrender everything to the guru and let the guru take care of everything.

"Of course, false gurus say, 'Give me all your wealth.' That's not what I mean. I mean to stop thinking that you are in control; stop thinking you are greater than nature—that no matter what happens, you can manage your life—and relax into the divine flow and accept what is, as it is, here and now. Ostensibly, the guru is plugged into this divine flow, this Process of Divine Evolution. Based on that, he is able to make available to that flow whoever plugs into him.

"It's sort of like when we set up for gigs, and the source of the electrical power is farther away than the speakers. Then you have a wire, and you plug the wire into the instrument and the wire plugs into the source of electricity, and then you have energy. It's sort of like the guru has an infinite number of plugs for whoever needs them, so whoever plugs in gets the juice, and everything else is secondary. But that's not the way we establish our priorities. When the cat jumps on your back, the truth goes out the window. Meaning, when everything is going well—kids are okay, your professional work is going well—then we're really like, 'The truth, the truth, accept what is as it is, say yes to life!' But then, when some tragedy happens, instead of relating to that tragedy and handling it from the context of the truth we've been talking about all along, we fall apart."

Lee talked about Carlos Castaneda, who was known to be quite a womanizer, and how he reacted when Don Juan pointed out to him that he was using women as objects to satisfy his own lusts. He continued, "I mean, love is complicated, messy, sticky, painful. It's beautiful also. If you're really interested in respecting a person, why give so much attention to their sex? 'Why doesn't that thing work? It had better work when I want it to work!' It goes both ways. The man says to the woman, 'How come you're never in the mood?' She says, 'How can I be in the mood when you attack me?' Because to a man, sex with a woman is like shooting a deer—you get it in your sights, shoot it, take it home and eat it!"

It was an air-tight indictment of the human condition. We were laughing in that amazing way that Lee's audiences have of enjoying the spanking, so to speak. He was chastising us, but we were totally on his side. Unfortunately, we were also laughing because we think we are the exception—it's all the other human beings who do that—when in reality we are still doing those same things, in one way or another.

"Because if you say, 'Oh, look at that magnificent animal! It's a female. I wonder if it has babies,' then it runs away! You shouldn't be a hunter if you're that romantic. To be a hunter you've got to just go and shoot the thing!" More laughter. The metaphor was working for us.

Lee continued, "American hunters just have to kill something! If they don't get a deer or a pheasant, they'll just shoot a cow or a horse or a bird in the trees! So Carlos was very insulted, because he thought of himself as a man who appreciated women. He said to Don Juan, 'You don't understand me, you don't know what I really feel . . .' Don Juan gave Carlos an exercise to prove his point. Carlos did the exercise and was shocked to find that it was true. Unfortunately, I'm all out of exercises. People are always saying, 'Give me something to do so I can realize this or that!' I say in my mind, 'How about practice?' 'No, I want a mountain to climb—I don't want to practice! Give me something I can do for three weeks and it will change my life forever!'

"Patanjali," Lee began, speaking of the father of Hatha Yoga, "said that practice is a threefold process: it requires consistency, meaning you have to do it on a regular basis, a regular basis, a regular basis; it happens over a long period of time—and sometimes there are immediate results, great, but that does not compromise the fact that practice happens over a long period of time; and third, practice requires ardent devotion. *Ardent* devotion: on fire, intense!

"We live in a time of instant satisfaction, and if we don't get instant satisfaction, we can get a kind of vicarious satisfaction from other people's activity by going on the internet. We can go on all the pornography sites or reality sites; people are even having their babies on the internet! If we can't get instant satisfaction, we can get 'sort of' satisfaction by knowing that somebody else is destroying their lives with fame and power, like we would like to do.

"To really practice we have to completely shift our worldview from 'me first,' to 'maybe my kids and family and then my friends' or to some, 'my country,' but that's a little old-fashioned. Remember 'One for all, all for one'?" Everyone laughed. "Because every time we take advantage of someone else to make an advantage for ourselves, we're actually losing."

Lee used the example of waiters in America, who work for a small wage and tips. He said that many people don't realize that if they walk out on a bill, the waiter has to pay the bill out of his or her own pocket. Furthermore, people who walk out on a bill don't realize that the money taken out of the waiter's pocket affects the person who walked out on the bill personally.

"So," he continued, "to really practice requires a complete shift in worldview, from 'me,' as an independent, isolated individual, to this idea that everything is in an interplay with everything else to varying degrees. It's easy to do in principle. When we are relatively taken care of it's easy, and when we have to make certain sacrifices we don't want to make, that creates an internal struggle which often makes that worldview, of truth and one for all and all for one, go out the window."

Shifting gears, Lee began to talk about the meal he had had the night before at Ceri's home, which led to extolling the virtues of pork as well as the fabulous, fat, juicy prunes he'd bought just this morning in the market in Prayssac. "Pork! It's fabulous food going in! It sits in there a while; takes it awhile to break down. So I started eating these prunes—two, three, four of them—and I couldn't stop! So if I have to *run* out of here . . .!"

The whole space seemed to be flowing; we were feeling easy and warmed up for a serious sales pitch. He plowed ahead, "I said to myself, 'I'm going to wait till tomorrow to sell stuff!' " He shrugged and smiled, a kachina in hand and three more beside him on the table with the flower arrangement. "I'm supposed to have discipline! 'The teacher doesn't have discipline, so I don't have to . . .' But I can't wait!"

He held up one bright, colorful kachina, bedecked with feathers, and said, "These are benevolent spirits to chase away bad spirits, promote fertility, promote kindness. This one is Buffalo Dancer, and this one is Eagle Dancer. The North Americans have a legend that if a white buffalo is born, then there will be peace in the world. And there was one born, not long ago! Let's hope it's true . . . Anybody interested? There are five of them up here, each one signed by the artist. They're made by the Navajos, but they are Hopi kachinas, exactly like the costumes the Hopis wear when they do their ceremonial dances. Take more than one and I'll make you a bargain—a *real* bargain! In fact, take all five and I'll make you a bargain you'll never forget!"

No one moved or made a sound but merely sat looking at him.

"Oh, I'm going to have to take longer to warm this crowd up! Nobody wants a bargain? You'll never get something this cheap from me again! But I'm not going to tell you the price until you tell me you want it."

Lee has made similar offers many times; the extent of his generosity in the "bargain" always hinges upon the degree to which the buyer trusts him completely. He has often said that trust really turns him on, in a way—it inspires him to flights of magnanimity. His sales pitch went on for some time while he held two of the largest, most colorful kachinas up in the air or danced them around playfully, like dolls.

"I love these things," he mused, looking at them. "They're fabulous! These will brighten up your space! Come out every morning and see these things—incredible!"

The audience remained unmoved for what seemed like a very long time. Just when it seemed like Lee was going to withdraw the offer for a bargain, Ceri, who was sitting near the back of the crowded room, spoke up, saying, "I'll take them all."

Lee said, "Do you want to know the price first?"

"Later," Ceri said. "I want them."

"Great! I'll tell you the price after the talk—but don't tell anyone in this room what you paid for them!" Ceri nodded.

Putting the kachinas down, Lee relaxed in the plush chair that had been provided for him and continued, "Ceri was telling me something last night, and I was thinking, in relation to *my* problem, this isn't so bad, because my problem is cynicism—a very big problem.

Don't ever become cynical—you always want to have the attitude, well, life goes on! It's another day! Let's go for it!

"There's a strange saying in English: 'God helps those who help themselves.' You have it in French too? Yes. Essentially that means, what is, as it is, here and now, and you have to try and try and try again and keep trying in relation to whatever it is. We just had a money seminar at Ferme de Jutreau. Purna really worked hard on it; he's been doing corporate consulting and giving personal growth seminars, and it was very inspiring and comprehensive. The first feedback I got from the seminar was from one of my students . . ."

Lee told the group about how he had sold his solo album, *Crushed by Love*, in lots of ten, twenty, thirty and fifty, so that people could re-sell them. One of his students, Sue Kali, who had taken a quantity of CDs, went to a seminar on Bengali music and offered the CDs; she had made fifty pounds in five minutes.

"She was terrified because the price of the CD was higher than the Bengali music CDs that were being sold there, and the music had nothing to do with Bengali music. She said, 'It's not my personality to sell,' etc, etc. But she did it anyway. She said, 'I was so happy, because it worked!'

"Okay," Lee continued, "so I have to change my context, my worldview. How? There is no formula. You have to 'just do it!' Some old sage thought of that, and Nike borrowed it! And it's sort of true in that domain too! If your worldview is 'I've gotta get mine,' in your profession or whatever, and you want to change your worldview, it's not going to happen."

Lee gave us an example of the kind of radical decision that we might have to make when we are wanting to change our worldview: a woman who was a fundraiser got a check for fifty thousand dollars, but she knew it wasn't right to keep the check, because it came with strings attached. She sent the check back. Fifteen years later she ran into the man who sent the check and he said, "I was so shocked when I got that check back that I started to look at my whole life and what I was doing with my life." She found out that his personal search led him to become a philanthropist, and all of his time and money went to speaking to groups and getting people involved in charitable projects. But, he said, he wouldn't have turned out that way if he hadn't gotten that fifty thousand dollar check returned.

"So," Lee concluded, "there is no formula to change your worldview; you just do it. Often that means acting in a way that contradicts the way we usually make choices in our lives. If we are really serious about practice, one thing we are called to do is to make choices based on a completely different criteria than we usually make choices."

After the talk was over people swarmed the Sacred Bazaar where Lee stood in the back at the several tables of bronze deities, books, CDs, and now, European *brocante*, especially of the sacred variety: antique rosaries, delicate crucifixes, bronze plaques wrought with the image of Mary, Queen of Heaven, holding the Divine Child. Meanwhile, Ceri stood nearby, looking excitedly at her new acquisition—five beautiful kachinas, dazzling in their creative power, rich with color and motion, decorated with feathers, carrying rattles and shields and other implements. If you were in a bad mood, all it would take is contemplating these images with even a little receptivity for a few minutes to turn things around. She said, "I've always had a very deep interest and feeling for the North American Indians!" She explained that she would have them all together in her house.

At four o'clock we reconvened for Lee's last talk of the first day of the three-day seminar. A woman asked a question about Lee's use of the phrase, "Pay Attention and Remember," which Lee used as a jumping off point for the teaching:

"When I visit other teachers there is either an agreement that we agree with each other or not. And the agreement has been with American Indian, Tibetan Yogis, Hindus, Sufis. Often the teacher will try to teach me, because they think I need teaching, which is always tremendous fun for me but very difficult for my students, because they get easily offended when someone tries to teach me."

Lee continued, "When I say 'Pay Attention and Remember,' it's based on an instinctual sense, not as a definition. So, my students have to keep beating their heads against the wall until they know what it means, and then I'll know that they've gotten it, the same way that teachers recognize each other: it's evident.

"We have a practice of daily meditation, study, exercise, and then specific breath practices, a specific phrase of Enquiry, which is an internal practice, and practices relative to a statement that we keep measuring our perception against (Just This); then we have all kinds of specific lifestyle practices based on childraising, relationship, use of money. In relationship to practice, nobody does all the practices all the time. There are too many, and some have to be earned. There are advanced practices—the use of breath and sexual practice and practices using the energy of the sun and moon. Who wants to do sexual practices? 'I do! I do!' everybody says."

Everyone burst into laughter; it's a familiar condition for us all, sex being one of the great fascinations; it is one of the primal arenas of life, and one of the most difficult to gain wisdom in relationship to. Lee smiled and chuckled along with us, then continued, "But we don't really, because to do the sexual practices you have to split your mind so that a part of your mind is doing something and the other part of you is just having sex. But we don't want to have a part of our mind observing the whole thing—it's embarrassing!

"Usually we just have sex—sometimes it's fabulous, sometimes it's mediocre, or wild or tame. It's always different—if we're lucky it's not always the same all the time. At least not exactly the same. There are minor variations . . . some people like major variations!" More laughter punctuated his words and held us all together in a strong but delicate web of knowing consciously our common bonds, our common humanity, our interconnectedness.

"When it gets wild," Lee continued with a big smile, "as all of you know, it's not very human. It's not dignified, respectful or polite. There is a whole part of us that's polite, respectful and dignified that doesn't want to see ourselves not being polite, respectful and dignified when we're having sex. It's embarrassing!" The laughter continued; everybody was enjoying Lee's candor, telling it like it is, exposing, without a trace of shame, the bare bones of experience.

"A lot of people think sexual practice is about bigger and better orgasms—or cosmic sex. But actually sexual practices in the Baul tradition are merely a means to an end, and the end is not better sex. So we don't want to split our minds, because how can we become absorbed and one with our partners if we are observing ourselves, because when we lose ourselves in the act of sex, it's a tremendous relief: 'Oh, *I* wasn't there for a moment—thank God! All my burdens, guilt, worries, gone for a moment!' So we have this idea that sex gets better and better until it's cosmic, we are one with Saturn and its rings and all the shooting stars in the sky . . . !

"Anyway. So, the practice. Nobody does all the practices all the time. Sometimes there is an ebb and flow to the practices. I used to have this religious practice about diet, before coming to France. Now I'm ruined, *completely* ruined—coffee, wine, meat! And the fresh *tomatoes*! Ohh!" Lee's passionate enthusiasm brought out a fresh round of smiles and laughter in the group.

"I haven't even been calling us vegetarians this summer, because I feel like a hypocrite! Look at what we eat!" More laughter broke out. "But we used to be vegetarians—a long time ago! Now we say, 'Oh, the law of hospitality comes first,' and we visit people. It's important to be a good guest! Somebody asked one of my students what I liked to eat and they said, 'vegetables,' and I got there and looked at all the vegetables and I said, 'Where's the meat?'" More laughter. "So I'm speaking with the hostess and she said, 'I asked one of your students what you like to eat, and she said, vegetables.' What?!

"I haven't been eating fish for a long time because it's all poisoned with things like mercury, because all the rivers are toxic. Purna has stopped serving fish on his ashram because of that; he's started serving beef. Their joke is, 'Beef is a vegetable!' " Laughter rolled over us again like wind over a field of wheat. The fine, well-honed blad of truth was wielded skillfully in the master's gentle hands as Lee continued with a fast commentary on the futile insanity of our desperation to avoid life as it is.

"The students are very happy! All those lifetime vegetarians! But how could you have a problem with that—just walk by the barbecue pit and smell that! It's better than lavender! By the way, we walked past a lavender stand today, and the advertisement said that lavender helps prevent wrinkles. I don't think so! Wouldn't it be great, ladies? But why even bother when every ten or fifteen years you can just get your whole face stretched by a surgeon? You won't look very human, but so what? You'll feel good about yourself! You'll have confidence when you look in the mirror—'I haven't aged in fifteen years!' "

It was classic comedy, threaded through and through with the tragedy of the situation. Where have all the wise elders gone? What has become of the Divine Path of Growing Old? One of the great tragedies of our times is that elders have no place in our society; they receive very little or no respect. We will do anything in our futile attempts to stay "young," as if growing old was a shameful and wrong thing, instead of a natural process of life in which one becomes wise and venerable.

"There are the practices, they come and go, sometimes strong, sometimes weak—that's natural. I haven't exercised all summer, I've been so busy. So I could eliminate something else; I could exercise instead of going to look for sacred artifacts. Forget it! Exercise has got to go!

"There are practices that take physical time, like meditation. They are sort of like natural supplements; it takes a lot of time to take natural supplements. The natural ones are really big, you have to take a lot of them, whereas the chemical ones you just pop one pill.

"There are certain practices that take a certain amount of time. Then there are the internal practices that you do during your day, that don't require any time; they are just done as you are living, but you have to remember to do them. And the mind does not want to do them, so you have to train the mind to do them. Like yesterday, there was an accident on the road. The car had turned over, it was completely crushed, and there were people in it. So probably most of the people in the van we were in, as we passed by it, shocked by the sight of the car, immediately thought of the internal practices that have to do with praying for others and sending the Blessings of our Master, Yogi Ramsuratkumar, to others. So we actually have to remember to practice. There are always people suffering in the world.

"There are basically two kinds of internal practice: those designed to serve others through prayer and invoking the Benediction for others, and those internal practices that are predominantly designed to clarify what is, as it is, here and now—the objective state of what is, as it is, here and now, not the subjective state. 'I'm a man,' 'I'm a woman,' is not what is. That is a projection that we have identified with, whose illusion has captured us in its shell. To really see what is here and now is shocking, because it's nothing the mind has given definition to. So we have internal practices to clarify all that, and as the clarification roots us more profoundly in what is, here and now, that ultimately serves others.

"Sooner or later you cover all the practices, internal and external. You start in the opposite direction and then everything is all mixed in the middle! The mind doesn't want to practice because realizing the fruit of those practices is for the mind to realize its illusion about itself. So a part of you is trying to remember, and a part of you is sabotaging that. The internal practices we do when we remember to do them. Hopefully, within our lifetimes, the internal practices have become so natural to us that we don't have to remember to do them; they just go on without any effort on our part. But for that to happen, you have to build up the naturalness of the practice by doing them with consistency over a long period of time. It's not as easy as it sounds, because the mind doesn't want to do it.

"That's the practices. Then there is Practice. When I say 'Practice,' I mean Context—a field of knowledge out of which all things arise. They say in the Gurdjieff teachings that you can see the Work from the eyes of the world, or you can see the world from the eyes of the Work. People predominantly see the Path through the eyes of illusion, and it can take years even to realize that we are projecting our illusory beliefs on the Path. I got a letter from somebody with a question; they gave me a little of their spiritual history. They used to be in a spiritual group, but the head of the group went to prison for pedophilia, and they lost faith . . . When your context is established in the Divine, you cannot act in a way that is inconsistent with intrinsic dignity and intrinsic nobility. When your context is established in the world of illusion, then you can take essential spiritual truths and superimpose them on your neurotic reality.

"For example, they say in the East that in a context of enlightenment or awakening, all action is good. You take all these faux gurus who think they're enlightened, acting without dignity or nobility, they're justifying their behavior, like pedophilia: 'This is good for the child.' That's seeing the Work through the eyes of the world. We look at our illusory lives as they are and fit those principles to our lives.

"One stream of the Work that I have plugged into is the stream that utilizes kundalini in a relatively transformational process. Sometimes spontaneously, people open up some little door in themselves and are flooded with energy that is ecstatic. When someone is ecstatic, but their context is still the world, not the Work, then they start to see their lives in terms of the world, not the Work. The second year this community was in existence there was a woman who had a kundalini experience for weeks and felt herself to be a goddess. In her view of herself as a goddess, she had the clarity to see the suffering of men. She thought, 'If Lee would give me the role of initiatrix,' then any man would be healed by her touch. She was a bit disappointed when I didn't see things the same way. She went on to leave the school and is still angry with me. That's viewing the Work through the eyes of the world. Because initiation by the divine feminine is a very real element of many paths, and that principle even has its anthropomorphic representation.

"Sometimes people have a dream that the goddess comes and initiates them; it happens to men and to women. It's easy to take an objective cosmic principle and project it onto our ordinary world. To view the world through the eyes of the Work is to see everything with a kind of unitive vision, understanding that an element of true unitive vision has an element of *distinction*.

"So, everything is one, literally, and within that oneness, one of the distinctions that is just to make is: 'This person is my husband, this person is my wife—all others are not.' "

This too brought out laughter among us, because Lee's tongue-in-cheek tone made it clear that he was pointing to a far-reaching subtext that was immediately recognizable. Distinctions create order, conscience, bring nobility and dignity to our lives, and must be applied at the most basic levels.

Lee continued, "So . . . and, we can understand all the implications of that—personally, financially, etc. What would we do, psychologically, if we weren't in some kind of antagonistic relationship with everyone on the planet, even with people we love? In America, it's a big problem when the woman earns more money than the man. Even if we love one another, the guy starts to feel emasculated. Then the man gets the job of staying home with the kids and preparing meals. Not everybody, but most, don't realize they're competing with their partners until something comes up to magnify some area for us.

"So, the mind, in its self-centeredness, doesn't want us to see things clearly; the mind is invested in keeping us divided and in illusion. To see the world through the eyes of the Work, in a very real sense, is unnatural, because you have to go against the natural process of psychology, of personality development, like you have to function in a domain that is meta-human or para-human. Our idea of enlightenment is to be super-human, not meta-human, to become the best human we can be. To see the world through the eyes of the Work, that whole program has to go—to be obviated. That's what is demanded.

"So, when I use the word 'Practice' as a principle, I'm talking about Context—living in a state that has become natural, which is seeing the world through the eyes of the Work. All of us have periods of that, but it fades back into seeing the Work through the eyes of the world."

After dinner, people gathered for tea in the upstairs room of the eight hundred year old stone building where Lee was giving his talks. Just when the gathering seemed doomed to be a superficial social space, Kathleen, an Irish woman who has lived in France for many years and was translating for Lee, began to engage Lee with some questions. When the talk turned to extreme violence in American movies, like *Kill Bill*, which Lee was enthusiastically describing as a "great movie," she zeroed in on a particular issue.

"Do you tell your students to see this?" Kathleen asked incredulously, due to the extremely violent nature of the movie.

"No . . . As soon as I say, 'Don't do that,' my students rush to it like lemmings to the sea."

After this statement on his students' disobedience, Lee returned to a more conversational tone on the further subject of movies, violence, emotionalism and cultural traits. Speaking about French and Japanese films, he said, "The French let their feelings hang out all over the place, and the Japanese keep all their feelings in. Between the two there is good balance."

It's an irony, someone said. In explaining this to another person, I ask what the French word for irony is. They answer, *ironie*.

"Same word!" Lee beamed, obviously having fun in the moment. "See," he said, turning to his American students, "they've stolen our language!"

Sian and Jean Pierre were speaking about some of the guests—spiritual teachers, well-known authors and spiritual friends—who have been invited to the upcoming eightieth birthday celebration of Arnaud Desjardins. One of the guests would be a Native American man who had also given some talks at La Source Bleue. Lee began to criticize the French tendency to assume that anyone with long braided hair, feathers and a peace pipe is a holy man of the Native American tradition, when in fact, as in all sacred traditions, there are only a few truly authentic medicine men among the tribal people of North America. Nonetheless, this particular Native American man was described as being a man of great depth, peace and, most of all, humility.

"I hope he's willing to talk to me," Lee jived brusquely, seeming irritated, "because I'm the *opposite* of humble!"

Lee laughingly commented that it would be very interesting having all these spiritual luminaries in one place together, intimating that there would definitely be some competition going on.

"You mean it's the same among spiritual teachers—the competition and power-tripping—as among us students?" someone asked.

"Of course!" Lee laughed genially. "What would life be without a few friendly rivalries here and there! You'd better not ever say 'Idaho potatoes' to the Irish!" He laughed again. I remembered how my Irish grandmother served potatoes every day, and they were called 'Irish potatoes' as a way to make a distinction between white potatoes and orange or yellow sweet potatoes, or yams.

"Do you remember what you say at different times?" Kathleen asked in her Irish brogue, softened by years in France. I assumed she was referring to the fluid way that Lee approaches any given subject: if approached from one direction, it's one thing, if approached from a different direction, it's another thing. This is a paradox that has absolute context at the center of its apparent mutability, and context never changes—only the outer appearances of things, which must be understood or apprehended on a situation by situation basis.

"Oh no! Maybe one or two things here or there. You know, Rita Mae Brown said, 'The good thing about telling the truth is you don't have to remember what you said.' Cause the truth never changes—you don't have to worry about what you said. You tell a lie, you have to remember what you said. Wasn't it Henry Miller who said, 'Don't let the facts get in the way of the truth.'? It's a very important point!"

Changing the subject, Kathleen asked, "Coffee doesn't keep you awake, Lee? Because you didn't drink coffee at all before." Kathleen had known Lee for many years and could remember a time when Lee was strict in his practice of abstaining from coffee.

"I disliked coffee intensely when I was younger. I started drinking it sweet with milk, and then just with milk. Now I get into espresso a little. In another ten years I'll be just like my mother and father, who drank coffee black."

Kathleen laughed and said, "They ate beef and pork too!"

Lee talked about how his parents lived through the American Depression, and after that, they always bought only the best food, especially meat—except for peas, which Lee's mother always bought canned.

"Do you see yourself continuing to travel around France and give seminars?" Kathleen pursued further.

"Next year, I'm cutting out four seminars that I usually do and giving them at Ferme de Jutreau, because I was hardly there at all this summer. Of course I'll always go to Hauteville—that's sacrosanct! I think the seminars will end at some point, because the teaching is so well documented, it's not necessary to keep generating more. We have thousands of hours of tapes to be transcribed and edited. I don't know how long it will take to catch up."

Kathleen continued with another question, "Do you see parallels in your own work with Arnaud and how accessible he is now and his changes?"

"I never thought of it," Lee said. "There could be some . . ." he shrugged.

"Denise Desjardins once said to Arnaud, 'You are a Gemini, and you can convince anyone of anything,' " Kathleen added.

"Well, I've been trying to convince people for twenty-five years with mediocre results," Lee snapped back. "I'm a Scorpio—it's worse!" Everyone laughed. "I try to beat people over the head with it! I try to force them to get it. Maybe, since I've been teaching that long, after that much time it's just time to do something different. We'll see how next year goes—it's kind of an experiment. And, it will wind down slowly. And if it doesn't go well, I'm back on the seminar circuit again, which would be unpleasant but necessary, until it's unnecessary."

Jean Pierre asked, "Where can you see hope?" It was a question that is in the consciousness of every thinking person these days, like a worm in an apple.

"Me?" Lee asked, as if surprised. "You're asking the wrong person!" Everyone laughed. Even though the topic of conversation was dark and foreboding, Lee kept the tone light and nonattached. We were basking in his compassion, which in this moment was showing up in his sense of humor.

"To me, the only hope is that history repeats itself, so the Sat Yuga will come again—we'll be there, but we won't remember this. So put in your order now! Write it down on a little leaf and send it out on the Ganges with a flame in it!

"Paramahansa Yogananda said that the integrity that can happen in small groups around the world is where it is at—large groups can't change anything. Little enclaves of true spiritual seekers will preserve things and keep the flow of the teaching going. But I think there were a few of those in New Orleans!"

When a number of people looked at Lee with non-comprehension, he said, "It's a joke!"

I wasn't so sure it was a joke. Among the serious voodoo practitioners in New Orleans, who come from a long line of tradition going back hundreds of years, there were bound to be some real adepts who work on the side of light, so to speak.[1]

Kathleen asked, "Do you feel someone like Yogi Ramsuratkumar will come back?"

"Of course He'll come back again, just like the Tibetans come back! I don't think any of us will recognize Him. I don't think He's come back yet . . . well, He could have . . . " Lee mused, "He said that He wants to come back. He's born a child, it takes thirty to forty years for Him to take responsibility for who He is . . ."

Jean Pierre asked, "Did he say anything about it?"

"He gave me some hints," Lee answered, perhaps intimating that Yogi Ramsuratkumar would take incarnation in the West.

Kathleen asked, "Arnaud said if he came back, he'd come back for the reason that he wants to be a father. What do you feel? Is it the same for you?"

"Well," Lee responded, "I'm happy with what I've done so far in this life." He paused for a moment, then said, "I think if I come back, I'd like to be all powerful!"

---

1 When I got back to Arizona in October, the underground news in the U.S. was that in the process of rebuilding New Orleans, government agencies and funding were trying to shut down the poor areas of the city where the voodoo culture proliferated. It was a shocking but not surprising development; the new New Orleans would be whiter, more affluent, less soulful. It seemed like the perfect opportunity to rid the city of a certain underworld element of the streets that, to the conventional mainstream culture, appeared unsavory, wild, scary, even pagan. It is not only an act of racism and classism, but an act of aggression on the part of the prevailing fundamentalist Christian bias against those cultures and spiritual milieus that threaten the absolute dominance of the right wing.

Laughter broke out among everyone, about twenty people, who were following Lee's dialogue very closely. It seemed to be his way of saying, "I am not going to answer that question." Why? There could be lots of reasons. Maybe the question was too threaded through with fascination, because after all, what good can it do? What can it mean to us, other than to distract us from the urgent necessity to tend to our own business—that is, our own practice, here and now. Meanwhile, throughout the conversation, the servers cycled back and forth through the room with coffee, tisane and banana bread.

Kathleen persevered: "Fathers aren't powerful enough?"

"No!" Lee responded. "Only to their children."

The server passed by bearing *tisane*. Lee exclaimed, "Oh boy! Temptation! What kind of tea?" Vervaine was the answer. "Okay, I'll take some!"

He laughed and continued tongue-in-cheek, "But Arnaud and I will be doing pretty good next to Prince Charles."

"Why?" asked Kathleen, taking the bait.

"Because he's going to come back as a tampon!" Lee retorted, a gleam in his eyes. Everyone who remembered the scandalous comment of Charles that hit the tabloids some time ago, "I want to come back in my next life as one of Camilla's tampons!" laughed heartily. Others had to have the joke explained to them. Immediately Sian, who is British, began to regale Lee with bad jokes about Prince Charles. The evening dissolved into talk of American and French movies, with Lee giving a rousing review of his favorite French film, *Ridicule.*

"Such a final and exact view of human psychology," he said. "It was just right there!"

La Source Bleue
September 24

"One of the things my Master liked about me was my facility with language," Lee was saying in the early afternoon session. "I used to write poetry, and He liked it. He told me to write as much of it as I could. He said we should read it everyday and it would sort of tune us in . . ." This was the entry point to a sales spree in which Lee sold numerous books and then started promoting a large number of singing bowls to his audience. The selling of the singing bowls was quite a ritual, in which he rang the tone of each one, held the bowl up to his ear, smiled in appreciation, looked expectantly out at everyone or breathed a sigh of satisfaction, "Ahhh!" at the various melodious tones of each bowl. Even with all this, no one was taking a bowl.

Lee smiled, "This will be good for my editors to write about: 'He played all the bowls and nobody took one!' It will be a chapter in the next 'Tawagoto'! Okay, the chapter is written! Now let's move on!"

The ringing of the bells continued with offering each one to the group, which kept its stance, as if, in a way, the audience had their arms across their chests in a "no way!" gesture.

"Ohh! This is tough!" Lee lamented candidly, which broke the silence of the group as people burst into laughter. "Lucky I'm used to this, or I'd play all the bowls, nobody would raise their hands, and I'd have to have two months in therapy. 'Oh, nobody loves me! Nobody buys my bowls!' "

Still Lee persisted in ringing the bowls, holding them up, scanning the audience for any sign of hope that someone might be interested. Suddenly a woman said, "I'll take that one," and then three more sold quickly to others who raised their hands upon the ringing of their special bowl.

He was just playing with us, I thought. Street merchant, liar, thief—who else is he? He sold one set of three bowls for a hefty price and they slipped out of his hands. Perseverance is one of Lee's strongest suits; the sales pitches kept coming, even in the face of the audience's reluctance.

"I'm glad I'm not teaching a seminar on business—then I'd really feel bad!" Lee laughed. "Okay, I'll throw this one in too—which one is better? You sell these to your friends and get this one for next to nothing! You say, 'I was at this seminar with this guy, and he was selling these, and I got a good deal . . ." Finally the blitz was over; things had been sold, or not. Lee asked, "Any questions?"

"I'm in a situation," a long-time disciple of Arnaud began, "where I meet married men, and they want to have sex with me. I don't want to do that anymore, but it's true these are men who are suffering, they love their wives, but are sexually frustrated."

"What's the reason they're frustrated, do you think?" Lee asked.

"Because they are with women who have been victims of incest," she answered.

"No! That's not why! Guess again," Lee prompted.

"But they have . . ." she started.

"No! That is not why they are frustrated. Guess again!" A short silence ensued before Lee started speaking. "They're frustrated because they don't know how to relate to their wives and awaken a healthy sexual appetite in their wives. They are really suffering because they aren't mature enough to bring their wives into relationship.

"If a woman has been sexually abused and the man she falls in love with and marries is so aggressive that it reminds her of the abuse, of course she's not going to have a normal sexual relationship. Their desire for affairs is because they think normal women would satisfy them, but they won't because it's entirely the man."

She said, "These are not violent men, they don't come across as abusive or aggressive."

"Of course they don't—they want to have sex with you! But it's very compassionate of you, very maternal!"

"I don't really want this to happen, so how do I drop out of this scene?" she asked.

Lee said, "I guess another twenty years and make yourself ugly!" Everyone laughed. "I think that's the only way out because I'm sure it's nothing you're doing. You're a normal, attractive woman. There's nothing you can do about these men.

"They may love their wives when they're not screwing another woman, but . . . Do you have another question? . . . Wouldn't it be easier if we were all dogs? Maybe you should pray to be a dog next life! No emotions, just a couple of sniffs, and it's yes or no!" More laughter. "No guilt, no jealousy. Life could be pretty good if you had a good family to take care of you! Some families don't let their dogs screw. Female dogs means puppies. They have them fixed, or keep them inside when they're in heat. They howl . . . all the boy dogs come out and bark, 'Let her out! Let her out!' That's really what they're saying!"

People were bouncing with laughter in their seats. I think we got the picture. Is our human sex drive really that much different than dogs?

"So, pray for a good rebirth next life. If not as a dog in a good family where you won't be abused, and if you pray right, you'll get what you want! You won't remember this lifetime of praying for it, but you won't have to. Usually when you're young, you take everything for granted, but when you get older, you see people get cancer, in America even people in their thirties and forties. Then you're grateful for not having that suffering.

"How you live now defines what will happen at some time later, and it doesn't matter whether you remember it at all, because when something good happens, you know it and are grateful and thrilled. So, it doesn't matter whether you remember your past lives; all that matters is what is, as it is, here and now. Other questions?"

A conversation ensued between Lee and Charlie, a young American living in France, about the perversity in contemporary sexuality. After the so-called "sexual revolution" of the sixties and seventies, now we are even more psychologically wounded and libertine in our need for sexual experience that goes further and further out there. Charlie concluded, "I can have sex with a horse, but am I really free?"

Lee retorted, "And even more important, is the horse free?" This poke at the absurdity of the whole issue engaged us immediately in another round of merry laughter. "We could start a whole race of centaurs! 'Hey, that minotaur looks like you! Oh no!' " More hearty laughter at this bit of theatre from Lee.

"I personally don't know what to do about the situation on a large scale," Lee began, "because people's aggression and perversities are very disturbing, but it's so wide-spread everywhere, like many things, I think the answer is education. In American they had this shooting in a high school—just kids! There was a tremendous outpouring of compassion for the families of the kids who were killed. The psychologists recommended family therapy for the killers' families, but the families refused to take responsibility for the behavior of their kids.

"My recommendation is always to spend time in Good Company, who have some integral aims and do the best they can to educate their children and grandchildren, so they won't perpetuate these things. Personally I don't think the system will change. I think the system will crash at some point, based on natural disasters and the human need to survive. In the New Orleans flood, of all the people evacuated, most had friends and families they could stay with, but three hundred thousand people who had no friends or families were thrown upon the charity and generosity of private foundations or the government.

"That kind of thing is likely to happen more and more, and the stress it will place on private families or agencies will create a breakdown that is even greater. When we hit survival a lot of the darkness will be transcended, just in our need to survive. So, my approach is education.

"Yogananda said that in the future everything would break down. In his book, *Autobiography of a Yogi*, a fantastic book, he said that the survival of the integrity of the human race will be in small groups, away from cities and industrial breakdown. On the one hand, I'm cynical; on the other hand, I have a natural optimism—I'm just going ahead with what the Work has given me to go ahead with, without any paranoia. I'm not putting aside dried fruit, water, toilet paper. What happened to washing with water, like in India?" Everyone laughed.

"In American when there's a scare, after bottled water, it's toilet paper off the shelves! So I don't need toilet paper, but I do need sugar, so when things break down in America, I'm coming to France!

"I'm just moving ahead with the plan the Work is giving me. We have two hundred acres in Arizona and we're talking about building a new ashram in a few years, and I'm just moving ahead as if it's all going to work out! And, I can move in a day. If I have to leave *everything* behind, I can move in a day. I can take my kids and my artifacts, get enough in the van, and I'm gone! When the breakdown comes, I'm taking care of my kids and my artifacts and if the adults want to come, they'd better get it together and be ready!" More laughter.

"I'd recommend that attitude to you all. So, I'm ready to go. You might need that attitude in five years, ten years, because we live in an extremely volatile time. It's really healthy to be able to move quickly, if you need to. Arnaud said in an impassioned way at Hauteville that he wasn't attached to any of it. Hauteville is a magnificent place, and the sanctuary of that place is undeniable. He really means that he's not attached to any of it!"

Lee recounted that a few of Arnaud's senior disciples had visited Yogi Ramsuratkumar in India with him. They would say to Arnaud, "You must meet Yogi Ramsuratkumar," but Arnaud never did. Lee said, "That's because Arnaud only moves the way the Work wants him to move, and enthusiastic students aren't necessarily the Work talking—know what I mean? If the Work says, 'Move,' Arnaud will move. It's a fantastic attitude for all of us to cultivate: the capacity to leave everything behind if necessary and move quickly."

We suddenly found ourselves in a very sobering and potentially rocky consideration with Lee, and yet, it was a topic that was on everyone's mind these days, with natural disasters coming at every turn of the wheel, it seemed.

Sara commented, "I agree with what you say, but I find it difficult to live with this without fear . . ."

"You have to just throw yourself into life and move as if there was no danger, no problem, without being stupid and naïve, of course," Lee responded. "You have to know the reality of the situation inside yourself and know you have the quality of strength and character to respond, should circumstances become dangerous. In America, the population is throwing away its freedom, practically begging the government to take its freedom away, which is completely designed by the government, which makes people think and believe that they have something to fear.

"So you have to trust your own inner quality of dignity and integrity, and trust yourself to move forward and not succumb to fear. Like being with a teacher. 'What if the teacher asks me to poison myself or put gas bombs in the Metro?' It shouldn't matter what the teacher asks you to do—you know your own integrity and dignity. If you know within yourself that you wouldn't kill anybody, that's all that's required.

"So I go a hundred miles an hour full speed ahead with one foot on the brake, with no security. If I have to say no, I can say no, and if I have to change directions, I can change directions. So, full speed ahead—I recommend it to all of you. Full speed ahead with our practice, with dignity, and develop the capacity to change direction at any time. I really mean it: if America gets bad enough, I'm coming here! I have no inherent need to live in America."

Someone said, "If it gets bad here, can we come to Arizona?" A few people chuckled or added their agreement to the question.

"Yes! You can! There's this thing among spiritual peers—'My house is your house.' That also implies, 'And your house is my house,' which depends on the teacher and the community as to whether that is good news or bad news, because some of these guys are pretty crazy! It's an unspoken Law of Hospitality—'If you ever need anything, you come to me. Always.' And we may all have to move to Tahiti! Which wouldn't be so bad!"

Ending doomsday considerations on a high note, with a sense of humor, is always for the best, and now everyone was laughing. Lee made one last comment: "I'm ready to run! I'm not a fighter! Things get tough, I'm on my way out! I'm a coward, I'm not fighting the system, because like in gambling, the house always wins in the end. So does the system."

The forecast had been for rain for the past twenty-four hours; instead it was warm and sunny all day for two days. The roses were having a final flurry of blooms at the end of the season, and the Virginia creeper, which covered much of the stone walls outside, was beginning to turn red. Instead of rain, brilliant light splashed and played about the bamboo and the tall trees by the river. In between talks people strolled the grounds or sat in the grass by the water. Many stood around the Sacred Bazaar and talked with Lee or looked for a long time at various artifacts, slowly making their choices.

At three-thirty in the afternoon we reconvened in the seminar room with Lee for the last talk of the day. Once again, he was selling books. The atmosphere was gentle and relaxed. Sun poured in through the southern window in the newly renovated seminar room, lighting up the arrangements of stargazer lilies and white gladiolus combined with bamboo leaves. The walls were adorned with *murtis* of Arnaud Desjardins, Lee and Yogi Ramsuratkumar. On a table beside Lee was a large photograph of the beggar king in his latter years.

The charm of the old stone of this place somehow communicates the wisdom of time, the inexorable teachings of time, while the old tile roof adds to its picturesque beauty. The hazy blue sky was skimmed over with thin veils of gossamer clouds, and it seemed to me like Apollo's heaven. The Greco-Roman gods had such a powerful influence in France for so many centuries that it sometimes seems they are still at play, here in deep France. We were surely in one of the remaining realms of paradise, surrounded by the gifts of the earth, the cornfields, vineyards, orchards and local gardens, the sunlight glistening the earthly green with gold and making magic upon it all . . .

"*Ecrasé par l'Amour*—if that doesn't describe Reality, what does?" Lee was asking rhetorically as he sold several copies of the CD to people in the group. "It used to be named *Dog's Day in the Sun*, which means the same thing as *Ecrasé par l'Amour*, but people weren't figuring it out. It was just too esoteric."

Lee plunged into a fast paced sales pitch, selling fifty, twenty or ten CDs at a chunk, exhorting people to sell them to their friends. "There just happen to be fifty in a box! Anybody want fifty! Let's start at the top! If you buy fifty, I want you to make money on them!"

No one moved or said a word. Lee was undeterred. With Lee, ego has no claim on his actions. He acts without attachment and then moves on to the next instant, demonstrating whatever is the new necessity of the moment. Whatever he is engaging in any given moment, he is completely committed to it; in the next moment, he is then completely committed to that.

Cajoling us sweetly, he said, "A little shy? Anyone for ten or twenty? Same thing. Give them away to your friends and family—*everybody* will like these!" Lee paused, holding up three CDs in a fan-shape in each hand, then he said, "Now I have to decide if I want to out-wait you. Ten! Ten! Ten! Twenty! Twenty! Twenty! Anybody want them? No? Okay, I'll have to wait till Paris!"

Then he put the CDs down and asked simply, "Any questions?"

The first question was about how Lee knew that Yogi Ramsuratkumar was his master. Lee said, "If I get three different signs that all point to the same thing, I think I'd better check this thing out. Like a book: if it comes to my attention three times, I'll look it up. Some people, when they meet their teacher, have an instant recognition. That's nice, but it didn't happen that way for me. A certain attraction was there, yes, but I figured because He was a great master. As I continued to visit Him, things He would say or do would remind me of something that nobody knew but me. The first time that happened I thought, oh neat, He's telepathic. The second time I figured, this Guy really knows something about me. The third time it happened, it's not like I decided anything intellectually; it just became clear."

Lee talked about a very wise German woman, Dina Rees, who was a friend of his; she had died of cancer many years ago. When she first saw a photograph of Yogi Ramsuratkumar, she said to Lee, "You must tell many stories about this man. People need to hear about him. People are suffering so much, they need to hear inspiring stories."

"So when I'm in America and Mexico," Lee continued, "I tell lots of stories of not only Yogi Ramsuratkumar, but also Arnaud Desjardins and Swami Prajnanpad. I was in India in 1979, before I'd realized that Yogi Ramsuratkumar was my Master, so I thought I was the greatest master on Earth. It's an error pretty much every teacher makes in the beginning, but some don't ever get over it—it's a problem! I got over it, with the help of Yogi Ramsuratkumar. Whenever Yogi Ramsuratkumar was happy, He would smack you . . ."

Lee told the story, which he has told countless times, of Yogi Ramsuratkumar asking Lee's companions what their names were. The three were named after persons associated with Lord Krishna: Radha (Krishna's chief consort), Balarama (Krishna's brother) and Mirabai (the great historical poetess who renounced everything, riches, marriage, children, respectability, to wander in a state of mad love for Krishna). Yogi Ramsuratkumar asked each one in turn, "What is your name?" And they answered, one at a time, "Radha," then "Balarama," then "Mirabai." Each time Yogi Ramsuratkumar would say, "Ooohhh!" as if that was the most miraculous thing He'd ever heard. Then he asked each one where they got that name, and they all pointed to Lee and said, "He gave it to me."

Finally, Yogi Ramsuratkumar turned to Lee and said, "And what is your name—Krishna?" And he doubled over in gleeful laughter. For the next hour, he would turn to Lee, smack him on the knee and say, "Krishna?" Each time he would dissolve into peals of laughter.

Lee continued, "He nailed me! And all afternoon he would turn to me, 'Krishna?' and die laughing! I wasn't stupid enough to call myself Krishna reincarnated! Like Christananda—how can anyone be so pretentious![2] But you know, we're sort of living out the Krishna lila in the twentieth century! And Yogi Ramsuratkumar just pushed the button, but with such humor and delight. Everyone was laughing, looking at me like, 'He got you!'

"I thought, 'This Guy has my best interests at heart. Everything He does is for me, and obviously for my students, since I'm leading people. Everything He is doing is for me! Because I would go to other teachers, and they'd try to teach me, but it was always about them, not about me, although I definitely had something to learn.

"I didn't follow up spending time with Anandamayi Ma, but I did follow up with Yogi Ramsuratkumar. So it was that kind of thing, where I'd be with Him and I'd know there was a connection—something was going on—and finally it just dawned on me. I'm a very dense character. Very gross. I don't have dreams, visions, I don't hear voices. People who are less dense are always having visions. I didn't wake up one morning and say, 'This is my Master.' I saw the murti of Him and I just knew. I made a personal commitment to be His student. When you approach a master there are two ways to do it: 'Can I be a student?' or 'Will you be my teacher?' These are very different. Ninety-nine point nine percent of the people say, 'Can I be a student?' But it's very different, because when someone is a teacher, a master, they have no self-interest.

---

2 Christananda was a self-named California spiritual scene teacher in the 1970s.

"Yogi Ramsuratkumar just followed the impetus of the Work and the catalyst of the Work. When it was time to accept a house from His devotees, He did; when it was time to have an ashram, He allowed the resources to be generated. He really had no personal attachment to anything. It was all the ongoing accessibility of His Blessing Work in the world. When you meet somebody like that, the question is not about what the teacher can do for you—because the teacher has no self-interest in you as a person; the teacher's interest is in the Work, in the Path. The real question is, do I have something that is of value to the Path and may I offer it? Because what the teacher is really interested in is how the Path can be served, not how the teacher or student can be served, but how the Path can be served.

"So how people decide who their teacher is is very personal, depending on whether we are outgoing or introverted. But the thing is, the more we know ourselves, the more we can throw ourselves into a situation and give ourselves entirely to the situation without losing ourselves. In the Eastern tradition the idea is to lose yourself in the Path. So when you know yourself, your tendencies, strengths and weaknesses, you can throw yourself in. Meaning if that is a temporary situation, you can give yourself completely, and when the permanent situation comes along, you can give yourself to it without conflict.

"Once I decided that Yogi Ramsuratkumar was my Master, I gave myself completely without any guarantee, and I tried to provide what He wanted. It turned out that He really liked my writing, particularly the poetry, so that was very easy—all I had to do was keep writing poetry, and He was thrilled. When I was in India, I would obey the protocol around Him instead of being a big pushy American. He appreciated that very much, because most Westerners intruded *their* protocol instead of going by India's protocol.

"All my eggs are in one basket, and if it hadn't worked out, I would've been able to change directions immediately. Once you make a commitment to a teacher, you should give as fully as you can to that commitment, always remembering that the essential you cannot be subsumed or taken over. The essential you cannot disappear, no matter how profound the teacher is. If you have a sense of who you are, you can give yourself completely no matter what.

"I was lucky because Yogi Ramsuratkumar didn't ask that much of me. He never asked me to compromise my Work. He was a pure renunciate, He ate very little, wore the same clothes all the time. He was a pure celibate. He never asked anything of me except to be devoted to Him and to bring integrity to my Work. When we find someone we believe to be our master, it's not that we close our eyes and that's the end of our questions. Any master, the most integral of masters, even Arnaud, sooner or later is going to do something to disturb the student. If you are with a real master, sooner or later they will push a button in you and get you aroused.

"Arnaud said of the first six years of his relationship with Swami Prajnanpad that he didn't have obedience. Hearing this was very upsetting to some of my students who have twenty years with me and still no obedience! Six years! Once Arnaud decided that he would obey his master, nothing compromised that.

"There is a period of time that is like a novitiate. In Pythagorus' work, when you decided you were committed, for the first three years there was no tolerance for error; you had to be totally in line with the lifestyle that he recommended. For three years all the teaching was done from behind a screen. So you got the teaching by hearing it. It might be three years before you even met Pythagoras . . . ."

So, Lee concluded, we should understand that there is an initial period of time when we are being tested and we are given the space to come to our own understanding and strength of commitment. Imagine, the resolve one would have to have to spend three years not even seeing the teacher, just hearing the teaching from someone else designated by the teacher and engaging the practices with faith and perseverance. We Westerners are quite spoiled in this regard; we expect the teacher to respond to our projections and expectations from the beginning, even when we are certain that we are not doing that. It takes a particular kind of compassion to teach others.

With the day of formal teaching coming to its natural close, Lee would spend the next hour, while we were waiting for dinner to be served, behind the tables at the Sacred Bazaar in the back of the room. Many people made their way there to linger and look, to talk with Lee and ask questions, and often, to acquire a deity. It's at the Sacred Bazaar that we hear the stories that people have to tell about the deities they've gotten from Lee in years past, the dreams they've had, the relationship that has developed with these symbols of the Divine. In listening to stories and watching, I noticed that gratitude seemed to be the natural outgrowth of the past three days.

The gorgeous weather had held out well so far. Dinner was a lovely affair held again at the long table about forty feet away from the river, with over half of the group sitting in small clusters on the grass or on benches here and there around the table and under the willow trees not far away. The air was warm, and the peaceful calm of the river mingled with the presence of the bamboo groves and the ancient voices of the spring, which gurgled and trilled happily as it merged with the river. There were two babies, two toddlers and Joachim, a seven-year-old, as well as the teenage and adult children of several people, making family a very strong element of the group. How incredible, to see three generations going strong at these gatherings in the spirit of the guru, the dharma and the community of practitioners. All this lent a certain sweetness to our time together in this marvelous setting.

A soft twilight fell on the land after supper while people were busy with clearing the dishes and cleaning the kitchen in the hotel. Lee went upstairs to play bridge with a few of his students and close friends, who came in and watched the game until eight-thirty, when tea was served and the rest of the group made their way into the space. About forty-five people, the babies and children were seated closely on the floor and in a few chairs that were scattered around the perimeter of the room. Right away people merged into small units of two, three or four to talk among themselves. As coffee, *tisane* and chocolate desserts were served and then consumed, the space became louder and louder with the chatter and social interactions of the group, while Lee sat in a chair by the wall and talked with Ceri, Benoit, Charlie and Florence, who were sitting near him in chairs or beside him on the floor.

Most people were too preoccupied with their own social conversations to be aware that Lee was talking and that the protocol around a master always includes the unspoken law that the disciple's attention should be on the master, even if not directly, certainly internally. It's not that it's unlawful to talk to each other, but inevitably we get carried away on the current, while the energy spirals on itself in the natural patterns of self-concerns and the imperatives of ego to be seen, heard and understood.

In the midst of this, Lee continued to reveal, in presence, word and gesture, life as it is in the moment, at that place in space and time. I was drawn to him like a magnet, and more than a little frustrated at the lack of attention in the space. Now and then someone sitting within a ten-foot radius of Lee would attempt to engage him with a question.

One woman asked, "What's happening with Ma Devaki?"

"She still lives on the ashram in Tiruvannamalai," Lee answered.

"And Mani?" the woman asked. It seemed that she had been to Tiruvannamalai and met them both. Lee answered her by saying that Mani is living in Bangalore, doing very well, retired and managing an apartment building; that he and his wife, Raji, have a huge shrine in their bedroom, which takes up over half the room. He said that they are devoted to Yogi Ramsuratkumar.

A conversation continued about the breakdown that groups of devotees typically go through when their master dies. Lee mentioned the splits among devotees when Meher Baba died, when Kirpal Singh died, and even when Ramana Maharshi died. What has happened among the devotees of Yogi Ramsuratkumar is par for the course in the human drama, it seemed.

Jean Pierre asked Lee if he had been to the ashram of Shirdi Sai Baba, and if there was anyone carrying on the lineage. Lee said, "It depends on who you talk to. We went in 1986, when there was the same original hut that Shirdi Sai Baba lived in, but so many pilgrims came that the town took over, and now the hut is inside a big brick temple, and it's mobbed with thousands of people. There are guards, and you can't stop and contemplate."

Jean Pierre asked, "Can you still feel something there?"

"Yes, you can feel something, but we were lucky to have been there before and made a connection with the place."

Charlie asked, "Do you think the way they do cremations in India will change because of Western influence?"

Lee began, "It's already changed. In Bombay they have cremation in an electric furnace for poor people; they just throw them in together and burn them. It's very expensive to have a traditional cremation."

The conversation moved from one subject to another involving India and what it's like to live there—the baksheesh system, and how things are done. Lee mentioned that many Westerners live in the West one or two months out of the year and work to make money, then go to India and spend the rest of the year there living on practically nothing, because it's still so cheap.

Kathleen asked Lee how he met Yvan Amar, and Lee told the story. Yvan was responsible for connecting Gilles Farcet with Lee, saying, "You have got to meet this American master—he plays rock and roll music, but he is really Saqi, the winepourer." Lee, of course, never says this—it's only that I remember Gilles telling us this when he first came to the Arizona ashram in 1991. I remember coming to France with Lee in 1992 and his meeting with Yvan; how Yvan introduced him to his gathering of three hundred people as "Saqi," the mythic servant of the Beloved, who pours the wine of the Beloved for all the lovers who wait and wait for the Beloved's kiss, or even the faintest whiff of a breeze as the Beloved walks past. I remember the beautiful gift that Yvan made to Lee that day of a very large, exceptional Shiva lingam, which Yvan had gotten in India. The Shiva lingam is in Lee's *darshan* hall in the Arizona ashram.

Kathleen and I continued to talk about Yvan Amar. He was a stellar example of bravery, courage, dignity and elegance in the face of his illness; as a human being, he was an example to us all in many, many ways.

Kathleen said, "Daniel Morin said that Yvan was the Mozart of spirituality."

The din of the large group was escalating again. I could hear Lee speaking about Chögyam Trungpa Rinpoche, telling stories of this amazing, enigmatic Tibetan Vajrayana master. Charlie told a story about a reporter who went to interview Chögyam Trungpa Rinpoche. When Rinpoche saw the reporter, he walked up to him and French kissed him. The man was nonplussed, completely thrown out of his usual way of thinking and being.

Lee continued, "Trungpa was in a different category from all the other Tibetans . . . . except maybe," he said a few seconds later, "Dzongsar Khyentse Rinpoche." As he had numerous times over the summer, he began to talk about this young Rinpoche and a new video that was produced by some of his students, *Words of My Perfect Teacher*.

Looking around at all the self-absorbed conversations going on while Lee was ignored by ninety percent of the people in the room, Kathleen turned to Ann and me and asked, "Why does he do this? What's the purpose of this? Why does he sit like this every night with people?"

We answered, "That's a good question to ask Lee."

We began to gather more closely around Lee to hear better and to bring more intention to our being with him. May and Roger, close friends from Hauteville, came to sit in vacant chairs nearby, while others moved in closer on the floor. Soon everyone had picked up on the trend, and the whole room had re-oriented itself to gather around the master. When he paused for a second, it suddenly became very quiet, as all the extraneous conversations had now stopped and everyone's attention was on Lee. He jumped and his eyes went wide in a sort of mock surprise. He smiled at everyone.

"They say, when it gets quiet like that, that an angel has passed over the room. Let's hope so. We could all use the help . . ." Then he went back to the subject he was on.

"Really, there are so few good teachers in the world today." Lee was in midstride, talking again about Dzongsar Khyentse Rinpoche when he looked and noticed the group of about forty people who were all now looking at him expectantly. He laughed. "I feel like I should get up and dance!" Our laughter broke the moment of social discomfort and seemed to release us all to be in a new space with Lee. He laughed again. "How anyone with my tendencies ever got in this position shows the true perversity of God!"

Silence took over again, and the only sound we could hear was the sound of my pen, scratching rather furiously on my notebook. Again Lee laughed and said, "I think if we do a video on my life, it should start out in the dark and all you can hear is the pen, scratching!" Again we all burst into laughter. Lee turned to Kathleen.

"Are you all out of questions, Kathleen?" he asked. Everyone laughed in a good-natured way, along with Kathleen, who smiled broadly, remembering her many questions at last night's tea space. "If it wasn't for you, last night really would've been a struggle!" Lee added.

With her usual Irish charm and pluck, Kathleen stepped up to the challenge. She said, "Well, yes. I was wondering, what's the use of this space? Why do you meet with people in the evening, because you say you don't have enough time for your family and children, but you meet here with us every night."

Lee interrupted, "Plus, I never sell anything!" Laughter burst forth from all the people who had been buying books, CDs and artifacts from Lee for two days. Then he seemed to click into a different mode. It was as if he changed channels from casual conversation to teaching mode. He began:

"Well, you know, everything I do, I do because it's given to me to do. It's not ever a personal choice. *This*," he said, referring to the evening gathering over tea that is held on both his ashrams every night, "started in a very significant way and continued and became a tradition. In Arizona I tried having one night a week a certain space with prayers and ritual practices, and after a couple of months people stopped coming. After a while there were three people there. Forget it! People don't want a defined, ritual, initiating space! So let's just get together and have tea."

The tone of Lee's voice was saturated with the weight of his maturity, the burden of his knowledge and insight, and his utter aloneness. The sound of his voice penetrated into my heart and struck me, imbuing the meaning of the words themselves with a depth of profundity that impacted me in a physical way. I remembered very well the Monday night "ritual tea space" as Lee had described it, disbanded by him in 1991. It was a very precious and rare space that he had created, which was not responded to in the way that its sanctity, as a pure gift to us, the body of practitioners, demanded and required. When Lee closed the door on this opportunity, there were a number of people, who attended regularly, who were crushed by its loss.

Lee continued, "As soon as I stopped having this ritual space, people were, 'Oh, I was just coming—can we start again?' Probably never! One chance, and it never comes again! So . . . this is nice," he concluded, indicating the evening tea and treats, the whole social aspect of it, the superficial conversations even, which seem to be what we really want.

Kathleen asked, "Don't you get bored?"

"No," Lee answered. "Other things bore me. Other people's conversations. People like to ask questions. I don't have any questions.

Andrew Cohen's students have all this 'investigation' into different issues; now it's immortality. Who cares? I know the answers, and the answers I have satisfy me, so questions totally bore me.

"So, when the Work gives an opportunity to practice, if it gets picked up, great, if not, forget about it. Swami Rudrananda died very young. Rudi was a big man, very fat. He used to eat everything. He said, 'Eat the world,' meaning eat energy. He knew he was going to die; in fact, his death could almost be called a suicide." Lee then described Swami Rudrananda's death: Rudi, as he was called, was in an airplane with a few of this students. When the plane crashed, Rudi's heart exploded and he died instantly. No one else on the plane was scratched; they all walked away completely unscathed.

"And the cool thing is, the name of the place where the plane crashed was 'Fat Man's Delight'!" Everyone laughed with delight at this, the meaning was so obvious. Lee continued, "Rudi was a great yogi. He was so tuned in that he kept getting revelatory practices all the time, and his students couldn't keep up. And so he died. I'm sure of it. He had enough power to call it on and terminate his life, because he was stuck. He had no interest in power . . .

"So, I get bored very easily if people don't catch on. Everybody says, 'I want to be initiated, let's have tantric sex.' But I give people breath techniques—there are three levels of them. People say, 'Gimme, gimme, gimme!' Then they do the practice for a week and that's it. So let people write poetry and have tea every night."

Sobered, maybe even a little shocked, along with everyone else who understood the untranslated English, Kathleen pursued, "What about the twenty percent?"

"They're still practicing," Lee said. He began to talk about the number of people in the meditation hall every morning in Arizona, and how he had asked for a minimum of twenty people to create a certain subtle magnetism. He said, "When people get together and meditate, it's like an energy generator. I suggested that we need a certain number in the hall to create a base. Fifteen years go by, people have kids, jobs . . . now, on a good day, it's fourteen or fifteen people. If people's practice means that little to them . . ." He shrugged.

Lee wasn't speaking cynically; he was speaking in absolute, ruthless terms. Rather he seemed more like the adjudicator of a higher law—something about reciprocity, paying for our work, or just karma. Too often we make certain decisions, turn away from opportunities and doorways without realizing the implications of our actions or non-actions.

"So, if practice means so little," Lee summed up, "then we can just get together and have tea. It's about consistency—if not on the meditation practice, then at least on tea. So, I'm just carrying on what was given to me—none of it was my idea. I could never think of these things! How do I know what people need? The Work gives me what people need. My personal choices would be very different."

Kathleen mused, "So Rudi terminated his life?"

"Well, he had so much to give," Lee answered, "and he was giving two percent of what he had, and he was receiving more and more—you can't live that way. There has to be someone to take what you're giving out, if you're at that level, so that there's one reason for your existence."

Kathleen continued, "That's the relationship between the student and teacher . . ."

Ceri, who was new to the scene, picked up the principle with the brilliance of beginner's mind and said, "You mean, you get fed by what you get back from your students, and it's reciprocal? Then when you see the changes in the person, it feeds you!"

Lee brightened visibly. "Exactly! So, if it's not received, then we try something else. The Sacred Bazaar is getting received very well—people are practically living in museums!" This brought a few chuckles out of the group. Lee continued without a break, "Nobody has to practice. Great! Just sit around and be radiated! I get to travel around and pick out little gems, and I don't get bored. It's all from Yogi Ramsuratkumar . . . If that's what people will involve themselves in, that's what we'll do!"

Sian asked, "Why is practice so difficult?"

"We think securing our little comforts means something. People have to have their coffee in the morning. As if it means something and is important. We have to shift our view of what's important. To us, in the Work, there should be a different level of priorities."

Kathleen asked, "Arnaud said he's capable of doing heart transplants, and he operates for appendicitis all day."

Lee smiled, "That's exactly what we're talking about. I haven't even gotten up to appendicitis—I'm still taking splinters out of fingers. Obviously there are exceptions—the few lovely surprises."

Sian said, "The Sufis say, 'Out of thousands, only one finds Me.' "

"We have to believe we're that one," Lee responded, "or we wouldn't ever practice. So many people are psychologically disposed to self-hatred, swearing they're shit, and they are some of the best students, but they won't take responsibility. This is what we're up against. And then every now and then someone relatively normal comes along who is completely capable, responsible . . . . It's not lack of love, because everyone loves the teacher. But if we can't be responsible as adults . . ."

Lee used the example of Purna's work with people in prisons, who are murderers, thieves, con men, gang members. Many of them have tremendous remorse about their lives. Lee said, "They're brilliant people with insight into the nature of reality, hearts of gold, but they can't rise above a psychological condition that says they have to lie and cheat and steal to survive. Purna meets guys who are completely amazing characters, but they are stuck in a loop. The attitude of the prison system is that they can't make it on the streets. The prison is not about rehabilitation; it's just about keeping these people off the streets.

"And then there are all the victimless crimes—in some places the punishment for selling marijuana is higher than the punishment for murder. Purna meets these amazing people, but when they get out, they have no place to go. There is a ninety-seven percent recidivism rate. All their genius and sincerity and goodness is completely dominated by their psychology."

Sian said, "Like us and practice."

Lee responded, "Exactly! That's us; that's the metaphor. So, practice, practice, practice! And if not—tea, tea, tea!" The tension of the space, trying as we were to take in the potency of Lee's communication to us, dissolved into laughter.

"Or coffee, as the case may be. And we do get some coffee. But then everybody goes, 'Oh, I can't drink coffee at night—I won't be able to sleep!' Here we are, with our guru, giving our lives to the guru; we'll be freezing in the barn at Ferme de Jutreau! You go into meditation in the morning and it's a riot, the clothes these people wear, bundled up against the cold to meditate. But they won't drink coffee, because they won't be able to sleep!

"Mani's wife Raji got concerned once because Mani wasn't sleeping very much at all—he was just working on the ashram all the time. She went to Yogi Ramsuratkumar and said, 'Mani's only sleeping two hours a night!' Yogi Ramsuratkumar thought about it and said, 'Two hours of sleep is enough for Mani!' "

Lee then told the story of how Mani wasn't allowed to come in the temple because he wanted to enforce the protocol of the space on people, especially insensitive, recalcitrant, disrespectful Westerners.

Lee said, "Yogi Ramsuratkumar wanted people to bring their own integrity to protocol, so He wouldn't let Mani tell stupid Westerners what to do." He talked about how the ashram staff wouldn't let the dogs on the ashram "screw in front of Yogi Ramsuratkumar," because he was a pure renunciate, and so they would beat the dogs and throw the male dogs out.

"Yogi Ramsuratkumar would never do such a thing. He just saw it as a natural part of life. He was very much, 'accept what is . . .'

His attitude was, 'You've got to learn your own lessons,' so He didn't interfere with other people. If people are going to bring a certain enthusiasm to practice, I'm happy and will give more, but my philosophy is: don't put anything out unless it's earned. People have to be able to hold it over time, or it's just pearls before swine. Of course, I wouldn't call you all swine. Jesus said that, so we can get away with it!"

A few chuckles, some laughter rolled through the space. One thing was for sure: there was no more idle conversation going on. Even though there were numerous people in the room who didn't speak English very well or even at all, the attention was riveted on Lee and the transmission he was making.

Lee continued, "So this is just a nice way to have a nice conversation and go to sleep feeling, 'Oh, that was nice.' "

Kathleen asked, "So what is the continuity in this?"

"The definition of any gathering of sangha is automatically a recognition of the Blessing Force of the Path. We would never be together, if we were not all on the Path. There is an automatic invocation of Blessing Force, which isn't always a ball of light in a room, but slowly, slowly . . ."

Lee referred to a conversation over dinner earlier that night, when Lee, Jean Pierre and Sian were talking about a mutual friend, Helen, who is studying to become the youngest female master sommalier in the world. Now Lee said, "Jean Pierre said that when you're a professional wine-taster, you have to taste wine every day because if you miss a day, your taste buds go to the dogs. Literally go to sleep. It's the same with this Work; once your system is running, to keep it up and running doesn't take much, but if it shuts down, it takes a tremendous amount of energy to start it up again. So, a little every day, it seeps in and gets into the cells . . . a little, a little . . .

"At least we can put ourselves into the field of Influence. It is the Kali Yuga, so you just earn merit, the Buddhists would say. You can earn merit by doing good works—you don't even have to meditate!

"So, I'm sort of coming to those conclusions. As fired up as we used to get—we used to say, 'I want everything in this life!'—now we all have kids and jobs, professions, homes. Now we're not saying, 'I've gotta make it in this lifetime,' but 'I've gotta pay my bills,' and 'My wife needs personal time with me.' Let people who are willing to work, work, and let the others hang out and enjoy. Why fight the wall of psychology? Some say that's disappointing. They say, 'I thought you were committed to our transformation!' I am committed to your transformation as much as *you* are. It used to be a big problem for me—not anymore. I'm categorically unwilling to use violence to get people to practice. What are the options? Relax. Capitalize on what there is, and relax."

Sian said, "It seems to me that Yogi Ramsuratkumar reached the highest point of that relaxation."

Lee said, "Yes, and anybody who was willing to practice heroically got plenty. I like to think I was in that category, because I got as much Work as I wanted—because I was committed. It could always change! But the Work has to dictate it. Arnaud could walk away right now; he could leave everything, as magnificent a sanctuary as Hauteville is, he could walk away from it right now if the Work dictated that. If it was left up to me, I'd be in New Zealand now!"

More laughter. What madness were we thinking of? Did we not hear the implications of what he was saying, or were we just grateful, fallen to our knees in thanksgiving, that he at least was still offering us tea?

"But I wouldn't go alone. If I got accepted by the New Zealand government, I'd have to have a few of my students there. I'd be in Napier Bay right now, watching the sunrise and eating papayas. I don't even like papayas!" More laughter ricocheted through the room. Lee smiled, "But when you're in paradise, you have to make some exceptions!" Another wave of laughter flowed over us. Once again he was softening the sting of his invective, rounding us out with laughter and the sheer joy of being in his presence. The last sounds of merriment were just fading as Lee said, "Bonsoir, Good-night, Gute nacht," got up and walked unceremoniously through the people and out the door.

La Source Bleue
September 25

At the beginning of the first session of the day someone asked, "You often speak of the broken heart. What does that mean?"

Lee answered, "It means to be completely and unequivocally realistic. To accept what is, as it is, here and now applies to our own condition, but to be honest about our own condition is not to be in denial about the currents of all. When catastrophe happens and homes are broken up, it's sad. You grieve, and at the same time, it's natural—a natural process in the world.

"On the other hand, the vast majority of human suffering is completely unnecessary and is created by human frailty, not by nature. The vast territory of therapeutic work, ninety-nine point nine percent of it, even when one has been abused, is unnecessary and a function of human error. The fact is that's who we are as a human race—violent and aggressive—and there are flashes of compassion and goodness.

"Brokenheartedness is a kind of recognition of the unavoidable human condition, as that condition is contrasted to the stainless, pure, brilliant beauty of the Divine as Oneness—not any facet of the Divine, like a beautiful sunset, but the Divine as indivisible, unitive. So we find ourselves in this crisis, where we're searching for God, for the teacher, for Reality, and we're in love with our family, kids, parents. We have human life, struggles, joys and pleasures, and on the other hand, we know if we find that which we are searching for, even though that will unify us with all things, on a human level it will irrevocably divide us from everything and everyone we love.

Not because we won't be able to live and serve them, but because they will not and cannot understand, unless they duplicate your condition, and who is going to do that? We'll be able to love them as they are, but we will not in any way be able to relieve their suffering. Because they will not understand.

"So, we're stuck in this dichotomy: our desire for Reality is the highest desire. It's the only thing to do. And, there are all the relative aspects of our lives. You love your children, but you can't stop them from making the mistakes they make . . . So, we know if we reach the goal, everything will change. We'll love people, but they will not understand unless they change, and the chances of that are—don't bet on it.

"That whole complex of 'what is' creates a kind of brokenheartedness, because whatever direction we go in—throwing ourselves into the spiritual domain and separating ourselves from those we love, that's a problem, and if we turn away from the Path, that's a problem—we are damned if we do and damned if we don't. We could also say we're Blessed if we do, and Blessed if we don't. That doesn't change the fact we're human and have minds and emotions, and we still suffer other people's suffering, although we are Blessed."

Lee used the rock artist Kurt Cobain as an example. He died from a drug overdose, and he was an incredible talent. All you could say was, "What a waste," and there was nothing anyone could do to save him.

Lee continued, "Purna works in the U.S. prison system, and as you all know, the abuses of justice in the justice system are too many to count and are unconscionable. The head of the mafia gets arrested and he gets a big cell, gourmet meals brought in, TV, and the guards say, 'Anything I can get for you, sir?' Whereas innocent kids are in for something like smoking marijuana and are thrown among the most hardened criminals, treated like hardened criminals—it's terrible! That's life.

"We're here. We start to get a little more conscious and we have to bear what we know. We have to bear it. So the more you try to get yourself in a cave and pretend it doesn't exist, it just doesn't work. You have to go forward. The more you go forward, the more you know, and the more you know, the more you have to bear . . . .

"The more sensitive you become in the real sense, the more the situation strikes you. I don't mean when every little thing freaks you out; that's not sensitivity, that's indulgence. The more genuinely sensitive you become, the more this situation strikes you in its inevitability. You're becoming more conscious, and the world's not changing—things are as difficult as ever. Usually we don't talk about it in such graphic terms; we say we are longing for the Beloved, and we're just heartbroken because we haven't found the Beloved, but really it's the situation I just described. So what to do, but buy lots of sacred artifacts and make your home a sacred space!"

Proceeding to accommodate that recommendation by selling several stone artifacts immediately, Lee then had a box of prints of Nara's paintings brought up. "Camunda!" he enthused, showing the gorgeous piece of art, "Eros, terror, death, beauty and transformation! Ahhh! Nice!"

Then he introduced another piece, "Gaja Lakshmi." The newest piece of work done by Lee's student Nara, it was a complex, highly detailed "breakthrough" piece in black, white and gray scale tones.

"This piece is incredible!" Lee grinned broadly, holding the print up for all to see. "You won't find anything like this anywhere! Only a hundred copies were made, all hand signed by the artist, and most of them are already sold. Lakshmi, goddess of light, wealth, success and intelligence! I recommend you frame it and hang it in a prominent place, so every time you look at it, the qualities of Lakshmi are manifested in your life."

The print was resplendent, magnificent; it was so gorgeous that more than twenty-five copies sold immediately. One by one they were passed through the crowd to their new owner. Buddhist deities and art in general is well represented in the West, but Hinduism remains obscure and esoteric for the most part. I had a strong sense in that moment of how Lee is infusing the East, and the Hindu tradition in particular, into the spiritual culture of the West through his love of Hindu art.

The next question was about how to deal with other people's criticisms of Lee and Arnaud, and the sadness that brought up for the questioner. Lee answered, "Whenever you hear criticism of Arnaud or me, you should feel compassion. Let the tenderness of sorrow wash over you for their suffering. You have to cultivate this, but that's the attitude you take. Don't say anything, don't do anything, don't argue—just feel compassion for them. If you do that enough, the compassion you feel will strike them at some point, more powerfully than any verbal exchange."

People left the space delicately carrying their precious art in their hands. The Gaja Lakshmi was one piece that didn't need a sales pitch—it had sold itself and literally flew out of Lee's hands to waiting recipients of Lakshmi's blessings.

Nara is a good example of how Lee empowers his students and brings out their native talents. Nara was painting before he met Lee in 1995, but he never imagined in his wildest dreams that his guru would take the seed of his interest in art, water it and shower it with sun, then protect it from wind and pestilence and vandalism. Nor did he imagine what would happen when Lee invested that growing creativity with Divine Influence, a magic so strong that a small vine would become a wish-fulfilling tree, an all-consuming passion, informed by the greatest Muse of all. It's as if those who compose music, paint, sculpt or write for Lee are an extension of Lee's hands, fingers, ears, heart. The art that Nara has produced in the past ten years under Lee's wing is the testimony of this process of reciprocity between guru and devotee.

Halfway through the morning session it had began to rain, which meant that Sian and Jean Pierre had to quickly change the brunch plan from outside by the river to upstairs in the old building, where the tea spaces had been the two nights before. By the time fifty or more of us had crowded into the room in a very intimate arrangement, seated mostly on the floor around Lee, it had stopped raining. The old stone walls added a certain ambiance and a touch of the rustic life to our excellent repast of fresh baked breads from the local *boulangerie*, an array of the most delicious *fromage artisanal, de beurre et confit de fruit*, greens, fresh grapes and figs, those being in season, *saucisson* and other delicacies. Coffee and warm cream topped it all off.

At one o'clock, when the talk began, it was threatening rain again outside. Thunder growled in the distance. The occasional patter of rain and the wind in the lush background of trees, willows and nearby bamboo forests, and the ubiquitous presence of the spring, *la source*, brought the *dralas* into clearer focus. After three days with Lee in this space—which had warmed us, heart and body, blood racing at times from the sheer intense truth of his presence that pressed on ego like the sword of Damocles—we were loosened up. There was a liquid mood, like cane syrup that has been held over a fire, so that we were melted and blended. It was a very pleasant atmosphere in which to be in an unexpected communion among good friends and strangers, acquaintances and unknowns.

Thunder rumbled again outside and the air became saturated, dense with the warm humidity and the weight of water. The water element is everywhere here in this beautiful place, but unlike in other places on the globe, it is peaceful. Sitting in the back, I could see out the double French windows to the sloping lawn, the trees and the river beyond. Lightning flashed in the gray sky, while the river flowed in its placid course; the rain began to fall gently, making a delicate dance on the surface of the river. People were laughing easily, flowing with Lee in whatever direction or quick turns he took.

"Any questions?" he asked.

One man, who Lee has known for several years, raised his hand to talk about his troubled teenaged son. He and his wife felt that their son, who goes to a Rudolf Steiner school away from home, became more withdrawn and troubled whenever he came home. He was unmotivated to do anything but sit at home and watch TV. He wouldn't get a job or interact with people. They were trying to deal with his inertia at home by only allowing him to come home once a week. It began to rain in earnest as Lee recommended that they drop that limitation and make their home totally, completely open to their son by cultivating an atmosphere of spaciousness, relaxation and acceptance.

"Give him all the room in the world, and give him the space and time to come toward you," Lee said. "Take the restrictions off his visits completely and say to him, 'Until you're twenty-one, do whatever you want, live with the family if you want, but when you're twenty-one, you have to get a job and take care of yourself. But then you can also come home and visit whenever you want.' If he just sits at home alone and watches TV, leave him alone. Make that deal with him.

"His mother needs to relax and trust that her son is a good person who will come into his own when it's time and just love him as her son. If you can tell her that without getting punched in the eye, tell her I said it. He will find himself, in his own time, and he needs the freedom to find himself. Keep being affectionate with him and let him know you respect him and trust him and that he has choices. Often the less we say, the better. And it's better to say something direct and powerful than to go on and on. What's his name?"

"Serge," the father replied. "Great," Lee said. I got the distinct impression that Lee had registered this young man very deeply, and that blessings were flowing in his direction.

The next question involved prayer. The man said, "I have a question about prayer. I don't know what it is. I was raised with no prayer. I try to be transparent, not forced, but then I find myself back in meditation and there is no prayer . . ."

Lee answered, "For most people, we find our way to prayer through experimentation. For everyone it's different. You try something and it feels like, 'This is not right, there's too much definition,' then you try something else. Then if *that's* not right, then you try something else. In your sincerity to discover what prayer is for you, you will find yourself there—you will be led to it. The exact form it takes will be specific to you, personal to you.

"Yogi Ramsuratkumar told everybody who came around Him to chant His name. Everybody was chanting His name, but Mani, who was the ashram manager. Mani was only working all the time. He asked Yogi Ramsuratkumar if he should be chanting and meditating, and Yogi Ramsuratkumar said, 'Mani doesn't have to chant this beggar's name. All Mani has to do is work.' That was his service and that was his prayer. Other people Yogi Ramsuratkumar would tell to do specific ceremonies or fire sacrifice. It was always very specific to the person. You will find your way to it. Keep trying, and if everything you try leads you back to meditation, then trust that in meditation. Whatever prayer will be for you will come, in some form."

Someone said, "In meditation I feel it's impersonal, like the people in New Orleans. In meditation it's not directed to some one person."

"Perfect!" Lee's lively response was further emphasized by a resounding clap of thunder in the background. Lightning flashed and cracked across the sky and the rain was now pouring down outside just as Benoit started asking his question, which began with a lengthy statement about his resistance to the dietary conditions and other practices that Lee recommends to his students.

Benoit spoke passionately about the hypocrisy in religions and in devotees of all paths, even those of Yogi Ramsuratkumar. He said, "An old prostitute, who knows the hearts of men, has a bigger heart than most practitioners . . . I eat like a pig! I don't see the logic in being a vegetarian . . . I try to think of the two most important things, the heart, the broken heart—and this I don't choose, life is nice enough to give it to me—and the form of practice . . . but I just don't see eating salad all year!" Benoit's presentation was quite humorous and yet serious at the same time. Everyone in the room was laughing along with him, including Lee, who chuckled at Benoit's dilemma.

"If something makes sense to you, you're willing to do it, and if it doesn't, you're not," Lee began.

Benoit broke in again, saying, "There is one practice—Who am I kidding?—that I don't understand at all."

"Of course," Lee said. "All the people who think they understand it, aren't practicing it." Another loud crash of thunder punctuated Lee's statement. He was picking up steam, and the weather was reflecting it. "People who *think* they understand only *think* they're practicing, but they're not! Outside of critical feedback that people get from my students who are particularly righteous—for whom the phrase, 'Lee said' is their mantra, which is always taken out of context—since ninety percent of the Work is hanging in, my recommendation is not to make a problem of something that isn't a problem for me."

Once again, thunder crashed as if to add an exclamation point to Lee's statement. There is nothing that irritates him more than students who have some years in the Work meddling with new students and laying a lot of trips on them. Lee has said many times that we have no idea what the inner life of another may or may not be; we always have to assume that everyone is working as hard or as much as they can.

"If it's not a problem for me, then you don't make a problem of it. So, we understand that we all come to faith in our own time. If we had to choose between no faith and idiot faith, no faith would be a better choice. Idiot faith is blindly following what the teacher says with no consideration or intelligence. As long as I'm not making a problem out of it, don't you make a problem out of it. This year, or next year, or next decade, if you want to practice 'Who am I kidding?' then you just do it. It's not a problem."

The thunderstorm was in full force now as Benoit went on railing about what he considered the ridiculous austerity of the diet as it is recommended in the Hohm Community.

"No wheat, no salt! I felt totally outside this!" he said, with some heat behind his words.

Lee's response was measured yet satirical. He said, "Have you ever been to a meal on our ashram when there wasn't salt on the table? There's always salt on the table. When I talk about Practice, I always talk about it in the highest sense, just in case somebody can connect. A few people really try to fit that role . . . wonderful . . . but I'm not under any illusions that everybody attracted to this school will fit that mold. We all practice at whatever level we are called to. No salt? That's crazy! Stick it on the shelf. If at any time it becomes a consideration, you study it and find out why it might be of benefit to have less salt in your diet. If it's not a problem for me, don't make it a problem.

"So, I always talk about Practice in the highest sense, but I don't expect everybody to fit into that mold. Every once in a while someone comes along who fits. We have salt on our table because we have people from my family who can't eat a meal without salt. Talk about frustrating! People who are supposed to be the best of the practitioners, the most senior of the senior students, suck down wine and desserts and anything else that comes along, any other little treat that they like whenever it's available—if it's off the diet, they love it, and everybody else follows their lead. So don't worry. There *is* no diet!"

This stinging invective was delivered with an acid wash that left me cringing. Outside the storm was at its peak; rain and thunder continued unabated. Lee was venting his frustration with his own students, especially his senior students and those who are most frequently in his physical company. Just as quickly as the demon wind had arisen, it subsided. His tone of voice was completely changed in the next instant, as he continued softly, yet with emphasis.

"However, if someone, just based on experimentation, wants to be a little more disciplined in their activities, they'll have my support."

Now a mischievous tone crept quickly into his voice; it was Lee Lozowick theatre at its best, and the thunderstorm was complying. He turned his humor and charm on Benoit, who is known for his attraction to women and casual sex, to make a point, saying, "Some of the best women students I have were brought to the school by philandering men! So just bring women to the school, and you'll have my gratitude! You'll be one of my recruiters!"

Everyone was laughing now. The heat was turned up, and we were enjoying it. "Are you relieved now?" Lee smiled, teasing Benoit a little more.

"How long have you been a student?" Lee asked Benoit. "Two years. Well, so, in another eighteen years, I'll be laying on my deathbed," people started laughing, "and you'll be banging on the door. I'll say, 'Who is it?' My students who will be in the room with me will say to me, 'Don't worry, we won't let anyone disturb you!' "

The laughter was quickly escalating as Lee went on, fueled by our response to his theatre. "They'll be yelling at me at that point, 'cause they'll think I'm deaf! They'll go to the door and come and say, 'Benoit,' and I'll say, 'Let him in.' "

Lee paused just long enough to deliver the next line: " 'Are you sure?' they'll say. 'Yes, let him in—hurry up, I'm dying!' " Another wave of laughter shook us; we were hanging on Lee's every word to catch the punch line.

"You'll come rushing in and say, 'I get it!' You happen to be in the room, and I'll go, '*Take over*!' "

Gales of laughter rocked the room. A steady soft rain poured outside, but it was hot and bright inside now. Practically wiping tears of laughter from our eyes, we settled down a little for the next question.

"I'm always serene and never disturbed . . ." a woman began.

"I'm never serene and always disturbed! She's got the better deal!" Lee laughed. That began a series of questions and answers that lead to Benoit asking a further question about the process of Enquiry, sparking Lee's discourse.

Lee said, "The instruction is, when observing your mind, you address your mind with the phrase, 'Who am I kidding?' and you keep doing it religiously, related to everything that arises in mind, related to every perception and sensation, and you know when the practice is successful: when all comparison and dualities dissolve. It's that simple. Understanding is irrelevant and counterproductive. We either practice it or we don't, just as an experiment, without understanding. Understanding comes through experience, not through conversation.

"We are a participant in this incredible ongoing process, and the thing that inevitably despoils this perfect landscape of paradise is the mind. So you want to get to Reality. You can practice it and just see what happens, and if not, it won't be a problem."

Another person said, "Swami Prajnanpad said, 'Let the mind have its play.' How does that fit in with what you are saying?"

"Well, I would guess something different, meaning, when we take the mind seriously, it begins to take itself seriously, and really it's just the mind. Let the mind do whatever it does, because it's going to anyway, but without identifying with that play as if it defines us and who we are."

This was followed by a dialogue between Lee and one of his newer French students, regarding his son. In the course of a lengthy exchange, it came out that the son, who is twenty-eight years old, had problems with money. He worked with his father, but could not manage money. The father was always helping him out of jams, and he was tired of doing it. Finally, when Lee questioned the wife who was also sitting there, she frankly stated that their son was a cocaine addict and dealer.

Once again, Lee counseled them to be careful not to rupture the relationship, but to trust that their son could work it out. He said, there is a gentle and easeful way to change the situation, but it may take some diplomacy. Staying in relationship with him was the most important thing. Finally Lee said, with great kindness, "I wish you luck. What is your son's name? I'll think about your son. Anything else?" He looked around the room for the next question.

Eva said, "Some years ago Daniel told me when you're with a master, don't talk much but try to be open to the master."

Lee asked, "How's it working?"

"It works well. Not just opens you to the master, but it also opens you to life, and it's a way of prayer even. But Daniel says also he uses the image that we are like a tube—when we're open, open on both ends, we're floating on air. I feel physically that something is happening that is more and more open on the front, but not yet open behind. Something is closed behind, and it's a physical sensation."

Lee retorted, "You need a good spiritual colonic!" Everyone laughed at this; we could see it coming. "So, I'll tell you the way I do things—keep pushing things in, and when you can't push anything else in, push some more in, and it'll open up the back end!" Lots more laughter burst out. The metaphor was working in a very human way for everyone.

"Relieve some of the pressure in the back," Lee laughed, then continued, "I was very touched when we were in Mangalam in Quebec last spring, because Arnaud was concerned for my well being, because I work so hard—because he knows what it is to work too hard. I work hard, but part of the reason I work so hard is to push things into the tube. I took Arnaud's concern very seriously in the sense of making the distinction about what's too much and what's not. But in principle, it's still the same process: push things into the tube.

"On a very real level, so you don't get a lot of sleep, then you sleep, make it up on a day you don't have as much to do. It's like having a restaurant that's successful—the work never ends. Especially if you're really concerned with the quality of the food—you don't just open cans and throw junk on the table.

"This opening is like that—a constant flow, and you just keep doing it, keep doing it, keep doing it. That's the way I do it; that's my recommendation. And, be able to make distinctions when it's too much. You keep cramming into the tube and there is time for the tube to expand and relax. Then you can put more in. Thank you."

The rain had stopped and the seminar was over. Lee spent the next two hours packing up the Sacred Bazaar and saying goodbye to the many people who came by to speak personally to him and receive his blessing, usually cloaked in a simple gentle clap on the back, sometimes a short embrace or just a warm smile and a few words. With the Sacred Bazaar all packed up, the Transporter was quickly packed. Dinner was early, held upstairs, but this time we sat at a long table, since our numbers were down to twenty or so. Afterward, we packed the last of the luggage into the van, along with a whole load of ripe plums from the neighbor's over laden tree, arduously gathered by Manuela, and zoomed back to Ferme de Jutreau.

Yogi Ramsuratkumar in the streets of Tiruvannamalai, 1980.

The Braderie du Lille.

Lille.

Lille.

Brussels

At Ferme de Jutreau.

*September 7, 2005—
Celebrating thirty years
of teaching.*

The graffiti has arrived.

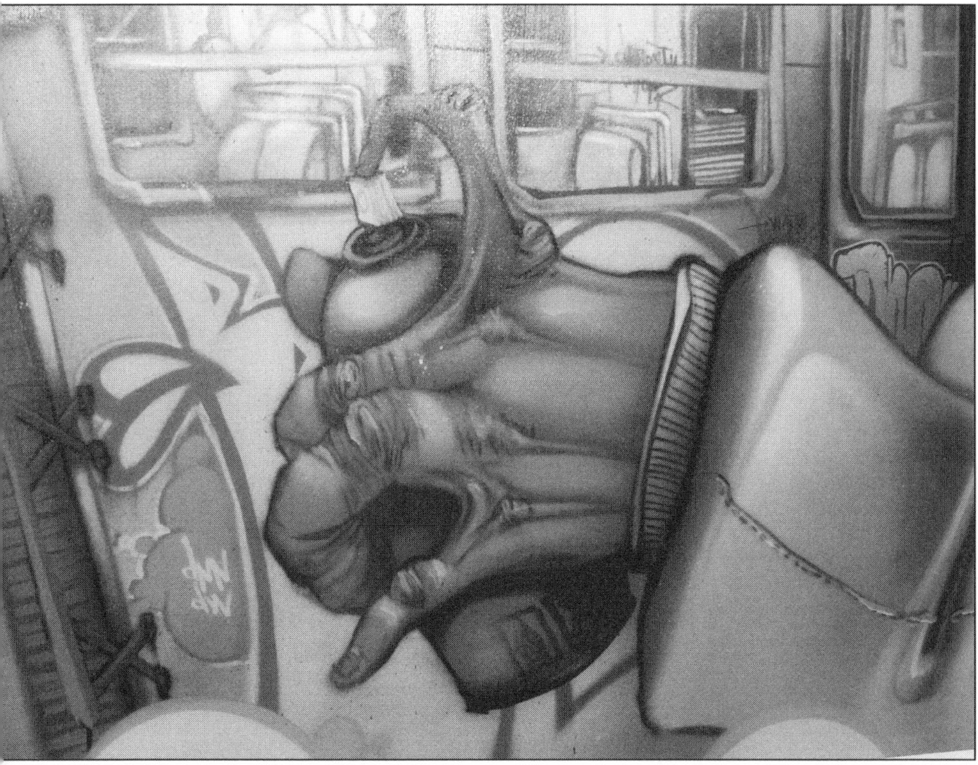

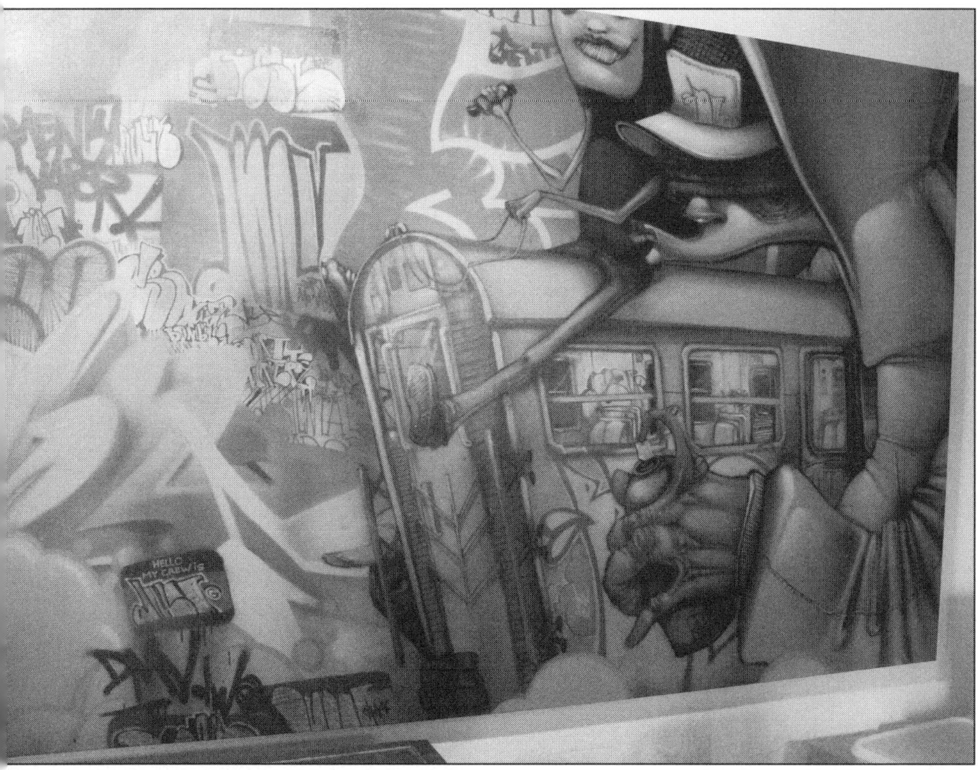

The Money Seminar at Ferme de Jutreau.

Soyez simple et restez-le.
Get Real And Keep It Real.

Darshan, September 18, 2005.

On the ashram.

In Paris with Philippe Coupey and students.

Paris, September 29, 2005.

Maison Raphael in Paris.

Yogi Ramsuratkumar and Lee, 1997.

Paris is Burning

Ferme de Jutreau
September 27, 2005

Tonight at the last after dinner talk of the summer at the ashram, Lee decided to show a video of his favorite poet, Charles Bukowski. What an inspiration! Afterward, over coffee and chocolates in the tea space, everyone was abuzz about Bukowski, including and maybe especially Lee. In the video, three of Bukowski's poems were read by the man himself. The one that seemed to have grabbed a number of people was "Bluebird." Everyone was talking about it, and how it so artfully captured the profound relationship to one's inner life, and the abuse that the tender essence of being takes in this world. It begins with a line, "I have a bluebird in my heart," and it leaves one with the hope that essence, the bluebird, can stay alive within despite the assault of cruelty and individual illusion in the world.

"That's the thing about not letting anybody into your inner life," Lee was saying. "If you do, they'll slaughter it, and then your work is dead. So honesty is not always the best policy; sometimes diversion is the way to go!"

Bukowski had spoken about keeping the fire burning inside, especially during his early years, when everything and everyone seemed against him. He said, "You have to keep the spark of the fire inside, and not let the fire go out." It's so true in *sadhana*, because there are many unforeseen blows, most of which come from seeing ourselves more clearly. Even so, others will do what they can, often unconsciously, to interfere and drag down someone they perceive as achieving something they themselves have not.

Not everyone gives into envy and jealousy and revenge. Another very inspiring aspect of the video was Bukowski's publisher, John Martin. Martin totally believed in Bukowski, started a publishing company, Black Sparrow Press, to publish his work, and stood behind him for years when he was an unknown artist. John Martin had a vision, and he made it happen; he created something out of nothing, to serve Bukowski's art, which most certainly falls gracefully into the rare genre of dharma art. It was a perfect end to the mood and flavor of the summer at the ashram; where art, in all its forms, was the *bhoga*—the enjoyment of sensual pleasure—we were celebrating with Lee.

La Roche Posay
September 28

Lee went to the village today to take some things to the shop that he wanted to display for sale. Tangore paintings, a fifteenth century stone Namalvar about fourteen inches high, and an eighteenth century bronze camel. It would be our last visit to the shop for the summer, and again I was struck by how much had been accomplished in the past three months, since we first arrived. The store looked absolutely beautiful, resplendent now as it was with fine things; it was a celebration of life, a tribute to the skill and craft and art of so many anonymous human beings.

Michelle Bompois, who was tending shop that day, mused, "When we first came here it was so dark, with this weird burgundy velvet stuff on the walls." I looked around at the merchandise: Mary and the divine child in bronze; several different renderings of the crucified

Christ, some with delicate wrought silver design work embellishing the figure of Jesus; hand beaten bronze and copper pots; hand cut wine glasses in jewel tones; the fabulous carved wood horses from eighteenth century India; a pewter tea service; the colorful Hopi kachinas; hand-painted large porcelain bowls; the ancient white marble Devi, Annapurna; a meter high Hanuman, covered in orange kumkum, giving a direct taste of devotional India; the many stunning bronze deities of the East, mostly Hindu, some Buddhist, and much more.

After carefully placing every new item and making tiny adjustments in many different pieces that he had placed here and there in the shop, Lee stopped, looked around at us and said, "Well, it's our last trip into La Roche Posay for the summer. We have to go for a final cup of coffee!" Off we went to the little café in the center of the village, where the market is held and we had bought the sweet pineau from a local vintner three months ago.

We gathered around a few tables at Lee's favorite café for a café crème, where he was joined by Benoit, Annette, Denise and Sari and a few others. It was a mellow scene, the last of the summer flower gardens in their profusion of blooms just across the street, framing the small park on the east end of the square, and us with our hot coffee, talking gently and informally about this and that.

The rest of the day for the Americans, who would be leaving in one week, would be spent packing—for Ann and I, it was summer's end and time to say goodbye. After dinner, there were two hours of bridge and a final gathering with the ashram residents and householders over tea, coffee and lavish servings of the sweetest chocolate cake I've ever eaten.

En route to Paris
September 29

With ten people, including an eleven-month-old baby, packed into the van, we left the ashram at five-thirty, in the predawn dark this morning, with Lee driving as usual. These early departures always remind me of traveling in India with Lee, when there are still a few stars twinkling here and there in the sky, and the yellow half coin of the waning moon riding low in the sky. We were driving to Paris for the final five days of our stay in France, where the activities would include a public talk and the last seminar of the summer, at Maison Raphael. Five of us would be leaving France on Monday morning, October 3, for the ashram in Prescott, Arizona. Lee himself would stay in France for one more week after our departure, to return to the States on October 10, after traveling to Hauteville for a special celebration of the eightieth birthday of Arnaud Desjardins.

The wheels of the van bounced over misty, bumpy roads as we bolted through the countryside and darkened villages, on our way to the autoroute. It was mostly quiet and contemplative, as if we were having our morning meditation now in the van, a little earlier than the usual seven a.m. ashram schedule. Breakfast would be hard-boiled eggs, dried figs and water.

After a long period of silence, now careening lickety-split down the autoroute toward Paris, the cell phone jingle could be heard. Ann answered the phone then handed it to Lee.

"Hello," he said, then quietly listened. "Okay, give them this number and have them call me. No, I'll call them. Okay, thanks. Bye."

He passed the cell back to Ann and told her to dial a certain number. When it started to ring, she handed it back to Lee.

"This is Lee Lozowick on the phone . . ." pause, "I'm in France going a hundred miles an hour on the autoroute!" Silence ensued while Lee listened very intently. The gathered force of his concentrated listening permeated the van, then he said, "Oh. Thank you. Tell him thank you for letting me know. Goodbye."

Handing the phone back to Ann, Lee said simply, unceremoniously, "M. died."

An inexplicable sadness washed over me in waves in the silence. He was talking about someone that he personally knew very well—a wonderful woman whom I had met a few times, who was a senior student of E.J. Gold, and who Lee had once called "a pillar of E.J.'s work." She had been profoundly involved with Mr. Gold's work, but she was struck with some form of Alzheimer's several years ago; the members of Mr. Gold's family had taken care of her at home until just recently, when her needs became so great that she had to be placed in a care facility for the terminally ill. It was merciful that she had been able to leave her body quickly after that, rather than to linger on, as so many people do, in situations where there is tremendous suffering for everyone involved. E.J. himself had asked T. to call Lee and inform him.

I thought about how implacable death claims us in its own time. M. was young by any standard—only around sixty years old. There was a time, not too long ago, when she was a vital, integral player in E.J. Gold's inner circle—she was an individual of great commitment to the Work, who had spent over thirty-five years with her teacher.

"We never know what the Work has in store for us," I mused into the dark, watching the illumined ribbon of the road and the faintest hint of dawn that lit the eastern horizon.

Lee responded, "Let's hope it's not too ugly!" He gave a short, ironic laugh. The implication was: it is all out of our hands, and in the hands of God. In the enclosed world of the van, silence welled up again and seemed to gather and settle in a pool as we reflected on the news. Outside, big trucks roared past us in the surprisingly thick early morning road traffic—and we still had Paris rush hour traffic to look forward to. After a while, Lee said, "It was a very good death. Her kids were with her."

"Is it possible that the work body is still functional, with Alzheimer's?" I asked Lee.

"Who knows? It's anybody's guess," Lee answered. He began to explain that in E.J.'s community, they will be reading from *The American Book of the Dead* for forty-nine days, twenty-four hours a day, for the deceased. We drove along steadily, and I noticed two nuclear reactors on the horizon, rimmed in red lights and streaming billows of smoke in the charcoal atmosphere of the lingering night, like something out of Tolkien—the war machines of the Dark Lord.

"Do you think E.J. helped her leave her body, I mean, helped her pass over sooner rather than dragging it out?" I asked, referring to Mr. Gold's prodigious skills as a shaman in the domain of bardo transit.

"Of course," Lee said in his laconic way, his simple response pointing out that I had, once again, merely stated the obvious.

We arrived at Café La Liberte well before ten a.m., earlier than expected, naturally, and settled into the usual seats where, for the past several years, Lee has met Zen meditation teacher Philippe Coupey—a disciple of Taisen Deshimaru and an expatriot American who has lived in Paris for over thirty years—for an annual visit. We ordered coffee and talked quietly in the cool, cloudy morning. Mira A. joined our party, pulling up a chair at one of the several tables we had appropriated on the sidewalk. The café, which inhabits a street corner in Montparnasse on a boulevard lined with trees, was quiet at this time of day.

About thirty minutes later Philippe and some of his friends and students arrived; three of them were also Americans living in Paris, while two were French and one was British. After handing over a copy of the new tattoo book, *Agony & Alchemy*, as a gift to Philippe, and receiving the book that Philippe gave to Lee, more coffees were ordered. As is often the case with Americans who meet in Europe, the conversation turned very quickly to the dismal reality of the overall degenerate atmosphere in the States. Everyone has grave concerns about what is going on, politically, socially, culturally, spiritually. With the New Orleans disaster and two massive hurricanes having decimated the Gulf Coast of the U.S. so recently, it was a sore and tender subject—rather like an unhealed wound.

After some time of lamenting the differences between the quality of life and culture in Europe and the States, and the general downward trend of culture in the West, the internet came up as one of the dominant aspects of postmodern culture that Lee abhors and rails out against regularly. He said, "The internet is cutting out more and more small businesses. People are afraid to go out of their houses anymore . . ."

Philippe said, "Afraid they'll get mugged?"

"Yes," Lee answered, "afraid of gangs. They're growing more and more."

"People are getting more afraid to interact with people in any way," I added.

"Yes," Philippe said, "they're just afraid of *people*. Is it that way all over the States?" he asked Lee.

Ellen asked, "Or just in Arizona?"

Lee answered, "It depends on where you live." Lee began to talk about the street culture in the States, which led to a more upbeat discussion of graffiti art.

"Our new thing now is graffiti," Lee began, which sparked a conversation among the ten or so people sitting around the tables, about graffiti art, what kind is illegal, how the crews work together, the difference between graffiti art and commissioned graffiti. Then Simon, a Zen practitioner, said to Lee, "I have a boring question."

Lee responded, "The only boring questions I get are from my students!"

Simon laughed and forged ahead. "How did you two meet?" he asked, indicating Lee and Philippe.

Philippe looked at Lee and said, "We met through Muriel and Jean Claud," referring to Muriel, a student of Arnaud Desjardins, and Jean Claud, a student of Deshimaru. "When was it?" he asked Lee, musing on the past. "Ten years ago?"

"It must have been 1992," Lee answered.

Philippe smiled and said, "Oh! We're getting to be old friends!"

Elaine asked, "How's the music going?"

"Fabulous!" Lee answered, brightening visibly at the mention of the music projects. "Next year I'm doing a tour with my own band, songs from my CD, *Crushed by Love*, some cover tunes, some old LGB songs . . . I'm going to have European musicians this time, though. I have everyone lined up."

Someone asked what the name of the band would be.

"The Lee Lozowick Band." He turned back to Mira and said, "When Mira plays you just sit there with your mouth open and tears running out of your eyes. I'm not kidding!" When she shook her head as if to say no and blushed a little, he said, "She's a little humble. She plays on the new Shri CD . . . We had a rock band years ago, and we'll be playing some of the songs we recorded then."

Philippe asked, "Your lyrics?" Lee answered yes.

The topic of Lee's public talks came up. We were speaking of how rarely he gives public talks when Elaine began to ruminate about how much she loved the public talk Lee had given last year at the Paris dojo to the Zen community.

She said, "Last year you were selling books and CDs, throwing them through the air and people were catching them—it was very unusual to have that going on in the Paris dojo!"

"Well, if people can't learn anything, at least we can entertain them," Lee commented mildly. I was wondering if we had fully registered his meaning, but the conversation immediately flowed on.

Philippe commented, "Really, your talk went very well. I wish I had written down the things people were saying afterward and sent them to you. Everybody was talking about it afterward in the cafés . . ."

Elaine added, "It was like a burst of energy for us, a breath of fresh air. People were very excited by it!"

The tattoo book was being passed around, and Blanche returned to the ever-fascinating subject of tattoos, saying, "It's very interesting, because tattoos are usually so violent, all warriors and terrible scenes."

"We do all sacred imagery," Lee responded.

While Philippe, Ellen, Elaine, Simon and Blanche continued looking at the photos in the tattoo book, Lee watched and commented on the photos as they leafed through the pages: "That's Sylvan, the guy over there with the baby. That's my daughter! She's the one who got me into the whole thing. That's her name."

Exclamations of surprise and appreciation come from our guests who were now looking closely at Aaron Funk's very graffiti-like, artful design of Gita's name. As Lee regaled them with stories of Aaron, the tattoo artist, and Nara, who drew many of the deities, they turned the pages. Music, tattoos, graffiti art, culture, practice, meditation—these were the topics of conversation, leading sooner or later back again to music and Lee's upcoming tour, 2006. Lee spoke about how fantastic it is playing the music festivals in France, the fabulous outdoor venues with one, two or three thousand people.

Another student of Philippe's asked Lee, "Do you play an instrument?"

"No. I sing. I'm not very musical," Lee answered candidly, with just a slender trace of a self-deprecating tone.

The student laughed and said, "Well, you're musical enough to sing!" Everyone laughed at the paradox of the situation. Lee laughed too, then said, "We don't tour in America; the pay is bad, the motels are dirty, in a bad part of town, the crowd is jaded. The band has some jobs, but Europe is where it's at for us."

The student asked, "When you tour, do you mix the music with other activities, like teaching?"

"I do," Lee answered, "but the band doesn't. Sometimes I'm giving seminars at the same time that we're touring. I also sell sacred artifacts, so I go shopping and buy things when I'm on the road with the band."

Just then the food we had ordered arrived and the conversation began to veer off onto other subjects. Philippe mentioned that he had an old video of Arnaud Desjardins and Deshimaru, and that he would like to get a copy of that to Lee.

"That is something that I would really like to see. Thank you," Lee replied.

"Did you see the Bukowski video?" Philippe asked enthusiastically. As a matter of fact, he was referring to the video Lee had shown at the after dinner talk two nights before at Ferme de Jutreau.

"I just saw it—loved it! Fantastic!" Lee answered. "Have you seen the documentary about him, done by a Frenchman some years ago? It's fantastic! In it there is a lot of him reading his poetry—breathtaking! No one can read his poetry like he does . . . He was an amazing man. He would write thirty or forty poems a day, totally drunk! Incredible!"

"How is he regarded in the States now?" Philippe asked.

"He's very popular," Lee answered. The Parisian Americans talked about how hard it is to get Bukowski books in Paris, and that they are terribly expensive. Lee generously offered to send Bukowski books to them from the States, where they are very accessible.

Inevitably, the conversation went to American spiritual teachers and the pervasive trend of false teachers, teachers who have fallen from grace, been involved in scandals or are known to be abusive with their students. A lot of the gossip that floats around is true, but as Philippe pointed out, some of it is not. His teacher, Deshimaru, was frequently lied about in the surprisingly conservative Zen world. One falsehood that was circulated about him was that he was so drunk that when he prostrated in the rituals, two monks had to stand on either side of him to pick him up.

"All lies!" Philippe continued, "They made this all up! And in Japan too . . . Deshimaru was one of the very few Zen masters who came into it without being born in it. The way it works in Japan is it goes from father to son—you basically inherit your father's 'temple' and his teaching . . ."

"Like being in a family business," Elaine added.

"Deshimaru left all that behind to come here," Philippe said.

"I would have loved that guy!" Lee smiled, obviously enjoying hearing stories of the great meditation master.

Philippe continued, "When I see other masters interviewed, I see that the dimension of Deshimaru was so much bigger than those who attacked him. And his books—remember that review in *Tricycle*?"

"Those people at *Tricycle*," Lee said, "are so condescending, except for their own brand of socially, politically correct Buddhism. Anything slightly different, they don't like it."

"But it's the biggest Buddhist magazine in the world!" Philippe said incredulously. "Their style is nauseating! We even wrote a rebuttal to their review of Deshimaru's book—you did too—and they said they didn't get it! Finally they said it came too late to publish . . ."

Philippe said that the *Tricycle* editors gave one flimsy excuse after another as to why they hadn't published the rebuttal to their bad review of *Sit*, transcripts of talks given by Deshimaru and translated from French into English by Philippe himself, published by Hohm Press. Finally, after being confronted several times, the editors simply said to Philippe, "Well, that's how it is."

A new Buddhist magazine, *Buddhadharma*, entered the conversation at this point. Lee commented that it was better at the beginning, although they are trying to hold the line of a more traditional Buddhism, rather than giving in to the new age, political, social, Western orientation that other Buddhist magazines have succumbed to. However, their depiction of dogs meditating was ridiculous. Do serious practicing Buddhists really believe that a dog can be in *samadhi*?

While Philippe and Lee exchanged views on the current Buddhist spiritual scene, a few drops of rain threatened a more serious downpour, then seemed to blow over. It was chilly, and we all sat with our coats on. I pulled mine a little tighter around. Once again the subject rolled back around to the lack of integrity in the Western spiritual scene.

"You now, all I'm interested in is being a disciple of Deshimaru. If you keep it small," Philippe was saying as he rolled another cigarette, "that seems to take care of it."

Ellen turned to Lee and asked, "Do you agree, it's a solution?"

Lee responded, "I wouldn't say it's a solution, but it is something I try to do—because the bigger you get, the more you have to manage property and publications and all that."

It was nearing time to part and go our separate ways. The waiter brought the check, and Lee took it. When Philippe offered money, Lee said, "It's on me . . ."

Watching that exchange, Elaine looked at Lee and said, "Thanks a lot."

"Yeah, there's a lot of people here!" Philippe smiled.

"The more, the better!" Lee answered, then turned back to Ellen and continued the conversation he was having, "And always, if you stay small, you avoid all the publicity—all the Buddhist movie stars and all that!" He laughed.

Elaine talked about how they have a small center and a small dojo, but it's not attracting people. She asked the question, "Are we happy with this? If we got more people and had to get a bigger place, it would be a big leap."

"Yes," Lee agreed. He began to talk about his plans for next summer, saying, "Next year I'm cutting out everything except two or three out of six or seven seminars I do in other places, and doing it all at Ferme de Jutreau. I'm just spending too much time away. So we're withdrawing everything except with Arnaud Desjardins and my students in Germany. We'll see if there is support for it. It's a big change."

"Is there anything else of interest going on in the States?" Philippe asked. When Lee mentioned that some of Chögyam Trungpa Rinpoche's long-time students were breaking with the Shambhala organization because they aren't using the teachings of Trungpa Rinpoche anymore, and instead are using the teachings of his son, who is the lineage holder, Philippe mentioned that he had met the new Sakyong, the eldest son of Chögyam Trungpa Rinpoche.

Lee commented, "The Zen establishment in the U.S. is completely superficial, with all these self-styled masters. They are watering down the lineages. The only really bright light in America is Sasaki Roshi. He had some monks come from Japan to train, and he was too tough for them! He's the real thing. Nobody likes him. Leonard Cohen was with him. They're still close, but Leonard Cohen doesn't live there with him anymore."

Philippe said, "I sent Leonard Cohen a copy of *Sit*, but he never answered."

"I saw an interview with Leonard Cohen a year ago," Lee said, "he is so articulate. I hope he goes back to Sasaki Roshi."

The visit came to its natural end with a couple of spirited photos snapped of Lee and Philippe, taken by Elaine. Once again we were back in the van and braving the Paris traffic to travel west across the city and out to the suburbs to a small town called Chatou, where a huge, weeklong brocante fair was in progress with seven hundred *vendeurs* set up. Lee spent the remainder of the day there—about seven hours—with his intrepid crew of the day, including Sylvan, Denise, Sari, Annette, Mira A., Dasya, Ann and myself. It was dark when we left Chatou to find our way to Maison Raphael, where we would be staying for the next four days.

Paris
September 30

The Friday morning market was in full swing at the Place d'Italie. Always happy to stroll through a market, Lee parked the van and we made a quick pilgrimage through the vendors, appreciating their products—*legumes et fruit frais, du pain, fromage* of all kinds, *poulet roti*. Lee bought bread, cheese and olives for our breakfast.

Lee spent the next two hours visiting his friend at the shop and buying Asian antiquities. As a gift, he brought a copy of *Agony & Alchemy*, which our merchant friends seemed to enjoy thoroughly as they looked through the book.

Unable to pull himself away, Lee ended up with a van-load of carved wooden Buddhas and devotional monks, about four feet high, as well as many other artifacts gleaned from the shelves and shop floor. Leaving the shop, we took the *peripherique interieur* toward Boulogne Billancourt, where we would unload the treasures at Maison Raphael. The traffic was grueling.

Finally, at about two o'clock in the afternoon, we headed along the river road, as we call the boulevards that run east and west across the city along the *quais* at the Seine. Soon we were headed north through horrific city traffic toward the bookstore, Espace Harmonie, where Lee would be giving his public talk that night. It took over an hour to navigate what usually takes about twenty minutes.

Brinda and Andrea were meeting us at the bookstore, having driven the Transporter up from the ashram and made a stop at the airport to ship something for Lee first. The Transporter carried the entire Sacred Bazaar—boxes of books and CDs, boxes and crates of bronze antiquities, deities, singing bowls, crucifixes and everything else that Lee had planned to lay out for his audience tonight and over the weekend at Maison Raphael.

We were still slowly making our way in dense traffic when Dasya called on the cell phone to say that he and Sylvan were waiting for Lee and had reserved a parking place right across the street from the bookstore on the rue de Petits Hotels. That meant that someone was standing in the parking place and literally safeguarding the space with their bodies. Should another car come along, there would be a confrontation. This was good news, because it is difficult to find parking on the one-way street in front of Espace Harmonie; all the streets in the area, with the exception of Magenta Boulevard, tended to be one-way, contributing to a complicated maze that was not easy to navigate, especially in traffic.

Dasya also warned us that the traffic in the area was fierce, and that we couldn't turn down the rue de Petits Hotel from Magenta Boulevard. Now, in addition, it was threatening to rain. Dasya's suggestion was to come down the one-way rue de Petits Hotels the wrong way, from the Place Franz Lizst, since you couldn't get to the bookstore at all from the other end of the street, due to construction on Magenta Bouldevard, which is not far from the Gare d'Lyon—a busy place on any day.

Lee pulled into the busy Place Franz Liszt, with its beautiful central fountain and old buildings, heavily adorned with stone sculpture and massive columns, and turned right onto the *rue*. Immediately we could see that a large delivery truck was blocking the street. Lee parked temporarily, and illegally, in a tiny alley on the left off the *rue*. After a short wait, when Sylvan spoke to the delivery man, who said he was going to be there for awhile, Lee assessed the situation. Rain was beginning to fall in light drops from a gray sky. As he pulled the van out of the alley to find another parking place on one of the many narrow side streets off the Place Franz Liszt, he asked Ann to call Brinda and Andrea on their cell and tell them to take everything to Maison Raphael and unload it there before coming to Espace Harmonie. There would be no Sacred Bazaar tonight.

Unheard of! Even before the bronze deities appeared on the scene, and then the European *brocante*, since Lee has been coming to Europe to give talks and seminars, he has always had an impressive spread of books and CDs at his talks. Not tonight. We parked the van three blocks away with no trouble and found a café in the Place Franz Liszt.

Taking his seat, Lee looked at us and instructed, "Go back to Espace Harmonie and tell everyone where we are so they can join us here. I'll stay here." His intense mood of urgency said that the energy was building toward a great talk. Ann and I were spurred into action. We walked down the street at a fast clip. Within seconds we saw Dasya standing on the sidewalk outside the bookstore and called to him, "Lee is at the café in the Place on the immediate right. Everybody's invited to join him." Seeing that Dasya had registered and would pass the message on within seconds, we turned around and headed back.

Less than a minute later everyone converged at the tables Lee had assembled. The waiter wouldn't let us gather around the tables; we had to sit in one long row facing the street. Somehow, we made this work as Alain René, who owns Espace Harmonie and was our host for the evening, Sylvan, Denise and Sari, Dasya, Annette, Ann and I crowded in as close as we could to hear what Lee was saying.

The conversation went here and there, and then seemed to settle in on a member of the sangha who has been misbehaving significantly in the past two years. It's hard to say exactly what happened, but it's enough to understand that he was in a position of worldly power that went to his head. One of the members of our group was reporting sins against the dharma perpetrated by this individual. She said that he keeps trying new things, and the more stuff he adds on top of his repertoire of tricks to gain power, the more bizarre it gets.

She added, "He says he's a healer now."

Lee laughed, turning back on his sense of humor in a way that completely dispelled the gossipy tone of the conversation, and said, "I should've sold him my shaman's cane! It's the coolest thing I've seen in years! I can't believe nobody bought that the other day . . . That iron tip on one end—it's like a nuclear vector! Did you see that phurba yesterday with the strings and rags and things tied on it? It had a meteorite tied on it too . . . They say in the teachings that those meteorites fall from heaven. The guy did not want to sell that to me!"

The rain was falling in earnest now. We sat huddled together in our long row, happy for the canvas awning over our heads, looking out on the busy *place* and the tall sycamore tree that stood like a sentinel in front of the café. People walked by with dogs, briefcases, big purses, bundles—university students, businessmen and women, old people. I got the sense of how it will be in Paris in another month or two—chilly, rainy, brooding and moody. When the rain slackened a little, we made a run for the bookstore, which was only one block away.

The little bookstore has a small-ish basement room, where Lee's annual late September talk is always given. There are no windows, no air and no sunlight. When we arrived the Paris bordello members were already in mode, setting up the space and prepping the food they had brought with them to host Lee and company for dinner. This too has become an annual informal ritual—the last impromptu feast of the summer with his sangha. It's an appropriate tradition that naturally evolved over time: the Paris sangha provides Lee's first sangha meal when he arrives in France and his last meal with the sangha before he leaves.

Three long folding tables had been put together to make one long table in the middle of the room. It was covered with a white paper tablecloth, set with plastic plates and cutlery, and then loaded down with roasted chickens, big bowls of green salad, plates of fresh bread, cheese platters, pickles and olives, Coke, wine, water and many other miscellaneous items. As it turned out, dinner was twenty minutes early, having originally been scheduled for six o'clock. About twenty-five people sat down to eat, since there had been numerous new arrivals while the prep was being done: Michel, Sabine and their two youngest daughters arrived; Ron Mukerjee came from Brussels; Brinda and Andrea from the ashram had finally gotten free of their various tasks and arrived; Danielle arrived from Nice and Evelyne from London.

Halfway through dinner Benoit arrived. Lee generously invited Beniot to sit directly across from him. All the seats were taken; clearly there wasn't room at the table for everyone. David H., who had finished eating, immediately offered his seat to the newcomer.

"We wondered where you went the other day, you were out of there so fast," Lee teased Benoit about leaving so abruptly, without saying goodbye, on Thursday morning when we'd arrived in Paris at Montparnasse for the meeting with Philippe Coupey.

Benoit, who lives in Paris, had spent the last week at the ashram and the seminar at La Source Bleue, then drove into Paris with Lee and company early that morning. He had volunteered to navigate for Lee as he drove through the thick traffic, first from the peripherique to Maison Raphael, and then to Montparnasse. Even for a Parisian, it was not an easy task to meet the master on his terms, while Lee drove like a house on fire through the streets. Navigating for Lee is an opportunity to be trained in attention and mindfulness, and everyone who does it gets a strong dose of medicine in terms of seeing the holes in one's ability to Pay Attention and stay present under pressure. Good natured as ever, Benoit took the joking in stride and settled into enjoying the repartee with Lee.

After a few minutes Benoit said, "Between seminars and the band, you're on the road all summer, aren't you? That's a lot of work!"

Lee smiled. "I wouldn't have it any other way." Then he looked around at us, his loving students, and said, "My students are all so lazy that I have to work even harder!"

I asked, half statement, half question, "You have to work for us?"

"Not *for* you; *instead* of you," Lee answered pointedly. It was an important communication of a crucial principle of the Work: until we can work for ourselves, the teacher has to work for us. It's a principle we hear for a long time without deeply registering what it means for the teacher; when the reality of this actually dawns on us with the clarity of the morning sun, it is a shock.

Another guest arrived, an expatriot American opera singer, Melanie, who first met Lee at Le Rozet this summer. Jennie got up to provide another seat across from Lee, and Lee began to chat about opera with the new arrival. A minute later I looked up and saw David Amar walking in; Mira, who was also sitting across the table near

Lee, got up and offered her seat to him. David walked around the table to embrace Lee, then took the seat across from him.

Spirits were soaring at this last supper. The celebratory mood was accentuated by the new people who kept coming and taking places at the table generously made available by someone who had just finished eating, so that many people got to interact directly with Lee over the course of the meal. Right away the subject turned to the graffiti artists who David Amar had hooked up with Lee. We spoke of Alain, Michel and Didier and the art for quite a while.

Remembering that we had a case of *Agony & Alchemy* in the back of the van, Lee dispatched Dasya to bring it to the bookstore. He had wanted to give David a copy as a gift, and we quickly realized that the tattoo books could be sold that night. In the meantime, Alain René was upstairs combing through his shelves and back stock to bring out every Lee Lozowick and Hohm Press book, CD and video that he had in the store, with which Lee could at least make an impromptu book table for the evening.

David began to talk about his sister, Anais, who we had met several times in years past at the home of her parents, Yvan and Nadege Amar. David had told us last year that Anais has several large tattoos, and in turn Lee had said, "Gita," who David knew well, "has lots of tattoos! Gita is the one who got me into them."

Like a messenger fresh from the Paris streets, David began to tell Lee about all the things happening in the counterculture arts scene in the city. He mentioned the Palais de Tokyo, a museum of modern art in Trocadero, in the sixteenth *arrondissement*, which had an exhibition of graffiti art recently. He spoke about the well-known graffiti artist, W.K., whose work was exhibited there. The Palais de Tokyo seems to have its fingers on the pulse, with exhibits not only of graffiti and street art, but of textile design, architecture and many other aspects of postmodern life.

David, who is an aspiring clothing designer, spoke further about people he knew in the world of street art. He said that he had some friends who painted a whole Boeing airplane with graffiti—they made the newspapers but didn't get caught. They also managed to paint a World War II plane.

He said, "The police know all the crews and their signatures. It's one hundred euros per fine, per signature piece. I know people who have been fined one million, two million euros, because their art is all over the streets." He talked about a famous Paris clothing designer, known as Agnes b., who has been a supporter of the graffiti crews for years. She once paid a one-and-a-half million euro fine for one artist.

After dinner, while the room was being re-arranged, Lee was ensconced behind his little book table in the small foyer of the basement room, where he usually manages to set up a small version of the Sacred Bazaar. David made his way over to the book table to talk with Lee and receive his copy of the tattoo book; Lee also gave him a second copy, a gift for Anais. Other people came over to buy a book and visit with Lee before the talk started. More people began to flood the basement room, which had now been turned into a talk space; the tables had disappeared, and rows of chairs and *zafus* had taken their place. In one corner was a padded high stool where Lee would sit. Next to it stood a small table with a large *murti* of Yogi Ramsuratkumar on it and a beautiful bouquet of red and white flowers. A single votive candle burned beneath the murti of Yogi Ramsuratkumar.

Many of Arnaud's students who live in Paris began to arrive and were eager to say hello to Lee. Ann, a former student of Andrew Cohen, arrived from London and greeted Lee with a dozen red and white variegated roses and a box of chocolates. Marilyn, a British woman who had hosted Lee's seminar in Aix en Province last summer, had come all the way from Aix to see Lee; an ardent devotee of Yvan Amar and now a student of Nadege, Marilyn was surprised and happy to see David, who she knew well.

People crowded around the little book table and an excited buzz began to fill the air. Blanche, who Lee had meet with Philippe Coupey the day before, arrived as well as Lee's long-time friend, François Fronty, a disciple of Arnaud's who filmed and produced two videos with Lee: "Sur La Route Avec Mr. Lee" (On the Road with Mr. Lee) and "Darshan," a video of Yogi Ramsuratkumar filmed on the ashram in Tiruvannamalai ten years ago.

Despite the rain that had been pouring off and on for the past few hours, the small basement room was quickly filling to capacity with old friends, Lee's students, Arnaud's students and some new faces. By the time Lee left the book table, the room was packed with people, hot and sweaty—the way he likes it. At least eighty people had crammed into the space. Most of them had been to Lee's talks at Espace Harmonie before, and knew that it was likely to be a wild ride through a riotous landscape, the ground of which is always the teaching, but where we meet many bizarre and unsavory characters—that is, ourselves, laid bare by Lee's comedy.

For some reason, giving a public talk in Paris brings this mood out in Lee, in which he plays the role of irreverent, heretical, funny but deadly clown. It's sort of like being on a roller coaster at a carnival. The audience seemed primed and ready as he strode up to his chair—a bar stool of sorts with chrome handles on it that looked extremely uncomfortable for a guest speaker. Lee moved the chair about a foot, then unceremoniously sat down and looked at his audience. People were seated in rows of chairs and then right up to his feet on *zafus* on the floor.

He gave one of his wry chortles and said, "I have to move the chair back to where I put it when I set the room up, because my students came in and moved the chair to where *they* thought it should be. Isn't that the way spiritual life goes? The teacher wants one thing, the student wants something else. The teacher wants *you*, the students, to be clear and healthy and happy and successful, and what do you think you want? Shit! So what to do? Buy a book!

"So I feel *terrible* tonight. Because three people tonight asked me where the Sacred Bazaar is, and it's not here. As any of you who have been to previous talks know, no Sacred Bazaar, no Lee Lozowick. So I've been *defeated* by the Paris city something-or-other, whoever decides to do this fucking work on the street! We come to the street, the street's closed, so we go around the other side to get in from the other side. So we drive in, and these two moving trucks just pulled in ahead of us, and they're unloading the trucks into this person's apartment!

"So we go up to them very nicely and say, 'We're trying to get down to the end of the street, would you mind just backing your trucks about ten meters, then we'll drive by and then you can . . .' And they said no. So we said, 'How long are you gonna be here?' 'At least two hours.' So we had this whole van full of bronze, maybe about five hundred kilos worth, and had to send them somewhere else. Now they've got a little table set up on the Champs d'Elysee, probably being chased away by the *gendarmes*, and here I am without my Sacred Bazaar, *naked*!

"*However*, I have one thing, because this was in the other van." Lee held up the *Agony & Alchemy: Sacred Art and Tattoos* book, with its glossy, full color cover. He had a small stack of about ten of them on the floor by his side.

"This is a book on tattoos. Okay. You have to see Andrea after the talk and pay her for these . . . This is called *Sacred Art and Tattoos*. So I figured, you guys are French, and you know, Americans think the French are kind of loose and free and relaxed and, you know, kind of 'with it.' Okay, I've been coming here for ten years. I know there are more therapists in France than in all the other countries in Europe put together!" Laughter broke out among this savvy crowd at the implications so clearly expressed in Lee's knowledge of cultural tendencies in the West. He continued, "Including Germany, which has got a *lot* of therapists. So I *know* something's wrong.

"You know, when I was a little kid, Paris was better than Tahiti, better than anywhere in the world! Paris was the way America used to be years ago, you know: streets paved with gold, the dream. Everybody wanted to come to America. When I was a little child, it was Paris. So I get here, and I figure, you people are cool, you're relaxed, you're chill, you can take a joke. So, I had five hundred of these tattoo books shipped over here at the beginning of the summer, figuring you're cool, you know what tattoos are about, there'll be no problem . . . Was I wrong!

"At the tattoo convention, they sell this t-shirt that says, 'Tattoos are not just for sailors and whores anymore.' But you guys don't know that yet. You guys are living fifty years in the past! You guys need to get with it, and tattoos are 'with it.'

"I got my first tattoos when I was fifty-eight years old, so don't give me this shit about you're too old!" Several people in the packed, hot room were already laughing heartily at Lee's jokes; some were squirming a little at this provocative "tattoo pitch."

Lee continued, "In fact, it's better to start thinking about tattoos when you're close to sixty, because then, guess what? You get a tattoo when you're eighteen, by the time you're sixty, you know what happens to your skin, right? And then the tattoos look like some kind of modern art—nobody can even tell what it is! But you get a tattoo when you're sixty, it'll be with you—beautiful, clear, crisp, obvious—till you *die*!"

Lee's tone was almost snide and derisive, as if he was speaking to people who were just clueless; at the same time, he was so friendly and engaging about it, and his theatre was so enthralling, that you couldn't help but listen attentively and even find yourself on his side, no matter what insult or threat he might be hurling your way. This was evidenced by the growing laughter and smiles that broke out here and there, which was the beginning of the almost constant laughter that would punctuate the rest of the evening. There was a great relaxation in the space, as if we knew we were in safe hands and had completely given ourselves over for the ride.

"There's some pictures in this book of people that are most of your ages. You know, their bodies aren't perfect—though we made sure that all the tits that we showed in this book are nice! And there's a few, but discreetly . . . I've had to waste a tremendous amount of time and energy explaining this book to people all summer, just so a few people would buy them, because people come up, and they see a book on tattoos and they . . ." Lee put his hands out to indicate that they were pushing it away.

"Tattoos are taboo. *Still*! I can't believe it! Tattoos are about as happening a thing as there is—except for the complete capitulation of the human race to the idiots who govern them."

Lee paused for the laugh, but everyone sat still. "Is that too subtle for those of you who . . .?" His voice was drowned out by the wave of laughter that flooded the room in a delayed reaction.

"Although if I lived in France, I might. I don't know what my politics would be if I lived here. Don't politics depend on situation? Sure they do! 'Cause most of you are still against *even the idea* of tattoos. So your politics depend on situation, not on *intelligence.* Ahhh . . . I'm glad those two people from New York didn't stay! Oh, this woman came in and she wanted to stay, and her husband came in and he said, 'You can't stay here because this is not about *Christianity*!' Whoa, if they were here, I would have been in big trouble! That guy was a Christian, but he had muscles!"

Everyone was laughing now, because no one in the room could be called a Christian in the terms that Lee was describing. His humor, which was so appealing, could in any moment turn deadly in the exactitude of its truth, as it did when he continued, "And you know how fundamentalists are; they're all for peace until you aren't about their ideas, and then they kill you or beat you up.

"So I've only got six of these here tonight. This is not a book about scarring your skin for life, and putting skulls-with-knives-through-the-eyeholes-and-blood-dripping-off-the-teeth type stuff on your skin. It's *sacred* art and tattoos. Now, to people that get skulls with knives sticking through the eyeholes and blood dripping from the teeth, those *are* sacred images, however. I have to say I have a different sensibility about the Sacred.

"This book is about how, essentially, sacred images of any tradition or culture can effectively and successfully help us on the Path. And it happens to use *tatouage* as a doorway into that consideration. Would anybody like one?" One by one, people began to raise their hands for a book. Lee tossed books to those close to him and passed them down to those who were further away.

"Thank you! One for Mona. These are too heavy to throw. Anybody else? Thank you! One for Evelyne. If I don't know your name, I can either just say, 'One for the person with the such-and-such color hair,' or I could give you a name, based on my first impression of you! No, I won't do that. Thank you, great! Good choice, this is a fabulous book. Okay, thank you. If you don't get one for yourself, everybody in this room must have somebody in the family who is into tattoos. One more, okay, great, thank you!

"The person from New York who came in was a very good-looking young woman, and I thought, fucking Christ gets most of them!" It was blasphemy, heresy, but for a Baul *khepa*, it said much more; it spoke of an intimate knowledge of the great yogi saint, Jesus of Nazareth, who probably also had a great sense of humor and was never the sexual and social prude the orthodoxy made of him. Stutifying organized religion has always drawn criticism from Bauls, who are innately revolutionary and iconoclastic. Laughter, the spirit of the night, claimed us once again; through mirth, we were being shaken free of the chains of the mind that bind us and lock down the body from the flow of life's great, healing passions.

"But every once in a while some decent-looking woman finds Buddha or somebody," Lee continued with a little smile. "Unfortunately, the good-looking women that find Buddha all go to the lamas, so where does that leave everybody else in Buddhism? And if they don't go to the lamas, the lamas *take* them anyway . . . in

Tibetan Buddhism, at least. I'm not sure how it goes in Zen, but . . . And they don't have lamas! That's the problem!" More unfettered laughter rocked the room. It was getting harder to catch everything Lee was saying as our laughter became the constant spice that heated and flavored the night.

"They have roshis, and senseis, and stuff like that. And *llamas* are known for having fantastic wool and being able to spit really toxic saliva at people that they don't like . . ."

This play on words stopped the translator, David H., in his tracks. He looked at Lee and said, "Lamas?"

"Yeah, you know *llamas*: l-l-a-m-a-s!" While Lee spelled out the word, delighted laughter broke out as the crowd followed the interplay.

"Un jeu de mots en Englais!" Lee explained in French. Hilarity reigned—the fun was out of control, and it felt great.

David, instantly thrown into the role of straight man, pursued, "It's a pun, right?"

Lee patiently continued, "No, it's a play on words in English. Translate that into English, because there are some Americans here and for Americans there's only one language." More laughter. Of course, everyone in Europe knows that Americans are notoriously uni-lingual.

"So, I didn't hear what the woman said because I was looking at her tits, but anyway," more laughter, "she said, 'What are you going to talk about tonight?' And I said, 'I don't know. I never plan. When I get up in front of the room, whatever I'm going to talk about happens, so I don't have a subject in mind.'

"So, I'm so crushed that the Sacred Bazaar isn't here. I'll probably talk about something meaningless and depressing. I had all of these fabulous Tibetan singing bowls from the seventeenth and eighteenth centuries, about fifteen of them. I was going to bring them up here and play them one at a time and sell them to you. Gosh, I feel terrible, because it's not about the money! This is the first bit of wisdom this evening, that is recognizable, of course, because we've been saying wise things since the beginning, but this is the first *recognizable* piece of wisdom, except for those who are particularly insightful and are able to *read* between the lines.

"But I also said to the woman, who was really sparkling and bright and young, very attractive, 'I might just insult people.' And she went"—Lee made a face of confused interest, then continued—"and that's when her boyfriend came in. If they had been here, boy, would they have been insulted!

"So, it's not about the money. Selling is what I do best. I've written a book on sex, I've written a book on child raising. I have had sex once or twice—I do have six children, so I have had sex eight or nine times." This tongue-in-cheek comment brought another torrent of laughs.

"I have six children, but I'm not a great parent, and I'm terrible at sex, but I'm a great salesman—when I want to be, which is most of the time. So when there's nothing to sell, it's difficult. How am I gonna have any fun? When I make jokes and insult you and share wisdom with you, it's sort of fun, but it's not like selling. If I was into Zen, I'd go, 'I can make jokes, but it's not like sitting!'

"You're feeling again. You're sitting there and your knees are killing you and your back is killing you . . . you have to be in Europe for this, because in America, no stick anymore. Oh, because Americans are such pussies, you know. Somebody's going to come in America and hit somebody with a stick and they're going to sue 'em for *abuse*!" More laughter.

"There you are, sitting, your back is killing you, your legs are killing you, and some sadist is walking down the aisle with this *stick*. And you know it's gonna hurt like hell . . . but the best part is coming up!

"You all have a parallel to this. For me it's sales, for you it's something else . . . art. If it's sex, I feel sorry for you, but it might be. Sex is okay, but what a thing to have your life center around, boy! Talk about wasting a life! It's nice, it's okay, you know, when it happens, just in the process of life itself. But when that's *it*: sex, sex sex! 'I only feel like a man when I'm having sex!' Ohhh man, come on! Grow up! That's the problem with not nursing when you're a baby. Okay . . . you've all had enough therapy, let's not get into that.

"So the thing is, I'm supposed to be a spiritual teacher, and I've been doing it about thirty years, with no scandals! Not only that, the reason there are no scandals is not because I hide it well; it's because there's nothing to have a scandal over! Unbelieveable! People get a big inheritance, they say, 'I want to give you my money,' and I say, 'No, put some in a trust fund for your children.' They look at me like, 'But, I love you, and you're my master, and I know the community is poor, and I want to give you this money!' And I say no. Do you believe that? And they call me a spiritual teacher! What century have I been born into?" More waves of laughter rippled through the room.

Lee forged ahead, "I should have been born three hundred years from now—in fact, I will! So will all of you. I hope we meet again. And the beautiful thing about it is, none of us will remember! Won't that be great! Imagine if we remembered! Here we are three hundred years from now, walking down the street and you go, 'You're the guy that was in Espace Harmonie! I bought a book and bronze from you!'

"That would be terrible, because I want to be unrecognized and unknown in the future. I want to just work behind the scenes, and have a little bookstore somewhere in the middle of Iowa, if there is such a thing. In three hundred years Iowa will probably be beachfront property, so . . . maybe in Viqc—that'll be nice—because France is going to do very well in the next couple of hundred years. That's why most of you are living here—good karma! Not because of the wine and the cheese, which *is* good karma," more laughter, "and the oral sex, which is also, you know, fair karma."

Lee paused ever so slightly as if to assess his audience. We had been laughing all along through his monologue but missed a beat at the "oral sex" joke. "Only a few people laughed! So you have no sense of humor about the reputation you all have around the world?" The audience responded now with plenty of laughter!

"Because 'Playboy' magazine did a—what do you call it?—survey on all different countries, and they asked all these questions about sex and oral sex and how many times a month and this, that and the other thing, and you all were the champions—oral sex!" More laughter. "'Playboy'! Maybe the interviewer was a man, and he only asked people that gave him oral sex. Obviously the survey was weighted. So, let's see, there was a thought I hadn't completed . . . so, ummm . . ."

Someone in the audience prompted, "Good karma for France!"

"Good karma for France!" Lee responded, gleefully picking up the thread again. "Yes! Not because of the wine or the cheese or the oral sex. Or your very, very, fine tattoo artists in France, and the very, very, fine graffiti painters in France—not because of that either. *Not* because of Baudelaire. *Not* because of Rimbaud. *Not* because of whoever you think—Picasso. Who wasn't French anyway . . . Just as an example, who's a good French artist?" The audience began to hum with people offering answers to his question: Monet, Manet, Renoir, Cezanne.

Lee continued, "Yeah, Cezanne. Monet, ah, not my taste. So, good karma, not because of all that, but because France is geologically situated—according to people who research these things—in one of the optimal geographic locations in the entire world, relative to being safe and secure from the natural catastrophe and turmoil that is going to go on for some years, all over the world. So, France is one of the sanctuaries. Which is why all of these fucking British and American and Dutch people are coming here!" Laughter broke out again.

"You know, they are forming little enclaves, not even learning your language! The Dutch even truck their own food in! Jesus Christ! It's unbelievable! And they're all coming to France—not because they're conscious; they're totally unconscious, they're as conscious as stone, like *you and I.* But everybody is telepathic with everybody else, and they *know* that France is going to be one of the sanctuaries in the world, according to people that research these things.

"So you live in a great place. And you know, maybe you'll even rewrite the Old Testament. Maybe even right where we sit, this very spot, will be the center of Sodom: 'Is there one citizen in the entire town who is not full of sin?' Something or other like that. I haven't read the Old Testament, but . . . One of my students is an ex-nun, and one of my students is an ex-priest—they happen to be married! First they left the church, then they got married. They didn't even know one another when they left the church. They met one another, one said, 'You're a priest,' and the other said, 'You're a nun,' and they've been very happy for many years."

Lee was happily engaged in busting the sacred cows of Western culture, both religious and secular, on many levels. These too, as he had let us know in a direct statement early on in the talk, were teachings in disguise; if fact, his entire hilarious monologue had been one, long teaching discourse, if we were able to get around the righteous, uptight, rigid mindset of our upbringing and just flow with him.

"So, I'm supposed to be a spiritual teacher. I've been doing it thirty years, so I've built up a bit of credibility, and I've managed to keep my student body small—and my reputation in the general public very small, but very large in the underground. So, things are great! Because as soon as you get popular, bad things start to happen. Sometimes just bad things happen, and sometimes bad things start to happen to you; your mind gets a little twisted.

"In fact, Corinne," Lee nodded toward a woman who was sitting nearby in the audience, "has—just this very day—had her book on psychosis come out. It's a little book, she tells me, and she didn't bring one to me tonight, so I was a little insulted, but I assume it was because of her humility. So then I figured, okay.

"So, you can read about what happens to you, how your mind gets twisted. In French! But if you can't speak French, her English is quite fluent, so you can speak to her in English, but her book is only in French. If you'd like to translate it and have it published in English, I'm sure she'd be very happy to accommodate you.

"So I'm supposed to be a spiritual teacher. After having done this for thirty years, things look really different to me than they did in the beginning, when you're in the blush of this—I call it a shift of context, but most teachers call it enlightenment, which I think is pretentious in the extreme. In the beginning you want to save the world, bring people into the wonder of this clarity and this light and love and . . . Very quickly you get the idea that everybody gives a lot of lip service to being brought into this domain of love and light and joy and all of that, but when it actually comes to *doing* something about it, that's a different story. Which you all should know about, 'cause you live in France!

"So, let's talk for a minute about the French and their *dogs*." People laughed again. Here was another topic of universal human standing: our attachment to our animals!

"You know how *that* goes: great big macho men with tiny little poofy dogs! And little old country men with gigantic fierce dogs that rip your face off, just for the fun of it. So what's that all about? I'll leave you to answer that. You're French, and all your friends have *the dogs*. But there's something wrong. There's something wrong in the way people relate to their *dogs*. It's worse in America, but I'm not in America—I'm in France. I'm talking to my students about some difficulty they have and this is what they do: they'll say, 'Well, so-and-so, what about so-and-so?' And I have to say, 'I'm not talking to so-and-so, I'm talking to *you*.'

"You know why I'm talking so loud? 'Cause I have a chest cold. What would you do if you had a chest cold? You would have cancelled the talk and stayed home and put on little warm compresses, if you were American," Lee switched to a whiney, pathetic little voice, "and drunk hot tea with honey and lemon!"

Dropping that characterization, he practically yelled, "FUCK IT! It's a piece of shit! You're going to lie down and kiss ass for a piece of shit? You have a chest cold? Fuck it! Go out and scream at the moon," he looked up, as if at the moon, and shook his fist in a play off Gurdjieff's teachings about feeding the moon, as opposed to feeding the sun with our states of being, " 'You're not getting me, you fucking piece of shit!'

"Don't let your body fuck you over, it's just a piece of shit. Okay, if you're on your back and you can't get out of bed, I understand that. But when you have a fuckin' little sniffle: 'How are ya?' 'I'm sick.' Grow up, people! So I figure the louder I talk, the faster this fucking thing is going to go away. I'm not going to lie down and roll over because I have a fuckin' chest cold. 'How are ya?' "

Lee made pathetic little coughing sounds and said in a weak voice, " 'I have a seminar this weekend, and I hope I can talk.' Fuck it! It's just shit! So don't lie down and roll over for this piece of shit, unless you have to, absolutely, one hundred percent have to.

"Chögyam Trungpa Rinpoche, who was a great Tibetan Buddhist master, died when he was forty-seven or forty-eight years old. He had been drinking two to three liters of sake a day for twenty years. When they did an autopsy on his body the doctor said, 'This guy should have been dead fifteen years ago; no human being could live with a liver like this.' That's how great a master he was. 'Fuck the goddamn liver; I'm teaching Buddhism!' That's the way you handle this piece of shit," Lee gestured toward his chest, indicating the body with all of its impermanence and fragility.

"And once in a while have some sex, so you get the idea that even though this is a piece of shit, it does have some utility. And if you have a good voice, *sing*—even if you have to sing in the shower alone! And if you don't have a good voice, spare the rest of us. Like if you're an artist, and you're a good artist, create, create, create! If you're a lousy artist, spare the rest of us.

"Do you think that people who have bad taste are going to learn to have good taste if they buy your shit and put it on their walls—no! And you know how many bad artists there are for every good artist?

Thousands! In Katmandhu, in Nepal, for those of you who missed the hippie revolution, there are twenty thousand painters of Tibetan thangkas. Twenty thousand painters, and there's less than twenty good ones; the rest are hacks. But it doesn't stop tourists from going there and buying tons of thangkas. The average person can't tell the difference. The average person can't tell the difference between a good therapist and a total psychotic. The average person can't tell the difference between a real spiritual teacher and an idiot, which is why there are so many law suits all over the world and so many people feeling betrayed and abandoned from some idiot having sex with them or taking all their money or beating them or starving them or—God knows what these idiots do!

"So in the beginning, after the shift of context, I thought, 'Oh this is wonderful, we'll save the world and I'll join forces with the 'Great White Brotherhood' and the forces of light and we'll go out there and really do something!' I should have known, after teaching for two months, when I made the gentlest of suggestions to the people around me at that time, we should start a conversation on vegetarianism. Fifty percent of the people left, that night! I should have seen it coming. But I was still a little innocent and a little naïve, and I thought, 'Oh well, those people just weren't serious about their work.'

"Then years went by, and years went by, and years went by, and we all fell in love with one another. The teacher falls in love with the students, and the students fall in love with the teacher, and it's all a big happy family, and everybody gets deeply bonded, even more bonded than you are with your own blood family—sometimes. And then what happens? People become more and more resistant. Not everybody, cause once in a while some practice hero shows up. And the teacher can go, thank God there's a couple of them around, who are really willing to practice. The rest just . . . you know, I put the chair where I want it, and they put the chair where *they* want it! Now I'm sure that whoever moved the chair is going to say, 'I didn't see you put it there. If I had seen *you* put it there, of *course* I would have left it there.'

"Let me tell you how it is: Every teacher is supposed to live in the now, right? If you're a student of a teacher, and you believe that your teacher lives in the present moment—you believe your teacher's enlightened, you believe they live in the now, right? So why is so much of your relationship with your teacher wrapped up in apologizing for things that are in the past? Ever thought of it that way before? Start thinking of it that way now, my friends.

"So, we want the Path, we want God, or if you're non-theistic, we want clarity or presence or Buddha-mind or something like reality, truth. Every one of us has our holdout. The fifty percent of the people that stayed when we started considering vegetarianism didn't have a problem with changing their diet, that wasn't where their holdout was. With some people, it's sex.

"I hang out with unusual people, or maybe not unusual. A lot of my spiritual teacher friends have a very unusual relationship to sexuality, so all my students hear the stories, because I love gossip, you all know that. I don't write any of it down, but I collect gossip like some people collect stamps, except I don't put it in an album . . . So, when there's no microphones on and no tape recorder running, I'll tell some of my students, 'Oh, did you hear this about this person or that person? Oooh, whoa . . .' Because some of these people are just twisted! What else can we say? They should be in therapy.

"Of course, my students, many of them, think that I should be in therapy. And since many of my students *are* therapists, they think that I should be in therapy with *them*!" Another outbreak of contagious laughter. "They'll even say to me, you know, to my face, 'If you would just do such-and-such and such-and-such, your teaching would be . . . you'd be happier, and . . .' But I was very happy. I was an ecstatically happy person before this work!" More laughter. "I had a wonderful life, I had my own business, I made my own schedule, I had freedom to travel . . .

"But listen, let me tell you what a nerd I was. I was in California at a conference once years ago, and this woman, this girl—I don't know, over eighteen, so she was legally a woman, but I like to call women girls 'cause it makes me feel younger. You know, who's a woman anyway? So, okay, there's this girl, and all the guys are sleeping with her, and she'll go out with anybody, so my turn comes around, and we go out to dinner and a movie and finally it's three-thirty in the morning and we're still *talking*!" Laughter was building up again.

"That's the extent of my social skills, back in the day. And then about four o'clock in the morning, I finally get up the nerve to say, 'Would you like to come back to my place?' Inside she goes, 'Jesus, I thought you'd never ask. I was ready five hours ago! What the hell is wrong with you? Why don't you grow up?' Anyway, so we get back to my place, and the first thing she does—this is to show you how really naïve I was—is she rips off her wig!"

Everyone was in on the joke now. Lee was being hilarious, his timing was perfection as he paused slightly, just long enough for the laughter to subside the right amount, then he continued, "And you know, that beautiful, long hair wasn't real! Oh my God!"

Another wave of laughter, so purifying, so right, came rolling through. It seemed that somehow, in some almost miraculous way, our laughter, spurred on by Lee's hilarious delivery and skewering of himself, his scatological and bawdy joking around about the human condition was paradoxically ushering us into a state of innocence and wholeness. I wondered, how does he do it?

"I was shocked, but I figured, fuck it man, it's four-thirty in the morning, I'm gonna get something out of this shit! I didn't care what her fucking hair looked like, things were going to move forward!" The room exploded with laughter.

"Okay, so I'm supposed to be a spiritual teacher, in spite of my language and everything else, and the thing is, after thirty years of laying out sublime dharma—it may not seem so tonight, but you know, when I get on a dharma roll, I can be eloquent. Sublime! Oh! And we've got some of this stuff on tape, so if any of you want to devote your life to being an archivist in my community, you'll be able to hear it. So after thirty years of laying it out, what happens? I mean, honestly! I put the chair here—after thirty years!—I put the chair *here*, and one of my students comes and moves the chair *there*.

"So, I still give talks like this for the fun of it, except I'm crushed tonight cause the Sacred Bazaar is not here. Alain, whose store this is, is an old friend, so he likes me to talk here. I like to do things like that for old friends. He's not a *real* old friend—ten years maybe? Eleven years, okay, not bad. So, we're very good friends. I don't see him that often, which is probably why we're such good friends." More laughs. "You know, people can get to be kind of *wearing* after a while . . . some people!

"So I do things like this, but really, the whole emphasis of my teaching work is completely shifting, and shifts of that dramatic a nature take some time to begin and progress and actually come into their own. All this enlightenment business is: if it happens, it's going to be an accident anyway, and there's nothing that you can intentionally do to make it happen. So instead of, 'Let's all try to be the new race that heralds in the New Age and have little enclaves of conscious beings sharing wisdom together,' I have a better idea. How about we start being *human*? 'No! I *am* human!' No, you're human based on your species, but you are not human based on the maturity of your feelings, your emotions or your mind. Maybe there are a few human beings in this room, but I mean, 'you' as a general comment. 'You/us'—I include myself. So how about we just try to be human, learn to be human, and then, if by accident enlightenment happens—great! No problem, capitalize on it, make use of it, do something with it.

"We become human, we live and we raise our children with some degree of genuine tenderness and affection. Most of the people in this room probably say, 'I do raise my children that way.' No you don't! You love them. You *love* them, but you wouldn't know how to raise your children with genuine affection and care and respect and regard if your *life* depended on it. Just because you love somebody doesn't mean you have any degree of understanding of how to express that love in a way that that person is able to receive the love you feel.

"Oh, I'm glad that woman from New York didn't stay—man, her brain would have been melted by now! Man, she would have peed in her pants!" Once again there was lots of laughter, the constant element of this talk. Lee continued, "Oh, maybe she should have stayed. Alain and I would have really liked that. Alain and I sort of have similar tastes. We would have remembered that one for a long time. Every time I'd see him I'd say, 'Remember that woman at your store last year who *peed*—whoa! Oh, yeah!' "

Lee turned to the table at his side, which held a large bouquet of red and white flowers and a beautiful *murti* of Yogi Ramsuratkumar, set on a silk brocade. "Look at these nice Indian silks that they put here. Wow. I hope I deserve it. Cause if I don't, bad karma for Alain, or whoever put this here. If I deserve it, good karma; if I don't, bad karma. Just putting an attractive piece of silk on a table! If I deserve it, good karma. If I don't deserve it, bad karma.

"So the thing is, to just be human produces a foundation of strength and clarity and dignity and nobility upon which God or Truth or the Universe is able to stand and feel steady and solid in its footing. That's a metaphor—you understand that. It's not like God is a creature and comes down . . . everybody got that? That's a joke! I know you're intelligent human beings; I'm *not* being condescending or belittling. That was a joke! I *know* you get it . . . if I wanted to be condescending, I would spin such webs around your minds you wouldn't even know I was being condescending, and all my students would be going, 'Oh man, he is fucking those people up tonight!' And you'd all be sitting there going . . . " Lee's face took on a look of blank incomprehension.

"What does all of this—what do you call it, stream of consciousness, rambling?—have to do with spiritual teaching, you might be thinking? Or you might be thinking, 'I didn't go to a movie for *this*?' " Laughter again. "Well, the thing is, as long as we are stuck in the orthodoxy of our psychologies, we cannot become human. We can animate a kind of neurotic human—something that sort of looks human—but we can't really be human, unless we are able to somehow manage our unmanageable psychology. The bad news is: it's impossible. Nobody can manage their unmanageable psychology. The good news is: some people have done it anyway.

"Of what value is trying to accomplish something that is possible? If it's possible, it's no great thing. If it's possible, you all can do it because you all are brilliant in a certain way. Take a look at your neurosis. What genius put together the flawless perfection of that manifestation? You! *You* put it together." More laughter. "Look at how perfectly self-hating you are—but perfectly! Your manifestation of self-hatred is pure genius. Your manifestation of vanity is pure genius. And who put it together? You!

"So certainly, whatever is possible, you can do, and you can do relatively easily if you really put your mind to it. What's really interesting and exciting, especially in the beginning, is going after what's impossible. After thirty years it's frustrating and maddening, but in the beginning it's very interesting and exciting—because it *has* been done. Even though it's impossible, by definition it's impossible, it *has* been done.

"I'm not just talking about people that get born in a certain state of brilliance and clarity, like Ma Anandamayi, or someone like that. I'm talking about people like my own master, Yogi Ramsuratkumar, or Arnaud Desjardins' master, Swami Prajnanpad, who by their own testimony and confession, started out as just guys, like any 'just guys.' Yogi Ramsuratkumar was a sort of a mad-yogi-just-guy and Swami Prajnanpad like a kind of intellectual-businessman-just-guy. Both of them realized what they realized, despite the impossibility of that realization.

"Yogi Ramsuratkumar was not born enlightened. He never claimed anything like that. He was just a guy, just an average kid, and He liked sports and He was a good student, and some inspiration drove Him to seek the impossible. And with the help of Sri Aurobindo and Ramana Maharshi, first, and then his final and abiding master, Swami Papa Ramdas, the impossible happened. So we have very real examples, contemporary examples, of people just like you and me. I used Indians as examples, but it could be Westerners, it could be Tibetans, it could be Japanese, it could be anybody who can realize the impossible. Because in human terms, by definition, it's impossible to do what any of us who have entered the Path, entered the stream of the dharma, are working towards. But we have to be *human*.

"When the energy of the Universe begins flowing into our system, any weak spot in that system will immediately be magnified to an unbelievable degree. So the things that are not truly human in us—like vanity, pride, greed, violence, aggression, hatred—if those things are still present when the entire energy of the Universe starts flowing through the system, those are the things that get magnified. Love has *nothing* to do with it. Some of the worst charlatan teachers in the world, the cruelest, the most violent, the most unethical, actually loved their students—whatever love means. You know, loved their students.

"Love has nothing to do with it. It's about being human, so that when the energy of the Universe starts flowing through *you*, when the switch gets turned and out it comes, the intensity of that energy gets expressed in service and compassion and in ethical ways, instead of in violence and abusive, manipulative sex. The likelihood of anybody in this room, including myself, realizing full enlightenment in this lifetime, is statistically insignificant. However, it happens. It's a phenomena. And should it happen to one of us, given the inviolability of the law of karma, we want to be damn sure that we aren't going to screw it up.

"The way to be damn sure that we're not going to screw it up is to become human. That was such a nice, neat little package I don't think I'm going to go on, because if I keep talking I know I'm going to screw it up. I'll start talking about women's sexual fluids, and you all will forget everything I just said. Or, you know, something interesting—sex with animals. That doesn't interest me, but when I was fourteen years old, one of the kids in my school class went to his uncle's farm for the summer, and his uncle had goats and sheep, and when this guy came back, boy did he tell some stories! That stuff was kind of interesting, kind of strange but fascinating in a certain way." Lee chuckled. "So I know if I keep going I'm going to start talking about . . ." The laughter was just subsiding as Lee asked if there were any questions.

"Not necessarily about anything I said in the last hour, but whatever might be . . . I know how to fry a really good egg! Well, if you put too much oil in the pan, no matter how good the egg is, it's too oily. And if you don't flip it properly, the yolk breaks and then you don't have perfect egg over easy. Yes?"

A woman had her hand up. The question was, "It's about the education of children . . ."

"It's a gigantic subject," Lee commented.

"I have a two-and-a-half-year old child. Are there activities to be done . . ." she began.

Lee interrupted her mid-sentence, "Give them as much freedom to explore and experiment as possible. With the exception of things that are physically dangerous, or psychically dangerous, like horror movies, let them explore and experiment and kind of be by their side. Like that. Give them lots of physical affection and always explain to them what's going on.

"Like if you're going to take a five-hour car ride, and the child has to sit strapped into a car seat, you always want to make sure that you tell the child ahead of time. By age two or three they have language, and they can understand, but even at six months old, you tell them, 'We're going to take a long car ride, and you're going to have to sit in the car seat, because that's the law.' Because it's important to obey the law. When they get older you can tell them that not all laws are just, but there are laws.

"Some laws are very stupid, but they are laws, and if we want to live our lives as freely as possible, we have to obey the laws. America and France both are full of stupid laws, but they are laws. Whatever we think doesn't matter so much, because we are not bigger than the state. If most of us were bigger than the state, the state would probably be even worse than it is now.

"Instead of hopping in the car, strapping them in, and then three hours later they're screaming because they didn't know what was going on, you *explain* to children ahead of time: 'I know you're going to have to sit in the chair for a long time, and it may be a little uncomfortable, but I'll do the best I can, and we can play and I'll talk to you.' Then, in their consciousness they know what to expect. Children should have their world explained to them, not in a stupid way, but in a very gentle and sweet way. 'We're going to visit Grandma, and you know how Grandma is: she always tries to stuff you with as much food as she can get down your mouth. You know, that's just the way Grandma is, and it's not a bad thing, so eat a little bit and make Grandma happy.'

"It's very important for children at that age to have their world figured out. Most children don't like surprises, things that are unexpected. You want to explain things clearly. It makes a one hundred percent difference in children's response to things. That should be useful. Anything else?"

"The question I have is that I have a seventeen-year-old daughter whose boyfriend is really quite hooked on drugs, and we'd like to know what to do about that."

Lee responded, "Mostly in situations like that I just pray. If children have been raised intelligently, with respect and affection, and if their family home is a sanctuary for them and not a hell realm, such children will experiment, and they will usually come back to a very sane and healthy life, after they experiment. It's very difficult to stop a child from experimenting.

"My children have experimented, and I've always let them know that I'd rather know about it than not know about it. But I've tried to make as few rules as possible, because when they're that age, they don't like rules. They're trying to find themselves. So you let your home be a sanctuary for them, so they can always come home. If a child feels ashamed because of their behavior, so ashamed that they don't want to come home, that's the worst thing. You always want to make sure that home is sanctuary.

"My mother never, under any circumstances, made me feel that I couldn't always come home, whenever I wanted, no matter how old I was. I had some really sick girlfriends. You know, when you're young and socially inept, you'll take anything. I had some *really* sick girlfriends. My parents never said a word, about any of my girlfriends, about any of my friends, never. Not one word. They never said a word about how I spent my money, and I could feel often that there was disagreement, but there was never any criticism. Only, 'Do you need some help? Do you need anything?' I'd always say no—end of conversation.

"So it's really important that your home be a sanctuary, so that whenever your children *need* to come home, they know that they won't be criticized, they won't be yelled at, they won't be given sermons, they'll just be welcomed: 'I'm glad you're home.' And pray a lot, which is what I recommend to everybody, you know. Most of our kids, they get to be teenagers and they're trying to find themselves, and the best of kids will experiment. It doesn't mean that they're not great kids; they're experimenting, they want to find out what the story is. If they've been raised well, in ninety-nine percent of the cases, they'll experiment and they won't hurt themselves too badly, and when the experiments are over, they'll go on about their lives. Sometimes covered in tattoos, but . . ." This brought on lots of laughter!

"Great. Thank you. So there are a few books on the back table, and a few tapes, because Alain has a publishing company and he's published a number of our books. So, even though I couldn't bring any, he had some of the books that he has published, and they're on the table in the back. He had some in the store upstairs, and a few DVDs on the Tibetans filmed by Arnaud Desjardins—which, if you haven't seen them, are magnificent—and some other odds and ends.

"So, I'll be behind the table in the back if you have informal questions you would like to ask. I'd be happy to talk with anybody, and to say hello to old friends. I'll see you next year. I'm leaving Europe in a few days, but I *will* be back, if the American government lets any of us out next year!" Everybody laughed but the Americans in the room. It was a sobering thought, the situation of personal freedoms being taken away so quickly in our own country.

Lee continued with an ironic smile, "It could go either way; it's getting very touchy. I guess they figure as long as we stay in the country our political sensibilities will not be *poisoned* by the evil ideas of foreigners!" Lee chuckled.

"When the shit comes down in America, I'm coming *here*, anyway . . . I'm a runner, I'm not a fighter! We've got our place here, and this is where I'm going to run to first. So . . .thank you for coming out in this weather, although I guess somebody said it's sort of like this in Paris in the winter, so I guess you're used to it. I'll be at the table at the back. Great. Thank you."

After the talk Lee was inundated by people as he stood behind the little table. Everyone waited their turn; forty minutes after the talk, people were still milling about and slowly leaving.

I ran into Alain René upstairs, who told me a little lila of Lee: When Alain René hosted Lee and Arnaud and their large party at his home near Hauteville back in early July, Lee had taken a minute to stop at a rose bush growing by the patio and swimming pool. Alain René had noticed that, for some reason, Lee had given that rose bush some attention, looking at it intently and touching its leaves. At the time, the rose bush was struggling for its existence; it wasn't really blooming. Now, almost three months later, that same rose bush was thriving and covered in roses—an amazing transformation! Hearing this story, I smiled. That is exactly what Lee does with all of us—he breathes life and energy into our potential, even when we come to him half-dead, struggling, wounded, not well-rooted in the soil of life, and in his company, the master gardener, we begin to bloom.

There were many exchanges of "À l'annee prochaine" and "au revoir" that night, as the members of the sangha who would not see Lee again until next July took their leave. We left the bookstore loaded down with bouquets of flowers from Lee's talk and walked through scattered raindrops the few blocks to the van. Lee would be leading a small caravan through the city to Maison Raphael, where people needed to pick up their luggage or backpacks that had been stored there for the day.

Once we were finally in the van with the two cars behind us, we immediately hit a traffic jam heading south toward the Seine in the maze of narrow, one-way streets. We were riding on the high energy of the talk, and Lee's mood was at the same time ebullient, expansive and fierce. When we found ourselves locked into a long line of traffic on a side street that seemed completely stuck, he snapped, "Find another way!" Even a three second hesitation in our response was too long. Gearing up to his speed to the best of our ability, we plotted an alternate route through the northern part of the city, heading west.

We were slowly making our way through the traffic on Magenta Boulevard when suddenly there was smoke everywhere in the streets, people running here and there, police cars, lights. A man stood in the middle of the street and waved us to the left; obviously there was a fire up ahead, and we couldn't continue down Magenta Boulevard.

Lee made a sharp left and barreled down the first available street. Immediately we had to find a completely different route. If we could just get to the Place Concorde and across the Seine, we could take the river road west to Boulogne. Once again we found ourselves in the maze of the city, navigating one-way streets, careening down them, as Lee would not slow down but seemed to speed up, as if the fire was actually in his hair and the only way to put it out was to get to the Seine. Ann would call out the names of streets as we flew past three, four, five, ten different small streets in twenty seconds' time, the van was moving so fast. Every move we made seemed urgent, fraught with importance. The egoic mind wanted to say, "Hey, what's the big hurry? Settle down. Can't we just slow down long enough to read the map?"

As Lee often says, he's got to have movement, momentum, and at this point in our Paris sojourn, after the long day and the liveliness of the talk and all the people at Espace Harmonie, Lee had a tremendous amount of momentum. Obviously he didn't want to break his speed in any way. How can we know what hangs in the balance in moments like these? Every morning on Lee's ashrams we sing the *Sadguru Ki Arati* chant in Sanskrit, and one of the verses translates into English:

Give us your grace, true guru,
to help us over the world;
show us the true path, dispel wrong ideas;
hail to the one who has revealed the eternal light
and whose existence is a divine play.

In circumstances like these, the phrase, "whose existence is a divine play" comes into focus, and we can glimpse that Paris is Lee's playground of the moment. To have momentum in the Work is to engage the Universe in its own game—to play at a high stakes level. Speed, in this sense, is a metaphor for light and sound and its power to create the world. The guru's momentum is one of the ways Blessing Power is made manifest in the earthly realm. At the same time that Ann and I were Lee's agents, enrolled to assist him in gaining and maintaining momentum, we were also being offered an opportunity to be trained by him; trained in how to function full-on, with all the senses engaged, totally alive to the moment, take the cues from the Universe moment by moment . . .

We had lost one of the two cars following us through the city. Ann kept making calls to Brinda—to let her car know what street we were on—and looking for the street signs, which was no easy feat in the dark. Juggling the map and the flashlight, straining to see the tiny streets on the map as we hurtled along, I momentarily gave up trying to locate us on the map and fell back on instinct. I knew if we kept going west and south, we would hit the river sooner or later.

"Which way do I go? Quick, quick, quick!" Lee insisted, urgency in his voice spurring me to act and act *now* as we came upon another intersection.

I spied a street veering off in the general direction we wanted to go and said quickly, "Take that one!" At one point Ann called out the name of the street ahead and I was finally able to pinpoint our location. "Yes! That's our street! Go, go, go!"

Ann remembered that we needed to find Madelaine. We drove helter-skelter through the streets that were illumined by the lights of the night and shining from the rain. People walked everywhere, and the cafés were humming with life. Brinda called on the cell and we were reunited just before Ann saw the street sign for Madelaine and steered us toward the Place Concorde. We were right on course!

It had been an unbelievable rollercoaster ride through the sensory panorama of the Paris night. There was no time to realize what an amazing *bardo* trek it was, or to assess how Lee was offering us the opportunity to function beyond ourselves and work as a team—and yet, there was no way that we could have done what he asked us to do without working together. We were riding a razor's edge, and it was incredibly exhilarating.

We crossed the Seine, still navigating our way along using the map and our memory of Paris. We took the river road west through the heart of the city. For the next ten minutes we got our last sight of Paris at night—the glimmer of lights on the Seine, the exalted architectural wonders and stone sculptures accented in soft pastel shafts of light, the wet streets—all these things made an almost psychedelic tableau of the City of Lights on this amazing wonderful night. I don't think I had ever felt alive in quite that particular way before.

After a few more navigational hurdles, we were almost at Maison Raphael. Lee turned to Ann and I and said, "Good work, navigators." That was unexpected! Exultant, yet in a very grounded and sober way, Ann and I looked at each other and smiled, breathing a small sigh of relief.

It was almost midnight as we reached Boulogne Billancourt. Finally settling down to rest, the images and impressions of the night were thick and active in my awareness. Driving home in the rain, the smoke and fire of the Paris night, soaking up the lights on the Seine, the beauty of the city, I realized again how much Paris has grown on me . . .

Truly, Europe gets under your skin. One of the many things I love about France is that it is a fertile field in which the esoteric underpinnings of Western culture slumber and ferment, like the fine wines produced in this extraordinary land. This can be felt in any given moment, even in the most ordinary of circumstances. As we travel and live in France, this power, so encoded in the culture, can be tapped like a bedrock source of protean fuel, which blazes hot when applied to the Work in the company of a real teacher. Paris is a unique source of energy in this way; despite its coldest and most aloof elements, this place—which has sheltered the likes of G.I. Gurdjieff, Ernest Hemingway, Henry Miller, and so many artists and visionaries and ordinary people—welcomes you and takes you to its vast and beating heart.

The Last Dance

Paris—Maison Raphael
October 1, 2005

Every year Lee gives his last seminar of the summer at Maison Raphael, located in Boulogne on the outskirts of Paris, on the first weekend in October. Maison Raphael was founded by three disciples of Arnaud, specifically for the purpose of providing a sanctuary in which therapeutic work and "Lyings" could be provided, under the auspices of Arnaud's teaching.

This year marked the ten year anniversary of the inception of Maison Raphael and the beginning of Lee's seminars there. To celebrate the event, Arnaud would arrive later this afternoon, and for the next two days Arnaud and Lee would be giving two, thirty-minute sessions of silent *darshan* in the main room to two different groups of students and friends. It had been arranged in this way to accommodate all the people who wanted to participate, many of whom were not enrolled in Lee's seminar, but were either members of the Hauteville association or friends of the Path.

Lee was up long before dawn this morning, setting up his Sacred Bazaar in the tiny office just off the salon where the seminar would be held. Before the first session, which would start at eight-thirty, Lee placed the four-foot tall Burmese Buddha and five monks in front of the room by the chair where he would sit to give his talk. He had also placed a two-foot tall, one-hundred-and-fifty-year old wooden Japanese Buddha directly beside his chair.

The relatively small group room of the center, typically used for group therapy, had white walls, a thick beige carpet and was appointed with photographs of sages and saints who have been important to Arnaud's work: Arnaud himself, Anandamayi Ma, Lee Lozowick, Swami Prajnanpad, Yogi Ramsuratkumar, Kongtrul Rinpoche. Two large windows opened out upon a disheveled green growth of courtyard, the presiding deity of which is the biggest, healthiest cherry tree I've ever seen. It's an island of sanity, of that which is organically good, surrounded by the concrete, asphalt, exhaust fumes and pollution of the city. The first time we came to Maison Raphael was in April, 1995. Bernard brought a large wooden bowl full of cherries from that tree to Lee and our small group. They were so delicious that we ate most of them at one sitting.

The cherry tree and greenery in the little cloistered space behind Maison Raphael added to the feeling of being in a sanctuary, providing shade and privacy to the seminar room. This room is always packed beyond capacity for Lee's seminars. This weekend would be no exception: there were about sixty people sitting on the floor on *zafus* in a tight arrangement, knee to knee, elbow to elbow.

Lee started out selling the marvelous artifacts that surrounded him. Their serene, devotional, compassionate faces spoke to us as he described them, saying, "They're really alive, and they don't like to be lying in a box with no affection or light. This guy," he pointed to the Japanese Buddha, "wants to radiate you with blessings. If you don't believe in God . . . actually, Buddha believed in God, but the Buddhists don't! . . ."

The first of many rounds of laughter moved across the room. Most of the people at this seminar had come to hear Lee teach many times in past years; they were familiar with his style and ready to get on his train. In some ways it was similar to Lee's week at Hauteville; we were just picking up from where we stopped last October.

"So, we're on the Path and we want to get enlightened! Doesn't that seem strange to you?" Lee charged ahead. "The highest aim! When I first started teaching I thought I wanted that. I thought I already had it! Ha, ha! That's a joke! And I thought I would guide others . . . Ha ha! I've had students for twenty-five years and they can't even get out of a car quickly! And we're going to get enlightened?! Because most of us are barely human. *Barely* human! Some of us are not even barely human . . ."

Okay! It was going to be Lee's familiar use of harangue, retort, declamation, blistering commentary, pointed sarcasm and occasional bombast, woven into a seamless whole with the fine threads of compassion, clarity, kindness, understanding and total empathy. Why do we keep coming back for more? Because Lee is only telling us the truth, and everything he does is for us, not for himself. He strives for our betterment, he carries the flame for us when we cannot; he is a beacon of clarity, holding the standard aloft and calling, "Over here!" Beneath his words there hums the mood of unconditional acceptance and even—dare I say it?—love for the human creature.

As he has so many times, Lee now spoke about how much his teaching has changed in the past thirty years. "So, my teaching has changed. The whole idea of enlightenment comes to me once a year in a dream, because the thing is, that happens anyway in its own good time, no matter what we do about it. We are looking for something real, something profound, to express itself in our world, as Swami Prajnanpad says, to reveal our 'intrinsic dignity,' our 'intrinsic nobility.' Once this clarity, this reality becomes true of us, we have to be human to start with, which is why Swami Prajnanpad came up with 'Lyings' to begin with—to make us human, not enlightened. Once we are human, then we can work.

"When you are in the light, to sound New Age, everything is brilliant; your intrinsic dignity and intrinsic nobility is brilliant and so are your neurotic qualities. If your neurotic qualities haven't been purified, they become magnified. Power, violence, sex . . . . When we find ourselves in this state of awakening, everything gets magnified. People tap into an ocean of energy that magnifies and intensifies everything—sadism, violence—so, if your tendencies have not been accepted and worked with . . .

"With more ordinary tendencies, like pride and vanity, you may look like a stupid ass, but you don't hurt anybody. Unfortunately, the darker side of most of us is not just pride and vanity. If during the Path you tap this tremendous source of energy, and you have not come to terms with the deepest neurotic part of yourself, then you will just as easily animate *that*."

Lee talked about the man who led his students to put poison gas on the subway in Japan. He loved his students. "Love is not the point. Love happens. It's very real and wonderful, but love just happens. Because these people love their students doesn't make them masters, or their love couldn't bring integrity to their relationships. The love of the master and disciple is the greatest love in the world—greater than the love of children and lovers."

Mentioning the visionary Wilhelm Reich, whose insights into the nature of the body and the basic life energies of the organic system revolutionized the psychological model of therapy and became the foundation of all body-centered therapies that evolved later, Lee said, "I'm a really armored person. I don't like to be touched! On the Path, when you live together, you get down to the bottom of things. You get intimately into the teacher's world. With the teacher and student this doesn't mean you have to be in the physical proximity of the teacher; you can be on the other side of the world and it doesn't matter, because the teacher is integrated into your world down to the base of things.

"They say, 'Absence makes the heart grow fonder.' It's true, with a certain amount of absence, but too much makes the heart forget. But, that's not so with the master. Absence makes no difference with the master because there is always reciprocity, no matter where our bodies are. So, the love of the master and disciple is the greatest love in the world. But love does not equate with Work integrity. I would like you to understand that should you realize yourself before you come to manage your psychology, it is possible that you could do more harm than good. Except that you have realized this cosmic revelation.

"So my work is not up here anymore," Lee indicated that "up here" meant sitting in front of an audience giving more or less formal teachings. "If I am the disciple of Yogi Ramsuratkumar, then His Blessings, His Grace, His Influence touches everything I touch. Like Arnaud and Swami Prajnanpad: the clarity and love and brilliance and genius of Swami Prajnanpad touches all that Arnaud Desjardins touches. That's how lineage works. If you are in a lineage, the whole force of it moves through your whole life.

"When I first started teaching it was the most sublime teaching, about realms of realization and dharma . . . People were doing what they always did—they were greedy, violent, vain—but they were *meditating*!

Continuing in this vein, Lee continued to warn us about playing with fire on the path and reiterated the need for ferocity in dealing with our own neurosis—we have to go deeper in seeing what motivates us. "One of the dangers of having a master is that we give all of our power and authority over to the master and assume that the master will take care of us. That's true, if we bring intrinsic dignity and intrinsic nobility to every thought, word and act." Lee mentioned again the reciprocity between master and student, emphasizing that the student has as much responsibility to maintain that reciprocity as the master.

Lee said, "I had an arduous practice, and I was very disciplined. I had the strong ability to place my attention and to intend and all that. That's what I brought to it, but the shift of context was all my Master. I had nothing to do with it. I didn't even know what it was.

"So this holding a sublime air over everybody's head, and I was there and they weren't, and there was a vast chasm between us had to change to getting down and talking on some level much farther down. Now I'm thinking, 'Let's see if we can teach people to get out of the vans quickly.' Let's see if we can understand how much space we take up and have the sensitivity to understand that when we are standing in a doorway, lost in thought and completely unconscious that we are standing in the way, if we can teach that, we'll have a start on sadhana!

"If the people of New Orleans were aware of the space they were in before the hurricane hit—because the space is more than the physical dimensions, it also includes the psychic space—they would have left in time to avoid some of the tragedy. There was a tremendous amount of human suffering because they didn't believe the warnings and were unaware of the space they were in."

Lee was taking this opportunity to speak out again about his own students and his teaching work, and the changes he has gone through, and especially the necessity and value of the Sacred Bazaar. Railing again about his American students was the segue into sharing with his new audience E.J. Gold's teaching, "Security is not the cure for insecurity," which Lee expanded to mean many things: love is not the cure for self-hate; success is not the cure for failure, and so on.

Lee continued, "E.J. is so full of energy, it's amazing he hasn't taken off into outer space yet! One of the things I've learned from him is how much extraordinary communication can be made over dinner. I don't need to be sitting up here with you out there. The most profound teaching lessons, across the board, with all of my students, have happened in informal situations when we were just hanging out and no fireworks were going on. So, the Sacred Bazaar and dinner parties . . . Thirty years of fantastic dharma all gets published and people study it and read it, and that has some effect, but people don't get altered in my talks. They get altered when we're just sitting together.

"I got this job as a spiritual teacher, sent in my resume last lifetime, and I didn't even know I'd gotten it! I want things to work. I look around and I see that my students are making huge sacrifices to work with me, but I know things aren't working to my satisfaction yet. When I walk into a room and two people have been viciously fighting, but I come in and they turn to me with beautiful smiles—I know it's not working, because if it was, they'd either keep fighting regardless of me walking in, or they wouldn't be fighting at all.

" ' God is gracious, God is good.' That's the same thing they say when they fly airplanes into buildings! Actually, God is quite heartless . . . " Lee said, not changing the subject, but developing a different aspect of it. The invitation was to follow his train of thought and connect the dots as he pointed to the Buddha and the monks that stood so serenely in front of the room. Each face was different, unique, and extremely beautiful to gaze upon.

He continued, "Look at those faces! There are feelings and emotions that go with the looks on those faces. If you look at those monks long enough, you can come to look like that too. I'm sort of like Santa Claus, you know. You have to pay me, but . . ." Everyone laughed, grateful, perhaps, for the comic relief.

"If you concentrate on this image long enough with the right attitude, you will become a person that looks like this. These came from Burma, from a temple where they were worshipped, and they absorbed that worship, and that worship radiates outwardly from them. They were made by practitioners for the purpose of transmitting sacredness.

"The point is, after thirty years of teaching and five years in metaphysics, which is why I understand the mechanics and physics of energy, it's often the most important transmission that happens in unexpected places. So that's why the Sacred Bazaar is here. There is an Influence that radiates from every object. It is not identical to the Influence of the master, but it is similar. It's never off; it's always on. It's more than art or reminding factors. When people buy these artifacts it creates a whole web of Influence. There is money involved, but that's life.

"E.J.'s gift, 'Security is not the cure for insecurity,' is a 'formulation' in the Work. If we want to bring our psychology into a manageable state, if we want to be deeply and profoundly effected by spiritual transformation, we have to deal with our psychology. The way we do that is by understanding the laws of psychology. Like Gurdjieff said, we are mechanical beings. Every once in a while we have to break out of our predictability. Usually that is due to a shock, like the death of a child or parent or sibling. You never get over something like that—like a child drowning. Shocks like that have the potential to throw us into a whole different domain not defined by our psychological script.

"So, the formulation is: Security is not the cure for insecurity; beauty, compliments and attractiveness is not the cure for self-hatred. Love is not the cure for unlove. We imagine if we had security we wouldn't be insecure, but it doesn't work that way. Just when we are about to make a big breakthrough, something happens—we get sick, or we back out, or we sabotage our own efforts in some way."

Lee stated that he knows people who have broken their arm, said the name of Yogi Ramsuratkumar, and had the bone knit instantly. This was a story I'd never heard before, and yet it did not seem unusual, since Yogi Ramsuratkumar had been the source of many miracles over the years of his life.

Lee continued, "Look at the incredible resources we waste on vanity! Cosmetic surgery—a desperate attempt to feel good about ourselves! Some people can't live with kindness. They have to do something to get their partners upset, so they will say something mean. So, God is good, and people are crazy!

"The only way out of our psychology is through it—directly through the storm. The eye of the storm is completely calm. What a metaphor! We are full of mad, whirling energy, but perfect equanimity is right exactly in the center of it, which is to be one with. But we keep adding things on top of it. The resolve to psychology comes from within us. Our therapist, lover, children cannot provide that. They try, but they can't. Even the pure, unconditional love of our children cannot make a difference because the solution is in here." Lee touched his chest.

"We have to find something in ourselves that outshines our psychological script. And when you do that, you have moved into a domain prior to your psychological script, so you can recreate yourself. Do you want to remain full of self-hatred? When you are one with who you are, in that place of perfect stillness, clarity, then you have a choice. Your psychological script is completely obviated, exactly in the middle of the storm. Two hundred mile an hour winds have no force there. In that space of oneness, even a lifetime of struggle is gone. You still remember your struggle, but in that space you have choice.

"That's why it's important to have a guide, because when we get into that space, we're so relieved to be relaxed, clear and calm, that we don't even think to have a choice. And the storm moves, so the eye of the storm moves. You become one with it, but it doesn't stay that way forever. It's now, now, now. In one moment you have choice because you are one with, but in the next moment you have to become one with all over again. So the energy of the guide helps you make the choice—now."

After a break for lunch we gathered again in the group room for the second session of the day. Lee was giving a serious answer to a question about women being in relationships with men who are psychologically little boys, when he stopped in the middle and more or less made an announcement about a new idea he had—pig cheese. This wasn't the first time the pig cheese idea had come up over the summer; possibly because Lee had playfully assumed the new identity of "Pig Man" during the tour with Shri, naturally because they were eating so much pork that he declared he was turning into a pig.

So, it must have been the pork—sausages, loin, sweet & sour, bacon, and more bacon—in pretty much every possible form. After all, Lee said, we have goat cheese, we have sheep cheese, we have cow cheese—why don't we have pig cheese? This humorous diatribe on pig cheese must have been inspired by lunch, which included—guess what?—sliced ham, prosciutto and *saucisson*.

The next thing I knew, he was talking about Krishna, Shiva and other forms of the Divine. Going from the ridiculous to the sublime has become, for me, one of Lee's trademarks in his talks. Today he created quite a juxtaposition of elements, in his fast, stream of consciousness flow of words that carried the seed teaching of tantra: There is only God, and it is that One, absolute Reality that is hidden or obvious in all these forms. On the fast path we find ourselves plunged into the infinite distinctions that can be made, appreciated and enjoyed in a unified field, where nothing is rejected.

Lee explained that in the Hindu tradition the God of love is called Krishna, who takes three forms—child, lover and warrior. You can worship Krishna in any of these. If you worship Shiva, you are worshipping the warrior aspect of the Divine, the force and masculinity; Shiva's weapons stand for his ability to chop and slice ego. Shiva is a dynamic force.

In Hinduism there are five forms of devotional relationship to the Divine, and each of us is moved more dominantly in one of those five forms. The five forms of devotion are: as a friend to the deity; as a parent to the deity as child; as a child to the deity as parent; as a servant to the deity; and as a lover. Some sects believe that to worship the deity as a lover is the highest form of worship.

Lee continued, "If your devotion takes the form of a parent to a child, like Krishna as Gopala, it doesn't mean that the Divine is infantile, but that there is a quality of love that a mother feels for her child, which is different than the love of a friend for a friend. This love has a protectiveness toward the baby that has a very fierce quality."

Lee was still answering the woman's question about being in relationship with men who are like children and treat her like a mother. He said, "It is possible to take the view of adoring the man as the adult with the quality of maternal love. It's delicate because there is nothing you can do about a man's response. One approach is to view the man as the divinity.

"In the Bauls tradition part of the esoteric relationship between man and woman is that each views the other as god or goddess, so that when we relate to the other person, we are relating on the highest level.

"The second approach is very simple and not easy. It's a process of relationship between the anima and the animus, the masculine and feminine poles of energy as manifested in woman and man. With luck, the man is the masculine pole and the woman is the feminine pole, although sometimes it's the opposite. There is the possibility when the man and woman can both rest in the ultimate masculine and feminine essence, that there is a relationship between mature adults, free of all quirky psychological struggles we have with each other and in our personal labyrinth. Woman, or the Feminine, because of its overwhelming feminine force, rests without manifesting because it's so powerful; if it were fully manifested it would burn everything up. For that force to manifest as sex or other, it has to be awakened and can only be awakened by the masculine pole. Only through adoration.

"When the masculine adores the feminine, not likes or appreciates but *adores,* that awakens the Feminine, which pours the creative fire toward the masculine. The only way the masculine can receive that force is to be mature, or it burns him up, so he appears childish, needy, or violent, because the power of the Feminine makes him feel meaningless and insignificant."

Lee's laughter communicated unknown worlds of knowledge built upon experience and the full interplay of irony and compassion. He continued humorously, "You've got to laugh at this stuff, because, we are sick fuckers! The chances of us being healthy are *so* small—you've got to laugh and enjoy the whole sick, humorous landscape of it. Like Woody Allen and other comedians.

"The ideal scenario is: man adores woman, Woman awakens, Woman's energy of awakening goes directly to the Source of Adoration, and that awakens Man. Because women are *already* awake, but they are asleep to that awakedness. Men are just lumps of flesh. Men are like, 'Huhh. Saucisson.' "

A number of people laughed in the crowded room. This is one stream of the teaching that always gets people's attention, for better or worse. Those who weren't laughing were looking a little worried. Many were just raptly listening and absorbing the exalted nature of the message as best they could.

He continued, "The best way to get a man to adoration is when he doesn't know he's doing it; he's getting it right because then it's pure. The woman can't say; 'Adore me, you prick!' Then he's just saying, 'Yes, Mother.' We don't want that. What quality of Mother is it that makes the child adore Mother?"

Lee began to talk about how children are always just pulling things down off the table and making a mess, but Mother is unconditionally accepting. A mother's unconditional acceptance makes a child peaceful and creates communion between mother and child.

"As long as we are trying to mold that child into something we want it to be, we don't have unconditional acceptance . . . If we are actively aggressing on that child so that they will be happy, the response will be rebellion. There are lots of other qualities, but I've never been a mother, in this lifetime."

Lee then told the story of the god Indra, who became so enamored with his own power that he decided to build a palace grander than any before it. He called in the celestial architect and said, "I want this and this and this—I want the greatest palace ever!" The celestial architect said, "Are you sure that's what you want?" Yes! And so, finally, as the palace was underway, one day a beautiful blue boy appeared and asked to see Indra. Indra let the blue boy in. The blue boy began to ask Indra about his fantastic palace, bigger and better than any palace that had ever been built.

The boy said, "So you want a palace that is better than any Indra before you?"

Indra was stopped in his tracks by this and asked, "Indras before me?"

Just then a long column of ants came crawling across the floor. The beautiful blue boy pointed to the ants and said, "Former Indras, *all*!"

Lee continued, "We've all been mothers before—men and women. We just have to remember. When we're unconditionally accepting, there is always a risk that you may start adoring the man and he becomes more childish, more demanding . . ."

However, the instruction Lee gave was don't hedge your bets. You have to just go for it. He said, "If we are always playing it safe because there is a risk involved, then we may be safe all our lives, but we have no idea what we missed because many times our risks will pay off."

Going back to the subject of our illusory search for enlightenment, Lee joked about talking of such exalted things as adoration. "We can barely have a moment of clarity, and we think we're going to be enlightened? Just because you don't think you're confused doesn't mean you're not confused!"

This struck me as an important point, because often when we think we aren't confused is when we are the most mired in the obscurations of the mind. How easily we can rationalize and justify our positions; until we have penetrated the depth of our illusions about ourselves, we cannot know when we are clear and when we are confused.

After a thirty minute break we reconvened for the last session of the day at two-thirty in the afternoon. Answering a question about "accepting that which is undesirable" led Lee into a discourse.

"As a general principle, when we find something undesirable, the overwhelming response to it is to reject rather than accept. We have the idea that to accept means nothing gets done about it: accepting what is, as it is, here and now means, 'I'll have this for the rest of my life and I don't want it.' There is a principle of energy that whatever we resist is strengthened. The instruction is to eliminate resistance. Even on the gross physical level, we build muscle through resistance. The more we struggle against something, the stronger it gets.

"It's the same inside us. In an objective sense, to accept is to eliminate resistance. When there is no resistance, the thing itself has no power, no authority. So the approach is to accept the fact that there is anger, not to accept 'I am angry.' We stop identifying 'anger is me.' The language we use is 'There is anger.' Yes, it's obvious, and 'I' am not angry; I am intrinsic dignity and intrinsic nobility. What stands between our ordinary experience and intrinsic dignity and intrinsic nobility are all our identifications. 'I am angry,' and 'I am smarter than anybody else.'

"So the process of beginning to accept is to dis-identify. There is anger, not, I am angry. You accept anger without implications. The implication is, 'I'm always angry, always will be, my father was angry, I'm angry too.' So, no extrapolations into the future or the past. When there is anger is when you work with it. When acting out starts, that's when you work on accepting: 'There is anger.' Purely, now there is anger, without all the extensions into the future. 'People don't love me when I'm angry,' or, 'I was angry when my children were little, how can I fix it?'

"Just accept that there is anger, without all the associations that go with it, and you will find—maybe you don't do it the first time you try, but you keep trying and you will find—that when there is anger without associations, there are lots of options, including not being angry. Ordinarily we act out or repress it and get sick or get depressed because it's negative, and we don't want to be negative.

"Just, 'There is anger,' without any emotional involvement. When you find yourself noticing there is anger, but *you* are not anger, that's the beginning of a complete shift."

A young woman named Valerie, who had been to Lee's seminar at Le Rozet a month before, was sitting near the front of the room. She looked very unhappy as she began her question, saying, "Lately I've noticed that I felt bored for some time. I find it absurd. So much is hidden in this ennui . . . ."

Lee said, "What do you do?"

She answered, "I'm a student of psychology." The room burst out in laughter at this point. Well, yes—everyone seemed to be in agreement—our psychological tangle is boring!

"Maybe you should study something *useful*!" Lee retorted, followed by another outburst of laughter. "Wow!" He chuckled, referring to the amazing numbers of psychologists and therapists in the room, but also in his seminars in general, "How can you all make money? There are so many of you!"

More laughter came on the heels of each comment he made as he continued to describe how she probably needed a hobby, like butterfly collecting—you know, you go out with those nets and catch a beautiful butterfly, you pour this poison on it to kill it, then you stab it with a pin and stick it on a board to look it. The metaphor was pointed and poignant; it seemed riddled with meaning for her, perhaps related to her childhood. It's often the case that pretty girl children are treated exactly like trophies. The metaphor worked on us all, as everyone can relate to having our life force thwarted or "killed" as we were forced into conventional forms of behavior, dress codes, and religious and social expectations. The young woman looked angry and upset.

After some further dialogue with her, in which she described her situation in more detail, Lee forged ahead, "When any of us find boredom hard to deal with it's because when we're not being entertained we're left with nothing but ourselves, and we are afraid of what we'll find. We're afraid we're going to find some terrible thing in there. Chögyam Trungpa Rinpoche says every human being has basic goodness; Swami Prajnanpad called that intrinsic dignity and intrinsic nobility. That's who we are essentially. Then there is this swirl of phenomena that we're all identified with—our psychological script, all the effects of childhood experience impinge on us, beatings and such, all that is what we're afraid of. We're afraid of discovering some dark something."

Crying now, she said, "I hear you, but I can't hear it all."

Lee replied, "Who can? That's not a problem. One American teacher said if we don't learn to live with boredom, we'll never have any spiritual realization because it's a basic human condition. If we take away everything we entertain ourselves with, what's left? We're not that interesting or that different from anybody else! So, 'I'm good-looking, I'm talented'—so what? We're really scared of that—of just being here and now without any crutches to lean on. Somehow we have to learn this lesson—that in Reality there is no ground to stand on; there is just this moment, and what is this moment? *Nothing*.

"A student of mine wrote a book titled *The Perfection of Nothing*. He means that the state of nothingness is impossible to describe; it's just what is. We have to figure out that the hopes and dreams we have are just phenomena, no matter what they are. Even if they are to serve humanity and heal people, they're all completely empty. And, we're human, we're going to live our lives and the things that feed us are empty—reading and movies and love and family and stylish clothing," Lee chuckled, "although it's better to realize that the person makes the clothes, not the clothes make the person, because if you have intrinsic dignity it doesn't matter what you wear.

"So, we have to come to this distinction that everything is empty and life is distinctions and love and beauty and children and so on. It's difficult to resolve because we're always trying to give substance to everything, because everything is insubstantial! We have to come to terms with what happens if we just sit with our boredom. If you just sit with being out of your mind bored . . . You don't feel that now, do you?"

Still looking somewhat miserable, she shrugged but said no.

"Lighten up!" Lee smiled brightly at her. She began to cry. "Why not?" His tone became very soft and tender now, as she cried with her hands over her face. "Can't you cry without your hands on your face? 'Cause I'm a male chauvinist pig, and to me it's just a pretty face! If you want an ugly face, I'll tell you how to have that karma. Do you still think I'm having fun at your expense?"

She answered no. Lee smiled, "Okay. That's generous!" He paused for a moment, then continued, "The next time you're bored, literally just stay there. Don't try to do anything about it. Just stay there. Don't do anything, if you don't have to go to class, until this boredom changes into something else. You know what I'm talking about? Okay, so just stay with the boredom. Don't dramatize or indulge it. Just stay there, as long as it takes—ten minutes, ten days—until it changes into something else. And when it changes into something else, you will be amazed—not horrified—at what it changes into.

"Before it changes into something else, you may have some scary thoughts go through your mind. Don't let those thoughts stop you from being bored—really bored. Because when you don't do something to shift the boredom, your mind is going to try everything it can to get you out of it, because the mind does not want what boredom will change into."

Tears were streaming down her face now as she looked at Lee. "Are you still with me?" he asked, very gently but firmly. "Okay. You set this up ahead of time. 'Next time I'm really bored, this is what I'm going to do.' You want the boredom to be pervasive, complete, total, so that when it changes into something else, it will be complete, total, pervasive. If you let your mind distract you from boredom, you'll never get to what you can get to. For most of us, the mind is the problem, because the mind knows exactly what scares us, seduces us, distracts us when we're trying to deal with some mood—fear, boredom, etc. The mind knows exactly what will distract us from breaking through.

"We're all telepathic. The mind says to a friend of yours, 'Call her now and invite her shopping.' We will create exactly the thing, we will mold reality, we will get our friend to call us . . . So we have to practice, practice, practice, time after time, to not allow the mind to take us away from the intention we have for transformation."

Lee talked about the Nobel Prize winner, Ilya Prigogene, and his theory of dissipative structures, which states that there is always breakdown before there is breakthrough. He said, "Before boredom changes into something else, the mind is going to break down. If we fall for it and get seduced, then we're never going to get to what boredom can change into." Lee used the discipline of dressage, and the principle of holding your seat on the horse, as an example.

"It's a principle of alchemy. You can't turn lead into gold until the lead disappears. The lead has to break down before gold can appear. What's the first thing we do? Run for entertainment. So you have to train your mind to keep your seat, when you're sitting with boredom and doing nothing.

"Look, Valerie, you're not going to blow up. Boredom, jealousy, whatever we feel is so intense we feel like we have to do something or we'll go mad, explode. No one has exploded yet! You will not go mad, have a heart attack. Will not.

"So we train the mind to simply stay in place until boredom changes into something else. It's a difficult thing to do, and nothing will happen except good things, but you have to not be distracted by the mind—because the mind can create nightmares. Stay with it, persist, until it changes, and what it changes into will not be horrible; it will be wonderful. But you have to persist.

"Like an athlete in the zone; if you keep running and don't stop, sooner or later . . . the zone! You're not tired, your breath comes naturally, like a panther, and you can run for days! Aahhh!"

Lee looked at Valerie with a smile. Obviously their interaction had come to a conclusion. She looked a little scared and sad, but she also looked brighter and like she'd just shed a big burden of some kind. He had given her a gift, an opportunity of much greater implications than she could possibly know at this point in her life. Such exchanges with Lee in seminars are never only for the person he is interacting with—it's almost always for most of the people in the room, and while one person has asked the question, many people benefit from the answer.

"Any other questions?" Lee asked.

A man raised his hand. "My problem is I get more and more excited as the day goes along . . . "

"Lucky man!" Lee joked with him. The man added that because of this, he had trouble meditating. Lee rejoined, "Don't meditate! Don't look a gift horse in the mouth." Lee explained what the English metaphor meant and everyone laughed. He continued, "If it's not broken, then don't try to fix it! If you're doing great as you are, then don't meditate. If the woman you are with says you have to meditate and it's the only way you can have sex—meditate!" We all seemed to relax into the laughter that spilled out effortlessly. The space was very rich and deep from Lee's interaction with Valerie, and now it was time to end. Lee got up and walked to the tiny adjoining room that held the Sacred Bazaar.

The dharma talks were over for the day at four-thirty. Around that time Arnaud arrived with Veronique. Lee and Arnaud spent some time together upstairs while the seminar room was re-arranged for the silent *darshan.* Women were seated on the left and men were seated on the right, with a narrow aisle between the men's and women's sides. When we went in to take our seats, the room was packed.

Promptly at five-thirty, the two teachers came in and took their seats in the rattan chairs that had been placed side by side, flanked by the windows that looked out on the garden. These were silent meditations, which could be done with eyes open or closed. Lee and Arnaud sat with their eyes open. To my perception, Arnaud was a mountain of awareness; he seemed to be looking beyond us, into a domain that exists here and now, while his eyes communicated a tremendous depth of joy and recognition. Lee was his radiantly ordinary self; I kept seeing him as garlanded in red roses—the earthy mystic, embodied, receptive, exuding wholeness and a certain feminine mystery.

The silence seemed to reverberate, to grow and build upon itself as spiritual power accumulated and thickened in the subtle dimensions of the space, felt as a palpable heat and pressure. Even though we were sitting in a group of people, it struck me as an extremely personal, internal process—profoundly intimate and profoundly impersonal, at the same time. It was soon over, there was a thirty minute break and then the second darshan started at six-thirty p.m.

Lee and Arnaud sat upstairs again afterward, waiting for dinner, which was served at seven-thirty in the same room, now transformed into a dining room with a large cloth laid out on the floor. About thirty-five people squeezed in around the huge rectangle to eat with Arnaud and Lee. A special feast of Indian food, provided by the study group of Maison Raphael and catered by a well-known Indian restaurant in Paris, was served. It was a celebratory dinner organized specifically to honor the influence of Arnaud and Lee on the inception and ongoing success of Maison Raphael.

When everyone had feasted, Sylvie, Christophe and Bernard—the three therapists who originally established Maison Raphael ten years ago and still run the center—each took turns speaking of their history and all they'd been through together. They each expressed their gratitude to Arnaud and Lee. I was surprised by the dominant nondual perspective of the path expressed in their speeches—perhaps because our own school is so specific in this regard. At one point Arnaud responded briefly to Sylvie; Lee said nothing at all, but listened to all that was said and seemed fiercely present.

When the three therapists were finished with their speeches, Arnaud spoke. He said that all the credit of the success of Maison Raphael should go to the influence of those sages whose pictures were on the walls: Kongrul Rinpoche, Swami Prajnanpad, Anandamayi Ma. He was referring to all the great masters who have helped so many people on the spiritual path. Arnaud's love of these great sages was so palpable in the space that it was like a live current that flowed from him. Then he said something rather unexpected. He cautioned, "In spite of the intellectual terrorism of the nondualists against this Being, don't be afraid to use the word 'God,' to reject a Being who could be of great help to us." I wondered if this strong comment was, at least in part, in honor of Lee's theistic tradition and lineage.

The evening drew to its natural close as Arnaud and Veronique left for their hotel. The next day the schedule would be the same: a dharma talk, brunch, two more short talks after which Arnaud would arrive for the two silent *darshans*. Afterward, Arnaud and Veronique would leave before dinner to catch their train.

Paris—Maison Raphael
October 2

Camille, who had come to hear Lee's teachings at Hauteville, Le Rozet and at Espace Harmonie, was speaking in the morning session, expressing her sadness and discomfiture that Lee was leaving Europe for the next eight months. She felt that her progress on the path would be interrupted with Lee away.

"You are leaving for America soon . . . You won't be here . . ." she said.

"How do you know I won't be here any more? That's just the mind. So slap your mind around and tell it to get back to work! Tell the mind you need to be here, to practice. It's a habit . . . a habit of thought. If you want to stop the habit badly enough, you just stop it.

"If you feel the Influence you felt at Hauteville and Le Rozet is not there anymore, it's you. Yes, you miss the physical circumstance and all that, but the real thing that draws you and magnetizes you is wherever you are. So you make that distinction between the pleasurable appearance of things and the essence of it. Either that, or give your life up and move to the ashram. Why not? Somebody's got to live on the ashram and wash the dishes! Why not somebody intelligent like you?"

She looked surprised, but seemed to accept his words of wisdom. Leaping from this point to what was next, Lee turned his attention to selling. All of the large wooden monks and the two Buddhas had been sold yesterday and were now gone. They had been replaced by a pile of books and CDs, which Lee proceeded to advertise. When he had sold an adequate amount, which created a certain movement of energy in the space, Lee seemed satisfied and began to talk about the three elements of practice according to Patanjali: consistency; it takes a long time; and ardent devotion.

Lee began to discourse, "Practice requires absolute consistency. I left absolute out yesterday," he was referring to having also talked about Patanjali the day before, "because this is the Kali Yuga, and we're all busy. But if we're really serious about practice it requires absolute consistency. If your practice is saying yes to life, then the practice is to live in the mood of yes. If your practice is mantra, consistency would be to repeat the mantra, 'Om Nama Shivaya,' or 'Om Sri Ram Jai Ram Jai Jai Ram,' like Ramdas said, twenty-four hours a day."

Lee talked about the practice of accepting what is, as it is, here and now, or saying yes to life, and how this can be done all the time. He said, speaking specifically to Arnaud's students, "You're lucky—you have no reason to fail at practice and every reason to be successful. For my students, it's the opposite: they have every reason to fail because their day has to be organized around meditation, study, exercise and remembering four or five internal practices! And we used to be vegetarians . . . ."

Lee went into a diatribe about how we can hardly call ourselves vegetarians anymore, because we eat so much meat, especially when we are traveling. He had everyone laughing again as he bombarded us with funny self-portraits: "I'm half pig already from eating pig all summer! For some reason, pig is good in France; beef is not so good—I don't know why!" Laughter reigned during this foray into the absurd, as Lee careened off on a tangent: "French beef is so stringy and tough, you can barely chew it . . . ah, but the pig!

"So, you say mantra until you don't need the mind for the mantra to be vibrating inside you. Absolute consistency with the practice of saying yes is not to have to remember to say yes to specific circumstances; it's to live in a state of being that *is* yes. That's absolute consistency of practice. It's better to practice as you can than to not practice at all, because you can't practice perfectly. We say, 'I'll start practicing when the landscape is clear, I'm not raising kids,' and so on, but you'll never start practicing if you wait until everything is clear for it.

"Each photo in this room represents aspects of Arnaud's work; people he spent time with. They are also reminding factors. Arnaud spent time in the Gurdjieff work too," Lee looked around at the photos, which seemed vivified by Arnaud's attention on them yesterday.

"Whenever you have a photo of Arnaud or any artifact associated with the Path, every time your eyes even briefly cross that object, you are reminded of the Path. One reason Patanjali said 'absolute consistency of practice is required' is because reinforcement, reinforcement, reinforcement is *vital* to ongoing practice. If you are a dancer or martial artist or yogi, you know when you practice on a regular basis that you have a certain presence and muscular tone. When you don't practice for two weeks, you have to build up the muscle again. So you have to keep reinforcing, reinforcing, reinforcing. When you stop, you'll stay at a plateau for a period of time, but then quickly start to deteriorate.

"My spaces are packed with reminding factors. Filled! You go into this space or Hauteville, if you had the psychic eyes to see you would see the space is filled with spiritual entities—gods, devis, demigods. They are drawn by this precious human life, because more progress can be made in the human body than anywhere else. Wherever there is genuine teaching going on, they all flock to that place—and they're having a party! When the teaching is going on, those people are up there dancing and partying and sexing!

"So, I like my spaces packed with reminding factors. One of my students called up and asked for Blessings for their mother. I asked how long she had had the problem, and they said four months. I'm practically tearing my hair out—I'm angry for days! If people call me right away, I can send the Blessings of Yogi Ramsuratkumar, but after four months, there's not much I can do. What's wrong with these people? Why can't they call me when it first starts? I'm angry for days! My students are always making me angry, but it's my fault—they're just being who they are. Slugs, slobs, rotten practitioners!

"So, I like lots of reminding factors, like these . . ."

Lee picked up two Burmese temple lions, sculpted in gilded wood. He began to extol their beauty and sublime qualities.

"That reminding factor is reinforcing our commitment to practice . . . . After twenty years on the Path, your life is pretty much the same as it would have been without your teacher—except for the extraordinary, profound benefits you have gotten from being with your teacher!"

Lee reminded us that at first on the path, things are extraordinary; after a while we adjust to the extraordinary. We become rather jaded or obtuse about the amazing golden shower of blessings in our lives; in fact, we are permeated with blessings, but our attitude is: what's the big deal? All because we have adjusted to living in the extraordinary. So, for this reason as well as many others, reminding factors are very helpful.

"In India the primary focus of the shrine is not the guru but mother and father. For the Indians, photos of their mothers and fathers have great power. Then there is the guru. So we give force to the artifacts, the reminding factors; every time we pass by the artifact in a room we are reminded, consciously or unconsciously."

Interspersing stories and pitching artifacts of various kinds, including throwing lots of books and CDs through the air to those who raised their hand to buy one, for the next hour Lee talked about Yogi Ramsuratkumar and his awakening.

Lee said, "Even when someone had a major shift of context, it takes a long time to integrate that shift fully. Yogi Ramsuratkumar repeated the mantra, 'Om Sri Ram Jai Ram Jai Jai Ram' night and day, twenty-four hours a day, not sleeping or eating, for one week, and he was thrown into a state of divine madness. He couldn't function anymore, and he even went to his wife and asked her to leave and wander with him. She said no, that she couldn't leave their children, which was much to her credit.

"It was a cataclysmic explosion of His ordinary reality," Lee continued, "He was so divinely intoxicated that He was disturbing Ramdas' ashram. Ramdas told Him to leave. He said, 'You've got to go somewhere else to worship God.' Because Yogi Ramsuratkumar couldn't stop. He wasn't acting out—His ordinary personality was obliterated. Where did He go? To Arunachala, the oldest natural symbolic representation of the Divine in the world. At least that's what the southern Indians say; the Indians in the north say something else. There was also a cave on Mount Arunachala where Ramdas had had his enlightenment experience.

"Yogi Ramsuratkumar went on the road for seven years before He came to Tiruvannamalai. He never told anybody about those seven years, but we do know two things: we know that He knew J. Krishnamurti. He had a great respect for Krishnamurti. And we know that He knew Nityananda. Yogi Ramsuratkumar went everywhere meeting every extraordinary person He could meet. In those seven years, whatever catalyst that shift of consciousness was for Him, that event matured and integrated and digested. It's not just that He had a shift and it was done. So, practice takes a long time to realize its aim, its goal—whether practice is intended to realize a state of consciousness or the shift of consciousness has already happened.

"Swami Nityananda was considered an avadhuta. He walked around naked." Lee proceeded to tell the story of how the locals complained and so the police locked Nityananda up for being naked in the street, but he kept appearing again, out on the street. Finally the police begged some of Nityananda's devotees to talk him into wearing a loin cloth, so their problem would be solved.

Lee concluded this session on the theme of how practice takes a long time, saying, "It might be five or ten years on the Path before you're actually *starting*. It took Arnaud six years to become obedient to Swami Prajanapad; only six years . . . . If you can come to perfect obedience in six years, you're doing great! But Arnaud was just a guy, just like you and I! We minimize the possibility of success by saying that the master wasn't like us. Don't put the master on a pedestal that separates the master's experience from us. It takes a long time, so be prepared to settle in and practice, practice, practice!"

After brunch Lee started the next session talking about the tattoo book. He said, "This book shows us there is help in areas of life we would never think to look for help." Even with a great pitch for the art and the symbolism in the book, and despite the t-shirts in the States that say, "Tattoos aren't just for sailors and whores anymore," it seemed that in the spiritual scene, tattoos are still taboo. Very few people were willing to buy the book on the chance that there might be something of value for them in it, when in fact the text includes a serious consideration of art, culture and the socio-political trends of our times, as well as the application of principles of alchemy and spiritual practice.

I think of the French as having a tremendous commitment to art. Considering the way many avant garde artists and art forms have been embraced in France over the years, I had assumed that the new tattoo craze would be, at the very least, of intellectual interest as a cultural and creative phenomena to many French people. In fact, there is a fabulous "tattoo culture" in France among many young people. But, like everywhere else in the West, the stigma of tattooing remains firmly in place; most people still think that you've just got to be a little crazy to get a Sanskrit mantra or a Hindu or Buddhist deity emblazoned on your skin! Off your nut. Lost it. Gone psychotic . . .

Or maybe just a little God-mad. Getting tattooed with sacred images in Lee's world is not a quixotic act. You've got to be committed in a completely different way. It is an act of abandon, of not caring anymore about your old identifications, and an act of serious devotion to the path. Once you have the tattoo, you will never be the same again—quite literally. Your skin will be different, and that difference will constantly remind you. You have to travel far off the grid of conventional, worldly life to have a deity, or Hari Om, or Om Sri Ram Jai Ram Jai Jai Ram, or the name, Yogi Ramsuratkumar, woven into your living flesh with a needle and colored inks.

Despite modern advancements in tattoo technology, getting a tattoo takes hours of breathing and practicing through an ordeal that hurts and confronts our delicate sensitivities about the impermanence of the body. It is an irrevocable act that puts the permanent commitment to your own ego's undoing, with the potential paradise or hell of that process, in your face. It is an act that becomes such a vivid and aching choice for you that you *do it*. You become a tattooed person, not with just one tattoo, but with many—like some of the crazy people in *Agony & Alchemy: Tattoos and Sacred Art*.

Andre, an elder and disciple of Arnaud who has come to Lee's seminars at Maison Raphael for many years, asked the question, "Why is the word 'agony' used in the title of the book?"

Lee answered, "Tatouage, in our context, is about alchemy. Alchemy is about the transformation of one substance into another: lead into gold. This is lead," Lee pointed to his body. "It could be gold. When you get a tattoo image on your body, part of the value of it is the pain. Now they have this anaesthetizing cream you can use—that's cheating! When you get this symbolic image on your skin, it's going all the way in. There are sects in India that say that tattoos are like money in the other world. The more tattoos you have, the more money you have! Some have Yogi Ramsuratkumar tattooed on their bodies, some want my name but I won't let them because it's Yogi Ramsuratkumar, not me. What do I want my name floating around on all this iron?

"Unlike other reminding factors, tattoos work on you all the time, because it's on your body all the time. In alchemy, for a substance to be created, the substance it is being created in has to break down. There are several stages of that: the first stage is disintegration. They make the acid that is water and moonlight and prayers—made during certain phases of the moon, with certain prayers—then the substance breaks down, then you have a solution. The solution is evaporated, then you have ash, then you add the mordant to the ash, and the mordant begins the process of creation.

"You take diamond, the most perfect, highest quality you can find: when you dissolve a substance alchemically you can't recreate it. You can only create something else. Once you start, you have to go to the end. Like us, on the Path. We find the master, the Path, and begin a process of human alchemy—we call it transformation, not change, but transformation. Sometimes we change transformationally, but not in the ordinary world. Once the habitual worldview is dissolved, you cannot get it back again. Sometimes students will say, 'I wish I could leave the Path! Why not? Because I know too much!'

"You cannot get it back again. You can't go back to being the liar, thief, hunk of lead you were. If you aren't willing to go to the end of the Path, don't start, because when you're in the middle of the Path, there is only one way to go. One of the things that happens in a process of dissolution is that your mind doesn't transform right away, so you're dealing with your mind. You're dissolved, but your mind is going on and on: 'You idiot! You'll never be the same! What are you doing, buying all those artifacts? Why are you doing all those retreats? Don't go to Hauteville—go to the beach!'

"So, the mind is the last thing that gets transformed—it fights right up to the end. There is dissolution and recreation, and in that process, there is agony. The agony and the alchemy. Alchemy cannot happen without that kind of agony—it can be a moment, or a lifetime. Please don't make it a lifetime. It can be literally a moment in which you have to deal with this kind of doubt, when you are broken down but not resurrected yet. 'Oh my God, what have I done?!'

"If it's just a moment—great! On you go! But if you have to live through that for any period of time, it's agonizing. And to some degree, it's really up to you. But you have to be willing to make a choice and stay with it.

"E.J. said when you are committed to the Path and you are struggling with your psychological character, you can't turn the psychological character into a disciple. The only way to eliminate the interference of all the other 'I's' that create this flurry of noise and distraction from the disciple 'I' is to put it down and walk away. Never come back. Don't think about it, don't talk about it."

Lee joked about when he first moved to Arizona from New Jersey with twelve students: "I felt like the Pied Piper, only it wasn't a bunch of rats that were following me, and we were going to an ashram!

"The only way to be free of all those other influences is to put them down, walk away, do not think about them. There is no formula, just do it. Like Nike! They stole the secret of the ages! We agonize over whether to buy Nike shoes or not, because they have such terrible business practices. You know, they pay little children fifteen cents an hour in the Third World; but then, if Nike didn't pay them fifteen cents an hour, they'd be making seven cents an hour anyways—oh my God, what a crisis!"

After the laughter subsided a little Lee concluded, "You gotta be flexible, because ethics are not written in stone. You live in France, but you go to India, and the cultural protocol is completely different in India than it is here."

Just then a cat jumped up on the ledge of the open window. She looked at Lee and around at all the people. Lee looked over at her and said, "Oh, hello. Come on in! There's some mice in here. Big mice. They look like human beings, but they're mice. Don't be fooled!" Everyone laughed along with Lee at the joke.

He continued, "We say, 'How do I do it?' You just do it! Or we say, 'I can't do it!' But you *can* do it. Your attachments are just illusions! Complete illusions! The thing you think is an attachment is not—that's just our definition of it . . . . To put it down is to sever all relationship with that thing forever. It's finished. There is no recidivism. Purna works in the American prison system, where the recidivism rate is ninety-seven percent. The guards, many of whom are sadists, will remind inmates of that regularly. If an inmate is studying to get a college degree, the guard will say, 'Why are you bothering? You'll be back here!'

"They say if a gang member is a junkie and goes back to the gang environment, they will go back to the addiction. They say, do not go back to the old neighborhood, which is a parallel to this principle of just dropping it. Like vanity: put it down, walk away. Finished, you know, no more looking in the mirror every time you pass by it, looking in store windows. If you put down vanity, it doesn't mean that you'll start looking like a bum and stop bathing and combing your hair.

"When you put something down, it doesn't mean your whole life is going to hell. Your choices will be different. You're not going to spend fifteen hundred euros on a red leather jacket because it looks good on you. You won't be stupid about it.

"So, how badly do you want it? How badly do you want to be clear enough to eliminate the complications that keep you from integrity of practice? And if that's what you want more than you want to maintain your mechanical psychological script, you will be able to put it down and walk away. If not, it's just not important enough to you—yet."

Lee described his second wife, who dropped alcohol and cigarettes: she used to go out and get drunk every weekend, that was her lifestyle, and one day she just stopped it all and never went back. She encountered the path; she was in Silva Mind Control, and she knew she had to make a choice. It was either keep drinking and smoking, or take this new direction that had opened up for her. He said, "When she set her feet on the Path, it was important enough for her to know that her habits would complicate and confuse her entering the Path. Her commitment to the decision was irrevocable."

Suddenly Lee switched tracks onto a different but related subject with a fluid ferocity: "Men may say they don't want to be with a younger woman, but if they come along—why not? They say it's because younger women make them feel young again—they want to have sex! Men come to me and say, 'My wife doesn't want to have sex with me' . . ."

Lee's voice was dripping with sarcasm as he charged ahead, as if someone had asked a question that hadn't been voiced, as if he was speaking to the unconscious in the room. His diatribe became more intense as he went on: "Our *wives* can make us feel young again. The only reason they don't is because of *us* . . . so whose fault do you think that is? One hundred percent of the time, it's always the man's fault if the woman doesn't want to have sex. Always, always, always, it's the man's fault one hundred percent of the time. That woman can be melted if the man is . . . Always, always the man's fault. Why do you think she doesn't want sex? Because you give her war—you attack her! That's not sex."

Shifting back to the track he had been on, he continued, "You cannot put something down and walk away from it if you still have an attachment to it. You have to put it down and walk away . . . "

It was time for another thirty minute break, after which Lee would give the last session of the weekend before we would adjourn for the silent *darshan* at five-thirty p.m. It had been a particularly rich weekend at Maison Raphael; quite often, because the center was focused on therapy, perhaps, the questions had tended over the years to be very psychologically oriented, rather than practice oriented. I noticed with some interest that Lee had given some particularly strong teachings, lifting the questions up to a different level.

The session began with another question from Andre, who asked, "Is 'Just drop it' the right attitude at the moment of death?"

Lee answered, "Absolutely. Any attachment we still have when we move over will hold us back, so we want to be able to go wherever we want to go, and not be held back."

After a practical discussion of whether or not a man should give up his job to open a bookstore, a woman named Marie, who has come to Lee's seminars for many years, spoke up.

"When I'm here the atmosphere is real, really real, but then I go out," she spoke slowly, "and nothing is real. I have the impression of being on another planet. I have to take the Metro every day, and people seem like alien puppets to me. I can't stand being around them, and I can't bring the two worlds together."

Lee responded, "So? You're not sleeping with all these aliens, and they don't know that they're aliens, so give them a break! Make it an act of theatre. You go on the Metro and treat them like they are human beings from your planet. Treat them as if they are real . . ."

Marie continued, "But they're far away . . ."

"That's all you," Lee spoke firmly, unequivocally. "You make them far away. And at some level, not at all, they have the same values as you. Everyone wants to be healthy, happy, have love in their lives. Okay, we want the Path too. We want health, happiness, love, the Path and God. They only want health and happiness and good air. When you sit down on the Metro, okay, they don't want the Path and never will, but they don't know about it. They're not separating themselves from you; you're separating yourself from them! Yes, if you walk on the Metro with rainbows on your head and wearing a sign that says, 'I'm on the Path,' yes, okay. But you're making the distinction; they're not. So give them a break. Treat them like human beings, because you don't have to live with them . . ."

She countered, "Yes I do have to live with them. Yes I do. When they're making love, they make a lot of noise . . ."

"On the Metro!?" Lee rejoined, as if incredulous, to which everyone in the room responded with a loud round of laughter. Marie explained that she could hear the people in the apartment next to hers.

When Lee stopped laughing, he said, "Yes, but those aren't the people on the Metro. So you hear a little noise come through the wall. What's the problem? Do they scream when they're having sex—making love, I mean?" The humorous tone of his voice kept everyone chuckling throughout this exchange.

He pressed on, "Would you scream if you were making love?"

Reluctantly she admitted, "If it was real intimacy, yes."

"Then assume they are you," Lee said with a smile. Then, addressing the whole crowd, he said, "She needs intimacy when she's making love—that's a lot to ask for from men!" More laughter broke out among us all. He turned back to Marie and asked, "How about just having great sex?" Another wave of laughter came rolling through the room.

"You are making definitions that separate you: 'I have no space, these people are aliens, I can't concentrate.' *You* are doing it. There is noise. We live on a noisy planet. People make love, blare their TVs. Imagine if you lived in Italy!" Another round of laughter burst out; we were feeling no pain at this point. We were just enjoying the moments of Lee's frank, easy, delightful play with us.

"Those people are *loud*! We played a couple of gigs in Italy this summer, and at one gig, in Solerno, we stopped at a rest area to get some chocolate or something—to get gas also, but the chocolate was the important thing—and I got out of the van and there was this *roar*, I mean *roar*! I realized the noise was everybody talking as loud as they could, all at the same time! Wow! I've never heard anything like that before. I found out that people aren't exaggerating about Italians. They weren't just talking, they were swinging their arms!"

Everyone was in on the joke—the French, of course, knowing the Italians quite intimately over centuries of history as neighbors. Lee was on a roll. He hadn't missed a beat; he was timing the onslaught of humor, rolling with the punches of laughter that intersected his comic monologue.

"I was afraid I was going to get hit in the head!" More laughter. "And everybody was *happy*! I really felt out of it! I was in my usual sour grapes attitude. Why don't all these people just shut up?" More laughter. Finally we wiped the tears from our eyes and settled down long enough for Lee to continue in an only slightly more serious vein.

"It's only *me* that wants everything a certain way—quiet, ordered. So you need to take responsibility for your projections. So they're noisy, so what? So you need to discipline your mind, however you can. When you get on the Metro and everybody looks like an alien puppet—I know exactly that perception—you take a deep breath and go sit down and read your book, and after a while, you realize they're just ordinary people. And maybe they wouldn't know the difference between a real space and a not real space, but so what?

"In many paths they say that you should be in the company of other disciples, but you can't drop your responsibilities, and you have to work. You have to make peace with the rest of the world. It's not going to go away. So when you can spend time here, you do. Nobody can spend their whole lives here—it's artificial."

Lee talked about a Harry Chapin song that tells a story of hippies who find out they could find genuine kindness and values among the straight people, and the straight people find out that the hippies aren't so bad either.

"Many of the people in this room have a certain sensitivity that even our families do not understand. When I first started teaching, I lost many close friends. I didn't ask them to be students—they just couldn't accept what I was doing. Those people on the Metro aren't asking anything of you; they're just going to work. Don't make a problem of it. Let them be who they are, and you be who you are. Okay, they can be scary sometimes, but at other times, they'll save your life . . ."

Marie commented, "It's not their fault, but . . ."

"But you're making it their fault by separating yourself from them," Lee repeated. "Yes, noise is disturbing. Ours is a noisy world, so it's our responsibility to adjust. We can't make what is unconscious conscious, so it's our responsibility to adjust. So, figure out when those people are making love, and don't be in your apartment."

"It's in the morning!"

"Then pretend you're with a man and scream back!" This suggestion from Lee got another big laugh from the group. "You might discover something! 'Oh, that was good! And I thought I needed a man!' " More laughter. The moment was over and it was time to move on. Several people raised their hands to ask questions.

"Okay. Simone?"

"I was touched by the cat . . . and what you said about dogs," she began, referring to Lee's rant earlier in the day about the common human neurosis in relation to dogs.

"Yes, the cat knew what I was talking about. Yes, people and their fucking dogs!" He laughed.

Simone continued, "I had a cat that died—I found this cat about a year ago. I was very attached to its presence . . ." She started crying. "So you were talking about how, through this cat, I'm discovering things?"

Lee said with emphasis, "I'm a cat man! Always was. I know exactly what you're talking about. My mother got me a dog once, when I was a kid and my last cat had died. After two days, it bit me! It's fine to be attached to the cat as long as you know you are attached, consciously, and you understand the implications: one day the cat will die. That's life. You can be as attached as you want so long as you are conscious in your attachment, and as long as that attachment does not interfere with your life going on.

"Attachment is a great thing as long as it's conscious and you know how deeply attached you are, and you are responsible for that attachment. It doesn't have to be a problem. If your life takes a turn and the cat can't make it with you, you have to go on with your life. Like your kids; they grow up and go on and live somewhere else. You know you're attached, and when life takes a turn, you turn. It's that simple . . . Say, there's an idea for Marie! Get a cat!"

Lee turned back to Marie, who said, in her uniquely Saturnian style, "I have a bird."

"A cat is a higher level of being," Lee retorted with enthusiasm. "Let your cat *eat* the bird!" She started arguing immediately with that idea. Overriding her protests, Lee raised his voice, "Let me finish!" People were breaking into unrestrained guffaws of laughter.

"Get a cat that yowls when the neighbors make love, and the guy will yell, 'Kill your cat!' . . . You yell back, 'Kill your fucking *bitch*!' " People were howling with laughter, rocking on their *zafus*, and Lee himself was grinning broadly, enjoying the whole scenario immensely. "Oh, that will feel good!"

While Lee poked fun at our aggressions toward other people who disturb our world in some small way, we were transported by the laughter into pure release.

"Not really," he said more soberly. "I was joking!" He smiled slyly.

Once again Lee played the wise fool's game, in which the comic, the clown, the witch doctor, the shaman, takes a deadly aim at the reality of our illusions and makes a direct hit, but does it while making us laugh. It's a sleight of hand trick as old as theatre, going back to the tribal campfire. Just to make sure we understood that this was all satire and comedy, Lee told the story of writing a piece of satire in a pamphlet that was widely distributed in New York City thirty years ago. People were extremely offended because they didn't know the difference between satire and reality.

"Anything else, Simone?" Lee asked, turning back to Simone, who answered no. Satisfaction was the feeling in the room; that is, we had been royally wined, dined and entertained. We'd been given the best of the dharma, delivered in Lee's peerless style; we had laughed, cried a little, been moved at the level of the heart, felt the pulling twinges of remorse—all within the skillful means of Lee's interactions with us.

Bringing the seminar to closure, he said, "It's time to end this part of the show!" Lee laughed. "Then we'll be back with another piece of theatre."

In a more sober vein, he commented on the quality of the teachings that had been given, saying, "That Arnaud is here this weekend changes the whole thing for me. If you found this weekend to be particularly useful, you can thank me a little, but you can thank Arnaud a lot. And thank you for your willingness to play the Sacred Bazaar game, and especially for your willingness to catch the books and CDs! I do appreciate it. Thank you."

After the last session of the weekend Lee joined Arnaud, who had just arrived, upstairs before the two periods of *darshan*, which were conducted in exactly the same manner as the day before. Afterward they spent some time together in Christophe's office before Arnaud and Veronique would leave to catch their evening train. They sat like two mountains, speaking little, now and then roused by a question or comment from someone. I sat down with my notebook, hoping to catch some of their words.

Arnaud began to speak with passion about the shocking degree to which his students, even long-term students, misunderstand the teaching. He said, "There is so much confusion about the teaching! 'We have understood that we are not to have any emotions.' " He looked pointedly at Lee with what was almost a grimace of disbelief at this kind of attitude. "What! We are not to be sick in the hospital?"

As is most often the case, Lee was in accord with Arnaud. "Yes, it's the same everywhere," he commented.

Perhaps to some small extent, I could understand the frustrations of the teacher, who holds out a solution to our confusion and suffering, but ego takes the very solution and turns it into another problem. Never have I heard Lee or Arnaud say we should not have emotions. The teaching is immanently sane, measured and practical in its application; it is all-embracing of life as it is. Emotions are a part of life; they are natural to the human being. It's true that one of the formulas of Swami Prajnanpad is: "To have emotions is to be a child. Only a child has emotions, not the adult." This teaching seems to point toward the need to discriminate as adults, to learn how to actually feel and know the difference between feelings and emotions. We will never be able to feel as adults if we, once again, take the child's position and believe that the spiritual authority has told us "not to have emotions," as if that is bad and unacceptable. Arnaud was addressing a crucial point in principle: we will not be able to practice if we continue to distort the teaching to fit our psychological cramp.

In this case, the teaching has been made clear: it is how we work with emotions that is the practice. Swami Prajnanpad also said, "Let the emotion have its full play and vanish." We could be accepting ourselves as we are, which allows the native instinct to discern what is basically good and true. Nonetheless, the mind insists on its perverse logic, a fundamentally fascist dialectic that all too often rules our thoughts. This kind of "letter of the law" mindset seems to be the default mode that we typically fall into when we are not able to summon the clarity to know the living truth of the "spirit of the law"—in all of its flexibility and permutations—which are lawful to the moment at hand. This rigid letter-of-the-law stance renders the teaching dead, lifeless and just plain wrong. Even worse, perhaps, is the student's twisted perceptions of the spiritual authority and the mess of things that is made by the projections we place upon the teacher.

Arnaud continued, speaking now of the timeless Eastern teachings that are being transposed into the West, and the implications of how this tendency to misunderstand and misinterpret the teaching will impact the purity of the teaching as it is incorporated into Western culture. He said, "It is sure that Buddhism, as it was practiced in Tibet, will be diluted more and more. There were many rinpoches of the highest level of realization. I met one and another in Tibet, and later when they reached India, Dharamashala or Sikkim.

"There are four or five Tibetan Buddhist centers founded in France, where the lama is trained for three or four years, but not at the same level as in Tibet. And there are many different influences in America, France and even in northern India for some years. So Tibetan Buddhism from the tenth century, for one thousand years, so strong, so deep, will not be the same in the future as it is today. There will be, like in Christianity, many changes made. Maybe I'm wrong, but I don't see how that can be avoided."

Lee agreed and commented that Buddhism in America has already changed; in particular that very thing has already happened in the Zen tradition.

Veronique came in and joined the conversation. I mentioned the heavy traffic that we had been caught in the night before, and that we had run into what seemed to be a fire in northern Paris, on Magenta Boulevard. She told us that there had indeed been a fire there yesterday that was reported in the newspapers; a large, very old tenement building of run-down apartments had burned. It was one of several such tenements that had burned recently; these were buildings that had been condemned, but had been re-opened to house the massive influx of African immigrants, who were living in very bad conditions in tiny apartments, with eight to ten people in one room. Rumor had it that some of them cooked over contained open fires in their apartments. At the same time, there was some talk of arson.

The stench around the whole issue of African and Arab immigrants in France—and in Germany and other First World countries as well—is not at all unlike the immigration problems in the United States. The issues are very murky, with just causes on both sides of the polemical fence. Typically, racism rears its ugly head to further obscure what justice might be brought to bear in the situation.

In France, it is strikingly noticeable that many of the village and inner city markets have been strongly influenced by an African and Middle Eastern presence; we have seen this situation countless times in the markets and wondered how immigrant people can make a living at all, selling carved wooden masks and animals of the bush, or trinkets and cheap, low-end household goods. Unemployment of the poor and immigrant population is running at a high of fifty percent in France. The fires didn't bode well at all, and the mood around them was troubling, signifying worse things to come.

I flashed on Lee's lyrics from an old song, "Burning," one that Lee wrote and performed fifteen years ago with *liars, gods & beggars*, years before Shri was conceived:

The museums, they are going first
No one wants the art
No one even cares no more
We've lost most of our heart
The librairies are following
So what, so few can read
There's more important business
There's avarice and greed

Rome, it is on fire, Paris it is too
London's also burning, yes it is too true

Cairo, it is going down, New York's already gone
The flames are taking Tokyo, it's not the only one

And we just stand here laughing
Refuse to see the signs
We hide our instinct good and deep
Covered with our crimes
The stench around us hidden by
The perfume of our lies
We're satisfied to sit and watch
As our world softly dies

We don't even realize
We're so consumed by fears
We refuse to come to terms
To cry our lonely tears
So here we are a-fiddling
Like Nero once before
Grinning like a Cheshire cat
Too numb to know the score

The conversation turned toward something more uplifting: the upcoming celebration of Arnaud's eightieth birthday, to be held next week at Hauteville. Many of Arnaud's friends and spiritual peers were invited for the weekend. A number of prominent Sufi teachers would be there also, and Veronique said that it was Ramadan, so the Muslims would only eat after the sun had set and before it rises.

I mentioned that Sian and Jean Pierre, who would be serving some of the meals over the weekend, had told us that Native American Jerry Dunson would be there.

Arnaud spoke, saying, "I remember Jerry Dunson in the festival in Fez. In the mornings there were meetings, and the title of the week was 'The Soul for Globalization.' Very big people from the

World Bank were there, the International Monetary Fund—those at the highest level! They were supposed to speak for one half hour, and they spoke for one hour. They were saying that people are more and more happy in the world!

"Jerry Dunson came up and said, 'In my Nation we cannot do anything serious or important without praying. Will you allow me to pray?' Then he said, 'In my nation when a young man asks to speak where there are older men present, he must first ask the permission of the elders. When a man speaks where there are women present, he knows that man is nothing without woman, so I must first ask the permission of the women to speak.' "

Arnaud continued, "When he started to speak, he was so clear, so deep, oh ho ho . . . I was amazed! I don't know how they got his name to invite him!"

I said, "I'll bet everyone was crying by then."

Veronique smiled and said, "Yes, they were."

Arnaud continued on the theme of the trends in modern spirituality: "I think in France there is more and more interest in religion, the spiritual aspect of life, and doubts about the values of the modern world, the materialists, the reactions of the pure scientists . . . It is a sickness we have to fight against—that technology will solve everything. I can see that in some weekly papers. It is going faster and faster in the wrong direction.

"To escape the vision of today—the future, the future, the future, let us proceed in this conquest of the space! So money is spent on these things and there is no money for the schools . . ."

Lee said, "In Prescott the schools all need money. They teach Arizona history, which is meaningless, and the first thing they eliminate is language, art, physical education. The educational system in America in general is terrible . . ."

Soon Christophe came in to tell Arnaud that it was time to leave for the *gare*. We said our goodbyes quickly. The image that stayed with me was of Arnaud saying goodbye to Christophe, Sylvie and

Bernard at the door downstairs by the cedar tree. His face was radiant with love, and his eyes beamed with kindness and beatitude as he warmly embraced each one, looking, one by one, into their eyes for a moment. He laughed and smiled, sharing a few last words, then he was off.

At dinner there were thirty-five people again crowded around the rectangle of cloth on the floor in the seminar room. After clean up, one by one or two by two, people slowly left Maison Raphael, embracing Lee and going out into the night—Christophe and his wife Muriel, Arnaud's daughter; Bernard and Marie Noelle, Sylvie; Evelyne from London.

Brinda, Andrea and Annie from the ashram, David, Mira Amadori and Annette stayed longer to help load the vans after the Sacred Bazaar was dissembled, carefully wrapped in newspaper and bubble wrap and packed away. By ten o'clock the Transporter was completely filled with the boxes of the Sacred Bazaar, and Andrea and Annie headed off for Ferme de Jutreau; Brinda would stay overnight and accompany Lee back to the ashram the next day. David, Annette and Mira headed out walking toward the Metro. We were ready for rest before midnight, knowing we would be up at five-thirty the next day; it was time for another early morning departure.

Paris
October 3

Lee saw Sylvan, Denise, Sari, Ann and I off at the Charles de Gaulle Airport this morning. We left in the dark, but by the time we arrived at the terminal building, it was daylight. After checking in, we sat in the airport café over coffee for almost an hour. We were in transition from the complex, multi-dimensional, rolling chamber of the guru's three-month summer sojourn in Europe to a reunion with the Arizona sangha—you could call them "old skool," to use a tattoo term—and the steadier, deep rooted, earthy months of autumn and winter. Then there would be the rebirth of spring at the mother ashram.

Poised on the brink of more changes, we were riding the momentum of the summer's immense wave, delicately balanced in the present moment on a peak between the appearance of a past and a future. Without doubt there would be many high peaks with Lee in the months ahead; we were moving toward a time of autumnal celebration with the Appearance Day Celebration, which centers around Lee's birthday on November 18, the Jayanthi Celebration of Yogi Ramsuratkumar on December 1, Lee's annual trip to India, and the midwinter Baul Feast, always held on the last weekend of the year. Lee's formidable travel schedule in the winter and spring already included New York City, San Francisco, Los Angeles, Las Vegas, Tucson, Mexico City and Montana.

But now, we still had a few minutes left in France. Sitting in the café, we listened while Lee brimmed over with enthusiasm for the band tours next summer. He spoke with candid excitement about the European musicians who would play with his band, and the Americans who would play with the Denise Allen Band.

We had heard that there would be transportation strikes in France on Tuesday, and the talk turned toward getting in touch with his guests who were to arrive at the ashram that day—old friends Rob and Stewart of the Tayu Center, a Fourth Way group in Santa Rosa, in northern California. Lee wanted them to come a day early to avoid the transportation shut down.

Lee commented, "They'll give the after dinner talk Tuesday night. I want to give people an opportunity to ask them questions about practice. Rob and Stewart will be gone when Purna comes in on Thursday—we leave that day for Hauteville for the weekend, and then I'll be home."

The summer had come to an end for the two of us who had arrived with Lee's original party of wayfarers back in late June, but unlike Lee's European devotees, we would see him in one week in

Arizona. Soon it was time to say good-bye, and we watched Lee and Brinda disappear into the crowd as they threaded their way through the lines of people in the busy airport. Finally, we boarded our plane and made our way to London, then crossed the Atlantic Ocean and the vast continent of North America to land in the middle of the Sonoran desert, in Phoenix, two hours south of our final destination in the high desert mountains of central Arizona.

Full Circle — Arizona

Prescott, Arizona
October 4, 2005

Disembarking in Phoenix unleashes a flood of relief that starts with getting out of the cramped quarters of a transatlantic flight. After making our way through U.S. customs, we were free to enjoy the first of many reunions with family and loved ones, many of whom we hadn't seen all summer. The drive north through the desert has always been a great pleasure for me on our return from long trips: the ancient hills and purple mountains, the living desert with its sentient saguaros, the ocotillos, chaparral and Palo Verde, the orange sherbet spread of sunset clouds across the sky. Then there is the moonrise and the thick diamond dust of stars blown across the endlessness of the night sky.

These were familiar sights on this night of return, and one that has become etched into my heart over the years, along with the first sight of the ashram. As soon as the tall Ponderosa pines began to appear we knew we were getting very close, but the first real sentinels of the ashram are always the cottonwood trees near the gate.

In the cottonwood grove at the front of the property there is a platform balanced across the top of a large, seven-foot high stump of cottonwood boles. This is where the ravens are fed every Saturday in a traditional ritual inspired by Robert Svoboda, the purpose of which is to propitiate Lord Saturn. In his book, *The Greatness of Saturn*, Robert extols the powers of the immense planetary body, second largest in our solar system, that the Romans called Saturn; through ancient Hindu stories and mythologies, he makes the convincing argument that one should pay homage to Lord Saturn by feeding any black scavenger birds on Saturdays—that is, Saturn's day.

As our car rolled to a stop at the ashram gate, one of the big pieces of news we heard was that in September the raven feeding had attracted over two dozen vultures that were migrating through the area. For two weeks on Saturday morning they perched on the living and dead cottonwood trees of our ashram grove, waiting for their offal and suet. Vultures, also known as turkey buzzards, are huge carrion birds that have been on the endangered species list for some time. They would sit up in the high branches with their huge wings spread out, sunning themselves and waiting for their treats. The appearance of these archaic scavengers of *smashans* and cremation grounds around the world was a highly auspicious sign that Saturn was pleased. This story itself seemed to open its arms and enfold us in a welcome.

We slipped back into the world of the ashram, which is Lee's world—the world we never want to leave, even when we range far away in miles, going here and there in our travels, across the ocean or on the other side of the world. For a Baul, everywhere we go is home because the refuge of the guru, the sangha, and the teaching—and our most sacred place, the ashram—is always inside us. In the travel prayer that Lee has given to us, we ask the question: "Where can we go where You are not?" Coming home to the Arizona ashram, this question was answered yet again, for we discovered that this blessed place had been with us all along . . .

The ashram was quietly humming with the presence of Yogi Ramsuratkumar. One of the places this was most evident was in the gardens. It's taken many years and a lot of work to develop our vegetable garden in this bare desert soil, but the garden has always been a priority for Lee. Now, the vegetable garden—a signature of thriving energies on any ashram—was overflowing with life. Dark greens in abundance, a wild tangle of tomato plants laden with jewel-like fruit, the yellow, orange and burnt red marigolds and the purple cosmos, huge heads of cauliflower and cabbages, a wide variety of winter squashes in many colors, all awaited harvest.

The rock flower garden in front of the office on the bottom floor of Arrakis—the main house of the ashram—was also spilling over with marigolds, huge winding bushy clumps of rosemary, African daisies and other plants that live and bloom well in formidable heat. All the plants were carefully tended, looking healthy and strong at the end of summer's long season. I walked around, soaking up blessings from the earth, taking everything in through my eyes. The hard work of the long summer was never more evident. Many projects on the property had been finished, like the beautiful flagstone path that leads from Lee's back door upstairs in Arrakis.

There had been ample rainfall over the summer, and the entire ashram was amazingly verdant. The silvery cottonwood trees were still green, and the evergreens—the hardy piñon pine, cedars, junipers and gnarled live oaks—were not dusty and drab as they can be at summer's end but vigorously alive, bristling with energy. The field in front of the ashram was actually green and had been recently mowed. The Ma Garden near the darshan hall had been vivified, and the stone Kwan Yin statue that is the center of this humble shrine seemed to be smiling beneath her garland of fresh flowers.

The ashram residents, companions on the way of deep bonds forged through many years together, were quietly and steadfastly focused on their work and going about the evening when we arrived. These were the heart-keepers, in a way—tenders of the flame, who kept the rhythm and flow of the ashram moving along while Lee was away during the summer. Smiles and greetings were exchanged, and with hauling luggage and boxes into the greenhouse and to our rooms, there was nothing that was unusual or strange or required any adjustment at all as we melted into the familiar environment. We would have one week to catch up on projects and work before Lee arrived like a comet, swooping through on its solar orbit.

Prescott
October 10

Lee arrived on the Arizona ashram tonight with Purna around nine o'clock. Coming into his living room looking tired but radiant, Lee almost immediately started talking about his visit with Arnaud at Hauteville.

"It was well worth the change of plans," Lee commented, referring to the fact that he had to change his original travel plans and plane flight to stay one more week in France. "It was fantastic. People really enjoyed talking to Purna. Everyone wanted time with him."

"Did you meet Jerry Dunson?" I asked, remembering what we'd heard about him from Arnaud.

"Yes. He seems very nice. I think he'll be coming here to visit," Lee answered.

Purna said, "He really liked Lee."

Lee spoke about some of the other guests, many writers and editors and teachers of various paths, including some Sufis and Muslim shaykhs. Lee was glad to see Alexandro Jodorosky, the well-known filmmaker and spiritual luminary, once again. Many people who were there had heard of Lee's work in France and were familiar with his books, but very few realized the depth of the relationship between Arnaud and Lee until this weekend.

Lee said very little else about the celebration at Hauteville, but Purna told us a *lila*: At one point during the weekend, Arnaud had turned to him and said in his passionate way, "When I looked into Lee's eyes, I saw Papa Ramdas and Ma Anandamayi!"

As always, when Lee and Arnaud are together, the quality of their relationship is a great inspiration to their disciples. Theirs is a friendship that shouts to us of intrinsic dignity and intrinsic nobility; based on their mutual dedication to their own masters, disciplined practice and commitment to the path, their relationship has continued to grow for over thirteen years. Despite the fact that he gave very few details of his weekend there, some of the power of Lee's visit at Hauteville seemed to arrive with him and flow into the earth and bricks and stones and walls of the ashram.

"I'm going to retire for the evening now," Lee said sweetly, with a gentle smile, then stood and walked toward his private quarters. Tomorrow he would greet everyone in the sangha, but for now, at ten o'clock at night after the long, wearying journey, our guru—who rarely gets what any ordinary person would consider a minimal amount of necessary rest—had finally earned, by his standards, a night of sleep. There is no time for jet lag in Lee's world; there's simply too much work to do. Tomorrow morning he will be up well before dawn at the latest. As usual, at seven a.m. he will be found sitting on the dais for meditation with everyone in the hall.

Prescott
October 11

Tonight the sangha gathered with Lee for a Return Feast, to celebrate his arrival after such a long absence. About eighty people came to stand in the long buffet line that had been set up outside the greenhouse for a potluck style feast offering an array of green salads, roasted chickens and lots of desserts. We crowded together in the long narrow "greenhouse" or porch that flanks the front of the ashram office and main building, eating shoulder-to-shoulder. Looking around at everyone, it seemed to me that our gathering was more sober than it has been in years past.

It has been ten years since Lee started spending his summers in France and away from his Arizona ashram. For some years his coming and going was marked by the evidence of strong feelings—some people openly shed tears or spoke of their longing or difficulty with the change when Lee was leaving or returning. The excitement and mood of high celebration when Lee came home was palpable; with Lee's return each year, people were visibly brightened and ecstatic.

Over time, the ashram in France also became "home." Roots were sunk very deeply into the fertile matrix of the ashram and sangha that was growing in Europe. Lee began to speak of wanting to spend more time in Europe, and there was an obvious difference between how he taught in Europe and how he taught in the States. In Europe the teaching was crystalline in its clarity, both sublime and ecstatic, and most of all, highly accessible to the mind.

Devotees in Arizona, many of whom had been with Lee for many years, were not evoking the same response from their guru. Instead Lee was usually cryptic, obscure or sometimes muted. There was no lack of teaching lessons and instruction being given, but understanding his communication required a lot more effort and clarity on our part. It could be said that we had earned this more inward and fiery form of teaching; the more cryptic or enigmatic the teacher is, the more the responsibility is on the student to see clearly, free of projections, and understand his communication properly.

At the same time, the sangha had largely stopped bringing burning questions to after dinner talks, which left Lee, a voracious reader, with reading to us and commenting from his current study materials. Lee began to travel more and more during the winter and spring every year as well, making annual trips to many different places, including San Francisco, Mexico City, Montreal, Quebec and New York City, where he would visit with friends, students and other teachers, conduct business and sometimes give seminars or public talks.

Simultaneously, those who stayed in Arizona summer after summer to tend the home fires—to be the actual ground of sanctuary out of which all this new growth in Europe could grow and be nourished—were overloaded with work, with a minimal number of residents tending to the ashram and keeping up with the demands of daily sadhana. The ashram residents were often disappointed at the lack of participation from the sangha members who lived in households in town. Morning meditation remained poorly attended on the ashram, and only a core group of householders were regularly coming to the ashram to participate in meditation and other programs or help maintain the property with *guru seva.* And yet tonight, with Lee returning, eighty or more people showed up for the Return Feast.

Although everyone was clearly very happy to see Lee, it seemed that for the sangha at large, the transition of his return was quieter, more ordinary than it had been in the early years of summers in France. On the positive side of that, it seemed that when he came back, it was as if he had never left. Lee has repeatedly cautioned us against too much attachment to his physical form, and in the same vein, he has constantly encouraged us to realize that space and time and miles do not change the fact of our oneness. Clearly the sangha had grown beyond the tears and feelings of loss that characterized summer's inevitable farewells; longing for the physical company of the master had become deeply internalized for many.

Lee has exhorted us to continue with diligent practice in every way, no matter how many years in the school we might have, and in many ways, the tangible, viscerally-felt spiritual power of the ashram is a manifestation of a solid group of strong, dedicated practitioners. Nonetheless, the law of gravity is what it is: as Lee has said before, now as middle-aged *sadhakas* and *sadhikas*, we have to fight the forces of crystallization and the tendency to become stodgy and stuck in our ways. The American sangha had become, perhaps, a little buffered to all the changes of the past ten years, especially since Yogi Ramsuratkumar left his body.

Upon returning to Arizona it was sobering, even disturbing, to encounter small pockets of serious disaffection and complaints among the sangha against other sangha members, specifically against long-time students, and even against the guru himself. Of course this can be found in every tradition, where enthusiasm for the difficulty of real sadhana waxes and wanes for us as individuals. The guru takes the brunt of our rebellion and projections of father and authority figure: forgetting that we have come to the school for radical transformation, when we do not live up to the task, we blame the guru when really our disillusionment is no one's responsibility but our own. We search for ways that the guru has betrayed us, when in fact we are the ones who have betrayed the guru and ourselves as we essentially are.

However, the Hohm Community is not a dangerous cult, where dissent or doubt is squelched at its slightest mention by the authority figures, including the guru—and thank God for that. Bauls are far too iconoclastic and heretical to suffer docile, blind following—although there is always something sycophantic or shame-based found in the human condition. These are shadow qualities that we seek to bring to the light of self-honesty through our practice of Enquiry and self-observation. Our teacher asks obedience of us, yes, but it is a mature obedience that comes from deep self-examination and direct personal experience of the teaching, the practice and the teacher.

In other words, we obediently attend meditation because we have discovered, for ourselves, that it is of great benefit to us. We obediently engage the dietary practice, exercise and study because these activities are nourishing to our whole being. We obediently practice self-honesty and self-observation because we have come to deeply desire right relationship and objective conscience. We obediently engage the core practices—Assertion, Enquiry and the Heart Breath—because these practices have profound virtue and build a matrix for transformation within. We pray, chant the name of Yogi Ramsuratkumar and practice kindness, generosity and compassion because we long for the touch of the Beloved in the inner sanctum of our hearts. These are things that we *know* to be true; not because an authority figure told us, but because we believe deeply in our guru and his teaching, and we have engaged these practices to discover them for ourselves. What we have found out is that they are the Names of God, exactly as he said.

Arriving in Arizona, burning with inspiration from the summer's heat on the road with Lee, it was never more evident to me that we have to continue to reinvent our *sadhana* and enliven our practice, to bring fresh enthusiasm and inspiration to everything we do. The common habit is to get dragged down by the obsessive ranting of our own undisciplined minds. Even after many years on the path, we are often plagued by the mind, which tells us that our illusions are reality, that our lies are truth. We can spend years wasting precious energy that could be used for the Work just spinning our wheels, dancing with our own demons and blaming everyone around us.

Many of our questions cannot be answered by the mind, which spins a web of doubt, confusion and separation. Our questions can only be answered by the heart; only the heart speaks with the voice of truth. How can we access the heart when the mind is running rampant, fueled by our own neuroses and psychological obsessions that separate us from others? Lee said recently that the mind is the last aspect of the being to become transformed; even when many other dimensions of the self have been alchemized in the transformational process, the mind is still carrying on its endless loop tape of misery, criticism and blame.

And further, we cannot afford to discount the degree to which we are affected by the collective unconscious. We need to gain clarity about the fact that we are feeling and then mirroring the restless, driven uncertainty and pervasive fear of our times. Authorities of all kinds—secular and spiritual—are suspect as misuse of power runs rampant in the world. Though we attempt to live in the world while not being of the world, we are still profoundly connected to the rest of humanity. The suffering of the world soul is our own suffering.

Lee was back on the ashram in Arizona to bring the steadying influence of compassion and absolute context to all this swirl of phenomena. Tomorrow he would be at his desk in the office, taking phone calls, receiving faxes, reading and answering letters. Tonight we will all gather in the darshan hall to tell and hear stories from the summer in France, with Lee commenting now and then and adding his own perspective. This process of "storytelling," as an important part of the oral tradition, will continue in the after dinner talks for the next few weeks.

In the weeks ahead, culminating in the Appearance Day Celebration in mid-November, a plenitude of community activities will enrich our time together. At Prescott Coffee Roasters this weekend we will once again be purified by the cleansing radiations and enlivening effects of Lee's music. The next night the Baul Theatre Company will stage the *John T.* production—Lee's rock opera about the life and death of John the Baptist—at a local theatre in Prescott. The next weekend there is another Shri performance at the Desert Botanical Gardens, a fabulous outdoor venue in Phoenix. In the meantime, Lee will be catching up on American movies every afternoon.

Stories of the summer would continue to be shared not only in the after dinner talks, but also in more intimate spaces, one on one, or in the evening gathering over tea and chocolates. Most of all, the teaching in the Hohm Community is: You never miss anything. If you are bonded into the subtle nervous system of the guru, then you receive the transformational impulse that is flowing through the sangha. Despite the occasional flashes of guerilla warfare—our grumbling and negative states—this year when Lee returned it was never more obvious that the *sampradaya* of Western Bauls is strong and alive; and most of all, there is no separation between us.

Arizona Ashram
October 16

Tonight Lee gave the first *darshan* in Arizona since June 5. Even so, despite the appearance of things—in which Lee has entered into the *lila* of a merchant who travels around the world in search of sacred artifacts and art; in which Lee insists he is just a businessman, and we enter into the world and the marketplace, working with desire; in which we cultivate an appreciation of beauty and a necessary skillful means that far exceeds anything this school has seen before—the fact is that we remain a very traditional path. What we have in the Hohm Community is the unique way that Lee has transposed ancient tradition, with the graceful guidance of Yogi Ramsuratkumar, into a Western community of practitioners who fully engage life as it is.

Yogi Ramsuratkumar came out of the timeless, fecund, spiritual culture of India, from which sprang the wild *avadhuta* poet-saint Dattatreya, who was deified as a god; the great poet Jayadeva who wrote the *Gita Govinda*; Vallabhacharya, who gave us the Pushti Marga and bhakti path, the devotional worship of Krishna; Chaitanya, ecstatic mystic and embodiment of RadhaKrishna; the Bauls of Bengal—wandering *tantrikas*, mystics, poets, singers and dancers, lovers of the personal Beloved; the ruthless, raw-edged Nath Siddhas, the ecstatic Shakti and Shaivite worshippers, the lovers of Ram; and all the great God-realizers of ancient India. This connection to Mother India through the lineage of Yogi Ramsuratkumar is, in essence, who we are as disciples and devotees. Because of this, Sunday night *darshan*—the opportunity to have the sight of the guru, or spiritual master—has always been the culminating formal event of our week.

Time may very well prove what we can sense: that we are part of the last generation of Westerners to know Mother India first-hand, before she succumbed to all the disasters of the West: a secular culture dominated by technology, the wholesale destruction of soil and water through industrial pollution, a killing context of materialistic rationalism, the false idols of television, media, fashion, greed, power, corruption and the degradation of humanity through the deterioration of family, clan, village and ancestral spiritual lineage.

Village life in India is dying, as it is in France and everywhere else in the world—in Africa, South and Central America, throughout

Asia. The United States, still a toddler in the world community, does not have the rich foundation of the village culture of our European forebears, and yet the United States is leading the entire globe toward massive destruction. All over the world countries are following America's trend toward monstrous business conglomerates that control money, science and politics. Ethnic, religious, cultural and racial differences are being assimilated into a white-washed, bland, tepid, soulless way of life, stripped of the unique character and art found in sacred cultures whose origins go back hundreds, if not thousands, of years and are rooted in relationship to the Earth itself. What terrible national karma we have engendered! Genocide, slave trade, war for profit, consumerism devoid of soul . . . these are the legacy of the United States. Music and theatre are some of the few good things America has to offer—gospel, the blues, rock & roll and American movies, many of which still reflect the sensibility and vision of the true artist. It seems, in some quarters of Hollywood, that the movie makers have far more integrity than the politicians.

Because of these urgent and pressing issues, it is our responsibility as practitioners on a true spiritual path—in fact, it is our obligation—to plant and nourish the seeds of sacred culture in the West and to preserve the precious teachings that have been given to us. Everything in our world today seems to work against that which we are working for as *sadhakas*; everywhere we turn there are serious seductions and fascinations and distractions. The denying force is in full play . . . How can we keep the teaching, the sacred culture of the Bauls of the West, alive and well in these turbulent and desiccated times? How can we preserve the fragile roots of ancient tradition and lineage that have begun to take hold in the West?

This is a prime question for Lee's apprentice practitioners. The answer seems to hinge on the guru's vision of building Triveni Ashram on the property owned by the community near Paulden, Arizona, in the desert hills northwest of Prescott. And yet, so many elements of bringing this vision into manifestation remain groundless, shaky, even unreal. Although spiritually potent, the land itself is arid and rocky, but all the water-witching tests have affirmed what the geologists also say: one of the biggest aquifers in the Southwest exists beneath the ground precisely below Triveni. Any hope of living off the grid at Triveni Ashram, as Lee calls it, in years ahead would depend entirely on our water source, water being an extremely controversial and touchy subject in the American Southwest these days.

The Colorado River has been drained by ruthless, profit-mongering development corporations and townships, from Colorado and Utah to Arizona and California, from Phoenix to Los Angeles. The same could easily happen with the mythical aquifer than runs beneath Paulden in central Arizona, as development corporations like Dell Webb—with its planned, cookie-cutter communities—have short and long term plans for massive, large-scale development of the Prescott area.

Everyone also knows that it will take a huge amount of resources to build the ashram that Lee has described, which in some ways is as immense an undertaking as the Yogi Ramsuratkumar Ashram in Tiruvannamalai. Like father, like son; Lee envisions an ashram that will contain and preserve the teaching and the transmission of the lineage for generations to come. As practitioners in this lineage, we too feel the pressure of a great desire to build a sanctuary from the ground up that will embody and emanate the teaching and transmission of grace and blessings that, through Lee, is Yogi Ramsuratkumar's work in the West. This is an objective impulse: The Buddhists *sutras* state that it is the responsibility of the practitioner to build a temple that will last for at least three hundred years, for the sake of future practitioners; it is said in the *sutras* that to build a temple is of great merit—to not build a temple is negligent.

Many questions about the future of Lee's work in Arizona had pressed upon those who stayed there all summer. The controversy was humming in the background as we gathered for *darshan* with Lee for the first time since he left for London almost four months ago. It was the fourth *darshan* he had given in nineteen weeks, something we all hoped would not become a precedent in the history of Lee's teaching work.

Like entering the temple on the Yogi Ramsuratkumar Ashram in Tiruvannamalai, when you walk into the *darshan* hall on the Arizona ashram, immediately you are impacted with the power of this place. The *darshan* hall has, over the years, become extraordinarily steeped in spiritual power and the presence of the lineage, not only through weekly *darshans*, but also because it is the meditation hall where practitioners gather every morning, year in and year out, to meditate together for fifty minutes then perform the *arati puja* to the lineage. In more recent years it has been used for Lee's after dinner talks on Tuesday and Thursday nights. It is a place that has the mysterious power to mirror your innermost self (or that which obscures it) back to you as soon as you enter it—which makes it one of the most potent reminding factors we have in the Hohm Community.

Upon walking through the door, you are struck by the mood that exudes from the walls, floor, ceiling. Two huge, bigger-than-life *murtis*, one of Swami Papa Ramdas and one of Yogi Ramsuratkumar, immediately penetrate the senses through the delicate medium of the eye. Between these two is another large *murti*, a color photo of Yogi Ramsuratkumar and Lee Lozowick, sitting side by side, in which Yogi Ramsuratkumar is holding something in his hand and showing it to Lee.

Often, when I have entered the hall in Arizona, I am vitally aware that I am not alone. In fact, I have entered the abode of Yogi Ramsuratkumar. This humble little temple, hidden in the high desert on our unobtrusive, funky old ashram, is one of Yogi Ramsuratkumar's constant dwelling places, where his name has been repeatedly sung in joyous sounds and rounds of chanting devotees every Sunday night for twenty-five years. He is alive in this space, and wherever a being like Yogi Ramsuratkumar resides, many other exalted beings in the unseen world flock like honey bees to a flower of rare beauty and exceptional fragrance.

Tonight as usual tall white tapers burn on either side of the dais. An impressive bouquet of large white lilies with five tall peacock feathers gleaming in iridescent blues and greens stand to one side of the dais, flanked on the other side by a vase of two dozen red roses. A larger than life, two-hundred-year old carved wooden Buddha sits in full lotus on the dais, on a special platform at Lee's right. His presence blesses the room; the eyes, which are open, look straight ahead and are cast slightly down, and yet they give the feeling of looking directly at you. The Buddha communicates the pristine quality of awakened mind—the peace and serenity of nondual realization—and the inward focus of meditation. At the same time, because his eyes are open and awake, this Buddha avails himself to you completely in that paradoxical flavor of impersonal relationship. Beneath the large wooden Buddha, the guru's time-darkened leather sandals rest in a silver tray on green Indian brocade, anointed with offerings of golden and orange marigolds from the ashram garden.

The Yogi Ramsuratkumar shrine is lit and beaming into the space. As always, my gaze is particularly captured by the *vigraha* of Yogi Ramsuratkumar, sculpted in 1994 by one of Lee's students. As always, this sacred image is vividly alive and seems to be laughing with childlike delight in the golden, dulcet tones of the beggar king of Tiruvannamalai. The *vigraha* is a reminder of how the sound of Yogi Ramsuratkumar's laughter lives in the heart of the *sampradaya*, the spiritual clan, as a precious memory. All of our collective memories of times and *lilas* and interactions with Yogi Ramsuratkumar exist now, almost four years after his death, as an active Grace within each of us who knew him in the physical form. This living memory is found encoded in many places: in the oral tradition of the Hohm Community, in its written literature, in the chants that are sung, many of them written and composed by community musicians, and most powerfully in Lee's poetry to Yogi Ramsuratkumar. As the heir and spiritual son of Yogi Ramsuratkumar, Lee is the primary embodiment of the beggar's living legacy in the West, as Ma Devaki is the primary embodiment of the beggar's legacy in the East.

The sangha, or body of practicing devotees, both East and West, is the second line of embodiment of the master's living spiritual blood. This principle is true of the devotees of any great master who has passed out of the body. This is the way with a true spiritual bloodline, where the "blood" is the subtle substance of a particular stream of Benediction or Divine Influence, the active manifestation of which is often referred to in Lee's words as "the teaching" or "the Work." Those who carry the seed power of the *sampradaya*, the spiritual clan, and are empowered to transmit the Grace of that line, are living artifacts. This is one of many reasons that we bow at Lee's feet every Sunday night to have his *darshan* and to share the gift of *prasad*, the symbol of the reciprocal relationship of Grace that exists between the guru and the disciple. We either live up to the spiritual gifts we have been given or we do not.

These were my thoughts as Lee walked in, dressed in white with a large blue-gray shawl—a gift from Yogi Ramsuratkumar—wrapped around his body. Visible beneath the shawl was the worn, dust and grime streaked *dhoti* that Yogi Ramsuratkumar once wore, which he gave to Lee many years ago. It is a priceless artifact of a great yogi saint and a powerful symbol of lineage; it is still tied in the same knot as when it was on Yogi Ramsuratkumar's body. On certain occasions Lee wears it in *darshan* beneath the blue-gray shawl. He also wore a strip of green cloth, another gift from his master, wrapped around his forehead. In his arms he carried a cardboard box full of *prasad* that he would give out tonight.

Many times I look at Lee and see Yogi Ramsuratkumar. Sometimes the image is so vivid that it catches me by surprise, even though Lee himself has said often that he is transparent to Yogi Ramsuratkumar. As taciturn and private as Lee is about his inner world, he shares his poetry with us—and yet we have Lee's poetry today only by the grace and gift of Yogi Ramsuratkumar, for without his intervention, we would have never known about it. In the poetry we have a glimpse into the real Lee Lozowick, in which appearances or personas are dropped, and it is the unveiled truth of the inner man that penetrates our senses. Tonight Lee was giving us a more traditional form of darshan.

The chanting began: "*Tvameva maataa cha pita tvameva*, You are my mother and my father; *Tvameva bhandhush cha sakhaa tvameva*, You are my relatives and my friends; *Tvameva sarvam Arunachalavasa*, You are my knowledge and my wealth; *Arunachalavasa, Arunachalavasa*, You are my Arunachala Shiva; *Tvameva sarvam Yogi Ramsuratkumar*; You are my everything, Yogi Ramsuratkumar; *Tvameva sarvam Lee Anjaneya*, You are my everything Lee Anjaneya; *Tvameva sarvam Mamadinabando*, You are the only source and solace that I seek . . ."

One by one, we came up to offer our gift of *prasad* and receive Lee's gift in return while the *kirtan* continued with singing the name of Yogi Ramsuratkumar in melodious call and response chants. Yogi Ramsuratkumar himself has instructed us to sing and chant his name. Countless times he has said, "Say this beggar's name one time, and he will be there." For many of us this is felt as a powerful organic pull to this practice of using the name of Yogi Ramsuratkumar as Blessing, reminding factor and even as mantra. On this night, the chanting was particularly sweet and impassioned, drums and bells making a complex polyrhythm underneath and around the voices, the sonorous chords of the harmonium resonating in the space.

At one point a sumptuous flower garland made of marigolds from the garden was offered to Lee and carefully placed around his neck. Each flower, red, gold and orange, was bursting with life, hearty and alive with sun, earth, wind and rain—all of the primal elements alive in their concentrated form within the petals and pollen of the flowers. The *prasad* trays, empty at first, quickly filled with jars of olives, cheeses, fresh vegetables and fruits, a bowl of lemons, an earthen bowl of fresh chard from someone's garden, a large crusty apple pie, a small pot of roses. The chocolates, candy, incense and small personal gifts Lee kept at his side on the divan. The Buddha sat with unblinking, heavy-lidded eyes looking straight ahead. The Yogi Ramsuratkumar *vigraha* seemed awake, wise, still laughing softly. After the exchange of *prasad* and the chanting was over, Lee began his talk:

"Many people asked how it was in Europe this year, and the response was always, 'Oh, it was fantastically great, a great summer, the most successful ever.' When I was in Europe, I was traveling so much and was so busy that I was only at two darshans at Ferme de Jutreau the whole summer. I didn't feel good about that. I didn't feel that was the way things should be going, so as most of you know already, I cancelled practically all the seminars outside of Ferme de Jutreau next summer except for three.

"With the exception of Hauteville, where I will always go, essentially everything else that is going on next summer will be at Ferme de Jutreau. Of course, the assumption is that people will come to us," Lee shrugged and chuckled, and everyone laughed with him, "if we don't go to them."

Lee paused for a fraction of a second and continued in a mildly self-deprecating tone, "That could be a big assumption!" Everyone laughed again. We were happy to have our guru home, and the ease with which everyone slipped into sync with his understated humorous banter on this evening was the evidence of our many years together.

"Georg Feuerstein, who is arguably the most well known scholar and author relative to the yoga traditions and yoga, spent years and years and years raising money to build a real school, and he finally got to do that. It was an hour and a half north of San Francisco. When he settled in and started offering classes, about eighty percent of the people that were committed to working with him and studying with him in San Francisco wouldn't make the drive—and that was only an hour and a half!

"There's a difference between what we're doing and what Georg is doing, but how many people know that? When we were going to Hilda Charleton's in New York City back in the seventies, people used to come from New York City and from as far north as Maine and as far south as Virginia. Every week, people from all over Pennsylvania and New York State and New England would come to her meetings. People were very committed, very devoted to coming to the meetings. At that time she used to give her meetings in this little church hall in Greenwich Village—St. Luke's. It was totally crowded, sort of like the way this room is on a Celebration weekend—absolutely choked with people. Everybody felt that they needed a bigger place, so they went up to one of the most ecumenical churches in New York City, St. John the Divine, just south of Harlem.

"They were in the main cathedral hall, which has enough space for a couple thousand people, and she was getting maybe four hundred people an evening. Overnight, the amount of people coming were twelve to eight hundred, and literally within a matter of weeks, the number went down—so far down that she started having her classes in the Synod House instead of in the cathedral, because it was much smaller. A very small thing—a change of space, a change of atmosphere, a change of mood—and everything changes.

"So, I'm hoping . . . I don't know if the people at Ferme de Jutreau are hoping, but *I'm* hoping . . . that people will come to see me if I'm not going to see them. I think we have a strong enough magnetic center in Europe so that will happen, but I don't know. I thought it was a really necessary move. I'm calling next summer's work in Europe an experiment to see what will happen.

"Of course people whose seminars I cancelled out of—one of which was La Source Bleue, where I've been going since the first year in France, every year for ten years—will survive without me, obviously. They survived before me, they'll survive quite well without me, but they're also very disappointed. So, I'm telling everybody it's an experiment. I'm telling them, 'If it works well, fortunately then I won't be going out and doing any seminars, but if it doesn't work, you're the first person I'll call.'

"So, when everybody asked how it went this summer, I say it went fantastically, it was an amazing summer. Nobody said, 'Under what criteria is that based?' I suppose everybody has some idea in their minds of what a great summer is. I suppose the way most people think is, 'Well, if I were teaching, a great summer would mean, how many people signed up to be students, how many people's lives were changed.' I don't know, everybody has their own criteria.

"I can articulate various things that, in a conventional sense, were successful about the summer. The Sacred Bazaar was very successful, even to the point that we had to hire a forklift to unload a truck that showed up at Ferme de Jutreau this summer! It wasn't just all the stuff on the palettes. Some of the individual pieces were maybe six hundred pounds; one of them was actually about a thousand pounds! I didn't sell that one—it's still there," Lee laughed, "in the storage room at Ferme de Jutreau. I'm not sure how we're going to move it out!

"One of the guys bought a piece that we loaded into a Volkswagon Transporter, which is a great, great vehicle for trucking around stuff. So we loaded that thing and sent it up to northern Germany, with all the other stuff in Germany. One of the guys who bought a couple of large pieces had safe movers come and carry the crates into the house, because the stuff is so heavy that he didn't want to risk his back!" Lee chuckled. "Or dropping the thing!

"So the Sacred Bazaar was great. As I was excitedly telling people in Europe this year, ordinarily, since the Sacred Bazaar has begun, every summer I find one treasure—one really completely unexpected breathtaking discovery of artifacts. This summer I found three, one of which will be an ongoing source of artifacts for us. The things we discovered were just amazing!

"The seminars were very well attended, and people were very enthusiastic. I think more people connected to the school in a very deep way this year, more than before. About the same number as usual asked to be students, four or five or six, which I look upon as a good summer. You know, if it was fifteen or twenty people asking to be students, I'd start to really get worried that I was doing something wrong . . . But the peripheral people who really connected deeply, who didn't ask to be students and weren't students of other teachers but really connected in, was very substantial this summer. So, that was good . . . And just the ongoing progress of the teaching was substantial.

"At the end of the summer, there was a gathering at Arnaud Desjardins' ashram, Hauteville. It was his eightieth year, so there were three celebrations for his birthday—one of them was back in June and another one was last week. One of the nice things is that his students are no more sensitive to his wishes than my students are to mine, so I think we can take heart in that! That's the good news for all of us," Lee smiled as he delivered this bit of "good news," then he continued his train of thought. "I don't know if it's good news for me, but it's very good news for you. Of course, Arnaud and I each, in our own way, has those students who are very sensitive and very fully aware of what it is that's not just needed but wanted.

"So, the program was a gathering of luminaries that Arnaud had known over the last thirty years of his teaching work. Most of them had never been to Hauteville and were not students, but were writers and editors and teachers. Alexandro Jodorosky was there and Stephen Jordain and a Native American man that Arnaud liked very much, who will probably end up coming here. He lives in Europe; he's from New Mexico originally, and comes to the States a couple of times a year. It was a very interesting weekend.

"Purna, Brinda, and I were there. Of course Purna, being the people person that he is, was constantly busy. People were relentless enough, and everyone wanted to talk to him, so a number of people asked him for private conferences that were really helpful for them." Lee laughed again. "He could have made a career out of it!

"One of the things that was really significant was how strong a presence we have in Europe. There were a lot of people at Hauteville last week that I had never met before, but everybody had read all my books, everybody knew who I was. Everybody was surprised at the relationship that Arnaud and I had. People didn't know that part of it, and they had wonderment about it. But people were very much . . . enthusiastic and interested in the work that we're doing. So that's the way the summer ended—that was the last weekend we were there, which is why I was home a week late.

"So, it was a very successful summer, and at the same time, I was hardly at Ferme de Jutreau. Even when I was there, I would arrive midweek, coming back from something on a Monday, and leave again on a Wednesday or Thursday. The people who live there were very heroic in their practice.

"I use the word practice in a very vague kind of sense, so when I say people are heroic in their practice I don't necessarily mean that everybody's meditating every day, using Enquiry, the Heart Breath, Assertion, exercising every day and studying every day; I mean they were practicing in the overall sense of working their way into a system of guru yoga in which there are practices and the essential practice is complete reliance on the stream of Divine Influence that flows through the lineage from Ramdas to Yogi Ramsuratkumar through us . . . and I don't mean necessarily through Lee Lozowick exclusively.

"So, even though I was hardly there, people's practice was heroic; there was less complaining this year than ever, and when there were complaints, they were couched in a sense of humor. There was laughter along with the complaints . . . We have a reputation now in the neighborhood that Ferme de Jutreau is a radical lesbian commune, because nobody lives there but women!"

Everyone laughed along with Lee at the incongruity of this and how it reflects the human condition: we project all kinds of things on that which we don't or can't understand—like a bonded group of people who are engaging esoteric alchemical work for the purpose of spiritual transformation. However, this was a new one!

"I'm very happy about that!" Lee smiled. "We were joking around this summer, and people were calling themselves the guru's dogs. The way it is here in the summer is the way it is there in the winter *and* in the summer, but in the summer there are more people than in the winter. It's just work, work, work, from morning till night—a never-ending stream of things that need to be done—and some of that is relatively subjective.

"For instance, taking care of the food: Western Europe is, generally speaking, so luxuriously full of fruit that a tremendous amount of food gets wasted. It drops off the trees to the ground, rots and becomes fertilizer, feeds the birds and the wasps and the worms . . . We were in Touzac at La Source Bleue this summer, and one of the guys that lived there had an orchard with probably a million plums. His wife and their kids and all their neighbors and everybody involved just could not pick up all the fruit on the trees so he said, 'Do you want to come over one morning and pick as much as you can?' A couple of people went over and picked boxes of plums. Even in our neighborhood at the ashram, the neighbor has pear trees and apple trees and we can barely keep up with our own orchard, let alone helping the neighbors out by picking fruit from their trees.

"So there's an overwhelming quantity of food, and even when we work full time, we can barely manage our own. There are students in the school everywhere who have neighbors who are always offering for us to come in and pick as much as we can. The orchards are full of massive amounts of apricots and peaches and plums and apples and nuts and every kind of fruit. So people work very hard, and often the rewards of their labors are not as evident as we might want reward for our labors to be.

"We had Rob and Stewart come to visit. They run the Tayu Center in Sebastopol, which was founded by Daniel Ennis, who some of you know. They'd been to the ashram in France several times, and they gave one formal and a couple of informal talks on self-observation, since they're a Fourth Way school. Their basic foundation practice is self-observation, and their group is very small; they only have a handful of students.

"They said thousands of people have crossed their path, but people don't stick because for a long time, if you're self-observing properly, the results of that self-observation are not tangible in the way that people generally need to keep going. We want feedback in order to keep going.

"If we're doing any kind of physical activity, one of the things we look for after a certain amount of time is—if it's hatha yoga, let's say—we can keep the posture a little bit longer. Or if it's a martial art or some kind of running, or swimming, or bicycle riding, we have a little more stamina. The breath flows more naturally, we're able to just persist for longer periods of time with a greater level of skill. In whatever we're doing, if we're a salesperson, then one of the things we look for as positive feedback is that we're selling more product, or whatever you sell, over time.

"We saw an interesting movie last week. *Lord of War*. Some of you have probably seen it. The state of the world is sad but true, or true but sad—I guess you could go either way. One of the elements of the movie is that war is good for business, and if there isn't a war let's start one, it's good for business.

"So, Rob and Stewart were saying in their talks that when we're self-observing, basically what we do is see ourselves more clearly. It's not like if you're self-observing properly you're having all kinds of mystical experiences, and you're feeling like you're getting enlightened, and all of a sudden there's more money in your life and more health in your life. It's not like that. If you're self-observing properly, you see more clearly but that's it, and sometimes the result of seeing more clearly is unpleasant. It's wonderful to be in denial! Ignorance is bliss . . . whoever said that surely knew what they were talking about! Sometimes the result of seeing more clearly, at least in the short run—not in the long run, but in the short run—can be unpleasant and sometimes can be *very* unpleasant, depending upon how pervasive our denial is.

"Rob and Stewart were saying that a lot of people come to their study groups and start to practice, but very few people stay around, because after a month or two or three, when people aren't having experiences, they get bored. They go someplace where they're going to have experiences. One of the things that is evident over long periods of time is that there are certain spikes of activity, in which we really feel particularly respected and honored and acknowledged for our efforts.

"There was a little show Saturday night at Hauteville, and it was pretty much kept to the more sophisticated arts, so there wasn't any rock n' roll. There were classical performances and a dance from the famous ballet that was the beginning of Nijinsky's descent into madness. One of the performances was a belly dancing performance from Mae, who visited here last winter. She was very insecure; she had choreographed a piece she had never done before, so this was the first time she had ever performed it, and she was very anxious. But of all the performances, Mae got the biggest round of applause, the loudest and most enthusiastic applause of anybody—and there were some really, really fine musicians and dancers and singers. There were some exquisite vocal performances, really amazing vocal performances, and she got the largest, most enthusiastic response.

"Afterward she was kind of walking around looking scared, not knowing if she had done well. I said, 'You got the biggest round of applause of any performance of the evening, so whatever you think about your performance, that's your feedback—from an outside view, you really presented something that touched people, and people really appreciated it.'

"Sometimes, at various times during the year or even once a year, we find ourselves in a situation where we're getting very direct, immediate feedback, and we feel, 'Okay, this is validation that my work is being successful and I'm needed here, and I provide some value to the school.' Often we feel if we aren't always getting that kind of direct feedback, we start to get a little insecure, or maybe a lot insecure—as many of you have noticed in the last several years, which may have to do with age." Lee laughed.

"Sort of like the midlife spiritual crisis instead of the midlife personal crisis, in which we think, 'My life is useless, and I don't even know what I'm doing here, and they can do without me, and I don't provide any value. I'm not Bala or I'm not Dasya or I'm not whoever,' whatever name we put on it. 'I'm not Steve or Dan, I can't do anything practical, and I don't even know why Lee lets me stay around,' and ' I don't feel anything anymore, and I was so passionate in the beginning and now I look around and I don't feel anything for these people and this place.'

"It's a very common experience. As Mr. Gold says, ninety percent of the Work is hanging in there—so, hopefully we have the tenacity to just hang in. It's a phase, and we pass through the phase, and often on the other side we feel very grateful that we weren't impulsive, and we didn't jump ship before it was actually sinking . . ."

The soft, tempered group laughter and chuckles that could be heard around the room off and on throughout the talk and the focused attention on Lee were a reflection of a rapport that went much deeper than our enjoyment and intellectual agreement; it grew out of a depth of understanding that had been forged over years on the path together. In many ways the sangha is like a family, but the bond is one of *sadhana* and service, not one of social or ancestral necessity. Tonight there seemed to be an easy relaxation in Lee, and that, combined with his intimate and soft-spoken address, made our kinship with him and each other a tangible presence in the room.

Lee continued, "A lot of our work is like that. I was feeling that one of the facets of our relationship that's very important to all of us—myself included—is the darshan evenings. I felt, 'My God, I was only in darshan on the ashram two Sundays the whole summer at Ferme de Jutreau, out of maybe sixteen Sundays, and that's just not right.' So I completely reoriented my schedule next summer, and hopefully that will be equally or more successful. I expect it to be. I'm not worried or in fear about it. I assume that the time is right, and the move is right, and however I define success, it will be wildly successful!

"It's also a sign, as many things are rapidly changing. One of the big conversations this summer has been relative to the tidal wave last December in India and the hurricane in New Orleans and all of the earthquakes in the world. Towards the end of the summer, New Orleans was a big shock in Europe as well as in America—a very big shock. People were stunned by the immensity of it. Of course, there were a lot of European journalists, so there was extensive photographic coverage all over Europe. At the end of the summer, one of the major conversations was, 'Is it going to get worse?' People were asking publicly, and quite a bit privately, 'What do you think? Is it going to get worse?'

"My feeling, when I was being honest, was that this is just the beginning. It will probably get much worse before it gets better. We'll pass through a certain global crisis; how long the global crisis will be, I don't know if anyone has any objective idea, but certainly it will not pass over in a year or two. Maybe the physical upheaval will pass through quickly, but then our human ability and willingness to deal with the consequences may take considerably longer—lifetimes, who knows? Generations, certainly.

"This is a large conversation. Everybody knows that we provoked this—'we,' meaning the human race, and our willingness to chop down every forest on the face of the planet for profit, and our willingness to pollute the air and the water on the planet. A lot of people that I meet, people in our circle, are saying that we created this, but people in our circle have no power and no authority. We have a vote, but as everybody was saying after the last election, somehow Bush still got re-elected. Where is that coming from? Those of us who have some degree of understanding don't wield the power required to change things.

"The human response to the natural and political catastrophe of the coming years may take lifetimes, because those of us who have some understanding are in the vast minority, and the majority will have to be educated. People are not going to come to terms with the reality of the situation overnight just because they lose their home or someone in their family is sent to war. That was really evidenced by the tragic glimpse into someone's personal life in 'Farenheit 9/11.' Those of you who saw the documentary remember the woman who was a total patriot until her son got killed in the war. Then she became vehemently anti-government, but she was anti-government because her son got killed. She didn't see deeply into the principles of karma and the principles of the Work. She wasn't raging against the machine; her anger was based on personal loss. It wasn't a shift of worldview based on understanding deeply into the nature of things.

"For a world population to be educated takes a long period of time. People can be provoked to react easily, like in the French Revolution—a perfect example of how people were easily inspired to revolt. The results of that revolution were a complete reversal of the power structure. The people who took over basically created a very similar power structure within a short period of time, because there wasn't understanding.

"People can be provoked to react and respond even in very positive ways, but to actually *understand* and have the ability to create a new world, to have the phoenix arise out of the ashes of the destabilization of the planet, that requires an education that doesn't happen overnight. People can be mobilized to serve a cause opposite to the cause they were serving, just minutes before, but *understanding* is a different story, and really only understanding will ultimately make a difference.

"What's the saying? Something to the effect of those who overthrow and become the leader soon become exactly what they've overthrown once the power is in their hands. People criticize world leaders, but we don't know what it is to be a world leader until we are one. Often people with a lot of integrity and some weaknesses, when they find themselves in a position of a certain authority, aren't able to maintain their integrity in the face of their weaknesses.

"So, essentially things are changing very quickly, and one of the ongoing questions that people in Europe were always asking was: What are we going to do if, in the worst case scenario, the American government breaks down, or if the Muslims take over the world, or if the earthquakes and the natural disasters become so pervasive that they destroy all mandate sources of energy? People are saying, 'What are *you* going to do if . . .? Are you looking at all that?'

"My personal view—not necessarily my community view, my *personal* view—is that I'm just going to keep going full speed ahead until I have to shift course. I suppose I'll have to stand for my words someday, but I feel that I can change direction quickly and easily without difficulty. I feel that if I *had* to, if there was necessity, I could easily leave. 'I' meaning 'we.' I could easily leave the comfort and security of our physical environments—the ashram in France or this ashram—if necessary.

"I could go on the road, become nomadic, if I had to. I could move to another country, even as deeply and obsessively attached as I am to the way things are now, our ashram in France and our ashram in Arizona. And by obligation, to our ashram in India; I'm not attached to the ashram, but I'm attached to it by obligation to Yogi Ramsuratkumar. I'm personally attached to *this* place, and you all and the French ashram and all of my students there. As deep as that is, I feel within myself—and I might be wrong, that has to be proven—that I could walk away tomorrow if I had to. I wouldn't want to, I wouldn't like to, but if I had to, I feel I could 'turn on a dime,' as they say.

"My personal plan is full speed ahead. I'm not in any way compromising the headlong avalanche of Vigraha and the Sacred Bazaar, so I'm buying everything I see at the right price whenever I see it. I'm just going full out, as if this thing were going to go forever. I don't believe it will, but I'm going full out. So, full speed ahead!

"I'm not in any way trying to cover my tracks or worrying about the future. I'm just moving as fast as I can, full speed ahead, through every door that's open. I feel that, if necessary, I could turn on a dime and move in a completely different direction. So that's the way I'm personally functioning.

"One of the things that Mr. Gold has talked about consistently is that what's important is the survival of the Work, not the survival of the teacher or the external form. What's important is that the Work survives, whether it survives in a continuous human stream through the ongoing survival of community as we know it, or whether the Work survives through the Tibetan Buddhist idea of *terma.* If there is a time in which the Work can't be freely practiced and lived, it is possible that it would have to be seeded into various cultural forms, to be in a symbolic seed form that could be discovered in fifty or a hundred or a thousand years, when it can be freely experimented with, investigated, practiced and lived."

Lee spoke about how a lot of the most valuable external influences in our Work have come from E.J. Gold and Arnaud Desjardins. However, he said, "The essential core is *always* Yogi Ramsuratkumar." He continued, "That's one of the reasons, I guess, that we're putting so much emphasis on art lately. All of you who have studied art to any degree—art that is two hundred, three hundred, five hundred or thousands of years old, the ancient Chinese and Egyptian art and so on—know that art maintains and conveys something of essential reality. What's to say that some of the art that we're producing won't have a similar impact?

"We've only met one crew of graffiti artists, but I was very intent upon telling these guys that I thought this was art. One of the guys actually had tears in his eyes, because I was very clear that there is money involved, and we're going to promote this thing. We are going to establish a major influence for graffiti in the world, but for me it's about art and the money is secondary. These guys were really touched because they've seen friends of theirs manipulated and used in commercial ways. These guys are really artists.

"So whatever we think of the style of their art, that's our business. To them, they're producing real art, and who's to say what form of art and how much of the art that we produce will convey something one hundred, two hundred or five hundred years from now. So, every time I see a manuscript that's four or five hundred years old, I think how miraculous it is that something as delicate as this paper has survived! There are massive archives in India, and India is full of termites or ants, I guess, and they just eat everything that's paper or wood. There are massive archives in India, really vital archives, that have just been eaten up, literally devoured—not just holes, but completely devoured—by termites! So every time I see something that's made of paper or wood that's been preserved, I'm amazed.

"There are thirteenth and fourteenth century wooden Buddhas from Thailand and Cambodia and Burma and Vietnam, and every time I see one of those, I say, 'Wow, this is amazing, that something so delicate has survived for so long!' Relative to the Sacred Bazaar, at one point Arnaud said to me that he was looking for a special Buddha for his ashram at Hauteville. I found something in Paris, and I just gave the name of my supplier to Arnaud. They did end up getting a Buddha from him—it wasn't the original one I picked, because that one had been sold by the time the machinery got moving. But they found a very nice fifteenth or sixteenth century Buddha about that big," Lee gestured to indicate about two or three feet high, "from one of the southeast Asian countries. They ritualistically installed it in Ranchi on the ashram. So, a sacred artifact that is five hundred years old is still valuable and useful in the *context* in which it was created, in the time and place in which there is a desperate need for this Influence, this Blessing Force.

"I think probably one of the reasons that we're falling more into the creation of art as time goes by is certainly for our own enjoyment: I think that the music we've created—from *liars, gods & beggars* all the way through whatever the newest permutations are—have provided a tremendous amount of enjoyment and pleasure and delight and many other things for all of us in the community. And, there are deeper and longer term possibilities for some of these things—who knows, when we'll be dead!

"I was thinking how really unfair the law of karma is. At least if we could remember who we were in past lives, we would have clear, linear feedback: 'Oh I did this, now I'm having to experience this . . . okay, I get the principle.' But it isn't like that. In many cases, we find ourselves almost victimized by the environment and raising our hands to heaven, saying, 'Why me, why did this have to happen to me?' and some people never get it. They're really, in a sense, innocent bystanders.

"If only we could remember! It seems like things would be much easier and more relevant. But we don't remember, so we find ourselves in a life in which our health is what it is, our financial situation is what it is, our personal relationship situation is what it is. Obviously, when we think about the victims of any kind of major crisis—famine or war or natural disaster, earthquakes or the water disaster—we feel tremendously grateful it isn't us. All those millions of people who are at the effect of such tremendous suffering, most of them will never know anything about karma. In a real sense, they're just innocent victims and, not knowing anything about the laws of karma, most of them are creating more karma, standing on the foundation of genocide in Africa.

"As soon as one tribe starts to get some weapons, they go kill the other tribe who was just killing them. So, it's not like we put an end to karma through a compassionate response to our circumstances; we are bearing the fruits of karma and creating, sowing the seeds of karma that, when those seeds blossom and sprout, are going to be hitting innocent victims again, who don't understand, who are just born in a certain place and are at the effect of a certain horrible suffering . . . So, I have no solution! I was just thinking how unfair it is!" Lee laughed.

"One of the things as the world changes is my feeling that, if necessary, I'm able to turn on a dime and shift directions—move, if necessary. One of the things that we're all called to embrace, of course, is: Can we, are we willing to, move with whatever changes happen to come? I shouldn't say this, it's depressing, but I was thinking about my enthusiasm for living out in Paulden. I was thinking, well it's a great idea, and we all want a new ashram, but look at the way things are now! Look at how many people live in Prescott, and how many people are in this hall for meditation every morning. Or let's give everybody the benefit of the doubt—how many people, by virtue of numbers, are regularly meditating every morning?

"There is a meditation space out in Paulden, so I assume that there is regular meditation going on. Okay, that covers a handful of people, but what about everybody in Prescott? And I was thinking, here I am, firing people up with enthusiasm about this place we're going to have, and who is going to do all the work? You know, the people who have given their lives to working here, none of us are getting any younger, and there's only a few of us. If we move to a place that's three times as large and has three times the physical facilities, are we going to get that many more people who are going to be willing to give five, ten, fifteen and twenty years of their lives without the glory?

"Let's use Dan as an example. Dan is not in a glory position, so it's not like everybody that comes here knows that without Dan—I could use many people as an example—would we even have vehicles that run? There are a lot of people who live on the ashram in France and on the ashram here who don't have the glory positions.

"The glory positions are like . . . Purna got the glory position, you think. If you look at the guy, you can see it's killing him. Or

Dasya goes to Europe and gives seminars. Okay, there are only five men at his seminar in Brussels, but those men were changed forever! Dasya's name will live on their lips, in their hearts, and fill their minds for the rest of their lives! So, that's a glory position.

"Really, the people who do the work, they don't have the glory positions. It's day in and day out, they wash the dishes, they take the rattlesnakes (if you're in Paulden) and throw them farther out in front of the dining hall, and repair the roof, and fix the wiring—and that's not a glory position. I'm thinking we're going to move out to this place, the new ashram is going to have facilities for two hundred people—who's going to do all that work?

"I was sharing that with somebody today and she said, 'Oh this person, that person, this person, yes this person—they need to move to Paulden so they can have their own house on the property.' All the people who build their own houses on the property, maybe they'll be in the meditation hall in the morning, but they're going to have jobs, they're going to have families, they're not going to have full time every day, seven days a week, three hundred and sixty-five days a year to serve the facility of the ashram.

"I suppose, as Starr Fuentes says, some big donation will come early next year, and I'll say, 'Oh boy, oh boy, let's start building!' But right now I'm thinking, 'Who's going to do all that work?' Somebody said, 'Maybe Jeff will move out there.' I said, 'Jeff has a family, he's got little daughters.' Jeff is not going to be able to do what somebody with no family would be able to do, even if he wants to. He's responsible to his family, thank goodness.

"Then somebody said, 'Well, Tom Lennon wants to move out there.' You think I'm going to tell Tom, 'Oh just get rid of your business, and come here and spend the rest of your life working like a mule!' He wants to move out and sell his house in Boulder and reproduce that house on our property.

"So, who's going do all the work? Ralph and Shukyo have said many times, 'Wherever you want us, that's where we'll be.' And I go out there and I look at the house that Ralph built with his own hands and I think, 'That's really nice of him,' I believe him, I think he genuinely means it. I don't have any question of his saying that out of some sense of obligation. I look at this house he built with his own hands, and I say, 'It is *just* that he lives here for a little while and absorbs a little bit of the benefit from all the labor, even if he's perfectly willing to move tomorrow,' and I believe that he is.

"Maybe all of that will come together. When it's time to move to Paulden all of it will come together. But it can't get much drier out there. There's a lot of water under that property, but then Del Webb's a big guy and he's very thirsty, and you know what happens if he moves in ten thousand homes and sucks all the water out of the ground! Then what? You can't get much drier than out there. There's water out there now, but you know, Prescott and Chino Valley and Paulden are not sitting still; they're booming developmentally, and that takes water.

"What if some industry comes in that requires a particularly high level of water? Where are they going to get the water? From our aquifers, those bastards! They can stick a pipe in this way and you know," Lee made a loud sucking noise to demonstrate just how fast the developers could suck the water from beneath Triveni, then concluded, "suck it right out!"

Lee continued, "I think the more pressure there is relative to the way the world is changing, the more personal pressure there is for us to be completely flexible and fluid. If I can be a little pretentious and talk about martial arts, it's almost like the more proficient you become, the more flexible you need to become, rather than resting on the strength of your accomplishments. There is a human tendency to think, 'I've accomplished all of this, now I can just protect my accomplishments.' The minute we start thinking that way, we start crystallizing, even muscularly.

"I think the more developed we become the more flexible we need to become, and certainly it's true here: the more we feel the tremendous stress that is taking place in the world—and I think the stress will continue for some time—the more flexible we need to become. Okay, we have this fabulous situation, this fabulous sangha that is really dedicated, and we're bonded to people who are dedicated to serving us and helping us, as we are dedicated to serving and helping them. How do we protect all of that, because in a very real sense there's no physical protection; this ashram and the ashram in France are as vulnerable as walking out on the street in the middle of Prescott.

"You know the new law in America? Any local, state or federal government organization can come in and take—they have to *buy* it, but they can *take*—any piece of property, *any* piece of property, even a piece of property that's been in your family for ten generations. They can force you to sell it to them based on the fact that this property, in the government's vision, is necessary to make a park or extend the road, or whatever they want to say. So even physically, your physical property is your sanctuary as long as the government lets you have it. If the government decides they want it, there's nothing you can do.

"The property at La Source Bleue in France has been in Jean Pierre's family for five hundred years. It's one of the most unique, special springs in their area in Southern France, and if the government wants to come in and say it's historical property, they can get it . . . It's in one of the largest areas for archeological discovery of ancient Roman sites, so the government can come in at any time and say, 'We've discovered this underground town and we need to take over for the government; it needs to become historical government site.'

"So we need to be tremendously flexible relative to how solutions get given, and when we need to know, solutions will be given, but we don't always know *how*. We have to have the willingness to be flexible and move in a way that the Work is requiring for its survival, which certainly does not exclude the sangha and our families. However, could we all move to Canada, to New Zealand, to Europe on a moment's notice? Of course we *could . . . would* we? Or would we drag our heels until it's too late?

"If you've been reading the news, France has a very liberal policy for all ex-French colonies in terms of immigration. A lot of the French colonies were in Africa, so there's a tremendous amount of Africans living in France. In the beginning the French were completely open to immigration, but then of course, as with many things, at first the Africans were culturally interesting and exciting, but now they've become completely socially counter-productive.

"In Paris there are certain apartment buildings where the immigrants live, and, like the Vietnamese when they first came to America, there are ten, fifteen, twenty people to an apartment. They're regular apartment buildings, and so they've got regular stoves, but when you're cooking for twenty people in an apartment designed for three, you've got to make some adjustments. So, towards the end of the summer there was a series of major fires in the immigrant buildings, and the buildings were burned down completely. There was not much loss of life, but a tremendous loss of property and homes. A lot of people think it was arson, because now the Africans that are wanting to come to France are being rejected. There's a reaction to the tremendous, gigantic influx of African people in France.

"So, what's to say that that won't happen here in the States? What's to say that the kind of social and cultural violence that takes place in India between Muslims and Hindus, and that is now starting in France and in Germany to some degree between the Turks and the Eastern Europeans, won't happen here? There has always been some animosity with the Turks and Eastern Germans swarming into Western Germany, even though it's all one Germany. Eastern Germany is still very oppressed, and Western Germany is still the place where everybody comes to get a good job and make a lot of money. What's to say that that won't happen here?

"Are we able to be flexible enough to move however we're required to move, in order to protect the teaching? Obviously part of that flexibility has to do with our relationship to one another. Are we willing to be flexible in relationship to one another? Not necessarily forgive and forget, but *be flexible.* Are we willing to make space for one another to serve the survival of the teaching, even when our psychological responses are crystallized? Whatever our psychological responses are—our sexism, our racism, our weightism, our ageism, whatever. Our inherent biases, our prejudices, are in place even relative to sangha.

"So, will we be able to be flexible towards other sangha members, relative to our prejudices, when the directive is to keep the Work alive and protect the teaching, rather than survive in an exclusive way? If keeping the Work alive means keeping the ashram, fabulous, that's what we do, we keep the ashram. For example, the farm in Tennessee was one of the most radical communal experiments in the twentieth century. It worked for years and years very successfully. At one point Stephen Gaskin, who is a brilliant personality and leader, moved away to do whatever he's doing now, and the physical way in which the farm was run was completely changed.

"They went from a place that was run completely communally to a place that became a land co-op instead of a commune, which is very different; the people had to buy their own land and were responsible in a certain way to everyone in the co-op, but legally and socially it was a completely different set-up. All the businesses were privatized, so the farm now has a very successful publishing company, a very successful health food production company, and the money feeds back to the community in a way, but not in the way it was when it was a community business.

"So, however the Work needs to be served . . . If, for example, whatever community business we had needed to be privatized—could we make an adjustment, be flexible, and flexible especially relative to one another? Could we be flexible so that however the Work is defining its survival through us, we are able to get on the train and move with how the Work needs us to move?"

Lee's discourse continued in the simple, friendly and intimate mood that had characterized the whole evening; at the same time, his words were tinged with a radical sanity and sobriety. On this warm October night, as Lee gave this overview of what the summer had been about from his perspective, he also addressed, in a very poignant, yet almost understated and gentle way, our spoken and unspoken concerns about the direction we are headed in. It seemed that his answer to the question, "Where were we headed next?" could be summed up as: we don't really know. Maybe there will be a new ashram in Arizona and maybe not. Maybe Lee will spend more time in France; perhaps he will move to France. Maybe he will go in a completely new direction, ranging farther and farther away from ashram life with his buying and selling sacred art and artifacts. Or, by necessity, we could take wayfaring to a new level in a nomadic existence.

On the other hand, we could easily return to a more traditional form, stricter practice and renunciate ashram life. We could build the Triveni Ashram in the dry boney hills north of Paulden and eke out an existence there amidst the rocks and piñon pine and juniper trees, becoming some kind of Baul desert mothers and fathers in our latter days. Without question, in the darkness of our era, the urgency to create a legacy of Lee's teaching and the lineage of Yogi Ramsuratkumar in the West is made all the more poignant by the dire need for temples and sacred places of all kinds to be built for future generations.

All that aside, Lee was clearly offering us an opportunity to practice: to live in the higher context of faith, to embrace his core teaching of Spiritual Slavery. Whatever may come, we find ourselves in a circumstance of not knowing, of groundlessness, not sure where the next step is, or if there is ground to stand on at all. This is the most creative place of all, the place of the most possibility, and the most terrifying to ego. It is also a place that forges faith, trust in God and radical reliance on the guru and the lineage. It's not for the faint-hearted, but for those who can gather courage from what they know to be true and stay in the crucible of that as the flames rise higher. To do that, we must win out over the pervasive cynicism in the world today. As Lee would later say, "The antidote to cynicism is faith."

Cynicism renders us into dark and opaque states of being; faith transforms us into radiant and transparent states. Since faith is what is required to transcend our cynicism, our tarnished innocence and harsh criticisms of others, or our despondency and dread about the general state of the world, then how can we cultivate faith? Faith is one of those sublime gifts of the spirit. Faith is not something that can be forced or faked. We may not be graced with faith, but we can pray. As Lee said at La Source Bleue, we pray in any way we can; maybe just a moment of silence, an appreciation of beauty, a remembrance of someone we truly love: our children or grandchildren, our life partners and friends.

Even when we are doubting and negative and cannot muster a prayer, we can still remember the name of Yogi Ramsuratkumar. In our lowest, darkest, most debased moments, we can say the name of Yogi Ramsuratkumar, for his name banishes darkness and invokes grace. As Lee often says in his poetry, we can sing, chant, whisper, think, speak, intone or shout the name of Yogi Ramsuratkumar. This is the road of faith. Maybe, if our prayers are strong enough, if our need is great enough, if we are consistent and persevering, then the impossible Blessing of faith will come to live in our hearts.

During the last five minutes Lee had slowly and deliberately picked up all the *prasad* that was on his divan and carefully packed it into the cardboard box that had held the *prasad* he gave to us. The end of tonight's *darshan* signaled the true completion of our summer sojourn this year. We were poised now for what would come next, as life would keep rolling along, unfolding and revealing where we most need to practice, showing us the way of the path.

"Okay! That will cover the news for tonight," he ended in his unceremonious way. Wrapping the gray-blue shawl more closely around himself, he stood up and said "Jai Guru!" Then, carrying the box of *prasad*, he walked out the door and into the night. We would see him again very shortly, in our evening gathering, for coffee, chocolates, tea and conversation . . .

Appendix

Finding the Baul Bards, East and West

Note on the Baul Path

The Vaishnava path has been the rich seed bed of many inspired teachings and visionary gurus, including the conventional, traditional Vaishnavas who constitute a popular organized religion in India. However, more relevant to Western Bauls are: the Sahajiya Vaishnavas, with their underpinnings in Bengali tantrism and deep connection with the Sahajiya Buddhists, out of which evolved the Bauls of Bengal; the Gaudiya Vaisnavism of Mahaprabhu Sri Chaitanya; and the Pusti Marga of Vallabhacharya.

All of these owe much of their religious mythology to the particular stories of Krishna with the gopis that have their origins in the famous poem, the *Gita Govinda*, written in the twelfth century by the Vaishnava poet, Jayadeva. This ecstatic poem of erotic mysticism tells the story of the relationship between Radha and Krishna, which is a metaphor for the relationship between the human soul and the personal Beloved or Divinity. It is a celebrated achievement that stands out in the genre of sacred erotic literature in the world, including the biblical "Song of Songs" and the hymns of Inanna and Dumuzi from ancient Sumer. Springing out of a vast transformational process that was occurring in medieval India at this time, Jayadeva succeeded in bringing the reality of the mystical realm back to this world of the marketplace and human need.

What was the cultural and religious milieu that provided the fertile ground for such a breakthrough of transcendent creativity? The ancient framework of Hindu culture in north India had been decimated by repeated Muslim invasions from the eleventh to thirteenth centuries. There was much plundering and razing of hallowed temples and seats of learning; ancient texts and sculptures were destroyed and Hindu culture was rocked to its foundations. Many Hindu monarchs, who had served the culture as patrons of the arts, disappeared at this time into the south, while poets, craftsmen, painters and musicians moved to the safety of mountains and forests in rural areas. Artists who had been trained in classical traditions discovered themselves almost in exile, in a new world among tribal and common people who "lived close to nature and expressed their innermost feelings in a language of refreshing simplicity."[1] This sweeping cultural upheaval had a far-reaching effect on the arts. Poetry was transformed from strict classical forms to a free-flowing vernacular style that was more connected to the earth and took on a new depth of unfettered, uncensored feeling.

Jayadeva came out of this creative outpouring. Like the Bauls of later times, he was born in the Birbhum district of Bengal. In his early life he wandered the roads of northern India, visiting Mathura and Brindavan, where he was deeply influenced by the enchanting scenery and tales of Krishna. A fervent Vaishnava, he went to Jagannath, where he camped under a tree near the Jagannath shrine. There, his life was changed forever.

A brahmin who lived at the temple and, after many childless years, had been graced with the birth of a beautiful girl child by the Lord Jagannath (Krishna), had a dream in which Jagannath instructed him to give the child to Jayadeva. Despite the reluctance of Jayadeva, the old man left the child with him and disappeared.

1 Ambalal, Amit. *Krishna as Shrinathji*, Mapin International, New York, 1987, p. 12.

That child became his famous dancing consort, Padmavati, whom he married and lived with happily for the rest of his life.

Inspired by Padmavati, Jayadeva became the visionary poet who wordsmithed language into this new, fresh form. For example, the original scripture on the love games of Krishna with the gopis in Book Ten of the *Bhagavata Purana* does not mentioned Radha; she did not exist until she was created by Jayadeva to represent the personified focal point of the archetypal gopis. The inclusion of Radha was one of the primary religious inventions of Jayadeva's *Gita Govinda*, which personalized this objective story as an event of the individual soul. Radha was a human person who became divinized, and everyone could relate with her.

Jayadeva and Padmavati found their way to the court of Lakshmanasena, the Vaidya king of Bengal, where they were renowed as poet and dancer. In India, poetry is almost always put to music, and when Jayadeva would sing his poems, Padmavati would dance. The *Gita Govinda* was considered a lyrical drama and performed as a play; this eight-hundred-year old masterpiece is considered the earliest example of the type of primitive dramatic play that still survives in Bengal.[2]

Jayadeva's poetry spread like wildfire and became so popular that "Poetry began to be written in the local languages based on the *Gita Govinda*, using the same symbolism and extolling love in all its varying moods."[3] The poetic metaphors and imagery of the *Gita Govinda* was reproduced in many different art forms: paintings, songs, rural ballads—all these began to reflect this evolution of expression.

---

2 Krishnamachariar. *History of Classical Sanskrit Literature*, Motilal Banarsidass, Delhi, 1937, pp. 337–338.

3 Feuerstein, Georg. *The Yoga Tradition*, Hohm Press, Prescott, Arizona, 1998, p. 388.

In the fourteenth century, northern India produced the great poet Candidas, who was considered the father of Bengali poetry. Candidas' love songs, which followed the style of Jayadeva, featured Radha and Krishna and are still sung in Bengal today. A brahmin by birth, Candidas was heretical and revolutionary; he is often considered a Baul because of the thematic similarities in his poetry and the fact that he rejected caste and rank, rebelling against religious law and social custom by falling in love with a low-born washer maid, Rami. The passion of their union was the inspiration that fueled his masterful writings of bhakti poetry.[4]

One hundred years later, in the fifteenth century when Vallabhacharya went to Vraja, the historical village of Krishna's childhood and play with the gopis, he further developed the eroticism of Jayadeva's story of Radha and Krishna with the added element of ecstatic devotion, and the *bhakti* tradition was born. With each of these developments, the worship of Krishna became increasingly intimate—a personal Beloved, a living God with whom the human person could have an immediate, direct relationship.

In the latter part of the sixteenth century, the dynamic son of Vallabhacharya, Shri Gosainji, added yet another element to the Pushti Marga: that of regal splendor, in which he formulated the *seva* (work) in which *raga, bhoga* and *shringara* (music, food, ornate adornment and rich attire) were offered to the deity. Furthermore, he emphasized *madhurya bhakti*, wherein Lord Krishna is known as the Beloved of the heart, and all of his devotees, whether man or woman, became gopis. In this path, worship of the deity included not only traditional *puja* but also painting, poetry, music, cookery, flowers and floral arrangements, sculpture, costumes and jewelry.[5]

---

4 Ambalal, Amit. *Krishna as Shrinathji*, Mapin International, New York, 1987, p. 12.

5 Ambalal, Amit. *Krishna as Shrinathji*, Mapin International, New York, 1987, p. 12.

The use of the image as *svarupa*, or real embodiment of God, became empowered in this tradition. The use of sacred images as invocational objects of meditation and prayer, was celebrated through the proliferation of many forms of art as pictoral visualization—or visualization of the deity—was further developed.

In the middle of this creative flowering of art, philosophy and awakened consciousness, the great contemporary of Vallabhacharya, Mahaprabhu Sri Krsna Chaitanya (1485–1533), was born in a northern region of Bengal. An ecstatic mystic who was disposed toward fits of devotional mood that were so intense they were alarming to those around him, his *mahabhavas*, or objective states of ecstatic love of God, were of such profound objectivity that he became revered as an incarnation of both Radha and Krishna.[6]

During this time, from around the fifteenth century to the present time, the Bauls of Bengal sprang up from the grass roots of Bengali religious culture and thrived as wandering beggars and mystic bard-poets; they were minstrels who brought joy and delight, along with exalted dharma and philosophy, to the common village people in return for a bowl of rice and dahl. Their renderings of these religious myths and teachings were couched in the language of the streets, spoken and sung in ways that everyone could understand. The Baul belief that every human being has an inborn divine potential fueled their insistence on turning away from rank and caste and accepting everyone into their communities. For the Baul, the human being is sacred and revered; thus, over the centuries, they have brought inspiration to the masses of people who have struggled to maintain their existence in the face of the fierce vicissitudes of rural life in Bengal. Because of this, the Bauls have always been the heroes of the common people.

6 McDaniel, June. *The Madness of the Saints*: Ecstatic Religion in Bengal, pp. 35–36.

From the beginning, the Bauls considered Jayadeva and Chaitanya to be their patron saints; at the same time, they were steeped in the tantric teachings and practices of the Sahajiya cults of Bengal. The Bauls were heretical, iconoclastic and revolutionary in their synthesis of tantric Sahajiya Buddhism and devotional Vaishnava Hinduism with music, dance and transformational mysteries of sexual yoga and breath practice. This syncretic way of life formed *kaya sadhana*, or the path to God-realization through the human body. They placed a very high premium on devotion and radical reliance on the guru or spiritual preceptor, which is at the center of their yoga. A further cross-pollination occurred between the Bauls and their Sufi counterparts, the Auls, which greatly influenced the Baul emphasis on longing for the illusive "Man of the Heart," or cosmic nondual Self, as personal Beloved.

The Baul ideal is to live from the authentic and original impulse that is called *sahaja* (innate) in the Sanskrit language. The *sahaja* principle might be summed up, if such a thing is advisable, in Lee's words: "We have to relax into the natural state in which the Divine, which is evolutionary, is free to live through us." This impulse takes the true Baul on the *ulta* or reverse path; it is a path that leads in the opposite direction of the rest of the world, or directly against the mainstream current:

[The Bauls] avoid all religion in which the natural piety of the soul is overshadowed by the useless paraphernalia of ritualism and ceremony on the one hand and pedantry and hypocrisy on the other. It is said in a beautiful song — "Reverse are the modes and manners of the man who is a real appreciator of the true behavior. Such a man is affected neither by the weal nor by the woe of the world, and constantly realizes the delight of love; it appears that his eyes are floating on the water of delight; sometimes he laughs alone in his own mood, sometimes he cries alone. Awkwardly wild are all his manners and customs—and the other extremely wonderful fact is that

the glory of the full-moon [Krishna] closes round him for all time; and further . . . there is no setting of the moon of his heart . . ." [7]

This is an accurate description of Lee's relationship with his master, Yogi Ramsuratkumar, who is the "glory of the full-moon," which never sets in the heart of the disciple. It is possible that Lee's greatest contribution to the dharma arising in the West is the *mahakavya* (great poetic work) of his poetry to his master, Yogi Ramsuratkumar, written from 1979-2004; these can be discovered in two large volumes titled *Death of a Dishonest Man: Poems and Prayers to Yogi Ramsuratkumar* (Hohm Press, 1998) and *Gasping for Air in a Vacuum: Poems and Prayers to Yogi Ramsuratkumar* (Hohm Press 2003) and in French, *108 Poèmes et Prièures à Yogi Ramsuratkumar* (2004).

As a Baul poet of the classic Indian devotional form of *ninda stuti*, or ironic praise, Lee's voice of radical devotion and worship of God in the human form of Yogi Ramsuratkumar as *ishta devata* (chosen deity), combined with a fierce call to the alchemy of inner work on self, is unparalleled in the contemporary world. Lee's teachings, music and poetry to Yogi Ramsuratkumar flow in the same stream of dharma as the Baul bards of Bengal; they transmit the truth for future generations who will long for the Beloved and seek the transformational mysteries. It is important to recognize as well that the introduction of sacred images through the tremendous influx of art that Lee has brought into the West vitally reflects the entire stream of the Pushti Marga, or Path of Grace, and the tantric dimensions of the bhakti tradition as it is appearing now in the Western Baul path.

---

7 Das Gupta, *Obscure Religious Cults*, pp. 162–163.

Bibliography

Ambalal, Amit. *Krishna as Shrinathji*, Mapin International Inc., New York, 1987.

Bose, Manindra Mohan. *The Post-Caitanya Sahajia Cult of Bengal*, Gian Publishing House, Delhi, 1986.

Das Gupta, S. *Obscure Religious Cults*, Mukhopadhyay Publishers, Calcutta, 1969.

Hohm Sahaj Mandir Study Manuals, Volumes I and II, Hohm Press, Prescott, Arizona, 1996.

Hohm Sahaj Mandir Study Manuals, Volumes III and IV, Hohm Press, Prescott, Arizona, 2002.

Lozowick, Lee. *Death of a Dishonest Man: Poems and Prayers to Yogi Ramsuratkumar*, Hohm Press, Prescott, Arizona, 1998.

Lozowick, Lee. *Gasping for Air in a Vacuum: Poems and Prayers to Yogi Ramsuratkumar*, Hohm Press, Prescott, Arizona, 2004.

Lozowick, Lee. *108 Poèmes et Prières à Yogi Ramsuratkumar*, Hohm Press, Prescott, Arizona, 2005.

Mani, with S. Lhaksam. *A Man and His Master: My Years with Yogi Ramsuratkumar*, Hohm Press, Prescott, Arizona, 2003.

Ryan, Regina Sara. *Only God: A Biography of Yogi Ramsuratkumar*, Hohm Press, Prescott Arizona, 2004.

Sarkar, R.M. *Bauls of Bengal: In the Quest of Man of the Heart*, Gian Publishing House, New Delhi, 1990.

Young, M. *As It Is: A Year on the Road with a Tantric Teacher*, Hohm Press, Prescott, Arizona, 2000.

Young, M. *Agony & Alchemy: Sacred Art and Tattoos*, Hohm Press, Prescott, Arizona, 2005.

Young, M. *Yogi Ramsuratkumar—Under the Punnai Tree*, Hohm Press, Prescott, Arizona, 2003.